WORLD DEVELOPMENT REPORT 2003

Sustai... ...pment
in ...ynamic World

Transforming Institutions, Growth, and Quality of Life

THE WORLD BANK

**A copublication of
the World Bank and
Oxford University Press**

About the cover:

A montage of two satellite sensor products, the cover image shows the lights of human settlements and (on May 14, 2002) variation in sea surface temperatures. The image illustrates several *World Development Report 2003* themes: the link between growth and environment (higher income correlated with greater energy use), the continuing socioeconomic challenge of inequality and poverty reduction (vast disparity in the energy use of industrial countries and that of developing countries), the interconnectedness and impact of human activity (fossil fuel-based energy use raising sea surface temperatures), and the need to gather information (such as that provided by satellite sensors) to anticipate and monitor problems if the world is to shift to a more sustainable development.

For more information on the concepts in this report, please visit
http://econ.worldbank.org/wdr/wdr2003/

City lights image courtesy of the Defense Meteorological Satellite Program Digital Archive, National Geographic Data Center, U.S. National Oceanic and Aeronautics Administration

Sea surface temperatures image courtesy of U.S. National Climatic Data Center

Inside art and typesetting by Barton Matheson Willse & Worthington, Baltimore

ISBN 0-8213-5151-6 (clothbound)
ISBN 0-8213-5150-8 (paperback)
ISSN 0163-5085

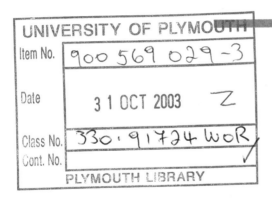

Contents

Boxes

Figures

Tables

ACKNOWLEDGMENTS

This Report has been prepared by a team led by Zmarak Shalizi and comprising Kenneth Chomitz, Christian Eigen-Zucchi, Gunnar Eskeland, Swati Ghosh, Christine Kessides, Linda Likar, and Robert Schneider. The team was assisted by Leena Datwani, Claudio E. Montenegro, and B. Bulent Ozbilgin. Valuable contributions were made by Matthew Stilwell and Paul Steinberg. Bruce Ross-Larson was the principal editor. The work was carried out under the general direction of Nicholas H. Stern.

The Report received useful advice from a three-person steering committee consisting of Nicholas Stern, Ian Johnson, and Vinod Thomas, and a six-person internal consultative group consisting of Michele DeNevers, Ian Goldin, Kristalina Georgieva, Steen Jorgensen, Odin Knudsen, and John Shilling.

Many others inside and outside the World Bank provided helpful comments, wrote background papers, and made other contributions, and participated in consultation meetings. These contributors and participants are listed in the Bibliographical Note.

The team undertook a wide range of consultations for this Report, from the initial outline to the final draft. These consultations included workshops in Berlin, Oslo, Paris, Washington, and San Jose (Costa Rica) and a series of video conferences with East Asia, Africa, and Europe. The participants in these workshops and video conferences included policymakers, academics, and nongovernmental organizations. The team participated in the United Nations' WSSD-related prepcoms in New York. In addition, it organized e-conferences with the help of the World Bank Institute. The Development Data Group contributed to the data appendix and was responsible for the Selected World Development Indicators. Much of the background research and external consultations were supported by a generous grant from the Norwegian government.

Rebecca Sugui served as executive assistant to the team; Leila Search, as program assistant and technical support; and Endy Shri Djonokusomo, Shannon Hendrickson, Joanna Kata-Blackman, Olivia Kurtz, and Ofelia Valladolid, as team assistants. Evangeline Santo Domingo served as resource management assistant.

Book design, editing, and production were coordinated by the Production Services Unit of the World Bank's Office of the Publisher, under the supervision of Susan Graham, Melissa Edeburn, and Ilma Kramer.

Foreword

This year's Report, the twenty-fifth, is about the growth in income and productivity required in developing countries to eliminate poverty in a way that is environmentally and socially sustainable. The core development challenge is to ensure productive work and a much better quality of life for the almost 3 billion poor people today earning less than $2 per day and for the 2–3 billion people to be added to the world's population over the next 30–50 years. To achieve this goal, while taking better care of our environmental and social assets, will require a global development process that does better than the one followed in the past.

Even though the world's population increased by 2 billion people in the last 30 years, there have been significant gains in human welfare in developing countries as measured by average human development indicators. But the development path has left a legacy of accumulated environmental and social problems that cannot be repeated. There are many drivers of today's socioeconomic and cultural transformations. Some are ongoing and continuous (such as technological innovation and income growth). Others are onetime and transitional, such as the demographic and urban transitions, which should be completed within this century—largely within the next 50 years. These historic transitions define the temporal and spatial context for managing sustainability. How it will be managed is critical.

Environmental and social assets matter greatly for well-being and productivity, but they are often neglected. That is why we need to think about managing a broader portfolio of assets. The 1992 World Development Report identified many policies to deal with environmental problems, but it underestimated the capacity of institutions to implement even policies that seemed on the surface to be win-win options. The failure to implement them is most often due to the social and political problems associated with distributing costs and benefits within and between groups and generations.

This Report integrates the findings of the last few WDRs into a broader and longer term framework to identify some elements of a process that might do better:

■ **The interaction between economic, social, and environmental problems and opportunities are manifested spatially—where people live.** For this reason, the report takes a spatial perspective on the social transformations and the opportunities for growth and poverty reduction—in fragile lands, in more favored agricultural lands, in urban areas. Some of the local problems can be handled locally—but others must be dealt with nationally or globally.

■ **Problems that require lasting solutions often are not susceptible to quick fixes.** Everyone could be better off if cooperative solutions were agreed on and implemented. But often the rules and organizations to coordinate human behavior do not yet exist, are undeveloped, faulty, or weak—especially for problems with high transaction costs and longer time horizons. To be able to coordinate well requires institutions that:

  • Pick up signals about needs and problems, especially from the fringes.

  • Balance competing interests.

- Ensure credible commitments and accountability in executing agreed decisions.

- **Institutions need to be improved at many levels—from the local to the global—to promote growth in ways that protect environmental and social assets.** The institutions to manage and protect environmental and social assets are not emerging rapidly enough to address the consequences of the growing scale and interconnectedness of human activity. Action is required now—even for problems that will unfold over a longer period. Societies need to ensure an enabling environment for creativity, initiative, and learning. These initiatives can come from the public sector, the private sector, or civil society. Partnerships among these various actors are needed within and across countries. Many innovative institutions are emerging which need to be strengthened. The key is to find ways to scale up these initiatives.

- **Strengthening the foundations for better institutions requires overcoming the inequitable access to assets and the pervasive barriers to inclusion.** The needed institutions (and the solutions to tough problems) do not emerge when some interests are dispersed or when some groups in society are poor or in other ways disenfranchised. This affects the evolution and quality of institutions and their ability to solve problems over the longer term. The reciprocal relationship between the quality of institutions and the distribution of assets can get countries locked into vicious cycles that require a special effort to break out.

Inclusive societies, within and across countries, ensure that signals of emerging economic, social, or environmental problems are picked up from all groups, and that they can cooperate to solve tough problems. Put another way, empowering poor people and the disenfranchised—the people "at the fringes"—and giving them a real stake in society is the key to building the stronger institutions required for longer term sustainable development.

James D. Wolfensohn

ACRONYMS AND ABBREVIATIONS

ANC	African National Congress
BRAC	Bangladesh Rural Advancement Committee
BSE	Bovine spongiform encephalopathy ("mad cow disease")
CCAMLR	Convention on the Conservation of Antarctic Marine Living Resources
CCD	Convention to Combat Desertification
CDF	Comprehensive Development Framework
CGIAR	Consultative Group on International Agricultural Research
CIDA	Canadian International Development Agency
CIESIN	Center for International Earth Science Information Network
CITES	Convention on International Trade in Endangered Species
CLRTAP	Convention on Long-Range Transboundary Air Pollution
CSOs	Civil society organizations
EDUCO	El Salvador's Community-Managed Schools Program
EPA	U.S. Environmental Protection Agency
EROS	Earth Resources Observation System
EU	European Union
EWG	Environmental Working Group
FAO	Food and Agriculture Organization of the United Nations
FDA	U.S. Food and Drug Administration
FONAFIFO	National forestry fund (Costa Rica)
FRA	Forest Resources Assessment
GEF	Global Environment Facility
GHG	Greenhouse gas
GIS	Geographic information system
GMO	Genetically modified organism
HIPC	Heavily Indebted Poor Countries
ICRG	International Country Risk Guide
IIED	International Institute for Environment and Development
IISA	International Institute of Applied Systems Analysis
IPCC	Intergovernmental Panel on Climate Change
IRRI	International Rice Research Institute
IUCN	Global Conservation Union
IWMI	The International Water Management Institute
MDG	Millennium Development Goals
MSC	Marine Stewardship Council
NEP	New Economic Policy
NEPAD	New Partnership for Africa's Development
NGOs	Nongovernmental organizations
NIC	Newly industrializing country
NOAA	U.S. National Oceanic and Atmospheric Administration
NSDF	National Slum Dwellers Federation (India)
ODESYPANO	Sylvo-Pastoral Development Authority (Tunisia)
OECD	Organisation for Economic Co-operation and Development
ORNL	Oak Ridge National Lab
PAN	Pesticides Action Network
PPP	Purchasing power parity
PRSP	Poverty Reduction Strategy Paper
RSDF	Railway Slum Dwellers Federation (India)
SINAMOS	National System for Social Mobilization (Peru)
SPARC	Society for the Promotion of Area Resource Centers (India)
TI	Transparency International
TRIPs	Trade-Related Aspects of Intellectual Property Rights
UCCI	Union of Capital Cities of Ibero-America
UNDP/GEF	United Nations Development Programme/Global Environment Facility
UNEP	United Nations Environment Programme
UNFCCC	United Nations Framework Convention on Climate Change
UNSO	United Nations Statistical Office
USDA	U.S. Department of Agriculture
USGS	U.S. Geological Survey
WCD	World Commission on Dams
WHO	World Health Organization
WRI	World Resources Institute
WTO	World Trade Organization
WWF	World Wildlife Fund
ZIES	Special residential zones of social interest

Roadmap to *World Development Report 2003*

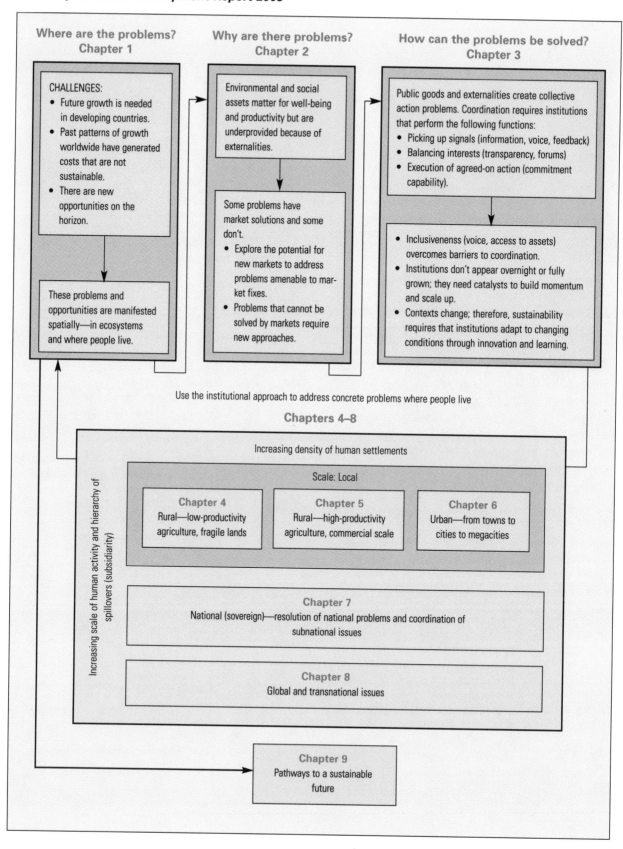

Where are the problems?
Chapter 1

CHALLENGES:
- Future growth is needed in developing countries.
- Past patterns of growth worldwide have generated costs that are not sustainable.
- There are new opportunities on the horizon.

These problems and opportunities are manifested spatially—in ecosystems and where people live.

Why are there problems?
Chapter 2

Environmental and social assets matter for well-being and productivity but are underprovided because of externalities.

Some problems have market solutions and some don't.
- Explore the potential for new markets to address problems amenable to market fixes.
- Problems that cannot be solved by markets require new approaches.

How can the problems be solved?
Chapter 3

Public goods and externalities create collective action problems. Coordination requires institutions that perform the following functions:
- Picking up signals (information, voice, feedback)
- Balancing interests (transparency, forums)
- Execution of agreed-on action (commitment capability).

- Inclusivenenss (voice, access to assets) overcomes barriers to coordination.
- Institutions don't appear overnight or fully grown; they need catalysts to build momentum and scale up.
- Contexts change; therefore, sustainability requires that institutions adapt to changing conditions through innovation and learning.

Use the institutional approach to address concrete problems where people live

Chapters 4–8

Increasing density of human settlements

Increasing scale of human activity and hierarchy of spillovers (subsidiarity)

Scale: Local

Chapter 4
Rural—low-productivity agriculture, fragile lands

Chapter 5
Rural—high-productivity agriculture, commercial scale

Chapter 6
Urban—from towns to cities to megacities

Chapter 7
National (sovereign)—resolution of national problems and coordination of subnational issues

Chapter 8
Global and transnational issues

Chapter 9
Pathways to a sustainable future

Roadmap to
World Development Report 2003

How can productive work and a good quality of life be provided for the 2.5–3 billion people now living on less than $2 a day—and the 3 billion people likely to be added to developing countries by 2050—in an environmentally and socially sustainable way? This report asks where problems and opportunities are likely to arise, why the problems arise, and how they can be solved (in fragile lands, relatively favored agricultural lands, and urban areas) and at different levels (local, national, and global). It argues that many appropriate policies are known but not implemented because of distributional issues and institutional weaknesses. Competent institutions pick up signals, balance interests, and execute agreed-on decisions. Inclusion of the poor and disenfranchised—giving them a stake in society through voice and access to assets—will enable more effective institutions to emerge.

Chapter 1
Achievements and Challenges

Provision of productive work and a better quality of life for current and future generations in developing countries will require substantial growth in income and productivity in these countries. This task will also require management of the social, economic, and environmental problems and opportunities accompanying the transition to a predominantly urban world (see figure 1); attention to the needs of the hundreds of millions of people living on fragile lands; reaping of the "demographic dividend" of declining depend-

Figure 1—Opportunities seized—or lost? Demographic and urban transitions

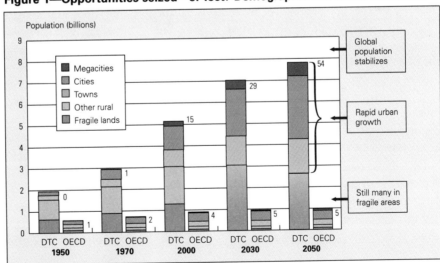

Note: DTC refers to developing and transition countries; OECD refers to high-income countries (and not all members of the Organisation for Economic Co-operation and Development). The numbers to the right of the columns show the number of megacities (cities in excess of 10 million people). Towns are classified as having a population of less than 100,000 and cities, a population of 100,000 to 10 million.
Source: Authors; global population projections are based on World Bank estimates; estimates of population shifts in urban and rural areas are based on United Nations data.

ency rates and slowing population growth; and avoidance of the social and environmental stresses—local and global—that might accompany achievement of the prospective, mid-century, approximately $140 trillion world gross domestic product (GDP). Although these problems and opportunities will play out differently in different places—in the ecosystems where people live and the social systems where they interact, at scales that range from a small mountain valley to a coastal metropolis to the planetary biosphere—many of the issues and the mechanisms needed to tackle them are common to all places.

Chapter 2
Managing a Broader Portfolio of Assets

Social and environmental assets are critical—but underprovided. Policy solutions are understood—but not implemented.

Societies need to manage a broad portfolio of assets—not just human and physical capital, but also environmental assets (such as fresh water and fish stocks) and social assets (such as trust). These assets are not perfectly substitutable. The immediate gains of depleting or degrading them can be outweighed by costs in productivity and lost options, as illustrated by forest conversion in Madagascar.

Productivity growth in agriculture is critical to poverty reduction in Madagascar, where nearly three-quarters of the population live in rural areas and where three-quarters of that population is poor. But conversion of Madagascar's biodiversity-rich forests, the potential focus of a future ecotourism industry, to mostly unsustainable, low-yield agriculture has been costly. Much of the new cropland is degraded, and hillside erosion clogs downslope waterways. The country has experienced a decrease in its per capita GDP from $383 (in 1995 dollars) in 1960 to $246 today. Madagascar is not the only country that has depleted or degraded forest assets without realizing gains in other assets. On average, forest depletion in low-income countries lowers net savings by 1.5 percent of GDP.

Why are environmental and social assets particularly threatened and underprovided? Because of externalities: the actions of one person may impose environmental costs (such as pollution) and social costs (diminished trust in institutions) on other people—costs that the responsible party does not bear. Free riders have no incentive to contribute to the maintenance of public goods from which they cannot be excluded.

The solution to these problems is well known: policies that align individual and social incentives, either through taxes, subsidies, and regulation, or through the deliberate creation of new market mechanisms. Failure to adopt such policies—even when they appear to be "win-win"—is most often the result of distributional problems and society's inability to make credible long-term commitments.

Chapter 3
Institutions for Sustainable Development

Problems that require lasting solutions are often not susceptible to quick fixes. Such problems require the coordination of many actors. Inclusion in the form of voice and access to assets facilitates coordination: more inclusive processes lead to more sustainable outcomes; voice and wider ownership of assets lead to more inclusive processes.

Avoiding inflation and protecting investors, ensuring labor and service delivery, maintaining environmental assets and systems for using them, preventing crimes and maintaining peace are all coordination problems. Markets work well for addressing some kinds of coordination problems—matching suppliers and demanders of goods, services, and physical assets—if supporting institutions such as property rights are in place. Mechanisms for other kinds of coordination problems, especially those in the social and environmental sphere, are often lacking, undeveloped, faulty, or weak.

Coordination mechanisms typically fail in three ways. First, *they fail to take the long view*. Cities grow without adequate provision for transport right of way. Short-term political fixes evolve into constituencies for perverse subsidies. Second, *they fail to represent dispersed interests*. The voices of the many who are affected by pollution may be less audible than the voices of those who pollute. Third, *they fail to commit to allow assets to thrive.* Wasteful destruction of forests, overexploitation of fisheries, plundering of people's savings through inflationary monetary policies—all reflect a lack of social mechanisms for restraint.

The collapses of the Newfoundland cod fisheries and of the U.S. energy and financial and risk management services company Enron illustrate these coordination failures—common problems in disparate realms. Potentially renewable assets—fish in one case, trust in the other—were depleted to the short-run benefit of some but the long-run loss of society (see figure 2).

Effective coordination requires institutions (informal and formal rules and organizations) that undertake the following functions: picking up signals (information, feedback, anticipation of future prob-

lems), balancing interests (transparency, voice, forums for negotiation), and executing agreed-on decisions (commitment and enforcement mechanisms). Such institutions are often lacking or are flawed, when some interests are dispersed or when some groups in society are poor or in other ways disenfranchised. Groups that lack assets tend also to lack voice, security, and a stake in the larger society, hampering institutions' ability to perform needed coordination functions. The result is a vicious cycle in which biased institutions implement policies that lead to an increase in polarization and unequal asset distributions (see figure 3).

That policies affect institutions and asset distribution is widely understood; less well known is that asset distribution affects the quality of institutions and policies.

This cycle can be broken. Certain mechanisms for promoting transparency, feedback, accountability, commitment, and negotiation of interests have been successfully applied in fragile lands, rural areas, and urban areas. These mechanisms do not change institutions overnight but help to build momentum for lasting change. Over the long run, fostering inclusiveness is essential. South Africa and Malaysia, among other countries, demonstrate that societies can make decisive moves toward inclusiveness when it becomes clear that failure to do so will be unsustainable.

Figure 2—Failure of institutions to protect assets

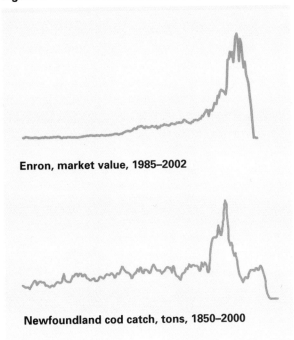

Enron, market value, 1985–2002

Newfoundland cod catch, tons, 1850–2000

Sources: Hannesson (2002); Center for Research in Security Prices, University of Chicago; New York Stock Exchange.

Figure 3—Policy-institutions-assets loop

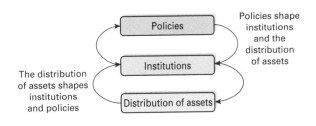

A local school and teacher enable girls to attend primary school for the first time in their village's history. *Photo courtesy of Robert Clement-Jones*

Chapter 4
Improving Livelihoods on Fragile Lands

Living on fragile lands—in arid zones, on slopes and poor soils, or in forest ecosystems—are an estimated 1.3 billion people, (see figures 4 and 5) a number that has doubled over the past 50 years. The inhabitants of these fragile lands account for a large share of people in extreme poverty. Living in remote areas and working in the informal economy, these people are invisible to decisionmakers.

Remotely located communities in some of the most fragile areas have a modest portfolio of assets that can help bring them out of poverty, but these assets are seldom nurtured by local or national institutions. Deftly combining resources for research and cost-effective services could enable these communities to catch up with more prosperous, less remotely located communities. Indeed, managing land to improve livelihoods underscores the strong link between traditional know-how and outside technical advice, which results in recognition of the land's potential and limitations.

By listening to grassroots organizations and testing ideas, governments, civil society, and donors can promote creativity, adaptable institutions, relevant policies, and workable solutions to address the social, environmental, and economic problems affecting one-quarter of the people in developing countries.

A Mongolian family moves camp for the winter. Mobility reduces overgrazing pressures, promotes sustainable grassland management, and ensures acceptable livelihoods. *Photo courtesy of Robin Mearns*

Figure 4—Fragile and nonfragile lands

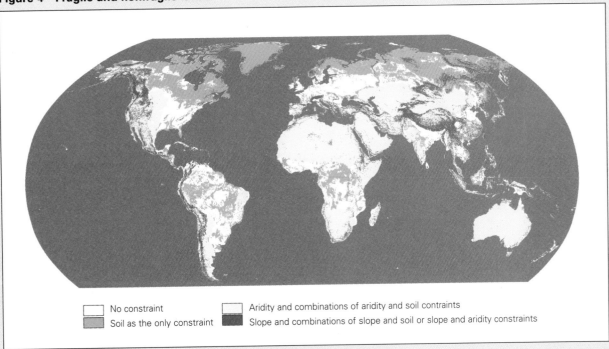

No constraint

Soil as the only constraint

Aridity and combinations of aridity and soil contraints

Slope and combinations of slope and soil or slope and aridity constraints

Nonfragile lands cover only a tiny fraction of the earth's surface, bear most of the world's population, and receive essentially all of the development attention. That the minority who live on fragile lands are nonetheless numerous, and are especially poor and voiceless, is a quintessential example of failure to balance interests.

Figure 5—Rural population on fragile and nonfragile lands

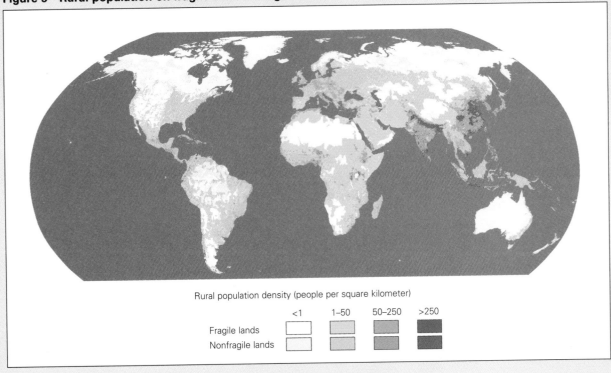

Rural population density (people per square kilometer)

	<1	1–50	50–250	>250
Fragile lands				
Nonfragile lands				

Figure 6—Projected water scarcity in 2025

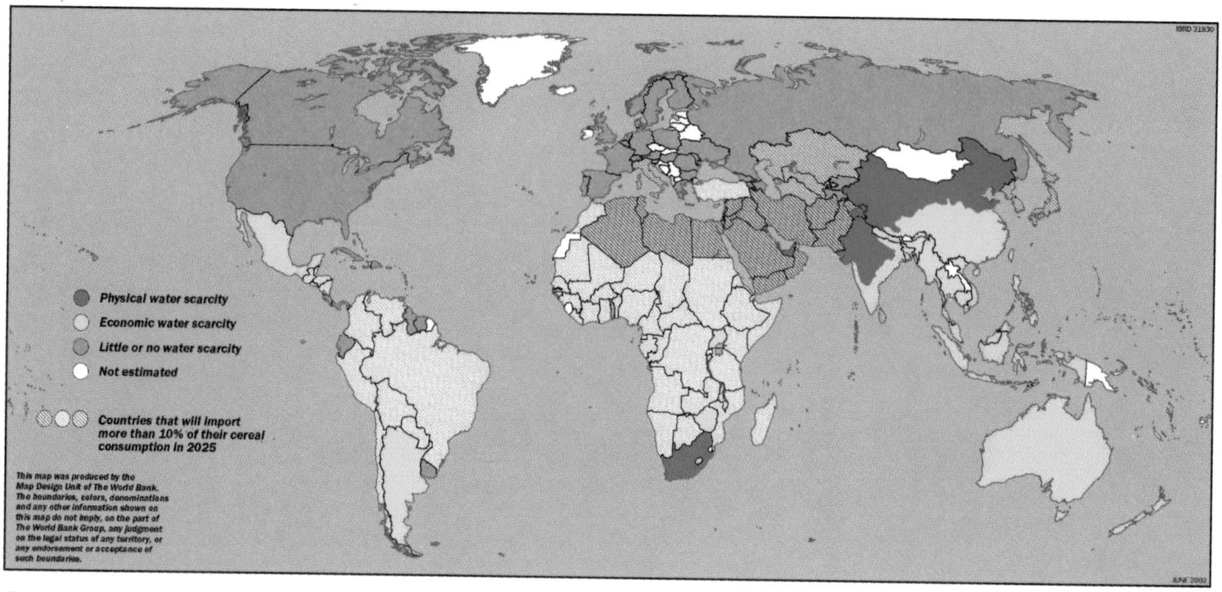

For countries with physical water scarcity, no reallocation of water or construction of water supply structures will satisfy all water needs. These countries will have to transfer water from agriculture to other sectors and import food, or invest in costly desalinization. Countries with economic water scarcity will have to increase their primary water supply by more than 25 percent through additional storage and conveyance facilities.

Source: Prepared by the International Water Management Institute as input for the World Water Vision, The Hague, March 2000.

Chapter 5
Transforming Institutions on Agricultural Lands

Over the next 30 to 50 years, the key development challenges for rural transformation are to eliminate rural poverty and strengthen rural-urban linkages, intensify agricultural production and sustainably manage land and water to feed a growing population, control wasteful land conversion, and create off-farm economic opportunities. In rural areas with potential for commercial agriculture, getting ahead of the "scarcity frontier" for both water and land is crucial. Many areas will experience physical or economic water scarcity by 2025 (see figure 6). Governments must establish institutions to equitably allocate water rights and ensure adequate stream flows to maintain aquatic ecosystems.

Similarly, governments must intervene to protect the environmental values of land before economic scarcity emerges. Mobilizing support for land management interventions, and implementing them, presents a host of institutional challenges. A promis-

ing new deforestation control program in Mato Grosso, Brazil, provides hope that these challenges can be met. An environmental licensing system uses satellite imagery and ground inspection to regulate land use by large landowners on five million hectares in the state of Mato Grosso. Through this system, the product of political will and technological and institutional innovation, Mato Grosso enhances enforcement of land use laws and deters wasteful conversion of Amazonian forest.

In the case of both water management and land management, two principles should apply. First, governments must anticipate and attempt to prevent resource management problems before those problems lead to severe environmental degradation. Second, where possible, allocation of rights to land and water should favor poor people. These principles ensure that non-market environmental values are protected as the economic frontier advances and that economic assets are put in the hands of poor people, developments that are good for the environment and for the evolution of local, regional, and national institutions.

A nationwide program to upgrade kampongs (slum settlements) in urban areas of Indonesia has provided basic infrastructural investments (water supply and sanitation, drainage, access roads and footpaths, lighting and other community service facilities) and security of tenure, dramatically improving living conditions for kampong residents and integrating their neighborhoods into cities. In this kampung in Banjarmasin in Kalimantan province, storm drainage works corrected chronic flooding. *Photos courtesy of James Fitz Ford, the World Bank*

Chapter 6
Getting the Best from Cities

Urban areas are expected to grow significantly in the next 30 years. The number of urban residents in developing countries and countries in economic transition will almost double through a combination of rural-to-urban migration, natural population increases in cities, and reclassification of adjacent rural areas as urban areas. The growth of urban areas will require physical expansion of the urban periphery as well as redevelopment and densification within cities.

The increase in share of national populations that will be living in urban areas (cities and towns) is one of the main forces of social and economic transformation. The massive new investment in the capital stock of cities required for the doubling of urban population by 2030 will be critical to environmental outcomes. Urban land use patterns, right of way arrangements, and building standards will affect energy and water use.

Some key urban development challenges are anticipating urban growth and guiding new settlements to prevent future slums, empowering the poor and excluded by providing access to assets (security of tenure), stimulating urban investment and job creation, and building informed constituencies to address environmental and social issues and anticipate risks. Institutions for urban governance need to link informal networks of social capital to formal structures so that together they can address the increasing scale and complexity of environmental and social assets in cities, while promoting a well-integrated labor market and improvements in the investment climate.

Often the urban poor have been left to fend for themselves, leading to the proliferation of large informal settlements without services (slums) where residents face serious environmental hazards. This neglect creates high private as well as social costs. These costs can be mitigated through corrective measures such as upgrading of investments through programs that involve slum residents in arranging their own resettlement when necessary to increase their safety and protect environmentally fragile areas. A more promising approach to upgrading of investments is to confirm the rights and responsibilities associated with the occupation and use of land, regularizing tenure status and thereby removing a major source of economic and political insecurity for households and communities. Tenure reduces some of the risks that discourage residents from investing in their houses and shops—and gives residents a stronger stake in urban society and an incentive to work with local officials to obtain services.

Chapter 7
Strengthening National Coordination

Because many externalities spill outside municipalities and regions, the nation is often the level at which interests can be balanced—directly or through facilitation of negotiation among localities. National actors help to create a framework and solve problems that cannot be resolved at local levels and are better placed than local actors to organize the provision of nonlocal public goods and to take advantage of scale economies when beneficiaries are spread among many subnational regions.

National concerns requiring coordination at different levels include the following: promoting inclusiveness (by fostering access to assets and voice), generating a sound investment climate (attending to macroeconomic fundamentals, strengthening governance, providing basic infrastructure), managing the environment (for instance, by regulating pollution and husbanding forests and fisheries), using aid and natural resources effectively (by avoiding natural resource depletion and degradation), and averting conflict.

Heavy reliance on natural resources (whether renewable, like forests, or nonrenewable, like minerals) for public revenues can, in many cases, retard the emergence of strong institutions (important for both economic performance and sustainable development) because this reliance weakens government accountability. Ensuring that development aid does not have a similar effect is a major focus in current efforts to improve the effectiveness of such aid.

The tragedy of violent conflict is more likely to visit countries with lootable natural resources and extreme poverty than countries without such resources and poverty. Poverty reduction and other forms of conflict prevention are essential, because the risk of conflict increases with poverty, economic stagnation, and a history of political turmoil. Providing public goods, reducing negative externalities, and avoiding conflict will require improved coordination at the national level by promoting inclusiveness and participation (through voice and improved access to assets) as well as creating the framework to foster partnerships among stakeholders from government, civil society, and the private sector.

Chapter 8
Global Problems and Local Concerns

Many local environmental and social problems spill over national borders. How can air pollution, water pollution, armed conflict, infectious disease, and other problems be addressed without a global authority? Some institutions are finding ways to align interests within and across borders to address the problems of stratospheric ozone depletion and transboundary acid rain. Other institutions are emerging to facilitate international coordination, including broader use of standards and certification and of "coupling institutions" that link policymakers and scientists, nurturing the development of creative new solutions to problems.

Figure 7—Population density in forests

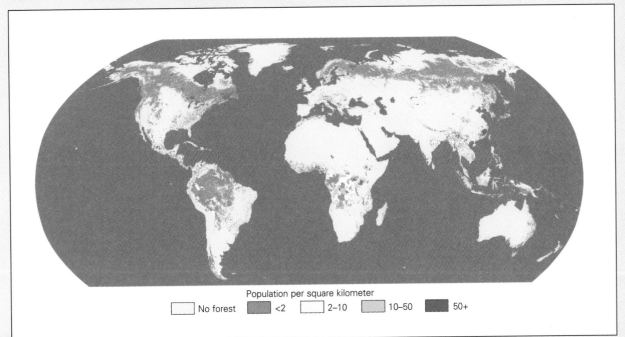

Population per square kilometer

☐ No forest   ■ <2   ☐ 2–10   ▨ 10–50   ■ 50+

Source: Authors' construction based on Columbia University's Center for International Earth Science Information Network's Gridded Population of the World dataset (version 2) and Global Land Cover Characterization. Mapped forests include deciduous broadleaf, deciduous needle leaf, evergreen broadleaf, evergreen needle leaf, and mixed forest; not mapped are savannas, shrublands, wooded wetlands, and tundra.

Two important global sustainability issues are deeply connected to local land, water, and energy use and have proven difficult to resolve: conserving biodiversity and maintaining ecosystems, and mitigating and adapting to climate change. Strategies for biodiversity conservation must operate at the level of entire ecosystems. The ecological and social issues related to sustainable forest management, for instance, will be quite different for vast, unpopulated forests than they will be for highly fragmented and densely populated forests (see figure 7).

Climate change, if unchecked, could have severe consequences. Long lead times, and concerted action at the required scale, are necessary to effect changes in both economic systems and the global climate system.

Chapter 9
Pathways to a Sustainable Future

Lack of assets and lack of an effective voice for large segments of the population block the emergence of competent institutions that can pick up signals early, balance interests, and commit to implementation of decisions. As a result, policies to avoid wasting of assets, particularly environmental and social assets, are not adopted and implemented. The more people heard, the fewer the assets that are wasted. These messages of *World Development Report 2003* inform a variety of recommendations and suggest some issues requiring further research and dialogue, including a global vision and accord on sustainable development.

CHAPTER 1

Achievements and Challenges

Worrld Development Report 2003 is about sustainable development. It is about people and how we deal with each other. It is about our home planet and its fabric of life. And it is about our aspirations for prosperity and posterity.

Any serious attempt at reducing poverty requires sustained economic growth in order to increase productivity and income in developing countries. But there is more to development than just economic growth—much more. This Report argues that ensuring sustainable development requires attention not just to economic growth but also to environmental and social issues. Unless the transformation of society and the management of the environment are addressed integrally along with economic growth, growth itself will be jeopardized over the longer term.

Environment and social issues, when not addressed, accumulate over time and have consequences that do not show up in the shorter time horizons typical of economic policymaking. That is why this Report adopts a longer time horizon of 20 to 50 years. Within this time frame it is possible to identify environmental and social problems—local, national, and global—that can have very costly or even irreversible consequences if not addressed immediately. For other problems, where the consequences are not irreversible, the longer time horizon provides the lead time to start changing attitudes and institutions and so make it possible to respond before the problems become crises.

In short, this Report takes a comprehensive, longer term, and dynamic view of sustainability, with a clear focus on poverty reduction.

The core development challenge

Most current estimates suggest that 2 billion people will be added to the world's population over the next 30 years and another billion in the following 20 years.[1] Virtually all of this increase will be in developing countries, the bulk of it in urban areas. In these same countries, 2.5 billion to 3 billion people now live on less than $2 a day.[2] The core challenge for development is to ensure productive work and a better quality of life for all these people. This will require substantial growth in productivity and incomes in developing countries.

The challenge may seem daunting—and it is. But over the past 30 years world population also rose by 2 billion.[3] And this growth was accompanied by considerable progress in improving human well-being, as measured by human development indicators. Average income per capita (population-weighted in 1995 dollars) in developing countries grew from $989 in 1980 to $1,354 in 2000.[4] Infant mortality was cut in half, from 107 per 1,000 live births to 58, as was adult illiteracy, from 47 to 25 percent.[5]

Looking back to the 1950s and 1960s, it was feared at the time that the developing countries—particularly China, India, and Indonesia—would not be able to feed their rapidly growing populations. Thanks to the green revolution in agriculture, the doomsday scenarios of famine and starvation did not materialize in these, the most populous, developing countries. In the 1960s and 1970s the Club of Rome and many other groups forecast that the Earth would rapidly run out of key natural resources. So far, this has not happened, again because changes in technology and in preferences have allowed the substitution of new resources for existing ones—for example, fiber optics in place of copper. Global action has also led to major strides in eliminating disease scourges (smallpox and river blindness), and in addressing new problems (ozone depletion).

But accompanying these achievements were some negative social and environmental patterns that must not be repeated in the next 50 years if development is to be sustained.

- *Poverty: declining, but still a challenge.* There has been a significant drop in the percentage of people living in extreme poverty (that is, living on less than $1 per day). Even the absolute number of very poor people declined between 1980 and 1998 by at least 200 million, to almost 1.2 billion in 1998.[6] The decrease was primarily due to the decline in the number of very poor people in China as a result of its strong growth from 1980 onward.[7] Since 1993, there have also been encouraging signs of renewed poverty reduction in India. Sub-Saharan Africa, by contrast, has seen its number of very poor people increase steadily. Yet in 1998, despite the decline in Asia and the increase in Sub-Saharan Africa, East Asia and South Asia still accounted for two-thirds of the world's very poor people, and Sub-Saharan Africa for one-quarter. Development strategies will need to do better in eliminating abject poverty. The estimated 1 billion very poor people is of the same order of magnitude as the independently generated figures on the number of people who are undernourished and underweight.[8]
- *Inequality: widening.* The average income in the richest 20 countries is now 37 times that in the poorest 20. This ratio has doubled in the past 40 years, mainly because of lack of growth in the poorest countries.[9] Similar increases in inequality are found within many (but not all) countries.
- *Conflict: devastating.* In the 1990s, 46 countries were involved in conflict, primarily civil.[10] This included more than half of the poorest countries (17 out of 33). These conflicts have very high costs, destroying past development gains and leaving a legacy of damaged assets and mistrust that impedes future gains.

The increased scale and reach of human activity have also put great pressure on local and global common property resources (water, soil, and fisheries), as well as on local and global sinks (the ability of the biosphere to absorb waste and regulate climate).

- *Air: polluted.* At the local level, hundreds of developing-country cities have unhealthy levels of air pollution (see chapter 3, figure 3.4). At the global level, the biosphere's capacity to absorb carbon dioxide without altering temperatures has been compromised because of heavy reliance on fossil fuels for energy. Global energy use traditionally has grown at the same rate as gross domestic product (GDP). Greenhouse gas (GHG) emissions will continue to grow unless a concerted effort is made to increase energy efficiency and move away from today's heavy reliance on fossil fuels.[11] In the past 50 years excess nitrogen—mainly from fertilizers, human sewage, and combustion of fossil fuels—has begun to overwhelm the global nitrogen cycle, giving rise to a variety of ill effects ranging from reduced soil fertility to excess nutrients in lakes, rivers, and coastal waters. On current trends, the amount of biologically available nitrogen will double in 25 years.[12]
- *Fresh water: increasingly scarce.* Fresh water consumption is rising quickly, and the availability of water in some regions is likely to become one of the most pressing issues of the 21st century. One-third of the world's people live in countries that are already experiencing moderate to high water shortages. That proportion could (at current population forecasts) rise to half or more in the next 30 years unless institutions change to ensure better conservation and allocation of water.[13] More than a billion people in low- and middle-income countries—and 50 million people in high-income countries—lacked access to safe water for drinking, personal hygiene, and domestic use in 1995.[14]
- *Soil: being degraded.* Nearly 2 million hectares of land worldwide (23 percent of all cropland, pasture, forest, and woodland) have been degraded since the 1950s. About 39 percent of these lands are lightly degraded, 46 percent moderately degraded, and 16 percent so severely degraded that the change is too costly to reverse. Some areas face sharp losses in productivity. Grasslands do not fare much better: close to 54 percent show degradation, with 5 percent being strongly degraded.[15]

■ *Forests: being destroyed.* Deforestation is proceeding at a significant rate. One-fifth of all tropical forests have been cleared since 1960.[16] According to the Food and Agriculture Organization of the United Nations (FAO), deforestation has been concentrated in the developing world, which lost nearly 200 million hectares between 1980 and 1995. In the Brazilian Amazon annual deforestation rates varied between 11,000 and 29,000 square kilometers a year in the 1990s. Deforestation in developing countries has several causes, including the conversion of forests to large-scale ranching and plantations and the expansion of subsistence farming. At the same time, forest cover in industrial countries is stable or even increasing slightly, although the forest ecosystem has been somewhat altered. According to a 1997 World Resources Institute (WRI) assessment, just one-fifth of the Earth's original forest remains in large, relatively natural ecosystems.[17]

■ *Biodiversity: disappearing.* Through a series of local extinctions, the ranges of many plants and animals have been reduced from those at the beginning of the century. In addition, many plants and animals are unique to certain areas. One-third of terrestrial biodiversity, accounting for 1.4 percent of the Earth's surface, is in vulnerable "hot spots" and is threatened with complete loss in the event of natural disasters or further human encroachment.[18] Some statistics suggest that 20 percent of all endangered species are threatened by species, introduced by human activity, alien to the locality.[19]

■ *Fisheries: declining.* The aquatic environment and its productivity are on the decline. About 58 percent of the world's coral reefs and 34 percent of all fish species are at risk from human activities.[20] Seventy percent of the world's commercial fisheries are fully exploited or overexploited and experiencing declining yields.[21]

None of these social and environmental patterns is consistent with sustained growth in an interdependent world over the long term. Given the social and environmental stresses caused by past development strategies, the goal of raising human well-being worldwide must be pursued through a development process that "does better"—a poverty-eliminating growth path that integrates social and environmental concerns in pursuit of the goal of sustained improvements in well-being.

Windows of opportunity

The development process is about change and transformation. Economies evolve. Societies and cultures evolve. Nature evolves. But they evolve at different speeds, creating stresses that need to be addressed and managed.[22] Moreover, in an era of globalization, the growing scale and speed of change in human activity are in some cases outpacing the rate at which natural processes and life-support systems can adapt.[23] Globalization and faster technological change are also altering the nature of social interaction and affecting the efficacy of existing institutions. Although globalization and technological change offer many benefits, they can have deleterious side effects if institutions at local, national, and international levels do not evolve fast enough to deal with the adverse spillovers. The consequences of previous patterns of development are also beginning to bind, restricting certain growth paths or making them more costly.[24]

But these processes, if managed well, can create new opportunities. Of the many interrelated drivers of change and transformation, four stand out: scientific and technological innovation, income growth, population growth, and urbanization. The first two are likely to continue changing preferences and providing new opportunities to satisfy these preferences. The demographic and urban transitions, by contrast, are one-time changes, and the opportunities they offer are perhaps less well recognized. These are discussed in the next section.

■ *Scientific and technological innovation.* The flow of information and ideas, boosted greatly by the Internet, can enable developing countries to learn more rapidly from each other and from industrial countries. It can also facilitate the emergence of networks to monitor a wider array of development impacts. Other technological changes can enable developing countries to leapfrog stages in the development process that rely on inefficient uses of natural resources. Science and technology can help address major socioeconomic problems. As noted, the green revolution was critical in enabling many developing countries to avoid widespread starvation. To benefit from these opportunities, institutions are needed that can stimulate and diffuse technological innovations and avoid or mitigate any deleterious consequences.

■ *Income growth.* A projected growth in global income of 3 percent a year over the next 50 years implies a fourfold increase in global GDP. Increasing income growth may place a strain on the environmental and social fabric if there is too little attention to shifting consumption and production patterns. But this future economic growth will also require major investments in new human-made capital to expand capacity and to replace existing capacity as it ages. Making these investments (many of which are long lived) more environmentally and socially responsible through appropriate investment criteria will go a long way toward putting development on a more sustainable path—an opportunity not to be missed.

Opportunities in the demographic transition
When today's industrial countries were themselves developing, their population densities and growth rates were much lower than those of developing countries today, and the pressure on their resources was consequently lower. They also had a more evenly distributed age structure and lower dependency rates, allowing social institutions to adapt gradually to the requirements of a changing population.

Populations in industrial countries as a group were fairly stable for most of the second half of the 20th century. As a result, the growth in world population in this period has been driven primarily by population growth in developing countries. The stresses and spillovers from this population growth are generally observed not, as was originally expected, at the aggregate level (for example, in large-scale famines and food shortages) but, rather, in more insidious ways—in many smaller interactions between population, poverty, and resources.[25] The outcomes are felt in greater pressures on fragile lands, in lower wages, and in persistent unemployment.

It is now clear that a global demographic transition is well underway, even if it is not yet complete. This is a major historic opportunity. World population is expected to stabilize by the end of this century at 9 billion to 10 billion people, 20 to 30 percent lower than forecast in the 1960s and 1970s. Many factors have contributed to this slowdown:

■ More educated, employed women and smaller families

Figure 1.1
Global population approaching stability

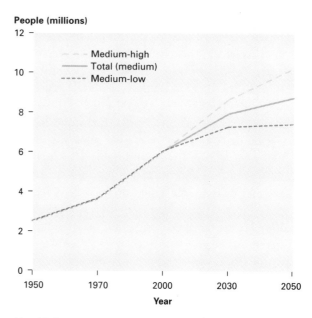

Note: Medium-high and medium-low variants based on U.N. projections of medium-high and medium-low scenarios scaled to World Bank aggregates.
Source: World Bank estimates.

■ Greater off-farm opportunities, creating a need for more education for children
■ Widespread dissemination of modern contraceptive technology, making it easier for people to plan childbearing.

Of the expected population increase, 85 percent (3 billion) will be born in the next 50 years (figure 1.1). But the speed of the transition, and the resulting population size and structure, will vary by region (figure 1.2) and by country. If fertility rates do not fall as rapidly as now projected, aggregate populations will be larger, putting greater pressures on natural resources and the social fabric. If they drop faster, many countries will have to deal sooner than expected with another problem—an aging population. This can have major consequences, especially for rural populations, for whom formal social safety nets are either nonexistent or not well developed. For example, one consequence of China's one-child policy—which dramatically and successfully lowered aggregate population—may be that by 2030 as much as one-third of the population will be over age 65.[26]

Figure 1.2
Some regions growing fast, others stable

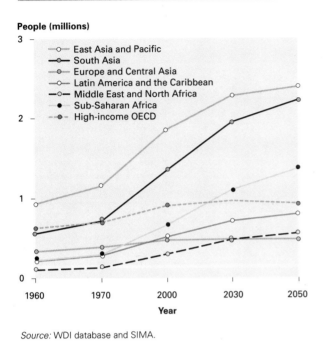

People (millions)

- ○ East Asia and Pacific
- ● South Asia
- ○ Europe and Central Asia
- ○ Latin America and the Caribbean
- ○ Middle East and North Africa
- ● Sub-Saharan Africa
- ○ High-income OECD

Year

Source: WDI database and SIMA.

Influencing the demographic processes in many countries is the growing incidence of HIV/AIDS, malaria, and tuberculosis. For example, current estimates and projections in Sub-Saharan Africa indicate increasingly large losses of working-age people to the AIDS epidemic. The economic impact of such high mortality is especially serious because enormous private and public investments have already been made in members of this age group. The loss of their productive lives leaves large and unpredictable gaps in the labor force. Malaria causes high levels of adult sickness rather than deaths, but this too inflicts heavy losses on labor productivity. Changes in the incidence of disease will have profound effects on health expenditures in these African countries.

With declining fertility, the age structure of the population changes, opening a window of opportunity in developing countries for a few decades—a window they can use for catching up and raising welfare for all. As figure 1.3 shows, the proportion of the working-age population rises in relation to the proportions of children (those under 15) and the elderly (over 65), enabling societies to spend less on school construction and on old-age medical expenses and to invest the savings in generating economic growth. But such benefits will materialize only if the

members of the working-age population are gainfully employed and have opportunities to expand their asset base. Eventually, dependency ratios rise again as these workers age, and the window of opportunity starts to close, as it will soon begin doing in East Asia and Eastern Europe (see figure 1.3).

Some regions, notably East Asia, have benefited substantially from the drop in the ratio of dependents to workers.[27] Investment in forming a skilled, healthy labor force, combined with policy and institutional settings conducive to using this labor force effectively, helped generate strong economic growth. Two keys to success were maintenance of an open economy and investment in sectors with high growth potential. Since most developing regions will continue to experience relatively low dependency ratios for some decades, careful preparation now can help make the most of their windows of opportunity.

Until now, populations have been growing too rapidly for fiscally constrained governments to expand the provision of jobs, infrastructure, and public services enough to keep pace with people's needs. This task will become easier now that the global population is approaching stability. Governments in both urban and rural areas can move from catching up with the quantitative need for services, to upgrading their quality. Much of the social tension and frustration arising from unemployment and poor public services can then be attenuated.

Lower rates of population growth will reduce pressure on natural resources, but this will be offset by the increase in per capita consumption. The latter trend makes it essential to adopt the technologies and growth paths for production and consumption that will ensure the sustainable use of natural resources. To benefit from the opportunities a stabilizing population provides, it is critical to anticipate problems and identify development strategies for getting through the transition period (the next 20 to 50 years) without creating conditions that generate further conflict or resource degradation.

Opportunities in the urban transition

As countries move from poverty to affluence, the required growth in productivity involves a shift from heavy dependence on agriculture as a primary source of employment and income to nonagricultural activities that do not make intensive use of land. This is generally accompanied by a major shift in population from rural to urban areas. Indeed, the most

Figure 1.3
Dependency ratios on the decline—for a while

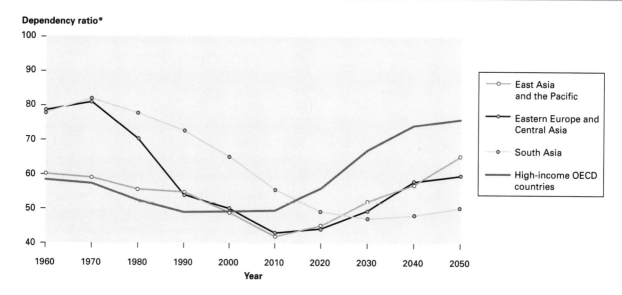

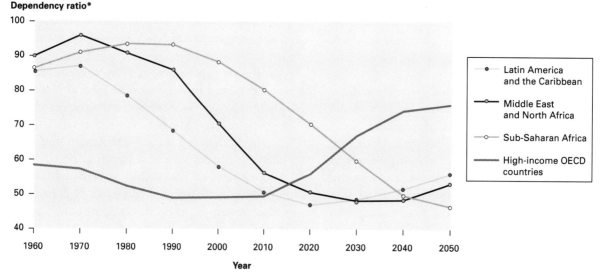

* The dependency ratio is the ratio of the non-working-age population (under 15 years old and over 64 years old) to the working-age population (ages 15 to 64).
Source: World Bank (2001g)

important socioeconomic and cultural transformation over the past 150 years has been the transformation of relatively closed, exclusive, custom-based rural societies into relatively open, inclusive, innovation-oriented urban societies.[28]

Rural communities, especially in less accessible areas, have long adapted to their circumstances, developing vibrant, self-sufficient communities. As long as risks could be absorbed locally, these communities continued to learn and adapt. Dependence on local

ecosystems, however, imposed limits on risk taking and innovation. This autonomous development path changes as rural areas become drawn into larger markets and strengthen their links with urban areas, making trade networks and distance from market centers more critical features of development opportunities and local resource pressures.

Increasing densities in towns and cities, and the greater connectivity between cities, as well as between urban and rural areas, increases the catchment area of markets and the returns to economic endeavor. If managed well, this transformation enables the emergence of new activities and productive job opportunities. Towns, as market centers for a rural hinterland, start the process of creating economies of scale for nonagricultural activities. Urban society also permits the spreading of risks over larger numbers of people and activities. Knowledge flows more readily, through increased opportunities for face-to-face contacts among various actors. And the need to accommodate diverse views and meet rapidly changing challenges stimulates innovation and new applications of technology. As a result, larger cities become incubators of new values—among them, risk taking and innovation.

Creativity, knowledge flow, the increasing scale of activities, and larger catchment areas are central to specialization and productivity growth. This is true not just for the production of goods but also for the provision of services. A village or neighborhood can support a primary school or basic clinic, and the local teacher or doctor can be a generalist. But providing higher, more sophisticated, and more differentiated education and health care requires more specialized skills. Because of the fixed costs of supporting these specialized skills, a larger catchment area (a town or a subsection of a city) is required. The higher population densities, lower transport costs, and lower communications costs in towns and cities make the more specialized operations possible. In moving further up the hierarchy of required specialization, the required catchment area also increases. So, the transition from villages to towns, and from cities to metropolitan areas, corresponds to the different functional capabilities of larger, higher-density conurbations. The potential benefits of higher densities and greater connectivity can be more easily realized if the investment climate is improved through better enabling rules and frameworks and better physical infrastructure. Stimulating and attracting investments—in particular, by the small and medium-size enterprises that provide most of the jobs for growing urban populations—is the key to accommodating the expected growth in urban populations and ensuring their ability to pay for needed urban services and amenities.

Seeing the socioeconomic transformations in spatial terms

Economists and engineers focus on the sectoral changes that accompany economic growth and technological innovations. This is understandable when focusing on GDP and the emergence or obsolescence of industries, but it is not very helpful for understanding the impact of these changes on society and nature. The most fundamental social and economic transformation—from traditional rural to modern urban—is manifested spatially. Except in the most populous countries, such as China and India, rural societies are relatively low in density and heavily dependent on agriculture as the primary source of employment and output. Modern urban societies are generally higher in density and dependent on activities that benefit from proximity and do not require a great deal of land, such as manufacturing and services. These activities and land use patterns generate different types of sociocultural and environmental problems.

Most ecosystems, too, are defined spatially. Much flora and fauna is locally unique and adapts gradually to changes in local circumstances. Local problems and stresses appear earliest, whether in the form of local extinctions, the reduction of the ranges of many plants and animals, or soil, air, and water pollution. These changes, the result of local development pressures, do not show up at national and global levels until they accumulate, but they provide early warning of problematic consequences of current development patterns.

The jurisdictions of many institutions that make or implement rules and laws (legislatures, constitutions, and government agencies) are also defined spatially. Often, the spatial jurisdiction of institutions does not match the spatial nature of the social and environmental problems generated by economic activity—one reason for the persistence of these problems.

Given our interest in people, where they live, and how they interact with each other and with nature, it is important to look at where people are now and where they are likely to be in the future. The world's population increased by more than 3.5 billion people in the past 50 years, and 85 percent of these added people were in developing and transition countries (see Figure 1 in the Roadmap). The number of people living in fragile rural areas in developing countries doubled, in stark contrast to the declining numbers in this category in high-income countries. The number of cities with a population of more than 10 million people went from 0 to 15 in developing countries but only from 1 to 4 in high-income countries.

In the next 30 to 50 years the 2 billion to 3 billion increase in the world's population will be almost exclusively (97 percent) in developing and transition countries, and virtually all of it will be in urban areas. The growth of the urban population is driven by natural increase, rural-to-urban migration, and the incorporation of high-density rural areas on the urban fringe. The number of megacities in developing countries is likely to increase to 54, while it will stabilize at 5 in high-income countries. It is not yet clear whether the number of people living in fragile areas will continue to increase, but it probably will unless migration opportunities change. As many as 2 billion people will live in two areas that are difficult to manage: fragile rural areas and megacities.[29] Dealing with these people's needs will be a major challenge, since there is not much experience in industrial countries that can be adapted to their needs.

The following are some of the key questions with local and global implications that will face the world's population over the next two to five decades:

■ Will rural populations—especially those on fragile lands, in more commercially active areas, and on agricultural frontiers—be able to overcome poverty, improve their livelihoods, and adapt to new opportunities, including opportunities in towns and cities?

■ Will the rapidly growing cities of the developing world live up to their potential as dynamic engines of growth and social modernization, or will they get mired in poverty, pollution, congestion, and crime?

■ Will renewable resources—particularly forests, soil, water, biodiversity, and fisheries—be depleted, or will they be managed as indefinitely sustained sources of livelihood and well-being?

■ Will societies be sufficiently creative, resilient, and forward-looking as they undergo sweeping transformations in patterns of growth and migration? Will they be able to promote more equitable development and cope with unexpected shocks?

■ Will poor countries be able to accelerate their growth without destabilizing social and environmental stresses? Will the prospective $140 trillion world GDP at mid-century generate fewer environmental and social stresses than the much smaller global economy today?

These are difficult but important questions, which this Report cannot answer definitely. However, it identifies an approach and process that should generate more dialogue and creativity in finding answers.

The interactions among society, economy, and nature vary in the different spatial arenas, although problems across locations are linked. Productivity increases in agriculture help feed the cities. Innovation and productivity increases in the cities help raise productivity and the quality of life in rural areas. Geography matters because of the characteristics of local ecosystems, such as the cost of overcoming local diseases.[30] Geography also matters because of geometry in the form of connectivity and distance to central nodes and markets; the cost of transport is more important here than that of communication.[31] Indeed, the strong association between rural poverty in remote and fragile ecosystems becomes more apparent when the problem is viewed through a spatial lens.

For this reason, the Report is organized by spatial areas that have different characteristics and require correspondingly different approaches to their development.

Fragile lands. The estimated 1.3 billion people living on fragile lands have modest assets that can help bring them out of extreme poverty, but these assets are seldom nurtured by local or national institutions. The people have land that is subject to many constraints, making it vulnerable to degradation, erosion, floods, and landslides. They possess human capital, which is handicapped by restrictive traditions, limited mobility, lack of voice, and poor access to services. This is even more true for women, who are thus the most marginal group. The mainly poor people on fragile lands also face circumstances vastly different from their counterparts on Europe's rural periphery 50 to 100 years ago. Today, international migration is highly restricted, and while rural-to-urban migration is important for them, there are limited numbers of jobs at above-subsistence wages for unskilled workers, especially in the low-growth economies. As a result, as noted above, instead of declining sharply, the number of people living on fragile lands is estimated to have doubled in the past 50 years—despite some outmigration.

Rural areas with potential for commercial crops. The problem of feeding a growing and more urban population calls for better management of the interaction with nature, particularly with respect to land and water (extensification versus intensification of agriculture). Whether or not rural families have land, water, and education is critical to their current livelihood, as well as to their ability to move to cities in the future. More egalitarian access to these assets is also crucial for determining the quality of society's institutions. A successful rural-urban transition requires the elimination of poverty for those who stay in the countryside and better preparation of those who move to the cities. It also demands protection of remaining natural ecosystems and habitats, given their central role in maintaining life-support systems and biodiversity. This latter requirement is one reason to intensify agricultural production in areas already under commercial crops and pasture. Intensification in such areas not only minimizes pressure on biodiversity and on marginal agricultural areas but also increases the food available to cities and leads to dynamic rural-urban linkages. Higher population density in these rural areas would also make investments in health and education more cost-effective and would increase the potential for off-farm employment and help farmers accept risk and innovate.

Urban areas. Cities of the developing world face a formidable undertaking, given the expected rapid rate of growth and sheer numbers of urban residents to be employed, housed, and serviced. The characteristics of periurban settlements, towns, cities, and megacities—higher density, large scale of settlement, and greater social diversity—facilitate the creation of productive employment opportunities, efficient provision of services, and access to ideas and learning. But having many people at close quarters also creates the potential for social problems—crime and social dislocation—and for environmental spillovers that pose health and safety hazards, especially for those living in neighborhoods without sanitation or drainage and in potential disaster zones. The long life of urban physical capital stock can lock in certain development paths, making changes costly. If managed well, urban areas can be the future engines of growth. If not, their environmental and social problems will be concentrated and difficult to fix.

The discussion of problems affecting fragile lands, rural commercial areas, and urban settings, and of possible solutions, is important because many public goods and externalities are local in nature and are, in principle, amenable to action at the local level. An enabling framework for local action and the principle of subsidiarity require that public goods and ex-

ternalities that affect wider catchments be addressed, at higher levels—national and global.

At the national level. The political, legal, and market domain for coordinating many activities is frequently the nation. Many externalities spill over beyond local communities and municipalities, and even across regional boundaries. The nation is thus often the level at which interests can be balanced, either directly or by facilitating negotiation among localities. National actors may be better placed to organize the provision of public goods and to take advantage of scale economies when the beneficiaries extend beyond subnational regions. Generating a strong investment climate, including sound macroeconomic fundamentals, good governance, and basic infrastructure, requires a framework that is typically national in scope. Dismantling perverse subsidies, husbanding forests and fisheries, and curbing water and air pollution in river basins and airsheds are major national challenges. Managing foreign aid and avoiding civil conflict are other key national concerns that determine whether development is sustainable.

At the global level. Many economic, environmental, and social processes—knowledge, conflict, disease, pollution, migration, and finance—spill over national boundaries. A few of these processes generate problems that are purely global: depletion of the stratospheric ozone layer is an example. But most global problems and opportunities are experienced at the local level as well. Automobiles that pollute local airsheds also generate greenhouse gases; wetland destruction that disrupts local water resources also undermines biodiversity of global significance; new ideas that are generated in one place can benefit people in other places, near and far. The public goods nature of many of these issues and the need to address the negative externalities requires coordination across boundaries. The distinctive challenge for global issues is to balance interests and commit to solutions in the absence of a global authority.

Act now—for long-term problems

Before proceeding to a discussion of local, national, and global issues, this Report sets forth a framework which argues that social and environmental outcomes have a bearing on human well-being both directly and through their effect on growth. When social and environmental issues are systematically neglected for long periods, economic growth will be affected. That is why improving the quality of life for those living in poverty today—and for the 2 billion to 3 billion people who will be added to the world's population over the next 50 years—will require a growth path that integrates environmental and social concerns more explicitly.

Some problems of sustainability are already urgent and require immediate action; examples are local ecosystems where population is pressing on deeply degraded soils, and forests and water stocks that have been nearly depleted. In such cases productivity is already on the decline and opportunities for correction or mitigation may even have been lost; abandonment of existing practices and outmigration may be necessary. The urgency of some of these problems has been overlooked because the people most affected are physically remote from centers of power, or because their voices are not heard, or both.

Some issues call for immediate action because there are good prospects for reversing the damage to the environment at relatively low cost, as in taking measures against air and water pollution. Even then, undoing some of the damage to the affected population (such as the respiratory damage caused by breathing air laden with particulates) may not be fully possible. But knowing the health impacts does create a moral imperative to protect those affected from further exposure, to compensate them to the extent possible, and to prevent others from becoming victims.

Another category of issues unfolds over a longer time horizon. The problems may not yet be urgent, but the direction of change is unmistakable. For these, it is essential to get ahead of the curve and prevent a worsening crisis before it is too costly. Biodiversity loss and climate change are in this category: there is already a need to adapt to the consequences of past and current behavior, but there is also still scope for mitigation, though not for complacency. Similarly, the need to anticipate urban growth by facilitating low-income settlements in safe areas and by setting aside major rights-of-way and spaces for public amenities makes it necessary to act now to avoid greater costs and regrets later.

What is clear is that almost all of the challenges of sustainable development require that action be initiated in the near term, whether to confront immediate crises, such as the health risks to children from unsanitary living conditions in existing slums, or to stem the tide of crises where concerted action in the near term could avert much greater costs and disruption to human development in the longer term.

In looking back over past successes and failures in solving development problems, it is clear that there have been more successes where markets function well (for example, in providing food to people with effective demand), even where the problems that markets have to solve (such as transport and communications) are relatively complex. The major problems that remain (inclusion, poverty reduction, deforestation, biodiversity, and global warming) are, however, generally not amenable to standard market solutions, although markets can help solve subsets of these problems.

One difficulty is that environmental and social assets suffer from underinvestment and overuse because they have the characteristics of public goods:

- Sometimes, ignorance of the consequences of action leads to overuse or underprovision. The ignorance is in part due to underinvestment in knowledge and understanding—itself a public good.[32]
- In other cases there are no mechanisms for facilitating cooperation among individuals, communities, or countries even when it is clear to those involved that the returns to cooperation (especially in the long run), exceed the returns to unilateral action (especially in the short run).
- In still other cases the gains from acting in the broader interests of society fail to be realized because correcting a spillover has distributional consequences and the potential losers resist change.
- Sometimes underprovision is a response to perceived tradeoffs between growth and the costs of correcting externalities. These tradeoffs may be the unfortunate outcome of having been boxed into a corner through a past failure of foresight. Or there may be genuinely difficult choices in balancing legitimate interests and assessing the value of nonmarket benefits and risk reduction, especially if those who would benefit are dispersed over current and future generations.

Environmental and social stresses reflect the failure of institutions to manage and provide public goods, to correct spillovers, and to broker differing interests. Because the spatial extent of spillovers varies by problem, appropriate institutions are needed at different levels, from local through national to global.

Getting to socially preferred outcomes requires institutions that can identify who bears the burden of social and environmental neglect and who benefits—and who can balance these diverse interests within society. This perspective helps in understanding why technically sound policy advice (for instance, "eliminate perverse incentives" or "impose charges on environmental damages") is so seldom taken up.

The emphasis of this Report is not on identifying a specific set of policies or outcomes considered advantageous but on the processes by which such policies and outcomes are selected. Outcomes emerging from strong processes are more robust. In many cases, and increasingly, institutions respond too late or too poorly—or without the capacity to commit to a course of action. In today's world the lag between the emergence of a problem and the emergence of institutions that can respond to it is too long. We need to see farther down the road. Why? Because institutions that facilitate and manage national economic growth, and even globalization, are still inadequate, yet where such institutions are in fact emerging, they are developing faster than complementary institutions that might be able to avoid or cope with the deleterious environmental and social consequences of economic change.

CHAPTER 2

Managing a Broader Portfolio of Assets

What we are doing to the forests of the world is but a mirror reflection of what we are doing to ourselves and to one another.

—Mahatma Gandhi

Sustainable development is about enhancing human well-being through time. What constitutes a good life is highly subjective, and the relative importance accorded to different aspects of well-being varies for individuals, societies, and generations.[1] But on some elements most people could probably agree. Having the ability and opportunity to shape one's life—which increase with better health, education, and material comfort—is certainly one of them. Having a sense of self-worth is another, enhanced by family and social relationships, inclusiveness, and participation in society. So is enjoying physical security and basic civil and political liberties. And so is appreciating the natural environment—breathing fresh air, drinking clean water, living among an abundance of plant and animal varieties, and not irrevocably undermining the natural processes that produce and renew these features. Indeed, peoples' self-reported happiness and satisfaction with life are closely associated with all of these factors.[2]

Society's ability to enhance human well-being through time depends on choices made by individuals, firms, communities, and governments on how to use and transform their assets. They might cut down forests to build dams and other physical infrastructure or to make way for commercial agriculture or urban expansion. They might clear mangroves to build shrimp farms. Or they may conserve forests and mangroves to maintain important natural processes or to support tourism. Enhancing human well-being on a sustained basis requires that society manage a portfolio of assets. Different assets have different characteristics that limit the extent to which they can substitute for one another in production and in human well-being.

This chapter discusses the broad concerns that need to be taken into account when balancing the objectives of economic growth and attending to environmental considerations and their social underpinnings in the short to medium term—recognizing that over the longer term prolonged neglect of environmental and social assets is likely to jeopardize the durability of economic growth. More specifically, it addresses the following questions:

■ What is meant by sustainable development and how can progress toward it be measured? Although the adjusted net savings indicator is a potentially useful headline indicator at the aggregate level, indicators are most useful when they can be disaggregated and used to diagnose and ultimately address specific problems.

■ Why the need to manage a broader portfolio of assets? What choices can and must be made between creating, maintaining, and restoring different assets as part of a long-term, dynamic view of sustainability? Although assets are complementary and substitutable to a certain degree, they all need to be managed, since once the quality or level of an asset falls below a threshold, there can be little further substitution without jeopardizing the productivity of other assets, as well as overall production.

■ What are alternative development paths to those followed by developed countries? What tradeoffs and priorities are justified, and when? By taking advantage of technological innovations and by learning from past mistakes of others, countries today have the option to manage their portfolio of assets in a different way to ensure they are on a more sustainable development path in the long term.

■ How to address the almost endemic overuse or underprovision of environmental and social assets while sustaining growth? Wherever spillovers (externalities) exist, there is a coordination problem that needs to be dealt with by correcting market and policy failures. This can be done by using a variety of mechanisms such as command-and-control regulations, harnessing market forces, and improving supporting institutions.

Sustainability—an evolving framework

What is meant by sustainability?

For any given technology, preference structure, and known resource base there are some utilization rates that cannot be sustained. Drawing attention to these unsustainable rates is critical to informing decision-makers and changing course toward sustainability. This will often require altering the pattern of preferences, the resource intensity of technologies, or the relevant time horizon for different decisions. Since none of these is constant or stable over time, defining sustainability in a broader sense is not easy—but there have been many attempts. The most commonly used definition is the one provided by the World Commission on Environment and Development (Brundtland Commission 1987): "progress that meets the needs of the present without compromising the ability of future generations to meet their own needs."

While the Brundtland definition highlights the need to balance the interests of current and future generations, it does not define the concept of *needs* or its implications. For instance, does the Brundtland definition imply that well-being (utility) should not fall below some minimum for any subsequent generation? Does it imply that each generation should enjoy a constant level of well-being? Alternatively, should well-being be nondeclining for each future generation? Most later definitions have retained the core ethic of intergenerational equity, emphasizing the current generation's moral obligation to ensure that future generations enjoy at least as good a quality of life as the current generation has now (Pezzey 1989).

Recent definitions have focused more explicitly on the three pillars of sustainability: economic, environmental, and social. These highlight the need to consider not only the environmental, or even the environmental and economic aspects, but also the social aspects of sustainability. The thinking about social sustainability is not yet as advanced as for the other two pillars. Societies do, and will continue to, transform over time. But it seems clear that significant social stress—and, at the extreme, social conflict—is likely to lead to a breakdown in the accumulation or preservation of all assets, thereby jeopardizing intergenerational well-being.

One concrete approach to thinking about sustainability and intergenerational well-being is to ensure that the flow of consumption does not decline over time. But what is needed for this? The academic literature shows that a country's ability to sustain a flow of consumption (and utility) depends on the change in its stock of assets or wealth. Intergenerational well-being will rise only if wealth (measured in shadow prices and excluding capital gains) increases over time—that is, only if a country's adjusted net savings are positive.[3,4] (See the section titled "Measuring sustainability.")

Not a steady-state concept

Does the composition of the asset base matter? In principle, this depends on the potential for substitutability among assets (see the section titled "The importance of a range of assets"). In the environmental economics literature (Pearce and others 1989) a distinction is made between weak constraints on growth, known as "weak sustainability" (which presumes that assets are fully substitutable) and strong constraints on growth, known as "strong sustainability" (which holds that assets are not fully substitutable because some natural assets, or more precisely some of the functions performed by these assets—such as global life support—cannot be replaced by others). Limits-to-growth type arguments focus on strong sustainability, while arguments in favor of indefinite growth focus on weak sustainability. So far the former arguments have not been very convincing because the substitutability among assets has been high for most inputs used in production at a small scale. There is now, however, a growing recognition that different thresholds apply at different scales—local to global. Technology can be expected to continue to increase

Box 2.1
Not yet able to fully duplicate natural processes

Biosphere 2—a sealed glass ecosystem that was built in Oracle, Arizona, at a cost of some $200 million in 1991—attempted to create a completely self-contained, human-made system to support eight people for two years. It could not.

There is still debate on how to conduct such an experiment. The idea was that there would be no exchange with the outside world except for the energy supplied to run appliances. The people inside the biosphere would grow all their own food. And the system would operate with a fixed volume of air and water, recycled and reused as they are on Earth, the original biosphere.

A year and a half after the sphere was sealed, the oxygen content of the atmosphere had fallen from 21 percent to 14 percent, a level normally found at 17,500 feet and barely sufficient to keep people in the biosphere functioning. Carbon dioxide (CO_2) and nitrous oxide levels surged. All pollinators became extinct, so agricultural production could not be sustained. Worse still, the drop in oxygen and rise in CO_2 meant that the biosphere's systems could not replicate the carbon cycle, the most essential cycle for life.

Source: Heal (2000).

the potential substitutability among assets over time, but for many essential environmental services—especially global life support systems—there are no known alternatives now, and potential technological solutions cannot be taken for granted (box 2.1).

The limits to substitutability among assets are likely to be greater for those assets that enter consumption untransformed (for example, natural forest scenery versus natural desert scenery) rather than as a produced output using the same materials (for example, a wooden window shutter or a glass pane). Ensuring that the well-being of future generations does not decline requires maintaining sufficient levels of some assets for the future, particularly when the drawdown or degradation entails irreversible losses and there is a possibility that these assets matter directly for the well-being of future generations. Of course, the mix of assets that supports improvements in human well-being is likely to change over time, as people's preferences and technologies change. So the concept of sustainability will itself evolve over time.

Proceeding with caution

What is more important for sustainability is how to manage risks by retaining options. There is considerable uncertainty about the consequences of human actions on complex ecosystems: small changes can sometimes accumulate and translate into losses of whole ecosystems (see box 2.5). There is also uncertainty about what technological innovations will be available and when. Where the costs of human actions today are uncertain, with potential for large and irreversible damage, there is a need for proceeding with greater caution in maintaining environmental and social assets.

Measuring sustainability

There are many important things that are not measurable, but in general, people value what they measure. One of the biggest challenges is how to measure all our assets and our progress toward sustainable development. Since the Brundtland Commission, there have been many efforts to develop indicators of sustainability. Much of the progress in developing indicators for measuring sustainability has been in the economic and environmental sphere (box 2.2). Social indexes, such as transparency, trust, and conflict are still at early stages of development. The fact that social indicators are less developed reflects the ongoing debate about the concept of social sustainability: what it means and what should be measured.

Green accounting

Early efforts to link economic and environmental accounting focused on the measurement of "a green GDP," motivated by the genuine concern that the traditional measure of gross domestic product (GDP) provides only a partial picture of changes in welfare—capturing mainly, if not exclusively, elements transacted in markets (only a few imputed services, such as owner-occupied housing, are included). Many environmental assets—especially those that function as "sinks" receiving pollution and waste, and those supporting life—do not operate in markets and are therefore excluded.

These early environmental accounting efforts tried to modify national accounts to include environmental damages, environmental services, and changes in stocks of natural capital. But that proved problematic mainly because of valuation difficulties and some conceptual issues. For example, should expenditure for environmental protection be treated as intermediate or final consumption?

Later efforts have been directed toward constructing "satellite accounts" that try to link environmental

Box 2.2
Indicators for measuring sustainability—a subset

Some of the main approaches to developing indicators of environmental sustainability are the following:

- **Extended national accounts**

  Green Accounts System of Environmental and Economic Accounts. United Nations. A framework for environmental accounting.

  Adjusted Net Savings. World Bank. Change in total wealth, accounting for resource depletion and environmental damage.

  Genuine Progress Indicator, Redefining Progress, and Index of Sustainable Economic Welfare. United Kingdom and other countries. An adjusted GDP figure, reflecting welfare losses from environmental and social factors.

- **Biophysical accounts**

  Ecological Footprint, Redefining Progress. World Wildlife Fund and others. A measure of the productive land and sea area required to produce food and fiber, and in renewable form, the energy consumed by different lifestyles within and among countries.

- **Equally weighted indexes***

  Living Planet Index. World Wildlife Fund. An assessment of the populations of animal species in forests, fresh water, and marine environments.

Environmental Sustainability Index. World Economic Forum. An aggregate index spanning 22 major factors that contribute to environmental sustainability.

- **Unequally weighted indexes***

  Environmental Pressure Indexes. Netherlands, EU. A set of aggregate indexes for specific environmental pressures such as acidification or emissions of greenhouse gases.

  Well-being of Nations. Prescott-Allen. A set of indexes that capture elements of human well-being and ecosystem well-being and combines them to construct barometers of sustainability.

- **Eco-efficiency**

  Resource Flows. World Resources Institute. Total material flows underpinning economic processes.

- **Indicator sets**

  U.N. Commission for Sustainable Development and many countries.

* Equally weighted indexes are those whose components are equally weighted and then aggregated, while unequally weighted indexes give some components greater weight than others.
Source: Authors.

datasets with (unmodified) national accounts information. In principle, environmental costs and benefits, natural resource assets, and environmental protection are all presented in flow accounts and balance sheets. But in practice, given the difficulty in valuation, the emphasis has often been on using information on physical quantities from environmental accounts. The drawback of this approach is the difficulty in making comparisons across accounts in different units to evaluate priorities or tradeoffs.

Adjusted net savings

The focus of more recent efforts to link economic and environmental concerns has been on determining changes in wealth (adjusted net savings) as an indicator of sustainability. Change in wealth, appropriately defined to include a comprehensive and complete set of assets, is a good measure of prospects for well-being as it indicates a country's ability to sustain a consumption stream—which is what matters for sustainability—not just the consumption flow at a particular time as measured in GDP or green equivalent. In principle, only if wealth (measured in shadow prices and excluding capital gains) increases

over time—that is, only if adjusted net savings is positive—will intergenerational well-being rise.

Ideally, measures of adjusted net savings would take into account human capital, natural assets, knowledge, and social assets.[5] But measurement difficulties and the lack of available data preclude this. Estimates of net savings currently account for some key elements of environmental stocks—energy depletion, mineral depletion, net forest depletion, and CO_2 emissions.[6] They also include education spending, as a proxy for human asset accumulation, but they do not yet include changes in the stock of (codified) knowledge or social assets (see table 2.1).[7] It is clear that adjusted net savings is an improvement over traditional savings measures; however, efforts to refine it further will need to continue.

In practice, also, additional adjustments may need to be made to deal with specific issues. First, when a country's population is growing, it is on a sustainable path on a per capita basis only if the percentage change in wealth (adjusted net savings as a share of total wealth) exceeds the population growth rate.[8] If the change in wealth is lower than the population growth rate, the country is "de-capitalizing" or run-

Table 2.1

Toward adjusted net savings, 1999 (percentage of GDP)

Income and region	Gross domestic savings	Consumption of fixed capital	Energy depletion	Mineral depletion	Net forest depletion	Carbon dioxide damage	Education expenditure	Adjusted net savings
By income								
Low income	20.3	8.3	3.8	0.3	1.5	1.4	2.9	7.8
Middle income	26.1	9.6	4.2	0.3	0.1	1.1	3.5	14.3
Low and middle income	25.2	9.4	4.1	0.3	0.4	1.2	3.4	13.3
High income	22.7	13.1	0.5	0.0	0.0	0.3	4.8	13.5
By region								
East Asia and Pacific	36.1	9.0	1.3	0.2	0.4	1.7	1.7	25.2
Europe and Central Asia	24.6	9.1	6.0	0.0	0.0	1.7	4.1	11.9
Latin America and the Caribbean	19.2	10.0	2.8	0.4	0.0	0.4	4.1	9.6
Middle East and North Africa	24.2	9.3	19.7[a]	0.1	0.0	1.1	4.7	−1.3
South Asia	18.3	8.8	1.0	0.2	1.8	1.3	3.1	8.3
Sub-Saharan Africa	15.3	9.3	4.2	0.6	1.1	0.9	4.7	3.9

(The columns Consumption of fixed capital, Energy depletion, Mineral depletion, Net forest depletion, and Carbon dioxide damage are subtracted (shown as "−" before the group); Education expenditure is added ("+"); Adjusted net savings is the result ("=").)

Note: Adjusted net savings are equal to net domestic savings (calculated as the difference between gross domestic savings and consumption of fixed capital), plus education expenditure, minus energy depletion, mineral depletion, net forest depletion, and carbon dioxide damage.

[a] Note that the energy depletion figure in the table is stated in terms of GDP. This translates to an annual depletion rate of about 1 percent of proven reserves.

Source: World Bank (2001h); for details on the methodology, see Hamilton (2000).

ning down its assets on a per capita basis. This would imply that it is on an unsustainable path to an eventual decline in welfare per capita. Second, if production processes are subject to thresholds (nonconstant returns to scale), then again an adjustment to net savings needs to be made, if measured net savings are to correctly indicate sustainability.

The adjusted net savings measure is a useful "headline" indicator for the economy. Like all national accounts or monetary-based indicators, it employs an integrating framework that permits weighting and aggregating disparate elements of the economy and the environment. In principle an aggregate indicator such as adjusted net savings allows for comparisons across groups of countries—by region or by income. Figure 2.1 presents a comparison by GDP per capita, and shows that adjusted net savings are negative in some countries—that is, they are de-capitalizing.

A system of indicators

As just mentioned, the adjusted net savings indicator is a potentially useful headline indicator at the aggregate level. But unlike GDP—which is affected by economywide prices, such as exchange rates and interest rates, and which can be influenced by economywide policies—there are no policy-relevant aggregate indexes on the state of the environment. For policy purposes, these indexes need to be disaggregated (as in table 2.1) and complemented by such biophysical measures as pressure-response indicators. Not only can the latter be disaggregated to a much greater extent, but they also have the added advantage that they can be used to identify the source of the problem.

While recognizing the need for an aggregate index as a headline indicator, it is important to note that indicators are most useful when they address specific problems. To catalyze change, information and signals have to be picked up by specific groups or institutions that can use them to diagnose specific problems, rally support for change, balance interests, and take action.[9]

A good example of this process is *Silent Spring*, the book Rachel Carson wrote in 1962 to alert the public that birds were disappearing or being silenced. She pointed to indicators that no government agency would have considered important in advance—DDT levels in falcons and the fragility of

Figure 2.1
Adjusted net savings rates by per capita GDP level, 1999

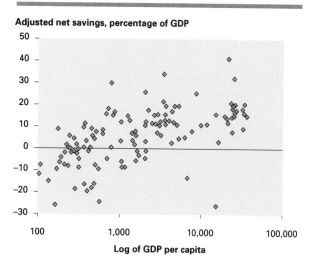

Adjusted net savings, percentage of GDP

Source: World Bank (2001h).

their eggs. This gave birdwatchers in America a new role and put environmental protection agencies on a track to monitor toxins in nature, industry, and elsewhere that might affect human well-being as well.

Policy-relevant indicators emerge and are continually validated and refined in an environment where there is a free flow of information and interaction. To avoid major regrets, there is a need for more credible information and networks that link experts, civil society, and decisionmakers.

The importance of a range of assets

Action to improve asset management need not await resolution of debates on how to define and measure sustainability, but does require a clear understanding of what assets matter and why. The capacity of any society to meet the "requirements" of individual well-being depends on the level and quality of a range of assets—and on how society deploys them. Broadly, these assets consist of the following:[10]

■ Human assets—the innate skills, talents, competencies, and abilities of individuals, as well as the effects of education and health.
■ Natural assets—both renewable and nonrenewable. These assets have source functions that enter as inputs into production and utility—forests, fisheries, mineral ores, and natural forces (such as air and water currents). They also have sink func-

tions to accommodate the unusable outputs of production and consumption—air, water, and soil receiving pollution and waste generated by human activities.[11] More fundamentally, nature performs critical life-support services on which the well-being of all life depends. So far—despite all the technological advances—no way has been found to fully replace these services through human-made alternatives (box 2.1).
■ Human-made assets—created physical products, particularly those used in production, such as machinery, equipment, buildings, and physical networks, as well as financial assets.
■ Knowledge assets—"codified knowledge," which is easily transferable across space and time (unlike "tacit" knowledge, which entails an individual's experience and learned judgment and thus cannot be easily transferred until codified).
■ Social (or relational) assets—interpersonal trust[12] and networks,[13] plus the understanding and shared values that these give rise to—which facilitate cooperation within or among groups.[14]

The importance of managing human, physical, and financial assets is well known, but how they interact with other assets is less well developed. Social, and environmental assets enhance human well-being *directly* through their very existence (e.g., the ability to trust another person or enjoy a natural setting).[15] They also enhance human well-being *indirectly* through their contribution to production and material well-being (figure 2.2). A tropical forest provides cut lumber as an input into the production of furniture and houses. A standing forest's environmental services—such as flood control and storm protection—can also improve the production of crops. And a forest's complex ecological functions support life for many species—that are important for the functioning and survival of the forest, which provides humans with material and aesthetic pleasures.

Why the need to manage a broader portfolio of assets?

The complementarity of assets
In improving human well-being, assets generally complement each other. For instance, human assets together with social assets can enhance a person's "freedom to be and to do." Assets can also be complements in the production process—that is, the productivity of one type of asset usually rises with

Figure 2.2
How society's assets enhance human well-being

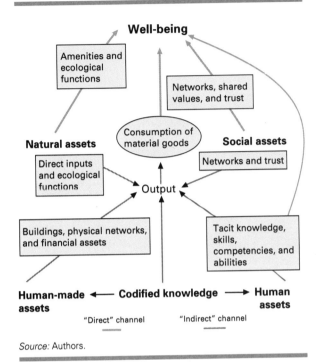

Source: Authors.

additional amounts of other assets.[16] For instance, there is now a growing body of literature that highlights the role of social capital (interpersonal networks, shared values, and trust)—an asset that has arguably received little attention in the economics literature so far—in the accumulation, preservation, and productivity of other assets—human-made, environmental, and human:[17,18]

- Social capital can improve the management and productivity of environmental assets. For example, the combined effect of attitudes about participation—and the actual participation in a collective enterprise, along with human capital (literacy)—has significantly improved the management of watersheds in Rajasthan, India.[19] Watershed management has, in turn, been crucial in raising incomes. Trust between technicians (agricultural extension agents) and farmers can generate increases in agricultural production. And the degree and nature of trust between the contact groups and the other members of the community can determine the effectiveness of the groups as catalysts for community development.[20]
- Social capital can enhance human capital accumulation: higher levels of trust have been associated with higher enrollment in secondary education.[21]

- Social capital can improve the productivity of physical capital. For example, interfirm social contact in the form of interpersonal networks in the clothing industry has a positive impact on learning.[22] Similarly, interfirm social interactions, as well as customer network ties, have significant effects through their impact on knowledge acquisition and on new product development in a range of high-tech industries, including pharmaceuticals, medical devices, and electronic instrumentation.[23,24] There is also a clear link between interfirm trust and firm performance (through conflict avoidance and lower negotiation costs).[25]

This complementarity generally applies to other assets as well. Cleaner air and water, for instance, improve human health and the productivity of human capital.[26] And the synergies from the complementarity of two or more assets raises overall productivity. But social and environmental assets are underprovided or overused.

Assets and diminishing returns
Most assets are also subject to diminishing marginal returns. The benefits to well-being or to productivity of an additional unit of an asset declines as the level or quality of the asset rises (all other assets kept constant). Why? As J.B. Clark said, "Put one man only in a square mile of prairie, and he will get a rich return. Two laborers on the same ground will get less per man; and if you enlarge the force to ten, the last man will perhaps get wages only."[27] As more people are added, the returns continue to drop, until someone is unable to cover his or her cost.

Only if there are very strong positive spillovers associated with an asset is the tendency of diminishing marginal returns offset. That is true for knowledge, particularly codified knowledge. Because new knowledge complements existing knowledge (there is no crowding out, as with the laborers), it is more valuable the more society already knows. Similarly, it is true for networks, such as telephones, where the advantages of owning a telephone increase with each new member in the network.

Limits to substitutability among assets
Because assets generally complement each other and because the returns to a particular asset diminish, the rate at which one asset can be substituted for another in production (while maintaining a given unit of

output) tends to diminish as well. As the level of one asset declines relative to another, the rate at which it can be further replaced falls. Moreover, when the quality or level of an asset falls below a threshold, there can be little further substitution without jeopardizing the productivity of the other assets, as well as overall production.

When environmental or natural assets are fairly abundant relative to human-made assets, substitution of the former by the latter can be expected to lead to higher returns. But there are limits to a long-term strategy that focuses primarily on replacing natural assets by human-made assets. Severely degraded farmland or fisheries will yield little wheat or fish, no matter how many plows or boats are used.

Development strategy to date has often relied on drawing down environmental resources and replacing them with human-made assets. This was the strategy followed by today's industrial countries.[28] Most developing countries' growth strategies continue to focus largely on the accumulation of human-made assets (physical capital). Indeed, a review of 60 countries in the late 1980s and 1990s shows that the growth of 16 countries considered to be serious policy reformers was accompanied primarily by physical capital accumulation. The increase in per capita GDP growth of this group of countries—rising from 2.8 percent in the late 1980s to 3.5 percent in the 1990s—entailed an increase in the rate of physical capital accumulation from 2.1 percent to 3.5 percent. In contrast, spending on education—a proxy for human capital accumulation—rose only slightly, from 3.2 percent of GDP in the late 1980s to 3.5 percent of GDP in the 1990s. And the rate of deforestation—a proxy for the depletion of natural assets—rose from 0.7 percent to 1.1 percent.[29]

The limits to focusing on physical capital alone are borne out empirically. An econometric study of 70 developing countries found that countries with low physical capital–labor ratios tend to experience a rise in their growth rates with increases in the stock of physical capital. But after countries reach a certain capital intensity, the contributions of further physical capital accumulation to growth—for any given human and natural capital—decline.[30] A separate study of 20 middle-income countries also found the marginal productivity of physical capital to diminish.[31] So although there may be economies of scale and technological spillovers for physical capital,[32] these do not seem to be large enough to continually offset diminishing marginal productivity.

The consequences of ignoring the complementarity of environmental assets and breaching thresholds

As an illustration of what can happen when the complementary role of environmental assets is ignored and certain thresholds are breached, consider the Yangtze Valley in 1998. Although China has always been susceptible to flood and drought, the 1998 floods were some of the most severe in its history. Rainfall from June to August that year was 38 percent above normal, but later analysis found that these unusually high levels could only partly explain the floods. The rest was perceived to be due to logging of the river's watershed, which eroded the soil. Deforestation had been so great (forest cover had decreased by more than half since the 1950s) that the watershed could no longer stabilize the water flow.[33] The resulting floods had very high costs in human lives—tens of thousands dead—and in lost production in the area.

Similarly, the degradation of the Aral Sea highlights what can go wrong when there is inadequate recognition of the role of environmental assets in the production process—and of the costs for human welfare (box 2.3). Expansion of irrigation schemes in the Aral Sea basin has generated billions of U.S. dollars in benefits and millions of jobs. But the overall costs of these schemes have been high, both in failing to generate the expected high levels of sustainable production over time and in causing serious health effects in areas immediately surrounding the sea. Today, avoiding further declines in the sea level is possible only if appropriate operational adjustments are made to the existing irrigation systems to improve their efficiency.

Some countries' experience with shrimp farming illustrates the costs of ignoring environmental services. Over the past two decades new technologies and production systems have enabled a dramatic increase in the intensity of shrimp farm operations—the production of farmed shrimp has grown at 20–30 percent a year.[34] Compared with traditional systems, however, the more intensive systems require large amounts of feed to support the shrimp and large amounts of water to flush out the wastes.[35] Because of the high concentration of farm units in areas of limited water supplies and inadequate flushing, the effluents in many cases exceeded the capacity of the receiving waters (sink), leading to pollution inside the ponds as well, which adversely affected production since these farms require a lot of water as an

Box 2.3

The Aral Sea—the cost of ignoring the role of an environmental asset

The Aral Sea watershed now spans the national borders of six countries. Over the past 40 years the excessive water diversion for irrigation along the Amu Darya and Syr Darya Rivers—the two main tributaries of the Aral Sea—caused the volume of the sea to fall by 85 percent, and the sea level by 18 meters, exposing more than 40,000 square kilometers of saline seabed and heavily salinating the remaining water (box figure). Today the Aral is divided into a smaller, less saline sea in the north and a larger, saline sea in the south.

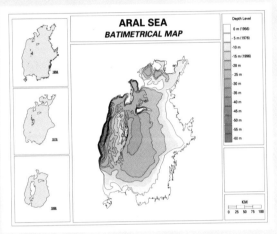

Shrinking sea, falling yields

Cotton yields in Uzbekistan, 1961–2000

Centners per hectare

Note: 1 centner is equal to 0.1 ton.

Loss of fisheries

Although Soviet planners realized that greater irrigation would lower the sea's water level, it was thought that the increment in agricultural output of the whole basin would yield significantly higher benefits than any damage caused. Not recognized, however, was that the excessive water withdrawal would make the remaining sea water so much saltier that it would become unfit for higher forms of aquatic life. The once fairly substantial fishing industry has now almost completely disappeared.

A drop in agricultural output

At the same time the combination of excessive irrigation and poor management of the irrigated land has led to waterlogging and increased the salinity of the soil in the entire basin. Almost one-third of the irrigated land is now degraded. Effective management in these areas, with an emphasis on environmental assets, could have helped avert the current problems and the environmental degradation surrounding the sea.

It is no longer possible to maintain irrigation and cotton production at levels experienced during the Soviet period. The land degradation, combined with the reduced availability of appropriate agricultural inputs for production after the breakup of the Soviet Union, has greatly reduced cotton production, both total yields and productivity per hectare. The original conversion of 7.9 million hectares of desert allowed a rise in Soviet cotton production from 2.2 million tons in 1940 to 9.1 million tons (at its peak) in 1980. Cotton production in Uzbekistan, which accounted for 70 percent of the total production (4 million tons) in 1960, peaked at 5.5 million tons in 1980. By 2000, it was down to 1960 levels—which may be more optimal and sustainable—when large-scale irrigation was beginning (box figure).

An increase in health costs

The exposed seabed and polluted downstream waters have also had high human and health costs. Winds carrying salt from the

seabed contaminate lands adjacent to the sea, and increased chemical and pesticide use upstream pollutes drinking water. The people hardest hit live in Karakalpakstan, at the end of the Amu Darya Delta. Reliable data on health costs are hard to obtain. But by some estimates maternal deaths in Karakalpakstan in 1994 were 120 per 100,000 live births (twice the national average) and infant mortality was 60 per 1,000 live births (three times the national average). In the past 10–15 years kidney and liver diseases, especially cancers, have increased 30- to 40-fold, arthritic diseases 60-fold, and chronic bronchitis 30-fold.

Full restoration too costly—how to avoid further decline

It may be too late to fully reverse the damage, but it is possible to stabilize agricultural production in the basin and mitigate negative downstream effects. Restoring the sea to its former level in the next 50 years would mean suspending all irrigation and other water uses in the basin—impossible today, when even water reductions of 3–5 percent meet with strong local opposition from people highly dependent on irrigation. Although the rates of return on the incremental irrigation have not been very high—ranging from 13 percent in the best case scenario (high cotton prices and low irrigation costs) to minus 10 percent in the worst case (low cotton prices and high irrigation costs)*—better returns can be achieved and agricultural production in the region can be put on a more sustainable path. Estimates put potential efficiency gains through operational improvements and greater participation and collective action in the use of irrigation water at 20–30 percent—this, at relatively low financial cost and without constraining production (World Bank 1998a). With these improvements, the decline in sea level could be arrested and some aquatic life could be reintroduced.

* The estimates of the return-to-irrigation investment are based on Uzbekistan, which accounts for more than 70 percent of cotton production in the region. The rate of return calculations are very sensitive to the average raw cotton price and the full cost of irrigation. Cotton prices fluctuated widely over the 1960–2000 period. The average cost of cotton is assumed to be $1,200 a ton (2000 prices) for the high-cost case and $850 a ton for the low-cost case. The average cost of irrigation is assumed to be $500 a hectare for the low case and $300 for the high case.

Source: Authors.

input (source).[36] The quality of the water in traditional shrimp farms is generally better because of the lower intensity of shrimp, which are thus less prone to disease.

The collapse of many shrimp farms in China, Indonesia, Taiwan (China), and Thailand has meant large losses in physical assets and in labor.[37,38] This was a direct consequence of not recognizing the importance of ensuring good naturally provided water quality in the production process, especially as the volume of shrimp and the capital intensity of farms increased.

Breaching thresholds through the cumulative loss of biodiversity can also lead at a localized level to a loss of resilience of an ecosystem—in its capacity to absorb disturbances without undergoing fundamental changes in functional characteristics. A run-down ecosystem, (one degraded by excessive use) can succumb to shocks that would not destroy a healthy ecosystem. A famous analogy made by Ehrlich and Ehrlich (1981) relates ecosystem components to rivets in an airplane.[39] One by one, biological species may disappear and not be missed. Eventually, however, the cumulative loss of biodiversity will lead to the crash of ecosystem functions just as the cumulative loss of redundant rivets will lead to the crash of an airplane.[40]

Thresholds are clearest when a renewable asset has been exploited beyond its capacity to regenerate or reproduce. When that threshold is reached, the productivity of other assets decreases—or if the degraded asset is the main input, production may cease altogether. The change is often sudden and discontinuous, as in cod fisheries in New England (see chapter 7).[41]

In some cases there may be no substitute for some of the functions of the environmental asset, so breaching thresholds can cause irreversible damage. An example of this is the ozone level: wearing a sunscreen lotion all day may protect skin from cancer caused by ultraviolet rays, but there is no known substitute for the protection ozone affords to our food chain.[42]

Thresholds can apply to all assets. Indeed, the experience of 80 countries during 1970–99 suggests that the probability of achieving a relatively high per capita growth of 2.5 percent a year for a five-year period is highly affected by the crossing of certain minimum thresholds of physical assets, human assets, and social assets.[43] That probability drops from 58 percent to 28 percent if the investment of physical

capital to GDP ratio is below 15 percent. Even when the ratio is above 15 percent, the probability falls by more than 23 percentage points if the level of social assets—proxied by an index of (the lack of) political and social tensions—falls below a threshold.[44] The probability of such durable growth also falls significantly (from 70 percent to 44 percent) if the education Gini—measuring inequality in the distribution of education—is greater than 0.30.

In sum, the long-term neglect of any set of assets—human, social, or environmental—can at some point sharply reduce the productivity of the other assets, whether for commodities, sectors, regions, or nations.[45] Therefore, while countries may be able to grow for a period based on a strategy of accumulating physical capital, the prolonged neglect of other assets is likely to endanger the durability and sustainability of the growth process—for example, allowing a country to fall into a state of high social and civil unrest (a drop in social capital) is likely to undermine sustained economic growth.[46,47] Similarly, if environmental degradation is irreversible, society can lose the option value of an asset that could make a serious difference to future productivity (box 2.4).

So far the concern has been with the potential for substituting assets in production. What about the potential for substitutions that affect human well-being directly? The need to manage all of society's assets may be even greater. The substitutability of assets that enter people's well-being directly is likely to be lower than the substitutability technically feasible in production. Some minimum bundle of social and environmental assets is likely to be needed if one is to achieve a given level of personal well-being.[48] This argument is just as valid for intergenerational well-being.

There will always be much uncertainty about the tastes and preferences of future generations—and about the technological possibilities open to them. But there is also much uncertainty about the consequences of our current actions. While many ecological problems are gradual, some can switch abruptly from one stable state to another (box 2.5). Such shifts can cause large losses of ecological and economic resources.

Very often, restoring the desired state would require drastic and expensive interventions. And sometimes the process of restoration is not even known. Technological solutions to these problems might be

Box 2.4
How keeping the option value of assets can make a serious difference

In 1970 a new virus—the grassy stunt virus, carried by the brown plant hopper—threatened rice production in Asia. The virus appeared capable of destroying as much as one-quarter of the crop in some years, making it critical to develop a rice strain resistant to the virus. This was done with the help of the International Rice Research Institute (IRRI), which researches rice production and maintains a huge bank of rice seeds—about 80,000 varieties of rice and near-relatives of rice. In this instance, a single strain of wild rice not used commercially was found to be resistant to the grassy stunt virus. The appropriate gene was transferred to commercial rice varieties, yielding commercial rice crops that were resistant to the virus.

Note that this strain was found in only one location, a valley flooded by a hydroelectric dam shortly after the IRRI took the strain into its collection. Without this strain—which apparently had no commercial value—the well-being of hundreds of millions of people would have been seriously affected.

Source: Heal (2000).

Box 2.5
Catastrophic ecoshifts

Recent studies highlight the possibility of catastrophic shifts in ecosystems. Usually the changes in outside conditions affecting ecosystems—climate, injection of nutrients or toxic chemicals, groundwater reductions, habitat fragmentations, losses of species diversity—occur very gradually. And sometimes the ecosystems will respond to such changes smoothly and continuously. But studies of lakes, oceans, coral reefs, forests, and arid lands show that these smooth changes can be interrupted by sudden, drastic switches to another state. The gradual changes in external conditions can lead to a loss of resilience and make the ecosystem more vulnerable to catastrophic shifts. Once a threshold is passed, the shift can occur suddenly, with little warning. So under some conditions the ecosystem can move from one stable state to another, separated by an unstable state.

Coral reef ecosystems can exhibit such dramatic shifts—from having high biodiversity to being overgrown with fleshy algae. Factors that make them vulnerable to such shifts include increased nutrient loading from changed land use and overfishing, and reduction of the number of large, and later the smaller, herbivorous fish species that control the algae. In the Caribbean, overfishing had already reduced herbivorous fish when a pathogen reduced the population of sea urchin Diadema (which also controls the algae). As a result, the reefs became overgrown with fleshy brown macro algae—the spread is now difficult to reverse because adult algae are less palatable to herbivores and the persistence of the former prevent the settlement of coral larvae.

Source: Scheffer and others (2001).

available in the future—or they might not be. When the potential damage can be very large—where the effects may be irreversible and where substitution possibilities may be limited—a "precautionary principle" applies: act more conservatively when you are uncertain about the effects (see chapter 5 and box 5.6 on the precautionary principle).

Tradeoffs and sustainable development

Balancing objectives and choosing how to act
Improving human well-being over time is a broader goal than increasing economic growth that focuses primarily on material comfort. This has some important implications. Since social and environmental assets also affect human well-being directly, a strict policy of "grow now, clean up later" has costs for today's generation, costs that often fall disproportionately on today's poor.[49]

Moreover, any serious attempt at poverty reduction requires, at a minimum, durable economic growth—not economic growth in fits and starts. This means paying enough attention to social and environmental concerns to ensure that durable growth is not jeopardized.

And while there is potential for substituting assets over a range, there are limits to such substitution (see earlier section on this topic), perhaps even more

from the perspective of people's well-being than of production. So to ensure that the well-being of future generations is not compromised, some attention has to focus on environmental concerns—in particular the avoidance of irreversibilities that may matter for future well-being.

The way the economy grows—the pace and pattern of growth—can matter for the well-being of both the current generation and that generation's children and grandchildren. Developing countries do not have to follow the path of development traversed in the last century by the industrial countries. Technological options have improved and it is now possible to avoid repeating the mistakes of industrial countries in their development (i.e., the use of lead in gasoline). On the other hand, some options open to industrial countries in their development phase are not open to developing countries now (land-labor ratios, extent of global competition, and so on).

What do these considerations imply for a country's development strategy—or how does a country balance the objectives of addressing environmental concerns and pursuing economic growth? Over the longer term, economic growth is unlikely to be sustained unless enough attention is paid to environmental assets. But over the short to medium term it may be possible to do so, on the grounds that such short-term growth could generate more resources for addressing environmental concerns later. Indeed, having limited resources usually makes it necessary to choose priorities between tradeoffs. But the priorities will not always favor growth over attention to environmental assets in the short run, or vice versa.

The appropriate ranking of priorities will vary by locale (region or nation) and at different times, depending on the issue and on several other factors. What environmental depletion or degradation has already taken place? How important is the asset in either the production process or in utility directly? Are the poor particularly vulnerable if the issue is left unattended?

Three broad cases can be distinguished for different emphasis and sequencing:

1. Simultaneously addressing environmental concerns along with economic growth, even in the short run
2. Placing a higher priority on economic growth, while addressing environmental concerns that can be dealt with at relatively low cost in the short run
3. Placing a higher priority on maintaining or restoring the environment in the short run.

Case 1. Win-win: preserve natural assets and keep growing

Addressing both growth objective and preservation or restoration of environmental assets can sometimes be critical to raising production and incomes, even in the short to medium term. That would be the case in Madagascar, where almost three-quarters of the people, most of them poor, live in rural areas. The bulk of rural poor people are in agriculture, and productivity growth in agriculture is critical to poverty reduction. Yet agricultural productivity has been stagnant for the past four decades.[50]

One of the deep constraints to increasing agricultural production in Madagascar is resource degrada-

tion and low soil fertility. The country has already lost 80 percent of its original forest cover, more than half in the past 40 years (see box 8.3 in chapter 8). In the east of the country, under the *tavy* agricultural system, rice is grown on steep slopes after slashing and burning of virgin or secondary forests. In the central highlands population pressure forces people from the valley bottoms to farm the hillsides, evident in the big increase in rainfed agriculture. The resulting erosion causes nutrients to wash off the already poor soil and to silt irrigation schemes in the valleys.

The annual cost of environmental degradation—from soil erosion, silting, declining soil fertility, and lost forest—is high, estimated at over 5 percent of GDP, and the agricultural resource base has not kept up with population growth. That is why arresting this cycle—through agricultural intensification to reduce the pressure of cultivating new uplands—is paramount. Today, little use is made of fertilizers and of new higher yielding varieties—for several reasons. The absence of secure land tenure reduces the incentives for investing in intensification. The lack of credit and liquidity hampers the use of inputs. And the very poor quality of rural infrastructure constrains the supply of inputs and makes it more expensive.

Indeed, for countries that rely heavily on renewable natural resources and have few alternatives in the short to medium term (because they are poor in human and human-made assets), it is especially important to contain environmental depletion or degradation. For these countries, maintaining natural assets is a critical component of economic growth. For example, in southern Africa, the Caribbean, and the Indian and Pacific Oceans, nature-based tourism has become an important source of foreign exchange and local income.

In some cases restoring or maintaining an environmental asset may not be critical for economic production (other factors of production could replace its functions), but it may be more economically efficient (box 2.6).

Case 2. Tradeoff: place more weight on economic growth and only address low-cost environmental concerns

When environmental degradation is reversible and has limited impact on economic growth in the short to medium term, placing greater weight on economic growth entails lower opportunity costs and should be

Box 2.6
Replacing natural assets with human-made assets can be costly

For years the Catskill watershed provided New York City residents with water of such high quality that it needed no filtration or chemical treatment. New York could even bottle and sell its water to other cities.

This began to change in the 1990s. The U.S. Environmental Protection Agency warned the city that it would soon have to invest in a filtration plant—for $6 to $8 billion, with annual operating costs of about $300 million. Given the huge sums, the city began to ask why a watershed that performed so well for so long was now beginning to fail. The main causes were uncontrolled land development in the Catskills and the intensified use of land in and around the watershed. The combination of pollutants from residential communities and farms was overwhelming the soil microbes that naturally filtered and cleansed the water as it percolated through.

Because there had been little deforestation or soil erosion, and because much of the natural infrastructure of the watershed was still intact, it was possible to reverse the situation. New York City then faced a choice: restore the watershed, or build and run a filtration plant. Costs of the first option—improving sewerage treatment in the watershed and buying lands to prevent development—were estimated in the range of $1 to $1.5 billion, one-fifth the cost of an artificial filtration system.

The choice was clear. As the commissioner of the city's Department of Environmental Protection commented at the time, "All that human-made filtration does is solve a problem. Preventing the problem, through watershed protection, is faster, cheaper, and has lots of other benefits."

Source: Heal (2000).

strong inverted-U shape relationship with income for sulfur dioxide and carbon monoxide, and even a one-for-one downward relationship between particulates and per capita income.[51] But for water quality the evidence is mixed. And for per capita emissions of CO_2 there is a steady worsening as per capita incomes grow.[52] Indeed, recent research concludes that, on the whole, there is little evidence of environmental quality getting worse with initial growth and then getting better at higher per capita incomes.[53]

Second, even for environmental assets that show a positive association with per capita income growth, the association is not structural. Instead, the better environmental outcomes reflect the impact of regulations and other polices put in place in response to public action and pressures from society as preferences for environmental quality become stronger with higher per capita incomes—not to any natural changes in the composition of production or consumption.[54]

It is important to recognize that, although the resource degradation or depletion may be reversible, its impact on human well-being is not (recall the degradation of Aral Sea described in box 2.3). Future remedial action cannot compensate the generation or generations that live during the transition to a better environment. Consider the costs of air and water pollution for human health. Recent estimates suggest that about 11 percent of illnesses and premature deaths in developing countries are due to environmental health risks from water supply and sanitation and from urban and indoor air pollution.[55] This is about the same as from malnutrition, which accounts for 15 percent of all illnesses and deaths. The poor are particularly vulnerable since they have fewer alternatives to polluted drinking water and are more likely to live near heavily traveled roads where air pollution is highest.

For this reason, there is little justification for not addressing at least some of these environmental concerns along with economic growth. And often a large proportion of the problem can be addressed at relatively low cost (see figure 2.4 on page 31).[56] Indeed, several cost-benefit studies have shown that the costs of addressing a sizable proportion of pollution can be relatively low—and that the benefits of doing so can often be very high. In such cases there would be grounds for stricter pollution control when pursuing a high growth strategy even in very low-income countries.[57]

pursued. But as discussed below, this does not justify ignoring environmental concerns altogether.

To justify a strategy of "grow first, clean up later," policymakers rely on the argument that is only partially borne out by observation—that environmental degradation gets worse initially and then gets better as a country develops—the environmental Kuznets curve. Often they also act as if the relationship is automatic—so that there is little need to actively address the problem. This could be the case if, say, shifts in the scale and sectoral composition of output and changes in technology within sectors result in a move away from pollution-intensive production to less pollution-intensive methods.

But it cannot be assumed that environmental quality will necessarily improve with economic growth. First, such a relationship is observed only for some environmental factors. For local air quality, there is a

Although policymakers often worry that pollution control measures hurt the competitiveness of firms, research does not support their concern.[58] What is observed is that countries can have quite different environmental outcomes while achieving the same economic growth rates. There is, for instance, a fairly wide range of environmental outcomes in countries averaging a 3 to 5 percent annual growth (figure 2.3).

Indeed, environmental outcomes at given incomes are strongly influenced by how parties (citizens, business leaders, policymakers, regulators, NGOs, and other market actors) react to economic growth and its side effects.[59] This suggests that there can be a demand in society for better environmental quality even at fairly low incomes. In a policy formulation setting that allows for participation, voice, and channels for feedback, countries are likely to experience better environmental outcomes at all levels of income (see chapter 3).

Case 3. Tradeoff: place more weight on the environment

When current depletion or degradation threatens to be irreversible—or when the degradation has signif-

icant and long-lasting implications[60] and having the asset may be important to the nation in the future—the environmental concerns need to be addressed today.

Forests rich in biodiversity may have little amenity value to the people in a poor country today. But as the country's per capita income rises, that value is likely to increase—making it important to have prevented irreversible losses. Since these assets often yield significant benefits to poor people in the country today, who rely heavily on it for their livelihood (food, fuel, fodder, and medicinal plants), it may be possible to address the environmental degradation and poverty reduction simultaneously through financing or cost-sharing from the larger community within the country or from abroad. Such schemes need to be appropriately designed to provide, where necessary, alternative livelihoods for the local populace.[61] By avoiding irreversible degradation, these schemes can also keep the option value of the resource for the nation in the future. Such cost-sharing schemes are interim proxies for economic growth insofar as they align the preferences of the current (poorer) population with those of future (richer) populations.

An example of such cost-sharing is Costa Rica's environmental services program. Costa Rica's forests are attractive to tourists worldwide, given the rich biodiversity there. But the rate of deforestation in the 1970s and 1980s was one of the highest in the world. To protect this asset, Costa Rica designed a very innovative scheme, the Payments for Environmental Services Program, in which those who benefit from the environmental services of the forests compensate those who bear the burden of maintaining the forests. Under the scheme, a market has been created for a variety of services, with carbon sequestration among the most successful (see box 8.5 in chapter 8).

Some assets are overused or underprovided—why?

From the preceeding discussions it should be clear that there is real value in designing development strategies based on better management of a broader portfolio of assets. A major problem in pursuit of this goal is that some assets (knowledge, environmental, and social) tend to have characteristics of public goods or externalities—that is, their use generates spillover benefits or costs to others that are not taken

Figure 2.3
Very different environmental outcomes with the same growth rates

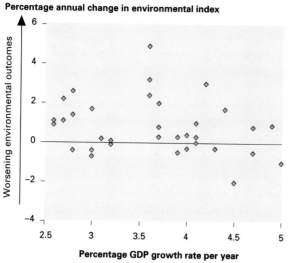

Percentage annual change in environmental index

Note: The environmental index is constructed by giving equal weights to annual rates of deforestation, water pollution proxied by emissions of organic water pollutants in per capita metric tons, and the increase in CO_2 emissions in per capita metric tons between 1987 and 1995.

Source: World Bank (2001h).

into account. As a result, the stocks of these assets are generally too small from society's perspective. This is a consequence of market or policy failures.

Market failures

It is difficult to exclude people from using many of the functions of environmental assets—they are nonexcludable. That means there are no well-defined private (individual or group) property rights, so markets cannot be used to ration the use of these assets or to expand their provision where that would be justified. Without property rights, it is not possible to charge others for the use of a good or service. Therefore not only does an individual or group have little incentive to preserve or provide the asset (since he or they cannot prevent others from using it), he or they have every incentive to free-ride on others' efforts to preserve or provide those assets. From the perspective of society, then, the assets will be over-used or underprovided.

Overuse. For some renewable assets that are common property goods (nonexcludable but rival) consumption by one individual or group will reduce the supply for others. Each individual or group can gain from overexploiting it in the short run, but lose in the long run as everyone else does the same and the asset falls below its regenerative capacity. Society then ends up worse off.

As an example of the common property problem, consider offshore fisheries, many of which are greatly depleted by overfishing. The fish biomass of several important fisheries is now a mere tenth of its pre-exploitation level—90 percent of initial stocks have been destroyed.[62,63] Although all fishermen would benefit in the long term from a flourishing fishery, individuals tend to act in their own interests and catch as many fish as they can. This is the "tragedy of the commons"—or open access, with users over-exploiting what would otherwise be a renewable resource as they race to get their share before others deplete the resource. The same behavior applies to ozone depletion and climate change—clear examples of global common property goods (see table 2.2). As discussed in chapter 8, the emission of ozone-depleting substances, or the use of fossil fuels (and, to a lesser but still important extent deforestation and other land use practices that release CO_2 and other greenhouse gasses), results in gases accumulating more rapidly in the atmosphere than natural sinks

can remove them. They change the climate in complex ways. Their global effect is the same regardless of where they are emitted. Again, individuals (and individual countries) do not factor in the spillovers of their actions on others.

Underprovision. Knowledge is a public good—since once generated, it is difficult to exclude others from using it (nonexcludable) and consumption by one individual does not reduce the supply for others (nonrival). Individuals or groups have less incentive to invest in generating information and knowledge than is socially desirable. There is a tendency to free-ride, expecting to benefit from a piece of knowledge created by someone else. And since an individual's use of a piece of extant knowledge does not reduce the knowledge available to others, the generation of new knowledge can have large positive externalities or spillovers to society that are not taken into account in decentralized decisions to invest in creating new knowledge. Thus knowledge also tends to be underprovided from society's perspective.

The existence of spillovers (externalities) that are not taken into account by individuals gives rise to the need for a "market for external effects" that can align the marginal costs and benefits to the individual with those of society as a whole—so that individuals take into account their impact on others (internalize the externality). When transaction costs are low, and property rights relatively well defined and perfectly and costlessly enforceable, all affected parties could get together to negotiate an outcome that is efficient from the perspective of society.[64] Under such circumstances, there is little need for policy intervention.

But generally transaction costs are significant, and for many environmental assets private property rights are difficult to define. The costs of transactions are likely to depend on the number of people involved and on whether the parties are concentrated or diffused groups. (Clearly, not all problems deserve being addressed—sometimes the transaction costs may be higher than the social benefits.) Usually, transaction costs are likely to be higher—and the problem more difficult to solve—when the effects of the spillover fall on a large, diffuse group. The problem is likely to be even more difficult to solve when a small concentrated group (that can organize itself at lower costs) generates the spillover, while the effect of the spillover is borne by a diffused

Table 2.2
Examples of types of externalities addressed in each spatial arena

Space/scale arena	Nonexcludability leading to market failures		
	Common property goods (rival)[a]		**Public goods (nonrival)[a]**
	Externality effect of many on many (dispersed interests)	**Externality effect of a few (concentrated) on many (dispersed, who could also lack voice or be otherwise excluded)**	**Usual case: externality effect of many on many (dispersed interests)**
Fragile rural	Wells and grazing land (chapter 4, box 4.2)	Mines (chapter 4, box 4.7)	Schooling for girls (chapter 4, box 4.6) Knowledge outreach in Tunisia (chapter 4, box 4.5)
Commercial rural		Groundwater (chapter 5, box 5.10) Frontier land (chapter 5, box 5.12)	
Urban	Disposal of solid waste in drains (chapter 6) Automotive air pollution <in wealthy countries>	Pollution in Cubatão, São Paulo (chapter 6, box 6.3) Automotive air pollution <in poor countries>	Public works in favelas in Brazil (chapter 6, box 6.5)
National		Cameroon forestry (chapter 7, box 7.8)	Public health services in Ceara, Brazil (chapter 7, box 7.2)
Global	Ozone depletion (chapter 8) Global warming (chapter 8) <individuals>	Global warming (chapter 8) <countries>	

Note: Nonexcludable means that a user cannot be prevented from consuming that good or service.

[a] *Rival* means that consumption by one user reduces the supply available to other users. Public goods are nonrival up to a threshold. Once that threshold has been breached they can become rival: for instance, a freeway, as it shifts from being underutilized to being congested; or the atmosphere once the pollutant concentration exceeds the atmosphere's absorptive capacity.
Source: Authors.

group that incurs higher costs to organize itself because it lacks the ability or voice to negotiate. Solving such problems requires policy interventions and supporting institutions (see the section titled "Correcting the overuse and underprovision of important assets" and chapter 3). And as discussed in the rest of this Report, where such institutions do not exist, it is necessary to find mechanisms or catalysts that may spur their emergence. Table 2.2 shows some examples that are taken up in each of the chapters of this Report, which is organized by space and scale.

Policy failures

The overuse or underprovision of an environmental asset can sometimes be the result of policy interventions to correct market failures that in turn have consequences for another set of problems—leading to a policy failure in the case of the latter. For example, countries may implement policies—to improve the competitiveness of certain products, industries, regions, or to support particular social groups—that have adverse environmental impacts. When the social costs outweigh the social benefits, this constitutes a policy failure, requiring offsetting corrections or even elimination of the policy intervention.

So-called perverse subsidies are an example. Many subsidies are introduced initially to stimulate the use of a good or service that is underutilized—fertilizer, electricity, water. But in the absence of sunset clauses and with the creation of a constituency based on perceived acquired rights, these subsidies can persist beyond their economically useful life and be detrimental environmentally. They can be economically costly if they sustain processes that would otherwise not be viable (for example, producing rice in California). They can also be economically harmful if they reduce the costs of environmental inputs to the point that eventual degradation of this complementary

Box 2.7
Perverse subsidies in India

Power subsidies in India have resulted in overpumping of aquifers, reducing the availability of drinking water, and encouraging water-intensive crops in areas where water is scarce.

In not distinguishing between peak and nonpeak tariffs, the implicit subsidy has also increased the incentive to overbuild capacity. (In fact, the World Bank estimated in 1991 that various measures to reduce peak power usage could reduce power generation requirements by about 12 percent in 10 years.)

In addition to facilitating the excess drawdown of aquifers, the subsidy is costly for poor people, who typically lack access to power but suffer the opportunity costs of having subsidies go to others. Since State Electricity Boards are not allowed to charge realistic tariffs, their accumulated deficits are at least partly serviced by deducting their dues from the Central Plan Assistance to the states. This reduced central assistance, along with the direct state subsidies to power, means that the poorest do not receive adequate basic services, such as health care and primary education.

Source: World Bank (2000e). Adapted from box 5.2.

asset affects productivity (for instance, power subsidies in India encouraging the overpumping of ground water—box 2.7) or if in attempting to benefit one activity, they harm others, so that their net impact is negative.[65]

Energy subsidies,[66] the bulk of which are directed to fossil fuels[67] in both industrial and developing countries, entail economic efficiency losses. But they also have highly deleterious effects on the environment, some reflected in higher economic costs.[68] Subsidies to fossil fuel and nuclear energy in Organisation for Economic Co-operation and Development (OECD) countries total $71 billion annually.[69] Studies that simulate the effects of removing coal and other energy subsidies—either for individual countries or the world—all find significant environmental benefits in reducing CO_2 emissions. And most studies that look at the economic effects also find real GDP gains.[70] The problem is not limited to industrial countries. While many developing countries significantly reduced their energy subsidies in the 1990s, they would still gain considerably by removing the subsidies altogether (table 2.3). Although it is often argued that these subsidies are needed to help poor people, the poor rarely benefit.

In general, subsidies encourage the use of the supported inputs, processes, or products—and reduce the incentives to find alternatives that may be more economically efficient. Fuel subsidies to fossil fuels reduce the incentive to develop renewable energy sources.[71]

Although dismantling perverse subsidies may be good for society, some groups would lose. For example, studies looking at the effects of removing energy subsidies in industrial countries point to a significant loss of jobs in the coal sector (although there would be real GDP gains associated with their removal).[72] Social considerations may thus call for incentive-compatible transfers and compensation (see chapter 7, box 7.7), as well as other support (vocational training for other jobs) to enable the transition out of perverse subsidies.

The costs and benefits of correcting underprovision or overuse

If environmental assets are generally overused or underprovided, how can society begin to weigh the returns to addressing an environmental issue against the costs? It depends on the starting point.

Starting from a moderately degraded state, it is often possible to make significant improvements at fairly low cost. Very simple low-cost measures to abate water pollution (for example, installing water filters) can often remove close to half the pollutants. The costs of additional reductions in degradation are likely to rise more steeply because more sophisticated measures are needed. Consequently initial costs are low and rise more steeply as the quality of the asset is restored.

In another example, consider the costs (estimated in the early 1990s) of reducing air pollution from transport in Mexico City. The cheapest emission reductions were found initially among the busiest vehicles, especially those that were driven downtown during most of the day. Further emission reductions required modifications for a larger part of the vehicle fleet—which became more expensive. (Emissions reductions for buses and taxis would have cost only $300 a ton because of their higher annual mileage, compared with $1,600 a ton for passenger cars.) The incremental costs of mandatory inspection and maintenance programs for vehicles in use would have been higher still (with costs rising as the standards

Table 2.3
The benefits of full-cost energy pricing

Country	Average subsidy (percentage of reference price)	Cost of subsidy ($ billion)	Effects of subsidy removal		
			Gain in economic efficiency[b] (percentage of GDP)	Reduction in energy consumption (percent)	Reduction in carbon dioxide emissions (percent)
Islamic Republic of Iran	80.4	3.6	2.2	48	49
República Bolivariana de Venezuela	57.6	1.1	1.2	25	26
Russian Federation	32.5	6.7[a]	1.5	18	17
Indonesia	27.5	0.5[a]	0.2	7	11
Kazakhstan	18.2	0.3	1.0	19	23
India	14.2	1.5	0.3	7	14
China	10.9	3.6	0.4	9	13
South Africa	6.4	0.08	0.1	6	8
Total	21.2	17.2	0.7	13	16

[a] Based on 1997 (hence, pre–financial crisis) prices and exchange rates.
[b] Transfers in the form of subsidies lead to increases in consumer and producer surplus (defined as the difference between what consumers are willing to pay for a unit of the good and what they actually pay, and as the difference between what producers actually receive when selling a product and the amount that they would be willing to accept for a unit of the good, respectively). These increases however are smaller than the total amount of the transfers (subsidy), which means that the subsidy entails a net loss in social welfare. Hence removing the subsidy would entail net economic efficiency gains.
Source: International Energy Agency (1999a); Myers and Kent (2001).

were tightened) and the additional reduction in emissions would have been lower assuming the cheaper alternatives had already been implemented. Improvements in the fuel mix are at the high end of marginal costs, providing even less additional reductions in emissions (figure 2.4).[73]

But if a resource is substantially degraded, the costs of restoring it can jump dramatically. For example, restoring water to the Florida Everglades is estimated at $7.8 billion. Sometimes, when the depletion or degradation reaches very high proportions, even if it is technologically feasible to address the problem, it may not be economically viable to do so. And when the problem is technically irreversible, the costs become infinite. For example, once substances such as oil, petroleum, and chemical solvents (which are part of a certain type of contaminants known as nonaqueous phase liquids) penetrate an aquifer, they are almost impossible to remove.

Complications arising from long time-horizons and uncertainty
One of the difficulties with environmental problems is that the costs and benefits of addressing the issue are sometimes highly uncertain. The problem is even more complicated when the costs and benefits are realized at different points in time—often benefits ma-

terialize in the long term while costs are incurred in the short term, as with climate change. Sometimes the costs and benefits that occur in the future at different points in time can be discounted or converted into an equivalent set of costs and benefits today, using the consumption rate of interest—the rate at which consumption tomorrow can be substituted for consumption today without changing social well-being. But the farther the benefits occur into the future, the greater the bias toward inaction, because discounting automatically reduces the valuation of these benefits.[74]

However, if one recognizes that a longer time-horizon also means that there could be significant uncertainty about the interest rate itself, and if the cost-benefit analysis takes this uncertainty into account, the valuation of benefits over distant horizons increases. (Since the consumption rate of interest depends in part on the forecast of future consumption, uncertainty about long-run economic forecasts would imply an uncertainty about the interest rate.)[75] As a nonrigorous but illustrative example, an exercise allowing for such uncertainty looked at the benefits of addressing climate change. Using the government bond rate (generally taken to be the best proxy for the consumption rate of interest) of 4 percent as the initial rate, the study assumed that future rates could either rise to 7 percent or fall to 1 percent, and showed

Figure 2.4
Reducing emissions in Mexico City

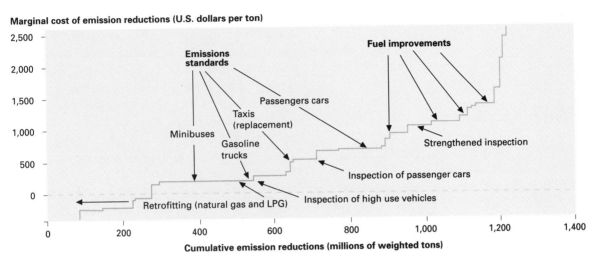

Marginal cost of emission reductions (U.S. dollars per ton)

Source: Eskeland and Devarajan (1996).

how allowing for this uncertainty could add about 80 percent to the expected present value of addressing climate change (carbon mitigation) relative to the valuation under a constant interest rate of 4 percent.[76] Thus, if a dollar's worth of benefits in the future is worth 25 cents under a constant interest rate of 4 percent, it would be worth 20 cents more (45 cents) allowing for this uncertainty in interest rates.

Reducing uncertainty generally requires the generation of knowledge and information. The possibility of hitting thresholds also highlights the importance of developing and monitoring key indicators that can signal coming problems. Unfortunately, as discussed earlier, such knowledge and information is also usually underprovided because individuals, in deciding whether to invest in knowledge and information gathering, do not take into account the positive spillovers that this can generate for society.

Correcting the overuse or underprovision of important assets

Developing indicators to determine how assets are being used is a challenge (see earlier section on measuring sustainability). Addressing the overuse or underprovision of assets is another. This section discusses the mechanisms to address the two main reasons for the overuse or underprovision of environmental assets discussed earlier—market and policy failures.

Addressing market failures

Whenever spillovers (externalities) exist, there is a coordination problem—private marginal costs and benefits diverge from social marginal costs and benefits, and policies that align the two are needed. While the focus is generally on formal policies or mechanisms, informal community institutions, which rely on informal norms and networks, can also be key means for addressing coordination problems.

It is usually most efficient to address market failures at the lowest level that can internalize the externality—this is known as the principle of subsidiarity. Note that this can have a bearing on the roles of informal and formal mechanisms.[77] Spillovers that affect people in a single community should be addressed at that level. But quite often spillovers extend much beyond a single community and must therefore be dealt with in a broader setting. For example, maintaining a hillside forest is of interest to groups at many levels. Local communities and those living near the forest may want to manage it to provide fuel and food. Communities in the larger watershed may have an interest in maintaining the same forests to mitigate flooding and siltation downstream. The nation may want to maintain the ecotourism potential of the forests. The world at large may be concerned about the forest's ability to support biodiversity and carbon stocks. This requires corresponding action at all levels.

Appropriate formal mechanisms to address a market failure can range from using command and control regulations and harnessing market forces to creating markets and engaging the public (figure 2.5). Usually a mix of mechanisms is required to address a problem, although occasionally one is applicable or sufficient. In general, the choice of mechanisms needs to be guided by the following:

- The effectiveness of the instrument in meeting the objective
- The efficiency of the instrument—including whether it ensures static efficiency (achieving the goal at minimum cost to society) and dynamic efficiency (providing incentives for innovation and the search for alternative, more efficient ways of meeting the objective)—while minimizing the implementation costs (monitoring, enforcement)
- The extent to which the instrument minimizes the costs of meeting other objectives when there are tradeoffs
- The effects on distribution and poverty.

Regulations—command and control

Regulations, or command and control measures, have traditionally been the means of aligning public and private interests. Such measures—which include licenses, permits, quality standards, emission standards, process standards, product standards, and prohibitions—have the advantage of targeting a desired level (quantity) or quality of an asset more easily than other mechanisms. For example, air quality can be addressed by process standards or emissions standards.

Similarly, management and planning, also a regulatory approach, can sometimes work. For urban pollution, zoning and land use restrictions can be important if, for instance, there are economies of scale in dealing with pollution when firms are in one place. Though blunt, zoning can be an effective tool in handling environmental damage when the spatial dimension matters. Experience suggests, however, that regulations are sometimes less efficient and effective than market-based instruments—and costly in the institutional capacity they require for implementation.

Using markets—taxes and subsidies

Pollution can also be addressed through such market instruments as a tax, but the impact of tax rates on the levels of emissions cannot be known before the fact. Only by trial and error would a regulatory

agency know the effect of a given tax rate. Increasingly it is being recognized that a combination of command and control and market-based instruments is superior to either alone. So if the interest is in reaching a desired quantity or quality at lowest cost, a target can be set for overall emissions, and permits or licenses would allow industry to emit up to the total but trade amongst themselves to achieve the overall goal at lowest cost to society.

Countries are thus moving to economic instruments to address environmental concerns. These offer more potential in terms of efficiency now (static) and over time (dynamic). They can offer more flexibility in meeting objectives. And they provide a source of government revenue that can address other public concerns. There are difficulties: many environmental assets do not have well-defined property rights, and operating in the market requires that property rights be assignable. Even so, some part of the depletion or degradation of the asset often takes place in the arena of markets—and is thus amenable to correction through economic instruments.[78] And technology can sometimes change whether an asset can have well-defined property rights and hence operate in the market (meters can foster water markets that would otherwise not be feasible).

For example, even though private property rights to clean air—the asset—are not assignable, it is still possible to deal with aspects of the degradation within markets. Emissions or fuels can be taxed, or vehicle use in the case of vehicles.

One proposal for dealing with global common–related concerns such as ozone depletion and climate change is to impose user charges or levies at the global level.[79] (Of course, curbing air pollution by taxing vehicle and industrial emissions in cities, as mentioned above, would also be an important component of a strategy to deal with climate change.)[80] User charges create incentives to reduce environmental pressures (the incentive function of user charges). They can also mobilize financial resources that can be earmarked to fund the conservation and restoration of global common goods (the financing function of user charges).

Creating markets: property rights and trading permits

Sometimes it is possible to define and allocate property rights that are supported through regulations and institutional arrangements, which then create markets

Figure 2.5
Mechanisms to address market and policy failures

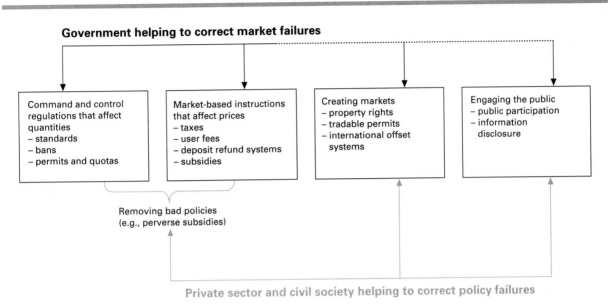

Source: Adapted from *"Five Years after Rio: Innovations in Environmental Policy,"* World Bank (1997a).

and allow the advantages of efficiency. Indeed, this approach (tradable permits for pollution emissions) has been a major innovation in the last decade.[81] The use of command and control to regulate the overall allowable pollution levels, together with tradable permits, creates a market for pollution abatement that would not otherwise exist. Making permits tradable gives firms an incentive to look for the most cost-effective solutions for pollution abatement, because firms that lower their pollution more effectively or at a lower cost than do other firms can sell their excess credits to those firms. Firms then face an opportunity cost of pollution, which creates incentives to find cheaper abatement methods, encourages less pollution in aggregate, and ensures dynamic efficiency.

In OECD countries, tradable permits are seen as a way of harmonizing environmental protection with economic efficiency.[82] The U.S. sulfur dioxide reduction scheme to reduce acid rain is an example, relying on tradable rights and credible threats in cases of noncompliance. Similarly, Iceland and New Zealand have revived fish stocks by assigning fishing rights at a sustainable level and allowing fishers to trade their quotas freely.

These arrangements, despite their advantages in providing the right incentives to adopt least-cost solutions, can still be costly to administer and im-

plement. Finding the right balance between giving free play to market forces and monitoring and enforcement is a big challenge.

Engaging the public: publicizing and sharing information

Civil society can monitor and ensure compliance with regulations. A good example is Indonesia's PROPER program, which discloses the noncompliance of polluting firms to the public (while rewarding compliance), encouraging local communities to put pressure on companies that score poorly. The program focused initially on water pollution. It ranked companies by their emissions, and disclosed the results in stages, recognizing good performers first and giving the bad ones six months to clean up. Within 18 months, half of the noncomplying firms were observing the legally established standards.[83]

Public participation and monitoring can also make voluntary compliance agreements more effective. Such agreements with the private sector are becoming popular in addressing environmental problems in many OECD countries, especially when regulatory structures cannot address specific issues. The agreements can be commitments devised by the government (or an environmental agency), with individual firms invited to participate. Or they can be negotiated commitments for environmental protection developed through bargaining between a public authority and industry. They can also be unilateral commitments initiated by the private sector. These agreements are not limited to environmental issues. For instance, tour operators have agreed with the City and Borough of Juneau (Alaska) to minimize any adverse impacts of tourism on the local community.

Voluntary approaches—designed, implemented, and monitored properly—can work. But they can also have problems. Control can be weak because industry does not provide adequate control mechanisms or because of a lack of sanctions. Free-riding is possible when other firms bear no cost of complying with the agreement while reaping the benefit. Then there is the possibility of regulatory capture—when powerful businesses exert undue influence on the process.[84] Encouraging the participation of civil society can help to mitigate these problems.

Addressing policy failures

Many environmental stresses today are not the result of ignorance about what policies to adopt. Indeed, 10 years ago *World Development Report 1992* addressed the complex issues of environment and development and concluded that several doable, "win-win" policy options were available (box 2.8). A decade later these policy recommendations remain valid, but many of them have, at best, been adopted or implemented only partially.[85] As discussed, the widespread use of subsidies remains high across the globe (for water,

energy, and food—especially in industrial countries). Damaging races for property rights abound (individuals or companies pushing to develop the remaining natural resources ahead of someone else: minerals, forests, fisheries). While the world is moving toward greater trade liberalization, trade restrictions (tariffs and non-tariff barriers) remain on precisely the goods in which developing nations are competitive, including agricultural products and textiles.

If the policy recommendations of a decade ago continue to be the best route to improving the welfare of millions of people, why have they not been implemented? In reality, even the win-win policies have been much harder to implement than initially thought—vested interests were much more entrenched, and institutional development was harder to foster. The persistence of policy failures even when society as a whole can benefit from their removal often reflects powerful interest groups blocking the necessary reforms. Just as participation by civil society, together with greater information disclosure and transparency, can help in monitoring the implementation of environmental regulations by individual companies, so too can it be an important means of improving the accountability of the public sector (see figure 2.5). The blocking of reforms by powerful groups represents one of the deeper barriers to the emergence of the institutions needed to support environmental policies.

This Report as a whole tries to show that environmental problems are, at their root, social problems. The distribution of assets, and of the costs and ben-

---

Box 2.8
***World Development Report 1992:* Development and the Environment**

World Development Report 1992 identified the challenge of pursuing development and poverty alleviation in a generation (1990–2030) that would see world population increase by 3.7 billion, food production double, and energy use triple. It called for actions that would mutually reinforce environmental protection and development: provide clean air, sanitation, and clean water; improve management of soils; and protect biodiversity. It saw great scope for win-win interventions that would simultaneously improve the environment and provide local economic benefits.

That report also called for improved institutions for environmental regulation, using market-based incentive principles where possible, and made a series of policy recommendations:

■ *Win-win policies.* Eliminating subsidies for energy inputs, pesticides, fertilizer, irrigation water, logging, and ranching (perverse subsidies); taxing urban road emissions

■ *Priorities for action.* Removing perverse subsidies, strengthening property rights over common pool resources, expanding service provision, increasing voice and participation, carefully evaluating environmental tradeoffs with special regard for long-term irreversible or large-scale damage, matching the government's role to its capability
■ *Policies for sustained development.* Where possible, relying on incentives rather than regulations; curbing the influence of vested interests
■ *Partnership for solutions.* Partnering with high-income countries to expand market access and to increase development assistance; partnering with high-income countries to finance the costs of global environmental priorities, especially those requiring the protection of natural habitats in developing countries.

Source: Authors; Acharya and Dixon, background paper for the *WDR 2003.*

efits of different policies, as well as the role of trust, are all critical to the ability of societies to develop competent rules and institutions (chapter 3) to address environmental, social, and economic problems.

This chapter has discussed the importance of managing and ensuring a better balance of assets to enhance human well-being on a sustained basis. It also covered the externalities and coordination problems that generally lead to the overuse or underprovision of some of society's key assets, detailing the policy instruments and mechanisms to address these externalities. As discussed, the nonadoption or nonimplementation of these policies reflect the fact that the supporting institutions—with the appropriate characteristics—have not yet emerged. Chapter 3 looks at the characteristics of appropriate institutions, the potential barriers to their emergence, and how these may be addressed; it focuses on catalysts that may increase the likelihood of the timely emergence of these institutions.

Institutions for Sustainable Development

We have to see individual freedom as a social commitment.

Amartya Sen[1]

The previous chapter made the case that for people to thrive—especially over a longer time horizon—a wide range of assets must also thrive. Managing a broader portfolio of assets can ensure that the growth process contributes to people's well-being on a sustained basis. Policies can be designed to improve the management of assets.[2] In practice many socially worthwhile policies are not adopted or implemented. The institutional perspective examines the forces that work to shape and implement policies.

If institutions are to protect people and a broad portfolio of assets, they must respond to and shape the major changes that will unfold over the next 50 years: urbanization, technological innovation, economic growth, shifting social values, changing scarcities for environmental and natural assets, and stronger linkages among nations. Institutions thus must be stable, but they also must be capable of changing and adapting, and new institutions must emerge.

Chapter 3 focuses on the coordination of human behavior that is required for people and assets to thrive, particularly institutions that sustain this co-ordination—by channeling interests, and by shaping the quality and effectiveness of growth. This chapter addresses four questions:

- What are institutions? They are the rules and organizations, including informal norms, that coordinate human behavior. They are essential for sustainable and equitable development. When they function well, they enable people to work with each other to plan a future for themselves, their families, and their larger communities. But when they are weak or unjust, the result is mistrust and uncertainty. This encourages people to "take" rather than "make," and it undermines joint potential.[3]

- What are the key functions of the institutional environment in promoting human well-being? It must *pick up signals* about needs and problems—particularly from the fringes; this involves generating information, giving citizens a voice, responding to feedback, and fostering learning. It must also *balance interests*—by negotiating change and forging agreements, and by avoiding stalemates and conflicts. And it must *execute* and *implement solutions*—by credibly following through on agreements.

- What are the barriers to the emergence of such an institutional environment? One is dispersed interests. Concentrated interests are often given too much weight, as in the assignment of property rights for land and water, and in the operation of government. A second barrier is the difficulty of forging credible commitments to protect and nurture persons and assets. And a third is institutions that are not inclusive. When societies and processes are unequal and undemocratic, it is more difficult to coordinate dispersed interests and forge credible commitments.

■ How can these barriers be overcome? Sometimes social and economic development offers opportunities for change. Structural changes—urbanization, the demographic transition, the redistribution of wealth (particularly increments of new wealth)— unleash dynamic forces and opportunities for institutional change. Initiatives to channel information can also serve as catalysts for change. Information can empower people by giving them more voice in public services and allowing greater transparency and accountability in the activities of governments and firms.

Institutions coordinating human behavior

Institutions are the rules, organizations, and social norms that facilitate coordination of human action (figure 3.1). On the informal end, they go from trust and other forms of social capital (including deeply rooted norms governing social behavior) to informal mechanisms and networks for coordination. On the formal end, they include a country's codified rules and laws, and the procedures and organizations for making, modifying, interpreting, and enforcing the rules and laws (from the legislature to the central bank).

Because institutions govern behavior, they are social assets (or liabilities, when bad or weak). So are the elements of social capital, such as trust and personal networks. The distinction between social capital and institutions can sometimes be blurred, and there are strong influences between the various social assets (see chapter 2, note 14). For example, the exchange of goods and services may be based on personal networks and other forms of social capital in the village, but on formal institutions in the city. Similarly, general trustworthiness in a society can be strong either because of strong personal networks— or because of good laws and judicial systems that are generally accepted. In fact, as societies become more complex, trust in individuals (based on knowledge of character and frequency of interpersonal contacts) is supplemented by trust in institutions (rules and organizations) when dealing with strangers.

Two very important dimensions of coordination are *others* and *future*. Markets are institutions with coordinating functions (box 3.1). A market coordinating the transactions of individuals and firms enables them to serve *others* and invest for the *future* (as when a baker builds an oven in response to greater demand). But markets need the support of other institutions to ensure confidence, control, and

Figure 3.1
Social norms, rules, and organizations for coordinating human behavior

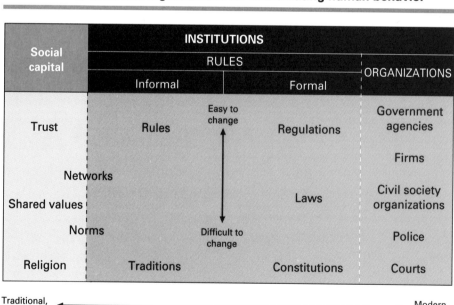

Box 3.1
The market as a coordination mechanism

Adam Smith, 1776, captures well how market forces coordinate human behavior for the common good with his famous "invisible hand" formulation: "It is not from the benevolence of the butcher, the brewer or the baker that we expect our dinner, but from their regard to their own self interest." Going beyond this, Friedrich von Hayek lucidly depicts the market as a discovery device. Through voluntary exchange, the market generates price signals, conveying information about scarcity. When markets are competitive and decentralized, the "knowledge of the particular circumstances of time and place" will help guide decisionmaking (Hayek 1945, p. 526). Hayek uses the example of a rise in the scarcity of tin. Users of tin will receive a signal through the higher price that "some of the tin they used to consume is now more profitably employed elsewhere, and that in consequence they must economize tin." Simultaneously producers receive a signal to seek new supplies. The system operates with remarkable economy of knowledge and gathers dispersed interests.

"The marvel is that in a case like that of scarcity of one raw material, without an order being issued, without more than perhaps a handful of people knowing its cause, tens of thousands of people whose identity could not be ascertained by months of investigation, are made to use the material or its products more sparingly; i.e., they move in the right direction" (Hayek 1945, p. 527).

Markets can perform these functions even when there are important public concerns, of course, but they need the support of other institutions to handle those concerns. For instance, an environmental protection agency issuing tradable pollution permits or charging for emissions (as with sulfur in the United States, or water pollution in Colombia), can use markets to find cheap ways to abate pollution. More typically, emission regulations fail to use markets as much as they could to challenge firms to find cheaper and more environmentally friendly ways to produce.

Source: Authors.

the right incentives. Economic agents face transaction costs, and institutions can coordinate to lower those costs. Traders may want to cheat each other—or to renege on their promises. But social capital and modern institutions—such as the rule of law and the enforcement of contracts—reduce this probability (a transaction cost), facilitating mutually beneficial transactions. Particular challenges for these other institutions are to commit to protect and nurture people and assets—and to serve dispersed interests.

World Development Report 2002: Building Institutions for Markets, looked mainly at human-made assets, and its focus was narrower than this Report's. But it looked deeper into what sustains investments and transactions. This Report builds on that foundation but expands the discussion to aspects of wellbeing that are not limited to income or easily amenable to markets, including services from environmental, natural, and social assets. The actors in society partly play under a given set of rules and they partly shape those rules. Firms, government, and civil society are positioned to act and to influence the actions of others, playing complementary roles in coordination.

Market players

Market participation enables people to specialize and work together, and to apply their skills and resources in the best way possible, as the price mechanism provides information to coordinate (see box 3.1, and chapter 7). But the institutional framework must ensure that markets function and deliver their expected benefits. Where formal institutions are weak, activity will locate in the informal sector—in many developing countries the share of workers in the informal sector is more than 60 percent.[4] This means that a substantial proportion of economic activity is deprived of potential productivity-enhancing support, and may also escape guidance from institutions that manage environmental and social aspects.[5] But market power can also give large domestic firms or multinational corporations potential coercive powers akin to the government's in terms of serving narrow rather then broad interests. Thus, a major challenge for government and formal institutions is to be more welcoming and supportive of private actors with appropriate safeguards to ensure the public interest is not compromised.

Government

In many areas, government plays a central role in organizing dispersed interests: meeting national goals and balancing competing interests. Unlike social norms and values, government operates a rulemaking process by which rules can be changed more quickly, with vision and design, and still be forceful. But if a government—with its socially sanctioned coercive powers—finds itself unbound by rules (e.g., by a constitution or equivalent with the separation of powers it brings), how can it commit itself as a partner? The private sector will be less willing to invest and do business if instability and risks of expropriatory consequence have not been curtailed. Unless institutions succeed in separating the powers of government and providing meaningful checks and balances, communities and the private sector will be less forward looking, and environmental and natural assets will be hurt through inappropriate investment and conservation.

Democratic forms of decisionmaking, despite their limitations, are associated with processes that exhibit desirable institutional features; they pick up signals, balance interests, and execute chosen actions. A growing body of literature finds that indicators of voice and accountability are closely associated with better development outcomes, including higher national income per capita, lower infant mortality rates, and lower illiteracy rates (chapter 7, and *WDR 2002*). Empirical evidence strongly supports Amartya Sen's finding that democracy—helped by free speech—plays a key role in eliminating famine and eliciting effective disaster relief.[6] Theoretical and empirical evidence also suggests that environmental commitment and related outcomes are positively correlated with democratic practices, though some countries have also done well environmentally using other channels.

Civil society

There has been a sharp increase in the active membership of civil society organizations in the past two decades (figure 3.2). During this period civil society organizations have become more capable, sometimes acting independently, sometimes influencing the activities of government and the private sector.[7]

Civil society's role has been most notable in mobilizing support for specific issues, supplying information, and providing third-party verification. Civil society organizations often take initiative and provide voice for unheard interests—building the trust, legitimacy, and knowledge needed. In West Bengal, India, the Ramakrishna Mission works with youth clubs in 1,500 villages, undertaking needs assess-

Figure 3.2
Growing participation in civil society organizations, 1981–97

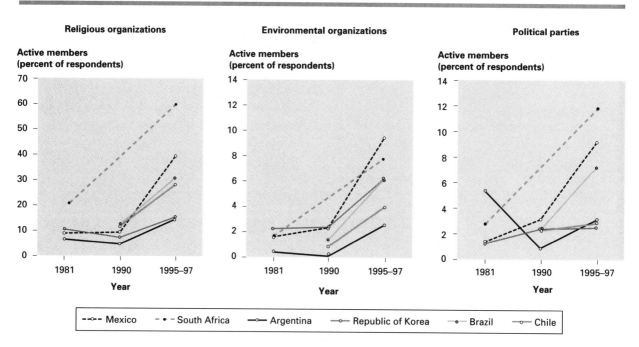

Note: Countries shown are the only developing countries for which longitudinal data are available. In the 1995–97 survey, participation data were collected in 11 additional developing economies: Bangladesh, Colombia, the Dominican Republic, Ghana, India, Nigeria, Peru, the Philippines, Taiwan (China), Uruguay, and República Bolivariana de Venezuela. Active group membership in these additional countries in 1995–97 averaged 25.1 percent for religious organizations, 8.5 percent for political parties, and 6.2 percent for environmental organizations. The survey was not conducted in South Africa in 1990 or in Brazil or Chile in 1981. As a result the true shape of the South Africa trend line may differ from what is shown.
Source: The World Values Survey.

ments and helping to identify external support for social welfare and development projects.[8] In Thailand the Appropriate Technology Association has facilitated collaborations among farmers, university scientists, and government authorities to reduce pesticide poisoning through the use of biological controls.[9]

Civil society and the media also play an important monitoring role—for example, improving accountability and reducing incentives for corruption in government. The commercial exploitation of natural resources is particularly susceptible to corruption;[10] for example, in Bolivia, a voracious illegal trade in endangered species in the mid-1980s was facilitated by customs officials who, in the absence of independent oversight, doctored export permits. An active civil society makes it easier for environmental officials and others to publicize mismanagement; for example, in Cameroon civil society plays a role in monitoring a promising new logging concession scheme (chapter 7). When citizens have access to independent sources of information, meaningful channels for political participation, and legal protection against retribution, they can become a strong political force for improved performance in public agencies.

Civil society organizations are particularly important for promoting environmentally sound development strategies. Environmental management often is about "downstream" spillover effects, and NGOs can often provide knowledge and links between geographically dispersed locations. The surge in civic environmental activity has often been part of a broad upward trend in civil society activity generally.[11] Opinion surveys consistently reveal levels of public environmental concern in developing countries equal to that in industrial countries.[12]

Institutions protecting assets

How can there be assets? Is it not easier to take than to make? Institutions that restrain the taking of assets—through norms or under threats of punishment—are essential for assets to thrive, whether the assets are human-made or natural, whether they are transacted in markets or not. For example, restraint is necessary for the forest and the aquifer to yield sustained benefits when population density, changes in technology or preferences, and other developments increase the demands on their use. Institutions ensuring such restraint allow assets to thrive; however, because they

yield dispersed benefits, such institutions do not emerge easily.

Protective institutions are those that define and support control rights in terms of access to and use of assets central to human well-being; for example, who can graze their cows where, who controls a factory, who takes home eventual profits—or who is allowed to discharge emissions—when and where, and at what price. A special subset of protective institutions are private property rights. They entail well-delimited (and not too limited) rights of use and decisionmaking for an owner, typically including rights to sell or lease an asset. These institutions include a commitment from society (extended family, neighbors, villagers, or governments) to help protect these rights. In a modern state, this commitment requires an active obligation of enforcement from the government (police or judges) and the assurance that the government itself respects those rights. For this reason, the security of property rights is closely associated with the rule of law—so that people can make assumptions about what will be respected as theirs.

But protective institutions also arise to manage assets that are not amenable to private ownership. A pollution control agency defines and protects control rights to the air. A central bank protects the integrity of a currency and financial system. And communities can solve coordination problems and allow assets to thrive, as the literature on *common property resource management* and *social capital* demonstrates (the important interplay between community cooperation and modern society's formal institutions can be beneficial or detrimental).[13]

In the broader institutional environment, firms, government, and civil society organizations together give force to rules and norms. For instance, civil society can help keep the judiciary independent. Indeed, rules and norms are typically backed by sanctions, and many are effective only when agencies and organizations back them up.

Some assets protect other assets—and some are more vulnerable to predation than others (box 3.2). Land is protected by formal institutions (property rights, courts, and titling agencies) in a modern urban setting, but it is relatively less protected under periodic, nomadic grazing. Fisheries turn from needing no protection when stocks are abundant—to needing costly protective institutions as fishing technology and demand develop. Savings under mat-

Box 3.2
Assets, threats, and protection

If not properly protected, assets cannot thrive and contribute to growth or human well-being. Assets are not all vulnerable to the same threats, but all assets—natural as well as human-made, in the village and the city—depend on protective institutions. In the examples here, the protection is weak.

With bandits, there is no use in bringing in oxen
In Uganda, animal traction for plowing is now promoted as a way to raise agricultural productivity. In the subcounty of Nambiti, the administration plans to provide selected farmer groups with trained oxen, in the hope that this will raise productivity and induce other farmers to put their savings into oxen. Farmers there are skeptical, however; the problem of mobile and armed bandits has not been resolved, and farmers expect that any oxen would soon be stolen.

With insecure property rights, incomes and well-being collapse
Massive transfers of state property to private agents have occurred in the postcommunist economies in the past decade. In almost all of these countries, the private sector went from having a very small share of the economy in 1989 to having the dominant share in 2000. But in many countries, these transfers were not accompanied by the development of institutions that would make private property rights well defined and secure.

A staggering 75 percent of firms in the Kyrgyz Republic, Moldova, the Russian Federation, and Ukraine were not "confident that the legal system will uphold my contract and property rights in business disputes." Among the six economies where property rights were least secure, income (GDP) fell in the decade of transition—by 40 percent or more. Many countries with contractions in GDP also had large increases in death rates.

Without commitments to law and property, well-managed exploitation is unlikely
Insecure property rights also hurt natural and environmental assets: fish populations are threatened, and trees are cut prematurely. Because people are not sure that they will be able to harvest tomorrow, they take what they can today—initiating a race for property rights.

For a cross-section of countries, the insecurity of property rights reduces investment in human-made capital and increases deforestation. Forests would benefit from reforms that strengthen the commitment to law and property. There are good reasons to believe that benefits will extend to other natural and environmental assets as well. But there will be exceptions, as when stocks are naturally protected by exploration or extraction costs. For petroleum reserves, exploration and extraction requires investment that is itself vulnerable to ownership risk. In these cases when more secure rights increase extraction or conversion, the likely effects will be more attractive, and not limited to reflecting short-term, narrow interests.

Source: Bohn and Deacon (2000); Hellman, Jones, and Kaufmann (2000); Hoff and Stiglitz (2002); EBRD (2002); World Bank staff.

tresses need some protection, but those in banks need good vaults and such credible institutions as independent regulatory agencies and central banks.

Higher national income can contribute to better institutional quality (for example, through more expenditures on courts). But more importantly, better institutional quality can also contribute to higher national income, as when good institutions facilitate investments or curb overfishing. A large body of theoretical and empirical studies concludes that there are strong causal effects from good institutions, measured by such variables as rule of law to higher incomes per capita (figure 3.3). According to one study, better voice and accountability would raise national income per capita by a factor of 2.5.[14] Another study suggests that per capita incomes would grow at least 2 percent per year in all countries if they would only protect property rights (public and private) and pursue more competitive market policies.[15]

So when institutions allow assets to thrive, an economy can flourish. But if good institutions are so important, why don't all countries have them?

Why would a politician or leader not take steps to strengthen the judiciary and protect property rights? Because a leader who takes steps to build stronger institutions would reap benefits from the stronger economy and the better environment only in the long run, and this requires a stable setting with broad political support.[16]

Valuable assets cannot thrive, and can be in wasteful decline, if there is no social commitment to developing protective institutions (box 3.3). For agricultural land, two facts facilitate the emergence of protective institutions, as they may have come about historically. First, when land becomes scarce, competing users cannot avoid meeting face to face, and can choose to fight or negotiate. Second, when neighbors are settled, they can help each other defend their land in a reciprocal fashion. Therefore, even without a state or feudal lord, transgressors will face some deterrence.[17]

To see how protective institutions form under more challenging circumstances, consider fisheries.[18] Fisheries account for 19 percent of total human consump-

Figure 3.3
The relationship between institutional quality and national income

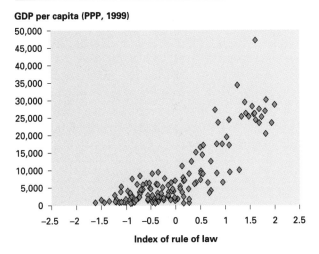

GDP per capita (PPP, 1999)

Index of rule of law

PPP = Purchasing power parity.

Note: As a measure of institutional quality, the rule of law includes considerations such as the security of property rights, or the confidence with which a group or individual can find tomorrow the fruits of what is planted or conserved today.

Source: Kaufman, Kraay, and Zoido-Lobaton (1999).

tion of animal protein, so good institutions for fisheries are important.[19] A typical story of fisheries development starts with the discovery of new fish stock. As fishermen make good money, more capacity rushes in. Though scarcity and wasteful competition ensue, fishermen do not coordinate management. Over time, the catch falls, first per hour of effort, then in total, with individual fishermen barely breaking even.[20] This wasteful race to exploit the resource wastes labor and capital, since fish that should have been allowed to spawn and grow are caught. Government involvement can make matters worse, if subsidies distort signals and prolong overfishing (chapter 7).

Contrast this story—of waste and no profit—with alternatives in which the value of the resource is maximized. A cooperative of fishermen could manage a resource well if it could control its members, if its members could control their organization, and if the cooperative could control entry into the industry—all big ifs. In theory, a private monopoly could also manage a fishing resource efficiently. More often in practice, government regulates by denying access or enforcing restraint. Restraints that start with and build on existing resource users are more likely to be credible and successful—as seen in New Zealand and Iceland (see chapter 7).

Box 3.3
Natural assets decline when protective institutions are weak

Poor institutions contribute to a poor investment climate and to the depletion of natural resources. It is also possible that some types of natural resources make institution-building difficult (chapter 7), while others support inclusive and development-friendly institutions.*

Consider a sample of 150 countries for which there are data (from the World Bank's adjusted savings table) on capital stocks, including human-made physical, mineral, forest, and agricultural capital. Adjusted savings are negative when this stock is declining. Of countries with low human-made physical capital stocks (less than 75 percent of national income), 24 percent (16 of 67 countries) had negative adjusted savings, compared with 10 percent (8 of 83 countries) for countries with higher stocks of human-made physical capital.

Thus, countries with high rates of depletion of natural resources also tend to be countries with low stocks of physical capital. For countries with negative adjusted savings, this perspective shifts the focus away from recommending policies to increase savings to recommending improvements in protective institutions. Their low accumulation of physical assets and the declining natural asset base are more the result of an institutional environment in which assets cannot thrive, than of low savings.

* The literature on natural resources as a curse makes this connection, as do recent studies such as Acemoglu, Johnson, and Robinson (2001); Engerman and Sokoloff (1997); and Woolcok, Pritchett, and Isham (2001). See also Auty (1997) and Hoff and Stiglitz (2002).

Source: World Bank's adjusted savings table.

The Law of the Sea, with 200-mile exclusive economic zones, reflects the idea that privatizing a resource can allow for better management—it "privatizes" ownership to coastal states, suitably linking the resource both to traditional interests and to a natural jurisdiction for enforcement. While not all fisheries' management problems are confined to national waters, nations can build on the law and negotiate. Many impressive fisheries management schemes would not have been possible without this law (chapter 7). In many other cases, however, management institutions have been only partly successful in limiting entry and stabilizing catches, and as a result there has not been enough reduction in excess capacity and harvesting to bring major benefits. The challenge is to win the industry's confidence that it can reap the benefits if capacity is reduced and profitability restored. If the commitment to rewarding restraint is not credible, overfishing continues.

Picking up signals, balancing interests, and implementing decisions

A good institutional environment must perform many functions. But to credibly and purposefully coordinate actions, three functions stand out—to pick up signals, to balance different interests, and to implement decisions.

Picking up signals

Fisheries being depleted, toxins poisoning children, corruption weakening emission testing, oppression hobbling indigenous groups, violence against women continuing—all these phenomena can be ignored willfully or accidentally in a setting that is not receptive to signals. Signals of social and environmental degradation (chapter 2) can be based on scientific measurements (as in the case of air quality), or voice and feedback, but they would be effective only if there are constituencies for information and action.

The ability to pick up signals is closely associated with the ability to balance interests. Creating and receiving signals range from the feasibility of detecting a phenomenon in a meaningful way, to the process of aggregating signals and getting the attention of decision makers. Receptivity to signals thus depends on social and political relations. Are they open and inclusive, or fragmented and discriminatory? Are they pluralistic, meritocratic, and free, or politicized and monolithic? Is there freedom and competition in individual expression, business, and political organization?

Both citizens and the air-quality protection agency need good information on pollution, and this information has many uses. Mexico City's IMECA index, published daily in the press, advises people whether to keep their children indoors and avoid exercise. And it obviously informs citizens on how well the agency is doing in improving air quality, strengthening their hand in holding politicians and agencies accountable.

But there are also other signals. *Voice* describes the signals from citizens, firms, and civil society to influence institutions (i.e., through complaints, votes, court proceedings, and the media). A lesson from recent research in developing and developed countries is that influence—including good-natured influence from citizens to the emission reductions by firms—can travel through many channels, strengthened by information.[21]

A message from chapters 4 through 6 is that urban as well as rural residents can have difficulty in being heard and served, and new institutional arrangements are evolving to overcome this problem (e.g., boxes 6.4 and 6.5, respectively on *favela* residents in Brazil and on railway station–dwellers in Mumbai). For marginal rural areas, two factors make receptiveness to signals from the fringes more critical now than before. First, outmigration is less of an option than it was when high-income countries were industrializing (chapter 4). Second, other developments, such as mining, happen faster, so that signals about their impact on the community and the environment need to move faster too (see box 4.7).

Many countries are rearranging the way they govern themselves at the local level. With political decentralization, institutions develop to receive more fine-grained signals—important, since problems and priorities differ from place to place. But decentralization, proceeding in both rich and poor countries, carries promises as well as risks. It can be hard to get the incentives right, and there may be issues of weak institutional capacity and elite capture at lower levels of government as well.[22]

Balancing alternatives—and interests

A protective institution such as an air quality protection agency operates within an authorizing framework that balances interests. It may impose an emission standard or a tax, or strengthen enforcement. This in effect strengthens the rights of beneficiaries to air quality—weakening rights of others, and this is one of the ways changing social priorities can be implemented. The balancing of interests takes place at many levels: in national legislatures, in court processes, in marketplaces, in individual norms and village interactions, in the seen or unseen processes in corporate boardrooms and branches.

Evidence shows how information provision (in an era of unprecedented quantities of information) can catalyze shifts in political balances and real world decisions. Thus, the term "transparency" dominates the current campaign for better governance. There is evidence from rich and poor countries that greater availability of information means better environmental performance.[23]

Figure 3.4 shows the 1,445 cities in the world—where, according to World Bank estimates—the pop-

Figure 3.4
Concentration of total suspended particles

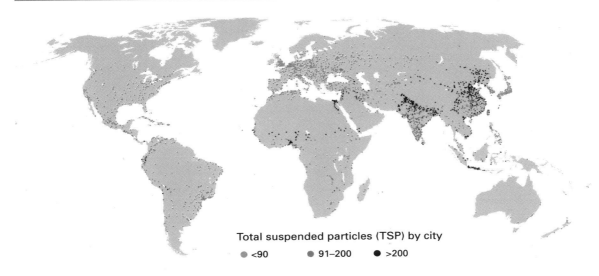

Total suspended particles (TSP) by city

● <90   ● 91–200   ● >200

Source: Bolt and others (forthcoming).

ulation suffers from exposure to concentration of dust particles, or total suspended particles (TSP) above traditional guidelines of 90 micrograms μ/m^3.[24] In less than 2 percent of these cities is air pollution systematically monitored, and in even fewer is information about that pollution made available to the public. A good working hypothesis—based on studies from industrial and developing countries—is that monitoring pollution information and making it public would help (in part through political channels) to improve air quality in these cities regardless of their level of income.[25]

But balance is not maintained by information provision alone. More open and democratic countries presumably give weight to dispersed interests, so there are reasons to expect that they would give more attention to environmental protection. The data are incomplete, but some results support this hypothesis (box 3.4).

One might expect a one-party system to have difficulty being receptive to signals, since unpleasant news might be easier to suppress in such a setting. But this is not always the case. In China two institutional features play a role in areas such as environmental management, where there has been noticeable progress in the last decade: a systematic approach to complaints, and national policies to make local environmental information available to the public (chapter 7). A complaints-driven system has many qualities, but may be biased toward immediately noticeable phenomena, such as noise. So the combination with objective monitoring data is valuable. Both mechanisms utilize the strengths of a decentralized system and recognize how national institutions (such as assurance of information) can be important for local accountability.[26]

In Europe information that helped establish a common understanding of who suffers from a problem and who contributes to the problem was essential in shifting the balance in favor of reducing transboundary pollution, even when negotiation—not authority—did the balancing (see box 8.1). For balance and for unbiased signals, it is essential to have supportive institutions in place. Corporations rely on laws and auditors for such traditional goals as protecting workers' pensions and shareholders' assets—and they now rely also on civil society for broader corporate social responsibility (chapter 8).

Executing decisions

As an environmental agency executes decisions through taxes, regulations, and enforcement, citizens

Box 3.4
Democracy and environmental policy: picking up signals, shifting the balance

There are strong theoretical reasons to think of democracy as conducive to environmental protection and economic efficiency in general.

Two plausible mechanisms can be observed:

- *Democracy helps give weight to dispersed interests.* In general, policies will be biased in favor of concentrated interests, giving less weight to equally important interests spread across a larger number of people. Benefits from environmental assets, such as from river water quality, are often considered public goods and are thus dispersed across many individuals, while the cleanup costs may be more concentrated.
- *Freedom of expression and association helps society pick up signals and adjust to change.* As population density increases, knowledge increases, incomes grow, or preferences change, the pressures on the environment change. As the problem of horse manure in London's streets declined, new problems—such as smog or lead contamination in city air or oil spills in the North Sea—emerged to beg for new management institutions and technical solutions. The accountability of politicians to the people and the separation

of powers are best envisaged in a democratic setting; these institutional features are also the key ingredients in putting new priorities on the table, rebalancing competing interests, and taking action.

It is not easy to accurately measure environmental commitment. Even so, democracies have a greater tendency to do the following:

- Put their land area under protection
- Sign and ratify multilateral environmental agreements
- Belong to environmental intergovernmental organizations
- Meet reporting requirements for the Convention on International Trade in Endangered Species of Fauna and Flora
- Have a National Council on Sustainable Development
- Have environmentally relevant information publicly available.

The study found that democracies are more likely to make an environmental commitment, regardless of their level of income.

Source: Neumayer, Gleditch, and Gates, background paper for the *WDR 2003.*

and firms change their pollution emissions. The agency will monitor these emissions and act on them, either by adjusting its charges for the emissions or by assessing penalties for noncompliance with regulations. Costa Rica's program to pay for environmental services program (see box 8.5) is an example where institutions shift the burden of protection, help to balance interests, and ensure better execution. There are many other examples, often integrated with development projects, such as the Global Environmental Facility (GEF) and the Prototype Carbon Fund (chapter 8). Box 3.5 discusses how locally negotiated solutions assisted in the implementation of water pollution reductions in Colombia.

Implementation is an extension of balancing. When the balancing is between suppliers and customers in a marketplace, the balancing and implementation functions may be one and the same (see box 3.1). Balanced decisionmaking in board rooms and national legislatures is not worth much if it is not implemented—or if the steps from policy to implementation are too far apart. In many countries, laws and protection through the courts are of little value because they are implemented by ineffective or corrupt courts—unless one has connections or money. In others, budget deliberations are not worth much because the budget is not followed.

It is not sufficient for society—or a development bank—to make a policy decision. Say society decides that forests should not be converted if the conservation benefits are higher than the conversion benefits. The implementation of this decision can be blunted by developers who press ahead and convert a forest, asserting that the conservation benefits are minor. The developers count on escaping sanctions—even if the losses turn out to be high—if society is known to lack the incentives, opportunity, or commitment to punish or undo wrongdoing.

How then does one ensure that policies are implemented? Good procedures and broad participation can help in the execution of high-level decisions. Procedures requiring ex ante assessments, participation, and public reviews can help. Routine social and environmental impact assessments, enforced with good quality information and public access to them, can expose consequences *before* development is irreversible. This can make it clear—to the public, to political leaders, to courts, and to civil society—that the proposed developments do not comply with broader social priorities. The information—and the supportive institutions—function as a commitment device.

In Uzbekistan, as part of the Uzbekistan Water Supply, Sanitation, and Health Project, a social assessment process was undertaken during project prepara-

Box 3.5
Local negotiations balance interests and commit parties to clean up Colombia's rivers

In Colombia, as in many countries, most wastewater is released untreated into waterways. With little enforcement, limits on pollution emissions have long been ignored. In 1997, the environment ministry implemented a new water pollution charge system that is cost-effective and enforceable. Facilitated under Colombia's decentralized structure, the system is implemented by regional environmental agencies. It brings together municipal authorities, polluting industries, and affected communities to negotiate local pollution reduction targets and charges. Polluters are charged per unit of effluent, and the parties agree to timetables for increasing the charges if targets are not met.

All the parties have received extensive capacity building from the national ministry, and the system holds together impressively: In the nation's 135 river basins, biochemical oxygen demand is already down by 31.5 percent, and suspended solids by 34.2 percent. Nationally the program has generated $9.7 million in revenues, funding pollution reduction projects and regional environmental agencies.

Lessons include the following:

■ *Use national commitment to facilitate locally negotiated solutions.* Regulated sectors participate because authorities have signaled their intent to enforce the program. But each region is allowed to set goals and timetables to reflect local conditions and aspirations. Firms can choose emission reductions—and method—in light of per unit charges.
■ *Devise innovative approaches to program administration.* A well-respected private bank collects the charges and administers the funds in return for a percentage of the revenues, reducing the burden of collection but not of auditing by government agencies.
■ *Enhance the community benefits of market-based regulatory tools.* Local business leaders were initially skeptical, perceiving the program as a new generalized tax burden. When it was agreed that revenues would fund monitorable benefits, such as local pollution reduction, this appealed to businesses and communities alike, and helped generate commitment to implementation.

Future progress will require greater compliance from recalcitrant sectors, such as municipal water companies, who use various pretexts to avoid paying and investing. If those who do not comply are seen to gain, it could threaten the more general commitment among polluters, a commitment that has proven to be a strength of negotiated approaches.

Sources: World Bank 2000d; Andean Center 2001.

---

tion. The government initially wanted to ensure that drinking water would have no more than one gram of salinity per liter, although international guidelines allowed higher salinity. The lower salinity level would have been costly and there is no known evidence that it would be healthier. So with the help of local social scientists, a taste tolerance survey was carried out. It found that salinity levels of up to two grams per liter were socially acceptable. The findings from the ex ante assessment were accepted by the Uzbek government, and consequent design changes freed up about $15 million dollars. Parts of the savings expanded the project's geographical scope and resulted in additional pilot projects.[27]

Many countries have a gap between the policy decision to teach children with public funds, and the implementation of that decision—to make sure learning is effective. Studies from Argentina, El Salvador, and Nicaragua show that empowering parents (through participation on school boards, for instance) can improve the delivery of educational services.[28]

Feedback—by and for institutions
The three functions discussed above of picking up signals, balancing interests, and implementing decisions are not always sharply distinguished. For private goods traded in markets, the market itself produces signals on scarcity—future and present, likely and plausible—while balancing needs *and* executing trades. But transaction between agents in a market can affect others (as with pollution). In this case, supplementary institutions (an air protection agency) can perform these functions and represent the interests of those affected (box 3.6).

Overcoming barriers to coordination

Institutions assist in coordination, but encouraging the emergence of good institutions is itself a coordination problem. Three barriers to building and supporting institutions are important:

■ Organizing dispersed interests—it takes more for people to come together and build a school than it takes for them to build individual homes.
■ Forging credible commitments—it takes more to commit to helping each other in the future and over a longer period than to helping each other today.
■ Promoting greater inclusiveness—it takes more to coordinate for the common good when access

Box 3.6
Policy accountability and accountable rulemaking

Consider an air-quality protection agency charged with balancing the need to pollute with the need for better air quality (see box figure a). It receives signals on pollution levels, damages, emissions, and preferences. It balances the interests of different stakeholders. And it implements policies through taxes and regulations, and through monitoring, enforcement, and publicity.

Accountable rulemaking

To handle new and evolving problems, the institutional environment must be adaptive, even though institutions also need to be stable and durable. The needs of coordination will change, and so must institutions. When the ozone layer was threatened, nations coordinated their actions by creating a new institution, the Montreal Protocol, to protect it (chapter 8). And most countries now have rules to keep lead out of gasoline since scientific evidence on its deleterious effects has accumulated and is widely available (chapter 7).

If the air is poorly managed, institutional analysis will likely find a weakness in the institution charged with adopting or implementing the policy to protect the air. For example, air quality interests may not have the information or voice they need to counter concentrated polluting interests. In these cases, monitoring and transparency can help shift the effective balance toward air quality. But maybe there is no air protection institution—or it is ill equipped or obstructed.

This brings the institutional analysis to a deeper level—to accountable rulemaking. At this level, rules will change and new institutions will emerge—if the overall institutional environment is picking up signals, balancing interests, and implementing policies. For rulemaking in an electoral democracy, elections are a powerful channel for signals to the legislature—the rulemaking process (box figure b, the intermediate loop). And when the legislature has done its balancing, it implements solutions by authorizing a new (or strengthened) air quality protection institution. For example, it could authorize the agency to justify its interventions by health benefits or more general

concerns for well-being. It could also give citizens access to information and the right to sue polluters (or the agency), or it could give the agency more powerful tax instruments. All these examples would shift property rights to the air toward the beneficiaries of better air quality.

Authorizing the rulemakers

The legislature is a permanent rule-making institution, but it is also a list of people who are there temporarily (changing with elections). The legislative process and the individual legislators earn their authority and powers from the authorizing environment, exemplified by values, religions, and constitutions (box figure b, the outer loop). In a strong authorizing environment—one giving strength to rules—the rules for rulemaking are fairly stable.

A key element in a strong authorizing environment can be a constitution that is respected, and likely short, which contains core principles only. If this is the case, when the constitution is tested against legislation, the executive, or the judiciary, the constitution typically stands unchallenged and unchanged. But more important than a constitution is a set of widely held values, so that support for sudden radical change is unlikely. Even knowing that the world is changing and that tomorrow's rules have many uncertain elements, some deeper values and widely held principles can provide stability and lend strength to the rulemaking. Countries with little commitment in the authorizing environment are more vulnerable to distributional conflict, as reflected in macroeconomic instability, lack of confidence, and credibility. Thus, the great penalty of low-quality institutions comes in the longer run, as is confirmed in empirical studies.

Sources: See Williamson (2000) for such a staggered hierarchy in institutional analysis. Rodrik (1996) emphasizes the role of institution in overcoming districtional conflict and negotiating reform. See also Acemoglu and others (2002).

(a) Policy accountability

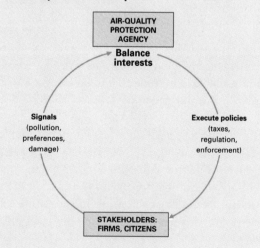

(b) Accountable rulemaking

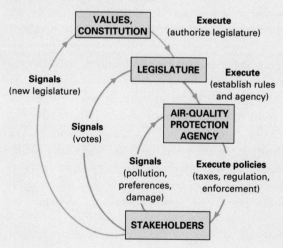

Source: World Bank staff.

to assets and voice are exclusive, unequal, and undemocratic.

Organizing dispersed interests

The brokering of political forces is often biased against dispersed interests. A trade regime may display protection even though many may lose from it, since the interests of those benefiting from it are more concentrated and thus more easily organized. Or policies may show an urban bias because the rural population is less vocal and has more difficulty organizing itself. Or the civil service may be overstaffed or overpaid because civil servants have a good grip on the policy process.

Institutions face challenges in organizing dispersed interests even if the counter-interests are not concentrated. Recall Mexico City: 20 million people benefit from air quality improvements, but there are also millions of polluters (vehicles, households, and firms). The collective action to generate institutions for air quality improvements may represent a tremendous challenge even when the interests of polluters are dispersed as well.

Protecting air quality requires coordination beyond what the market would accomplish unassisted. But how is this coordination accomplished? In many contexts a government intervenes with taxes and regulations. But in many others, coordination is accomplished without state intervention. Communal grazing grounds and irrigation systems are managed, sometimes well, by village norms and councils.[29] What is the process that enables such coordination?

Freedom of expression and association, trust, and political accountability provide some institutional machinery to coordinate dispersed interests, both in picking up signals and in giving them balance. Democratic institutions and the popular vote, despite many weaknesses, lower the costs of coordinating dispersed interests (see boxes 3.4 and 3.8).

Forging credible commitments

Society may have an interest in not polluting the water, and it may even prohibit excess discharges in the water. But if the water is already polluted, aggrieved parties may find it difficult or impossible, for political or other reasons, to punish polluters.[30] Such failures to deliver on commitments encourage transgressions by those who are well positioned, and are detrimental to accumulating and protecting assets.

Similarly, a government might want to protect an area from settlement, but it will have difficulty doing so if many settlers can arrive and dig in before the government gets there. A prior action (assigning and paying for suitable guards to protect the area) can serve as a commitment device. For example, the United States posted the U.S. army to protect Yellowstone National Park against incursions before the park service was established.[31]

When assets can be degraded or destroyed without risk of sanction, they are more likely to be depleted, often in a wasteful fashion. But the cultivator settling beyond the agricultural frontier traditionally has not asked for permission. At low levels of human impact on the environment, anyone can use something that nobody else uses, so this regime makes sense. It allows institutions to advance geographically at a pace with (or slightly behind) settlements, which is both economic and realistic.[32]

But there may also be times when it is important to get ahead of the advancing frontier of settlement, either because there is scarcely any forest, land, or water left, or because selective preservation has become a priority (chapter 5). In many developing countries the area under agricultural cultivation will stop expanding or may even reverse in the coming 30 to 50 years, so selective preservation now can yield lasting benefits at modest cost. As incomes rise, a time arrives when the forest has value not only to a potential cultivator (or those who depend on it as an ecosystem for their livelihood) but also to citizens far away. If these interests can find a suitable channel for expressing their interests the first-come, first-serve regime can be taken off the table selectively.

It is often difficult, however, to fight the tendency to reward early movers. When fish quota systems are put in place, the race for quotas can become a race to the shipyards, or to government offices—races that can be just as wasteful as the race to fish the declining stock (chapter 7). Preventing waste in environmental matters and natural resources requires confronting those who choose to deplete natural assets with the full social consequences of their actions, whether through informal mechanisms, taxes, or regulations. Similarly, loggers and fishermen must be induced to act as if they faced the consequences of others who might use the forest or the fish.

When commitments to protect are not credible, it is highly profitable to move early to manipulate the (supposedly) protective institutions. Tradable conservation obligations, such as those in Brazil (chapter 8), reduce the costs of compliance, and are thus one way to make conservation commitments more credible. As discussed above, information also helps, as when participatory procedures ensure that consequences are known beforehand. Box 3.7 draws the parallel between commitment by institutions protecting natural assets and by those protecting people's savings in a modern financial market.

Box 3.7
When protective institutions fail: the collapse of Enron and Newfoundland's cod fisheries

Like a forest that has been logged behind a nice facade of trees and billboards, the Enron corporation crumbled and filed for bankruptcy in 2001. At $60 billion in market value before it perished, the darling of financial markets became one of the largest bankruptcies in U.S. history. The assets had disappeared over time, shielded by misrepresentation.

Even in a private corporation such as Enron, the dispersed interests of thousands of owners are potentially threatened by well-placed individuals. Just as a contracted logger can either log sustainably or wastefully, managers and auditors can—by legal or illegal means—serve their own interests rather than those of dispersed owners. Norms and culture, and of course protective institutions (laws about property, accounting, and auditing) protect dispersed interests, but the protection will never be perfect. The Enron case is still in its fact-finding phase, but the list of techniques used by well-placed officials covers what one would expect in any other public sector or private sector institution that has been corrupted: concealed, misrepresented, and ghost transactions aimed at the enrichment of a few.

Why, one might ask, if well-placed individuals can abuse an asset by taking out more than their assigned incomes, would they overdo it, killing the golden goose? They may of course have lost or overtaxed the asset by accident. However, the path of Enron's stock market value looks suspiciously similar to that of another failure of protective institutions, the collapse of Newfoundland's cod fishery, hinting at how failing protective institutions lead to wasteful races.

Newfoundland's rich cod catches were growing slowly but steadily for about 100 years, until they increased steeply in the 1960s and 1970s, and then collapsed (chapter 7). In fisheries, as technology and equipment develop, the stock of fish in the sea starts declining. And if protective institutions fail to curtail overfishing, a wasteful race among fishermen follows. Fishermen understand that the fish they do not catch today may be someone else's tomorrow, and a frenzy of harvesting may end in collapse. Collapses are rare, however. It is more common that weak institutions result in steady and sustained losses, for both natural as well as produced assets. For instance, many fisheries steadily yield zero profits, and many managers and workers in overstaffed firms and public agencies add little value for their pay.

A system of protective institutions lies behind the success of mobilizing savings through financial institutions and stock markets, undoubtedly one of the great achievements of the United States. Such a system rests on checks and balances and introduces independent veto players, many of whom must look the other way for improprieties to occur. But Enron officials commanded impressive contacts and influence. Though the potential watchdogs were many, Enron went down without a peep from uneasy auditors and with enthusiastic "buy" recommendations from the world's best paid stock analysts.

For the United States, the Enron incident is a sobering one but not earth-shattering, and it has not eliminated the credibility of the protective institutions. Valuable assets—be they trees and fish, or people's savings—need protective institutions to thrive. When those protective institutions are successful, trees and fish and air quality and savings will thrive—to the great benefit of widely dispersed interests. But as assets grow, pressures on institutions grow—testing their commitment. Protective institutions are essential for people to make their savings available for banks and business people. The real cost of weak institutions is not that they result in more fraud and theft, but that, as a result, most people are not forthcoming with their savings. Potential is left unrealized. Ownership is concentrated and business is constrained by lack of depth and little competition—serving everybody poorly.

Source: CRSP, University of Chicago, original data from New York Stock Exchange; *The Economist,* February 14, 2002; Hannesson, background paper for the *WDR 2003.*

Enron, market value, 1985–2002

Newfoundland cod catch, tons, 1850–2000

Promoting inclusiveness

The third barrier to coordination mentioned in the previous section is fundamental enough to deserve expanded discussion. While it is well recognized that the quality of institutions affects the management of assets, it is less well recognized that the distribution of assets and voice affects the evolution of institutions in the long term (see figure, roadmap). Poorly distributed assets can affect adversely the quality of institutions and their ability to solve problems. Because of this reciprocal relationship between institutions and the distribution of assets one can get locked into vicious or virtuous circles. These circles are not deterministic, but extra effort is needed to break out of a vicious circle. This is easier when greater inclusiveness in access to assets is assured from new additions to the asset base, such as with broad investment in primary education.

The importance of voice and participation

A community that wants to improve air quality—or protect trees—may or may not find a channel to express its interests.[33] Individuals in the community could form an association and negotiate with polluters. Or they could lean on government to do this—in other words, voice and participation are important. A society in which the majority has no voice can lose out big in two ways. First, it can lose because the potential creativity and productivity resting in the majority of the people is ignored or valued only in part. Second, because beneficiaries to communal and natural assets are not heard, the potential of these assets may be wasted, too. Institutions such as the law necessarily involve coercive powers, and one of the potential benefits of broad-based voice—an inclusive democracy—is that it better commits these powers to serving society at large. Box 3.8 relates the remarkable and very promising transformation in South Africa toward a more inclusive society.

But even very basic protective measures, such as shielding families and savings from abuse and theft, often fail to materialize. Poor people have to accept very costly outlets for their savings, as when they buy gold, are hurt by inflation, or must pay others for safekeeping.[34] And the police and courts, responsible for enforcing the law, often fail to assist or adequately protect poor or disenfranchised groups. Indeed, many institutional development initiatives are geared to making police and judges more attentive to the needs of the poor and disenfranchised.[35]

Box 3.8
Fostering inclusiveness: South Africa's new democracy

One of the more remarkable examples of institutional transformation toward an inclusive society is South Africa's transition from a system of white rule to a pluralist democracy founded on the principles of human rights and reconciliation. When national elections were held in 1994, black South Africans, comprising three-quarters of country's population, were able to vote for the first time. In addition, they were able to exercise long-denied rights to travel freely and to live and work where they please. This transformation has required uprooting the entrenched institutional foundations of apartheid and creating a host of new and more inclusive institutions—from the 1996 Constitution to reformed security agencies, provincial governments, and health and education ministries. How did South Africa manage this transition?

From violence to negotiations
Under apartheid, legally sanctioned discrimination backed by violence permeated every aspect of society, as blacks were denied the most basic liberties and were the victims of widespread human rights abuses. In 1961 Nelson Mandela and the African National Congress (ANC) abandoned their strategy of nonviolent protest and resorted to armed struggle. Mass demonstrations and violence continued throughout the 1980s and early 1990s. The transition to a new path in South Africa began with a series of conversations, initiated by Nelson Mandela from his prison cell, involving the ANC and National Party leaders in the mid-1980s. At the same time, work stoppages and uprisings in overcrowded urban slums were exacting a toll on the country and prompting the flight of skilled workers. Western nations that had long supported the apartheid regime became more vocal in their criticism, and eventually tightened economic sanctions. Following the collapse of the Soviet Union, the Cold War logic of support for the staunchly anticommunist regime was also abandoned.

Leadership and a commitment to reconciliation
These developments alone could not ensure a successful transition from apartheid to a new set of institutional rules. The process depended on the vision and skills of political leaders. Mandela went to great lengths to reassure his supporters that he would not act without the consent of the rest of the ANC. This earned him the trust and respect of his followers, a re-

(Box continues on next page).

Box 3.8   *(continued)*

source he drew on when it came time to reach difficult compromises with the National Party. Leadership was also demonstrated by President de Klerk, whose decision in 1990 to free Mandela and lift the ban on major black political organizations involved great risk.

Mandela and other ANC leaders were adept at combining tough negotiation with a strong public commitment to national reconciliation. This allayed the worst fears of National Party leaders and facilitated compromise. The mechanisms of reconciliation included broadly participatory negotiations over the new constitution, and a government of national unity that gave former rivals the experience of governing side by side. The Truth and Reconciliation Commission, established in 1995 under Archbishop Desmond Tutu, provided a high-profile confidence-building mechanism for addressing past atrocities while restraining fears and pressures for retribution. And the new constitution devolved significant powers to the provinces, which further allayed white concerns over majority rule at the national level.

The transition to democratic rule

These and other measures facilitated the transition to democratic rule while preventing capital flight and preserving valuable social assets such as the skills and expertise of the mostly white civil service. A commitment to human rights and reconciliation provided the winning formula that ensured the success of the transition despite efforts to derail the process.

South Africa's transformation to an inclusive society is an example to the world—but not because it was timely, smooth, or bloodless; it was none of those. But South Africa underwent the most difficult of institutional transformations in the most trying of circumstances, and did so while fostering a political culture that emphasizes human rights and reconciliation. Many challenges of governance and development remain, and aspirations will continue to create tremendous pressures for change—a positive force but also a challenge to institutions and leaders.

Source: Sparks (1996); personal communication with World Bank staff.

Protecting people—and the emergence of protective institutions for assets

When institutions such as the law, and the agencies supporting the law, become more inclusive, more people are given protection, voice, and support. And when institutions are more inclusive—listening to and supporting more people—a broader range of assets can thrive (boxes 3.4, 3.8, 3.9, and 3.10 illuminate different aspects of this). The reason is that assets need guardians and spokespersons. Assets therefore may fail to be served if the people who benefit from these assets are not well served by—or represented in—institutions. For private assets, more inclusive institutions facilitate development and asset accumulation as more people feel safe in their homes and find promising outlets for their savings. For communal and natural assets (roads, water, fish, or forests), more inclusive institutions deepen the support for their provision, so that their quality and quantity can rise. Consider what happened in Cubatão, Brazil, where inclusiveness in the form of democratization and the end of media censorship shifted the balance toward civil society and a cleaner environment (box 6.8). In many countries, social movements pressing for democratization and environmental improvements have reinforced each other (box 3.9).

How can protective institutions be formed to give dispersed interests effective channels? In a wide range of cases, society relies on guardians, or custo-

dians, to look over something of value. An example is when participatory approaches in projects ask people to speak their mind. The presumption behind this empowering people's voice is not only that people have a right to speak on their own behalf. It is

Box 3.9

Mutual reinforcement: environmental movements and democracy

In many places environmental movements arose in the 1980s in the midst of broader social movements for democratization. Democratization and environmentalism have developed together but in diverse ways. In the Republic of Korea social movements for democratization, labor, and environmental protection joined forces in opposition to authoritarian rule in the 1980s. In Taiwan (China) the environmental and prodemocracy movements were the two strongest social mobilizations. An estimated 582 environmental protests occurred there between 1983 and 1988—one-fifth of public protests during this period. In Brazil disparate environmental organizations that had kept a low profile during military rule were animated and united when they helped draft the environmental chapter of the new national constitution during 1985–88. In the former Soviet Union, civic environmental organizations flourished in the early years, were crushed under Stalin, resurfaced in limited form during the political liberalization of the 1950s, and exploded as a central component of mass movements for democratization in the late 1980s.

Source: Mirovitskaya (1998); Anbarasan and Yul (2001); Lee and others (1999); Hochstetler (1997).

also that city people, for example, can benefit from hearing from people in more remote areas about what goes on in the forest, about the effects of cutting trees or damming rivers.

For people to be functional guardians, they must be well-endowed and feel safe. As an illustration, all societies rely on parents to protect and nurture children. It happens that this protection fails—as when children are sold into slavery or prostitution. This is not because parents are not their guardians—they are—but because of the family's poverty and despair.

This need to have well-endowed guardians places broad-based development and poverty reduction at the heart of concerns for environmental and other communal assets. More inclusive access to assets (human capital, a piece of land, or a plot for housing) can change people's perspectives, allowing them to be more forward looking and engaged in their communities. When people have assets—and thus a stake in the future and in the community—it is also easier to build support for institutions, public goods, and publicly provided goods such as rule of law, watershed management, and schooling.

What does inclusiveness in access to assets have to do with sustainable development?

In important ways, high levels of inequality and deprivation can be harmful to efficiency and growth. The presence or absence of inclusiveness in institutions and in access to assets tends to have *long-lasting effects* (box 3.10).

Economic forces that create differences in income and wealth serve a positive function by creating incentives to allocate resources efficiently. But poverty and inequality can be harmful through other important mechanisms; at the macro level, damage can be done in the political process. Institutions and government policies are essential for assets to thrive, through the rule of law and macroeconomic stability. An equitable distribution can facilitate the emergence of institutions to negotiate change and thus help adopt and implement good policies—particularly to address externalities and public goods. At the micro level, sharp differences in income and wealth are also costly. Imperfections such as those found in capital markets may allow individual potential to be wasted when individuals are very poor. Examples are when a talented child goes uneducated (chapter 7), or a worker stays with an employer, or with an asset

with low yields only because she cannot finance migration or a job search (chapter 4).[36] Another example is when agricultural potential is wasted because of distorted and highly concentrated land-ownership and contracting problems.[37]

Inequality in land assets has been found to be harmful to growth.[38] Good institutions appear to facilitate long-term growth, and more egalitarian societies appear to have better institutions. Furthermore, good institutions work in part directly, and in part through schooling and openness.[39]

An ambitious quantitative study tested the role of inclusiveness and institutions using a 500-year perspective.[40] For colonized countries (not limited to the Americas), a major break in power structures and institutions happened under colonization. Those that were richer and more densely populated in 1500 (before colonization) are poorer now. This reversal of fortune came about because colonizers in richer, more densely populated areas could force a large supply of labor to work in mines or plantations. Under these extractive institutions, political power was more concentrated. The lower quality of these institutions for growth reveals itself after 1700, when *asset creation* became important, rewarding countries that had institutions better suited for savings and investment.

Long-lasting harmful effects of institutions that concentrate ownership are also found in a recent study of India.[41] The British colonization in India lasted for 200 years. Where they implemented a landlord-based revenue system (by implication, with concentrated property rights), yields were higher than in areas where they implemented cultivator-owned rights. In post-independence India, the landlord-based revenue system was abolished, so only the historic traces of the institutions remain. Yields have grown significantly faster in the areas where, historically, cultivators themselves had property rights. The differences prove to be particularly important from the 1960s onward, as districts with smallholders benefited more from the green revolution, with significantly higher application of fertilizer, high-yield varieties, and irrigation. Districts that historically had smallholder institutions also had higher investments in human capital.

The proposition that ownership matters is supported also in other studies. Before 1977 sharecropping contracts in West Bengal, India, generally in-

Box 3.10
Inequality: its long tails in the Americas

Many of the former European colonies that offered the best economic prospects in early colonial times (based on their national resource endowments) are today among the poorest in the world. They started to fall behind at the outset of the Industrial Revolution. In 1700, Mexico and the colonies that were to become the United States had very similar per capita incomes, and the sugar-producing islands of Barbados and Cuba were far richer. Indeed, before the 19th century, the North American mainland was widely considered to offer poorer economic prospects than the Caribbean and Latin America. All of Canada, which Voltaire once characterized as "a few acres of snow," was considered by the colonial powers to have a value comparable to that of the small sugar-producing island of Guadeloupe.

The rapid rise of national income per capita in the United States and Canada after 1800

	GDP per capita relative to the U.S. (percent)			
Economy	1700	1800	1900	2000
Argentina	—	102	52	36
Barbados	150	—	—	44
Brazil	—	50	10	22
Chile	—	46	38	28
Cuba	167	112	—	—
Mexico	89	50	35	26
Peru	—	41	20	14
Canada	—	—	67	82
United States (GDP per capita in 1985 dollars)	550	807	3,859	34,260

— Not available.
Source: World Bank (2001); Engerman, Haber, and Sokoloff (2000).

Once industrialization began in North America in the 19th century, the United States and Canadian economies diverged sharply from the rest of the hemisphere. Why did the areas previously favored fall behind? Development depends not just on having productive opportunities—*it depends on creating a never-ending supply of new opportunities.* One key to early industrialization was the ability of the broad population to invest, accumulate human capital, and participate in commercial activity. In the Americas, only the United States and Canada provided the laws, institutions, and government policies to make such investment and participation possible.

In the New World colonies of Spanish America, the core natural resources—high-yield ores and agricultural land—were susceptible to large-scale operations. This made possible a high inequality in income, wealth, and human capital at the beginning of colonization. This inequality had a great influence on the evolution of institutions. In particular, the institutions that emerged in these colonies blocked effective access to opportunities for economic and social advancement for a broad cross-section of the population. This persisted long after colonization ended and slavery was abolished. These institutions inhibited the accumulation of human capital, the spread of entrepreneurship, and the creation of a mass market—factors viewed as important in industrial development.

Why should inequality hundreds of years ago matter for development today? As just noted, societies that had high inequality in the ownership of assets at the outset generated institutions that placed restrictions on individuals' opportunities for future economic advancement, and this may have tied these economies into low growth paths.

Note: Klenow and Rodriguez-Clare (1997) attribute only 3 percent of the variation of growth per worker across countries to variations in the growth of capital per worker, while variations in technical progress accounted for 91 percent. Other studies conclude differently, in part because technical progress and capital accumulation move together. But there are few studies that place major emphasis positively on initial endowments. In chapter 7, the "natural resource curse"—the idea that certain natural resources can be harmful to growth—is discussed in more detail.
Sources: Engerman and Sokoloff (1997, 2001); and Hoff, background paper for *WDR 2003.*

volved 50 percent output shares to the tenant for the approximately 2 million sharecroppers in the state. In 1977 a new administration gave high priority to a law giving security of tenure to tenants. The reform increased most tenants' share of output from 50 percent to 75 percent. In the decade after this reform, West Bengal broke through: Annual growth in the production of food grains rose from 0.4 percent to 5.1 percent, while that for all of India rose only from 1.9 percent to 3.1 percent. The tenancy reform program explains about 30 percent of the added growth.[42] Tenancy reform in urban slums in Brazil seem to also have unleashed growth potential and improvements in the urban environment (see box 6.6).

At early stages of development, owners of land may benefit from booms more than others (so ensuring broad-based land ownership and smallholder agriculture is likely to be more effective in reducing poverty—see chapter 5).[43] In a similar way, owners may be best positioned to benefit when a community performs better, as when schools and roads are in good repair. For this reason, having narrowly based ownership and many citizens without land or secure tenure can be an impediment to forward-looking and constructive collective action, whether for environmental protection or for other purposes.[44]

The cited studies show how greater inclusiveness in access to assets—or lower inequality—can assist in making development more sustainable. One mechanism is direct and micro-economic: Ownership matters, and access to assets can help a poor family realize its potential. Another is political: A person with land or a house is more likely to support institutions protecting assets (rule of law and secure property rights, for instance) than a person without a house or hope of having one. So insecure property rights—with costly policy swings where shifting groups expropriate each other's assets—are less likely if access to assets is broad and inclusive.

In figure 3.3, the observation was made that protective institutions—such as the rule of law—are typically stronger in high-income countries. It was also noted that there are causal effects in both directions: Not only can protective institutions allow assets to thrive and incomes to grow, but a society strengthens its institutional capacity as incomes grow. In a similar way, there will be causality both ways between inequality and good institutions. Countries with greater inequality have a weaker rule of law (and lower incomes). The key point of this section is that highly unequal access to assets can be punishing to asset creation, preservation, and improvements in well-being if institutions are not rock solid. Groups without assets see themselves as unsupported by property rights, and are thus less supportive of property rights politically. This undermines support for the evolution of institutions that enable growth and sustainable development.

A narrowly based elite is often concerned about the risks of more inclusive political empowerment. One concern is that they might be expropriated. Just as unequal access to assets can be an obstacle to the emergence of good institutions, improperly designed and balanced, *redistribution* of existing assets can also be harmful to the emergence of good institutions. If a person without assets is more likely to support expropriation of assets, then a group that has lost through expropriation is also likely to become less respectful of the law and property. It should be clear that it will be easier to improve inclusiveness through access to new types of assets (as when land for agriculture replaces the importance of natural resources—minerals, forests, fisheries; or when education replaces muscle power, etc.) and through the expansion of assets that come from the growth process. Redistributive measures must be designed and balanced to avoid undermining the emergence of good institutions that enable people and assets to thrive.

The studies cited in this chapter represent, but do not exhaust, a still-young literature on the deeper institutional preconditions for economic growth. Important questions are whether institutions are everything, whether policies—in part determined by institutions—have separate and important effects, and finally whether high inequality itself is a major and important obstacle to sound institutions. At a practical level, there are many points of agreement: A key element in the success of East Asian economies was a focus on shared growth, inclusive schooling, and how this served to give political stability and investor confidence (box 7.10, Malaysia). An important element in political discourse in Western Europe and North America in the 20th century has been "to give everyone a stake in society," supporting policies to strengthen social safety nets, to subsidize general education, and to make home ownership more inclusive. Finally, policies that are frequently pursued—wasteful protectionism, unsustainable macropolicies, a bloated public sector—are best understood as short-term redistributive games that are costly in the long run. These games are played at greatest cost in nations with poor institutions, giving them low ability to negotiate and to commit to mutually beneficial change.[45]

Catalysts for change

Institutional reform happens when the actors take advantage of opportunities for change, and use instruments of change at their disposal. The institutions that mediate social interaction must foster both stability and change. A measure of stability and predictability in the rules governing society is necessary for the people to have confidence to work together, to challenge each other to improve their communities, and to invest in their future. A vibrant civil society and such institutions as a democratic legislature can provide for dynamism—including that in rulemaking. In a society founded on broader consensus and certain ethical principles, these institutions are simultaneously given force and anchored to give predictability and confidence.

A seeming paradox is that democracies—despite their frequent leadership changes—can better commit to the longer run, and do the right things. When characterized as a stable democracy, countries benefit from predictable successions, as if the democratic institutions themselves have taken on the role of an owner with a long-range perspective.[46] However, studies show that young democratic states have problems similar to those in autocratic states, in terms of protecting property rights to allow assets to thrive, at least until democratic institutions have taken root. This is a challenge for fledgling democracies.

Many East Asian countries have done well in the last 30 years in stability and asset creation, but not necessarily through democratic institutions. What these countries had in common, however, was broad access to land (some had experienced historical shocks that gave them land reform) or other characteristics that made them emphasize shared growth, such as through broad-based rural development and broad provision of health and education.

Some institutions—such as constitutions—are designed to make change exceptionally difficult.[47] Constitutional changes typically require a much higher degree of voter consensus than do lesser legislative reforms. And a two-chamber legislature requires that coalitions be built in alternative ways for changes to pass. Other institutional means of providing stability and commitment are so-called checks and balances, that is, independent veto players. High court justices appointed for life, and systems with separation of power among branches of government can ensure that radical departures from the norm are not made

in haste. Institutions may also be designed to facilitate change in one direction and not in another. In many Latin American countries a national park may be created with a simple presidential decree, but dismantling a park requires the approval of both the president and the legislature. Some countries have anchored their commitment to the environment in the constitution by linking the environment to the rights of their citizens. Others, such as India and Pakistan, have supreme court decisions serving the same purpose.[48] The stability provided by all these institutional mechanisms depends on whether they rest in shared values, so that relevant actors abide by them. In general, multiple review procedures and systems of checks and balances work only when political and economic power are not too concentrated.

Opportunities

Improvements in social conditions and in the institutions that shape them often seem unbearably slow. But significant and sometimes sweeping institutional reforms do occur, as with democratization in South Africa, the successful anticorruption campaign in Hong Kong (China), and decentralization in Latin America (figure 3.5).

Figure 3.5

More mayors in Latin America are elected locally—by citizens or by elected city councils

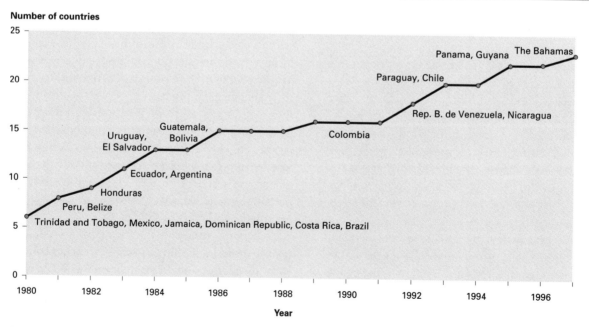

Source: IADB (1997).

Opportunities for reform often arise from economic or political crises that inspire civil society or political elites to demand changes in the status quo and to search for new solutions to long-standing problems. In Latin America, perceived crises in the legitimacy of governing institutions have inspired substantial democratizing reforms that give greater voice and power to local communities (chapter 7). On a more routine basis, opportunities appear as a result of elections, changes in agency leadership, or discretionary decisions by national leaders. And opportunities for reform arise with changing public preferences, and with changes such as education, urbanization, technological change, and income growth. For example, new generations of individuals raised in conditions of material prosperity and stability tend to place greater emphasis on freedom of expression and quality of life.[49]

The demands that societies place on their institutions also change as a result of observing other societies. In recent years the transnational social movement for indigenous rights, the sweep of independence movements across Eastern Europe, and the multinational campaign for transparency in governance show that new social demands can spread rapidly across borders.

Information and forums as catalysts for change

A suite of tools is available for catalyzing changes in institutions: tools that provide information to enhance the voice of neglected stakeholders, and forums held for collective problem solving. Unaccountable power structures are often vulnerable—and thus potentially responsive—to the exposure of information, so having more information available can be a catalyst for change used by reformers, entrepreneurs, and civil society. A broad set of studies shows the power of information disclosure in environmental performance, in both developed and developing countries (chapter 7).[50] A growing number of firms and NGOs provide investors and markets with information on the social and environmental performance of companies (chapter 8)—information that facilitates decisions by investors and customers, and catalyzes changes in the behavior of firms. In the realm of governing widely held corporations for profits, better financial accounting is sought to improve actual behavior. Also, public disclosure of weakness drives pressure, both for adherence to rules and for better rules (see box 3.7).

Enhancing the voice of stakeholders can dramatically shift the balance of forces that favors institutional reforms. Cultural translators (see chapter 4) can bring new ideas and ways of working together that increases the self confidence and voice of groups previously excluded from participating in or authorizing institutional change. In Cubatão, Brazil, the state environmental protection agency was able to reduce pollution by joining forces with a vocal citizens' movement during Brazil's transition to democracy (box 6.3). Stakeholder forums can facilitate conflict resolution and the sharing of ideas, and the consensus building associated with international environmental treaties has allowed steady progress on issues ranging from wetlands conservation to preventing oil pollution at sea (chapter 8).

A spatial approach

Some changes come about easily, some only with other structural changes—such as changes in technology, endowments, and values. Changes in labor market conditions, combined with public and government action, have contributed to phase out slavery and elevate women's status. And women with more voice, clout, and knowledge have delivered fertility declines and better-educated children. Economic growth, better transport, and the successful growth of cities give poor people a broader choice of employers, neighborhoods, and service providers. Today, perhaps the most significant structural change is the information revolution, with the potential not only to increase knowledge and the use of knowledge but also to improve accountability.

Dynamic development is sustainable when it is forward looking and responsible. Therefore it must be assessed not only by such indicators as poverty, natural resources, forest coverage, and ocean temperatures but also by the institutional environment that helps this information emerge, gives it weight, and ensures that it is acted on. This chapter proposes a checklist of functions for the institutional environment: to pick up signals, to balance alternatives and interests, and to execute decisions. It also highlights some barriers to institutional development: dispersed interests and commitment problems. These barriers are more easily overcome by fostering inclusiveness.

The main messages of this Report are that sustained development requires that a broad portfolio of assets thrives in order for people to thrive, and that managing this broad portfolio well requires better institutions.[51] In this chapter it has been argued that the quality of institutions themselves influence, and are influenced by, the distribution of assets. As a result, more inclusive access to assets and more inclusive authorizing institutions allow implementing institutions to better protect assets and people, and to facilitate well-being. In short, the more people that are heard and the more diverse interests that are voiced, the fewer assets that are wasted.

Inclusiveness can be increased in a number of ways. With greater access to education, agricultural land, and security of tenure, people are better-endowed citizens. They have something to lose, and something that can grow—they can be more forward looking, trusting, and see greater value in creating and supporting good institutions. In such a setting they can better accumulate, manage, and protect a variety of assets, including environmental and social assets. As stakeholders they can become more cooperative, creative, and willing to take risks—all necessary for the transformations described in the rest of this Report.

In the next few chapters (chapters 4, 5, and 6), these ideas are applied in spatial arenas—marginal rural, commercial rural, and urban areas—where people live, enjoy life, and engage locally, before the ideas are applied at the national and global levels.

CHAPTER 4

Improving Livelihoods on Fragile Lands

The test of our progress is not whether we add more to the abundance of those who have much; it is whether we provide enough for those who have too little.

—Franklin Delano Roosevelt

Inclusion, innovation, and migration

One-quarter of the people in developing countries—1.3 billion in all—survive on fragile lands, areas that present significant constraints for intensive agriculture and where the people's links to the land are critical for the sustainability of communities, pastures, forests, and other natural resources.[1] They account for many of the people in extreme poverty, living on less than $1 a day. The size of this population is a signal that our assumptions about the extent and speed of outmigration have been flawed. The least productive areas should have been abandoned first, as people migrate out to better opportunities. While some people have left, many remain behind and others are migrating in (the estimated population on fragile lands has doubled since 1950—chapter 1, figure 1.5). Improving their livelihoods is essential for meeting many of the Millennium Development Goals for the coming decades.

People living on fragile lands are vulnerable but have a modest portfolio of assets that can help bring them out of poverty: the land (albeit with constraints), traditional social capital, human capital, and indigenous knowledge and know-how. However, the potential productivity of even these assets has not been fully developed by either local or national institutions. Living in dispersed settlements and working in the informal or subsistence economy, people on the rural periphery are largely invisible to decision-

makers. Because it was assumed that they would move out of these areas, few governments took the initiative to gather information about their activities. As a result, institutions have not been picking up social and environmental distress signals from the periphery—nor have these institutions been able to balance interests (particularly dispersed interests) in setting their development agendas. For the past 50 years the government and private sector have focused the bulk of their attention and agricultural spending on the development of lands with commercial potential—even though much of the rural population remains on marginal land.

This focus is beginning to shift. Returns on more productive land are diminishing.[2] And boosting yields in fragile areas is becoming more pressing—and feasible. But to address the needs of people on marginal land requires more research on appropriate technologies and services and more information on their conditions. Many of the households are headed by women, constrained by poor education opportunities, little access to information, and no legal land tenure. Population pressure, lack of knowledge, and simple fear of change lead to destructive patterns of asset management. Understanding the problems and finding ways to help these people out of vicious circles of degrading existing assets, damaging livelihoods, and blocking paths out of poverty are major challenges.

People are more likely to break out of vicious circles when change is introduced gradually but steadily over long periods. And change is more likely when the risk factors are addressed openly, in ways that make the costs less burdensome to those who have most to lose. Long-term advice and grant money to experiment with innovative institutional solutions should be part of the package—to mitigate risks. Introducing high-tech mining operations in remote areas disrupts communities and can harm the environment. Setting up community-based schools is a major shift from the centralized system and often perceived as a threat by ministry officials. But countries can benefit from long-term partnering with experienced institutions to help them think through the process. Successful strategies combine outmigration of a few family members, organization of community associations, and national programs that upgrade the community's modest portfolio of assets.

This chapter looks at what governments, communities, and the private sector can do to promote growth and improvement in the well-being of people inhabiting fragile lands. The emphasis here is on arid areas (because of the many people living there) and on mountain slopes (because of the links with water, forests, and mineral resources). How can public and private (national and local) institutions promote in situ upgrading and/or outmigration? Some of the options explored in this chapter include:

■ Allowing voice and the inclusion of these groups in the decisionmaking process. Only in this way can institutions pick up the signals of what is happening at the periphery so they can design appropriate solutions.
■ Nurturing all the assets available to poor communities—sharing of know-how, upgrading the status of women, applying research on special crops, and sharing revenues from mineral and other assets that have national benefits.
■ Creating environments that motivate entrepreneurial people to come forward with ideas that address grass-roots realities.
■ Establishing long-term public-private-NGO partnerships that promote transparency, accountability, the transfer of knowledge, and solutions that balance everyone's interests.

Managing fragile land to improve livelihoods

Half a billion people in developing countries live in arid regions with no access to irrigation systems. Another 400 million are on land with soils unsuitable for agriculture, 200 million in slope-dominated regions, and more than 130 million in fragile forest ecosystems.[3] These areas (table 4.1), covering an esti-

Table 4.1
Environmental fragility in developing countries

Characteristics	Number of people (millions)	Share of population on fragile lands (percent)	Share of earth's land surface affected (percent)
Aridity	**518**	**40**	**35**
Only	350		
Arid, slope	36		
Arid, poor soil	107		
Arid, slope, poor soil, forest	25		
Slope	**216**	**17**	**7**
Only	149		
Slope, poor soil	26		
Slope, forest	41		
Poor soil[a]	**430**	**33**	**22**
Only	386		
Poor soil, forest	44		
Forests (only)[b]	**130**	**10**	**7**
Total	**1,294**	**100**	**73**

Notes: a. FAO data on soils unsuitable for rain fed agriculture.
b. Total estimated number of people in forests is 237 million, of whom 130 million live in forests that have no other geophysical constraints. These forests are part of fragile ecosystems, mainly in remote tropical areas (Amazon, Central Africa) and the boreal forests of Asia. Conversion to private commercial use needs to take into account the forest's private and public good values.
Source: Averages of CIESIN and LandScan (see Endnotes, chapter 4, note 1). The constraints were classified according to dominant constraint, ranking first aridity, followed by slope, poor soil, and forest. This does not include fragility due to weather-related factors.

mated 73 percent of the Earth's land surface, face significant problems for agriculture investment and have limited ability to sustain growing populations. Sensitive to land use patterns, they are particularly vulnerable to degradation, erosion, floods, and landslides.

Rapid population growth, fragile land, and conflict
East and South Asia have the most people on fragile land, and Sub-Saharan Africa and the Middle East and North Africa the largest shares, at nearly 40 percent each. All regions have several countries where people living on fragile lands make up half of their total populations. Between 1950 and 2000 several countries with a large share of their population on fragile land saw their rural populations triple or quadruple. And more than three-quarters of the 42 countries in civil conflict in the 1990s have significant populations on fragile lands (tables 4.2 and 4.3).

The size and speed of population growth in developing countries over the past 50 years were unprece-

Table 4.2
Regional distribution of people living on fragile land

Region	Population in 2000 (millions)	Population on fragile lands by region	
		Number (millions)	Share of total (percent)
Latin America and the Caribbean	515.3	68	13.1
Eastern Europe and Central Asia	474.7	58	12.1
Middle East and North Africa	293.0	110	37.6
Sub-Saharan Africa	658.4	258	39.3
South Asia	1,354.5	330	24.4
East Asia and Pacific	1,856.5	469	25.3
OECD group[a]	850.4	94	11.1
Other	27.3	2	6.9
Total	**6,030.1**	**1,389**	**24.7**
Total less OECD	**5,179.7**	**1,295**	**26.9**

a. OECD: Australia, Austria, Belgium, Canada, Denmark, Finland, France, Germany, Greece, Iceland, Ireland, Italy, Japan, Luxembourg, Netherlands, New Zealand, Norway, Portugal, Spain, Sweden, Switzerland, United Kingdom, United States (23 original members).
Source: Average of CIESIN and LandScan measurement methods (see Endnotes, chapter 4, note 1).

dented—faster than the rate experienced in the OECD countries at any time in their history. In two generations the working-age population increased 3.5 times in North and Sub-Saharan Africa, and in Latin America and the Caribbean, and nearly 3 times in Central and South Asia. Rural population growth rates even now remain higher in countries where 30 percent or more of the population are on fragile land (figure 4.1). Many people are on marginal land because of their higher fertility rates and because of overcrowding on the better land. Refugees and displaced persons have also been forced there, because they have lost their homes—from floods, fires, hurricanes, conflict, civil war, or high urban unemployment.[4] Some of the people in these marginal areas are the estimated 250 million indigenous people with distinct languages, cultures, and attachment to the land.[5]

Living on the edge—the arid plains
Dryland ecosystems are characterized by extreme rainfall variability, recurrent but unpredictable droughts, high temperatures, low soil fertility, high salinity, grazing pressure, and fires. They reflect and absorb solar radiation, maintain balance in the functioning of the atmosphere, and sustain biomass and biodiversity. Although the biodiversity of drylands is low relative to that of forests or wetlands, the ecosystem services they provide are considerable. Despite its fragility the Serengeti Plain of East Africa currently supports the largest tonnage of animal wildlife assembled on land, as did the equally fragile Great Plains of North America in the past. Dryland species and eco-

Figure 4.1
Rural population growth rate relative to share of total population on fragile land

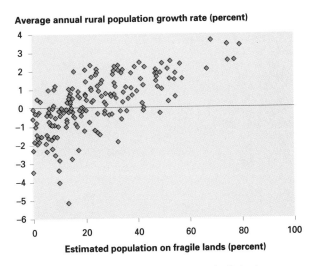

Average annual rural population growth rate (percent)

Estimated population on fragile lands (percent)

Source: World Bank estimates for population on fragile land; average rural population growth rates from 1995–2000, U.N. secretariat.

systems have developed an array of coping mechanisms that provide resilience and recovery in case of fire, drought, and pressure from wildlife. These mechanisms are important for climate changes, which are expected to intensify drought and the variability of rainfall in Africa.[6]

Of the 500 million rural people on arid and dry semi-arid land,[7] most are in Asia and Africa, but there are also large pockets in Mexico and Northeastern

Table 4.3

Share of population on fragile land, countries in conflict, and rural population growth

Sub-Saharan Africa	South Asia	Middle East and North Africa	Latin America and the Caribbean	Europe and Central Asia	East Asia and Pacific
>70 percent *Eritrea*[a] *(2.77)*[b] Niger (3.62) Cape Verde (1.19)	*Bhutan (2.7)*	*Yemen, Rep. of (3.4)*			
70–50 percent *Somalia (3.22)* Burkina Faso (2.47) Namibia (2.62) *Sudan (2.31)* *Mali (2.47)* Swaziland (2.62) *Zimbabwe (3.33)* *Congo, Dem. Rep. of (2.0)*	*Afghanistan (2.21)*	Egypt, Arab Rep. of (2.5)			*Papua New Guinea (2.48)*
50–30 percent Uganda (3.96) *Sierra Leone (1.54)* *Guinea (2.27)* Lesotho (2.02) Comoros (2.83) *Chad (2.35)* Senegal (2.85) Equatorial Guinea (1.25) *Rwanda (3.43)* Botswana (1.97) *Angola (2.26)* *Kenya (3.47)* *South Africa (2.76)* *Ethiopia (2.95)* Mauritania (1.40) Cameroon (1.89) Nigeria (2.38) Tanzania (3.11) *Central African Republic (1.98)* The Gambia (3.35) Benin (1.86)	Pakistan (2.70) Nepal (2.44)	Morocco (1.99) Syrian Arab Rep. (3.04) *Algeria (1.77)* Iran, Islamic Rep. of (2.19) Tunisia (1.34)	Guyana (1.54) Costa Rica (3.66) *Guatemala (3.28)* St. Vincent and the Grenadines (0.9) *Haiti (1.83)* Grenada (1.07) Belize (3.5)	Kyrgyz Rep. (2.7) Turkmenistan (3.93) *Tajikistan (4.08)* Uzbekistan (3.62)	Lao PDR (2.48) Vanuatu (3.49) Solomon Islands (4.38)
(30–20 percent) Togo (2.45) Côte d'Ivoire (3.56) *Liberia (2.24)* *Burundi (n/a)* Ghana (2.84) Madagascar (2.88) Guinea-Bissau (2.01) *Mozambique (1.81)* *Congo, Rep. of (n/a)* Zambia (2.83)	*Sri Lanka (2.26)* *India (2.44)*	Jordan (4.11)	Bolivia (1.85) Jamaica (1.10) Honduras (2.67) *Peru (1.42)* Panama (2.26) Ecuador (1.81) Dominican Rep. (1.63) *El Salvador (2.71)* Trinidad and Tobago (1.46) Mexico (1.59)	Kazakhstan (1.72) *Azerbaijan (2.21)* Albania (1.89) Armenia (1.47) *Bosnia and Herzegovina (0.99)*	China (1.78) Vietnam (2.6) Indonesia (1.8) *Cambodia (2.82)* Malaysia (1.95) Korea, Rep. of (0.53) *Myanmar (2.31)* Mongolia (1.5)

Notes:

a. *Countries in bold italic were reported to be in civil conflict* during the 1990s, defined as war that has caused more than a thousand battle deaths, challenged the sovereignty of an internationally recognized state, occurred within the country's recognized boundary, involved the state as a principal combatant, and subjected the state to an organized military opposition that inflicted significant casualties. Countries in Civil Conflict in the 1990s from Sambanis (2000).

b. Numbers in parentheses are ratios of rural population in 2000 to 1950, U.N. Secretariat www.un.org/esa/population/demobase.

Source: Country estimates of population on fragile land: Average of CIESIN and LandScan (see Endnotes, chapter 4, note 1).

Brazil (figure 4.2). The low volume and extreme variability of precipitation limit the productive potential of this land for settled farming and nomadic pastoralism. Many ways of expanding agricultural production in the drylands—shifting cultivation from other areas, reducing fallow periods, switching farming practices, overgrazing pasture areas, cutting trees for fuelwood—result in greater environmental degradation.

Both state-driven and market-driven agricultural investments neglect dryland agriculture, with its lower returns and higher risks, concentrating instead on agriculture in more productive areas. Research and development (R&D) funding for temperate agriculture is 70 percent of total public and private funding for agricultural research. R&D funding for tropical agriculture accounts for 28 percent of the total (mostly on rice). And R&D that focuses on the problems facing people on fragile lands accounts for only 7 to 8 percent of total R&D funding.[8] Without the capacity to migrate, and without major financial and technical support, poor rural inhabitants in arid areas have few prospects for meeting their nutritional needs.[9]

The Southern Plains of North America, Africa's Sahel, and the inner Asian grasslands face similar climatic and soil characteristics but different political, financial, and institutional constraints. The case of the Southern Plains is an example of the dismissal of indigenous knowledge followed by its recognition, the near-extinction of the plains bison and subsequent efforts to preserve it, the partial understanding of climatic variability followed by technology to neutralize many of the effects of climate, and poverty followed by massive outmigration and measures to expand the resilience of the ecosystem to withstand drought and generate wealth (box 4.1).

It is also an example of a heavily subsidized, energy-intensive model that is unlikely to be sustainable in the United States, and is not replicable in other grassland regions. Few countries are of continental size, enabling easier outmigration to better-endowed areas. Few economies are large enough or diversified enough to enable extensive cross-subsidization from other sectors to pay for the technical solutions to the problems of the fragile grasslands. And few have the political and financial commitment to sustain such a high level of support over such a long period. The solution to preventing and offsetting Dust Bowl consequences required massive transfers from the rest of society. Each affected state alone could not have solved the problems with only its own resources.

Rain, floods, or drought? Africa, north and south of the Sahara

Throughout much of Africa the plowing and monocropping on fragile soils of colonial times continued

Figure 4.2
Arid lands of the world

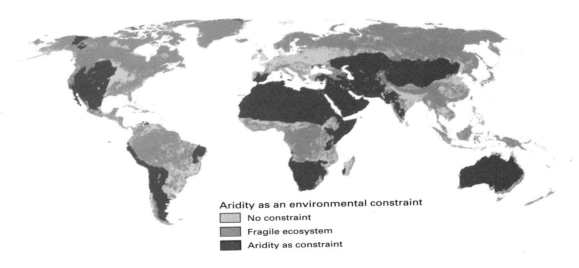

Aridity as an environmental constraint
- No constraint
- Fragile ecosystem
- Aridity as constraint

Source: FAO Global-AEZ Aridity Map; covering hyper-arid, arid, and dry semi-arid. See note 1.

Box 4.1
From degrading soils to degrading water—managing natural assets on the Southern Plains

Many indigenous people in the Southern Plains of North America and around the world recognized and accepted the basic constraints of drylands that forced a pattern of ecological restraint on their behavior. They also designed rules to alter destructive behavior. Complex and evolving institutions—traditions, rules, laws, habits, and a conservation ethic—guided indigenous cultures to conserve scarce natural resources and to survive in hostile environments by getting the incentives right. The colonial settlers on the Southern Plains saw the traditional use of productive land by nomadic groups as inefficient. They converted prime grazing land into intensive agricultural uses (monocropping, usually wheat). This pattern was badly suited to the lighter soils of the Southern Plains. Deep plowing dislodged soils, and monocropping mined soil nutrients.

Degradation, poverty, and migration
Large-scale farming in the 1920s pushed the expansion of wheat cultivation further onto native grasslands. By the next decade overgrazing, overplowing, and monocropping were exacerbated by the worst drought in U.S. history. An area of about 50 million hectares was affected each year in the "Dust Bowl" of the 1930s. The government mobilized a range of experts to find solutions—scientists, agronomists, civil engineers, political and social historians, local farmers, businessmen, and politicians. The scientists' solution was to bring back indigenous methods of planting a variety of plant species, replanting grass on the looser soils, and limiting grazing. The business view was against giving up the profitability and ease of monocropping wheat on large farms. While hundreds of thousands of destitute people migrated out of the area, the New Deal Conservation program spent an estimated $500 million on drought relief in the 1930s ($6 billion in 2000 dollars) and introduced a series of measures:

■ Federal Emergency Relief, zoning laws for the most fragile areas, repurchases of submarginal private land (it was deemed easier to buy problem areas and move the people living there to better land than to regulate and rehabilitate

lands under private ownership), cash payments for leaving land fallow, and farm loans tied to approved land practices;
■ The Civilian Conservation Corps, planting of shelterbelts with 220 million trees, soil and water conservation techniques such as the introduction of contour plowing, small dam and pond construction, mixed cropping, replanting of grasses, and state and federal protection of the remaining open grasslands under the Bureau of Land Management.

Beginning in 1940, normal rainfall patterns resumed, and outmigration reduced the farm population and increased farm sizes (about 1 million people migrated out of the area between 1930 and 1970). But in the 1950s Dust Bowl II hit, followed in the 1970s by Dust Bowl III. Conservation practices had helped, but to achieve reliable production for the agroprocessing industry, the United States needed to achieve a "climate-free" agriculture on the plains. It needed to get rain by pumping from deep, underground aquifers.

Financial transfers, technology, and "underground" rain
The government responded with an unprecedented and sustained political and financial commitment at the national and local level to address the human and environmental impact of degradation. The strategy reflected the conviction that ingenuity and technology must solve the puzzles of nature that our ancestors learned to live with as immutable forces. One striking feature has been the reliance on fossil fuel–intensive agricultural production with deep pumping of underground aquifers (up to 600 feet), and heavy reliance on chemical fertilizers and mechanization. The vast aquifer is being pumped faster than replenishment rates, with a net depletion rate of 3.62 million acre-feet (4.5 billion cubic meters) a year. Government net spending per head in the Southern Plains is higher than anywhere else in the United States, with state farm subsidies estimated at a cumulative $350 billion from 1960 to 2000.*

*The *Economist* (2001) December 15th.
Source: Worster (1979).

---

after independence.[10] National governments viewed common tenure claims as impediments to getting access to more agricultural land for growing populations. But when traditional common forests and lands managed by village elders were broken up, they were not replaced by alternate tenure arrangements and the state could not protect the areas. Neither individuals nor communities owned the land or forests, so there were no clearly defined or direct consequences of misuse.[11] So the lands were misused.

Changes in land use can rapidly lower soil quality, and intensive cultivation can deplete soil nutrients. Deforestation can cause erosion, washing away the layers of soil most suitable for farming. Two patterns are typical in Africa (and the world):

■ Growing populations convert higher quality pasture land to grow cash crops. Herders lose the better grazing land, their security against drought. Migratory movements for herders are reduced, lower quality land is more intensively grazed, and overgrazing leads to degradation.
■ Poor subsistence farmers have to reduce fallow periods to feed growing families. The reduction in fallow increases vulnerability to drought and without sufficient inputs, depletes soil nutrients. Degradation and soil erosion get worse.

More people and animals are concentrated on semi-arid and arid lands that can sustain cultivation or more intensive grazing only when rainfall is higher

Figure 4.3
Rainfall in the Sahel, 1950–2000

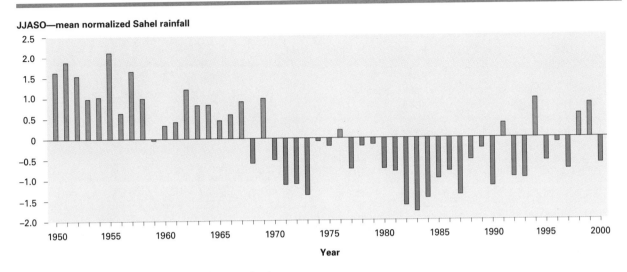

JJASO—mean normalized Sahel rainfall

Note: JJASO stands for June, July, August, September, October.
Source: National Center for Atmospheric Research, World Monthly Surface Station Climatology. Available on-line at http://tao.atmos.washington.edu/data_set/sahel.

than normal. In the Sahel favorable rainfall from the 1950s to the mid-1960s attracted more people. Rainfall reverted to normal low levels after 1970 (figure 4.3), and by 1974 an estimated 250,000 people had died along with nearly all their cattle, sheep, and goats. Some 7 million people had to rely on emergency food aid. The devastation prompted the United Nations to call a special conference on desertification in 1977 in Nairobi, Kenya.

The possibility that the Sahel could enter another period of favorable rainfall poses the risk of repeating the same tragedy—as poor people are drawn back to the land. Scientists do not have enough information about the effect of climatic disturbances on the resilience and long-term viability of dryland ecosystems; nor do they know the human and natural stress that these ecosystems can handle.[12] One difficulty in distinguishing between human and natural causes is the lack of data on the extent of grasslands before human disturbance and the loss over time.

The Intergovernmental Panel on Climate Change (IPCC) reports that Africa is highly vulnerable to climate change.[13] Although the equatorial region and coastal areas are humid, the rest of the continent is dry subhumid to arid. Global warming will reduce soil moisture in subhumid zones and reduce runoff. Already, water storage has been reduced to critical

levels in some lakes and major dams, with adverse repercussion for industrial activity and agricultural irrigation. Given the diversity of constraints, Africa faces daunting challenges in adapting to the effects of climate change (chapter 8).

The poor quality of soils is another constraining environmental factor. Phosphorus deficiency, low organic content, and low water infiltration and retention capacity on much of African soil have been limiting factors in agriculture. Unlike climate variability, this problem can be addressed: soil quality can be augmented through careful management and soil nutrient supplementation. More difficult to address are the recurrent droughts (box 4.2).

The Asian drylands: Managing competing land-use pressures

Population pressure on arable land in Asia is considerable—and growing. Severe land degradation affects some 35 percent of productive land. The result has been to put more population pressure on the Inner Asian drylands. Most affected are Afghanistan, China, India, and Pakistan,[14] and Inner Asia's high steppe, the largest remaining pastureland in the world, which includes Mongolia, northwestern China, and parts of Siberia. Over thousands of years, these grasslands have been home to nomadic herders of horses, camels, goats, sheep, and cattle, practicing elaborate systems

Box 4.2
Traditional knowledge and voice: sustaining livelihoods on the grasslands of the Sahel

Traditional survival know-how in Nigeria, grass-roots management efforts in Burkina Faso, and high-efficiency rangeland management in Mali all illustrate important livelihood strategies in the Sahel.

Seasonal migration and hedging techniques in Nigeria

In Nigeria, as in much of the Sahel, traditional social and institutional mechanisms have allowed pastoralists to adapt to fluctuations in rainfall and other natural changes.* Dryland people migrate in response to scarcity and environmental change. For some, migration is seasonal, as between the dry and humid areas of Nigeria. After the short rainy season Fulani pastoralists migrate south to graze livestock and avoid the tsetse. On their return, they bring back root crops grown in the south. Other arid land farmers and pastoralists recognize the value of diversity in their hedging strategies against environmental variability and water scarcity. They plant a variety of crops adapted to different stresses and graze a mix of animals. These strategies help people manage risks by understanding the resilience that biodiversity contributes to dryland ecosystems.

Inclusion and grass-roots development in Burkina Faso

The communities inhabiting the Sahel are poor, and erratic weather patterns make them just a growing season away from destitution. Providing for basic health, education, and food security under such vulnerable conditions remains very difficult. Service-asset management organizations are development committees formed to manage local infrastructure assets and indigenous associations that collaboratively manage resources such as land, forests, water, livestock, wildlife, and some village production activities.† They scale up the internal organization of villages and provinces by implementing a culturally coherent strategy that balances equity and enhances productivity, using mechanisms for inclusion, equity expansion, and com-

pensation. Water committees, for example, make decisions that ensure that a maximum number of working boreholes or water ponds are within walking distance of the community during the dry season, with adequate backups. (See also box 5.5 on zais.)

There is hope that locally based rural organizations could make a difference in coping with the climate problems and service delivery. Local institutions in Burkina Faso start with equity and solidarity and aim for growth and development. They are reducing poverty with little or no outside assistance.

Mali's high-efficiency traditional pastoral systems

Earlier research depicted traditional pastoral systems of the arid tropical areas as inefficient. More recent findings highlight the efficiency of those systems in using their resources.‡ A pioneering study in Mali showed that the mobile pastoral system produced 1.5 to 8 times more protein per hectare in meat and milk than beef cattle systems under similar climatic conditions in the United States and Australia, with essentially zero input of fossil fuel. The more settled, sedentary systems in Mali were less efficient. Later work in Botswana and other countries confirmed these indications of higher biological efficiency.

The findings shift thinking about rangeland management under the highly variable climatic conditions of arid tropical regions. Under those "nonequilibrium" systems livestock producers need to be able to "track" available forage or find new grazing areas for their animals, which usually requires access to large areas that encompass a diverse range of landscape niches. This calls for mobility and flexibility that enable rapid destocking in times of drought and restocking when the rains reappear.

Source: * See Niamir-Fuller (1998); † See Donnely-Roark, Ouedraogo, and Ye (2001); ‡ See Breman and Wit (1983); Behnke, Scoones, and Kerven (1993).

---

of seasonal pasture rotation across wide stretches of land in response to climate fluctuations. Herd rotation has helped sustain the fertility and resilience of grassland ecosystems and improve the health of livestock.[15]

Over the past decade population pressures and competing uses on these fragile lands have made it hard to find the right balance between traditional land management and demand for higher agricultural productivity. Government policies that discouraged a nomadic lifestyle, herd movement, and temporary use of patchy grasses led to dependence on agricultural livelihoods and sedentary herds, which created greater pressure on local ecosystems, and degraded fragile grasslands. The contrasting experiences of Mongolia and northwestern China illustrate some of the problems and possible solutions.

Mobile pastoralism—Mongolia.[16] Mongolia has retained many traditional herding customs and customary tenure with land management as a commons. Herders rely on local breeds (which are stronger and more resilient) that graze year-round on native grasses. These customary practices were effectively supported by the collectives between the 1950s and 1980s. The policy environment allowed people and herds to move over large areas and provided the possibility of sustainable grasslands management under controlled-access conditions. Until 1989 the state helped move families around to different grazing areas and provided subsidized schools and clinics. The state also set up several public enterprises that offered employment outlets, reducing the numbers of herders and keeping herd sizes relatively stable.

The economic transition since 1990 has not been conducive to sustainable management. Livestock mobility declined significantly. Many public enterprises closed. Having few alternatives, people turned to herding—often for the first time. The numbers of herders more than doubled from 400,000 in 1989 (17 percent of Mongolia's population) to 800,000 in the mid-1990s (35 percent). Poverty also increased to 36 percent of the population by 1995 from a very low base in the 1980s. Herds went from the traditional 25 million head to about 30 million. State subsidies for health, education, and relocation services were halted, making migration and the acquisition of human capital more difficult. Today, an estimated 10 percent of pastureland is believed to be degraded, causing noticeable increases in the frequency and intensity of dust storms.

The problem is considered manageable in Mongolia because population pressures are not too high. Rural population increased by about 50 percent from 1950 to 2000 (compared with a 700 percent increase in neighboring northwestern China). The government is responding to the consequences of the last 10 years by promoting secure livelihoods in the pastoral livestock sector through asset diversification, risk management, microfinance, and assistance to improve population mobility. The state is setting up a fund to finance service delivery in remote areas and is trying to foster growth and new jobs in other parts of the economy, reducing the number of herders. Having fewer more mobile herders should reduce overgrazing pressures, promote sustainable grassland management, and ensure acceptable livelihoods.

Mixed farming and intensifying livestock production—northwestern China.[17] As in Mongolia, the grasslands in China are state-owned. But settled pastoralism and the conversion of grasslands to arable cultivation were more common in northwestern China than in Mongolia, beginning in the 1950s when state-owned pastureland was allocated to "people's communes." The concentration of people in villages meant declining pasture rotation and expanding agriculture. Policies encouraged conversion of prime pasturelands into arable crop land, leading to salinization and wind erosion in some areas. Common policies were applied to highly diverse circumstances, resulting in perverse outcomes and higher degradation in some places. Subsidies encouraged mixed farming systems, which put more pressure on fragile land than the traditional mobile pastoralism.

Economic reforms in the early 1990s granted households nominal shares in the collective land pool. Shared areas were fenced off, making herd mobility more difficult. Subsidized inputs, income transfers, and deep pumping of underground aquifers encouraged a rapid increase in farming. From an estimated 3 million indigenous pastoralists in the 1950s in the "Inner Mongolian" part of northwestern China, farmers and livestock producers today number 20 million, and cattle doubled from 17 million head in 1957 to 32 million today.

China's western development plan shares two characteristics with the policies followed in the Southern Plains of the Unites States: intensify agricultural production and create "climate-free" agriculture in the grasslands through irrigation from underground aquifers. The objective is to make the area a bread and meat basket to provide for China's growing demands for improved local diets. But unlike the Southern Plains—where about 1 million farmers left between the 1930s to the 1970s, enabling reconsolidation of land holdings and conversion of vast grassland areas to protected areas—population pressures have continued to increase in China's grasslands. Poverty rates in these degraded and ecologically sensitive areas are well above the national average (25 percent in some provinces, compared with the national average of 6.3 percent). There is little empirical scientific research on what is happening to the land and the aquifers. The frequency and intensity of dust storms are increasing. Estimates of degradation are 50 to 75 percent, compared with 10 to 15 percent in the grasslands of Mongolia.

Combating desertification and a way forward for the drylands

The environmental problems of the coming century will almost certainly arise from the worsening of current problems that are not receiving adequate attention. Some scientists rank desertification and deforestation third among environmental issues requiring attention, after climate change and water resources.[18] Many emphasize that the links between climate change and other environmental problems (water, ecosystems) are likely to be important. And as demonstrated repeatedly, sector policies taken in isolation may solve one problem while aggravating others, particularly over a long period. We may know more about these links now, but we still do not understand exactly how these issues interact or what the most effective measures are likely to be.[19] More applied research and organized dissemination of lessons and techniques are needed.

With the 1992 Rio process and under the auspices of the United Nations, the Convention to Combat Desertification (CCD) was negotiated and entered into force in 1996.[20] With 178 signatories and 115 countries directly affected by desertification, the convention reflects a global commitment to combat the problem. It is one of the few conventions that incorporate socially and environmentally sustainable development objectives. Recognizing the disconnect between the wealth of local experience in dryland management and the cutting-edge science that connects global environmental changes to societies, the convention established institutional arrangements that link national goals and global interest in land and water management.

The convention also recognizes the need to share the risk and management of solutions over a much larger group of countries (the U.S. Southern Plains example illustrates the limited options available to a small jurisdiction in the absence of wider burden- and risk-sharing). It promotes partnering of national and international groups and linking indigenous communities with the scientific community to develop solutions to desertification by integrating partners, financial resources, and land degradation concerns into ongoing programs.

Agricultural research in China and India shows diminishing returns to investments in many high potential areas, but investments in drylands can produce large returns in reducing poverty, even if yields are modest.[21] Governments, researchers, and donor organizations are beginning to pay some attention to R&D on crop breeding varieties for people on marginal lands, but much more needs to be done by the public sector to replace antiquated crop varieties (see notes 7 and 8). In partnership with South African institutions, the CGIAR's International Maize and Wheat Improvement Center has developed two maize varieties for small farmers in South Africa's drought-prone, acidic, nutrient-depleted soils. Both varieties are drought-resistant, and one matures early, when farm food supplies are at their lowest. Trials from Ethiopia to South Africa have shown yields that are 34 to 50 percent higher than currently grown varieties.[22]

There are opportunities to achieve sustainable livelihoods in quite a few areas. But developers must recognize that the drylands are not homogeneous and cannot be made to function sustainably as nondrylands. Since large numbers of people are likely to remain in the dry grasslands for at least a few more generations, a range of strategies is needed to identify the attributes of the land that can be harnessed to provide inhabitants with a livelihood:[23]

- New technologies for drought-resistant crops
- Better water harvesting
- Some intensification, including the use of fertilizers
- Advice on better farming and grazing practices
- Innovative insurance schemes (such as those established in Mongolia, Kenya, and Ethiopia)
- Community-based early warning systems (such as those in Kenya)
- Local knowledge and new initiatives.

Some arid areas can take advantage of solar energy potential; others may have scenic value worthy of ecotourism development. The Mozambique Transfrontier Conservation Area Program and Burkina Faso's wildlife reserve development are two attempts in the direction of ecotourism that combine local and international cooperation. Research and innovations for appropriate service delivery—combined with policies that link human activities (farming, herding, and settlements) with natural processes (vegetation distribution, seasonal growing cycles, and watersheds)—help sustain vulnerable ecosystems while enhancing productivity to support growing populations.

Living on a precipice—the mountains

Mountains provide most of the world's people with fresh water and a substantial portion of their timber and minerals.[24] They shelter more than half the world's biodiversity and nurture varied cultures in a wide range of latitudes, from the polar regions to the temperate, subtropical, and tropical zones (figure 4.4). But their slope, altitude, relief, temperature, isolation, and rainfall make them one of the most highly variable and differentiated ecosystems. The concentration of people dispersed in many small communities in rugged areas has implications for

Figure 4.4
Mountainous areas of the world

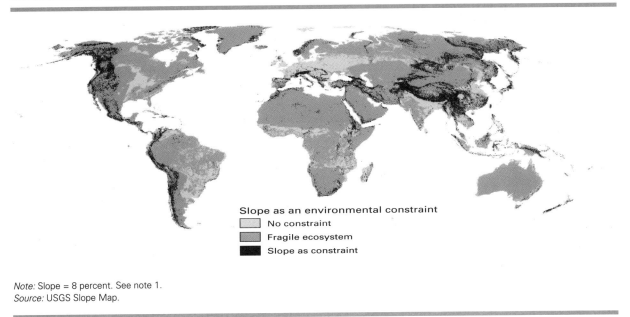

Slope as an environmental constraint
- No constraint
- Fragile ecosystem
- Slope as constraint

Note: Slope = 8 percent. See note 1.
Source: USGS Slope Map.

their subsistence and for the sustainability of mountain production systems. Agricultural potential in mountains is limited by the small size of arable plots, climatic variability, and more difficult growing conditions, including shorter growing seasons, which contribute to higher levels of poverty. The people living in these fragile areas are surviving by deftly managing the mosaic of land available to them.[25]

Mountain transformations

Mountain environments help to even out the rate of water flow between wet and dry seasons. But human activities, such as forest conversion, can disrupt normal flows and increase siltation, with costs to downstream users. Mining and fertilizer use can contaminate mountain water before it goes downstream. So in some places downstream users have begun to compensate upstream users to mitigate the negative impacts (for instance in Costa Rica).[26] Many of the commercial activities in mountains contribute to income generation and growth. But mountain people have not always benefited appropriately from the goods and services provided by mountain areas. The objective here is not to stop change in mountains; it is to manage resources in ways that provide sustainable livelihoods for mountain dwellers and provide the goods and services valued in lowland areas.

Deforestation in mountain areas has contributed to lasting changes in land productivity. Large areas of European mountain forests were cut and have not grown back because of changes in land use and soil loss. Some mountain areas in Africa have been stripped of vegetation by overgrazing and are no longer capable of supporting sustainable livelihoods. Land conversion (deforestation) and species depletion can often be spread over time spans longer than a normal human life, so impacts may not be immediately perceptible. Institutions need to be improved so that they can pick up these signals before it is too late. Some mountain attributes change over even longer periods, through gradual erosion or uplifting due to tectonic processes. Glacial retreat due to global warming is already occurring and over the next 50 to 100 years, nearly all mountain glaciers are likely to have melted, affecting downstream water flows. Some environmental fixes, such as restoring glaciers or reforesting in higher altitudes where trees grow slowly, may be impossible in any humanly relevant time span.

Mountain resources: Forests, minerals, biodiversity, and sustainable livelihoods

Logging generates employment and income—as well as inputs for production. It can also disrupt local cultures and production patterns. Unless forest dwellers control their own resources and gain the revenue from their exploitation, logging may not raise the income of mountain people—and may even impoverish them over the medium term (as happened in India and Indonesia), even in high-income countries (West Virginia).[27] It may provide short-term income at low wages for loggers, but once an area is logged out, timber companies move on, leaving the local populace without traditional sources of livelihood in the now-depleted forests. This often leads to destructive cutting of the remaining wood for other uses, which is not sustainable.

Minerals, like forests, are distributed unevenly among mountain areas and are often extracted by enterprises (foreign or national) from outside the region. The impacts of mining are more localized than for logging, but usually more intense due to the potential for social clashes and possible environmental problems. More recently, there has been progress in addressing sustainable mining.

Biodiversity and amenity benefits are among the most widespread of mountain values and among the most difficult to assign market prices. Although individual species attract attention, most biodiversity and amenity benefits stem from the integrated functioning of mountain environmental systems. These ecosystems provide important sources of livelihood for mountain dwellers. A steady livelihood can be earned from the sustainable use of mountain forests, for example from tourism and recreational uses, or from combining biodiversity preservation and commercial crop development (box 4.3).

Integrated mountain systems have aesthetic and economic benefits of global value. They reduce risks of landslides and protect biodiversity, which preserves genomes for food crops and the development of new medicines. Mountain forest areas can also be important for sequestering carbon dioxide. It is difficult to translate these benefits and values into market prices and transactions, but work is under way on a carbon trading system (one example is the sequestration program in Costa Rica—see box 8.5).

Mountains are involved in many ecological processes: water management, biodiversity, weather influences, and cultural, recreational, and amenity values. Human interventions can alter these relationships in ways that may harm (or benefit) different populations. Just as on the arid grasslands, when population and economic pressures are low and resources abun-

Box 4.3
Balancing public and private goods: biodiversity and coffee production in Chiapas

The El Triunfo Biosphere Reserve has remarkable biodiversity conservation value, with relatively large tracts of still-intact cloud forest and a high diversity of native animal and plant species, including many which only occur in the Sierra Madre of Chiapas and Guatemala.* Inside the El Triunfo Reserve's 120,000 hectares of pristine forest are some of the poorest people in Mexico. At 40 percent, the incidence of extreme poverty in Chiapas is more than twice the national rate (17 percent) and more than six times the incidence in Mexico's northern states (6 percent). Some 14,000 people in a buffer zone of private land inside the reserve had been clearing forest to plant mountain-grown coffee, cutting down some 17,000 hectares of forest in the last 20 years. Coffee producers were unaware that tree cover protects the coffee plants and improves the quality of the coffee.

In July 1999 the Global Environment Facility (GEF) provided grant funding ($750,000) for a Habitat Enhancement Project. A local NGO was put in charge of fostering community cooperatives and local leadership in 20 villages, helping local leaders prepare natural resource and development plans. The NGO brought together for the first time local government officials, communities, and NGOs to coordinate activities, learn about shade-grown coffee, and improve access to credit and technical assistance.

The El Triunfo farmers were among the first to test an emerging market for environmentally friendly coffee. The organic shade-grown coffee and the producer organization's skill in marketing the superior quality coffee allow farmers to earn a premium of 40–100 percent over ordinary mountain-grown coffee (and over what they were earning before). Investing in knowledge, local leadership, and grass-roots cooperation gave poor farmers an incentive to protect their natural resource base as one of their best assets.

Source: Pagiola and Ruthenberg (2002).

dant, use of the public good does not usually pose a sustainability problem. As pressures increase, overuse and abuse may arise, usually requiring some type of institution to manage the scarcity. Threats can result from degradation due to open access exploitation, from insufficient protection of valuable assets, and from imperfect pricing of the goods provided. Managing mountain environments often requires more elaborate consideration of the systematic secondary effects than is the case for lowland areas.

There are often competing demands on mountain resources for increasing resource extraction or preserving in-place and downstream services. Like drylands, mountains are not homogeneous. Each area requires a different strategy based on its inherent potential, the mix of natural resource values, and the commercial value of some of its renewable and nonrenewable products. All strategies need to incorporate the land's potential and the voice, capabilities, and aspirations of the people living there.

Nurturing assets by listening—and by enabling communities to act

In addition to the geophysical constraints, other socioeconomic constraints leave many people in the rural periphery with little to protect themselves from shocks. Poor health care, limited access to education, information and technical assistance, and high urban unemployment reduce the opportunities for outmigration and lower the remittances sent back to the village communities. Many developing countries have been ill prepared to help people on their rural periphery address problems and get connected to the economic mainstream.

Lacking access to information, education, and training, subsistence-based communities have difficulty improving their health and diversifying their off-farm activities. The costs of addressing malnutrition are manageable, yet micronutrient deficiencies remain serious in an estimated 85 countries, reducing mental capacity and the ability to learn. Schooling deficiencies are poorly measured, since most systems focus more on enrollments rather than on completion rates or the relevance of curricula. Poor access to health and education services increase the incidence of mental handicaps and low productivity, blocking opportunities for marginalized communities to advance.

This section looks at how communities can nurture their assets and find ways out of poverty through a combination of public sector or centrally initiated and top-down policies (as found in Tunisia), and locally initiated and bottom-up changes that work their way up to power centers (Morocco). Peru's mining sector, for instance, looks at a recent attempt at shifting to shared development among communities, companies, and the government. The way marginal rural groups in some European countries got out of poverty 100 years ago also reveals important lessons, showing how much more difficult it is for developing countries today (box 4.4).

Industrial country institutions never had to deal with many of the problems facing developing countries today. The institutions that developing countries inherited were not geared to addressing the problems of large, dispersed groups living in remote, fragile areas. Today, in many cases government spending for social services is highly skewed toward the better-off in urban areas—even when a large share of the population inhabits rural areas, marginal lands, and the urban periphery (chapter 6). Many countries have highly centralized and standardized education and health delivery systems that simply do not fit the needs of remote areas—and are costly to administer. Agricultural investments and services are concentrated on the more favorable lands, even when the majority of farmers are on fragile lands. Countries are slowly changing these approaches.[28]

Nurturing women's human capital

Studies of a wide range of societies find that women are an important engine of growth and development.[29] Their ability to save and invest in their families is well documented. As the family's nutritional gatekeeper, women fight hunger and malnutrition. Their largely unrecorded role in agriculture explains the survival of many traditional subsistence communities on marginal lands. Yet in many places, traditions, limited mobility, and lack of voice or access to information make women the most marginal group. With the men seeking work elsewhere, women tend the fields and look after the children, the elderly, and the farm animals. Traditional communities depend on women and girls to fetch fuelwood and water, and to produce and prepare food. Are national and local institutions investing in this engine for growth, or are they handicapping it?

Some 80 percent of economically active women in Sub-Saharan Africa and South Asia are in agricultural activities—largely subsistence farmers in female-headed households or day laborers on larger commercial farms. These economic realities are beginning to give women more influence. Forward-looking institutions are responding with changes in attitude and service delivery. Bangladesh's Grameen Bank and Morocco's Zakoura Foundation offer microcredit for women and schools for girls; women contribute to the design of water, health, and education projects in West Africa, Central America, and Baluchistan. Agencies and communities, recognizing the high returns from raising women's status, are teaming with NGOs, local anthropologists, sociologists, and

Box 4.4
What worked then (Europe, 1900) is much harder now (developing countries, 2000)

At the turn of the last century, many of Europe's poor peasants inhabited marginal lands. They got out of poverty traps thanks to ingenuity, to inclusive and flexible institutions, and to favorable circumstances that do not exist for the rural periphery today. Technical innovations attracted unskilled workers and encouraged the migration of peasants from Europe's rural periphery to factory jobs in North America. A vibrant civil society brought about sustained and wider participation in income growth.

Migration then . . . but not now
Institutions never targeted policies to deal with people remaining on fragile lands, because most of them left. Open migration from Europe between 1870 and 1910 reduced pressures on Europe's poor rural areas and boosted productivity in the New World. Some 13 percent of Europe's labor force migrated to the New World during those 40 years. For Italy and Ireland, as much as 45 percent of the labor force migrated—for Scandinavia, about 25 percent. Some 80 percent of migrants were peasants or unskilled laborers with no more than primary education, but they found jobs in factories and mines. The transition took place with few legal restrictions, and government facilitated the assimilation through public education and health.

For developing countries today, outmigration from the rural periphery is toward coastal urban centers and the peri-urban shantytowns, not North America, Western Europe, or other developed countries. Cumulative migration to the United States from 1970 to 2000 accounted for less than 2 percent of the labor force in Sub-Saharan Africa and less than 5 percent in Latin America and the Caribbean (the region with the highest migration ratio). Unlike 100 years ago, when peasants made up 80 percent of migrants, today professionals, skilled workers, and those with some university training make up more than half the migrants into the United States. The lowest skilled workers came from Mexico, the highest skilled workers from Asia and Africa.*

Technology, wages, and jobs then
The factories of the early 1900s employed unskilled workers with little schooling, at subsistence wages (under well-documented Dickensian working conditions). Henry Ford took the unprecedented decision to improve working conditions by pursuing his own interests within the context of the interests of a wider group. Increasing labor's access to assets is a distributional initiative that has efficiency gains, recognized even by hard-nosed businessmen.

In 1908, after designing a reliable and affordable automobile, Henry Ford wanted to bring the unit cost down to expand sales to a mass market. In 1913 Ford and his engineers introduced the assembly line, reducing the time to assemble a car from 12 hours to 2 with the same amount of labor. Productivity shot up, and the labor required no education and little training (half of Ford's workers were poor immigrants from Italy and Eastern Europe's marginal lands). After a year of record profits, Ford more than doubled unskilled wages and reduced the work day from 10 hours to 8—even though workers were waiting in line for jobs at the lower wage.

Ford's decision meant that poorly educated workers could begin to accumulate capital and savings—enabling unskilled workers to lift themselves and their families out of poverty. He reduced labor turnover from 300 percent to 23 percent and increased productivity by another 50 percent. What motivated him? He wanted to sell more cars (wages were so low at the time, that few but the wealthy could afford them). And he wanted to block the establishment of a labor union.

In the following 50 years, interest groups in the United States and other OECD countries pushed for shared growth, creating institutions to include more people in a wider prosperity circle. Top-down measures (such as universal public education and health care) and bottom-up measures brought about wider participation in income growth. Labor unions obtained higher wages through a combination of collective bargaining, increases in productivity, and some tightening of the labor market. Women's rights organizations gained for women the right to vote and later to become active participants in the job market. Social safety nets helped the elderly and unemployed. These and other policies all served to bring more people into managing, distributing, and benefiting from the countries' growing wealth. The policies supported inclusiveness and helped create better institutions.

Technology, wages, and jobs now
By the end of the 1970s production methods in all countries started changing with diminishing returns to unskilled labor and increasing returns to skills. Today, unskilled workers in developing countries face legal migration restrictions and higher skill requirements. The limited number of jobs with above-subsistence wages makes it difficult to improve the incomes of the globally large uneducated, unskilled work force. Since 1990 the high supply of unskilled workers has pointed to a global stagnation and convergence of wages at subsistence levels in many developing countries. This makes it difficult for outmigrants from rural areas (both the periphery and the overcrowded commercial rural areas) to find gainful employment in urban and peri-urban areas.

Even though the informal sector accounts for the largest share of employment for the working-age population, it is not visible on the economist's radar screen. Data on the informal sector are not systematically collected. Wage rates reported in the 1990s for farm labor and unskilled construction workers (the two most likely jobs for people migrating from the rural periphery) remained low and flat in many countries (box figure).

Only the Republic of Korea (at $500 a month) and the Czech Republic, Mauritius, and Tunisia saw unskilled wages approach $250 a month. Average purchasing power parity (PPP) wages for unskilled work in most of the other countries remained very low, at under $100 a month for the past decade. Farm wages show a similar trend. The average PPP equivalent wage in the OECD countries for *similar work* was 16 times higher for farm labor and 22 times higher for unskilled construction work.† Such a difference in wages for farm work is partly explained by legal migration restrictions and barriers to agricultural trade in

Box 4.4 *(continued)*

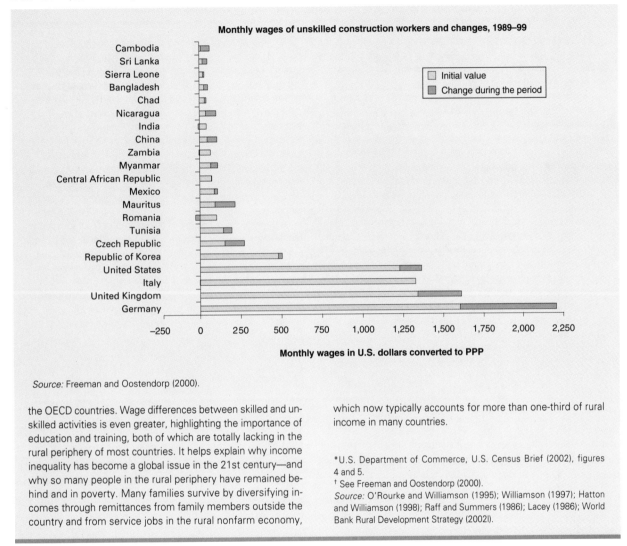

Monthly wages of unskilled construction workers and changes, 1989–99

Source: Freeman and Oostendorp (2000).

the OECD countries. Wage differences between skilled and unskilled activities is even greater, highlighting the importance of education and training, both of which are totally lacking in the rural periphery of most countries. It helps explain why income inequality has become a global issue in the 21st century—and why so many people in the rural periphery have remained behind and in poverty. Many families survive by diversifying incomes through remittances from family members outside the country and from service jobs in the rural nonfarm economy, which now typically accounts for more than one-third of rural income in many countries.

*U.S. Department of Commerce, U.S. Census Brief (2002), figures 4 and 5.
† See Freeman and Oostendorp (2000).
Source: O'Rourke and Williamson (1995); Williamson (1997); Hatton and Williamson (1998); Raff and Summers (1986); Lacey (1986); World Bank Rural Development Strategy (2002l).

economists to reach women directly—with information, education, and access to credit.[30]

By tailoring service delivery to local circumstances and empowering remote rural communities, some countries are finding affordable ways to improve services and help people get out of poverty traps. This starts with a good understanding of a community's values and capabilities. It requires people who can marry an appreciation of modernity with an understanding of local traditions (cultural translators).

Tunisia illustrates the combination of national leadership, long-term commitment, and cultural understanding to achieve broad-based improvements in the quality of life of all citizens. Soon after independence in the 1950s Tunisia's President Bourguiba began introducing legal reforms to improve the status of women. He routinely visited villages, explaining the changes he wanted. The education ministry transported boys *and girls* in remote areas to school, and the health ministry sent midwives out to villages to discuss preventive health care and family planning, and to inform women of their rights.

Decades later Germany's technical assistance agency, Gesellschaft für Technische Zusammenarbeit (GTZ), recognized that one of Tunisia's public agencies would be a good candidate for its participatory development approach. The Sylvo-Pastoral Development Authority (ODESYPANO) had been administering a tree-planting program, with mixed success, along the barren hillsides in northwestern Tunisia to reduce the erosion that silted up dams farther downstream. GTZ wanted to fund a project that would

Box 4.5
Addressing risks, changing institutions, and reaching subsistence families in Tunisia

The families in the semi-arid mountainous region of northwestern Tunisia are poor, with an annual average per capita income of $220. In the mid-1990s GTZ approached the Tunisian government with a $1 million grant to finance a project that integrated female participation at the village level. The director of ODESYPANO saw several problems and risks in introducing female agricultural outreach workers. There were few, if any, trained female agricultural specialists. Families would not want young women to go with male agents to villages in remote, rugged areas. And the villagers would have difficulty accepting female agents. GTZ argued that this approach had brought good results in other countries and that the women in Tunisian villages had important farm responsibilities. After a year of discussions on how to minimize the risks, in 1995 the director hired seven women for a staff of 40 outreach workers.

One of those selected, Leila, 25, was an unemployed university graduate in Arabic literature. GTZ put her and the others through a six-week training program and teamed her with Ali, an agent with a degree in animal husbandry who had already been working in the villages. On her first visit to a village, Ali requested the men to allow Leila to talk with their wives. They refused. She sat quietly listening to the discussion and continued to accompany Ali to his meetings with the village men once every two weeks, but never spoke, only listened to the men discuss the problems of the village.

After their third meeting the men brought along their wives and told Leila they trusted her. The barrier had been broken. Leila taught the women animal hygiene, better milking methods, and how to make cheese, plant caper bushes, cultivate saffron flowers, and plant and braid garlic—all products they are beginning to sell in the local market and to resort hotels along the coast. Several activities were introduced as team efforts for the men and their wives, including rabbit husbandry, improved poultry pens, and better water harvesting techniques. Having the women hear the same messages that were being given to their husbands reinforced the know-how and application of new ideas—significantly improving outcomes.

A development dynamic is changing traditions, increasing family incomes (up 7 percent a year from 1996 to 2000), and promoting social cohesiveness. It is also reinforcing partnerships between husbands and wives and among families who are starting to pool resources to create larger commercial activities. The number of female agricultural workers has nearly doubled, from 7 women in 1997 to 13 women in 2001.

Source: Bank staff field visits, interviews with ODESYPANO staff, June 1997, and World Bank (2001d).

incorporate women. The idea of having female outreach workers accompany male agents had not previously been considered. The director of ODESYPANO was supportive of the idea, but saw many risks that are difficult for a civil servant to assume. The experience showed that persistence, grant funding, and partnership can overcome an agency's deep-seated aversion to risk taking (box 4.5).

Transforming institutions and individuals: The role of leadership

Tunisia's political leadership improved the status of women through decades of persistent public pronouncements, changes in the laws, and concrete actions. These policies have continued and been consistently applied even after a change in government in the late 1980s. Adding female outreach at ODESYPANO fit in with these efforts, but it entailed risks that needed to be addressed up front. The director emphasized changing local traditions by strengthening women's position in the context of lifting up the entire family.

Tunisia has made major progress in transforming a master-servant relationship into a partnership between husbands and wives—even in poor, remote villages. Thanks to consistent efforts by Tunisian leaders over a long period, women enjoy equal rights in almost every respect under the law except inheritance. When the women in the Tunisian mountain village were asked to reflect on what change had the most important impact on their lives in the past 10–20 years, they responded that it was "the way the men's behavior toward us has changed . . . they are nicer to us—less demanding, more appreciative. Now they call us by name, and we have the right to refuse our husbands."

It is difficult for economic analysis to capture all the benefits of bringing remote communities into the mainstream. The costs can be high and easy to calculate, but the benefits are more difficult to capture. It is possible to have some idea of the costs of not undertaking investments that include minorities and remote groups in the development process. Drug cartels in Colombia, the Shining Path movement in Peru, rebellion in Mindanao in the Philippines and in Chiapas in Mexico—all are partly attributable to the discontent and poverty of disenfranchised communities in remote areas. Unless ways are found to meaningfully bring these groups into the mainstream, they sow the seeds of later conflict.

Building on traditional social capital

Dispersed settlements, far from urban centers, make it costly and physically difficult to provide services. Public servants, especially teachers, are recruited from urban centers and are reluctant to live in villages. Absenteeism is high, and villagers often distrust outsiders. Agricultural experts sent to marginal rural areas sometimes view the local people as too poor or uneducated to develop themselves. The result is either benign neglect or costly (and only partially successful) interventions. By building on long-standing traditions, one poor village found a way to improve its quality of life.

Solving collective action problems in the community

By combining traditional assets of trust and sharing with modern assets—educated men and women—the villagers can move beyond survival to development. Local leadership blended a keen understanding of the village culture with technical, managerial, and fundraising skills acquired through education and experience outside the village. The project's technical design matched the community's financial capacity and engendered a strong sense of community ownership box 4.6). It was important that everyone contribute, maintain, and benefit from a project. The villagers in Ait Iktel had to be able to afford the project and subsequent maintenance costs. As Ali Amahan explained, "the grant from the Japanese Embassy for the electricity generator was vital. We could not have done the project without it, but it was important the villagers work hard to get that grant." If a project is designed, built, and entirely paid for by an outside entity, the community will have little sense of ownership.

Achieving unanimity is difficult, but in this village it was important for sustaining the dynamic and guiding traditional social capital in the direction of development. When consensus is lacking (as for the girls school), it is better to move forward on activities on which everyone agrees (the access road and electricity). Goodwill has time to develop, making it easier to reach consensus on the next project. By listening to, understanding, and addressing each family's objections to the school, the village reached a consensus, and the association prepared a highly successful project with locally appropriate features not found in the state education system.[31]

Scaling up community-driven development to a large number of villages requires visible commitment from the communities. It cannot be forced. Mo-

hamed Amahane now works full time in 14 villages on community development, but he advises other villages only when they initiate the contact. He helps them identify "cultural translators," and helps them come up with projects that are within the village's means and capacity to manage. A national effort to support such activities and expand voice in local communities is gradually emerging.[32]

Support from the top

Formal government institutions could have blocked the community development process, but the late King Hassan II allowed some political loosening in the mid-1990s that enabled local advocacy NGOs to emerge. Without this opening, Ait Iktel could not have set up an association or sought external grant funding. Another boost came in 1997 when the minister of basic education introduced a pilot program of community-based schools. The program's budget is less than 0.01 percent of the ministry's budget, but it allowed local NGOs to set up schools, benefiting the many girls for whom the public system was not a viable alternative. It also allowed communities to adapt rules to local conditions, identify teachers, and promote stronger community involvement in education. The cost of these schools is 25 to 50 percent that of public schools, with impressive results. The program has remained a small pilot. The ministry, cautious about the initiative, is taking time to consider the many changes the program introduced.

To reach remote populations in cost-effective ways, national institutions need to be flexible—open to new ideas and to learning by listening.[33] Because government administrations can be highly risk averse, changing behavior is extremely difficult. Prominent leaders and international agencies can play a catalytic role in raising awareness and promoting promising initiatives.

In 1998 a well-known Moroccan writer, Fatema Mernissi, published a book about the development dynamic in Ait Iktel. Her book was featured at the international gathering of the Mediterranean Development Forum in Marrakesh. In 1999 a Moroccan businessman launched a rural school program, drawing on the lessons of Ait Iktel. In 2000 King Mohamed VI honored the Ait Iktel Association with a national merit award and cited Ait Iktel's development philosophy for the activities of the Mohamed V Foundation for Solidarity (a national grant facility established in 1998). In 2001 the association received an international award from the Aga Khan Foundation. Such

Box 4.6
"Cultural translators" as catalysts to upgrade livelihoods in Ait Iktel, Morocco

Ait Iktel is in the High Atlas Mountains about 100 kilometers from Marrakech.* Per capita incomes are low, 2,500 dirham ($250) a year, much of it from migrant remittances. In the mid-1990s the village had no electricity, and in drought years potable water was a 3-kilometer walk. Primary enrollment was 5 percent for girls and 20 percent for boys, who attended the state public school about 5 kilometers away.

The village's most valuable asset was its traditional social capital, characterized by village elders managing by consensus-building and an equitable, shared distribution of the limited resources (brush forest, water, and communal grazing land). The village's social capital enabled the community and its social, musical, and religious traditions to survive over the centuries. More recently, it has enabled the community to shift toward a development dynamic unprecedented in this region's history.

In 1995, when Ait Iktel faced a third consecutive year of drought, the villagers pooled remittances and two of the villagers (Ali Amahan, then director of the National Monuments of Fez, and his cousin Mohamed Amahane, a mechanical technician at a phosphate mining company in Casablanca) organized the men to construct a well. Assuming the vital role of "cultural translators"—people who understand modern management methods and are also steeped in the local traditions—the two men noticed how spontaneously and efficiently the women organized the water distribution and maintenance of the well and decided the community was ready to do more. The water project's success set off a development dynamic that continues today.

The villagers established an association, Ait Iktel pour Développement, working under the village assembly's traditional authority. The village assembly, a traditional patriarchal authority structure that brings together all the chefs de familles, manages village affairs, resolves disagreements, and makes decisions based on unanimous agreement. The association mobilized the migrant remittances for community development projects and set up a "village work bank." Each family contributes five labor days a year on projects.

After constructing the well, Mohamed and Ali asked the assembly about building a school for girls, but the village priority was to upgrade the access road and purchase an ambulance to help reduce maternal deaths. After these two projects were completed, Ali and Mohamed again raised the possibility of setting up a girls school. Again the village assembly had another priority: electricity. Mohamed designed a project that fit the income levels of the villagers: a small generator for all the homes in the central village and solar panels for more remote locations. It was critical to the building of social capital that everyone contribute to and benefit from the project. In 1997, on the night they all celebrated lighting up the village, the assembly agreed to a school for girls.

The villagers were not opposed to sending girls to school, but they were dissatisfied with the schooling provided by the state. The poor quality of instruction did not prepare students for jobs in the village or the city, and it cut children off from local agricultural and artisanal roots that could provide them some livelihood. The association selected an unemployed university graduate from the village to be the teacher. The villagers refurbished an abandoned house for the school room using their own materials and set school hours to allow time for girls to do their chores. They also wanted year-round classes (with vacations coinciding with village events, planting, and harvesting).

Classes were taught in the native language, and the curriculum was Arabic, French, math, and on Fridays handicrafts taught by the village women. These represented major changes from the state system. By the second year enrollment of girls ages 6 to 20 went from 5 percent to 90 percent. To accommodate demand the villagers built a second school in 1998. After three years, many girls had graduated but had no prospect of continuing to the next level. In 2000 a national NGO (Support Committee for Rural Girls' Education)[†] set up a scholarship program for girls to continue their education.

Over a period of three years, each project contributed to a development dynamic that expanded the villagers' modest asset base, and that continues to this day. Incomes increased somewhat, but the time budget increased dramatically, so that people had more time to devote to advancement rather than to survival. Electricity allowed children to study at night, women to continue working on handicrafts, and the villagers to afford an electrically operated irrigation pump. Readily available water and electricity cut down on girls' time for fetching water and wood. Health advice is now available on video in the community center (65 percent of families have begun using family planning). The irrigation system has doubled summer crops during the dry season and allowed for some crop diversification. Thanks to the ambulance, there have been no maternal deaths in childbirth.

Total project costs of $300,000 ($300 to $400 per person) were covered by a grant from the Japanese Embassy (60 percent), savings from remittances (25 percent), and the villagers' labor (15 percent). Maintenance costs are covered by the villagers, and teachers receive their salaries from the association through a transfer from the education ministry. The grant cost of scaling up this level of service nationwide would be roughly $1 billion a year over five years. The ministry of agriculture's annual budget is about $2 billion, most of it devoted to investments for farmers on more productive land, even though the majority of farm families inhabit marginal lands.

Source: * See Amahan (1998); Mernissi (1997); interviews, field visits with Association Ait Iktel du Développement, 2000; † http://www.cssf.ma/.

recognition is important, especially if the authorities back it up with concrete actions. Transforming hierarchical national government agencies into institutions that listen, devolving some decisionmaking to communities, and responding effectively at the local level is a long, complex process. Such transformations are being prompted by internal and external political and economic pressures from local NGOs—and by easier access to satellite news and information which make people aware of the possibilities.

Scaling up community-driven initiatives

In several countries, government ministries and civil society are working together to strengthen and expand community-based initiatives. The Bangladesh Rural Advancement Committee (BRAC) is the largest and one of the most impressive scaled-up examples of community schools. Other promising projects include the Community Support Program for primary education in Baluchistan and El Salvador's Community-Managed Schools Program (EDUCO). In Nicaragua, with its diverse and hard-to-reach populations, the ministry of education devolved managerial and budgetary autonomy to local school councils with reasonable success. Private companies are also getting more involved in education promotion and in "adopt a school" initiatives.

Health outreach, microsavings, and credit are other badly needed services in remote areas.[34] Donors and health ministries are teaming with NGOs to get trained midwives and health visitors (rather than expensive clinics staffed with doctors and nurses) out to villages on a routine schedule with medicines, family planning, and nutrition advice. Other examples include the following:

■ In Orissa, India, the international NGO CARE is setting up microenterprises to produce insecticide-treated mosquito nets to reduce malaria and to help poor villages generate income.
■ A community-based health and antimalaria program was launched in 1992 in Tigray, Ethiopia, with 714 volunteers serving more than 1.7 million people in some 2,000 villages.
■ Private banks in Lebanon are sponsoring NGOs to promote microsavings in remote mountainous areas. Vans go to villages, collecting savings, making small loans, and depositing the savings in the nearest bank branch. A few combine mobile banking with health outreach services.

Scaling up community-driven development to a large number of villages is critical to improving livelihoods on fragile lands. Some government ministries are embracing new approaches, but often the leadership, will, and know-how of government officials are lacking—keeping promising initiatives at a modest level. Local motivation and capacity for collective action are the main prerequisites for scaling up successful community initiatives, but an enabling national environment combined with grant funding are critical complements.

There is a long history of qualitative studies on community development, but careful econometric evaluations are more recent. The results of the econometric research on the effectiveness of community development initiatives are still sketchy but the findings indicate that community-based projects are directed to the poor and can improve service delivery. Much depends on the village context (homogeneous groups have a higher success rate), on whether the design is sensitive to and scaled to local realities, whether the government is committed to the projects, and whether the approach is gradual, monitored, and adapted as necessary.[35]

The use of nonrenewable local resources— balancing interests

In all countries, marginal rural groups living on or near potentially rich natural resources often have the least voice in matters that concern them, their land, and other resources. But how the environmental and economic costs and benefits from resource extraction are managed and transformed into other types of assets is critical to sustaining the livelihoods of poor communities in fragile mountain areas. Are the revenues from natural resources shared with the local community? Are the revenues used to transform the local and national asset base by investing in new human, physical, and financial assets? For some developing countries resource revenues have been an important opportunity for accelerating development (for instance in Botswana, Chile, and Malaysia). For others (Algeria, Angola, Liberia, and Peru), mineral and oil resources have not generated sustained, broad-based economic growth. Institutional rules make the difference (chapter 7, figure 7.3).

In the late 1990s attitudes, approaches, and laws concerning the extractive industries began to alter the rules of the game to give more influence to local communities. In countries as varied as Australia, Canada, Nigeria, Peru, Turkey, and the United States, local communities have been making their voices heard, organizing themselves to achieve sustainable benefits from large extractive operations. Social and environmental considerations are being woven into decision-making to avoid harming the community or the environment and leaving behind wasted lands and dysfunctional communities after an operation closes.

Poor communities in remote areas have high expectations that extractive industries will offer them a chance to climb out of poverty through jobs, infrastructure, and tax revenues. When these expectations are not met, and when social and environmental costs are incurred, local communities often revolt. In recent years community protests have led to the interruption, or even closure, of extractive industries operations—with high direct economic costs to the private sector, the public sector, and everyone else (examples include a copper mine in Papua New Guinea; a gold and copper mine in Iryan Jaya; a gold mine in Bergama, Turkey; oilfields in the Niger delta; and a gas pipeline in Malaysia and Thailand).

Done well, extractive activities can help transform a society's asset base, generate growth, and serve the interests of all stakeholders. Local communities want to get out of poverty. Central governments want foreign exchange and tax revenues to meet fiscal obligations. And companies want to maximize the returns on their investments. But in many cases, governments have difficulty balancing the different interests: institutional capacity is weak, officials are insufficiently trained, local communities are poorly organized, and companies are left to manage potentially chaotic situations that go beyond their traditional areas of expertise. International and local NGOs are putting pressure on mining companies and governments by helping local groups organize to demand transparent disclosure, environmental cleanups, and fair treatment. Companies—and governments—have begun to develop strategies to respond (box 4.7).[36]

Balancing interests among governments, companies, and communities

The community's lack of voice at an early stage of mine development at Yanacocha meant that signals did not get picked up, and problems and mistrust accumulated. Diverging interests became more difficult to balance, and problems were much harder to solve. Inclusive institutions, transparency, access to information, and attention to the decisionmaking process are now recognized as key elements of good practice and social corporate responsibility in the extractive industries. Shifting from bilateral relationships to tripartite partnerships among companies, communities, and government shows promise. In the mid-1990s the Canadian government adopted a partnership approach based on "a fair distribution of net benefits, local participation, and respect for the environment."[37]

Governments

Governments have difficult roles in regulation, revenue balancing, and national and local development that are particularly apparent in the extractive industries sector. Getting the structure of fiscal arrangements right to achieve all of these objectives is not easy, and solutions need to be tailored to local circumstances.[38] Central governments need to put aside tax receipts legally targeted to the regions, establish transparent procedures on how the revenues will be used, and assist local officials to organize themselves to spend these funds efficiently—with accountability. Each of these tasks is difficult, even for countries with well-developed institutions. Governments have several objectives in setting the fiscal terms:

- Protect tax revenues from commodity price fluctuations
- Ensure some distribution of wealth to affected communities
- Support investment decisions that generate the highest returns
- Avoid corruption and prevent misuse of funds
- Allow some share of tax revenues to be set aside, either for emergencies or for future generations.

The central government can legitimately be asked to provide the legal and regulatory framework for the environmental and social impacts of extractive industries and for institutions that monitor and enforce compliance on the ground. Even if mines use clean, modern processes, they can still create environmental and health problems that are technically difficult to address. Communication and emergency plans are needed to respond to accidents and employees and local communities need training in the steps to be taken.

The agency responsible for environmental monitoring and enforcement needs to have autonomy and professional credibility. In Peru this responsibility rests with a specialized unit *within* the ministry of mines. This ensures technical capability, but also sets the agency up for conflicts of interest, since the ministry's mandate is to promote mining as well as regulate it. Conflict of interest could be diminished by a more autonomous environmental unit with some industry and community representation (similar to the

Box 4.7
Learning to balance interests: two big mines in the Andes

The Yanacocha and Antamina mines are 4,000 meters (13,120 feet) above sea level in the Andes Mountains of Peru. At this altitude, agriculture is not viable except for small-scale grazing. More than 90 percent of the predominantly rural people in these two regions live below the poverty line. Malnutrition, infant mortality, and illiteracy rates are high, at two to three times national averages.

Exploration of the Yanacocha mine began in 1989 and operations began in 1992, while explorations in Antamina began roughly in 1999, and operations began only at the end of 2001. The experiences of these two mines illustrate the degree to which—globally—expectations and industry practices in socially, environmentally, and economically sustainable mining are beginning to change. And they show how institutions (governments, companies, and communities) need to learn to adapt behaviors, anticipate or avoid clashes, and promote broad-based development.

Yanacocha—turning collision into cooperation over gold in Cajamarca?

By early 1990 gold and other minerals were detected in the Cajamarca region, and Buenaventura, one of Peru's leading private mining companies, teamed with U.S.-owned Newmont, one of the world's largest mining companies, and the International Finance Corporation (IFC) to form Minera Yanacocha, SRL.

The deposit is near the city of Cajamarca, a site of symbolic and historical importance. Inhabited by descendants of the Incan people, Cajamarca is where, in 1532, the Spanish conquistador Francisco Pizarro and his hundred or so men ambushed and killed thousands of native Incan warriors and captured their emperor Atahuallpa. Pizarro held his captive for eight months "while extracting history's largest ransom in return for a promise to free him. After the ransom was delivered (enough gold to fill a room 22 feet long, 17 feet wide, and 8 feet high), Pizarro reneged on his promise and executed Atahuallpa."*

Gold has once again become a source of tension in the region. Community expectations for the mine as an escape from poverty were understandably high. But from the outset the company was preoccupied with security, fearing the activities of the Shining Path (Sendero Luminoso). The company believed it had little choice but to keep a low profile to protect its employees and others in the community who supported the operation. The company thus refrained from organizing extensive consultation meetings and stayed away from the more urban areas, focusing instead on development activities in the rural areas near the mine and limiting consultation to selected representatives of the community. The feeling of distance between the company and the town of Cajamarca was difficult to change even when the Shining Path was no longer a threat after 1995.

The Yanacocha mine was a remarkable financial success. It is the most profitable, lowest-cost gold mine in the world, owing largely to the excellent gold reserves. Under full operation export earnings have reached $500 million a year in the past few years, and corporate income taxes amount to $45 to $55 million a year (30 percent of profits). A 1992 law *(canon minero)* required the central government to return 20 percent of the annual corporate tax collected (about $8 million) to the local region, but Cajamarca appears to have received only a part of these funds. Whether and in what form the money was received is unclear. Transparency of accounts at different institutional levels remains an issue.

In June 2000 an accidental mercury spill proved to be a "wake-up call" for the company, as well as the community and the government, prodding them to reexamine the project's impact on the local community. The spilled mercury did not reach the water system, and the company undertook remedial action. (There has been some dispute about the circumstances and number of contamination cases.) Much concern remained in the community regarding Yanacocha's commitment to protect the environment and the community's health.

Concerned for some time that the expansion of the mine could affect the source of water for Cajamarca, the Cajamarca community organized itself by November 2000. To prevent the company from mining the large remaining deposits next to the existing mine, the municipality of Cajamarca passed an ordinance declaring part of the basin a reserve for water recharge (the ordinance is being appealed to the Constitutional Tribunal by Minera Yanacocha).

The company now realizes the importance of a wide-reaching "social" license for its operation in addition to its "legal" license. Consultation has shifted to a broad process that includes community validation of local development projects, formalization of the information and complaint systems, and multistakeholder dialogue. The company is embarking on an urban development program involving investments that will be added to the ongoing rural programs. Since the mine has at least another 20 years of operation, it is not too late to forge a socially and environmentally sustainable development compact.

Antamina—building a development relationship with local communities

Antamina is a new mining venture in the central north Andes Mountains, about 300 kilometers south of Yanacocha. Owned by a consortium of three Canadian companies (90 percent of the shares) and a Japanese firm (10 percent), Antamina is expected to become the world's third largest zinc producer and seventh largest copper producer. Export earnings were initially projected at $950 million a year and corporate taxes at $83 million (with 20 percent to go back to the region).

The Antamina operation came along some 10 years after Yanacocha, but the two mines share several similarities. Both have high economic profiles as modern operations contributing valuable revenues to the Peruvian economy. Both are in areas with poor indigenous people who have little or no previous mining tradition. But the communities around Antamina have had much less contact with the modern, outside world than those in the Cajamarca region. For both operations the central government's capacity to address social, environmental, and other institutional development issues has been limited. But Antamina wants to avoid some of the problems experienced by Yanacocha and is fortunate to begin its activities at a peaceful time when more inclusive rules of the game are becoming internationally recognized.

*See Diamond (1997).
Source: McMahon and Felix (2001); interviews with World Bank and IFC staff.

environmental agency in Chile). In exceptional cases, responsibility may need to be vested in an impartial external agency.

Companies

Large mining operations are capital intensive, requiring skilled technicians, who are often from outside. With few jobs available for locals, communities increasingly look for other compensations. One option is for the company to provide intensive training for locals and small enterprises at the earliest stages of development, enabling them to sell goods and services to the mining company. Given the opportunities for local outsourcing, such training can have an important impact on the local economy, fostering entrepreneurship. The goal would be to transfer skills—to have a larger share of locals working for the company, directly and indirectly—and to create more social cohesion between the company and the local community. Because mines are a finite resource, the revenues need to be invested wisely to create alternatives for the community when the mine closes.

The arrival of skilled workers from outside and the availability of higher cash incomes often clash with local customs. Companies would benefit from hiring cultural translators, who can link the modern commercial world with the local culture, language, and traditions. If cultural translators are part of the decisionmaking team alongside the engineers and financial specialists, they can play a vital bridging function to help the community and the company understand each other and resolve problems. Antamina's consortium of local mayors and NGOs and its early engagement of three international NGOs working full time on development issues show promise. Yanacocha is now strengthening its community relations, training, and outsourcing program. It is also setting up a foundation to promote income-generating activities, which will help improve communication and trust with the local community.

Large mining and other extractive industries require extensive land areas. How the land is acquired (and whether the inhabitants have clearly demarcated titles) affects the negotiations and the trust of the local community. The price of the land needed for mining is also difficult to determine. Farmers who sell early at lower prices—even though they received agreed prices—later feel cheated when they

see their neighbors' land selling for much more. Often, farmers spend their sale (or resettlement) proceeds quickly and find themselves destitute shortly thereafter. Companies may need to propose ways to assist local farmers in managing cash incomes. Where possible, land sales or rental agreements should take place between the company and organized groups of farmers rather than individual farmers.

Communities

Company and NGO efforts to help local communities develop advocacy and operational capabilities are beginning to bear fruit. Local communities have begun to learn how to organize and find their voice, a major change that has gained momentum in the past decade. They need to make sure that their views are understood and that their goals are geared to protecting and developing their communities. Like the companies and government, they need motivated leadership, open access to knowledge, and a willingness to learn. Around the world a workable approach appears to be gradually emerging around "sustainable mining paradigms" that combine business strategy and ethics. In a case as complex as Yanacocha, things are moving in the right direction, but much remains to be done.

Deeper institutional support

Many governments are struggling to fulfill demanding and complicated roles in these three-way partnerships. When government cannot meet its obligations—and companies, local officials, and communities cannot agree on their responsibilities—it is difficult for extractive resources to be developed in a way that is sustainable. If mineral extraction is likely to continue anyway, given the overwhelming interest of most parties in moving forward, then providing short-term technical assistance for institutional strengthening—while necessary—may not be sufficient. There must be more substantial support and genuine learning-by-doing at an appropriate scale and duration. Managing tripartite arrangements effectively involves a long and costly learning process, but it has a potentially high payoff for everyone concerned.

Partnering for change

Several initiatives have emerged to integrate local consultation in decisionmaking. The Latin American Organization for Energy for the oil-producing countries of the Sub-Andean Basin emphasizes communication among governments, industry, and indigenous communities on how to use and distribute oil rents. It also strengthens social and environmental standards for oil and gas in Latin America. The Chad-Cameroon pipeline project addresses how oil revenues will be used, with procedures for incorporating community views and regulations on environmental and social impact (box 7.10). The Nile River Basin initiative tries to get all parties to focus on the potential benefits of cooperating by thinking not only of their country's interests but also the interests of neighboring countries that share the resource (box 8.4).

Donors can do much to help governments set up the right institutions by supporting long-term partnering, but it will require a greater scale of support, for example, than what is currently practiced for scientific exchanges or for the CGIAR. Long-term institutional efforts are needed at all levels. Donors can substantially increase the volume and reliability of funding for long-term expert advice, timely technical support, technology transfers, staff exchange programs for key personnel, and international training scholarships (chapter 9).

Combining know-how, information, and grass-roots understanding

Many developing countries copied institutions from the West, but few adapted them to local circumstances, which led to adverse environmental, economic, and social consequences. Centralized administrations had difficulty adapting public services designed for urban settings to vastly different conditions in remote rural areas. Institutions have changed—but slowly, particularly relative to fast-growing populations and a fast-changing world. They need to adjust services to local conditions, to listen to and understand the people they are trying to help, and to empower communities to help themselves.

Governments need to encourage open interactions among government, universities, business, and civil society. Problem-solving institutes (think-and-do tanks) focusing on concrete challenges facing communities are needed. At present, many countries are badly underserved. Think-and-do tanks can help to make sense of imported ideas and adapt them to

country circumstances. By listening at the grass-roots level and testing ideas against reality, they can promote creativity, relevant policies, and workable solutions that help governments govern better (chapter 9, box 9.2).

Nurturing assets in the community. . .

Communities in the rural periphery have assets that need nurturing. Combining local know-how with stepped-up research and outside technical advice can help increase their land's productivity and sustain critical ecosystems. Such communities have indigenous knowledge that has guided them to conserve scarce natural resources and survive in hostile environments by getting the incentives right—and national institutions need to listen and learn from these insights and combine them with modern technological approaches. They also have women who are potentially strong engines of development but whose contribution is too often handicapped. And they have social capital—and some savings from remittances, which, if mobilized, can launch a development dynamic. Villagers who have experience outside the area can help the community guide its traditions toward the design of projects that fit their means, and governments need to find ways to promote and encourage this type of work.

the nation . . .

Governments (and donors) can fund knowledge networks, dissemination and village exchanges, enabling local community leaders and government counterparts to learn firsthand about creative solutions—such as Burkina Faso's service-asset management groups or Morocco's Ait Iktel Association. Developing countries receive various volunteer programs from donor countries and NGOs working in marginal rural areas. To ensure that the knowledge transmitted stays with a country, governments could set up national volunteer organizations for local graduates (often fresh out of university and unemployed) to team with the foreign volunteers to work on projects together.

By working with NGOs, public institutions can expand their reach and improve the relevance and cost-effectiveness of their services. Civil servants are often risk averse, perhaps reluctant to cooperate with outside associations. Behavioral changes are sometimes easier to introduce when senior officials launch pilot initiatives that are followed up with clear evaluations and results-oriented incentives that promote learning, changing, working with local groups, and scaling up positive experiences. Better monitoring of appropriate indicators will help governments track what is happening in the rural periphery. For example, what share of public expenditures actually reaches the rural marginal areas? Is health, agricultural, and environmental advice routinely reaching village communities? What share of the nation is employed in unskilled, low-wage jobs, and how have these wages changed?

and the world

There is often the potential for local upgrading contingent on realizing that upgradings requires significant change from the bottom up and the top down, and both approaches take time. Many people on fragile lands have begun to organize themselves to move beyond survival—and onto grass-roots development. They are at the cutting edge of social, economic, and environmental advances. But they need adaptable and flexible national institutions and global commitments for funding, support, and partnerships for the long term.

Long-term partnering of institutions—experienced civil servants helping their counterparts in other countries implement difficult reforms—could become a much larger part of donor development assistance. The long duration of these relationships increases the relevance of the advice and could include donor-sponsored exchanges between agencies, think tanks, academics, and business advisors. More grant funding (combined with advice) can help national governments overcome the aversion to risk taking. Sharing risks and burdens across a larger number of better-endowed countries offers the best chance for addressing some of the most difficult problems trapping communities in poverty.

Donors can do much in learning what seems to work in community development dynamics and in disseminating this information through hands-on village exchanges and support for setting up practical problem-solving institutes. They can also take the lead in R&D and technology dissemination for renewable energy, suitable crops for fragile areas, land management techniques, and medicines. They should expand scientific and empirical studies on what is happening to fragile lands and the climate—proposing economically feasible scientific and technological remedies as and where appropriate. Because fragile lands are heterogeneous, improving livelihoods is not always easily replicable. But there is substantial scope for adapting innovations across countries and regions; such innovations include community schools, outreach advice, drought-resistant plant breeding, and other productivity-enhancing technologies developed in one region with good applications in other regions.

This chapter explores opportunities for improving *in situ* the well-being of the many people living on fragile lands and ecosystems. At present they have few options but to remain. International migration is highly restricted, compared with 100 years ago (see also chapter 9). Even internal migration is uncertain, especially in economies where the numbers of rural unskilled workers are very high, or where urban-led economic growth has been low. To address population pressures in fragile areas, outmigration must be encouraged both by better preparing rural inhabitants to take on nonrural jobs, and by improving the ability of commercial rural areas and urban areas to provide these people with more productive opportunities (see chapters 5 and 6). For the people living on fragile land, as well as for those in the commercial agricultural or urban areas, developing their human capital is critical for expanding their options for improved livelihoods.

Transforming Institutions on Agricultural Land

The previous chapter focused on people living in remote, low-density settlements on fragile lands, and how, with new institutional improvements, they can better manage their portfolio of assets to increase productivity and sustain critical ecosystems. Chapter 5 is about people living in areas with commercial agricultural potential, either in frontier areas where market-driven agriculture is newly emerging, or in areas closer to larger and increasingly urban markets. These areas will help feed the growing and increasingly higher-income world population. This chapter focuses on the management of and interaction of assets such as land and water and the environment; how to help the poor get better access to land and water; and the importance of asset distribution for the development of good institutions (as described in chapter 3)—especially in near-market areas where intensification can generate considerable equitable growth. Population in rural areas totals 3 billion people, and more than half of them live in areas with commercial agriculture potential (see figure 1.1). Some of these people will migrate to cities, and many will live in areas that will be reclassified as urban when the areas' densities increase. The total number will remain in the range of approximately 1.5 to 2 billion people over the next three to five decades. Despite widespread concern over the past 20 to 30 years about food shortages, the rural developing world has exceeded expectations in food production (box 5.1). Will past trends continue, or is there a real cause for concern? For the world to make a smooth transition to relative population stability 50 years from now, its rural areas will have to meet a range of challenges.

Chapter 5 addresses the key development challenges for rural transformation over the next 30 to 50 years:

■ *Eliminate rural poverty and strengthen rural-urban linkages—including preparing outmigrants for a productive urban life.*

As discussed in chapter 4, rural populations are expected to grow in most low-income countries. In much of the world, the combination of subsistence food production and cash earnings in the hands of poor people is not enough to yield an adequate diet. About 820 million people lack access to enough food to lead healthy and productive lives, and about 160 million children are seriously underweight for their age.[1] Some 2 to 2.5 billion rural people will become urban residents between now and 2050. Whether their families have land, water, or education before they urbanize is critical to their future, the future of the cities they move to, and the quality of their societies' institutions.

■ *Intensify agricultural production and manage land and water to feed a growing and increasingly urban population.*

Over the next 30 to 50 years, rural areas will have to feed an additional 2 to 3 billion people globally, and substantially improve the diets of the 2.5 to 3 billion people living on less than $2 a day. That will require tilting institutional rules to move assets into the hands of smallholders, halting nutrient mining, reducing soil erosion, and adopting agricultural practices that restore soil fertility. It will also require sharing rural land and water to serve the expanding urban population and meet environmental needs.

Box 5.1

More food, greater intensity of land use, fewer farmers per urban resident

Global food availability has increased. Global food availability per capita is at an all-time high, with variations among countries and regions. Doubling grain production and tripling livestock production since the early 1960s, the world's farmers now provide about 2,700 calories per person a day. India and China, widely considered two decades ago to be Malthusian disasters in the making, satisfy their own demands for cereal. For the developing world rising incomes enabled increased consumption of meat and poultry. And despite growing demand for grain, the prices for maize, rice, and wheat came down 50 percent or more over the past 20 years. Perhaps most important, the proportion of children who suffer from malnutrition fell sharply—from 45 percent in the 1960s to 31 percent in the late 1990s—though not yet sharply enough.

Agriculture has intensified. For most of the world, reduced availability of agricultural land has induced a transition from land-increasing to yield-increasing technology. Africa and South America are the clear exceptions; they both have large remaining areas of unexploited land. However, that land may not be very productive. Although the trend in South America is toward intensification, the extensive margin continues to expand into the Amazon forest. In Africa there are pockets of intensified production, but the larger story is one of new frontiers of crop production opening areas previously devoted to communal grazing of livestock—and of shortening the fallow period under shifting or bush-fallow cultivation. In the more marginal areas these changes have created new problems (as noted in chapter 4).

Many countries have made the transition from rural to urban human settlement, with fewer farmers feeding more city folk. In developing countries in the 1960s, there were three farmers per urban resident—today, there is one and one-half.

Source: Pinstrup-Andersen and others (1999); Rosegrant and others (2001); Crosson and Anderson (2002).

■ *Get ahead of the agricultural frontier to control wasteful land conversion.*

The expansion of agricultural land has taken a large toll on the world's repository of biodiversity, with one-fifth of tropical forests cleared since 1960. The remaining biodiversity is concentrated precariously—more than one-third of it now confined to 1.4 percent of the world's land.[2] Some new agricultural land is of high quality and yields important local benefits in agriculture. But much of the newly converted frontier provides little opportunity for the advancement of locals, despite imposing large national and global social costs in GHG emissions and the loss of biodiversity and amenity resources.

This chapter argues that although the rural "sector" has done well in meeting aggregate food needs, it has done less well in meeting the broader needs of the rural population and preparing many for an urban future. It also highlights issues surrounding the conflicts and complementarities between promoting rural development and protecting the environment. For both, good institutional rules are critical. Because of this focus, the chapter covers issues dealing with property rights in land and water, and intellectual property in agricultural knowledge. It does not try to give a complete, or even a balanced, treatment of the problems of rural development. The purpose is to illustrate the importance of thinking more deeply about the institutional rules that govern behavior and support policies, and how they might be improved.[3]

The main message of the chapter is this: Countries should, where still possible, give a high priority to creating egalitarian endowments of land, water, and human capital for its people as they make the transition from rural to urban human settlement. The smooth emergence of land and water institutions is of fundamental importance to a country—because the rules sanctioning property ownership determine the later character of the state and society. Countries that have distributed rural property equitably before urbanizing have developed more egalitarian and democratic societies than those that put assets in the hands of relatively few rural elites. Put another way, countries with rapidly growing populations that have concentrated land in the hands of the few have urbanized prematurely, educated few, and developed extremely inegalitarian societies. Experience and research show that creating widespread land ownership is critical to the later development of inclusive institutions.

Land and water constraints

Food production increases are slowing. Land is becoming increasingly degraded. Scarcities of land and water are more evident. These problems are best addressed by thinking of them not as problems of global resource scarcities but as problems of poverty among plenty.

Global food abundance, yet hungry poor

The prevailing view among agricultural economists is that the world food problem is one of insufficient purchasing power in the hands of poor people, not of global constraints on aggregate food production—even with an expanded global population. The aggregate data support this view, but some poor regions have too little food. And it is true, as many point out, that annual increases in food production have been falling. But annual increases in demand are falling faster. Evidence at the global level—that the growth of yields (as opposed to production) is slowing—is extremely weak.[4]

What is incontestable is that a slowdown in food demand relative to production—much of it inappropriately subsidized in OECD countries—has depressed food prices to record lows. With an ever-larger portion of the world's people fed well, rising world incomes induce smaller increases in food consumption. Falling rates of population growth are also slowing the growth in food demand.[5] With higher incomes, food consumption patterns do change. But simulations of the world food economy suggest that even a rapid increase in meat consumption in China (underway) and India (less likely) would not significantly alter the balance of world food supply and demand.[6]

In short, food will continue to be abundant at a reasonable price for those people with the income to purchase it. Eliminating hunger tomorrow, however, will require the same solution as eliminating hunger today—raising the productivity and incomes of poor people. And here the world must do better. For the more than 70 percent of the world's poor people who live in the countryside, this means increasing their ability to produce food to consume and food to sell in markets.[7]

Land degradation—also a poverty problem

It is widely reported that erosion, salinization, compaction, and other forms of soil degradation affect 30 percent of the world's irrigated lands, 40 percent of rainfed agricultural lands, and 70 percent of rangelands. The effect of this degradation on overall productivity so far is limited, in part because cultivators bring new lands under cultivation. Cumulative global productivity loss due to land degradation over three decades has been estimated at 12 percent of total production from irrigated land, rainfed cropland, and rangeland. This yields an average annual rate of productivity loss of 0.4 percent.[8]

The underlying degradation estimates have weaknesses, however, because most attempt to estimate losses through time without data on degradation through time.[9] Empirical studies based on actual time-series data on soil samples (taken throughout China and Indonesia over 50 years) find no overall loss of agricultural soil depth or quality for China or Indonesia.[10] Time-series data for 1971–93 from the India and Pakistan Punjabs, by contrast, suggest that intensification of land and water use has resulted in resource degradation that is lowering overall productivity growth. For Pakistan these data indicate that resource degradation has reduced overall productivity growth from technical change, education, and infrastructure investment by one-third.[11]

Studies based on cropping patterns and fertilizer use in Africa indicate that failure to replace the soil nutrients removed through cropping (nutrient mining) is grave, widespread, and poverty induced.[12] All but three countries in Africa show negative balances of nutrients of more than 30 kilograms of nitrogen, phosphorus, and potassium per hectare annually.[13]

African farmers have traditionally practiced bush fallow and shifting cultivation to maintain production, as decreasing soil nutrients begin to affect yields. This practice is becoming unsustainable as rising population density shortens the fallow period, which lowers fertility. So more land is needed in cultivation each year, partly because of higher population and partly to offset the effect of a decline in yields. Poverty-stressed farmers face three choices, with mixed outcomes:

- Expand into forests, permanent pasture, hillsides, or wetlands.
- Continue to intensify labor inputs on existing land.
- Complement labor on existing lands through the use of inorganic and organic fertilizer and land and water conservation infrastructure, such as grass strips, anti-erosion ditches, hedgerows, bunds, and terraces.

The first puts farmers on a collision course with other land users, such as cattle herders, commons holders, and biodiversity reserves. It also begins the vicious cycle of land degradation anew, condemning farmers to work on increasingly marginal lands (because of agronomic conditions, disease, and distance from markets). The second is unsustainable in the absence of new fertility-augmenting soil management, hastening the downward spiral of falling yields and shorter fallows.[14] The third choice has been prohibitive in the past because it requires that farmers assume additional risk in the form of purchased inputs.[15] As discussed below, new adapted techniques are becoming available that can improve soil fertility using resources naturally available in Africa.[16] These techniques offer the promise of breaking out of this downward spiral.

Land and water: Serious regional scarcities globally abundant

Land and water, now globally abundant, are projected to remain adequate throughout the 30- to 50-year time horizon of this Report—even while meeting the needs of a growing population and improving nutrition.[17] But the aggregate picture masks serious local and regional water and land shortages in all continents—as well as a lack of financing and institutional capacity to develop and sustain Africa's water resources potential. The World Commission on Water predicts that water use will increase by 50 percent over the coming 30 years and that 4 billion people—half of the world's population—will live under conditions of severe water stress in 2025.[18] Conflict over land and water will worsen, especially in areas already suffering from water stress in South Asia and the Middle East and North Africa. In addition, bat-

tles are looming between direct economic use and environmental needs. And in many urbanizing semi-arid regions, conflict between high-value (usually urban) use and low-value irrigation will worsen.

Land availability. Additional land available in the developing world is of three types (figure 5.1):[19]

- Land in use for annual and permanent cultivation
- Land lost or no longer usable economically for cultivation
- Land reserve still unused but suitable for sustainable agriculture.

"Lost" land has been either consumed by urban sprawl or degraded beyond the point of economic recovery.[20] Globally, agricultural land has been lost through degradation at the rate of about 0.5 percent a year—and from new infrastructure at 0.1 percent a year. Severe degradation comes from water erosion (particularly in Southeast Asia and Central America), soil nutrient mining (particularly in Africa), and salinization (particularly in some areas with large irrigation schemes). Note that almost as much land has been lost (303 million hectares) as is now in use (307) in Africa and Latin America. Some of this is from shifting "slash and burn" cultivation pat-

Figure 5.1
Regional variations in land scarcity

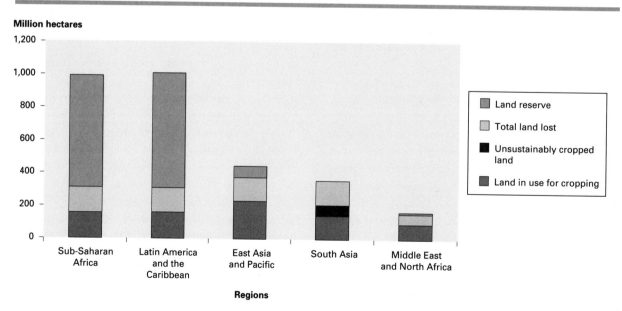

Source: IBSRAM (2001).

terns (based on nutrient mining) and may recover after an extended fallow period.

The land that is available (and tillable) varies widely from region to region. Latin America and Africa stand out as having extremely large reserves of tillable land: 700 million hectares and 680 million hectares, respectively. At least 45 percent of the 1,400 million hectares of reserve land is in forests. East Asia and the Pacific and the Middle East and North Africa have little additional tillable land. And South Asia is already farming soils that are not sustainable for cultivation.

Much of the potentially tillable land in Africa is either not accessible for commercial agriculture, is subject to human or animal disease, or is already being used for animal grazing. In Latin America, new land is mostly in the Amazon, predominantly uneconomic to exploit. But some of it is potentially economic and therefore the subject of considerable dispute between environmentalists and rural development interests. Clearly on both continents this remaining uncultivated land has extreme limitations relative to land already under production, from the agronomic perspective and relative to markets. Much of it can be farmed only at high environmental cost.

Water availability. Like land, water resources are also unequally distributed around the world.[21] Africa and Latin America again have large unexploited water resources. According to the International Water Management Institute (IWMI), in Africa only South Africa has exploited more than 20 percent of its potentially usable water resources, and in Latin America only Cuba (48 percent) and Mexico (27 percent). Despite the modest exploitation of water resources in Africa and Latin America, future irrigation development is expected to be limited. Most good sites for irrigation—flat, close to water, near good markets—have already been developed.

Data from IWMI reveal China as the most water-stressed country in East Asia, exploiting 44 percent of its usable water (in the aggregate) and projected to exceed 60 percent by 2020. Primary withdrawal of more than 60 percent is widely considered by water experts to exceed the environmental carrying capacity of a river basin system. Although China's aggregate use appears still to be reasonable, it has several basins that are severely stressed environmentally, and it faces a serious groundwater overdraft in the North China Plains. According to IWMI data, withdrawals already exceed environmental limits in Afghanistan and Pakistan and will exceed limits in India by 2020. Irrigation already exceeds recharge rates in India's northwest plains (the major site of its green revolution). In the Middle East and North Africa only Morocco has unexploited water resources. All the rest have exceeded environmental limits, and many are mining groundwater aquifers (figure 5.2).

Africa is relatively well endowed with water resources. It has only 1–3 percent of its agriculture under irrigation, compared with two-thirds in Asia. The potential for expansion in Africa is limited, however, because more than 60 percent of the irrigation potential is in humid regions, where, because of high rainfall levels, irrigation would be at most supplementary to well-managed rainfed agriculture. In many of the regions where irrigation is most needed more than 60 percent of the potential renewable water resources are already exploited, and most of the highest potential areas are already under irrigation.[22]

Figure 6 in the Roadmap shows the projected water scarcity worldwide in 2025 grouped in three categories: physical water scarcity, economic water scarcity, and little or no water scarcity.[23]

Eliminating rural poverty and preparing outmigrants

The social challenge of the rural sector over the next 50 years is enormous. Not only must it feed the world and prepare some 2–2.5 billion people to become productive urban citizens but it can also create the preconditions for the evolution of responsive, inclusive local and national institutions (as discussed in chapter 3).

For poor developing countries with large agricultural sectors, rural growth has a powerful effect in pulling people out of poverty.[24] In rural economies, the more equal the incomes and assets, the more powerful the growth effect in poverty reduction.[25] As inequality increases, the linkage of growth to the poor weakens, and in the most unequal of rural economies, growth tends to bypass poor people completely. The quality of rural development is thus a basic determinant of the quality of the future social development of a country. Countries that let rural incomes and assets become concentrated in the hands of a few find it extremely difficult to lift poor people out of poverty later (box 5.2). They have painted themselves into a corner.

Figure 5.2
Regional variations in water scarcity

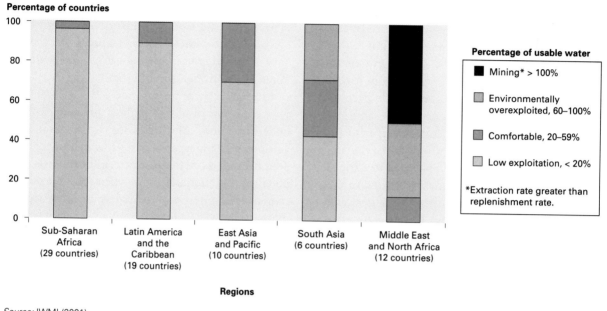

Source: IWMI (2001).

*Breaking the poverty cycle
and preparing outmigrants*

The conditions to break the poverty cycle and bring the rural poor out of poverty are overwhelmingly associated with increasing rural-urban interactions and more intensified use of existing agricultural land. In more dense rural areas with towns, credit markets are more apt to exist, and land is more likely to qualify for collateral. Higher farmgate prices associated with better roads and proximity to urban markets, and more opportunities for spreading risk, encourage higher-input agriculture. This in turn leads to greater value produced per unit area and generally to more off-farm jobs in food processing, transportation, and in the agricultural service industries. A more diversified economic base, dynamically linked to farm towns—and eventually cities—provides more stability of incomes throughout the economy. Education and health services can also be provided more efficiently.[26]

The first pillar of rural-led economic growth that reaches poor people is a "virtuous employment multiplier" and a transition to urban life through rural nonfarm jobs.[27] Driving the virtuous employment multiplier is the tendency of the rural poor to con-

sume goods of predominantly local origin, produced by people who are also poor. This sets up a chain of increased demand and incomes that cascades through the hands of poor people in the rural and urban sectors. An extra dollar of income in the hands of a poor farmer might lead to 50 cents worth of demand for products and services from other rural poor, 40 cents of demand for products produced by poor urban residents, and only 10 cents of demand for products produced in the formal urban sector or imported from abroad. In the hands of a rich farmer, nearly the whole dollar escapes the economy of poor people.

The second pillar of rural-based economic growth is the training effect of rural nonfarm employment. Besides allowing the rural family to diversify income sources and reduce risk, rural nonfarm employment is an important stepping stone to urban skills. A young rural man or woman who gets a job with the fertilizer or farm implement dealer makes a smooth transition to a rural town economy—developing the urban skills and often the opportunity to later move to the city. This process of transformation and growth has the added benefit that it leads to greater support for schools. As parents observe children in the com-

Box 5.2
Poverty, equitable growth, and path dependency

Inequality reduces economic efficiency and traps societies in bad development paths through inequality-perpetuating institutions in three ways:

■ Inequality reduces the participation of poor people in political processes, both directly and indirectly. This in turn reduces the likelihood that poor people have access to education, health care, and other services that would contribute to growth.
■ Inequality can hinder the establishment of independent and impartial institutions and the enforcement of binding rules, because they might reduce the benefits of the privileged.
■ Inequality makes it easier for the wealthy to hold out in political bargaining, either directly or through capital flight. It therefore makes it more difficult for societies to respond quickly and optimally to external shocks.

Each of these effects prevents the emergence of institutions that would distribute incomes, assets, and opportunity more widely.

Source: Binswanger and Deininger (1997).

munity successfully negotiating the rural-urban dynamic, they place a higher value on better education.

Governance and the distribution of rural assets

As chapter 3 showed, path dependency arises when institutional rules lock countries into bad development paths that prevent them from meeting future challenges. For example, the sharpest drops in growth after the economic shocks of the 1970s were in countries with divided societies and weak institutions for conflict management.[28] Similarly, the recent stagnation in Argentina and the República Bolivariana de Venezuela can be traced to an inability to settle distributive conflicts. Investigations into the determinants of growth have consistently found a negative relationship between initial inequality (usually unequal distribution of income or wealth in the rural sector) and subsequent growth.[29] This effect can be traced through the short and medium terms, as discussed above in the context of the virtuous employment multiplier, as well as through the very long term (relevant for the 30–50 year time horizon here). As discussed in chapter 3, differences in inequality in wealth, human capital, and political power stemming from colonial experiences account for much of

the variation in the records of growth of North and South America.[30] While in North America, early settlement experience led to a virtuous cycle of inclusive institutions, in Latin America inequality and exclusive institutions became the rule (box 5.3).

Increasing the value of smallholders' assets

Urbanization has been rapid over the past several decades, and in many countries, especially countries in Latin America, most rural residents have already migrated to the cities without physical or financial assets or human capital. At the same time, institutions have not evolved to include them in the development process. In Asia and Africa, however, most people still live in the countryside. And it is from these countries that a substantial part of the 2 to 2.5 billion increase in urban populations expected in developing countries by 2050 will occur. In these countries a strategy to enhance the range of assets to which rural people have access would simultaneously strike a blow against rural poverty, stimulate an inclusive orientation in institutional evolution, and prepare migrants to become good urban citizens.[31]

Water control is critical to ensure and minimize climatic risk—and to allow farmers to safely invest in increased production. Unlike Asia, where 30 to 35 percent of agricultural land is irrigated (producing two-thirds of the agricultural output), Africa irrigates only 1 to 5 percent of its agricultural land (depending on the classification of traditional water management).[32] Without mechanisms to control risk, on-farm investment will be restricted to intensifying labor inputs. Farm and landscape-scale investments may be needed to enrich soil nutrients and organic matter, to protect fields from water and wind erosion, and to regenerate natural vegetation to provide local ecosystem services that also benefit agricultural production. Where investment can take the form of improving water control, and the water-retaining characteristics of the soil, climatic risk may be lowered considerably (box 5.4).

A broad-based attack to help African farmers break out of the vicious cycle of poverty will require increased investment on all fronts, including more attention to low-intensity agricultural techniques and genetically modified crop technology in areas remote from markets. And it will take major public investments in water control, transport, and technological advance aimed at staple food crops.[33]

Box 5.3
Land distribution and path dependency

The powerful impact of initial land allocations on subsequent agricultural development is well illustrated in Brazil. In most of the country in the late 19th century land could be titled only in lots of 4 square kilometers (988 acres) or more—an area much larger than a family could work. Restrictions on subdivision kept landownership highly concentrated. As a consequence, Brazilian agriculture became dependent on wage labor, characterized by relatively low efficiency and investment. Investment and productivity rose only after government subsidies brought about rapid capitalization of the sector.

Land sales were unable to significantly reduce inequality in the size distributions of the holdings. Brazil became a largely urban society without ever having developed a significant presence of appropriately sized family farms. As a result, much of the rural population moved as wage labor to the cities, without assets and unprepared for urban life—and over half the remaining rural population is in poverty. Undoubtedly, the dynamic of this rural-urban transition is a major contributor to Brazil's having one of the world's highest levels of income inequality. Recently, Brazil has invested heavily to overcome this early inequitable start. From 1995 to 2001 Brazil invested more than $10 billion in land reform, settling some 584,000 families on nearly 20 million acres.

In the United States the Homesteading Acts limited to 160 acres the plots that families could acquire. To retain ownership rights, individuals were required to cultivate the plots for a specified number of years. Owner-operated farms dominated agricultural production, with rentals and sales merely reallocating land to more efficient farm families working plots of comparable size. U.S. agriculture became one of the most productive systems in the world—and remains so today.

Based on an agrarian structure consisting predominantly of family farms, the major Southeast Asian economies—Indonesia, Malaysia, and Thailand, following the earlier lead of Taiwan (China) and the Republic of Korea—and China reduced agricultural taxation in the 1970s and started to support smallholders. These countries, in addition to establishing favorable macroeconomic policies, invested in rural infrastructure and social services. They also provided research and extension services and supported viable smallholder credit systems. Agricultural output grew rapidly, and the number of rural households living in poverty fell dramatically.

In 1978 China abandoned collective agriculture and assigned most agricultural land to families, giving each a very small holding. It also sharply increased the prices paid for agricultural goods. Over the next 15 years farm output grew more than 6 percent a year. This dramatic increase in agricultural productivity precipitated China's long-running economic boom and reduction in poverty.

Source: Based on Binswanger and Deininger (1997).

In Africa improved agricultural institutions may depend on first strengthening asset value through water and transport infrastructure and fertilizer (box 5.5). Many countries will follow a two-pronged strategy—encouraging intensification and commercialization through purchased input-intensive agriculture in productive areas near urban markets and transport (and in more distant areas with dense rural populations) and low-external input agriculture in more remote areas. With the predominance of constrained soils, high production levels in Africa will require use of both inorganic fertilizers and inputs to maintain soil organic matter and structure. In peri-urban farming areas where high levels of fertilizer inputs (inorganic or organic) are used, water quality issues may become a concern (as they have become in intensive production areas of Asia and Europe), requiring use of filter strips and other waterway protections.

A soil fertility replenishment approach, developed over the past 10 years by researchers from the International Center for Research in Agroforestry has been adapted by tens of thousands of farm families in Kenya, Malawi, Mozambique, Tanzania, Uganda, Zambia, and Zimbabwe. This approach uses various combinations of fallow, phosphorus, and biomass transfers with consistently good results. A program to scale up these practices from tens of thousands to tens of millions of African farm families would cost $100 million a year for 10 years.[34]

How deep institutional structures impede research on the needs of poor smallholders

Genes are already available that could help food production in the poorest countries if they were to be transferred into poor people's crops. These include genes that improve tolerances to salt, aluminum, and manganese in soils; give plants greater resistance to insects, viruses, bacteria, and fungi; enrich beta carotene to correct vitamin A deficiency; create more nutritious oils, starches, and amino acids; and improve fatty acid profiles and digestibility for animals.[35]

Despite this promise for poor people, biotechnology in general and transgenics research in particular have barely begun to be put to work to address the problems of poor people. So far large commercial

Box 5.4
Breaking out through *zais* and *tassas*—low-input traditional technologies

Since the early 1980s a technique for reclaiming degraded land has spread rapidly in Burkina Faso and Niger and was recently introduced into Ghana. This technique—called *zai* in Mossi and *tassa* in Hausa—originated in the Yatenga region of Burkina Faso. It involves digging holes that are 20–30 centimeters deep and filling them with crop residue, household compost, and manure.

Many lateritic soils of the area had become impermeable, sealed by a thin crust, hardened by wind and water. The *zais* attract termites, and their underground tunnels increase water infiltration. Millet is planted in the holes, which protect seedlings from wind damage. The number of *zais* per hectare varies from 12,000 to 25,000. Digging that hectare takes about 60 days (averaging five hours a day) in the dry season when work demands are low.

This technique has tripled yields and greatly reduced yield loss in dry years. On the central plateau of the Yatenga some 100,000 hectares have been restored, promoted by Projet Agro-Forestier (funded by the Oxford Committee for Famine Relief), and the German-funded Projet Agro-Ecologie. In many cases farmers spontaneously adopt the technique after seeing the results on others' fields.

The reaction of visiting Ghanaian farmers to what the Burkanabé had accomplished bears noting:

"We are very much blessed and yet we are complaining of our poor soils. A large proportion of our soils we have even discarded as 'dead' but, to our surprise, such soils are being used here [in Burkina Faso] to produce something even better than we are doing on our best soils."

The *zai* is a response by farmers to population and climatic stress. The Yatenga region of Burkina Faso has some of the highest population densities in the country. Earlier versions of the *zai* were used in the Yatenga prior to the 1950s, but on a much smaller scale. They were abandoned in the 1950s and the 1960s because rainfall was much above average and the water harvesting properties of the *zai* were not needed. Re-emerging in the drought of the 1960s and 1970s, they began to be rapidly adopted following improvements in the techniques around 1980 by Yacouba Sawadogo, a farmer from the village of Gourga. The role of donors in dissemination, especially through field visits and farmer trials, has been critical.

Source: Reij, Scoones, and Toulmin (1996); Millar (1999); Meitzner and Price (1996); and IFAD (1999).

Box 5.5
Breaking out through fertilizer: the next green revolution?

During the 1960s the fundamental cause of declining per capita food production in Asia was the lack of short-statured, high-yielding varieties of rice and wheat. Asian food security was only effectively addressed with the advent of improved germ plasm. Then other key aspects that had previously been largely ineffective (enabling government policies, irrigation, seed production, fertilizer use, pest management, research and extension services) came into play in support of the spread of the new varieties. The need for soil fertility replenishment in Africa now is analogous to the need for the "Green Revolution-type" germ plasm in Asia three decades ago, a belief that is supported by two of the "fathers" of the Green Revolution: Norman Borlaugh and M.S. Swaminathan.

Source: Sanchez and others (2001).

plantings of transgenic crops have been restricted to Argentina, Canada, and the United States, with other countries planting less than 2 percent of the world total.[36] This is partly because much of the research supporting this technology is locked into patents held by a small number of multinational, vertically integrated life-science organizations, which have had little commercial interest in working on crops with limited markets, or funding research for the needs of poor producers. It is also because the rules that make this technology available worldwide—about the sharing of proprietary knowledge, products, processes, and genes—are being defined in U.S. courts, based on U.S. case law. The other high-income countries are catching up, but the developing countries, where needs are greatest, are being left behind.[37]

The use of modern biotechnology (genetic engineering) in agriculture has left the world sharply divided, though not always along predictable lines.[38] Some applications generate little controversy, such as marker-assisted genetic selection. Others, such as transgenic organisms, cause much concern. Comfort with the new technology is determined in large measure by a society's comfort with its scientific and food safety institutions, as well as its feelings about emerging concentrations of economic power in multinational life-sciences corporations.[39] Poor farmers and poor consumers have not yet been given significant voice in the decisions on agricultural use of these new technologies.

The current controversies over biotechnology result from twin revolutions in science and in property rights:

- *A scientific revolution* in understanding the structure of genes and regulatory gene sequences (genomics) and in bioinformatics has created an unprecedented opportunity to improve the characteristics of plants and animals, either through more rapid and efficient marker-assisted breeding or through the insertion of new genes into plants by genetic transformation.
- *An institutional revolution* in the coverage of intellectual property rights (IPRs), especially in the United States, has resulted in rapid growth of the private sector in crop genetics.

These revolutions have generated associated concerns about food and environmental safety, and ethical and equity consequences, all within a context of society's lagging institutional capacity to keep up, especially in the developing world. These concerns

have a foundation in related earlier experiences (see box 5.6 on pesticide stockpiles in Africa).

Transgenics and developing countries. The slow progress in applying transgenic research to the problems of poor farmers is due to the exclusionary aspect of IPRs, as well as issues of biosafety, food safety, consumer choice, trade, and the publicly funded research network. Solutions to these complex issues are all playing out against a backdrop of globalization-related uncertainty that leaves many people unsettled about their incapacity to control their lives and their environment.

Deepening IPRs have created a revolution in agricultural science and a race for (exclusive) property rights for agricultural and biological knowledge. This race has led to greater concentration of the life-sciences industry, including massive buyouts of seed companies in all countries. These global giants raise

Box 5.6
Science, technology, and institutions to solve the challenges of nature: obsolete pesticide stockpiles in Africa

Science and technology are important tools to address the forces that damage livelihoods and affect quality of life. To take advantage of these tools requires effective supporting institutions. In Africa, weak institutions, unable to regulate and distribute pesticides, have left a legacy of dangerous, obsolete pesticide stockpiles.

In agriculture, insects and other pests have a potentially devastating impact on crop yields throughout the world. One of the most dramatic examples is locust infestation in Africa. To address this and other pest infestation over the past 40 years, the donor community has provided loans, grants, and other transfers to cover the procurement of pesticides as important components of agricultural projects. However, for this action to be successful, ministries of agriculture, port authorities, transport and handling networks, storage agencies, shopkeepers, extension agencies and farming communities need to know how to manage the timely purchase, transport, storage, application, and disposal of these chemicals. If this coordination is done well, the chemicals contribute to well-being. If not, they become a social and environmental liability.

Coordination problems combined with misguided advice or ineffective development assistance from donor agencies and pesticide manufacturers have resulted in a stockpile of more than 50,000 tons of extremely toxic and now obsolete pesticides, some dating back 40 years, and tens of thousands of tons of severely contaminated soils that have to be shipped out. An estimated 30 percent of the pesticide waste is believed to be made up of highly persistent organic pollutants (POPs), which have seeped into the water tables and oceans, and which are moving around the globe through ocean currents, contaminating the food chain of many marine species far from

Africa's shores. The stockpile problem went from being a local problem to being a local and global problem, with shared responsibility among all parties. African countries do not have the specialized industrial facilities to dispose of the pesticides, hence the stockpiles need to be collected and transported back to hazardous waste disposal centers in industrial country locations, mainly Europe.

Donor agencies underestimated the institutional prerequisites necessary for the correct application of pesticides, which would have allowed African countries to realize the beneficial effects while minimizing the negative impacts. Donors have also underestimated the difficulties in mobilizing global action to address the problem. At the initiative of the FAO and a few other donors, modest clean-up activity began nearly a decade ago, but has moved slowly. Less than 5 percent of the estimated stockpiles have been disposed of, and new additions of obsolete pesticides continue to accumulate faster than the disposal rate. Recognizing that a gradual, piecemeal approach would not solve the problem, in December 2000 two NGOs (WWF and Pesticides Action Network, or PAN U.K.) launched the idea of major clean-up actions under an "Africa Stockpiles Program." The 15-year program, estimated to cost $250 million, would be donor funded and managed in cooperation with the partners and member governments. The program includes country level inventories, clean-up and disposal, and extensive technical assistance to avoid recurrence of the problem. The challenge now is to coordinate the process among the different parties involved.

Source: GEF, Africa Stockpile Program; interviews with World Bank staff, 2002.

fears about biosafety and food safety, heightened by tragic institutional failures in the areas of feed, food, and drug safety in Europe.

Who has the greatest need to access these new agricultural technologies? The rural poor in developing countries. The precautionary principle tells us that we should err on the side of caution, look at alternatives, and ensure a fully transparent and democratic process. Applying this principle suggests doubt about the need for genetically modified organisms (GMOs) in high-income countries, where oversupplies of food and low food prices are associated with subsidies of $360 billion a year. It will certainly lead to a different decision in countries in Africa, where the rural poor depend critically on one or two crops grown under precarious conditions.

Poor people need a stronger voice in international discussions of these matters, and science and governments must find mechanisms to improve the quality of the debate. This requires sorting more clearly what is known in current science from what is not, so that the political process can act more effectively on what is not known. If informed, representative stakeholders decide to move forward with genetic engineering, that would also require credible and independent monitoring—and systems to identify and intervene early, when unforeseen problems arise. The worldwide problems with invasive species should serve as a warning on the need for due diligence in introducing new organisms to nature.

The twin revolutions in science and property rights have created challenges and opportunities for public research institutions, life sciences departments in universities, national agricultural research institutions, and the international agricultural research centers of the CGIAR. The opportunity is that stronger IPRs have unleashed an extremely dynamic race for exclusive property rights in agricultural knowledge. And public research is in the race.

The race has generated new agricultural knowledge at an unprecedented rate. But the challenge is twofold. First, how can research be channeled to benefit poor people in developing countries, who really need it? And second, how can this be done in a period of declining public financial support for public agricultural research? This situation calls for new public-private research—and new institutional models for regional cooperation.[40] Ensuring that this research reaches poor people also calls for a consid-erably strengthened public sector role in doing and directing basic research.

Proprietary agricultural science and the dominance of the private sector. The dominance of the private sector in agricultural bioscience is relatively new. As long as farmers could replicate improved plant and animal varieties in the field, there was little scope for the private sector to recapture the costs of investment in improved varieties. So, to promote the public interest in higher yields and food quality, the public sector has traditionally borne the bulk of agricultural research spending. It was only with the introduction of hybrid technology in the 1930s that the private sector became interested in investing in crop biology. Why? Because hybrid varieties lose their high-yielding characteristics if seeds harvested from them are used for planting. Farmers who want the benefits from high-yielding hybrids must purchase new seeds every year if they want to maintain high yields. This makes it possible for seed companies holding the parent lines to appropriate the benefits from research-induced increased crop yields.

Incentives for private-sector agriculture R&D were strengthened in 1980 when the U.S. Supreme Court decided that although patent protection could not be extended to naturally occurring living things, it should apply to living organisms that had been altered by human intervention.[41] Later interpretations extended this coverage to new processes, which may or may not give rise to a new product. The 1995 Trade-Related Aspects of Intellectual Property Rights (TRIPS) agreement has further established an international institutional framework of minimum standards for international trade involving intellectual property, including for proprietary agricultural processes and products.

Three factors explain the private sector's dominance:

- *The deeper protection of intellectual property*, which allowed firms to move into more basic research, traditionally left to the public sector.
- *The race for property rights* among firms and between firms and the public sector, strongly influenced by eager capital markets.
- *The weakening of taxpayer support for public sector agricultural research*. Indeed, with annual agricultural subsidies in excess of $300 billion, glutted world markets, and record low prices, the case for

public support of agricultural innovation was, for many taxpayers, weak. The prevailing mood has become "leave it to the private sector."

A divided public. Support for the application of transgenics to the food needs of poor people has been nearly unanimous among the major agricultural development institutions.[42] Even so, discussion of the use of transgenics to address the development needs of poor people has been heavily influenced by public concern, especially in Europe, and the use of transgenic agricultural technology has been overwhelmingly geared to the needs of large, mechanized agriculture.

In Europe consumer groups, led by Greenpeace and Friends of the Earth, have driven genetically modified foods off the shelf—and subsequent domestic production and imports of genetically modified products have largely halted.[43] In a European Commission survey 56 percent of the respondents felt that genetically modified food was dangerous.[44] Similarly, consumer groups and NGOs prevented genetically modified soybeans from entering Brazil, despite the support of the minister of agriculture and the head of the national agricultural research agency, EMBRAPA; local and international NGOs have also led resistance in China, India, and Kenya.[45] In North America, by contrast, the public attitude is optimistic about the promise of modern biotechnology, though with concern over possible environmental effects.

Clearly the perception of risk differs strongly between scientists and the public in Europe, and between the general public in Europe and North America. Caught in the middle are the rural poor, especially those on dry or degraded lands who could most benefit from the new technology.

Explaining the differences in perceptions of risk. The differences in risk perceptions between North America and Europe appear to be due in large measure to differences in their confidence in their life-science institutions to accurately pick up risk signals and to communicate them to the public. These differences have a base in experience. While North America has had no catastrophic failure in the food and drug protection system, Europe has experienced numerous failures, especially over the past decade. Rightly or wrongly, the U.S. public's confidence in its food and drug safety institutions has been constantly reinforced. Beginning with Thalidomide at the end of the 1950s, it has avoided the food and drug

tragedies that occurred elsewhere.[46] This confidence has enabled the U.S. Food and Drug Administration (FDA) to resist industry pressure to reduce its scrutiny of new products.[47]

Europe, by contrast, has been buffeted by a series of food and drug safety issues, precisely as genetically modified foods were beginning to enter the market. "Mad cow disease" (bovine spongiform encephalopathy, or BSE), suspected of killing at least eight people and leading to the slaughter of herds in Britain worth $5.5 billion, rocked public confidence in government and the agri-food industry's credibility and capacity.[48] According to a British parliamentary report released in February 2000, BSE created a "crises of confidence" in both science and government.[49] It was observed that British citizens were more likely to trust science they see as "independent," with university scientists ranking at the top and government at the bottom. The rest of Europe has also suffered recent crises of confidence in government's ability to protect them. France suffered from government failure in its scandal over AIDS-tainted blood, which infected 3,600 people receiving blood transfusions in the mid-1980s. Belgium, too, experienced high-visibility food and agricultural scares in the 1990s.[50]

European distrust of government food-protection institutions has led to demands to be directly informed and directly involved. Given this desire, the precautionary principle (box 5.7), widely supported in Europe, has three attractive characteristics. First, it slows the commercialization of new crops. By putting a greater burden of proof on promoters to show that new organisms will not create environmental or food hazards, the precautionary principle,

Box 5.7
The precautionary principle

- When an activity raises threats of harm to human health or the environment, precautionary measures should be taken even if some cause-and-effect relationships are not fully established scientifically.
- The proponent of an activity, rather than the public, should bear the burden of proof.
- The process of applying the precautionary principle must be open, informed, and democratic, including potentially affected parties. It must also involve an examination of the full range of alternatives, including no action.

Source: Adapted from The Wingspread Consensus Statement on the Precautionary Principle (http://www.sehn.org/ wing.html).

as implemented in some national laws, slows the approval process and allows more time for the public to become informed. Second, the principle calls for more transparency in environmental, food, and health-related public sector decisionmaking. Third, where substantial scientific uncertainty exists, it requires that decisions be made through an informed political process. References to precaution have been adopted in the Cartagena Protocol on Biosafety, which regulates the shipping of certain genetically modified organisms (referred to in the protocol as "living modified organisms") across national borders.

Poverty and the precautionary principle

The precautionary principle requires analysis of the alternatives to introducing new technology and organisms, not just the risks inherent in their use. In Africa, in many marginally viable agricultural areas, the range of alternatives is currently minimal. For farmers in these areas, modified crops that can better survive prolonged drought, or that improve diets through micronutrient enrichment, may be among the few critical options, to be supplemented with investment in farm- and landscape-scale soil and water improvements.[51]

Efforts to improve the lives of farmers in arid and semi-arid borderline areas through conventional breeding programs have had limited success. Crop breeders have had limited success in either raising the yields of robust but low-yielding millet or getting improved resistance to moisture stress from fragile but higher-yielding hybrid maize. Both these objectives have resisted traditional breeding programs but have become credibly feasible with genetic modification.[52] The precautionary principle requires weighing the alternatives and the costs and benefits of helping these farmers. As noted above, the development community supports a broad consensus that alternatives that can be adopted on a large scale are few and that risks from transgenics can be managed. The challenge is to focus research and promote knowledge sharing for improving "orphan crops"— crops important to poor people but that have not had the benefit of significant research because of limited market potential.

Disentangling the elements. The ethical, moral, and social dimensions of biotechnology challenge society's institutions at all levels, from the field to the planet. They challenge notions of property and property rights institutions, the national and international institutions responsible for biosafety, the institutions concerned with food safety and consumer choice, the rules for international trade, and the organization and role of public sector research (table 5.1).[53]

For biosafety, food safety, and consumer choice and trade, active sensing mechanisms are in place, largely through NGOs and formal and informal networks. The Internet has greatly increased the power of networking. Mechanisms to balance interests are weak across all five dimensions. Much greater attention is required to frame the debate so that the public can better understand the benefits and risks by making independent positions, agreed on by scientific leaders, accessible to the public. Implementation of institutional remedies in each of these areas is taking place within a global context, and frameworks are emerging to forge international agreements. Because these frameworks often do not reflect satisfactory consensus at the national level, their implementation path can be expected to be rocky.

More importantly, to successfully introduce more science and technology into neglected areas of developing country agriculture, a long-term commitment to the development of agricultural knowledge and supporting institutions must be in place—particularly in Africa (see box 5.8).

Intensifying the use of land

Creating more dynamic, input-intensive agricultural communities in near-market areas, where price incentives make intensification attractive, requires sustained effort on several fronts.[54] First, conditions must be established to activate the land market and make land affordable to smallholders. Second, smallholders must have access to credit to make the holding a viable economic unit. And third, smallholders must have enough protection from risk to be able to afford investing in yield-increasing inputs, such as fertilizer and improved seed.

Three activities are important to move additional land into the hands of smallholders: clarify and adjudicate property rights, improve the functioning of land sales and rental markets, and where necessary, redistribute land through land reform.

Clarify and adjudicate property rights as land scarcity dictates. Countries making the transition from communal to more individual forms of land ownership need to set up a legal framework that permits evolution of land rights toward individualized

Table 5.1

The capacity of institutions to sense problems, balance interests, and implement solutions

	Where we are in identifying problems	Where we are in balancing interests	Where we are in implementing solutions
Problems with intellectual property rights regime	Innovators (especially in pharmaceuticals) felt investment threatened by weak property rights. Legal costs of innovative research now a barrier for public sector researchers. Concern about effect of strong IPRs on concentration in life sciences industry.	IPR debates not well accompanied or understood by public. Minimum standards of IPRs established in the Uruguay Round. Menu of acceptable IPR options large.[55] Many developing countries and NGOs believe that IPRs, based on Western concepts of law, are unethical or impractical in developing countries.[56]	IPR implementation varies widely, as a function of national income.[57] IPR implementation will strengthen as countries become potential exporters (to meet intellectual property (IP) standards of importing countries).
Biosafety	Old concern over invasive, exotic, wild species. *Nature* documents Bt-maize pollen threat to Monarch butterflies.[58] Monsanto sued for Bt "creep" into organically grown neighboring crops. Subsequent research shows low threat to Monarchs under field conditions.[59] Genetically modified crops found poorly competitive outside of cultivated conditions for which designed.	Developed countries have minimal voice regarding tradeoff of biosafety risk against food security. Arguments are inaccessible to lay public. Precautionary principle accepted in Cartagena Protocol on Biosafety, but mechanisms to resolve disagreement weak.	United States screens GMOs using same standards as non-GMOs. U.S. Department of Agriculture (USDA) responsible for implementation—except for Bt products which must also clear EPA. European legislation tends to require screening hypothetical risk. European public pressure halts new approvals in 1998.
Food safety and consumer choice	No documented cases of human health problems from eating commercially marketed GMOs. Normal testing catches potential allergy problem. Scientific opinion in Europe and the United States agrees: "there is no problem with GMOs over and above any other food."[60]	European public pressure pushes a "strong precautionary principle" requiring screening for hypothetical risk. U.S. Academy of Science declares no scientific basis for tougher screening processes for GMOs than non-GMOs. European preference for non-GMOs drives down price of GMO crops. U.S. corn acreage in GMOs falls. Liability concerns arise for pollen contamination.	U.S. FDA applies the same standards of food safety as for non-GMO crops.[61] EU adopts labeling based "on consumers' right to know." GMO food safety low priority in developing countries compared with clean water and uncontaminated meat.
Trade	Developed country consumer and environmental groups question trade in GMOs. Concerns related to globalization-related "loss of control" and multinational industry concentration, as well as to specific food and environmental safety issues. Industry concerned with disguised protectionism and theft of IP.	Contradictory positions. World Trade Organization (WTO) requirements, based on Uruguay Round (SPS agreements), require restrictions to be based on scientific assessment of risks. Cartagena Protocol on Biosafety, endorses "precautionary principle"—that "lack of scientific certainty due to insufficient relevant scientific information and knowledge" should not prevent states from banning imports.	Protocol establishes Biosafety Clearing-House to exchange information on living modified organisms and to assist countries to implement. Calls for assistance from developing countries in capacity building.
Public research investment	With food abundant, prices low, and agricultural subsidies high, developed countries' support for public agricultural research is weak.	Difficulty balancing (a) "pure research," (b) research on improving the productivity of crops without significant commercial markets, but of importance to poor people, and (c) research on yields for major staples where yields are approaching genetic maximums.	Must develop national and international public sector research programs that (a) are oriented toward clear national objectives, and (b) complement (through partnerships), and do not duplicate other public sector and private sector activities.[62]

Box 5.8

Institutional commitment and African agriculture: lessons from Asia and South America

The current pessimism about a continent's ability to feed itself has been seen before—in Asia. The pessimists were proved wrong about Asia. But it took a long-term, coordinated commitment to agricultural research, extension, and agricultural higher education. These are the lessons to be learned from the Green Revolution in Asia and South America.

"Asia's development experience reveals that a bleak economic future for Africa in the 21st century is not foreordained. There are scores of cracked crystal balls in economic forecasting. Even Nobel Laureates such as Gunnar Myrdal can widely miss the mark. Myrdal was pessimistic about Asia's development prospects in the late 1960s because of corruption, 'soft states,' rapid population growth, and the gloomy prospects for agriculture. But Myrdal failed to anticipate Asia's Green Revolution, which was taking root at the same time that his book, *Asian Drama,* was rolling off the press in 1968. The rapid spread of Green Revolution wheat and rice varieties in Asia in the late 1960s and early 1970s, and China achieving the fastest rate of agricultural growth in the world from 1980 to 1995, highlight the perils of economic forecasting." Even Bangladesh, long considered a "basket case," has recently emerged as an agricultural success story. In Latin America, Brazil and Chile have become aggressive competitors in global food markets.

What these countries have in common is a long-term commitment to agricultural research, extension, and higher education—to the development of what Carl Eicher has labeled the "Agricultural Knowledge Triangle." The time for the success-ful development of agricultural knowledge is measured in decades, not years, and requires long-term national and donor support. The complexity of agricultural systems in Africa have foiled attempts to "jumpstart" a Green Revolution in Africa. Success in Africa will require local adaptation, piloting, and dissemination. Where agricultural institutions are strong, success has been achieved. Zimbabwe's Green Revolution in maize, which led to a reliable maize surplus and generated maize exports for 19 of 21 years during 1970–91, was based on 28 years of indigenous research, which in 1960 produced the high-yielding maize variety SR-52. Unfortunately the technological leadership that made this possible has been allowed to erode.

The long-term commitment required to develop agricultural knowledge institutions does not resonate comfortably with today's aid climate. Today's climate favors rapid "results on the ground," and prefers direct field involvement, often through NGOs. Donors are right to demand accountability for aid resources. But experience shows that there is no shortcut to agricultural knowledge. Sustained agricultural progress in developing countries will require a long-term commitment from donors and partnering with local agricultural research extension and higher education institutions.

Sources: Carl Eicher, *Institutions and the African Farmer,* CIMMYT Economics Program third distinguished economist lecture. On the Web at http://www.cimmyt.org/Resources/Publications/cat-log2001/Pub Cat2001-Economics.htm; *Zimbabwe's Maize-Based Green Revolution: Preconditions for Replication,* World Development, vol. 23, no. 5, pp. 805–808, 1995.

tenure as the need emerges with increased commercialization and land scarcity. Where tenure arrangements have been severely disrupted by civil strife and war, collectivist land reform, or land-grabbing by influential individuals (Bolivia, Cuba, Ethiopia, Honduras, Nicaragua, Tanzania, Uganda, and Vietnam), an approach is needed that adjudicates among overlapping claims and establishes clear ownership rights at minimum cost.

Where insecurity of tenure already affects incentives, land titling should be initiated. Area-based titling is important where the insecurity results from attempts by the powerful to wrest land from the less powerful. Under these conditions an "on-demand" program may increase the ease of land grabbing, and an area-based system is more appropriate. An example would be the rehabilitation of an irrigation scheme in Somalia—where land values will increase greatly with improved water access and where the rule of law is tenuous, exposing those less powerful to loss of land to individuals with strong political connections or power positions.[63] Experience in Bolivia, El Salvador, Peru, and Thailand demonstrates that area-based titling can be accomplished by introducing titling in combination with a mechanism for dispute resolution.

An on-demand approach can be justified under four conditions. Commercial agriculture is just beginning to emerge as a profitable enterprise for the most innovative and progressive producers. Traditional community values and norms are still strongly enforced. Local political power in the formal governmental structure is constrained effectively by traditional political structures and traditional authority. And national administrative systems extend the rule of law to the local areas.

Under these conditions the emerging entrepreneurial commercially oriented producers may need more security of ownership than the majority of farmers who are still largely subsistence producers. For example, the emerging entrepreneurial group may need access to formal credit markets, which typically requires greater security of ownership. Under such circumstances an area-wide titling project would be expensive and inefficient because the cost would exceed the benefits for most parcels. Further, it may be possible to use the political strength and local support of traditional authorities to certify boundaries in an equitable manner without area-wide titling. Communities of exactly this type exist in many areas in central and western Uganda.[64]

Improve the functioning of land sales and rental markets. Restrictions have often been placed on operations of land markets to compensate for failures in credit and risk markets—and for policies that raise the price of land above its expected value in agricultural use, such as the use of agriculture as a tax loophole, and agricultural credit subsidies directed to large land owners. These restrictions on tenancy and sales contracts typically reduce the willingness of landlords to make land available to smallholders through sales or rentals and so should be removed. Underlying market failures must be addressed directly. Taxing land can reduce the incentive for large landholders to hold unproductive land (box 5.9). A lump-sum local tax on land has the advantage of maintaining incentives to produce, and it provides revenue to local governments. In addition, by capitalizing local amenities in land values, a local land tax establishes a direct link between tax levels and benefits received by taxpayers.[65]

Depoliticize land reform and stress sustained productivity and poverty reduction. Because many land reforms have taken place in response to political crises, with little sustained commitment to making the smallholders' farms productive, the outcomes have often been disappointing.[66]

Transforming a large farm into a workable set of smallholder enterprises requires a new pattern of production, subdivision of the farm, and construction of infrastructure.[67] So, realizing the productivity benefits of redistribution requires a shift from ad hoc political objectives to productivity and poverty-related objectives. Brazil, Colombia, and South Africa are implementing a new model of "negotiated" land reform. Although it is too early to draw definitive conclusions, initial evidence is encouraging. Key elements of this approach are:[68]

- Emphasize sustainable poverty reduction through elaboration of integrated farm projects by poor people (which are then supported by a land purchase grant).
- Decentralize execution and integrate into development objectives at the local level, with an overarching emphasis on beneficiary training and human capital formation.
- Involve the private sector in project development, financing, and implementation.
- Work to build and maintain a broad-based constituency, including landowners, rural workers' unions, agribusiness, and agricultural research and extension.

Intensifying the use of water

With water scarcity rising, markets tend to emerge—formal or informal, legal or illegal, peacefully or through violence. And the tendency will be for water to go to its highest-value use given the infrastructure in place. Although this provides some comfort, because the scope for improving efficiency of water use through better pricing is great, the institutions underlying those markets will determine the social cost of the transition to markets and the efficiency and

---

Box 5.9
Weakening the interest of landholders in unproductive land

In 1995 Brazil transferred collection of its land tax from the land reform agency (INCRA) to the ministry of finance. With this change, the tax began to be seriously assessed for the first time. In addition, Brazilian Federal Banks began foreclosing on bad debt collateralized by land, and land prices fell because of Brazil's entry to the Southern Common Market (MERCOSUR) and the ending of hyperinflation (which had led to a flight to real assets).

These events began a process of weakening the interest of landowners in holding unproductive land. With this weakened interest it became possible to mount a major campaign against irregular holdings. In the past few years INCRA reclaimed more than 50 million hectares of irregular holdings. Of these holdings 10 million hectares in the Amazon region were turned over to the Brazilian Institute for the Environment to create protected areas. The rest became available for redistribution. According to the minister of land reform, there is now no constraint on land available to be distributed to Brazil's landless. The constraint is budgetary resources required under the Brazilian Constitution to help land reform beneficiaries set up workable production units.

Source: World Bank staff.

equity of infrastructure put in place to make water transport and water markets possible.[69]

As for land, emerging legal protection of property usually confers rights on the first users. But gaining truly secure property rights is more complicated with water than it is for land. Physical distance and different legal and administrative jurisdiction (states, regions, nations) complicate agreements between upstream and downstream users. Guaranteed quantities become meaningless as quality is degraded. And the complexity of hydrologic systems and unpredictability of climate make "ownership" a contingent concept. For these reasons, property rights in water have emerged only in situations of scarcity, and the nature of the rights varies according to the water basin's peculiarities.

The competition for water has two stages: one for access to cheap water and one for rights to water. The competition for access takes the form of competition for property rights for land that is well endowed with water (box 5.10). This means purchasing good, easy to irrigate land; land above shallow aquifers; or land on which the government can be persuaded to provide low-cost water. In each case rights to water are less of an issue—in the early stages—than rights to land. Only as water scarcity emerges in a second stage, often from conflict with urban or public use, does the irrigator seek to convert traditional uses of water to property rights. This principle of prior appropriation—the squatter's rights to water—tends to be accepted in most settings.

Prior appropriation has pluses and minuses. A plus is that it tends to reward entrepreneurial behavior and investment in productive resources. A farmer who fears losing rights to water is much less likely to invest in land leveling and irrigation infrastructure than a farmer who is sure that water will continue to be available. Communities also prefer to see investment and economic activity than to see a resource lying idle.

There are two minuses. First, prior appropriation sharpens inequalities in incomes and assets by rewarding those with the initial capital to invest. Second, unless well administered, it leads to a destructive race for property rights and loss of environmental services of water.

Nonvoluntary redistribution of existing water use and associated rights has been proposed but found to be impractical—both in industrial countries such as Australia and the United States—and in develop-

Box 5.10

The race for water—and land—and the displacement of the poor

In some arid regions of Sub-Saharan Africa, land rights are less important than rights to use water at specific locations such as an isolated waterhole. Rights to graze land might be open to the entire community or even several communities, but rights to water were restricted. Control over the water meant de facto control over the land, just the reverse of the frontier setting of the Americas. So having a water right was far more important than having a right to graze the land.

With the advent of a modern technology—the borehole well—the constraints to grazing were suddenly relaxed, and it became possible for wealthy or powerful individuals to gain access to land and grazing opportunities through implementation of the new borehole technology. The tribal lands grazing policy (TGPL) program in Botswana promoted private ownership of grazing land and borehole water points under the theory that individual ownership would provide incentives to maximize the returns from grazing, maintain or improve the quality of the range, and increase the rate of herd offtake and national income. The result was that many of the private ranches came to be owned by wealthy individuals, and grazing, hunting, and gathering opportunities for poor people declined.

Source: Richard Barrows, personal communication.

ing countries with strong central governments such as Mexico (where redistributing water rights would, in the words of a prominent reformer, "require a revolution"). It is also problematic even in developing countries with a strong redistributional mandate (for example, South Africa). The benefits of formalizing the de facto rights of water users, and working with these users to manage the resource in a sustainable manner, have in most cases been judged to outweigh the drawbacks of reinforcing existing inequities.[70]

If the settlement of rights becomes protracted, negotiation strategies of individual claimants will lead to a wasteful drawdown of the resources—and to premature investment. A property rights regime that does not allocate rights expeditiously not only risks wasting water, but also leads to uneconomic infrastructure designed to "lock in" water claims before other claimants do so—often years if not decades before it is justified by emerging demand. For example, pressure for a 2,000-kilometer conveyance system taking water from the San Francisco River to Brazil's northeast—even though most of the urban demand justifying the project will not begin to emerge for more than 10 years—comes in part from a concern to guarantee Brazil's poor and arid northeast a claim on the San Francisco's limited water. Similar pressures exist between states in India.[71]

The environmental use of water will not be protected without specific institutional intervention. In the absence of protective institutions the environmental use of water is priced at zero—every other use will establish a prior claim. If estuaries and freshwater ecosystems are to be maintained, institutional solutions have to be put in place to take into account the public goods nature of water.

What are the major institutional issues for rural communities in controlling the race for water? The first, "institutional" principle for water resource management, is that water management should be carried out at the lowest appropriate level—and be as participatory as possible. The second, "ecological" principle requires the holistic management of water, including management of watersheds and guarantees of maintenance of environmental values. And finally the third, "instrument" principle requires that water be managed as an economic resource. Widely known as the Dublin Principles, for the 1992 Dublin conference where they were first developed and agreed on, these are the three principles that water specialists agree that water management must respect.

Picking up signals of environmental decay. Water problems are environmental and economic. Signals of environmental decay are picked up by rural communities as a gradual loss of fisheries and the recreational and aesthetic value of water, as well as the quality and supply of water for domestic use, and the presence of water-borne human diseases. These signals are often missed or interpreted incorrectly. If environmental flows are to be protected, basin-level expertise must be mobilized prior to the emergence of economic conflict for water. The economic signal is a growing disparity among the values of water in irrigation and in urban and industrial uses. For groundwater the early signal of a problem is falling levels, often noticed by local communities with shallow drinking water wells long before it becomes a problem for irrigators.

Balancing the interests of all of water's claimants. Balancing competing water interests requires a consensus on the technical nature of the problem. This requires basin-level expertise. It is critical that envi-

ronmental flows be established early. If environmental needs emerge only after economic conflict is already emerging, the problem of balance becomes much more controversial. The function of a water agency is to provide quality analysis and technical information about the hydrological characteristics of the basin, including analysis of alternative water sharing, trading, and pricing scenarios.

Interests need to be balanced where they conflict—the Dublin institutional principle. Where problems are local, such as managing an irrigation district, and the actors homogeneous, communities typically find mechanisms to resolve the conflict.[72] Conflicts among widely differing claimants—for example, the irrigation district and urban water supply, with the hydropower dam an added complication—require basin-level mediation. Water parliaments, or a similar institutional structure representing all basin stakeholders, become essential. Water parliaments must have technical backstopping from a strong and respected water agency (box 5.11).

Box 5.11
Water parliaments in France

Since 1964 water policy in France has been made at each of six major hydrographic levels by a *comité de bassin,* an authentic river basin water parliament. The number of seats varies from 61 to 114, with the composition fixed by ministerial order and comprising three groups:

1. Users, qualified local dignitaries, and representatives of socioprofessional groups (40–45 percent of seats).
2. Representatives of the regional authorities (*régions, départements, communes;* 36–38 percent of the seats).
3. Representatives of the state (19–23 percent of the seats).

This organization deliberately limits the influence of the state and reflects the desire to promote the role and responsibility of the different actors—users and elected representatives—in each basin and to encourage them to reach agreement. The basin committee must give its approval on fees and the basis for their calculation.

The basin committee's executing agency is the water board *(agences de l'eau),* an administrative public body under the responsibility of the state. It has a dual role:

■ Taking part in the financing of general works in the basin.
■ Carrying out water-related research studies.

Source: Chéret (1993).

Executing arrangements to share water. Action requires either sharing available water better or building new infrastructure to bring in additional water, or increasing the flow and quality of water through rainwater harvesting and landscaping improvements. Water management institutions have historically developed to address allocation of existing flows; much more attention is needed to enhance institutional action on water production and use efficiency. Water, even in industrial countries, tends to be very poorly allocated.[73] So the scope to share water better, without resorting to new sources of supplies, is generally great, but incentives have to be in place. Where the number of competing users is relatively small, ad hoc solutions can be sought. For example, the water utility can purchase high-efficiency irrigation devices for the irrigation district (such as the Imperial Valley, California). Or the utility can pay the farmers not to irrigate at all (California water market and others). As the number of players increases, or as all easy solutions become exhausted, water markets become most efficient for water allocation and coordination.

Water basin commissions, or water agencies, must be established to open the dialogue for win-win opportunities in water sharing. Eventually water markets will emerge through this process of ad hoc negotiation and comparison of value.[74] Water markets ensure that water in each basin gets to its highest value use. They also ensure that price differentials clearly signal the potential benefits of augmenting flows through dams, reservoirs, or interbasin transfers.

Moving to market allocations of water requires two important acts, however. First, property rights must be assigned: it must be decided who will have to pay whom for water. Second, environmental allocations must be made—how much water has to be set aside to maintain environmentally critical flows in the basin? The market will not make these decisions. The first must be determined by existing law and prevailing notions of fairness, and the second through a combination of technical and political criteria.[75] In the absence of appropriate balancing mechanisms, many major rivers stop flowing into the ocean or inland lakes.

Water markets will eventually price low-value users out of the market. This can have two bad outcomes. If the community of low-value users is strong, well represented, and politically strategic, it can block market reform—delaying or even preventing badly needed improvements in water allocation. If they are weak, they risk losing their economic base without clear alternatives, as irrigation water becomes priced out of their reach.

But if the rule of prior allocation were to assign property rights to rural users, the transition to market allocation would be greatly smoothed. When local farmers are owners of the water, they are unequivocally made better-off by the market-induced increased value of the water. They have a range of choices; they can continue farming as they were, sacrificing the income they could get by selling water; or they may upgrade by investing in water-saving irrigation equipment and higher-value crops and sell the surplus water created; or they may decide to sell all the water and invest in alternative livelihoods. Similar property rights would have to be assigned to institutions protecting the environmental services of the basin.

Getting ahead of the frontier

What drives the expansion of the agricultural frontier into different wildernesses? Poverty and opportunity. In this section the forest frontier is discussed. But the pattern also applies to the conversion of wetlands, grasslands, and other agriculture—or wilderness—boundaries. The settlement in the eastern Amazon of Brazil has been shaped by Northeasterners fleeing periodic droughts. Western settlements, by contrast, tend to be populated by smallholders who sold farms in southern Brazil during the booming land market of the mid-1970s and early 1980s to seek opportunities by buying cheaper land in the Amazon, often gaining 5–10 hectares of land in the Amazon for every hectare sold in the south.[76] Similar stories of expansion into the forests of Indonesia, Malaysia, the Philippines, and Thailand have elements of poverty-induced flight and profit-driven opportunity.[77] The frontier's expansion highlights the importance of institutions to address a race for property rights.

Many forests were originally claimed by local communities, but these claims were granted to governments during the colonial or postcolonial period. While governments have often faced great difficulties in managing these (often huge areas of) forest, lack of local rights and economic benefits from forests have reduced local incentives to protect them. The past 15 years have seen a major shift in forest tenure in developing countries back to local communities and indigenous peoples, such that 14 percent are now owned by communities and indigenous groups, and another 4 percent are still publicly owned but reserved for exclusive use of communities and indigenous groups.[78] This shift in forest ownership, plus the dramatic shift in many forest-scarce countries to tree growing on farms, means that commercial forest product and ecosystem service markets could potentially contribute much more in the future to rural livelihoods than they have in the past, particularly with reforms in market policies.[79]

The process of conversion to agriculture usually begins with logging. As roads advance and markets develop, forests become worth seizing. In Asia and Latin America there are typically waves of logging, successively removing more valuable to less valuable trees, followed by the burning of residual noncommercial trees, and finally the establishment of large, commercially oriented ranches or farms. In Africa the closed forest is more likely to be converted to smallholder farms. These are nonetheless often commercially oriented (chapter 8, figure 8.1).

Rational occupation of the frontier and conservation of its biodiversity require better national governance and policies. Project interventions to improve community welfare are well meaning and potentially useful, but they do not address the scale of the problem.[80] Countries need first to rein in unregulated logging, which catalyzes conversion and degradation and appropriates rents to private individuals that belong to the public or to indigenous people. It is technically feasible to do this, but more influential vested interests can resist change. Large-scale logging often benefits government leaders or other powerful interests—sometimes for personal gain, but often because the forest provides an off-budget source of revenue for projects.[81]

The people and wildlife of the world's great transfrontier forests—the western Amazon, parts of the Congo Basin, Siberia, and New Guinea—are protected, only partially and for the moment, by their inaccessibility. These are the last places where large ecosystem processes represent preindustrial experience, and they are home to many indigenous people, plants, and animal species. Today they are also subject to increasing threats. Roads built for oil and gas development, for extraction of mahogany, or for mil-

Box 5.12
The Amazon rancher's decision to deforest

Pasture in the Amazon often degrades beyond economic use in some 10–15 years. The rancher then has to decide whether to restore the pasture through plowing, fertilizing, and planting new pasture grasses or to plant on newly deforested land. The decision depends largely on the relative cost of new land (net of sales of commercial value logs) and the cost of fertilizer and limestone to reclaim degraded land.

In intensifying areas where the cost of new land is above $300 per hectare, farmers will generally choose to reform pasture. But where land values are between $20 and $100 per hectare, farmers find it more profitable to deforest new land and abandon degraded pasture. By a conservative estimate of the value of the carbon storage, the value of a hectare of Amazon forest in sequestering carbon is over $800. So, although deforestation generates value to the rancher of less than $300 and costs society more than $800 in lost carbon storage benefits, no national or international arrangement has yet succeeded in developing institutions to influence the rancher's decision.

Source: World Bank estimates.

itary purposes can open these regions to encroachment—and often wasteful exploitation by loggers, ranchers, and farmers—and to destructive fires. The combination of conversion and sloppy logging provides a deadly recipe for forest fires: open canopies leading to dried-out soil, highly flammable logging waste on the ground, and escaped land-clearing fires.[82] The catastrophic forest fires in Indonesia in 1999 caused $7.9 billion of damage to the Indonesian economy and additional health and tourism damage to neighboring countries.[83] Without intervention these areas are likely to experience, over the next 5 to 50 years, the social and environmental problems of earlier frontiers.

The frontier trap. The race for frontier property creates a sharp disparity between what is good for an individual landholder and what is good for society. First, the rancher or farmer opening new land is unlikely to take into account the loss of biodiversity and carbon storage (box 5.12). Second, holdings at the extensive margin tend to be associated with low density and transient communities—raising the costs and lowering the quality of government services and creating little opportunity for building human and social capital. So an extensive and predatory agricultural economy either has a sharply higher cost to the state to provide equivalent human services, or has services that are poor, leading to a corresponding loss in human potential.

Weak institutions to support communities and protect biodiversity

Whatever the motive driving settlement onto new lands, important institutional and economic conditions are constant. First, the combination of abundant, inexpensive land and high-cost agricultural inputs (owing to high transport costs and poorly developed markets) creates economic pressure for land-extensive techniques. These include mining the soil nutrients and failing to control soil erosion. Second, government and governance are weak, with much of the frontier population involved in unilaterally staking out claims to forested land. Third, the loss of valuable biodiversity and contribution to global warming do not enter the economic calculation of farmers opening new land.

Under these conditions rapid farm turnover and transience for poor people are nearly inevitable. Poor people lack assets—collateral, access to credit, access to other, nonfarm sources of income, and urban skills—to navigate formal sector input and output markets. As a result a speculator or entrepreneur will almost always, sooner or later, make a purchase offer that the poor homesteader cannot refuse—generally under distress, such as crop failure, death of a family member, or illness.[84] Some poor families escape poverty through repeatedly settling new lands, improving them, and selling out and moving on as the frontier advances. Many more stay locked in perpetual poverty.

The process through which poor people occupy and gain squatters' rights to land, and later sell out to entrepreneurial agents is repeated in many forms and settings. In the *pa boei* system in the Chon Buri hinterland in southeast Thailand, poor small farmers are paid by local entrepreneurs to establish homesteads on federal forest land, with agreements that the land will be turned over to the sponsor after three to five years.[85] Whether formally arranged in advance or resulting from distress sales or different implicit discount rates, this pattern of poor people gaining informal property rights through clearing the forest, and later selling out to the entrepreneurial agent, is common throughout the developing world.[86]

This cycle of transience is embedded deeply in both the educational and social status of the poor settler and the institutional environment of the extensive frontier. Education is rudimentary at best, so the poor homesteader, lacking education and urban skills, has few alternatives. To make matters worse, the predominantly low-input and low-population-density pattern of frontier expansion sharply limits off-farm opportunities. So poor settlers lack insurance and risk-management alternatives, except selling the farm and migrating farther out on the frontier. This generates a destructive cycle for the poor and for forests.

Although social capital might be substantial in frontier settlement areas—especially in settlements where immigrants have moved together from the same community—the capacity to pool risk through collective action is low. Since nearly all poor settlers are engaged in the same activity, they are all subject to the same risks of pests, drought, sickness, and are unable to self-insure as a group.

Getting institutions ahead of the frontier

Most remaining large wilderness areas are in remote areas of low agricultural potential. In these areas measures to remove land from the land market—by establishing parks, indigenous reserves, or biological reserves—reinforce complementary efforts by the national authorities to encourage more intensified production on lands already under cultivation. Setting this land aside has important public benefits. It protects critical ecosystems, and it reinforces economic forces to intensify land use closer to markets. To the extent that it closes the frontier and raises land prices (reflecting decreased land abundance), it discourages nutrient mining, stabilizes communities, and promotes intensified land use. Park creation, the focus of most conservation projects, has achieved considerable success: 13 percent of the world's lowland rainforest is already protected.[87] Such parks can be effective, especially when guards are present and local people are involved or compensated.[88]

Financing the maintenance of protected areas is a concern everywhere. Frequent criticism has been voiced about "paper parks," without adequate infrastructure or staffing. But recent research shows that the mere designation of parks has an important impact on future settlement patterns.[89] Where protected areas are established well ahead of the frontier's advance, a light official presence is enough to stop intruders. Over the next 30 to 50 years, the pressure on the frontier is going to increase initially and then abate as global population stabilizes, and

higher incomes and education create better job opportunities. Avoiding irreversible losses during this
ebb and flow will likely have a high payoff for future
generations.

*Major institutional needs to establish protected
areas ahead of the frontier*

The major institutional needs are (a) pick up signals
of biodiversity loss; (b) balance interests of communities with biodiversity protection; and (c) execute
activities to protect biodiversity.

Pick up signals of biodiversity loss. Signals of ecosystem or species loss are difficult to identify locally because the loss is often a part of cumulative effects on
a much larger scale. Warning signals of biodiversity
loss, such as forest conversion, are being increasingly
monitored by government environmental agencies
and universities. Specialized monitoring organizations, such as Global Forest Watch, increasingly play
a vital role. The Global Environment Fund has been
instrumental in developing biodiversity assessments
and action strategies in many countries.

Initiatives to promote transparency can help catalyze change. The combination of voice for forest
dwellers, better communications technology, and advances in remote sensing means that forest activities
are now more visible than before. NGOs and reform
groups in government can use this information to call
for greater accountability on how logging is conducted and how forest revenues are used. Transparency in the award of concessions and in monitoring concessionaire performance are important steps
toward better forest regulation. Recent efforts in
Cameroon show both the challenges and the benefits
in moving toward transparency (chapter 7, box 7.10).

Balance the interests of communities and developers.
Ultimately though, these tools can be applied only if
there is popular consensus on regional development
strategies and support for policies that set up the necessary incentives and disincentives. Provinces and nations need to debate, for instance, the desirability of
intensifying and upgrading rural road networks in
densely populated rural areas while restricting the
construction of new roads in areas important for biodiversity but poorly suited for agriculture. There are
few good examples of this kind of large-scale land-
use planning, which goes far beyond the discredited
technocratic approach to zoning. It is an area where
international resources may be crucial in helping to
facilitate domestic agreement on biodiversity-friendly,

Box 5.13
Brazil: getting ahead of the frontier

One hundred forty million hectares of the Brazilian Amazon, or 28 percent, are in protected areas—national parks,
biological reserves, extractive reserves, or indigenous reserves. Analysis based on satellite imagery and field surveys to detect signs of occupation, forestry potential, and
high biodiversity values shows that without competitive
use, 46 million new hectares (9 percent of the Brazilian
Amazon) could be put into biodiversity protection and 70
million hectares (14 percent) into national production for
sustainable forestry.

If this were to come about, more than half the Amazon
would be dedicated to either preservation or sustainable
forest use. Government has pledged to put a representative 10 percent of the Amazon forest (41 million hectares)
into new protected areas through the WWF–World Bank
Forest Alliance program. And it is developing a National
Forest Program to strengthen the forestry system, creating new national forests. The long-run goal is to create a
mosaic of land use to control the advance of the agricultural frontier, support communities through sustainable activities, and ensure a strategic buffer for areas of high
biodiversity value.

Source: Veríssimo and others (2000).

economically sensible, and socially sustainable regional development approaches. But the agenda has
scarcely begun to take shape.

Experience shows that balancing interests in creating individual parks, protected areas, and forest production reserves is much easier than building consensus on more comprehensive zoning. This is largely
a matter of getting far enough ahead of the frontier
that development pressure has not yet emerged.
Once the protected or reserve area is a going concern,
little presence is required to keep it intact.

Even so, setting aside land beyond the frontier
will generate resistance from development interests
and from local traditional communities. By providing both economic and environmental benefits, a
land-use pattern based on a "mosaic" of land use—a
mix of production forests, extractive reserves, indigenous lands, and fully protected areas—can help
build a constituency of environmentalists, foresters,
and forest dwellers, including indigenous peoples
(box 5.13). Large protected area initiatives, by contrast, unaccompanied by job-creating alternatives,
face formidable politics.

Execute ecosystem protection activities. Areas beyond the frontier can be protected through biological reserves, indigenous reserves, extractive reserves,

or production forests. International resources are helping governments sustain land use and protect biodiversity. For example, with the goal of putting a representative 10 percent of all forest ecosystems into fully protected status and 200 million hectares into certified production forest, the World Bank and the WWF are working with governments and local NGOs to create parks and to create and certify sustainable logging reserves.[90] Brazil's pilot program to conserve the Brazilian rain forest, jointly financed by Brazil, the Netherlands, and the G7, has set the standard for NGO and local people's participation in forest protection activities.

Technical solutions are at hand to ensure the rule of law in areas of difficult access, in part owing to rapid technological advances. Brazil's Proarco and Amazonia Fique Legal programs have shown the technical feasibility of detecting large-scale illegal deforestation through coordination of remote sensing and ground-based inspection. Using satellite detection the state of Mato Grosso has moved vigorously to prosecute illegal deforesters. Brazil and Indonesia have used the Internet to post the location and identities of lawbreakers.[91]

Conclusion

This chapter reviewed some key development challenges for rural areas over the next 30 to 50 years: get ahead of the frontier with biodiversity protection and environmentally and socially sustainable activities in frontier areas; intensify agricultural production; and manage land and water to generate growth, eliminate rural poverty, and prepare outmigrants to be productive urban citizens.

Getting ahead of the frontier

In many countries the frontier's advance reflects a failure in land tenure policy, and the race for property rights leads to excessive farm sizes, underutilization of land, and lack of opportunity in the more favorable areas nearer cities. It also creates incentives to open new land on the frontier.

The results are nearly all negative. First, because of distance, cost, and transience, the ability of governments to provide for human development on a frontier is extremely limited (and thus, frontier people are the big losers). Second, the low cost of land at the frontier leads to extremely extensive agriculture. As long as biodiversity and carbon values are not taken into account in the farmer's decision to open new land, the environmental costs are high. Third, there is a high probability that marginal frontier land being opened up today will be abandoned as uneconomic in the future. This is becoming more evident now than ever, as global food projections indicate little need for additional land to meet anticipated growth in population and incomes.[92]

Getting ahead of the frontier with parks, reserves, and production forests helps end this cycle of transience and low-value land conversion. It stabilizes the frontier economy. It provides incentives for more intensive development nearer to cities. And it reduces needless loss of biodiversity.

Intensifying agricultural production

Intensifying agricultural production and increasing overall agricultural productivity is critical in much of the developing world, in response to rising populations and food demand. It can also be highly desirable. It can reduce pressure for expansion in wilderness areas and remaining areas of natural habitat within settled regions (in conjunction with conservation initiatives)—thus reducing pressure on biodiversity. It increases the food available to the cities and it leads to dynamic rural-urban linkages. Higher population density and strong rural-urban linkages make investments in health and education more effective in rural areas, increase the potential for off-farm employment, and help farmers accept risk and innovate. These arguments all support a tenure policy promoting relatively small, owner-operated farms.

In areas closer to rural towns and cities, nonfarm rural employment will be a powerful force for diversifying income, allowing greater risk and investment. It can also act as a stepping stone for the rural worker to enter productive urban employment. Rental arrangements should thus be encouraged to allow young "starter" farmers access to land and often to credit. Shareholding arrangements, effective for starter farmers to share risk with the landowner, should not be discouraged.

Eliminating rural poverty and preparing outmigrants

In poor developing countries with large agricultural sectors, growth led by the agricultural sector has a powerful effect in pulling people out of poverty, especially when the incomes and assets of the rural sector are somewhat equal. Smallholders with assets develop voice and become political players. History has shown that this generates an inclusive development path that helps countries face later challenges. But getting assets into the hands of smallholders requires good land and water policies. These policies also enable poor people to get access to opportunities for building their human and social capital.

The value of assets is enhanced through agricultural research directed to poor people, and through better agricultural institutions. In Africa improving agricultural institutions may depend on strengthening the asset value first—with water control and transport infrastructure, and with a concerted program of fertility enhancement. A reasonable estimate for the cost of a program to scale up currently successful models is $100 million annually for 10 years. Many countries will follow a two-pronged strategy that encourages intensification and commercialization. This strategy would also promote intensified research to adapt staples for high-input agriculture in productive areas near urban markets and transport, and encourage minimal chemical fertilizer supplements for low-input agriculture in more remote areas.

This strategy will require reforms in both developing and developed countries, however. The developing-world farmers produce in a world market where world agricultural prices are depressed some 12 percent by tariff barriers and agricultural subsidies worldwide—but mainly in industrial countries. For many farmers in high-transport-cost developing countries, this may translate into a difference in farm-gate prices of 50 percent or more.[93] Similarly, developing countries' farmers suffer from lack of agricultural knowledge. As noted in chapter 4, only 28 percent of public and private agriculture research and development is applied to tropical agriculture. Sustained agricultural progress in developing countries will require a long-term national and donor commitment to the agricultural "knowledge triangle"—agricultural research, extension, and higher education. A development strategy based on strengthening rural institutions and a strong smallholder sector will also facilitate eventual migration to cities. As will be discussed in chapter 6, cities must also be prepared to deal with new migrants.

CHAPTER 6

Getting the Best from Cities

Cities of the developing world face a formidable undertaking, given the rapid rate of growth and sheer numbers of urban residents to be employed, housed, and serviced. Cities offer proximity, which generate externalities both positive and negative. On the positive side, proximity is a source of productivity; industrial and service activities emerge in cities because entrepreneurs and small firms can share markets, infrastructure, labor, and information. Cost savings and productivity advantages that accrue to firms when they locate near each other in the same industry or near other economic activities derive directly from physical proximity or indirectly from less tangible interaction among economic actors (learning and networking, leading to innovation). However, large groups of people and activities in close proximity also generate negative externalities: poor sanitation, pollution of air and water, congestion, crime, and so on. This puts a premium on the quality of institutions—both formal and informal—to ensure the positive externalities and to cope with the negative externalities.

As the previous two chapters have noted, the development of urban areas will have to be better coordinated with the development of rural areas by providing markets for rural products, by subcontracting activities to expand nonfarm rural employment, and by helping rural migrants adapt more rapidly to city life. Cities and towns facilitate society's transformations in knowledge, institutions, and economic activity. By bringing together diverse people and activities, urban areas offer great opportunities for improving the quality of life.[1] For cities and towns to realize the promises of a better life—especially for poor people and for migrants from rural

areas—they need stronger institutions to provide wide access to assets and to balance interests that ensure the provision of public goods. Such institutions are central to an urban governance that is inclusive of all residents, responsive to their needs, and conducive to careful management of natural resources and wastes.

This chapter first describes the opportunities and challenges for urban life and then asks the following questions:

- How can informed constituencies be built to address spillovers and anticipate risks? Providing information, building knowledge, and mobilizing dispersed interests are key to creating constituents that act together to anticipate problems and to prevent and manage disasters.
- How can competing interests be balanced and dispersed interests articulated to provide urban public goods? Foresight, political will, and a governance system that is accountable to a wide array of stakeholders are key ingredients for achieving credible commitments.
- How can inclusion and access to assets be encouraged—one key to a city's sustainability? Security of tenure and guidance of new settlements to prevent future slums will lessen the inequitable access to assets, thus empowering and enabling poor people to become productive members of urban society.
- What institutional mechanisms are necessary for good urban governance and sustainable urban development? These include an appropriate sharing of responsibility and coordination across stake-

holder groups; wide participation in strategic planning; and networking among practitioners and stakeholders.

City lights: beacons of hope and warning flares

The rising share of people in urban areas and the corresponding economic growth of cities and towns are two defining experiences of economic and social development (box 6.1). Urban areas offer possibilities for greater welfare because they give individuals the opportunity (through a myriad of functioning urban markets) to develop a wider and larger portfolio of assets—and to achieve higher returns to their labor. They also exist because of collective concerns to share culture, learning, religious observation, and mutual protection.

Yet across cities in all regions of the world there is evidence that the potential benefits, both individual and collective, are not being fully realized, and are clouded instead by myriad problems. The inadequate provision of jobs, housing, and other goods and services stems from imperfections in markets and policies. For many environmental and social concerns, markets cannot provide the coordination needed to reveal interests and minimize transaction costs. In many countries institutional failures mean that markets are less effective than they could be, while alternative solutions and innovative uses of market instruments to address the threats to sustainable development are inadequately developed. This chapter does not examine the full range of good urban policies.[2] Instead, it focuses on the conditions for building institutions to protect urban assets—particularly environmental and social assets—because these conditions shed light on the potential for identifying and adopting good policies, and determining society's ability to respond to future concerns.

The role of cities in sustainable development
Over the next three decades the urban population of developing countries will grow (from natural increase, migration, and reclassification of formerly rural areas) by 60 million people a year—equivalent to the population of the Arab Republic of Egypt or Ethiopia. Urban areas will need to perform a few key functions to support sustainable national development:

■ Facilitate social and institutional change, by improving access to ideas, knowledge, and technol-

Box 6.1
The focus of "urban" in this chapter

Two categories of urban issues are relevant to this Report: the spatial system of urban areas in the country and the performance of urban areas. The first topic is discussed in chapter 7. This chapter takes the second category of urban issues—the city and its governance—as its unit of analysis. Focusing on the city spotlights the impacts of urban living (good and bad) and how the relevant institutional framework, both national and local, affects these outcomes.

Although the analysis of this chapter applies both to cities and to towns, as their smaller counterparts, the discussion mainly refers to cities. Most of the benefits of agglomeration and most of the diseconomies appear as towns become recognizable cities.

The Report examines changing opportunities and challenges that appear as population moves along the settlement-size continuum, but it does not argue that the prospects for sustainability are a function of scale. Very large settlements (cities of multimillion inhabitants) are neither necessarily the best nor the worst cases of sustainable development.

■ In some countries urban air quality tends to be worst in medium-size cities (populations between 100,000–500,000).*
■ Crime and vulnerability to disaster often become problems in urban agglomerations well below 1 million inhabitants, but do not increase proportionally with population size.
■ Congestion tends to worsen with city size but also depends on such other factors as public transport, traffic management, and road space.
■ Many of the economic benefits of urban productivity, such as higher wages and increased human capital, appear positively correlated with city population, at least to a fairly large threshold.

What is most clear is that the quality of urban governance and management is critical to gaining the benefits and reducing the negative aspects of cities of any size. As chapter 1 notes, the projected trend of increasing numbers of people (and possibly shares of urban population) living in very large cities over the coming decades in developing countries will put a premium on building institutions to address the problems of those cities.

* Observation based on countries with most extensive data by cities. Lvovsky (2001), annex B.

ogy and by creating both the impetus and opportunity for innovation.
■ Provide employment and services at a scale sufficient for current residents and new arrivals. Productive employment is critical so that the fall in demographic dependency ratios projected in most developing countries over the next 20–30 years can translate into increased savings and investment.

■ Ensure a healthful and attractive environment for the urban population while protecting natural resources and reducing deleterious impacts on wider regions and later generations. The massive new investment in the capital stock of cities required for the doubling of urban population by 2030 will be critical to environmental outcomes.

What enables urban areas to promote change and improved quality of life is their scale and density—and their social and economic diversity. Proximity and heterogeneity make urban areas mechanisms for knowledge and learning, for productivity and market development, and for improved choice and quality of services. And they do this even more when the institutional conditions are right.

The urban stimulus to social transformation and innovation. The shift from rural to urban society, with greater mingling among diverse people, transforms social attitudes and behaviors. It reveals the limits of traditional values and institutions and intensifies pressures for change in local governance and intergovernmental relations. Traditional social norms that perpetuate inequalities for women and for certain minorities tend to be less strictly enforced in the urban environment.[3] Urban households are generally more motivated to limit family size, because of economic alternatives and lifestyles.

The ferment of urban life generates new forms of collective action to address the challenges that arise. Urban-based constituencies have been the driving force behind many of the environmental causes that pertain to national and global public goods—creating national parks, protecting biodiversity, and managing coastal zones. More than 90 percent of China's environmental NGOs are located in cities of the relatively well-developed eastern coastal region.[4] A recent study of Indonesia proposed that the best way to save the tigers was to teach urban children about them.[5]

Historically, cities have been centers of learning and innovation. The growing intensity of knowledge exchanges arising from globalization and the information technology revolution has the greatest impact where there is also occasion for interpersonal communications.[6] Informal information or tacit knowledge, important to productivity and to social relationships, thrives on face-to-face contacts.[7] Research among Mexican firms, for example, shows that access to informal networks (business lunches

with local buyers, suppliers, competitors, and government officials) has a significant and positive effect on their productivity.[8] And proximity to higher education institutions provides firms with opportunities to commercialize research ideas, often through university-enterprise partnerships.[9]

Sources of urban productivity. Urban employment and services benefit from the economies of agglomeration—from cost savings and other advantages that accrue to firms when they locate near others in the same industry, or simply near other economic activities to share markets, services, infrastructure, labor, and information. The productivity advantage means that urban investment has strong multiplier effects in stimulating other high-value activities. The benefits extend to rural areas, which need access to urban markets to expand and diversify both farm and nonfarm production.

As a rule, larger urban areas are the most productive since they allow for greater specialization in labor use, better matching of skills and jobs, and a wider array of consumption choices for workers and ancillary services for producers.[10] As long as this greater productivity outweighs higher costs for land, labor, housing, and other necessities, the city can thrive. Once the diseconomies become too great, larger cities may lose their edge in creating jobs or improving the welfare of residents, unless they can shed some activities (those that are more mature and standardized) to smaller cities to make room for others (more innovative and higher value industry and services) and change land uses.

For cities to fulfill their potential as engines of national economic growth, they need to ensure that the labor market is not only deep but well integrated and inclusive—with accessible workplaces and residences. A city can improve its investment climate. However, cities in general can only improve the national investment climate if their overall legal and regulatory framework complements the national framework to minimize risks, uncertainties, and transaction costs to investors. This is especially important for small and informal sector enterprises, which provide most urban employment, rely more heavily on publicly provided infrastructure and information, and are particularly vulnerable to institutional and policy failures.

More affordable and higher quality services. The greater scope for competition and specialization in all goods and services enables urban areas to provide consumer benefits in the form of greater choice and quality.[11] But the advantage is especially important for services with high fixed costs (increasing returns to scale), such as middle- and higher-level education and health facilities, and network infrastructure.[12] The cost advantage explains some of the manifestly better social indicators in urban areas and in countries that are more urbanized.[13] That is, urbanization has a large positive impact on a country's efficiency in achieving health and education outcomes.[14] Even where more expensive services are required for environmental and health benefits (as for waste disposal, sewerage, water treatment, and mass transit), the added cost can often be justified by higher economic returns.

Migrating for choice and change. The offer of new opportunity and a better life is often what draws migrants to towns and cities (the pull factor). Limited employment options in rural areas, whether from agricultural dislocations arising from natural and social disasters, or from increased agricultural productivity that reduces the demand for farm labor (chapters 4 and 5), also contribute (the push factor).[15] Cities and towns allow individuals to substitute their human capital (work effort and skills) for natural, financial, or physical assets they may lack—and to

more steadily transform and expand their portfolio of assets than is possible in many rural areas.

Those who migrate to cities are often better off than their neighbors back home;[16] in cities they receive more education and better skills, and in the longer run they catch up with established urban residents.[17] A recent survey in Latin America finds a potentially large private gain from migration to urban areas, in part because the returns to human capital tend to be larger there.[18] A study of the urban labor market in the Punjab State of India found no evidence that migrants remain confined to marginal jobs or are disproportionately unemployed.[19] Migrants frequently obtain work, housing, and urban services through the informal sector, and they often depend on supportive social networks to do so (box 6.2). Nonetheless, imbalances in the demand and supply of jobs, housing, and urban services can contribute to urban poverty initially and for long periods.

In the short term, the influx of migrants can sometimes overwhelm some urban areas, particularly when the pace is sharply accelerated by civil conflict or national disaster. In the medium term, as part of the natural development process, rural-to-urban migration and the resulting return flow of transfers

---

Box 6.2
How social networks help the urban poor manage risks and get ahead

Urban areas are often said to lack social capital. Yet social networks are important to the survival and mobility strategies of urban poor people and to decisions about migration from rural areas. Risks in the urban context arise mainly from weak property rights (which can result in loss of assets and involuntary resettlement), inadequate sanitation, exposure to violent crime, and unemployment or other effects of macroeconomic shocks. The urban poor, like their rural counterparts, cope by using their social networks and personal assets.

Social networks in the city are based more on reciprocal links between individuals and friends, than on familial obligations (as in rural areas). Yet, maintaining close links between rural and urban social networks can be crucial to preserving one's identity. As in rural areas the ability of urban communities to engage in collective action is often instrumental in obtaining public services. This is particularly the case in large cities (for instance, Jakarta or Manila) where the urban poor—because of their numbers, and the relative ease of organizing them—are an important political constituency that can also be manipulated by officials promising services.

Recent field research in the slums of Delhi confirms that the major source of risk to the home and asset base for residents of squatter settlements is insecure land tenure. The slums with

the least security are usually those harboring new migrants and others with relatively limited social networks, who are unable to negotiate with bureaucrats and politicians. Social networks among slum residents assist with survival (coping with emergency needs), similar to traditional rural networks, and to upward mobility of individuals and the community. The transition from an "unrecognized" to a "recognized" slum affords access to water and sanitation and immunity from demolition. Similarly, networks are used to get ahead occupationally, whether through formal sector employment or informal self-employment. Slum-dwellers also use relationships with local leaders to obtain citizenship status and strengthen their legal protection.

The urban poor, including migrants, move from their initial inherited networks to ones that link them to external benefits and resources outside their original community. While these networks are a useful resource, the energies of poor people would be used more productively if basic services and security of tenure were provided more consistently and transparently, thus removing both the need for exhaustive negotiations to acquire basic entitlements and the opportunity for rent-seeking by local officials.

Source: Rao and Woolcock (2002).

raise incomes and living standards in both areas. Circular and temporary migration to and from cities or towns help manage risk for both rural and urban households.[20] Openness to new ideas and learning acquired by urban migrants are transmitted to rural communities through social and family links—and through the use of remittances to introduce technology to rural activities.[21] In the longer term, once the urban transition has been completed, natural population increase in cities, rather than rural-to-urban migration, will account for most urban growth. Migration among cities will continue in response to changing economic opportunities.

Making the environment work for urban residents—and saving it for others. Urban living poses environmental hazards, which affect the current population (especially poor people) through immediate, local impacts on health and safety. It also causes environmental degradation, with longer-term, wider-area, and intergenerational consequences.[22] Variations in the incidence and relative severity of a range of environmental problems across cities at different levels of development suggest differences in priorities for action (table 6.1).

In low-income cities fewer than half the households are connected to water and sewerage, and per capita water consumption is half that of cities with lower-middle income ranking (table 6.2). Less than one-third of solid waste in the poorest cities is disposed of properly; only the richest cities provide comprehensive wastewater treatment. Partly reflecting environmental risks, the average mortality of children under five in the poorest cities is more than twice that in the next city-income category, and 20 times that in the richest cities.

Especially in cities at low levels of development many residents face environmental risk because of their living conditions and location. These households are least able to afford protective or mitigating mechanisms—or to assert claims for improved services. Most vulnerable are children and women, the elderly and disabled, and homeworkers, who are continuously exposed to hazards in their immediate environment.

In the poorer cities badly managed urban growth degrades natural resources, especially watersheds, soils, and coastal environments—because of untreated sewage discharge, poor solid waste disposal, and a lack of storm drainage. In contrast, many of the issues of environmental degradation in richer cities, such as greenhouse gas emissions from hydrocarbon fuels, stem from lifestyles entailing high consumption and associated waste of natural resources.

Despite these differences in the incidence of risks and their links to income and consumption, urban residents of middle-income countries suffer environmental insults both traditional and modern (such as exposure to hazardous wastes and chemical pollutants).[23] International travel and changing global weather patterns are bringing environmental profiles of cities in industrial and developing countries closer together by spreading some risks (of disease and natural disasters, respectively) to both groups of countries. For the full range of concerns, institutional reform is required to protect poor people and environmental assets in cities both today—and in the future.[24]

Allowing the urban potential to transform society and to improve welfare, while also protecting the environment, may appear to be harder for the developing world today than it was for industrial countries at similar points in their urban transition. Why? Because of today's faster urban population growth rates (figure 6.1) (approximately one-half from migration and the rest from natural growth and reclassification of contiguous areas) and the sheer numbers of urban residents to be employed, housed, and serviced over the next few decades. Urban population growth rates, especially in Sub-Saharan Africa, have been unprecedented, though as in other regions they are projected to slow. Despite the deceleration, almost 20 million new urban residents a year are projected through 2030 for East Asia.

The same characteristics of urban areas—density, scale of settlement, and social diversity—that can bring about the positive potential of more jobs, services, and learning also create the negative potential and the need to balance interests. In addition to environmental spillovers, urban areas are associated with other threats to sustainable development and livability. Problems of land use and accessibility (including congestion) impede the utility, inclusiveness, and enjoyment of urban life, while physical insecurity results from poorly managed risks of natural disasters, crime, and violence. All of these problems affect poor people even as they reduce the welfare of all urban residents.

None of these threats is driven primarily by the rate of urbanization, by the size of city, or by the lack

Table 6.1

Urban environmental issues and status by level of city development

Sector or problem area	Low	Lower-middle	Upper-middle	High
Water supply service	Low coverage, high bacteria contamination, inadequate quantity for hygiene (high risk of food contamination and infectious diseases)	Low access by poor residents and informal neighborhoods	Generally reliable, but rising demand causing shortages in resource supply	Good supply but high total consumption; some concern with trace pollutants
Sanitation	Very low coverage, open defecation in some neighborhoods and low ratio public toilets to residents; high risk of diarrheal diseases	Better coverage of latrines and public toilets, but poorly maintained; low sewerage coverage	More access to improved sanitation, but still large numbers of residents in large cities not covered especially in informal settlements; most wastewater discharge untreated	Full coverage; most wastewater treated
Drainage	Storm drains very inadequate, poorly maintained; frequent flooding, creating high risk of water-related disease vectors (mosquitos)	Somewhat better than in low income	Better drainage; occasional flooding	Good drainage; very limited flooding
Water resources	Mixed sewerage and storm water runoff to water bodies causing bacterial pollution and silting	Risk of groundwater contamination from poorly maintained latrines and untreated sewage	Private wells drawing down groundwater; severe pollution from industrial and municipal discharge	High levels of effluent controls and treatment to reduce pollution
Solid waste management	Little organized collection; recycling by informal sector, open dumping or burning of mixed wastes; high exposure to disease vectors (rats, flies)	Moderate coverage of collection service, little separation of hazardous waste; mostly uncontrolled landfills	Better organized collection; severe problems but growing capacity for hazardous waste management; semicontrolled landfills	Increased emphasis on total waste reduction, resource recovery, and preventing hazardous waste; controlled landfills or incineration
Air pollution	Indoor and ambient air pollution from low-quality fuels for household uses and power generation	Growing ambient air pollution from industrial and vehicular emissions (high per-vehicle, due to inefficient fuels and vehicles)	Ambient air pollution still serious (but greater capacity to control especially industrial sources)	Ambient air pollution mainly from vehicles (due to high volume of vehicle kilometers)
Greenhouse gas emissions	Very low per capita	Low but growing per capita	Rapidly increasing, mainly due to motorization	Very high per capita
Land management (environmental zoning of fragile sites and preparation for new settlements)	Uncontrolled land development; intense pressure from squatter settlements on open sites	Ineffective or inappropriate land-use controls, pushing new settlements toward urban periphery; continued high population growth	Some environmental zoning	Regular use of environmental zoning; little population growth, but rising incomes press for more land consumption for existing residents
Accident risk	In-home and workplace accidents due to crowding, fires	Increased risks of industrial workplace and traffic accidents (pedestrians and nonmotorized vehicles)	Transport accidents increasing, but some mitigation and emergency treatment response	Rate of industrial and transport accidents reduced despite increasing travel (vehicle kilometers)
Disaster management	Natural disasters produce massive loss of life and property especially in settlements in disaster-prone areas; little capacity for mitigation or emergency response	Somewhat better than in low-income, although with increasing risk of industrial disasters	Increasing awareness and capacity for disaster mitigation and emergency response	Good capacity for mitigation and response

Note: Cities grouped by estimated city product (city average income calculated by national accounts methods). Sample is of cities (including in OECD countries) with available data and is not statistically representative. Low income defined as city product below $750 per capita a year; lower-middle as $751–2,499; upper-middle as $2,500–9,999; high as above $10,000.
Source: Adapted from Leitmann (2001) and Hardoy, Mitlin, and Satterthwaite (2001).

Table 6.2
Environmental health, welfare, and living conditions vary by city product

Indicator	City product category			
	Low	Lower-middle	Upper-middle	High
Household connections (percent)				
water	48.0	78.8	92.9	99.9
sewerage	45.6	68.7	84.3	99.9
electricity	72.3	93.6	95.0	100.0
Water consumption				
liters per person per day in all settlements	88	161	232	247
Wastewater treated				
percent treated	29.4	56.7	68.2	97.4
Solid waste disposal (percent)				
sanitary landfill or incinerated	30.7	41.4	37.6	77.7
other (open dump, recycled, burned)	65.9	58.3	62.2	22.3
Under-five mortality per 1,000	104.2	39.7	25.8	5.2
Households below the locally defined poverty line (percent)	31.7	23.2	16.0	6.9
Sample size (cities)	49	36	25	20

Note: Cities grouped by estimated city product (city average income calculated by national accounts methods). Sample is of cities (including in OECD countries) with available data and is not statistically representative. Low income defined as city product below $750 per capita a year; lower-middle as $751–2,499; upper-middle as $2,500–9,999; high as above $10,000.
Source: United Nations–Habitat Global Urban Indicators Database 1998.

Figure 6.1
Many developing countries are undergoing urban transition with relatively high urban population growth rates

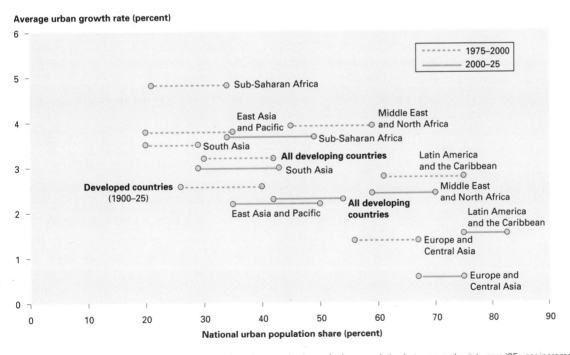

Note: All averages weighted by population. Lines indicate increase in share of urban population between end-point years (25-year increments).
Source: Developed country data from Brockerhoff and Brennan (1998); other data and projections from U.N. (1999).

of fiscal or other resources—though these factors (and such others as geography, local culture, and historical legacy) can make problems harder to manage. Cities need not suffer crippling diseconomies whatever their size or income (see box 6.1). Shanghai, one of the world's largest urban areas in one of the poorest countries, devotes more than 3 percent of the city GDP to environmental protection. And it has managed to achieve better outcomes (green space, improvements in air quality and sewage treatment) than most other developing-country cities.[25]

The growth of urban poverty in many countries, evidenced especially by the increase in populations residing in extremely poor environmental conditions, is partly a reflection of the pressures on limited city resources.[26] It also underscores the failures of institutions and their unresponsiveness to certain constituencies. As urbanization plays out, growth rates will slow, easing the pressure on cities. But catching up over several decades is not satisfactory. Measures are needed now to accelerate the rate of improvement in cities and to avoid making it more costly to close the gaps later. There are now technological and institutional options that need to be explored more vigorously.

For cities to contribute to sustainable development, they need to maximize the positive while minimizing the negative externalities. The favorable economic and social impact of cities can exceed their "ecological footprint."[27] Cities can get themselves into vicious or virtuous circles that become self-reinforcing, and triggers for change can often be found in institutional innovation. A key institutional catalyst—information—can increase urban benefits and reduce diseconomies and risks.

Building informed constituencies to address spillovers and anticipate risks

The spatial concentration of people and economic activities in urban areas creates spillovers with significant impacts on residents—and increasingly on wider regional and global populations. Mobilizing for action to solve such problems (for example, pollution) requires that the parties affected gain access to credible information on costs and benefits and that they perceive a common interest in finding a solution. Building an effective constituency can be more difficult where the impacts are uncertain and infrequent, as in disaster mitigation. Advances in technology and knowledge help, and local and na-

tional governments need to play important leadership roles in both cases.

Credible information and incentives—curbing air pollution

Air pollution generates large social and economic costs. In many developing and transition countries, the damage reaches 4 to 6 percent of urban income, and has serious adverse affects on human health. Between 500,000 and 1 million people die prematurely every year as a result of air pollution–induced respiratory problems.[28] Vehicle emissions create the greatest damage to human health because they occur near ground level and in dense population centers, while smokestack sources disperse pollutants more widely at higher elevations.[29] Urban residents in low- and middle-income countries have greater exposure (well above WHO guidelines) to some localized air pollutants, such as suspended particulates, than their counterparts in high-income countries, even though the latter consume more energy per capita.[30]

Countries do not have to suffer worsening air quality as they industrialize, motorize, and become richer. Many technologies and behaviors for curbing urban air pollution are cost-effective even at low levels of economic development and limited institutional capacity, as long as there is political commitment and public understanding.[31] While action by industrial countries to eliminate leaded gasoline, for example, took a decade to implement, sharing knowledge and demonstrating workable solutions have permitted developing countries to phase out this fuel much more rapidly (chapter 7).

Curbing stationary sources of urban air pollutants (concentrated interests) is institutionally easier than curbing mobile sources (dispersed interests) because there are fewer polluters.[32] That the fuel supply was the main source of airborne lead made it easier for countries to implement the phaseout administratively. Pressure from an informed public has been more instrumental in getting governments to rein in other types of pollution and in motivating regulatory or other action. In China the educated urban population has been an important force for such reforms. But the national government's willingness to make information on health costs and risks publicly available was an essential precondition.[33]

Curtailing mobile sources of pollution and large gas guzzling vehicles is most challenging because the middle- and upper-income groups are the beneficiaries of increased motor vehicle travel, and the main source of growing emissions with global and regional impact. These stakeholders are a more influential interest group than the general public, and especially more so than poor people suffering from the resulting pollution and accident risks. Collective action to reduce transport-based GHG, (especially CO_2) is further complicated by the nonlocal and longer-term nature of the damages.

Growth in motor vehicle ownership in developing countries could overwhelm improvements in fuel or vehicle efficiency. Effective approaches to reduce transport-based pollution therefore involve a range of interventions at different scales (local, national, and global), forming part of the integrated transport strategies discussed below.[34] These measures include improved information on levels and sources of, and damages from, pollution, educational campaigns, incentive systems (including taxation of vehicles and fuels), and technological measures, such as replacing high-mileage, heavy-polluting vehicles and installing computerized inspection and maintenance regimes.

It is also necessary to manage supply and demand across transport modes, through better public transport, improved conditions for nonmotorized transport, traffic-management, traffic-calming measures,[35] and road and vehicle user fees. These measures require coordination between jurisdictions within urban areas and across levels of government.[36]

Creating constituencies—for clean water and wastewater management

Even though inadequate neighborhood disposal of wastewater has unavoidable negative impacts, solutions are often limited by weak organizational capacity for collective action. Technological innovation, spurred by a professional association of progressive-minded civil engineers, was behind the introduction of a low-cost approach of shallow, small-bore sewerage networks in Brazil a decade ago. Compared with conventional systems, this condominial sewerage reduces investment costs by half but requires a strong commitment of households to maintain it collectively. Condominial sewerage systems have worked well where this cooperation was sustained and participating households understood their responsibilities. But since it can be difficult to get individual households to commit to take part, a more organized institutional arrangement, through community associations that would contract for the maintenance

work, is being considered for any future extensions of the system.[37]

While communities and NGOs can work together to provide household and neighborhood sanitation facilities, the social costs are lower and benefits greater if disposal and treatment of wastewater are citywide. Few cities in developing countries treat their wastewater, contributing to the pollution of downstream water bodies and corruption of fragile coastal environments. Because investment costs are high and impact areas can extend across many jurisdictions, solutions require cooperation among local governments and across levels of government.

Water pollution charges have been much less effective in making municipalities cut their emissions than industrial and agrobased polluters. The Watershed Cap and Charge System in Colombia has induced industrialists to reduce effluents, yet two-thirds of local governments, which create 70 percent of the water pollution, have been unresponsive.[38] Rising public demand for improved water quality will be needed to press for such changes, aided by income growth and good water-system management to reduce waste and sustain net revenues, since treatment is very costly.

For both air and water pollution, public awareness and citizen pressure on governments and polluters are possibly the most important factors motivating environmental reform in the face of entrenched interests or official indifference. Political democratization and the freedom to associate can be catalytic in making dispersed stakeholder groups see their common concerns and collective strength (box 6.3).

Mobilizing dispersed interests to anticipate problems—preventing and managing disasters[39]

Urban disasters (natural and industrial) can cause large loss of life and have enormous economic and financial costs. They are especially devastating to poor people, who often live and work in precarious conditions. The drive for mitigation increases as the effects of disasters, and the costs of failures to take action, become more immediate and widely perceived. Institutions are needed that can motivate action in advance of crisis and share the costs and benefits of preventive measures among citizens in a fair manner. Hazard mitigation requires improving knowledge, building constituencies for risk reduction, and strengthening institutions and partnerships across levels of government and the private sector.

Box 6.3

Political reform and stakeholder alliances overturning pollution

The city of Cubatão, in São Paulo State, Brazil, was castigated in the country's press in the late 1970s as the "valley of death" because of the extreme industrial pollution of its water, air, and soils that had occurred under decades of military dictatorship. Poor people lived in the midst of toxic waste dumps in an area also prone to natural disasters. In 1983 the state environmental protection agency (CETESB) initiated a pollution control program that significantly reduced pollution levels in less than 10 years. The agency managed to challenge the privileged position of entrenched industrial interests and make industrialists bear most of the costs of pollution control.

How was this achieved? A citizens' association of "victims of pollution and bad living conditions" (APVM) focused the public debate on the human toll of pollution and attracted widespread support for reform. While the program was advanced by high-level support for environmental improvement in the state government and aided by international opinion, three

changes at the national level in the early 1980s were key: the transition to democracy that allowed the emergence of independent social activism, free elections at the state level, and the elimination of media censorship.

In executing the program, CETESB relied on a suitable legislative framework and its status as the only agency with both the mandate and expertise for pollution control in the state. Still, the environmental clean-up of Cubatão was possible only after changes in the political rules of the game meant that progressive bureaucrats could ally with informed citizens to challenge the powerful economic elite that had stymied previous reform efforts. The experience of APVM forged a collective identity among victimized residents that moved them to act and set new terms for a collaborative relationship between the citizens and economic powers of the city.

Source: De Mello Lemos (1998).

Climate change and natural disasters are closely related. Global warming, projected to raise sea levels as much as 0.8 meter this century,[40] is particularly threatening to coastal cities—where most of the megacities in developing countries will be located by 2025[41]—as well as to small island states.[42] Climate-related events directly affecting urban areas include floods, mudslides, heat inversions, wind storms, and storm surges. Much of the economic and human toll will strike at the advancing frontier between the built environment and nature in the cities of developing countries, which also serve as reception areas for environmental refugees.

Although earthquakes claim fewer lives than weather-related events on an annual basis, between 40 and 50 of the fastest-growing cities in developing countries are in earthquake zones.[43] Exposure to such hazards and the reduced ability to provide basic services after a crisis can jeopardize a city's attractiveness as a business location.

Building knowledge. Knowledge about the hazards may be scant or absent, even among residents most at risk, yet community awareness of physical hazards is fundamental for mitigation efforts. Comprehensive vulnerability assessments using remote sensing, satellite imagery, risk and loss estimation modeling can help document and reduce physical, social, and economic vulnerability. Changing physical infrastructure and innovative techniques for retrofitting buildings can improve disaster prevention. So can "soft," nonstructural methods—those that increase

hazard information, create new knowledge, build the capacity of institutions, and train and raise the awareness of decisionmakers and the communities at risk.

Estimating losses can make the financial case for preparedness. Memphis, Tennessee, calculated a $0.5 million cost for retrofitting water pumping stations to be disaster resistant—compared with $17 million to replace each pump and $1.4 million for each day the system is out of service.[44] But developing countries rarely have well-documented, location-specific, and hazard-specific costing of hard and soft mitigation measures. Even more rare is costing used systematically for public education. Without an educated constituency collective decisions on disaster policies are usually dominated by better-off members of the community. Their priorities can differ greatly from those of poor people, who risk a larger share of their assets in a disaster.[45]

Creating incentives and constituencies for risk reduction. Indispensable for mitigation strategies are strong disaster prevention proponents and the political will to lead regulatory changes and financial appropriations. With limited resources developing countries must rely on partnerships of all actors. In the United States disaster prevention started with coalitions of scientists, emergency relief organizations, professional associations, and other civic groups who lobbied governments to fund research and hazard mitigation strategies. This movement received impetus when the Federal Emergency Management Agency (FEMA), armed with a federal mandate and incentives, took the lead and promoted local and state initiatives (such as the regional Earthquake Preparedness Projects in California), but still worked through civic and professional partners.

The public needs to decide on acceptable levels of risk, comparing the immediate benefits of expenditures on other social priorities with the delayed benefits of reduced loss of life and asset replacement cost following a potential disaster. These tradeoffs can be eased when well-designed incentives change private behavior to help prevent hazards. Examples include reducing insurance premiums on residential property when basic hazard-resistant steps are taken, offering disaster insurance with strict enforcement of building code provisions, or providing tax holidays or grants for mitigation.[46] Poor residents, for whom insurance or fiscally based incentives may not be practical, would benefit from urban planning for slum prevention, enforceable environmental zoning in cities, and resettlement combined with community-based upgrading and tenure regularization schemes (discussed below).

Recent disasters can motivate countries to undertake some of these measures and instill longer-term thinking. Gujarat State in India is trying to establish effective disaster management institutions following the January 2001 earthquake that killed 15,000 people. The state has a new disaster management authority to coordinate all aspects of the response, working with NGOs, the private sector, universities, local communities, and external donors. The program includes predisaster preparedness and postdisaster response, reconstruction, and disaster prevention. Incentives are being introduced to build constituencies for disaster prevention by capitalizing on the population's heightened awareness and willingness to change.

Adapting to climate change. Adapting to climate change may be more difficult since the risks mount gradually and less visibly—but no less urgently.[47] Coastal cities and other population centers (especially small island states) will need to invest in protective barriers and possibly to relocate residences and essential public facilities through managed retreat. Priorities for such adaptation should be given to built areas and infrastructure that require urgent attention in any case, such as vulnerable informal settlements and outgrown sanitation and drainage systems. Adaptive expenditures will place a significant burden on the public sector, private utility companies, and, indirectly, on the urban economy. Low-income residents living in harm's way will need particular assistance.

Balancing interests to provide urban public goods

Urban areas can enhance and enrich social integration through the provision of public goods and cultural and environmental amenities. Achieving these benefits requires institutions to channel dispersed interests of a pluralistic public—to give expression to the social value of equitable access to publicly provided assets, and to identify future needs in land development and redevelopment—and sometimes to overcome powerful vested interests. To provide other urban public goods, similar mechanisms are needed to balance competing interests (for a well-integrated transport system, and sanitary solid waste disposal),[48] and to express dispersed interests (for drainage). Foresight, political will, and a governance system accountable to a wide array of stakeholders are key ingredients for achieving credible commitments.

Balancing private and public interests in land use and committing to priorities in the public interest
The challenge in anticipating urban population growth is to focus on the most socially, environmentally, and economically important aspects of future land uses, and commit to credibly executing these public choices. New settlements in or near existing urban areas require the following actions:

- Setting aside rights of way for primary transport arteries
- Proscribing settlement or other development of areas that are unsuitable because of environmental fragility or vulnerability to disasters (steep hillsides, flood zones)—and protecting fragile environmental resources (urban watersheds, wetlands)
- Reserving areas for amenities, especially parks, and developing other public spaces with social and cultural value.

This effort has to take into account emerging supply and demand and avoid overdetermining the city's future. A frequent problem is that city master plans may exclude large high-value sites, especially at the periphery, from urban development, while failing to fence off environmentally vulnerable or risky sites in an enforceable way. Although urban expansion into agricultural areas may pose real social welfare trade-offs, much so-called agricultural zoning around cities is outdated. It neglects the greater economic and fiscal benefits of urban land uses and fosters opportunities for corruption and speculation. Urban municipalities often have much less say over land conversion at the periphery than do national governments or powerful elites.

To identify minimal, high-priority, and enforceable limits on land use, local institutions must first identify the socially desired outcomes for urban development (such as which environmentally sensitive areas to protect—recall the Catskill example in chapter 2, and how much green space to set aside) and then commit credibly to achieving them. In Conakry, Guinea, the municipality developed a basic structure plan for the city in the early 1980s. Thirteen years after the plan was adopted to create the primary roads and infrastructure networks essential for urban mobility and productivity most of the networks are in place. Now the city's focus is on upgrading densely populated neighborhoods by providing internal and secondary roads linking to this network, and basic municipal services (drainage and solid waste collection), as part of an integrated citywide program.

Urban redevelopment for public goods. The economic and social vitality of cities is enhanced by promoting and protecting their cultural characters, developing public spaces and other amenities as equitable social assets, and converting abandoned and degraded land and waterfronts to new uses. Civic groups and private entrepreneurs can motivate such collective action, but often formal partnership and political leadership from local and national government are needed.

A city's historical heritage and social culture embedded in its neighborhoods and structures are valuable assets.[49] Vision and voice for dispersed and future interests are necessary to give appropriate weight to such intangible values, to counteract pressures to rebuild and modernize for commercial or high-income uses, and to prevent the gradual degradation of the built environment because of poor households' need for affordable places to live. In the early 1980s the city government of a historic Chinese city, Ping-yao, almost demolished the old city wall to build a wide road. Protests by scholars and residents, with help from officials and news media elsewhere in China and abroad, persuaded the government to locate new development outside the old city. The

city's economic decline has been reversed and it now enjoys a new distinction for tourism as the only city in China preserved within old city walls.[50]

The use and reuse of public spaces provides an opportunity to cultivate a city's natural resources—by preserving or creating parks, architecturally distinctive streetscapes and squares, and waterfronts. Such urban amenities are part of a city's portfolio of assets and broad access to them enhances well-being and strengthens social capital, since poor and wealthy alike can enjoy them. In the fast-growing cities of the developing world reserving open spaces requires strong commitment (championship) and forward thinking to speak for these dispersed interests. A former mayor of Bogotá saw in the hundreds of kilometers of drainage canals crisscrossing the city a way of connecting all parts of the city by converting them to walkways and bikeways. Despite resistance from some quarters, the city realized this vision, creating one of the world's largest pedestrian paths lined with trees, lighting, open sculptures, and benches—and linking some of the poorest neighborhoods of the city with golf courses and parks.[51]

Remediation of despoiled sites and abandoned structures (brownfields) can also present many benefits to a city. Overcoming the institutional and financial barriers to brownfield redevelopment is important to correct the environmental and social blight in surrounding areas and to prevent the flight of new (greenfield) investments to the urban periphery. Extensive experience in industrial countries underscores the social and economic benefits when brownfields are redeveloped as an integral part of neighborhood renewal processes.[52] Public–private investment partnerships require clear legal frameworks for property rights, risk sharing, and assigning liability for pollution clean-up. Efforts in Budapest to identify a redevelopment program for the Csepel steel works on an island in the Danube River in the middle of the city have been delayed by difficulties in negotiating with more than 200 owners of the site, which was hastily privatized during the post-socialist transition.

Leadership and foresight are also key to urban renewal. In the mid-1980s the mayor of Istanbul led an initiative to clean up an inlet of the Bosphorus, known as the Golden Horn, which had become putrid from the dumping of sewage and solid waste. The program—part of a large metropolitan sewerage investment to extend sanitation to some 300,000 low-income residents and treat municipal water—also relocated the polluting industries and warehouses. The water quality of the Golden Horn has been restored. Recreational and tourist activity has reemerged. And public and private investment has rejuvenated the area's historic and cultural assets.[53]

Balancing competing interests for accessibility[54]

Urban transportation is closely tied to urban land development and can create both positive and negative externalities as cities grow. Urban transport is best addressed as part of integrated urban strategies that can attend to the interests of all user groups (including poor people, women, and the mobility-impaired) and anticipate long-term needs that have no vocal constituency. Most cities in developing and transition economies are sufficiently densely populated to support extensive public transport,[55] and often include (depending on physical and climatic conditions) walking and cycling as major modes of travel. It is important that institutions are developed that balance and give weight to these interests. And since motorization is still at an early stage, it is likely that an urban transport strategy will emerge in such an institutional setting that focuses on balancing roads and private cars with other alternatives within a broader urban perspective.

Traffic congestion is one of the major negative urban externalities. As cities grow and become richer, vehicle ownership and use increase more rapidly than available road space. Expanding road space tends to stimulate more car use, so the imbalance continues. Experience shows that more road building is not the route to a congestion-free future. Most important is how the space devoted to roads is used and managed—for example, it should be organized hierarchically to separate traffic flows for different purposes. Managing demand, through taxes and impact fees on road construction and use, is politically much more difficult once car dependency becomes entrenched. Cities need a minimal amount of space for circulation relative to their size to operate efficiently, and early reservation of rights-of-way for major transport routes is essential to good urban planning.[56] Transport infrastructure costs rise sharply as cities become more densely developed, and the investments are large and "lumpy," so requirements need to be considered well in advance of actual demand.

Although the environmental and efficiency costs of motorization and related traffic congestion attract vocal (and often competing) lobbies, the interests of poor people are less well expressed politically.[57] Yet poor people lose when the dominance of private vehicle traffic undermines support for public transport and space for nonmotorized options. Poor people become more restricted in their mobility—and as pedestrians, they suffer most from road accidents. High-speed roads often carve up low-income neighborhoods, increasing noise and ground-level pollution. During the construction of the U.S. interstate highway system in the 1950s, for example, the planning criterion of selecting "least cost" sites caused intrusion not only into environmentally sensitive areas (wetlands and so on) because their market land value was low, but also into the poorest urban neighborhoods, severing them from the rest of the city and hastening their deterioration. The massive public spending on the highway system, unbalanced by sustained support for other transport modes, accelerated the flight to the suburbs of wealthier city residents and the economic decline of older inner-city areas, contributing to persistent social problems in U.S. cities.

Urban transport strategies that focus on the mobility of all residents, not just a few, to make transportation more sustainable environmentally, socially, and economically contain a balanced array of measures:

- Managing the existing road infrastructure to improve the traffic flow and calm speeds around densely populated areas
- Giving weight to the effects of induced traffic and impacts on nonmotorized transport and the environment when evaluating new road projects
- Internalizing the social costs of road use by charging land developers impact fees to finance new roads, introducing road congestion pricing (or some proxy), and charging the full social costs of parking
- Improving the viability of public transport by giving priority to buses on restricted lanes, ensuring adequate financing, and improving operational efficiency through regulated competition
- Protecting pedestrians and nonmotorized transport users by providing safe walkways and bicycle paths
- Providing rail-based mass transit in very large cities with high transport demand, where it can also serve low-income users, as in some Latin American cities.

Box 6.4
Meeting environmental, social, and economic objectives through urban transport strategy in Bogotá

Since 1998 Bogotá has implemented a comprehensive urban mobility strategy that includes promotion of nonmotorized transport (bicycle paths), restriction of automobile use during certain hours and days (approved by public referendum), and a bus rapid transit system (Transmilenio). Using exclusive busways on central lanes of major roads and a network of feeder buses and stations, the system provides express and local services and carries 45,000 passengers an hour per direction. Vehicle operations, passenger access, and ticketing services are carried out by private companies through competitively tendered concessions. The new bus system is attracting ridership by former car users and restoring respect for public transport.* By mid-2001 the system had achieved high productivity (630,000 trips per weekday) at a fare that fully covers operating costs, with no traffic fatalities. Some air pollutants have been reduced by 40 percent, and user travel time is down by 32 percent.

Bogotá's transport strategy benefited from strong mayoral leadership in articulating a long-term vision and representing the interests of noncar users despite the resistance of motor vehicle lobbies. The program also required partnership between the private concessionaires and the municipal government, which financed and implemented the physical infrastructure and provided the dedicated road space.†

* Presentation by Peñalosa (2001), updated April 2002.
† World Bank (2002a), box 8.2

Planning and managing transport requires balancing conflicting interests in an environment of uncertainty and risks. Many decisions have long-term impacts and high costs, so coordination across the various modes of transport is needed. Cities that have managed to execute a comprehensive transport strategy, such as Curitiba, Bogotá, and Singapore,[58] have combined political will and leadership with technical and professional competence (box 6.4). Similar integrated approaches are necessary to ensure traffic safety.

Reaching a consensus and compensating losers—sanitary solid waste disposal

The production of solid waste (including hazardous waste) increases as economic activities shift from agriculture to industry, incomes rise, and lifestyles change. Its improper disposal can have environmental consequences. Managing waste removal and dis-

posal is a coordination problem. Waste collection is usually the responsibility of municipal government, but in many cities the formal service covers at best half the waste generated. Informal private operators do much of the pick-up, sorting, and recycling of garbage, and communities sometimes provide the service for themselves.[59] But these informal solutions are rarely well integrated into a safe disposal system. Improper disposal of solid waste damages drainage systems, contaminates groundwater, and releases methane, a potent greenhouse gas.

A key constraint to collective action and coordination is the NIMBY syndrome ("not in my back yard")—no community wants the waste disposal site. Disposal is then neglected, or a facility is located without public discussion near the population with the least political clout. Successes in public decision-making on solid waste disposal facilities (sanitary landfills or incinerators) suggest several lessons:[60]

- First, public discussion should be early and open, with site selection based on transparent criteria agreed on in advance by candidate communities.[61]
- Second, communities adversely affected should be compensated, through financial transfers or access to other desired investments. In Canada and the United States the selected community typically receives "host fees."
- Third, the project sponsor needs to be credible in meeting commitments to minimize environmental impacts, through proper operation and management. The facility should be monitored by the local community and local authority—and designed to retain functions for informal collectors, so that they can acquire less risky livelihoods.

The problem of safe disposal is particularly acute in large cities and metropolitan areas where several municipal governments need to reach agreement on siting and cooperate to share costs and reach economies of scale. Many large cities have been stymied by the absence of an appropriate governance arrangement. In Monterrey, Mexico, a special-purpose metropolitan authority runs a public company to operate a sanitary landfill serving eight municipalities. In Santiago, Chile, 14 communes created a jointly owned corporation to build and operate a landfill and gas recovery system through voluntary cooperation rather than a formal metropolitan authority. These examples show that collective action by governments, as by other social entities, requires goodwill, trust, and a conviction that interests are fairly balanced (in this case, reflected in burden sharing of costs and environmental spillovers from the disposal facility).[62]

Finding voice for dispersed interests—drainage
Many cities also lack effective storm drainage systems, and ill-planned construction closes off natural water courses. In Algiers, where massive flooding in November 2001 caused 800 deaths (700 in densely populated neighborhoods), a natural water runoff channel in the city had been converted to a paved road. Overflowing of clogged storm drains and sewers during high rainfall is projected to become a greater source of disasters in major cities than river flooding.[63]

The key institutional issue is that drainage has no clear constituency until major problems occur. Local governments may become motivated to act on drainage issues when flooding affects the business district, as in Cabanatuan in the Philippines, where the local business community put pressure on the mayor to invest in drainage infrastructure. In Kampala the local authorities had neglected for years to protect past investments in the Nakivubo channel from settlement encroachment and obstruction with solid waste. There, and in communities in Ethiopia, recent reforms expanding local democracy have raised the profile of drainage as a priority for public expenditure.

Inclusion and access to assets: Challenging the institutional roots of urban slums

As noted in chapter 3, the evolution of good institutions to solve coordination problems is itself determined by the extent of inclusion and access to assets by a wider public. Access to urban land—the city's scarce natural resource and most durable asset—is key to a city's economic, social, and environmental sustainability. Institutions need to allow people to settle securely, so that they can envision a future for their families and their city, while allowing for flexibility in land use. Informal, illegal, or quasilegal neighborhoods with seriously substandard living conditions, often generically called slums, are an obvious manifestation of inequitable access to physical and financial assets, to secure land tenure, and to po-

litical representation. They also reflect the failures of government to guide and facilitate the growth of low-income housing and basic services for incoming migrants through appropriate policy and planning. These communities grow through the enormous entrepreneurial energy of residents who build the city and provide its labor. With the right institutional environment they can evolve more quickly into safe, healthful, and hospitable urban neighborhoods.

Geographical and environmental manifestations of exclusion
Poverty and its many manifestations in cities can be appreciated only by looking at disaggregated (especially spatially detailed) data. In Cali, for example, the incidence of income poverty is highest in periurban neighborhoods with precarious environmental and infrastructural conditions. The eastern area (formerly a lagoon) and the western zone (steeply sloped) are settled mainly by poor migrants and minorities living in very crowded housing (figure 6.2).[64]

Figure 6.2
Poverty in Cali, Colombia: 1999 headcount rates

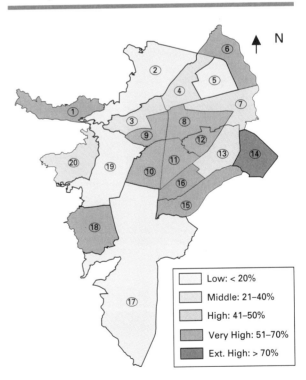

Low: < 20%
Middle: 21–40%
High: 41–50%
Very High: 51–70%
Ext. High: > 70%

Source: Departamento Administrativo de Planeación Municipal de Cali, Colombia, 1999.

Reducing the disparities in welfare among residents within cities is one of the starkest challenges to a sustainable urban future.[65] These disparities are often masked by official data on access to water and sanitation, which do not accurately reflect problems with the quantity, quality, and reliability of services—or the numbers of people sharing facilities in dense settlements. In Accra, Ghana, for example, only 12 percent of the richest quintile of the population, but more than 66 percent of the poorest quintile, share one toilet or latrine with more than 10 other households.[66] Some 44 percent of households in Mysore, India, have water connections, but only 8 percent of those in informal settlements do.[67]

Such inequities help account for infant mortality rates three or more times higher among the low-income households of many cities than among high-income households (figure 6.3).[68] Poor people in Accra and São Paulo have higher death rates not only from communicable diseases of childhood but also from respiratory and circulatory diseases and injuries from traffic accidents and homicides. The threats affect all age groups, creating a web of insecurity.[69]

Local groups and agencies concerned with environmental health problems and epidemiology in cities are combining census data and household surveys with a geographic-referenced information system to map service access and health outcomes by neighborhoods. In Porto Alegre, Brazil, for example, the local authorities use a detailed environmental atlas for planning and management and for education in schools.[70]

The multiple environmental health and safety risks in urban areas are related largely to the conditions and location of settlement. Hundreds of millions of urban dwellers have few affordable options other than to live on sites (usually public lands) where development has not been approved and where residents are therefore not officially entitled to urban services or protections. Such informal neighborhoods remain in squalid condition for decades. Since the home is also a major source of income (both from rental and home-based industry) and the household's main private asset, the social and economic burden of such physical conditions is profound. Many slums are also disaster-prone sites—on hillsides or floodplains, or near factories. Monsoon flooding in Mumbai claims hundreds of victims among the illegal occupants of hazardous areas—including the canals meant to drain the excess water.

The population of urban slums is estimated by U.N.-Habitat at 837 million in 2001. Based on 1993 regional breakdowns, more than half are in Asia accounting for one-third of the region's urban population. Slums house more than one-half of all urban residents in Africa and about one-quarter in Latin America and the Caribbean.[71]

Slum neighborhoods typically have disproportionately high concentrations of low-income people (though not necessarily the extreme poor, such as the homeless). They may also house middle-income residents in cities where formal provision of infrastructure and housing markets are very weak. Residents of inner-city slums, typically settled for many years, generally have better availability of infrastructure (though it is often poor in quality and unreliable). They also have more established communities and less physical isolation than residents of newer settlements, usually on the outskirts. Both groups suffer from the stigma of their neighborhood that impedes their access to employment and to wider networks of social capital.[72]

Factors associated with crime and violence are also common in zones of deprivation within cities. The

Figure 6.3
High inequality in health outcomes in urban areas

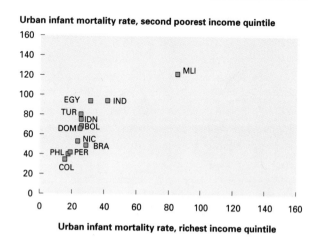

Urban infant mortality rate, second poorest income quintile

Urban infant mortality rate, richest income quintile

Note: Data shown for all countries with data base for which adequate size sample is available (lowest quintile inadequately represented to be shown). Infant mortality rates measured as deaths before one year of age per 1,000 live births.
Source: Demographic and Health Surveys (see www.measuredhs.com).

highest homicide rates in Cali are found in its poorest neighborhoods. Surveys of urban residents in Guatemala and Colombia identified tensions over access to water as a cause of violence.[73] Analysis of administrative regions or municipalities in São Paulo State categorized their territorial exclusion based on physical hazard, provision of urban services, and security of tenure. Municipalities with the most precarious living conditions had the highest homicide rates, and those with the least territorial exclusion were the least violent. The regions with the worst outcomes also had very high income inequality.[74] Such exclusion contributes to frustrated expectations, defeated hopes, and mistrust in society's future.

Even in some transition economies many of the urban poor live in severely substandard, quasilegal settlements (for example, 15–25 percent of urban residents in the Former Yugoslav Republic of Macedonia, many of them ethnic minorities).[75] But not all informal settlements feature low-quality housing. Some illegal or irregular housing is produced by commercial developers or politically influential parties who speculate that property investments will be regularized later (akin to the race for land rights at the agricultural frontier described in chapter 5). Such land speculation is encouraged when countries lack clear policies on tenure security, and authorities are unable to balance interests and articulate public choices regarding land use, or commit to enforcing them.

Empowerment through access to assets: security of tenure

Although slums reflect institutional failures in housing policy, housing finance, urban planning, public utilities, and local governance, one of the most fundamental failures is the absence of tenure security. Security of tenure means "protection from involuntary removal from land or residence except through due legal process."[76] The emphasis is thus on preventing forcible and arbitrary eviction, whether of individual households or entire settlements. The significance for urban poverty underlies its inclusion under the Millennium Development Goals (MDGs) as indicator 31 ("Proportion of people with access to secure tenure"), related to Target 11 ("By 2020, to have achieved a significant improvement in the lives of at least 100 million slum dwellers") and Goal 7 ("Ensure Environmental Sustainability"). The issue is also a focus of the U.N.–Habitat Global Campaign for Secure Tenure and the Cities without Slums program of the multidonor Cities Alliance.

Lack of secure tenure in urban areas has not been systematically measured. Even the designation of residents as homeowners or tenants does not convey protection from summary eviction when land registration and the rule of law are poorly enforced.[77] Secure tenure is part of a country's hierarchy of rights, ranging from legal titles and contracts to customary recognition of use rights.[78] Providing secure tenure therefore does not pit the rights of squatters or tenants against those of private property owners and landlords, who should be protected under contract law. But countries permitting arbitrary eviction often also fail to enforce private real estate contracts and otherwise obstruct the private rental market, further disadvantaging low-income citizens.

By confirming the rights and responsibilities associated with the occupation and use of land, regularizing tenure status removes a major source of economic and political insecurity for households and for communities. It reduces some of the risks that discourage residents from investing in their houses and shops—and gives them a stronger stake in urban society and an incentive to work with local officials to obtain services. A study in Indonesia found that stronger tenure security increased the probability of demanding garbage collection.[79] And surveys of slum dwellers in Bangalore reveal that better tenure status has a significant and positive impact on willingness to engage in collective action to obtain urban services, even in culturally heterogeneous communities.[80]

A growing commitment by city, state, and national governments of Brazil to regularize slums or *favelas* has put in train a process of transformation (box 6.5). A key turning point was the 1988 federal constitution, which strengthened the role of local government and encouraged municipal policies to legalize and improve tenure conditions in these informal settlements. A groundbreaking new city statute enacted at the federal level in July 2001 provides a legal underpinning for municipalities to regularize *favelas* as part of concerted plans to combat spatial segregation and social inequity—and to create more inclusive and democratic urban governance.[81]

Security of tenure is both a collective good and a private good in the urban context.[82] Whole communities are threatened when shanty towns are bulldozed, while residents individually gain security

Box 6.5
Regularizing *favelas* in Brazil

In many cities in Brazil, large shares of the population—25 percent of the residents of Rio de Janiero and 40 percent in metropolitan Recife—live in informal or illegal settlements, often on public lands. These *favelas* are home to an essential workforce—a workforce subject to terrible health conditions, frequent natural disasters such as mudslides and floods, and crime. Official policy toward *favelas* in the past was that of neglect (with occasional introduction of services when politically expedient or necessitated by emergency) and threats of eviction. Not until the 1970s did most municipalities begin to even include such settlements on planning maps as provisional, despite their existence for decades in many cases. Transformation in these settlements has started to occur in recent years where local governments, supported by their state and the national government, have made commitments to sociopolitical as well as physical inclusion of the *favelas* into the city.

Beginning in the early 1980s a number of cities, most notably Belo Horizonte and Recife, initiated efforts to regularize or integrate the *favelas* into the urban fabric and give them legal recognition. New planning instruments were introduced at the national level to permit designating certain settlements as "special residential zones of social interest" (ZEIS), which permitted planning and zoning regulations to be adapted to the land use requirements of these communities. In Recife, a further mechanism (PREZEIS) was established in 1987 to institutionalize, for the first time, the process of integrating irregular settlements into the formal planning apparatus, with community participation, and allow for the provision of services and infrastructure to reduce disparities. Under this law Recife created a land tenure legalization commission charged to identify and address specific problems in each ZEIS through participation of multiple stakeholders—a device credited with enforcing the government's commitment to follow through with its regularization program despite resistance from conservative sectors. The state of Pernambuco has joined Recife's efforts by bringing investment resources to help cover the settlements designated for regularization across the metropolitan area.

Programs with similar objectives have been adopted in other Brazilian cities, including Porto Alegre, Rio de Janiero, and São Paulo. The Rio program (where the state government has also reversed its past resistance to *favelas*, by providing finance for building materials for residents without requiring collateral) is notable for its scale.* In Belo Horizonte and Porto Alegre the programs entail a strong emphasis on participatory budgeting and planning for investments in the settlements. A 1998 study by the Brazilian Institute for Applied Economics indicates that at least 794 municipalities have some kind of *favela* or informal settlement upgrading program and about 506 of these include some form of land tenure regularization.

Where tenure regularization policies have intended to transfer full individual freehold titles to the occupiers of public or private land, as in Belo Horizonte and Rio, this aspect of the program has been problematic to implement and less successful than the physical upgrading and service provision. Other municipalities, such as Porto Alegre and Recife, have used an innovative alternative legal instrument to promote individual and community security of tenure. This formulation, the "concession of the real right to use" (CRRU), is a leasehold that confers private property rights to publicly owned land for a period of up to 50 years, either for an individual or a community.† Combined with the designation of settlements as "zones of social interest," the CRRU protects residents from eviction and gives them broad property rights. This instrument permits the state to protect access for the low-income communities to land they occupy in order to promote socioeconomic integration of the city; it also serves to preserve scarce public land for current and future social uses. Settlements granted such use rights have gained physical improvements from private and public investment in housing and infrastructure, and increasingly take on the appearance of working class neighborhoods physically integrated with the adjacent areas.

Though still largely untested, the new national City Statute gives municipalities the tools to go even further in regularizing informal settlements. The Statute includes, for example, provisions for facilitating the transfer of privately owned land to the existing occupiers in cases where occupation has gone uncontested for at least five years. To complete the transformation in the quality of life and social inclusion of the urban poor, these political and legal commitments and investments need to be supplemented by a broader set of policies that also promote economic opportunity and counter other dimensions of poverty.

* The first phase upgraded about 60 *favelas* and 20 irregular subdivisions, affecting some 250,000 people, supported by an Inter-American Development Bank loan in 1995. A second phase and loan in 2000 applies to 56 *favelas* and 8 irregular subdivisions, for about the same number of residents. The total costs of upgrading under these projects average $4,000 per household, which compares favorably to most housing programs and to many sanitation and social services projects. Brakarz (2002).
† In Brazil, the CRRU can be registered, allows transfer of right to legal heirs, selling, renting and use of land as collateral. It can be used as both individual and collective right (a form of condominium), and has a gender dimension, as women are given priority treatment in granting of use rights (Payne and Fernandes 2001; Fernandes 2002).
Source: Cira, background note for the *WDR 2003.*

when their settlement is accepted as an integral part of the urban fabric. Often there is enough stability of inhabitants that they confirm each others' rights to residence. Community organizations in informal settlements use their strongest asset (social networks) to protect their area from encroachment by new entrants, to resist involuntary resettlement, and to push for associated rights as urban citizens.[83] The Railway Slum Dwellers Federation in Mumbai (RSDF) successfully managed the resettlement of member households to permit a transport project with citywide benefits (box 6.6).

How important is a legal title? Experience in many developing countries confirms that households and

Box 6.6
How railway dwellers in Mumbai managed their own resettlement

In Mumbai, the commercial capital of India and home to 12 million people, some 24,000 families have lived for almost two decades along heavily traveled suburban rail lines, with some huts hardly a meter from the tracks. Besides risking death and injury, these residents suffer from a near-total absence of basic services.

A project to improve the city's traffic and transportation system required the resettlement of these slumdwellers. To represent civil society in the resettlement plan, the Maharashtra Government task force sought the participation of an alliance of The Society for the Promotion of Area Resource Centers (SPARC; a registered NGO), the National Slum Dwellers Federation (NSDF), and a savings cooperative of women slum and pavement dwellers. A constituent unit of the NSDF is the RSDF, made up of the Mumbai families who would have to move for the railway project.

By June 2001 the alliance had resettled 10,000 families, in just over a year, without force, to accommodations with assurance of secure tenure and basic amenities of water, sanitation, and electricity. How was this done? The Mumbai Metropolitan Regional Development Authority in charge of the railway project was willing to give up some of the powers normally held by government agencies in resettlement and rehabilitation—determining eligibility, obtaining baseline information on the community, allocating housing. Such functions, which provide opportunities for rent-seeking and corruption, were ceded to the NGO alliance.

Long before the railway project was initiated, the RSDF had collected information on the railway dwellers as a means of community mobilization and had the trust of its own members as a resource for the resettlement process. The households agreed on the criteria for allocating permanent and temporary accommodations. In the new settlements the families have formed lending cooperatives to compensate for income forgone as a result of the move.

The experience shows that a mobilized and self-governing community of poor people can act collectively for its own good and for the good of the larger urban society when there is mutual trust and flexibility on the part of the community and government agencies.

Source: Burra (2001a).

communities realize significant benefits in moving from highly insecure tenure to de facto tenure (more secure though not fully legal).[84] Granting individual legal titles (freehold) is sometimes expected to confer additional advantages, such as greater access to housing loans and a more active housing market.[85] But this requires supportive banking and real estate institutions, which have often not materialized because of other limitations, including low incomes and the reluctance of lenders to finance incremental home improvements, the main way poor people provide their own housing.[86] In the transition economies of Europe and the Former Soviet Union, some of the incentive effects of housing privatization have been limited by the informational and financial impediments in the real estate markets.[87]

Titling can even worsen poor people's overall access to affordable land and housing. That can happen when titles are extended only to certain settlements, when tenants are forced out by higher rents after titling, or when slumdwellers are resettled into new neighborhoods with deeds of ownership but no assistance in acquiring infrastructure services.[88] Effective demand for legal titles is therefore often less than would be expected by observed increases in land values.[89]

Legal titling can also have significant administrative costs, especially since many cities lack good cadastres, leading to protracted legal battles over ownership status. The COFOPRI program in Peru achieved a much higher volume of legal titling (one million deeds issued in four years) than did similar efforts in other countries. But this has been possible because of the large tracts of government-owned land on the urban periphery. Titling in older urban areas of the country has progressed more slowly because of ownership disputes.[90] An alternative to formal titling and cadastres that can be quite effective and easy to implement to aid service delivery and acknowledge occupancy is street addressing—the mapping and naming or numbering of streets and homes in informal settlements. This system, used in 15 West African countries, aids utilities in billing for services and permits the simple taxation of plots.[91]

When residents in informal neighborhoods do not fear arbitrary eviction, they can devote their social capital to negotiate claims for services with local government or utility companies and take collective action to improve their settlements.[92] In Pune, India, a residents' organization used similar techniques of community mobilization and self-assessment as in Mumbai to respond to their own demands for sanitation, after these had been long neglected by the municipal authorities. The Pune slumdweller alliance (mainly the women) assessed the needs of residents, managed the construction with innovative designs to meet the needs of different user groups, and set up effective payment and maintenance arrangements. Their efforts resulted in a record outturn of latrines in just a few years, serving about half of the city's 1 million slumdwellers.[93] In Santo Domingo, the Dominican

Republic, residents' associations of three low-income settlements took similar steps. These settlements, located on the sides of ravines are vulnerable to frequent landsides. Association members, mainly the women, designed and managed their own disaster mitigation program by building retaining walls and making other infrastructure improvements.[94]

Institutions for sustainable urban development

Good urban governance requires institutions to reveal and balance divergent interests and to commit to solutions for collective welfare. Some institutional arrangements are particularly important to ensure performance of these functions across the range of urban issues:

- A structure of responsibility sharing and coordination that links the community, local government, and provincial and national levels of government and empowers the appropriate actors to address problems at each level
- A forum for wide participation in strategic thinking, to enable common understanding and consensus, motivate actions, and assess progress
- Networks for communication and capacity building among practitioners and stakeholders.

As noted, some informal arrangements that work in rural areas can be paralleled in urban communities, especially in neighborhoods. But such informal institutions are often asked to do too much. They can stimulate private enterprise but not enable firms to grow. And they can provide support to households but not confer all the services, economic security, or political legitimacy that the population deserves at the scale the city requires. The greater scale and complexity of urban life thus require effective formal institutions that operate with greater predictability, transparency, and adaptability.

What prompts such institutions to emerge and grow? Often major changes seem to come about through sudden crises—a disease outbreak or natural disaster—or the rise of a charismatic leader. In recent years democratization and fiscal decentralization have given new legitimacy and authority to local governments (chapter 7).[95] And globalization has been creating new opportunities, bringing in new knowledge, and raising new expectations for addressing urban challenges.

Empowering the appropriate level of actors and ensuring coordination

The environmental and social assets needed for sustainable urban development get more complex with increasing scale of settlement. Moving from neighborhood to city, to region, and to nation implies more extensive environmental and social linkages and impacts, increasing the divergence of interests and potential for conflict, and greater technical and institutional requirements for coordinating those divergent interests.

Taking responsibility for urban services and spillovers at the lowest practical level—the principle of subsidiarity—is a basic condition for mobilizing collective action. Subsidiarity empowers those with most at stake and strengthens the legitimacy of higher government through power sharing. Decentralizing urban services to local government is desirable for enhancing the voice of urban citizens and the access to credible information, but it requires the respective authorities to be accountable and have the means to address problems at their level—and that depends on the framework of intergovernmental financial relationships.[96]

Political tensions across levels of government are common. Central governments frequently impose unfunded mandates on local governments, and local governments may innovate without getting adequate support from central governments. Local governments can also be less progressive than central governments and obstruct needed reforms. In China, some local governments resisted disseminating information on city environmental conditions well after the State Environmental Protection Agency had authorized it, while others (in Jiangsu province) moved on disclosure policies—experimentally—in advance of the central government's commitment.[97]

Collective action in neighborhoods. Local environmental problems, such as removing solid waste from the neighborhood, can often be addressed by coordination at the community level. The commonality of interests makes collective action possible either to solve problems internally or to obtain what is needed from other parties (government or utilities). Grassroots and community organizations that move beyond confrontation to engagement with city government have greater prospects for obtaining sustainable benefits for the urban poor.[98] Experience in Pakistan, the Philippines, and Thailand with programs for basic infrastructure and housing improvements in low-income neighborhoods demonstrates what community associations can achieve as key players in partnership with government and the private sector. Those partnerships, however, require a long-term commitment to sustain them.[99]

The main weakness in many such programs has been the lack of continuity in financial and political support from formal institutions. In particular, city agencies and utilities need to assume responsibility for scaling up and maintaining infrastructure networks and such services as drainage, lighting, and parks beyond the neighborhood. Links with off-site infrastructure (roads or solid waste disposal sites) are often inadequate because of weak coordination with responsible government agencies, reducing the environmental and other benefits.

Many urban neighborhoods have also used their internal social networks to create protective institutions to ensure local public safety, such as through community "crime watch" activities—but this also requires the close collaboration and support of formal institutions, such as the police. In the Warwick Junction district of Durban, South Africa, 50 traders from the community voluntarily patrol around the clock. The group was trained by metropolitan police on citizen's arrests, constitutional rights of individuals, and court procedures to ensure successful prosecutions. Their efforts have contributed to a reduction in crime, and new trust between the community and police has improved the rate of successful police investigations and prosecutions. But relations are still strained by the citizens' perceptions of inadequate formal policing in the city.[100]

Strong local (municipal) government. Most issues of sustainable development in urban areas extend beyond an individual neighborhood and require a permanent formal mechanism of collective action, through effective local government that works with communities but shoulders broader responsibilities. This is where clashes of interests among larger and more powerful stakeholder groups—and tradeoffs about priorities and who gets served—begin to occur, underscoring the need for representative governance.

Reforms to make municipal governments and their agencies more accountable and transparent to all constituents are thus at the core of improving sustainable development in cities. The reform agenda comprises:

- Increased democratization (electoral processes)
- Good practices and incentives for sound financial management
- Public participation and access to information in budgeting and investment planning
- Upgrading of skills and professionalism of government staff
- Monitoring and evaluation based on benchmarking and client feedback.

Many cities demonstrate innovative relationships between civil society and local government to increase pressures for performance in the execution of basic functions. Reform initiatives often gain ground through collaboration on concrete activities of the local government—such as the public review of municipal budgeting and procurement in Obninsk, Russia,[101] and the citywide referendum to affirm residents' willingness to pay for infrastructure improvements after flooding in Tijuana, Mexico.[102] Such initiatives can then launch wider, deeper processes of reform in other areas. Obninsk is now influencing reforms at the provincial level, and Tijuana transformed its disaster recovery plan into a series of innovations linking taxation and public work improvements. Participatory budgeting, which was initiated in Porto Alegre and has now spread to over 80 cities in Brazil, has dramatically transformed relationships between civil society and local government.[103]

As part of urban capacity building and decentralization in Senegal and Guinea some local governments have institutionalized public consultation in the production of their public investment and maintenance programs and embedded these programs in a contractual agreement between the city and the central government. This municipal contract commits the authorities at both levels to enforcing the agreed financial implications and reform measures promised to constituents.[104]

Collaboration across jurisdictions—metropolitan management.[105] The wide impact areas of many environmental spillovers, and the interdependence of major economic activities sharing spatially contiguous infrastructure networks and other services, require collaboration among local governments, as well as regional and national governments. This is especially true for systems implying economies of scale—citywide transportation, water resources management, pollution control, landfills, and wastewater treatment. But this next level in the hierarchy of collective action presents an even greater potential divergence of interests, especially over sharing costs and benefits. And fragmentation and excessive competition among municipalities are more the norm. In the more than 70 countries undergoing decentralization, with the notable exception of India, municipal laws and constitutional reforms have had the largely unintended effect of weakening the prospects for metropolitan solutions to large city problems.

A variety of organizational arrangements—formal and informal, in developing and industrial countries—have evolved over the years to meet the challenges of managing large cities. In one common pattern (as in Dhaka and São Paulo), jurisdiction for specific functions is assigned by geographic area, creating many general purpose local governments that may cooperate for specific purposes, such as gathering regional data or sharing the costs of expensive equipment and facilities. Sometimes this collaboration results in a specialized metropolitan area or district service, in which limited powers—usually for planning or preservation, as of watersheds or regional parks—are ceded to special authorities.

Formally constituted metropolitan authorities, created or authorized by national law, are less frequent. In a pattern called functional fragmentation, lower-tier governments are limited to basic functions such as water distribution and street lights, while a second tier handles areawide functions, such as freeways and water trunk supply lines, as in Mexico City (box 6.7). These second-tier governments can be autonomous bodies, sometimes with executive powers to carry out projects such as the development authority in Kolkata. In other cases, as was common in Latin America in the 1970s and 1980s, the metropolitan agencies have only a consultative role. The most formal arrangement—that of centralized metropolitan organizations as in Bangkok, Kuala Lumpur, and Seoul—is fairly rare and usually imposed by central government to manage a capital city.

Some cities, such as Johannesburg, have blended these models—and the original prototypes are also changing as demands shift. Globalization exposes cities to forces requiring a wider basis for management and planning—and more strategic direction. Metropolitan arrangements also seem to be responding to the need to connect voter-taxpayers with mechanisms of public choice. In the past few decades, London, Montreal, New York, Ottawa, and Toronto have

Box 6.7
Mexico City's search for metropolitan management arrangements

Mexico City has explored several organizational arrangements in recent decades. The urban agglomeration in the Valley of Mexico starts with the Federal District, the seat of the central government, an area with 10 million people divided into 16 boroughs or *delegations*. Surrounding the Federal District, but seamlessly connected in functional terms, are 12 contiguous municipalities (another 7 million people) in the State of Mexico. An even more encompassing definition (the Mexico City Region) covers nearly 100 municipalities in five states.

Various metropolitan commissions have been created to cover key areas of need. A water commission was formed more than 30 years ago to plan and implement a mammoth system of interbasin transfers to supply water to Mexico City. Similarly, an air quality commission has steadily grown to manage mobile sources of pollution. The commission has successfully eliminated lead from fuel and is working to reduce the volume of traffic and to improve vehicle operating efficiency.

A persistent problem, despite half a dozen planning and special purpose commissions, is coordinating the city's growth with water and transport infrastructure—for example, having mass transit connect residential areas to key concentrations of employment. Recent political reforms making the office of the mayor an elected position have sparked an active political debate about creating an entirely new metropolitan authority for Mexico City.

Source: Campbell, background note for the *WDR 2003*.

all followed an iterative path, moving first (in the late 1980s) from formal metropolitan bodies with executive authority to a system of fragmented, independent municipalities. By the end of the 1990s these cities had shifted back to various centralized systems, but with more democratic input from elected or appointed citizen groups.

As these and other arrangements evolve, international sharing of experience will be important. Leadership from national or provincial governments is often necessary to provide functional assignments and funding for metropolitan arrangements, since local governments do not cede powers easily, especially when it involves redistributing tax revenues across jurisdictions.[106]

Building consensus and strategies for sustainable urban development

An essential condition for coordination is having a shared understanding of the problem, knowing the costs and benefits of alternative solutions, and accommodating the concerns of different stakeholders. Two relevant sources of experience in revealing interests and reaching a consensus on what to do are local environmental action plans and city development strategies.

Since the Earth Summit in 1992 some 6,400 local authorities in 113 countries have either formally committed or actively undertaken to produce local environmental action plans (called "Local Agenda 21s").[107] These initiatives integrate environmental objectives into development plans, emphasizing participation and accountability. They articulate local concerns and motivate local stakeholders around shared priorities for the area's future. And they provide a basis for coordinating the work of different levels of government and sectoral agencies.

The city of Manizales, Colombia, with about 360,000 inhabitants, has formulated a local environmental action plan with wide consultation and integrated it into the municipal development plan and budget. The plan included measures to revitalize the city's architectural heritage, improve public transport, strengthen watershed management of the Chinchina River which provides water to the city aqueduct, reduce risks of landslides, create ecoparks, and define community environmental action plans. The plan also devised an innovative indicators program of "environmental traffic lights" to signal progress.[108]

Not all Agenda 21 exercises have been as participatory as planned, and the momentum for longer-term implementation has often waned—the difficulty of forging long-term commitments being one of the barriers to successful coordination noted in chapter 3. Success has been greater with sustained support by successive mayoral administrations, strong participation by a local NGO or university, and efforts to mobilize funding for local economic development. Most Local Agenda 21s have been undertaken in smaller cities, perhaps indicating the difficulty of consensus-building at a metropolitan scale. National government leadership has also been instrumental in replicating Local Agenda 21s within countries.

City development strategies are similar efforts in participatory strategic planning, but with a potentially broader focus of integrating environmental and productivity concerns within a propoor perspective.[109] They have been used to build consensus on a vision for the city and on the steps to achieve the vision. These strategies typically include a participatory assessment of the city's economic, social, and en-

vironmental conditions and prospects, and spell out priorities and action plans for both policy and investment. Some examples:

- A city development strategy in Cali, Colombia, helped explore stakeholder views on major public projects and led to changes in the city's investment priorities. The first phase, which also prompted discussion of violence as a key issue for the city, pointed out the need for better understanding of the local economy and employment constraints.
- In San Fernando, in the Philippines, a city development strategy helped reorder investment priorities for sanitation, among other outcomes.
- Santo Andre in São Paulo State focused its strategic planning on social inequities and exclusion—and undertook social mapping to target and monitor actions to reduce disparities.

A good practice for institutionalizing city strategies is to incorporate their key elements into the regular systems of city planning. While sustaining and implementing strategic planning remains a challenge, such efforts can reveal the priorities of various stakeholders and contribute to public pressure for change.[110] Two items that should be on the agenda of most city development strategies are: Getting ahead of the expanding urban frontier; and making urban density affordable and livable.

Getting ahead of the expanding urban frontier—guiding new settlements to prevent future slums. Cities and towns in developing countries will need to accommodate the projected doubling of urban population over the next generation. Even with institutional reforms to upgrade and integrate existing slums, new ones may form. Local governments have often shied away from acknowledging the need to anticipate and facilitate the growth of low-income settlements, instead letting them fend for themselves. Providing infrastructure networks after the fact is much more costly, however, especially for very dense settlements with irregular layouts or requiring resettlement. In Bogotá the urban development agency estimates that installing drainage networks is about three times more expensive in informal settlements than in planned neighborhoods.[111]

Political will is essential to create an institutional environment that senses and anticipates the demands from new entrants and permits forward thinking and partnership among government, pri-

Box 6.8
Leading the advance on urban settlement growth in Lima

Lima, Peru, 1977—As we stood on a hill overlooking a new settlement on the edge of a vast desert plain about 10 kilometers northeast of downtown Lima, the boy, about 7 or 8 years old, said he was an engineer. An engineer? "Well," he said, "I am helping the people draw the lines for the lots and build our barrio." The settlement, which consisted of little more than chalk lines and shanties of woven reeds and plastic sheets, was growing day by day, as new arrivals were trucked in by the National System for Social Mobilization (SINAMOS). The settlers helped the surveyors lay out the plots and clear areas for playgrounds and community facilities.

The core group of settlers had initially organized itself to squat on public land under high-tension power lines. They had come mostly from slums in the city center, where they rented rooms or lived with family. On the agreed-on night, walking in small groups and with plastic sheets wrapped around their bodies, they converged on the selected site and built their tents and shacks overnight. Having established themselves as a squatter settlement, they knew SINAMOS would remove them to a permanent, if unserviced, settlement, one of the new *pueblos jóvenes*, or young towns.

SINAMOS, staffed mostly by young and deeply committed engineers, architects, and social workers, was established in the mid-1970s. Armed with enthusiasm and an understanding of the dynamics of settlements that John F.C. Turner had developed in Arequipa and Lima, SINAMOS set out to meet the challenge of rapidly growing squatter settlements on the outskirts of Lima.* They called the low-income communities *pueblos jóvenes*, which gave the squatter settlements a positive image.

SINAMOS developed a two-pronged approach. It upgraded existing *pueblos jóvenes*, relying on community participation and relatively little public investment. Then, as squatter settlements continued to appear, it began a massive slum prevention program, providing surveyed plots to meet anticipated demand for low-income housing. The first minimal structure plan was gradually detailed down to neighborhood layouts and engineering studies for trunk infrastructure.

Twenty years later the *pueblos jóvenes* had become well-consolidated, low-income and low-middle-income neighborhoods with most urban services, schools, clinics, markets, and other amenities. The key to the program's success was picking up signals of demand, balancing interests, and committing to implementation—matching social coordination with the aspirations of poor people.

*Turner and Fichter (1972).
Source: Chavez, background note for the *WDR 2003.*

vate investors, and households. Valuable experience in planning low-income settlements has come from sites and services programs, usually initiated by local government or its agents, to provide basic plot layout and minimal infrastructure (such as core sanitary facilities) in advance of spontaneous development. Such a program in Lima aimed to prevent the growth of squatter areas by anticipating demand (box 6.8).

Forging long-term commitments is key to successfully getting ahead of the frontier. A strong supply response is important in making such schemes sustainable. Many well-meaning programs have been stymied by the lack of affordable land and housing—even for the middle-income groups. This has reduced political support for minimal design/minimal cost approaches, and poor people have been pushed to the end of the service queue. In Conakry the municipality's basic structure plan aimed in part to set aside periurban areas for new settlements and to test public-private partnerships for the production of serviced plots. The government planned to facilitate connection of the sites to infrastructure networks while the private investors, through payment of an "equipment contribution," were to ensure replication of the scheme. But the authorities could not commit to fully implementing this part of the plan when no private developers joined in, and resulting delays led to land disputes as squatters moved into the area. In El Salvador, however, a private commercial company (ARGOZ) has carried out a profitable land development scheme for low-income households for more than 25 years, with the help of a conducive legal framework for urban land conversion and a determination to keep design standards affordable.[112]

Making urban density affordable and livable. Accommodating the growth of population in cities will involve both physical expansion at the periphery and, in many cases, increased density of settlement in the city. Average urban densities are already vastly greater in major cities in developing countries, especially in Asia, than in North America and Europe—for example, Mumbai has almost 400 persons per hectare and Shanghai 500, compared with about 170 for the Barcelona metropolitan area, and 40 for New York.[113] The key issue for mature cities of developing countries is to provide the infrastructure and services (especially sanitation, public transport, and green spaces such as parks and playgrounds) needed to make already high densities livable and efficient, with ease of access to homes, work, and other places. The challenge for cities that have not yet filled in is to avoid making such spatial development unaffordable to their growing population.

Governments often try to control city size and influence the spatial form of city growth by regulating land use—through rules on minimum plot sizes and road widths, for example. It is common for cities to present inconsistent signals to investors: an official stance extolling compact urban form, countered by regulations and financial practices promoting low density land uses that favor middle- and higher-income groups. At the start of the economic transition in Cracow, Poland, municipal officials advocated higher density development of the inner city—yet rigid zoning persisted, inconsistent with both the planners' intentions and the market incentives.[114]

When land-use regulations aiming to limit densities are strictly enforced, as in Brasilia, they drive up the cost of inner-city housing and force poor people to the periphery, where infrastructure services and transport are unavailable or expensive.[115] Even cities that try to encourage development around public transport zones (such as Curitiba, Brazil) or to curb periurban expansion by imposing a green belt (such as Portland, Oregon) have seen denser land uses shift to the outskirts. In Mexico, the lack of financing for rehabilitation of existing housing or for most multi-family units, as well as vestiges of rent control, deter improvement of inner-city neighborhoods and promote development on the urban periphery.[116]

Urban growth controls aimed at tightly regulating densities and building codes can make access to urban assets of land and housing more inequitable.[117] Zoning that permits mixed land uses—consistent with how low-income neighborhoods develop naturally—is more advisable to keep jobs, services, and housing accessible. Fiscal and other policies that charge developers the full costs of providing the incremental infrastructure required for new settlements are also necessary to internalize the social cost of expanding urban development. These charges, which should be introduced before spatial expansion patterns are locked in, can be a combination of development impact fees and general taxation linked to property values.

But such charges will not reduce the demand for low-income settlements at the periphery in developing-country cities. Residents in these areas are not subject to formal taxation as long as they lack tenure security, and they already pay dearly for whatever infrastructure they are able to acquire from informal markets. So, regularizing informal settlements and facilitating low-cost land and housing development should be the highest priorities to ensure more equitable access to urban assets and more healthful, attractive living conditions in developing-country cities. These measures, coupled with appropriate allocation of urban land for public purposes—right of way, environmental easements, and so on—can transform the institutional basis for the evolution of urban form.

Promoting institutional learning and leadership through networks

Institutions for sustainable urban development need to embody incentives and processes for learning to better solve existing problems, and anticipate and prepare to deal with new problems. Increasingly this stimulus occurs through networking by local government and nongovernmental groups, through both associations and Web-based communications. Networks foster communication among peers, disseminate innovations, and enhance reputational pressures for change. They can also instill professionalism and high standards of performance, cultivating leadership. Increasing forums for public feedback also helps identify mistakes and make mid-course corrections.

A prime illustration of networking is the association of local, national, and international NGOs promoting the empowerment of communities and women in India and other countries. Through the alliance of SPARC, Mahila Milan (a women's savings cooperation), NSDF of India, and Slum Dwellers International (see box 6.6), practitioners and the urban poor share experiences on housing, urban services, and security of tenure. And by distributing information gathering methods (such as a self-census of slumdwellers), negotiating skills, and encouragement across the city and country and communicating with similar groups elsewhere, the alliance is increasing the scale and sustainability of its efforts.

Local governments are also networking internationally to learn from each other. National, regional, and international associations of local governments diffuse technical assistance, training, and ideas to member cities on a wide range of planning, operational, and fiscal issues.[118] The Union of Capital Cities of Ibero-America (UCCI) runs workshops and a Web site to help member cities learn about municipal modernization, solid waste management, urban transport, cultural heritage protection, and other issues.[119] The first cohort of Philippine cities that carried out city development strategies is helping others do the same, as part of a growing urban knowledge network involving the Philippine League of Cities, the China Association of Mayors, and other national groups in East Asia.[120] The Clean Air Initiative, a consortium of donor and private funding, is helping build capacity among cities in several regions—for example, to extend to African cities the Asian and Latin American experiences with removing lead-based fuel (chapters 3 and 7).

Networks also help to create incentives for sustained collective action by building reputational pressures within peer groups. Professional associations of local governments provide advice and standards on performance indicators that can be compared or benchmarked among member cities. Numerous external rankings of cities on quality of life or attractiveness to investors have been widely publicized—and have sometimes provoked corrective action.[121]

Conclusion

Achieving sustainable urban development requires forward-looking institutions that sense emerging problems, balance interests (especially by heeding the disadvantaged in society), commit to effective execution of agreed solutions, learn, and adapt. To make such institutions emerge and function well, it is necessary to confront basic inequities in access to assets, to empower dispersed interests and balance them against vested interests, and to build constituencies that can represent and commit to longer-term concerns.

Priority actions to reveal problems and divergent interests include developing disaggregated datasets, such as mapping environmental hazards within a city. Wide dissemination of such information, along with the costs and benefits of alternative solutions, is essential to building constituencies for action. Balancing interests and forging consensus can be facilitated through participatory strategic planning, aided by networking among practitioners and local governments for sharing local and global knowledge, innovations, and reputational pressures that stimulate leadership. These measures to strengthen the workings of institutions are fairly low in cost and can be implemented in the short term with existing capacities and resources. Support from the central government can help, but city stakeholders should take much of the initiative.

More fundamental changes would have wider and more lasting impact—and would be more instrumental in building new institutions. These deeper reforms include granting secure tenure, which can transform the balance of power between urban poor people and the rest of the urban society. Increasing the openness and accountability of local government, through democratic processes and participatory procedures, would also increase the responsiveness to the interests and problems of poorer constituencies and the legitimacy of government actions. Although these reforms are long in impact, experience shows that they can be initiated fairly quickly—provided there is political will. More complex measures—such as devising metropolitan management arrangements, and helping cities mitigate disaster risks and adapt to threats from climate change—may require more creativity, leadership, and resources. They also require greater and sustained support from national institutions.

Much of the future physical development that cities require can come at a lower cost when problems are recognized sooner rather than later; for example, setting aside rights-of-way for primary transport routes and parks and green spaces, facilitating new low-cost settlement, and guiding land development away from precarious or environmentally fragile areas. Investments to protect environmental health locally can also be made effectively and cheaply with the participation of residents to identify and carry out appropriate solutions. Significant advances in the quality of life of the less advantaged urban residents are possible when there is a shared commitment to integrating them fully into the life of the city; when there is flexibility on the part of government and private service providers; and when there is an openness by formal institutions to creative solutions developed by a diverse array of residents, actors, and networks in a city. Many activities in one location or community have consequences that affect other locations or communities. The principle of subsidiarity requires that these spillovers be addressed at higher levels—a principle based on matching the span of the spillover with the span of the jurisdiction best able to internalize the problem. The principle of inclusion ensures that people's well-being is a priority to be addressed at national and global levels, as discussed in the next chapters.

CHAPTER 7

Strengthening National Coordination

The biggest gains to society cannot be picked up through uncoordinated individual actions.

—Adapted from Mancur Olson

Many welfare enhancing opportunities can be realized only through coordinated activity, guided by institutions and policy.[1] Because of differences in laws, norms, and systems of government, the political and legal domain for coordinating activity is frequently the nation. Much private sector activity is national in scope and currencies, trade policies, safety regulations, and the like substantially circumscribe the markets. Furthermore since many externalities spill outside municipalities and regions, the nation is also the level at which interests can be balanced—either directly or by facilitating negotiation among localities. In fact, the national government plays a special role in providing a legal framework and in creating an enabling environment for partnerships in which the private sector, civil society, and all levels of government can contribute. Partnerships between government and think-and-do-tanks are one example (chapter 9); those between loggers, NGOs, and local and national government, to create mosaics conserving the productive land uses ahead of the agricultural frontier are another (chapter 5). The smooth evolution of property rights from communal to private (chapter 5) or the enhancement of tenure security in urban slums (chapter 6) depends critically on a facilitating national framework of norms, laws, and organizations. National leadership, including parliamentarians, can be fundamental in directly bringing about change, as with Tunisian President Bourguiba's support for the rights of women (chapter 4) and

Nelson Mandela's contribution to the formation of a modern South Africa (chapter 3). National actors also engage in and frame the pursuit of international goals, as elaborated in chapter 8.

This chapter focuses on the reasons that better outcomes emerge when the institutional basis for coordination is strong, encouraging the *make, exchange, and preserve,* which leads to growth and sustainable development, and discouraging the *take,* which leads to waste and conflict. The emphasis is on coordination at the national level—to manage a broader portfolio of assets (chapter 2). The national concerns analyzed here are critical for sustainable development and highlight the institutional levers that can strengthen coordination:

- Promoting inclusiveness and the participation of poor people (fostering access to assets and voice)
- Generating a sound investment climate (attending to macroeconomic fundamentals, strengthening governance, and providing basic infrastructure)
- Managing the environment (dismantling perverse subsidies, husbanding forests and fisheries, and curbing air pollution)
- Using resources effectively (avoiding the natural resource curse and ensuring that external aid does not undermine government accountability)
- Averting violent conflict (using natural resources well and confronting extreme poverty, thereby limiting their inciting effects).

Reducing poverty and providing a sound investment climate strengthens the incentive to work and build communities, and fosters the better use and protection of the environment. Strengthening the management of natural resources, especially certain concentrated resources, helps confront widespread destitution and reduces the likelihood of conflict.

The treatment of each of these issues will attempt to answer three questions:

- Does the institutional environment perform the key functions of picking up signals, balancing interests, and executing decisions?
- What institutional levers might improve the process of organizing dispersed interests and forging credible commitments?
- Do today's processes permit the emergence and evolution of more inclusive institutions over time?

Whether the development process is strong, sustainable, and responsive to new challenges depends largely on the answers to these questions.

Promoting inclusiveness

As noted in the previous chapters, the growth of assets, the production of assets, and the sustainability of social transportation depends on the quality of institutions whose evolution depends on voice and inclusivity of all members of society. There are not many simple adjustments that can be implemented in a 3- to 5-year period, but over a long period, sustained broadening is possible if it starts now and is steadily reinforced at the national level.

Promoting inclusiveness can help realize the potential of a nation more broadly. Poor or excluded people often cannot seize opportunities because of high barriers to participation. Without a stake in the social, economic, and political system, they do not have the incentive to partake, contribute, and be forward looking. Promoting wider participation, with greater access to assets and voice, is a pillar of steady growth and sustainable development, and the institutional environment is central to how national actors address this pressing issue.

Fostering access to assets and services
Much human potential is wasted because of the underprovision of services. A recent study of primary and secondary education based on surveys from 41 countries shows major gaps in educational attainments associated with gender and family income.[2] There is a large female disadvantage in education in

South Asia, North Africa, and western and central Africa, and poor people have limited access to education in almost all countries studied.

The study also shows that educated adults, especially women, tend to have fewer, but healthier and better-educated children. Beyond the generalized productivity gains associated with schooling, the surveys suggest that major opportunities are missed in poor countries. The expected returns to a nation of expanding education, particularly for girls, are now well documented, and education is a key part of the MDGs.

The wider extension of access to assets and services will help realize people's potential and improve dynamic efficiency. The institutional environment is central in redistribution through growth. Partnerships with donors are a promising avenue for financing greater inclusiveness, including spending on education and market-based land reform projects where the landless poor receive help in buying land and establishing farms (see chapter 5). This shifts the potential disincentive among taxpayers to higher-income countries, where the effect is easier to absorb. Regardless of source, national or international, the support for assistance from rich to poor will be more feasible politically when resources to provide public services are used more efficiently. In the case of international development assistance, for example, this means mitigating the negative incentive effects that aid can potentially generate, such as weaker government accountability (as discussed in greater detail below). Levers for addressing such incentive issues and improving services include involving the private sector and civil society in delivery; promoting decentralization (fiscal, administrative, and political); and facilitating parental and community influence in schools (voice and other means to raise transparency). Such measures also encourage the emergence of better institutions over time (chapter 4).

Strengthening voice
Mechanisms that strengthen voice—such as a free press, elections, and participation in civil society organizations—are keys to including the disenfranchised, building mandates, and generating consensus. Those excluded, without voice, will not take ownership of a process, action, or outcome. This effect also applies at different scales—local, national, global. Voice can do much to channel dispersed interests (chapter 3).

Box 7.1
Democracy, leadership, and decentralization in Latin America

Between 1989 and 1994 the República Bolivariana de Venezuela and Bolivia implemented sweeping institutional reforms that decentralized political power and enhanced opportunities for participation. In the República Bolivariana de Venezuela, citizens were given the right to vote for mayors and governors for the first time, reversing a long trend toward centralization. In Bolivia, the Law for Popular Participation created hundreds of municipalities and granted them 20 percent of government revenues.

In each case, institutional change resulted from a combination of three factors: widely felt social problems, political leadership, and ready-made proposals crafted by small groups of analysts. In the República Bolivariana de Venezuela, riots in Caracas forcibly demonstrated to political elites the depth of public dissatisfaction with the country's governing institutions. President Pérez responded by proposing a package of democratic reforms designed years earlier by a commission established under his predecessor. The creation of municipalities in Bolivia was an idea developed in a think tank associated with the party of President Sánchez de Lozada. The president became convinced that such an initiative held promise for addressing the concerns of increasingly vocal indigenous groups and local communities.

Leadership played an important role in the decision to decentralize power and in the choice of specific institutional approaches. Political leaders exercised substantial discretion in seeking to balance interests through decentralization, overcoming opposition from vested interests. In Bolivia, for example, powerful unions and departmental civic committees opposed the idea of municipal empowerment.

In addition, political leaders had at their disposal a stock of specific, ready-made proposals that they could offer as solutions for addressing general social dissatisfaction with the performance of public institutions. The proposals were devised by technical analysts in think tanks and presidential commissions that were intimately familiar with national conditions—in many cases through direct contact with grass-roots organizations. Often the proposals were developed many years in advance and were kept alive in discussions among experts and social leaders who made the proposals available for adoption when the political opportunity arose.

Source: Grindle (2000).

Opportunities for reform often arise from economic or political crises that inspire civil society or political elites to demand changes in the status quo and to search for new solutions to long-standing problems. In Latin America, perceived crises in the legitimacy of governing institutions have inspired substantial reforms that give greater voice and power to local communities (box 7.1).

Organizing dispersed interests for improved coordination depends largely on voice. In the form of votes, voice increases accountability and responsiveness, as policymakers in competitive democratic contexts are concerned about reelection. A good example is famine—perhaps the worst sort of coordination failure. In observing that India has not suffered a famine since independence, Nobel Laureate Amartya Sen notes that "with the present political system in India, it is almost impossible for a famine to take place. The pressure of newspapers and diverse political parties make it imperative . . . to organize swift relief."[3]

The proposition that newspapers in a competitive democracy elicit swifter disaster relief has been investigated empirically in 16 Indian states, showing that newspaper circulation strongly increases public food distribution during shortages.[4] The effects are large, robust, and significant, even after controlling for income, urbanization, and population density.

The study shows that information, political accountability, and an educated and informed public are critical for picking up dispersed signals of distress. Ensuring a free press and democracy also represents a commitment device to acting. Unfortunately, this mechanism has limitations. As noted by Sen, "the deprivation has to be dramatic to be 'newsworthy' and politically exploitable. The Indian political system may prevent famines but . . . it seems unable to deal effectively with endemic malnutrition."[5]

Education is another example of the importance of voice. And it is a good example of the challenge hinted at by Sen: how can institutions be geared to ensure commitment to activities that are longer term, less visible, but as important? One resounding message from research on education systems is that the participation of families and communities can increase inputs and discipline. Decentralization and the promotion of private sector and NGO involvement can help society meet educational goals. In El Salvador, decentralization encouraged greater family and community involvement in schooling, expanding educational opportunities for the poor in rural areas.[6] In Colombia, a government voucher program used the private sector to expand secondary school enrollment and choice for poor children in a cost-effective way.[7]

Box 7.2
Brazil: changing the rules of the game for better public services

The state of Ceara—in Brazil's poorest region, the north-east—was legendary for clientelism, patronage, and poor public administration. In 1987 a newly elected reformist government, led by Tasso Jereissati, took the reins. Only a few years after the new government launched a public health program, vaccination coverage for measles and polio had tripled to 90 percent of the child population, and infant deaths had fallen from 102 per 1,000 infants to 65. How could a long tradition of clientelism and political opposition be overcome so rapidly? How did reputedly mediocre state agencies deliver and sustain better performance spanning several years and changes in administration?

The governor and the state administration had to compel reluctant mayors to join the program. Pressure on the mayors came from neighboring *municipios* that had joined the program, and from an unusual and unending flurry of publicity through radio and other means. By creating an informed and demanding community, the state had initiated a dynamic in which the mayors saw political rewards for supporting the program. In so doing, the government contributed to replacing the old patronage dynamic with a more service-oriented one, exploiting an opportunity as a strong third party to improve municipal accountability.

Source: Tendler (1997).

Studies on secondary schools in Argentina show that institutional features, such as school autonomy and parental participation, make a substantial difference in educational outcomes.[8] Parental participation (such as through a school board) empowers families to influence how the school is run—and anchors the school's commitment to serving their children's needs. Autonomy and participation are found to have a positive and significant effect on student learning, as measured by test scores. Interestingly, the effect is at least as strong for children from poor households as it is for the general population.

Voice combined with transparency and access to credible information is a powerful lever for improved coordination. This makes new technologies that promote transparency and bring relevant information closer to all stakeholders all the more exciting. Voice also plays a major role in creating a setting that is conducive to the emergence of better institutions over time (box 7.2).

Creating a sound investment climate

Institutions are crucial to fostering a sound investment climate that favors make over take and enables a broader portfolio of assets to thrive. Whether planting rice saplings in a field, making furniture on the side of a road, setting up a new enterprise, or buying securities on a stock exchange, investors like return and dislike risk. Aspects of the broader investment climate, such as the rate of inflation, the extent of corruption, or the cost of shipping, help determine the incentive to invest.[9] Institutions will be important in addressing these, affecting not only the drive for new investment, but also the productivity and value of the existing stock of assets.

The investment climate encompasses:

- the macroeconomic fundamentals (including sound money, strong fiscal accounts, and stable exchange rates),
- the operation of government (emphasizing effective corruption control and a sound regulatory framework that promotes private sector competition while addressing negative externalities), and
- basic infrastructure (underpinning commerce and the development of human capital).

Set in a broader context that facilitates initiatives like self-regulation through the adoption of the triple bottom line to evaluate a company's performance (gauging profits, social impacts, and environmental effects), these components are critical determinants of transactions costs that shape what is produced and how.[10] Improved criteria are especially important in guiding investment that is long lived (lasting 20–50 years), or where impacts are irreversible. The investment climate will also play an important role in the emergence of better institutions over time.

Attending to macroeconomic fundamentals

Sound management of macroeconomic variables is necessary but not sufficient to foster sustainable development. Macroeconomic crises—especially financial and budget crises—can undo development and undermine sustainability. The macroeconomic landscape is broad, and only a few elements are touched on here: inflation, fiscal balances, and the exchange rate.

Inflation—particularly unexpected inflation—weakens the incentive to produce. There is an extensive literature on inflation, with commitment problems as a major feature: can the government or central bank commit to not printing money? Some institutional remedies involve granting the central bank independence and adopting transparent targets and rules in managing the money supply. Other commitment devices include tying the exchange rate to an appropriate nominal peg.[11]

The fiscal accounts are also an important part of the investment climate. Public finance research has addressed many important aspects of fiscal management, such as spending countercyclically, building a safety net, redistributing income, providing public goods, and the like. One important aspect that illustrates well the approach taken in this Report is fiscal decentralization, which has attracted increased attention based on the promise of improved accountability and the more responsive provision of services and public goods financed closer to the level of the ultimate beneficiaries.

The potential gains from decentralization, however, face several pitfalls, especially the problem of "soft budget" constraints.[12] If localities feel confident that a higher-level government will bail them out in the event of a financial crisis, spending may be excessive, creating uncertainty and gyrations that undermine the incentive to invest. In the extreme, regional fiscal profligacy can lead to national fiscal problems that precipitate inflation and exchange rate crises. So institutions are important in generating a "hard budget constraint" that protects the dispersed interests of taxpayers in other municipalities, and facilitates commitment by the higher levels of government.[13] For example, in 1996 Hungary adopted a law establishing formal bankruptcy proceedings for municipalities. Such arrangements are central to enabling the sound fiscal management that contributes to a strong investment climate.

The exchange rate is another macroeconomic fundamental, important for international transactions on both the current account (trade in goods and services) and the capital account (borrowing and foreign direct investment). Large gyrations in the exchange rate can undermine the incentive to invest. In addition, poor people perceive adverse effects disproportionately, because they have little access to the sophisticated financial instruments needed to protect or hedge against exchange rate movements. Much depends on confidence. Although a lively debate continues on how best to manage the exchange rate, maintaining strong fiscal and monetary policy is essential. And many governments have sought institutional commitment mechanisms including fixed exchange rates, the gold standard, currency boards, and even using the U.S. dollar.

Strengthening the operation of government

The incentive to invest is strongly influenced by maintaining property rights and the rule of law, enforcing contracts, regulating activity, and engaging in other interventions that support make over take. But regulation, for example, can be captured by concentrated interests to the detriment of the many. Similarly, bribe seeking by government officials typically motivates arbitrary harassment, also harming broader interests and the incentive to invest. And once someone has accumulated wealth through judicious investment, it may be subject to seizure, either by private individuals (crime), or by government (expropriation). Can government commit to protecting assets and avoiding predation? If not, much activity will be discouraged, relocate to where it is protected, or move to the informal sector.

As noted in earlier chapters, substantial growth in productivity and employment is required over the next 50 years in order to improve the quality of life for growing populations in developing countries. Small- and medium-scale enterprises are often the most dynamic segments of developing economies, and are central to the expansion of employment opportunities, especially for poor people.[14] Yet these enterprises face many hurdles in difficult business environments. For example, seminal research on entry regulation was done by Hernando de Soto and his team by opening a garment shop with one employee in Lima, Peru. They found that it took 289 days working 6 hours a day to legally register the business, and the cost was more than 30 times the monthly minimum wage.[15] A similar study subsequently looked at the obstacles and costs of formally establishing a business in 85 countries, to see whether the quality of public and private goods—ostensibly the justification for regulation—is better in countries with more regulations.[16] If the quality is better, government works in the public interest—if it is lower, government has a grabbing hand. The authors find that the quality of goods is not better in high-regulation countries; instead, the additional regulation leads to corruption and forces activities to locate in the informal sector, hampering more productive arrangements. The authors conclude that where government institutions are weak it is better to have a smaller government that intervenes and regulates less.[17] This is consistent with one of the main themes of the *World Development Report 1997,* arguing for "a good fit between the states' institutional capabilities and its action."[18]

Another important avenue for broad-based investment is housing and land. Formally acquiring land for housing often involves many steps and takes years.[19] The result again is discouraged investment, the inefficient location of activity in the informal sector, and corruption. Institutional responses include better tenure arrangements, streamlining formal registration procedures, and introducing more transparency and accountability into the process.

Corruption is a major risk entrepreneurs face, because government officials seeking bribes can undermine the viability of an entire investment. Paying bribes to continue business operations also lowers returns, reducing the incentive to invest. A series of World Bank–sponsored surveys of businesses in developing countries show that corruption is a major concern, frequently imposing additional costs on smaller enterprises disproportionately. Ongoing research continues to illuminate the deleterious effects of corruption, and suggests potential remedies that are mainly institutional, including partnering with civil society (box 7.3), providing access to information,

Box 7.3
Civil society and governance

Civil society has emerged as a major force in efforts to improve governance. High levels of corruption are associated with poverty, inequality, reduced domestic and foreign direct investment, and weak overall economic performance.* Corruption control that ensures a well-functioning government is substantially a public good and an intermediate input into the provision of other public goods. This collective action problem is aggravated by difficult incentives: not only would beneficiaries prefer to free-ride and not contribute to governance if others are contributing, but the incentive to defect and engage in corrupt practices is stronger when other actors curb their own illicit activities.

International aspects of corruption further complicate the issue. When the United States enacted the Foreign Corrupt Practices Act of 1977, prohibiting the payment of bribes by U.S. citizens or companies and their subsidiaries, no other nation followed suit with similar legislation. In many countries, foreign bribery was so commonplace that bribes were treated as tax-deductible business expenses. Government subsidies through export financing and insurance accommodated foreign bribery as an unpleasant but necessary ingredient of doing business in emerging markets.

Civil society organizations (CSOs), such as Transparency International (TI), helped change attitudes towards corruption in the 1990s. This organization's basic approach is a nonconfrontational effort to build "national, regional, and global coalitions that embrace the state, civil society, and the private sector to fight domestic and international corruption."[†] The objective is pursued by building public awareness, lobbying governments, and facilitating agreements to reduce corruption. One of TI's most important and enduring contributions has been to help place corruption firmly on the agenda in both developing and developed countries. This was accomplished mainly by emphasizing the negative effects of corruption (falling disproportionately on the poor), and generating publicity through the annual publication of the Corruption Perceptions Index.[‡]

The cornerstone of TI's efforts to foster agreements curbing corruption is the integrity pact between governments and companies bidding for projects.** While the details vary depending on the project, the basic idea is a commitment by the authorities not to demand or accept, and by firms not to offer, any bribe or gift in exchange for an advantage in the project award process. These pacts are currently forging coalitions among bidders, government agencies, and CSOs in about 50 competitive situations around the world, and are underpinned by transparency and disclosure procedures, independent third-party oversight, and specific sanctions for noncompliance.

TI has also promoted international collective action to curb corruption, most significantly the OECD Convention. With the support of business leaders, governments, and CSOs, the OECD Convention on Combating Bribery of Foreign Public Officials in International Business Transactions was signed in 1997, went into force in 1999, and, at the end of 2001, had been ratified by 34 of 35 signatory states, including several non-OECD members.***

The Convention is an attempt to make a coordinated escape from the corruption trap, such that firms are not disadvantaged by refraining from corrupt practices. It has no formal mechanism of punishing signatories who cheat and do not contribute to controlling corruption by enforcing antibribery laws, but publicity and national and international condemnation are expected to ensure good faith efforts. It does stipulate an elaborate monitoring system, however, aided in part by CSOs, to further reassure signatories that other participants are complying with the agreed requirements. The experience with international efforts to combat corruption is an important example of how CSOs can contribute to development.

* Lambsdorff (1999).
† Galtung (2000, p. 26).
‡ For a discussion of how corruption impacts the poor disproportionately, see the World Bank (2001c, p. 102).
** TI (2000). Source Book 2000: Confronting Corruption—The Elements of a National Integrity System. Berlin. [http://www.transparency.org/sourcebook].
*** See the OECD Web site for the text: http://www.oecd.org/pdf/M00017000/M00017037.pdf.
Source: Eigen and Eigen-Zucchi (2002).

creating anticorruption agencies, ensuring media and judicial independence, and decentralization.[20]

Providing basic infrastructure

Infrastructure, the third main part of a sound investment climate, is analytically distinct from other investment in that it tends to exhibit a substantial public goods component and economies of scale in production. It also requires the coordination of networked facilities and a sound regulatory regime. Hence, it is often cheaper to provide infrastructure services—sewerage, piped water, power, telecommunications, ports, and roads—in ways that capture scale economies. Greater population density raises the returns to infrastructure investment.[21] Infrastructure also has profound long-term effects on development, with significant path dependence in energy efficiency, mode of transport, and the spatial distribution of activity.

Proximity matters.[22] Not all areas have the same potential. As a result, the spatial distribution of economic activity in general, and of urban centers in particular, is important to sustainable development (box 6.1). The spatial view of urban settlement as a system of cities and towns (linking urban and rural activities) deals with the extent to which the urban population is concentrated in the largest city (measured as "primacy"), and how smaller urban units and secondary cities are dispersed across regions. Excessive primacy can have real economic efficiency costs to countries. Poor accessibility of the rural hinterland to urban markets—caused by a weakly developed system of towns and cities reflecting a thin rural to urban and intercity transport network—also limits options for growth and diversification of the rural economy (chapter 5), and weakens the incentive to invest.

Disproportionate urban concentration often results from an imbalance in national institutions for signaling and balancing interests, especially across regions and levels of government. Democratization, fiscal decentralization, and investments in intercity roads, waterways, and communication can significantly reduce such concentration, permitting wider access to urban assets across the country (box 7.4).[23]

By providing access to urban opportunities and assets, and linking spatially dispersed activity across the country, basic infrastructure helps determine the return on other investments. Farmers need roads to bring produce to the market. Exporters require tele-

Box 7.4
National policy can generate excessive urban concentration

Urban concentration is positively associated with economic growth in the early stages of development. Focusing development in a few urban centers generates scale economies in production and consumption and conserves scarce infrastructure such as roads, skilled workers, and managerial resources. But excessive concentration is costly, as these gains are increasingly offset by congestion and diminishing returns to additional investments. Further, disproportionately high concentration of economic activity in a few urban areas is likely to have an adverse effect on the interregional distribution of opportunities and welfare. Empirical research shows that urban concentration rises and then falls with economic development. For example, recent work provides evidence that countries' urban concentration increases with growth at low levels of income, peaks at low-middle levels of income (around 1987 PPP income per capita of $2,500), and then declines at higher levels of income.

Policy and politics also influence urban concentration. Moving from the least to the most democratic regimes reduces urban concentration by 10 percent from its mean. Urban concentration is also lower in countries with higher levels of fiscal decentralization (box figure). This relationship holds even when controlling for the scale of the urban population. Infrastructure investments in waterways and roads, usually driven by national policies, also help reduce primacy, as these investments open the hinterland to external trade, domestic and international.

Urban concentration declines with fiscal decentralization

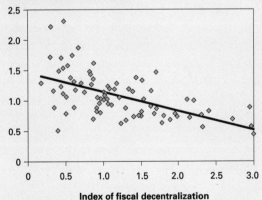

Index of urban concentration (y-axis), Index of fiscal decentralization (x-axis)

Note: The graph shows that urban concentration (as measured by the size distribution of cities) falls with greater fiscal decentralization (as measured by the share of sub-national revenues in total revenues). This note draws on findings reported in Ades and Glaeser (1995); Henderson (2000); Henderson and Davis (2002); Lall (2002); and Wheaton and Shishido (1982).
Data Sources: World Bank, WDI, and Government Financial Statistics.

communications and ports to make and execute trans-actions. Small industrial enterprises demand electric-ity to run equipment. In addition, the reliability of these infrastructure services is a major determinant of risk. Farmers, exporters, and entrepreneurs are exposed to large losses in the event of infrastructure failure. Recent research emphasizes the importance of infrastructure for economic performance, especially in the long run—and its positive spillovers on private investment.[24] Institutional remedies for improving the delivery of infrastructure services include commercial management, competition, stakeholder involvement, and public-private partnerships in financing infrastructure projects.[25] These will be central to building the basic infrastructure underpinning a strong investment climate for sustainable development.

Managing the environment

Many developing countries are responding to environmental concerns sooner than industrial countries did at similar levels of development. Indeed, as noted in chapter 2, the development approach of "grow first, clean up later," and the notion of an environmental Kuznet's curve is increasingly being challenged in recent research.[26] For some pollutants the relationship holds, but for others, like carbon dioxide, emissions continue to grow as per capita incomes rise.[27] New technologies and the spreading knowledge about the impacts of environmental degradation also mean that developing countries can make better environmental choices, as in the case of switching to unleaded gasoline (see below). Still, the environment remains a major challenge for national actors and institutions. Managing forests, water resources, coastal zones, fisheries, and airsheds pose several well-known coordination problems involving externalities and public goods. In many cases, when fisheries, forests, bodies of water, and air are treated as common pool resources, efforts to preserve the environment are underprovided; if coordination were implemented, the gains could be large.

Public finance approaches to these problems are to tax the activities generating negative externalities, subsidize the activity yielding positive externalities, or regulate the activity directly (chapter 2). The tendency to underprovide public goods can be remedied by using the political process to determine the type and the level at which public goods are to be provided—and then levying taxes and subsidies to strengthen the incentives for the supply of public goods or providing the public goods directly, financed out of tax revenues. But these remedies are typically difficult to implement—complicated by disputes about burden and benefit sharing and the nature, importance, and value of the externalities and public goods.

Many environmental issues were not recognized in the early stages of the activities that precipitated the problems. Furthermore, powerful constituencies have emerged to obstruct change and relegate environmental concerns to lower levels of priority. Not only does policy often fail to discourage environmentally damaging activities, but, in the form of perverse subsidies, it frequently encourages such activities. The governance and institutional challenges of effectively managing the environment are examined here by elaborating on perverse subsidies before turning to three environmental concerns at the national level that illustrate well the importance of nationally supported institutions for coordination—managing forests, fisheries, and airsheds.

Dismantling perverse subsidies

Perverse subsidies encourage activities that are harmful to the environment and the economy.[28] Subsidizing coal, for instance, can hurt the economy by allocating scarce tax revenue to an activity that is not competitive at international prices, and damage the environment by encouraging the use of one of the most polluting sources of energy. Subsidies have been instituted for a wide variety of reasons, including many laudable ones such as alleviating poverty or addressing market failures. However, they often fail to achieve these aims or achieve them only at exorbitant cost. The removal of perverse subsidies would simultaneously benefit the economy and the environment, releasing public funds for other purposes. *World Development Report 1992* described such policy actions as win-win.[29]

Unfortunately, policy reforms are often very difficult to implement because in reality the situation is win-win-lose. Once in place, constituencies develop to keep subsidies in place past their publicly useful role. Some politically important stakeholders stand to lose. Another factor obstructing the removal of subsidies—mainly in industrial countries, is the transitional gains trap, whereby the expected subsidy stream becomes capitalized in the associated asset.[30] The removal of an agricultural subsidy, for example, would reduce land prices and hurt current farmers, who may perceive no special benefit from the subsidy program once the higher price they paid initially for the land is included in the calculation. The biggest beneficiaries of the subsidy stream were the farmers who owned land at the time the subsidy was first introduced. So, current farmers can be expected to resist the removal of subsidies strenuously (compensation in exchange for greater dynamic efficiency is very difficult to address).

Agriculture is subsidized worldwide for a variety of reasons—among them ensuring the supply of food, reducing the variance of farm prices, maintaining the farming sector, and supporting rural communities. The bulk of global subsidies to agriculture are dispensed in OECD countries (most developing countries impose net taxes on their agricultural sector), where they are estimated to have exceeded $325 billion in 2000 (compared with official net resource flows to developing countries of about $37 billion in 2001), and much of this is perverse.[31] Agricultural production spurred by subsidies degrades the environment by encouraging the following practices:

- Overly rapid conversion of forested land or wetlands for agricultural use
- Overgrazing on range land
- Excessive application of pesticides and fertilizers
- High water use and aquifer depletion.

Many agricultural subsidies were intended to be temporary—to provide assistance in a farm crisis, for example (see chapter 5). However, their removal has proven difficult, even in cases in which the initial legislation contained a sunset clause. Agricultural subsidies benefit a concentrated group and hurt dispersed interests, including consumers, taxpayers, and those who bear the environmental costs, especially in the OECD countries, where farming is a small part of the economy (box 7.5).

Perverse subsidies to agriculture also seriously undermine development. Those in the North distort domestic economies and depress world prices, blocking trading opportunities in agricultural commodities that generate more than half the export earnings for 40 developing countries.[32] Perverse agricultural subsidies in the South primarily involve specific inputs like water, fertilizer, and pesticides, but can have similarly adverse environmental effects, as shown by

Box 7.5
Perverse sugar subsidies in the United States

Sugar in the United States is an extreme case of perverse subsidies, and the classic example used by Anne Krueger to help spawn the literature on rent seeking.* Because of a program of price supports and import quotas, American consumers pay at least twice the world price for sugar. More than $3 is lost to consumers and the economy for each $1 transferred to the sugar growers, and the subsidy to each grower is more than twice the average family income in the United States. Furthermore, most sugar production is concentrated in southern Florida, drawing water from the Everglades and returning it with fertilizer, leading to eutrophication.

The U.S. Army Corps of Engineers and the South Florida Water Management District have developed a plan to reverse some of the environmental degradation in the Florida Everglades, at an estimated cost of $8 billion and to be implemented over 20 years.† Generating information about the environmental and economic cost will be central to organizing dispersed interests to overcome the vested interests surrounding current U.S. sugar policies. Some institutional progress is being made. The Environmental Working Group (EWG), an NGO, is publishing the amount of subsidies received by agricultural producers and others, which may eventually help catalyze a change in policy.‡ International pressure is also growing for liberalizing trade to promote sustainable development, because the U.S. policy, and similar policies in the EU that protect sugarbeet farmers, undermines the development prospects of more competitive sugar growers in developing countries.

* Krueger (1974, 1996).
† See http://www.discovery.com/news/features/everglades/everglades.html for details.
‡ See EWG's Web site at www.ewg.org.
Source: Myers and Kent (2001), p. 47.

the underpricing of water in the Aral Sea basin (box 2.3 in chapter 2).

Perverse subsidies also abound in energy (box 7.6). Much of the production and distribution of energy is controlled by governments. When the fiscal and regulatory framework fails to price energy in a way that internalizes the full social costs of its use, consumption is excessive, with high costs of pollution. Developing and transition countries provide subsidies of more than $120 billion to electricity production, and in eight large developing countries, total energy subsidies exceed $83 billion.[33] In the OECD, as noted in chapter 2, total energy subsidies in this group are about $71 billion, and coal subsidies are about $8 billion a year.[34] The dispersed interests of those who bear the environmental and other costs are not captured adequately in the decisionmaking process. While energy

Box 7.6

Perverse energy subsidies in the Islamic Republic of Iran

The Iranian economy is heavily distorted, such that reforms would yield welfare gains estimated at about 19 percent of the GDP. A large part of this stems from petroleum prices that are only about 10 percent of world prices, with an implicit subsidy to petroleum products that amounts to more than 18 percent of GDP. Such subsidies encourage excessive and wasteful energy consumption, with substantial foreign exchange earnings forgone.

Poor people usually do not benefit from these subsidies and their removal would release vast resources that could be redirected toward environmental, social, and other expenditures underpinning sustainable development. The prospects for reform hinge on the opening of the political process, allowing greater voice and participation. The first step in addressing fuel subsidies is to display them explicitly in the budget. This would highlight their magnitude in relation to other priority areas, and facilitate a process of gradually lowering the subsidy to allow fuel prices in Iran to rise to world levels over a 3-year period once reforms are initiated.

Source: World Bank (2001d).

Box 7.7

Aid and compensation to address obstacles to reform in the Russian Federation's coal sector

The Russian Government's coal sector restructuring program is aimed at reducing subsidies and redirecting resources from loss-making production (among other reform goals). It illustrates how aid combined with increased transparency and effective institutional arrangements can help overcome obstacles to reform. Total subsidies to the coal sector in Russia were $2.76 billion in 1994 (1.02 percent of the GDP), and production was inefficient. Initial efforts to restructure the coal sector by redirecting government support ran into difficulties, mainly due to a lack of transparency in the transfer system, and implementation problems in the early phases of transition. During the second stage of the restructuring program, supported by the World Bank, new institutional mechanisms, including checks and balances, were put in place with the explicit aim of bringing transparency into the allocation and transfer of support. This included funds for the social protection of laid-off workers, physical works at closing mines, job-creation programs, and safety measures. The World Bank also provided a separate technical assistance loan to the Russian government in advance, in order to build capacity and help address implementation problems more effectively. This loan was instrumental to the success of the larger sectoral restructuring program, which led to a fall in total coal subsidies to $0.28 billion in 2000 (0.12 percent of the GDP). After 10 years of lowering subsidy-induced overproduction, the output of coal began to grow again in 1998, and the industry's production is now increasingly market-driven without distortive subsidies but not yet subject to externality-correcting taxes.

Source: Kudat, Ozbilgin, and Borisov (1997) and World Bank staff.

use is broad based, the subsidies generally benefit high-income groups disproportionately. The impact of such subsidies is also felt for a long time because the stock of capital with low energy efficiency (transport, buildings, and production processes) takes many years (and some- times decades) to change.

Perverse subsidies also exist in other sectors, such as water management, roads, fisheries, and forestry. And debate continues on how some of these subsidies serve such policy goals as reducing poverty and inequality. Still, the staggering sums suggest that policy reform could substantially improve environmental conditions, strengthen economic performance, and release vast resources for more equitable development. There has been some progress in the last decade and international development assistance can facilitate the process (box 7.7). Indeed, reforming policy to stop encouraging environmental degradation is the first step to implementing broader measures to ensure that environmental assets such as forests, fish, and airsheds are not squandered.

Getting the most from forests—governance, markets, and partnerships

Natural forests are being converted at an unprecedented 12.6 million hectares net a year.[35] The value of forests for maintaining biodiversity and sequestering carbon needs to be more fully recognized as an integral part of sustainable development strategies. Forest resources underpin the livelihoods of 90 percent of the 1.2 billion people living in extreme poverty—and are important to the agriculture and food security of almost half the people in low-income countries.[36] Illegal logging and mismanagement lead to substantial losses and forgone government revenues that are larger than total World Bank lending to these countries.[37] In addition, at present, much of the carbon emitted by developing countries, between 10 and 30 percent of global emissions, is from burning forests.[38]

When traditional methods of managing forest resources are supplanted by mechanisms that are formal but weak, the resource is squandered, often because those who are in and near the forest perceive less secure future control. Races for property rights can be very damaging to forests, accelerating the rate of conversion into agricultural land (chapter 5). And perverse subsidies to industrial forestry—through tax breaks, underpricing for commercial loggers, infrastructure spending, and lack of enforcement of regulations—are substantial.

Institutional levers to correct this include the following:

- Improving the policy and legal frameworks to establish and maintain the property rights of local communities
- Promoting partnerships with local groups and CSOs to integrate forestry, small-scale enterprise, and conservation activities into rural development and watershed management
- Seeking reforms of governance and timber concession policies
- Building international markets that channel funds to countries providing the global public goods of preserving biodiversity and sequestering carbon
- Fostering partnerships with private actors and CSOs to move to sustainable harvesting and forest management with credible performance-based certification by independent third parties.

Each of these levers is important for strong forest management that recognizes the different benefits to different stakeholders, and performs the functions of picking up signals, balancing interests, and executing decisions. When property rights are well specified, it is more likely that actors will be receptive to signals about the state of their asset, and will weigh tradeoffs between present and deferred uses. When transparency and governance are strong (i.e., the public is an active partner of government and bureaucrats are not accepting bribes), government will have a greater capacity to balance broader societal interests with the narrower interests of loggers. The relevant government agency is also better able to implement informed concession policies that mobilize fiscal revenues. Forest management requires nested institutions that can ensure that property rights, assigned to local communities for food, fuel, and shelter, do not overlook the regional or provincial watershed benefits of forest conservation, nor global interests in a forest's carbon and biodiversity services. The latter set of dispersed interests can be channeled with funds from around the globe through newly created markets (including initiatives such as the

World Bank's Prototype Carbon Fund, discussed in chapter 8). Partnerships with CSOs and private sector actors can also encourage sustainable forest management practices by rewarding responsible behavior, driving rent seekers and corrupt actors out of business, and creating the basis for credible, independent certification by internationally recognized bodies. Many of these features are illustrated in the promising steps taken toward reforming forest management practices in Cameroon (box 7.8).

Getting the most from fisheries—overcoming the tragedy of the commons and improving information
As discussed in chapter 3, fishery resources present major opportunities and challenges. Managing this renewable resource to maximize well-being in a sustainable way is critical for development. About 30 million people living in developing countries are engaged in fisheries, and "coastal fishing communities are frequently among the poorest of the poor."[39] For about 1 billion people living in poor countries, fish are also a vital source of protein, and an important component of food security.[40] Yet, as noted in chapter 1, 70 percent of the world's fisheries are being overexploited or are at capacity. Subsidies in fishing are between $14 billion and $20 billion a year globally, of which half are given in OECD countries, leading to substantial overcapacity.[41] By some estimates, the maximum sustainable yield worldwide could be caught with half the existing fishing fleet.[42] The two main reasons for the difficulty in managing fisheries are the open access or common pool nature of the resource, and the lack of information. This leads to spectacular coordination failures in the form of waste and sometimes even in the collapse of fish stocks. The institutional framework is key to preventing such failures and in underpinning strong fishery management.

The common pool nature of fisheries gives rise to dispersed interests and commitment problems. In the absence of clear property rights, individual fishermen are unable to manage fish resources effectively and commit to limiting the catch to a sustainable level. The gains from reduced fishing effort by an individual fisherman accrues to the whole group, and cooperative arrangements are complicated by strong incentives to cheat. The inability to forge credible commitments undermines cooperation, and the common pool is overfished. When fish stocks and fishing incomes fall, the problem is compounded by politi-

Box 7.8
Cameroon: The path to improved forest governance

As Africa's largest wood exporter, Cameroon generates substantial income from the exploitation of forest resources, and the rich biodiversity and other environmental services provided by these forests make them important globally. As in some other forest-rich nations, logging has been poorly regulated. Until the mid-1990s, logging permits were awarded through an opaque administrative process linked to deep-seated patronage. Permit holders were not required to adhere to forest management plans. There was little enforcement of basic logging regulation. Furthermore, the five-year license provided no incentive for long-term care of forest resources. Without enforcement, loggers built roads deep into the forest. This opened previously inaccessible areas to agricultural conversion and facilitated the bushmeat trade, imperiling rare wildlife and the forest's long-term ecological integrity. The system of allocating forest permits was prone to corruption and was generally insecure for long-term investors. Moreover, the forests yielded very low, unsteady revenues for the state, local administrations, and local communities.

A new law to auction concessions
After years of policy dialogue with donors, Cameroon's executive branch brought to parliament a new forestry law in 1994, providing for the auction of forest concessions on the basis of per-hectare bids by prequalified bidders. This was intended to increase transparency, discourage unnecessary expansion of the logging road networks, and encourage high value-added industrial activity. The law also required management plans and allocated half the revenues to local governments and communities. But the law's implementation decrees ran into public opposition, both from those who perceived it as benefiting foreign companies and from those who preferred the status quo. In the end the proposed reforms were adopted to comply with structural adjustment loan conditions but without strong initial local ownership.

Support builds
After a slow start, the reforms developed local support and began to yield results. The first round of concession allocations, in 1997, was flawed and drew criticism from the World Bank and from local and international NGOs. Soon afterwards, a third World Bank–supported structural adjustment operation provided a new, more flexible framework for debating and supporting the implementation of the forestry law. Progress was due in part to the emergence of constituencies for reform, including a strong team of reformers in government, and the communities that began to benefit from increased revenue sharing.

Consultations among stakeholders have intensified. And transparency has increased: newspapers publish details describing which companies are authorized to operate in which locations, helping local residents identify illegal operators. Also important was the widespread formal use of independent observers. Respected Cameroonians are hired to observe the concession allocation process. Cameroonian and international NGOs are contracted to assist in verifying concessionaire compliance with logging regulations, both through on-the-ground inspection and through the use of satellite imagery. This helps to ensure that the bidding system does not encourage overexploitation of the forests.

Progress so far
- *Improved transparency.* Global Forest Watch Cameroon concluded, "The June 2000 round of concession allocations was far more transparent than those of 1997 . . . the new allocations appear to be in compliance with government guidelines, which have recently been clarified. This change attests to Cameroon's commitment to develop a complex market-based auction system aimed at increased transparency and rents captured from logging." The annual area fee per hectare increased from $0.14 in 1996 to $6.00 in 2002, and the total value of multiyear contracts awarded since June 2000 exceeds $600 million.
- *Introduction of the first legal framework for community forestry in central Africa,* including priority access to forest land secured to local communities.
- *Clarification and simplification of forest management regulations,* resuming field inspections and prosecuting illegal logging, with fines up to $15 million being levied on a single company.
- *Gradual exit of short-term speculators* and increase in long-term investors with a positive impact on high value-added industry and local employment.
- *Enhanced revenue capture in the interest of the nation and rural communities,* as annual forest revenues increased from less than $3 million in 1995 to more than $30 million in 2001 (excluding timber export taxes and duties). Fiscal revenues accruing to local communities increased from negligible levels in 1998 to $8 million in 2002.
- *Stronger commitment for biodiversity conservation, including* the creation of new protected areas and ongoing negotiations on conservation concessions with international NGOs.

Time will tell if these reforms hold up. An encouraging sign is that the forest sector's lessons in negotiating reforms, dealing with vested interests, and increasing transparency are now being applied to other sectors including the national procurement system. This may prompt emulation elsewhere in the Congo Basin, and suggests that the existing process is conducive to institutional strengthening over time.

Sources: Bank staff; Essama-Nssah and Gockowski (2000); Brunner and Ekoko (2000); Collomb and Bikié (2001).

cal economy dynamics that frequently enable the concentrated interests of fishermen to elicit government subsidies, harming dispersed interests (other taxpayers) and prolonging overfishing (see box 3.4).

Poor information is also a major problem. Not only is it difficult to monitor fishing and landed catch, but it is also hard to monitor stocks. The concern about reliable fishery statistics is illustrated by the ongoing debates about whether the total world catch has peaked (in part depending on the accuracy of Chinese fishery data), and the extensive efforts made by governments and international organizations to ensure dependable statistics.[43] Such data form the basis for establishing maximum sustainable yields and other key aspects of fishery management. Aggregate data on caught fish by weight mask the composition of the fish, making it hard to account for changes in the quality of fish. There is also little information on the relationship between fishing and marine ecosystems, an area that is generating growing interest.[44]

The challenge of sound fishery management is magnified in developing countries, where fishing often represents employment of last resort, "attracting increasing numbers of poorly remunerated fishworkers who have to resort to damaging fishing practices to make a meager living."[45] When fishing is on a small scale and done by poor communities in the informal sector, authoritative intervention is more challenging administratively and politically, and the capacity for monitoring and enforcement is likely to be weak. A broader development process that creates alternative employment opportunities is important not only for reducing poverty, but also for improving fisheries management.

Institutions are central to improving coordination in the management of fish resources. Mechanisms need to be found to restrict fishing to levels that maximize the value of the resource. Such improvements would significantly raise the total value of landed fish. This will depend on stronger protective institutions, including improved monitoring and enforcement of fishing rules. For example, the Thai government has made extensive efforts to improve fishery management during the 1990s, more than doubling related expenditures to reach 1.6 percent of the total gross revenues from marine fish landings in 1999.[46] Still, a ban on push-net fishing from 1972 remains unenforced. The same fishery management–spending ratio in Iceland is 3 percent; in Norway it is about 8 percent, and in Newfoundland, Canada, it is estimated to be 20 percent of the catch value.[47] Improving monitoring, enforcement, and research capacity is costly, but a growing trend in fisheries management is to use part of the increased wealth generated by strengthened management of the fishery to finance this capacity. This is a marked change from financing those activities from general taxation.

A major difficulty in restricting catch for improved fishery management is the international race for property rights over marine resources. The Third U.N. Conference on the Law of the Sea (passed in 1982, ratified in 1994) brought an important institutional change in this regard, giving coastal nations a 200-mile exclusive economic zone.[48] This facilitates more productive use of fishery resources since most fishing takes place within this zone and responsibility for good management falls to a smaller group of stakeholders. Although many types of fish migrate between the territorial waters of different countries, and swim into international waters outside the exclusive zone, cooperation is easier when it involves fewer nations, and fishery issues can often be resolved on a bilateral basis.

While establishing property rights over fish stocks is rare, efforts to address the common property problem have focused on some form of exclusive use rights, such as individual transferable quotas, licenses to own and operate fishing vessels, and territorial use rights.[49] These mechanisms exhibit varying strengths and weaknesses, depending upon the context, but they generally aim to improve the private incentives faced by fishermen to ensure sustainable management, sometimes by creating tradable fishing rights. These practices have generated some success stories (Iceland and New Zealand), but were unsuccessful in other instances, such as the collapse of cod stocks off Newfoundland, Canada, in the early 1990s (box 3.4).

Although fishery priorities vary—with developed countries seeking to reduce capacity and allow the regeneration of fully or overexploited stocks, and developing countries aiming to develop new resources and improve technology—all nations are trying to maximize the benefits from this great renewable resource.[50] Actors must be able to pick up signals about the status and trends of fisheries, develop confidence in each other, and commit to restraint. The FAO is involved in improving reporting and strengthening capacity in developing countries.[51] A Code of Conduct for Responsible Fisheries, promoting stronger fishery management in national legislation, underpins the efforts of governments, civil society, and private sector actors.[52] There is also a growing recognition that balancing the interests of fishermen, present and future, requires consensus and partnerships among all stakeholders, and that CSOs working through the market can play an important role (box 7.9).

Box 7.9
Partnership for sustainable fisheries

As one of the world's largest buyers of fish from around the globe, Unilever shares the growing concern about the sustainability of fishing practices in many areas, especially since a reportedly stable gross tonnage of landed fish masks a fall in recent years of white fish, the type used most in Unilever products. In response, Unilever joined with the WWF to found the Marine Stewardship Council (MSC) in 1997. The MSC's mission is "to safeguard the world's seafood supply by promoting the best environmental choice."* Through extensive negotiations with key fishery stakeholders around the world, the MSC developed a set of strong environmental standards. The MSC encourages the certification of fisheries to this standard, provides an ecolabel for products from certified fisheries (pictured at right), and promotes sourcing from MSC certified fisheries. The MSC became fully independent in 1998, and continues to refine the MSC standard, accredit independent third party certifiers, and build public awareness. Unilever supports these initiatives and seeks to promote sustainable fishing practices in part through its sourcing decisions. At the end of 2001, 5 percent of Unilever's fish inputs were purchased from certified sustainable fisheries (through the certification of the Hoki fishery in New Zealand). By the end of 2002, Unilever hopes to increase this share to 25 percent (as certifications expand to cover larger fisheries), and by 2005, all fish are to be purchased exclusively from sustainability certified fisheries.

MSC illustrates how partnerships between private sector actors, NGOs, and government can generate an institutional response that improves coordination for sustainable development. A large private sector firm recognizes the threat to its core businesses from overfishing, and partners with an NGO to generate a credible, independent certification agency. By establishing environmental standards and promoting an ecolabel, the new agency connects the consumer to the management of fisheries, helping to underpin government efforts to establish, maintain, and enforce sound rules for exploiting fish resources. While some of the certification decisions have been controversial, the partnership process offers some hope that the management of fish resources will improve over time. The example of the MSC may also spark ideas for how partnerships can help in other areas as well.

* See the pages on vision, mission, and values within the MSC Web site.
Source: MSC Web site at: http://www.msc.org/, and Frozen Fish International GmbH presentation "Verpflichtung des Marktes zur bestandserhaltenden Fischerei—Fortschritte und Herausforderungen," at the Berlin Forum—Committed to Sustainability, Berlin, May 20–23, 2002.

Curbing air pollution at the national level: the role of information

As noted in chapter 6, air pollution causes serious damage at the local level in many developing and transition country cities.[53] Air pollution is mainly an issue about externalities, where the dispersed interests of people negatively affected are not accounted for by polluters. Although many actions and initiatives are taken at the local level, control strategies, such as standards for fuels and new cars, generally have—and need—support in a broader national framework. National level actors are also engaged in addressing air pollution problems, such as ground-level ozone and sulfur, that affect larger regions and neighboring countries (see chapter 8 for a discussion of sulfur in Europe). In the absence of broader institutional support, traditional public finance approaches are often not adopted or implemented. The role of information is critical.[54]

As noted in chapter 2, developing countries do not need to go through a prolonged period of hazardous air quality on their path to development. They can benefit as latecomers at many levels. First, cost-effective, low-emission technologies have al-ready been developed. Second, institutional mechanisms and policy approaches, developed elsewhere, can help countries and communities avoid mistakes and escape some regrets.[55] Third, and perhaps most important, in a realm where political economy considerations are paramount, the increasing global flow of information about people's experiences elsewhere strengthens the position of those adversely affected in any given country.

Lead in gasoline: latecomers escape some regrets.[56] Leaded gasoline is a good example. By the end of the 1990s, most developing countries outside Africa had made substantial progress switching to unleaded gasoline, and about 16 had completely phased out leaded gasoline.[57] Tetra-ethyl lead is an inexpensive additive used to raise the power of gasoline. It was introduced in the United States in the 1920s, and was not removed until more than half a century later. Initially, there was scant information about the effects of lead, and over time, industry interests became entrenched and blocked efforts to remove lead from gasoline. As the United States switched to unleaded gasoline, however, it quickly became clear that removing lead from gasoline is associated with

Figure 7.1
Lead in gasoline and in blood in the United States, 1975–90

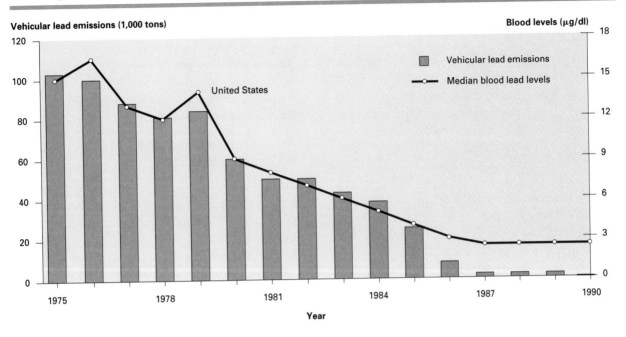

Source: Lovei (1999).

falling lead levels in human blood (figure 7.1), lowering hypertension and heart attacks, and avoiding harm to children's intelligence (removing lead from paint also played a role).

The phasing out of leaded gasoline in Vietnam is a good example of how an institutional context that encourages actors to pick up signals, balance interests, and execute decisions can help address a difficult challenge, even at relatively low levels of economic development.[58] Initial attempts to phase out lead in gasoline began in 1995, but were resisted due to concerns about the cost of switching and the impact on older vehicles. A workshop was held in December 1999, which included representatives from government, the military, the police, industry, academia, and the media, as well as experts from neighboring countries (such as Thailand) with fresh experience and experts from other countries with earlier experience. The "South-South" consultations were very important to allaying continuing concerns. Following the meeting, the government of Vietnam started re-evaluating more carefully the costs of switching, and launched a program to raise public awareness. Consultations with various stakeholders indicated that a

rapid switch would be technically feasible and cost-effective, and Vietnam switched virtually overnight to unleaded gasoline on July 1, 2001. Leaded gasoline was banned in September 2001. Vietnam was well placed to switch, since competitively priced unleaded gasoline was already available on international markets, and the absence of substantial refining interests within Vietnam also meant that there was little opposition from this sector. Still, information dissemination and stakeholder involvement to help overcome misperceptions about leaded gasoline were central to the process and may be replicated to address other similar challenges.

Information helps curb air pollution in China. Information was important to the process of switching to unleaded gasoline, described above, and can catalyze significant improvements in air quality more generally, as evidenced in China. Air pollution in China is a serious problem. Thousands of city-dwellers die prematurely from it every year. Millions more are ill with pollution-related diseases. Despite problems in Chinese policy for air pollution, there have been successes, and new tools are being developed to improve the process. These tools are based on experience gained with information disclosure programs about firms' environmental performance, which have "been characterized as the 'third wave' of environmental regulation, after command-and-control and market-based approaches."[59]

Chinese policymakers and institutions clearly recognize the value of environmental monitoring and how it can shift balances and strengthen accountability. "One of the strongest elements of the State Environmental Protection Agency's environmental strategy has been its work on public participation, public dissemination of environmental information, and environmental information at all levels."[60] The central government explicitly emphasizes openness, and Premier Zhu Rongji stated in the spring of 2001 that all environmental information should be public.[61]

The province of Jiangsu is a good example of how access to information can improve environmental outcomes. A pilot industrial performance rating and disclosure program was established in the city of Zhenjiang in 2000.[62] After a series of workshops, the provincial government scaled up the initiative to cover the entire province of Jiangsu. By mid-2002, about 2,500 industrial companies, responsible for in excess of 80 percent of the total industrial pollution in the province, were included in the program.[63]

In these programs information is generated in order to promote the involvement of the wider community in the regulatory process, to help put pressure on polluters with "informal regulation."[64] Where formal regulatory capacity is weak, as in many developing countries, information catalyzes the participation of civil society, political leaders, and the private sector. Concerns about environmental liabilities may also induce private creditors to avoid making loans to heavy polluters, and consumers to avoid their products. In addition, consumers and CSOs in industrial countries pay close attention to the activities of multinationals. Firms that face social, political, and economic sanctions are more likely to negotiate with local actors.[65]

Environmental outcomes are sensitive to institutional arrangements. This highlights the need to avoid focusing exclusively on emission standards and pollution taxes and instead to complement the latter with the voice of the environment's beneficiaries and other mechanisms to improve environmental choices.[66] Such initiatives are not substitutes for efforts to develop more formal institutions and official policy instruments, but clear complements which lower the eventual cost of adopting and implementing policy measures. Information empowers dispersed interests through multiple channels: product markets—labeling and certification; legislatures—increasing voter pressure for reform; capital markets—shareholders; courts—citizen suits, tort actions, and complaint processes. None of these channels works without adequate information.

Managing natural resources and using aid effectively

The exploitation of natural resources is often a major challenge for national actors and institutions. The exploitation of natural resources creates revenue for government that in a weak institutional context makes it less accountable and responsive to citizen taxpayers, encourages rent seeking and other unproductive competition, and can lead to macroeconomic imbalances, weaker economic performance, and in extreme cases, violent conflict. It thus has the potential to impair the emergence of good institutions, which in the longer term are critical for strong, sustained growth. International aid can have similar effects in impeding the emergence of inclusive and responsive institutions. The challenge lies in avoiding these negative potentials from being realized.

Natural resources—blessing or curse?

There is much discussion about whether and under what circumstances natural resources are "treasure or trouble."[67] Will the exploitation of vast new-found oil in central Asia be a source of great wealth and economic dynamism, or will it bring misfortune? The importance of institutions has emerged as a key aspect of the debate. In the context of a viable social contract, based on widely agreed formal and informal rules for the allocation of resources and the settlement of grievances, institutional arrangements can be sufficient to restrain opportunistic behavior and the violent expression of grievance. An extensive World Bank study on natural resources in Latin America "found . . . that the key to success is to complement natural resource wealth with good institutions, human capital, and knowledge."[68] Where institutions are weak, however, exploiting natural resources can have negative consequences, with some authors even pointing to a "resource curse."[69] One central mechanism is that the availability of revenue from such resources may free the government from developing institutions that are accountable to the populace at large. For example, the question of whether oil and minerals hinder the emergence of democratic institutions has been tested empirically and found to hold for a panel of 113 countries between 1971 and 1997.[70]

The adverse effects are magnified when the natural resource endowment—say, petrochemicals and minerals—is "point-sourced," meaning that its production and revenue patterns are concentrated.[71] Coffee and cocoa take on point-source characteristics when shipped, and are similar to petrochemicals and minerals.[72] When governments control the revenues from resource extraction, their activities can be financed to a greater extent without the consent of taxpayers, reducing accountability. Where government is less open, easily appropriable rents weaken governance and institutions, both of which are critical for long-term economic performance (see box 4.7 on mining in Peru). In a context where government is responsive to its citizens, these adverse effects are muted.

Data on real per capita GDP show that developing countries with few natural resources grew 2–3 times faster between 1960 and 1990 than natural resource–abundant countries, an observation that appears to be robust with regard to alternative methods for classifying countries as natural resource–poor or natural resource–abundant.[73] Indeed, figure 7.2 presents a list of 45 countries whose growth was not sustained, in that they achieved their 1999 level of GDP per capita in an earlier decade—many as far back as the 1960s.[74] Of these 45 countries, all but six are point-source economies.[75] The majority of the countries with point-source natural resources also suffered violent conflict in the 1990s (indicated in bold in figure 7.2).

Angola is a striking example of this tragedy. Civil strife has persisted in Angola since the mid-1970s,

Figure 7.2
Unsustained growth performance is closely associated with point-source natural resources, and conflict*

COUNTRIES WITH UNSUSTAINED GROWTH

1999 GDP per capita (1995 US$) was reached:

In 1960 or before	During the 1960s	During the 1970s	During the 1980s		
Senegal *Somalia*		Honduras *Mali* *Philippines* Zimbabwe			
Angola *Cen. African Rep.* *Chad* *Dem. Rep. of Congo* Ghana *Haiti* *Liberia* Madagascar Nicaragua Niger Nigeria *Rwanda* *Sierra Leone* Venezuela, Rep. B. de Zambia	Bolivia Côte d'Ivoire Jamaica Mauritania Togo	*Algeria* *Burundi* Cameroon *El Salvador* Gabon *Guatemala* Guyana Iran, Islamic Rep. of Malawi *Peru*	Ecuador *Ethiopia* *Iraq* Jordan Kenya Paraguay *Rep. of Congo* Tanzania Trinidad and Tobago	Benin Botswana Brazil Burkina Faso Chile *Colombia* Costa Rica Dominican Rep. Egypt, Arab Rep. of Fiji Guinea Indonesia Mauritius Mexico Morocco	Oman *Papua New Guinea* *South Africa* *Sudan* Syrian Arab Republic Tunisia *Uganda*

COUNTRIES WITH POINT SOURCE NATURAL RESOURCES

* Countries in italic were reported to be in civil conflict in the 1990s; civil conflict is defined as war that has caused more than 1,000 battle deaths, challenged the sovereignty of an internationally recognized state, occurred within its recognized boundary, involved the state as a principal combatant, and subjected the state to an organized military opposition that inflicted significant casualties (Sambanis 2000).

Note: Countries for which data are available show unsustained growth if their 1999 per capita GDP (1999 U.S. dollars) was reached in some prior period (Murshed 2002). Countries are categorized as point-source economies if their two most important exports are of fuels, minerals or plantation crops (with some judgments made where there was some ambiguity) (Isham and others 2002).

Source: Authors.

Figure 7.3
Angola: real GDP per capita, 1960–96

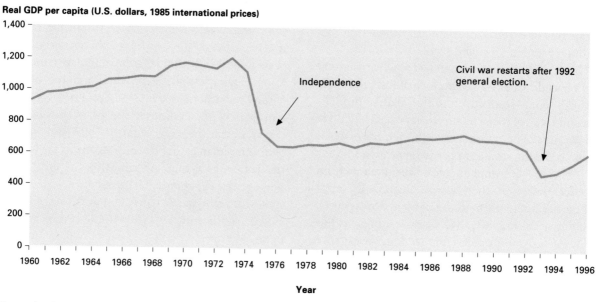

Source: Araujo and Costa (1999).

and "has been associated with weak (sometimes non-existent) institutions—political instability and violence, little rule of law, and an underpaid and corrupt bureaucracy—which have presided over an average annual change in GDP per capita since 1973 of –4.3 percent" (figure 7.3).[76] This, in a country with abundant diamond and oil resources.

The institutional context is crucial. Where norms and rules are weak, greater endowments of natural resources lead to worse economic performance in the long run, compared with countries that have smaller resource endowments. Existing institutions are eroded, and the emergence of new institutions is hampered.[77] There are two key issues in dealing with natural resources: how are *resources managed,* and how are the resulting *proceeds deployed*?

Effective natural *resource management* hinges on property rights, whether ownership is held individually, as a group, or by government. While there are exceptions involving some multinational corporations promoting sustainable practices due to concerns about reputation, in general when property rights have not been established or are poorly defended, time horizons are short, and damaging races for control ensue. As chapter 5 noted for forests, if private sector actors and

other claimants are uncertain about future control over the resource, they are likely to extract the resources as fast as possible—with little regard for market conditions, the impact on local communities, the environment, or sustainable yields. In the midst of violent conflict, resource management is even less likely to be optimal, because future control is very uncertain. If it is inherently difficult to establish property rights and the resource remains in a common pool, management is also likely to be wasteful.

While formal participants enjoying property rights typically are able to receive market signals, exploiting natural resources involves substantial externalities with wide social and environmental impacts. Implementing standard remedies, such as regulation and taxes, is difficult. Where accountability is weak and government leaders have short time horizons, the resource is again likely to be extracted as fast as possible—with little regard for the broader ramifications.[78]

In these instances, the institutional context is central to the ability of national actors to improve coordination. Secure property rights rely on an enforceable commitment by all stakeholders, especially the government and other nexuses of power that employ force, to refrain from looting. Only then will the resources be husbanded in the process of extraction. The same goal will be served by finding ways of formalizing the rights of those who have de facto control, such as landless farmers in the Amazon forest (chapter 5).

Managing natural resources also involves major problems in channeling dispersed interests. As a result of resource extraction, communities may need to move or the local environment may suffer substantial degradation. There is an important role for government in managing these impacts—setting a framework for responsible private sector participation and facilitating the efforts of CSOs. Social cohesion and institutional development will be served by using resource wealth to promote the participation of poor people and to share the benefits broadly (even though it is more difficult to compensate affected communities that operate outside the cash economy). The Cameroonian forests project described in box 7.8 and the Chad-Cameroon oil pipeline described in box 7.11 are promising examples of how broad partnerships can improve the process.

Another set of problems arises with *deploying the proceeds* from natural resource exploitation. The availability of associated funds in government coffers complicates the relationship between government leaders and the citizenry. When government must finance its activities through general taxation, it must interact and negotiate with taxpayers, giving citizens greater opportunities for holding their leaders accountable. But having funds available from natural resources, especially when production involves a concentrated few, enables government leaders and others with de facto control to pursue their own agenda. The funds confer power, facilitate patronage, and provide a basis for co-option. And the country is likely to experience more corruption, rent seeking, and other unproductive activities in the costly competition for the resources, including civil conflict.[79]

Such a country is also likely to end up with macroeconomic imbalances stemming from price volatility and "Dutch disease," whereby the real effective exchange rate appreciates, increasing the relative price of nontradables and impairing the production of tradables. Domestic manufacturing loses competitiveness and is undermined, weakening the opportunities for human capital development and generating unemployment. The phenomenon also slows urbanization and the demographic transition to slower population growth.[80] And by inhibiting competitively honed industrialization and urbanization, it also impedes the emergence of favorable institutions that ultimately are more important for long-term economic performance and the creation of a continuous stream of new opportunities.

In the presence of large accumulated funds, can budget constraints still be binding? How can government leaders commit to honest use in the interest of broader sustainable development? Overcoming short-term rent seeking is a major challenge, requiring a strong "no bailout commitment" for struggling sectors of the economy or local governments. Transparency, independent audits, and open dialogues with all stakeholders are central to effective processes—especially when creating investment funds (sometimes offshore) for future generations as part of a long-term strategy to ward off Dutch disease–type problems.[81]

Once the share of total revenues to be placed in these investment funds is determined, their effective management would benefit from an independent board whose sole objective is to maximize returns. Civil society can perform a key monitoring function, as in Cameroon (box 7.8) and Chad (box 7.11). And reaching broad agreement on corporate codes of conduct can be important, as with the attempts by some international oil companies to improve accountability by publicizing the beneficiaries and accounts of their royalty payments in Angola.

That natural resources can undermine institutions and hamper their evolution is not destiny. Malaysia (box 7.10) and Botswana have both leveraged their natural resources to foster development.[82] In addition to sound macroeconomic policies, the "good" examples of resource-rich countries point to the importance of shared growth—or inclusive access to assets—by which resource rents are invested in education and agriculture improvements targeting the poor. Taking advantage of resource rents to promote inclusiveness in access to assets also encourages social cohesion and institutional development, where such initiatives financed from taxing the affluent might have been more difficult. Reducing polarization and fostering a capacity for negotiations and coalition building as well as an ability to commit to and sustain reforms, can also be decisive in responding to external shocks.[83] When managed and deployed well,

Box 7.10

Malaysia: ethnic diversity, conflict resolution, and development

Despite the rich natural resource base (tin, rubber, forestry products, oil and gas, and large tracts of cultivable land), Malaysia's successful economic transition was not obvious in the years following independence from British colonial rule in 1957. A communist insurgency raged in rural areas, Singapore separated in 1965 in acrimony, and urban centers simmered with ethnic tension.* There was a strong perception in the majority Malay ethnic group that they had lost out to the Chinese in securing well-paid urban jobs and in benefiting from high-income growth.[†] In the federal elections of 1969 political parties promoting non-Malay interests did well, and Malay frustration ended in riots with hundreds of deaths. Parliament was suspended, and a state of emergency was declared. Malaysia's future looked bleak.

Response to crisis

In response to the crisis, the government announced the New Economic Policy (NEP) in 1970, a 20-year program aimed at sharply reducing poverty, improving living standards through the expansion of education and health services, and eliminating the identification of race with economic function. Employment and output growth were to be sustained by large investments in land development programs, and smallholder agriculture, an expansion of the public sector, and a welcoming foreign investment regime.

By 1990 many objectives were met. The incidence of poverty fell countrywide from 44 percent in the early 1970s to 15 percent in the late 1980s, with Malays registering the largest decline. Primary education was made universal, and life expectancy at birth increased from 58 to 71 years, with all ethnic groups registering impressive gains. Unemployment in peninsular Malaysia was reduced to less than 4 percent, and Malays and Chinese had an equal opportunity of securing a well-paid urban job. Annual GDP growth during the NEP period was sustained at an average of 6.5 percent and the structure of the economy was modernized with manufactured goods replacing natural resources for the bulk of exports.

What were the factors that largely enabled Malaysia to avoid the resource curse, defuse complex ethnic conflict, and successfully transform the economy?

An egalitarian ethos

One explanation is the absence in Malaysia of a feudal elite that might have siphoned away rents and prevented institutional development. As a result of legislation enacted during the British colonial rule, 60 percent of the agricultural land on peninsular Malaysia was owned by smallholders and 30 percent was under estates owned mainly by non-Malaysians at the time of independence.[‡] While reservations and smallholdings discouraged Malays from playing a role in urban life, they promoted an egalitarian Malay ethos that contributed to the success of NEP.

Furthermore, Malaysia developed a sultanate system that cooperated with the federal government in consensus building and conflict resolution. The British had a protectorate agreement with the Malay sultans whereby the resident British officer did not interfere with the sultan in matters of Malay religion and customs even though the sultan's status was that of a titled courtier.** This set a good precedent for the cooperative

relationship after independence between the federal government and the states and blunted potential competitive claims to natural resource rents.

Good distributional solutions

Malaysia's delicate ethnic balance was also a strong incentive for the Malay political elite to seek out distributional solutions that delivered resources to low-income Malays. Even a small shift of the Malay vote could undermine the parliamentary majority and control of government, and tilt the balance toward non-Malay elites. Strengthening the civil service and other political, economic, and social institutions for cost-effective delivery of resources to poor Malays was thus a political necessity.

The pragmatic political leadership was committed to an outward orientation of Malaysia in trade and investment, requiring a long-term perspective on development and distributional outcomes, and a consensual approach to decisionmaking. This was acceptable to the electorate because the Malay political leadership enjoyed credibility stemming from success in steering the country to independence from colonial rule.[#]

A critical but less well-documented factor in Malaysia's success lay in fostering ethnic harmony through a tacit understanding with Chinese citizens on distributional mechanisms. The NEP strategy was to redistribute growth in favor of ethnic Malays, while avoiding expropriation of existing assets for redistribution.[††] Furthermore, while natural resource rents helped fund public programs aimed primarily at low-income Malays, taxation of income, trade, and commerce continued to be light, primarily helping Chinese groups whose presence in activities that generated such tax revenues was stronger.[‡‡]

While several important challenges persist, Malaysia's substantial development success lies in fostering inclusiveness by using natural resource rents to create an ethnically diverse middle class with a stake in conflict resolution and economic progress. Contributing factors include the absence of a feudal class, a delicate ethnic balance, and a credible and forward-looking political leadership.

* With about 55 percent Malays, 35 percent Chinese, and 10 percent Indians, Malaysia is an ethnically diverse country.
[†] In the 1960s, average Malay per capita income was half that of the average Chinese, 80 percent of Malays worked in rural areas in agriculture, and the incidence of poverty among rural Malays was high (Ross-Larson 1980).
[‡] The legislation was the Malay Reservation Enactment of 1913.
** Steinberg (1987). Independent Malaysia's Constitution continues to protect the privileges of the Sultans. The hereditary rulers and governors constitute the Conference of Rulers. The hereditary rulers elect one of their number to serve a term of five years as the Supreme Head of State or *Yang di-Pertuan Agong*.
[#] Parliamentary government resumed in Malaysia after launching the NEP and elections were held every four years starting in 1974. Barisan Nasional (National Front), a pragmatic multiethnic alliance constituted along the lines of the alliance that launched the independence struggle in 1951, was voted into power throughout the NEP period.
[††] Chinese per capita income was 64 percent higher than Malay per capita income in 1973; in 1987 it was still higher but by a more moderate 44 percent.
[‡‡] World Bank (1992a).
Source: World Bank staff.

the rents from natural resources present an important opportunity for accelerating more sustainable development.

Ensuring that aid does not make government less accountable

Development assistance can help governments leverage domestic resources to bring about change. However, aid and natural resource rents share a key attribute: the potential for weakening the accountability of government to its citizens. Aid provides a source of funds to government leaders, again without the need for interaction and negotiation with members of the polity. This effect is clearly identified in research on odious debts, where government leaders raise international loans—and proceed to misallocate funds to poorly conceived projects or, in the extreme, to steal and squander the funds without the consent of those in whose name the obligations were contracted.[84] That the loans are still extended and debt service is still demanded from subsequent governments, despite a weak relationship between the initial contracting government and its citizens, shows that in a weak institutional context, official lending can have damaging effects. The 1998 World Bank aid effectiveness study and other research offer sobering observations:[85]

- In the past, countries with poor policies received as much aid as those making positive reform efforts.
- Aid has sometimes prolonged bad policies.
- Aid is fungible: Funds for schools may facilitate the acquisition of planes.[86]

The study found that aid amounting to 1 percent of national income contributed 0.5 percent to growth in countries with good policies, zero percent in countries with mediocre policies, and –0.3 percent in countries with bad policies. Other studies find evidence that less corrupt countries were not preferentially funded by donors, and that foreign aid eroded the quality of governance, as measured by indexes of corruption, the rule of law, and bureaucratic quality.[87]

Similar to the natural resource curse, development aid gives rise to commitment and dispersed interest problems. But as with natural resources, it is possible to find innovative solutions to increase aid effectiveness without incurring undue transaction costs. In a weak institutional context, donors need to ensure that the limited accountability of government officials to their constituents is enhanced (or temporarily offset) by other accountability mechanisms, such as detailed project involvement or conditionality, until the development of more permanent domestic measures based on transparency and participation. Donors and other creditors need to be receptive to signals from the dispersed interest of the populations shouldering the debt service, for example, when providing funds to concentrated interests—those who control the proceeds from new international obligations.

Donors have become more selective, directing aid to countries with good policies and institutions ("institutional conditionality").[88] International financial institutions increasingly seek to promote the emergence of better institutions and participatory approaches, aiming to strengthen coordination by directly addressing the problem of finding channels for the dispersed interests harmed by ill-conceived policies. Debt relief seeks to encourage reform and channel funds to development. Recipient governments as well as donors are permitting greater transparency in the process, especially in providing access to information and facilitating the participation of civil society (box 7.11). Support is growing for the preparation of Poverty Reduction Strategy Papers, which aim: "To strengthen country ownership of poverty reduction strategies; to broaden the representation of civil society—particularly the poor themselves—in the design of such strategies; to improve coordination among development partners; and to focus the analytical, advisory, and financial resources of the international community on achieving results in reducing poverty."[89]

Averting violent conflict

Violent conflict breaks down the institutional framework that enables people to get the most out of life and to work together toward sustainable development. When death and destruction are widespread, prevention, reconciliation, and reconstruction must be the first order of business. Since 1990, more than half of all low-income countries have experienced significant conflict, generating substantial transnational spillovers that demand a response from the global community—for example, in helping refugees, providing third-party mediation, underpinning commit-

Box 7.11
Improving the process: the Chad-Cameroon Pipeline Project

The development experience in Chad suggests that aid can be made more effective in reducing poverty. The exploitation of oil is a major new opportunity to accelerate development in one of the world's poorest countries. To facilitate extraction, contribute to poverty reduction, and avoid adverse environmental and social impacts, the World Bank is supporting the construction of the Chad-Cameroon oil pipeline through three projects.

But the institutional environment in Chad is weak. Extracting point-source natural resources and managing the associated revenues often add to the institutional challenges. Moreover, part of the pipeline passes through forest areas and is close to indigenous communities in Cameroon.

International aid to facilitate the exploitation of oil in Chad aims to address these concerns with the following measures to strengthen the management of oil revenues and to mitigate any negative environmental and social impacts:

- By law, direct net incomes (dividends and royalties) are to be deposited in an offshore escrow account to ensure annually published audits according to international accounting standards.
- By law, 10 percent of revenues will be deposited in a Future Generations Fund. The remainder will be allocated as follows: 80 percent for priority sectors, including public health and social affairs, education, infrastructure, rural development, environment, and water resources; 5 percent for development in the producing area (Doba); and 15 percent for government operating and investment expenses.
- An Oil Revenues Control and Monitoring Board, established to authorize and monitor disbursements, comprises nine members, four of whom are representatives from civil society and one who is a parliamentarian from the opposition.

- The World Bank is also committed to monitoring the use of oil revenues, and violations of agreements could trigger accelerated repayment of loans under the program, and affect the level of development assistance more generally from the World Bank and other donors.
- The project will comply with World Bank safeguard policies for environmental assessments, natural habitats, indigenous peoples, cultural property, resettlement, and forests.
- A small area of tropical forest (10–15 square kilometers) will be lost as a result of the pipeline construction, but to compensate for this loss two large new national parks (5,000 square kilometers) have been created in Cameroon, to be managed for better biodiversity conservation in those areas.

These measures, which emphasize capacity building, transparency, and accountability, combined with continuous civic engagement in spending decisions, should help ensure that revenues are targeted to the poor.

The program still faces challenges. Some of the first payments received by the government of Chad in mid-2000 were used for military purposes. Since these funds were "prepayments"—and therefore not included in the framework of the project—they did not violate the letter of the pipeline agreements but they highlight the potential difficulties in improving aid effectiveness. The military spending was made public, provoking debate, and the government later took steps to make spending plans for the remainder of the signing bonus more transparent. The hope is that the process will enable further institutional strengthening over time.

Source: World Bank staff.

---

ment guarantees, and supporting reconstruction.[90] In Africa major conflict has visited virtually every country or an immediate neighbor over the last decade.[91] Although some aspects of security may be resolved at the local level, the formation of the state and challenges to the state are national in scope, making conflict a major national issue.

Chapter 3 argued that people and assets—human-made and natural—need to be protected to thrive. Threats to people and assets are held in check by informal norms, values, and sanctions, but also by such institutions as laws and a state that upholds them. This protection may fail on the small scale, leading to extortion and crime—or on the large scale, resulting in challenges to the state and civil war. It is worth noting that in addition to destroying lives and physical assets, violent conflict also assaults social capital, undermining trust and social networks, and devastates the environment, wasting natural assets. As ar-

gued in chapter 2, there are interdependencies in the portfolio of assets, and their destruction can spawn vicious cycles, as evidenced by the greater likelihood of conflict returning to areas that have recently suffered conflict.[92]

Civil conflict and homicides (table 7.1) stem from similar underlying factors, including the potential gains from violence, such as the available loot—and from the breakdown or weakness of defensive structures, such as traditional norms, sanctions, and government-enforced rule of law.[93] Table 7.1 shows that:

- For the world as a whole, the average number of annual deaths from civil wars was four to five times greater than from homicides between 1944 and 1996.
- In Sub-Saharan Africa, both civil conflict deaths *and* homicides are higher than in other regions.

Table 7.1
Civil conflict and reported homicides
(per 100,000 people)

	Total civil conflict deaths per year (1944–96)	Total homicides per year
All regions (population-weighted average)	10.3	2.3
Sub-Saharan Africa	30.3	7.4
East Asia and Pacific	10.1	0.6
Middle East and North Africa	9.4	1.2
South Asia	7.4	1.9
Europe and Central Asia	3.4	1.8
Latin America and the Caribbean	3.2	4.5

Sources: Sambanis (2000); Jacobs, Aeron-Thomas, and Astrop (2000); Fajnzylber, Lederman, and Loayza (2000).

- East Asia and Pacific, and the Middle East and North Africa, by contrast, have relatively high civil conflict deaths and low homicides. This suggests that state institutions have less success in mediating tension and containing civil violence than norms and sanctions do in limiting homicide.
- In Latin America, where incomes and inequality are somewhat higher, civil conflict deaths are relatively low, but homicides are high. This suggests that the state has been well "defended," partly through periods of military rule, but that factors such as high levels of inequality continue to fuel homicides.[94]

"Atypically severe grievances" and religious or ethnic divisions in society have been cited as important causes of civil conflict.[95] Studies by Easterly (forthcoming) and others suggest that the institutional framework is central to constraining the divisive effects of such social characteristics, and that other factors may be more important.[96] Empirical findings suggest that two other factors are important to the incidence and duration of civil conflict: the presence of natural resources, and the incidence of extreme poverty and unsustained growth.

Natural resources and civil war
There is evidence that dependence on natural resources increases the likelihood of conflict, especially if they are location specific and lootable, giving opposition groups funding opportunities.[97] This is distinct from the broader impact of point-source, natural resources elaborated earlier.[98] There is also a link between natural resource extraction and civil war based on grievances related to "land expropriation, environmental damage, and labor migration."[99] The potential access to resource rents makes it easier for private armies or warlords to acquire the arms that contribute to the incidence of civil conflict.

Similar mechanisms may affect the duration and intensity of conflict.[100] Resource wealth makes it easier for weak groups to continue rather than be crushed, and their leaders might derive greater resource rents during conflict than they would obtain in peace.[101] The presence of natural resources may also make it harder to reach peace accords, because leaders have difficulty controlling looting by subordinates. For 13 cases of civil conflict—in countries such as Angola, Sierra Leone, and the Democratic Republic of Congo—these mechanisms were evident.[102]

In addition, the government and the international community may be unable to convince violent rebel groups that they will not benefit from the resources extracted. To the contrary, rebel groups successfully pay for weapons and other support with "booty futures," trading diamond concessions for mercenary services, for example, before the conflict has even begun.[103] Rebels agree to peace in exchange for regional autonomy only if the government can credibly commit to its promises, but the presence of natural resources increases the incentive for the government to renege on peace agreements.[104]

Institutional remedies are emerging, but they need to be strengthened. Civil society organizations continue to focus international attention on the practices of failing governments and violent rebel groups. The publicity is also encouraging private actors to adopt codes of conduct for resource extraction, illustrated by efforts to label diamonds and exclude "conflict diamonds" originating in Sierra Leone and Angola from the market. International pressure is growing to curb the looting by neighbors, now fueling conflict in the Democratic Republic of Congo, and to promote democracy and participation to help prevent the accumulation of grievances that boil over into violence. Indeed, as noted above, recent research on the "resource curse" suggests another less direct mechanism by which resources raise the probability of violent conflict—by undermining the institutional framework that is critical to economic growth and poverty reduction.

Extreme poverty, inclusiveness, and civil war

The high level of conflict in Africa can be largely explained by low incomes and poor growth.[105] Still, the likelihood of conflict rises as poverty is concentrated in a group—distinct by ethnicity, religion, or region. Systematic discrimination, denied access to public services, "extreme poverty and poor social conditions (including refugee camps) also facilitate conflict by providing more readily available combatants."[106]

The concentration of poverty in a particular group suggests that decisionmakers are not receptive to signals, especially from the fringes, and national potential is being wasted. Government leaders may also be politically unable to take better care of aggrieved groups to prevent violence. Adapting institutions, by expanding democracy, for example, can help. Rulers of England strengthened the hand of the nobility by creating a parliament.[107] Indeed, democracy (or a dramatic extension of suffrage to new groups) can be a commitment to redistribution. In many states democracy has been extended in response to social tensions—bringing about successive reductions in inequality.[108] After the cessation of hostilities, the decentralization of power is sometimes sought to reduce tensions by allowing greater autonomy. But it does not guarantee peace.[109] It can also allow regions to drift farther apart, and the center often reasserts its powers over time. For this reason, offers of greater autonomy often suffer the same commitment problems as other elements of peace proposals.

Governments need to move to nondiscriminatory policies and help those in extreme poverty. Recall Malaysia, which used natural resource rents (rather than aggressive asset redistribution) to finance an improvement in poor and excluded people's access to assets, helping overcome ethnic and socioeconomic conflict (see box 7.10). International aid agencies may be able to contribute in a similar way, by providing aid to leverage a new base of assets for poor and excluded people that enables greater participation. In addition, by helping to guarantee agreements, the international community can help overcome the serious commitment problems associated with laying down arms. The resolution of conflicts

and commitment to reconstruction is thus facilitated not only by moving from the local level to engaging institutions at the national level, but further by inviting global participation.

Conclusion

Fostering sustainable development requires the effective management of broad portfolios of assets—human-made, human, natural, intellectual, and social. This requires improving coordination across communities and localities at the national level, particularly for assets with beneficiaries that are widely dispersed or poor. The institutional environment is central to this process, enabling government as well as private and civil actors to be receptive to signals, balance divergent interests, and execute collective decisions. Good processes also promote the emergence of better institutions over time—discouraging the propensity to take, and providing incentives to make, exchange, and preserve.

Motivated by the take, and engendered largely by extreme poverty and unproductive competition for natural resources, conflict breaks institutions down. But strengthening voice, broadening participation, and ensuring more inclusive access to assets can limit the tendencies to take. It can contribute to better institutions—with support and reach that are broader and deeper. Inclusive institutions can liberate creative potential by extending protection to groups and assets previously unprotected. Discouraging the take hinges on rendering institutions more inclusive and receptive to dispersed beneficiaries, which is crucial for better management of the environment. Encouraging the make hinges on fostering a sound investment climate that provides the conditions for growth and for assets to thrive, which is crucial for reducing poverty and generating innovations to reduce the demands on the environment.

Partnerships among government, civil society, and private sector actors offer substantial promise for improving development outcomes. These nexuses of interests, especially national governments, also play key roles in addressing transnational issues, and improving global coordination, as will be elaborated in the next chapter.

CHAPTER 8

Global Problems and Local Concerns

Social and environmental problems often spill over national boundaries. Many of the issues described in earlier chapters—risk management in the fragile lands (chapter 4), races for property rights in water and land (chapter 5), urban pollution (chapter 6), and conflict (chapter 7)—have international ramifications. Dealing with them requires the same kind of institutional apparatus described in chapter 3: problems must be detected and diagnosed, and interests must be balanced within and across borders. However, there is one big difference: at the global level, there is no central authority to enforce agreements. Nations have to devise ways to keep themselves on agreed paths.

This chapter cannot treat in detail the long, varied, and growing list of challenges that require international cooperation: transboundary river basin management; international fisheries management; control of infectious diseases; mitigation of acid rain; and prevention of armed conflict and terrorism, to name a few. Instead, it draws general lessons from the experience with some environmental problems regarding the design and development of institutions that can handle more difficult transnational issues.

Chapter 8 features progress on two transnational environmental problems: protecting the stratospheric ozone layer, and mitigating acid rain in Europe. It applies these lessons to two fundamental but unresolved sustainability issues that are the subjects of controversy and emerging global environmental conventions: mitigating and adapting to climate change, and conserving biodiversity. (A third issue, desertification, is addressed in the context of chapter 4.) Though usually characterized as environmental issues, these problems have causes and solutions with deep social and political roots, and lessons for nonenvironmental global problems.

Designing institutions to solve global problems

Who would have thought that leaky refrigerators, fire extinguishers, and aerosol spray cans could seriously damage the entire biosphere? The story of how stratospheric ozone depletion was diagnosed as a problem, and how the global community organized to address it, illustrates how *adaptive, learning institutions* can successfully address global issues.

Refrigerators began using chlorofluorocarbons (CFCs) around 1930.[1] By 1970 the world used about 1 million tons of these substances each year as coolants, as propellants in aerosol cans, and for manufacturing. In that year, James Lovelock used recently invented techniques to detect trace amounts of CFC in the atmosphere over London. His request for a grant to measure CFC concentrations over the Atlantic was denied: "One reviewer commented that even if the measurement succeeded, he could not imagine a more useless bit of knowledge."

Lovelock persisted, though, and showed that CFCs were detectable far from land. Four years later, chemists F. Sherwood Rowland and Mario Molina realized that even tiny concentrations of CFCs could, theoretically, erode the stratospheric ozone layer that shields life from ultraviolet radiation, an insight that won them the 1995 Nobel Prize in chemistry. It was known, too, that CFCs had a long lifetime in the atmosphere and that increased exposure to ultraviolet radiation would increase the risk of skin cancer. Although a definitive cause-and-effect relationship had not yet been demonstrated, circumstantial evidence was strong enough in the early 1980s to support a precautionary approach to the threat of ozone depletion. The Vienna Convention (1985) committed the nations of the world to addressing the problem, but imposed no obligations.

Meanwhile, scientists had been monitoring stratospheric ozone since the 1920s in a widening global network that extended to Antarctica in 1957. A scientist at the British Antarctic Station, noticing declining ozone readings in the late 1970s, published definitive data by 1984. Shortly thereafter, dramatic satellite images of the Antarctic ozone "hole" captured public attention. This deepening evidence prompted the Montreal Protocol of 1987, an outgrowth of the Vienna Convention, to impose obligations on developed countries to reduce the use of ozone-depleting substances. The Montreal Protocol also set up panels to assess the impacts of ozone depletion and the technology and economics of mitigating ozone-depleting substances.

By 1990 there was firmer evidence of a causal impact of chlorine and bromine compounds on ozone. In that year the London Protocol to the Vienna Convention took effect. Under this protocol, developing countries agreed to take on obligations, with a grace period, and developed countries underwrote a trust fund to assist them.

The process remains dynamic. Two more amendments to the Vienna Convention have been adopted. Technical panels, involving multistakeholder cooperation, have helped identify technological approaches to phasing out ozone-depleting substances. More than $1.3 billion have been committed to help developing countries. The result: a foreseeable reduction in atmospheric concentrations of ozone-depleting substances and an eventual recovery of the ozone layer.

The problem of protecting the global ozone layer was, for a variety of reasons, easier to tackle than other global problems. The production and use of ozone-depleting substances is not central to any economy—unlike greenhouse gases, whose production is deeply embedded in the energy and transport sectors. It has been easy to find less harmful substitutes for most substances, at modest cost. The political economy of reaching agreement has also been favorable. At the national level, the wealthy industrial nations responsible for most production were also those at the greatest risk from skin cancer, in part because ozone depletion is far more severe at temperate than tropical latitudes. And the corporations that produced most ozone-depleting substances also produced most substitutes.

The record of success in tackling this problem provides both hope and inspiration for other global initiatives. It also shows the key components in global problem-solving:

- Pick up signals of the problem and agree on its nature.
- Build local capacity and international networks to support adaptive learning.
- Reconcile domestic and international interests.

These components are explored in detail below, together with an emerging fourth:

- Harness decentralized mechanisms to establish incentives for socially responsible actions.

Pick up signals of the problem and agree on its nature

Solving problems requires some consensus on the facts and on the costs and impacts of action (or inaction). The first step is to detect the problem and put it on the public agenda. Initial detection of environmental problems is often by scientists, sometimes drawing serendipitously on information gathered for entirely different purposes. Acid rain, for instance, was taken seriously in Europe only after a Swedish scientist, Svante Odén, in 1967, used data from a longstanding network of precipitation monitors to link foreign emissions to acidic rain in Sweden, and to link the rain to deteriorating surface water quality.[2] But detection is not enough. Especially where dispersed interests need to be mobilized, activists (sometimes including scientists) can put a problem on the public agenda. NGOs such as TI, Global Witness, and Global Forest Watch gather and publicize evidence on corruption and human rights abuse, especially in relation to management of forests and natural resources. In the future, the new Aarhus Convention on Access to Information, Public Participation in Decision-making and Access to Justice in Environmental Matters may facilitate detection and discussion of environmental and social problems.

The next step is achieving some consensus on the problem's gravity, threats, and potential solutions. At the outset, activists use data to demand action, and defenders of the status quo attack the data and interpretation as inaccurate, incomplete, and biased.

Progress in resolving the issue requires better information and some consensus on the diagnosis. This is not always easy. To understand such problems as acid rain and global warming, we need to understand how thousands of factories and millions of households behave—and how chemicals mix and react across the entire atmosphere. These processes can be understood only through sophisticated simulation models, and the models can be validated only against rich and accurate observations of physical, biological, and social systems. There is scope for honest disagreement on interpreting data and models. And naturally, each stakeholder group will promote interpretations favorable to its own interests. What is needed is a credible, legitimate forum for fostering consensus on diagnosis and action.[3]

Combining credibility and legitimacy in a policy institution is a fine balancing act, especially for global issues. Credibility requires scientific and technical input, insulated as much as possible from political pressures. Legitimacy, by contrast, is properly political. Parties to an international agreement need to legitimate and accept the scientists' interpretations. So do the citizenries who will be asked to comply with the agreement. Mediating institutions need somehow to broker problem analyses that are politically palatable and yet have scientific integrity. How can this be done?

The IPCC is one example. The IPCC was chartered by the World Meteorological Organization and the United Nations Environment Programme (UNEP) to assess the risk of human-induced climate change. It has produced three large assessments, carried out by an international team of volunteer experts, who evaluate and synthesize the vast and sometimes contradictory scientific literature through an elaborate set of working groups, subgroups, and reviews. Because the reports are thick, densely technical documents, attention focuses on distilling summaries for policymakers. Each summary is approved, line by line, by representatives of all IPCC member governments in a forum where scientists can defend their conclusions. The process results in political buy-in to scientific findings. Over the past 10 years, the IPCC's work has contributed greatly to promoting consensus on the nature and causes of climate change.

The World Commission on Dams (WCD) is another pioneering assessment effort, emphasizing social issues. The commission's goals were to review the effectiveness of large dams, to provide a frame-

work for assessing options and decisionmaking processes for water resource development, and to produce guidelines related to all aspects of dam development. Convened by the World Bank and the IUCN, the commission's members represented a broad range of stakeholders. It succeeded in producing a consensus report whose core values and strategic priorities have been widely endorsed. But the informal authorizing environment has resulted in weak engagement of national governments in the result, according to an independent evaluation.[4] And there is less consensus on the WCD's specific recommendations for implementation. It remains to be seen whether the report will be a one-off outcome—or will have initiated a sustained process of learning and engagement.

Learning and adapting

The diagnostic process is most effective when it feeds into an adaptive process of balancing interests, setting goals, taking actions, and learning from results. The Convention on Long-Range Transboundary Air Pollution (CLRTAP) illustrates adaptive learning (box 8.1). This Convention has forged increasingly ambitious agreements among European nations (including economies in transition) on reducing emissions that cause acid rain, eutrophication, ground-level ozone, and other environmental problems. It has done so in part by encouraging the collection, harmonization, and analysis of data on emissions and environmental conditions. This process has fostered communication among policymakers and scientists, facilitated agreement on an operational definition of goals, and promoted a rational, cost-effective approach to achieving those goals.

The CLRTAP and the Montreal Protocol illustrate the appeal of adaptive learning in forging international agreements. Countries are averse to taking on binding commitments when there is great uncertainty about the costs or impacts, about their ability to induce citizens to comply, and about the compliance of other parties. Adaptive learning allows countries—and groups whose behavior is targeted for change—to understand the problem and to acquire confidence in their own ability and others' to deal with it.

Two routes are available:

■ One route is through "soft law": nonbinding statements of principles and sometimes targets. By grad-

Box 8.1
An adaptive, learning institution

The CLRTAP has concentrated mostly on mitigating European pollution, though it includes North American parties. Its first substantive agreement, the Helsinki Protocol (1985), required parties to reduce sulfur emissions by 30 percent relative to those in 1980. Many observers consider this to have been a modest goal. But it established a track record of cooperation that has so far resulted in six subsequent (and increasingly more ambitious) protocols on emissions reductions.

In setting, refining, and implementing reduction targets, CLRTAP has been aided by the Cooperative Programme for the Monitoring and Evaluation of the Long-Range Transmission of Air Pollutants in Europe (EMEP) and the acid-rain modeling group at the International Institute of Applied Systems Analysis (IIASA). EMEP was established in 1977 with a U.N. mandate, but was "adopted" and given permanent funding by CLRTAP in a 1984 protocol. EMEP has worked to compile data on emissions and air quality—and to model atmospheric transport of pollutants. Several reviews by political scientists have pointed to EMEP as catalytic in promoting better understanding of the pollution problems and facilitating agreements on more stringent emissions limits. Over more than a decade,

EMEP worked to ensure consistency in data collection and reporting methods among its diverse members.

By 1990 the data were deemed good enough to support a credible simulation model, RAINS, to assess the costs and impacts of alternative emissions reductions scenarios. This model, developed at IIASA, was used by negotiators in setting commitment levels for the Second Protocol on Sulfur Reduction. It and subsequent analyses have shown that the near-term cost of fully meeting environmental goals was unaffordable, facilitating agreement on achievable interim measures.

The process of data-gathering, model-building, and model application facilitated communication among scientists and policymakers, fostering a virtuous cycle of continuous refinement of data and models. This has helped the Convention tackle additional pollutants and provides a basis for all stakeholders to monitor nations' compliance with the protocols, increasing mutual confidence in the Convention. Integrated assessment modeling has now been formally incorporated into EMEP, though it remains based at IIASA.

Sources: Jäger and others (2001); Jäger, van Eijndhoven, and Clark (2001); Di Primio (1998); Chayes and Chayes (1995).

---

ually establishing norms, soft law lays the foundation for negotiation on binding arrangements. Nonbinding but ambitious targets can also encourage experimentation that would be too risky under a binding regime.[5]

■ The other route is to start with a binding agreement that is easy to achieve, but that sets up a process that allows parties to learn more about costs and benefits and to build confidence in their partners' behavior and in newly created institutions.

For both routes, the seemingly mundane requirement of reporting can be key.[6] Reporting—for greenhouse gas emissions under the Kyoto Protocol, for consumption of ozone-depleting substances under the Montreal Protocol, or for compliance with labor standards under the International Labour Organisation—deepens domestic understanding of the problem and strengthens external confidence in the country's commitment to compliance.

Build local capacity for assessment, negotiation, and action

How can a hundred or more governments, representing billions of people, forge sustainable agreements that touch those people's lives? These agreements need to balance the diverse interests of groups that cut across national boundaries. International labor stan-

dards affect the workers, owners, and customers of low-wage assembly plants. The Montreal Protocol touches multinational and local chemical companies, people who risk developing skin cancer, and poor families that dream of affording a small used refrigerator. Negotiations on climate change affect coal miners, oil companies, Sahelian herders, atoll dwellers, car owners, and wind turbine entrepreneurs.

To work, these agreements must reconcile interests within and between countries. This requires mobilizing concern, and demands for action, among the many who would gain some benefit from the agreement, but who are less vocal than the few who perceive their main interests to be at risk. It thus requires creative ways of framing problems and solutions to increase the perceived congruence of interests, within and across countries. And it often depends on strengthening the capabilities of people and organizations in the developing world to assess options, to negotiate provisions, and to finance and undertake actions.

Bolivia and Costa Rica have countless pressing domestic concerns, yet both have taken the lead in pursuing biodiversity conservation goals with global implications. Their experience illustrates the critical role of networks of experts and policy entrepreneurs in mobilizing domestic concern and finding creative ways to link civil society, domestic policymakers, and global interests. In both countries, research or-

Box 8.2
"Coupling institutions" and policy entrepreneurs in Costa Rica and Bolivia

In Costa Rica and Bolivia strong communities of policy entrepreneurs have grown around a unique brand of environmental research organization that serves as a site for collaboration and intellectual exchange between national and foreign environmental experts. The Tropical Science Center, The Tropical Agriculture Research and Higher Learning Center, the Organization for Tropical Studies, and the Ecology Institute provide training in tropical ecology. They also facilitate networking among environmental scientists who wish to apply their knowledge toward creating institutions such as environmental laws, agencies, and protected areas. These same experts have taken the lead in building national support for sustainable environmental management, creating environmental education programs in schools and helping to "mainstream" environmental concerns in their societies.

The institutional accomplishments in Bolivia include the world's first debt-for-nature swap, the world's largest forest-based climate mitigation project, and some of the world's most innovative approaches to park management, involving indigenous peoples, NGOs, and local stakeholders. Among Costa Rica's successes are its national park system and innovative explorations of environmental finance, including its environmental services payments system, forest-based carbon offsets, and biodiversity prospecting agreements.

Three characteristics of these research institutions are noteworthy:

- They are physically located in the countries of interest. This is essential for networking and community building among national scientists, and produces a cadre of experts who often assume leadership roles in environmental agencies and NGOs.
- They ensure extensive participation by both domestic and foreign scientists, which encourages international cooperation in support of national goals.
- They are nonpartisan, which facilitates constructive working relationships among experts and reformers associated with diverse political parties—a key ingredient for ensuring that policy reform efforts continue across administrations.

Source: Steinberg (2001).

ganizations linking national and international scientists nurtured a group of policy entrepreneurs who could blend scientific knowledge and international financial resources with the domestic political skills and experience needed to usher through and implement major policy reforms (box 8.2). Attuned to ideas from abroad but deeply immersed in domestic social movements and policy debates, these countries have been at the forefront of an impressive record of environmental policy innovations. And they have helped to stimulate national dialogues on environmental quality and sustainable development.

Capacity building of this kind is important for developing countries to assess, negotiate, and implement international agreements. Lacking experts and money, poorer countries are often at a disadvantage in international negotiations. For instance, lower-income countries fielded substantially smaller delegations at the sixth Conference of Parties of the Kyoto Protocol, handicapping their ability to participate in the wide range of simultaneous, technically specialized sessions.[7] And without a pool of experts, it is difficult for these countries to design policies and implement projects. For these reasons, it is important to develop expert networks and organizations within developing countries (and in some cases shared between developing countries)—and sustain them over the long term. It is not enough to assemble teams for temporary assignments.[8]

Reconcile domestic and international interests—with commitments and cash

International agreements are possible because of the overlap between domestic and global interests—and because participating nations agree that the benefits they gain outweigh the costs that they accept. But environmental and social agreements usually involve balancing opposing domestic interests, often supporting a broad constituency of dispersed interests against one that is more narrowly focused but influential. And national compliance is not usually achieved with the simple stroke of an executive pen, requiring instead the cooperation of a multitude of citizens, government officials, corporate leaders, and others. Think, for instance, of the issues surrounding worker rights, pollution, and protection of privately owned wetlands or forests. A nation that agrees to international commitments on these issues has to deploy domestic carrots and sticks to coax its citizens into compliance. However, international agreements themselves can help provide some of those carrots and sticks.

Sometimes, international agreements can be a welcome tool to reinforce domestic legislation and regulation. The Ramsar Convention on wetlands requires that each participant commits to the conservation and sustainable use of at least one wetland site of "international importance." (Almost 1 million square kilometers of wetland are now listed, in both developed and developing countries.) Listing may restrict the ability of farmers or developers to drain and convert wetlands—or that of factories and waste-treatment plants to pollute them. But these restrictions may also confer domestic benefits such as groundwater recharge and flood prevention, while also providing global benefits such as maintenance of migratory wildlife populations.

Although the Ramsar Convention has little enforcement power, preliminary analysis shows that protection of listed wetlands has improved. This suggests that listing with Ramsar helps strengthen domestic commitments to wetlands protection. Similarly, accession to human rights conventions can strengthen implementation of domestic laws on human rights.[9] The Aarhus Convention, for example, appears to strengthen domestic commitments to freedom of information on environmental issues.

Financial transfers are often designed to align local actions with global interests. Many international agreements recognize that developing countries may be unable to finance their commitments to improve the global environment, even when those commitments provide some domestic benefits. The GEF has approved about $2.7 billion in grants to reduce ozone-depleting substances, mitigate climate change, protect biodiversity, and protect international waters. Depending on how the Kyoto Protocol is implemented, developing countries and economies in transition could get billions of dollars annually in market payments that would promote clean energy technologies.

Standards, certification, and performance reporting—inducing socially responsible behavior
How can society reward people, firms, organizations, and governments that behave well? Locally, a community might patronize merchants who are friendly, civic-minded, and environmentally responsible—and do so happily even if their prices are a bit higher than those of less respectable competitors. Outside the community, the scope for doing this diminishes, as information about reputation thins. Citizens may appeal to the government to regulate or tax bad behavior, and sometimes that works. But it does not always work—it fails at the global scale, or when government is unresponsive. An emerging set of institutions and networks tries to fill this gap by gen-

erating information about performance, using that information to set up incentives for socially responsible behavior.

Intentional oil pollution at sea was curbed through clever use of standards and performance reporting. The problem had long been intractable: empty tankers filled their still-oily tanks with water for ballast, then discharged the polluted mix. The 1958 International Convention for the Prevention of Pollution of the Sea by Oil prohibited this practice, but enforcement was impossible on the wide dark seas. A new convention, MARPOL (1978) tackled the problem afresh, requiring that all new ships have a ballast tank separate from the oil tank. Independent verification bodies inspect ships and issue certificates of compliance. Ships find it hard to get insurance without a certificate. The problem was partially solved[10]—though the lack of port facilities for oil disposal remains a problem.[11]

Private firms have great leeway in their choice of production processes. These choices have environmental and social consequences, both local and global. They affect the quantity of industrial and agrochemical pollutants dumped into waterways, the care with which fish and timber are harvested, the treatment of low-wage workers, the release of greenhouse gases. But these choices are generally not easily observable by outsiders.

Systems for environmental and social performance reporting (or certification) might help shift firms toward more socially responsible production processes, for a variety of reasons. Consumers may preferentially patronize more responsible firms—for instance, those that produce sustainable timber or fish products. Communities may apply pressure to firms that flout legal or social norms.[12]

Perhaps most importantly, financial markets may reward companies with good performance indicators. Why? A growing literature suggests that better environmental and social performance is no burden and at best is associated with higher profits.[13] One econometric study found that multinational firms that apply self-imposed higher-than-U.S. standards throughout their global operations had higher market value than otherwise comparable firms.[14] Another study, of 614 U.S. firms, found that a 10 percent reduction in waste generation was associated with a 0.3 percentage point increase in the return on assets.[15] These associations may be causal: good practices reduce waste of valuable materials, improve worker morale and productivity, smooth community relations, and reduce liability. And it may be that managers who deal well with complex environmental and social issues are also good at other aspects of running a business. Either way, if environmental and social performance is a proxy for profitability, then financial markets will welcome and act on improved information on such performance.

Various initiatives are beginning to publicize information about environmental and social performance—and there is some evidence of firms responding. Indonesia's government-led PROPER program, which instituted audited self-reporting of firms' pollution levels, has now been emulated in China, India, the Philippines, and Vietnam (see World Bank 2000d and Wang and others forthcoming). Nongovernmental evaluation and certification systems are developing quickly. The International Organization for Standardization has formalized certification for environmental management processes—systems that give firms the kind of internal feedback mechanisms that figure prominently throughout this Report. Some NGOs have developed certification systems for timber, labor standards in shoe and apparel assembly, organic food production, and other products and processes.[16] For instance, the NGO-initiated Forest Stewardship Council has set up criteria for sustainable forest management and now accredits private certifiers. By 2001, 25 million hectares of forest (mostly plantation) were certified. Several private investment firms have developed "triple bottom line" rating systems to assess firms' social, environmental, and financial performances. And the Global Reporting Initiative, a UNEP-sponsored organization, is trying to develop auditable standards for environmental and social reporting, analogous to those for financial reporting.

There has been rapid growth in mutual funds and other investment vehicles that screen investments on social and environmental performance. In 1984, $40 billion in professionally managed assets were socially screened; in 2001, $2 trillion, of $19 trillion in professionally managed assets.[17] The growing demand for socially responsible investment and the growing supply of environmental and social performance indicators can interact in a virtuous circle. Better

information enables more discerning investment; greater interest in ethical investment elicits better information. Similarly, as certification starts to become the norm in an industry, noncertified products find it harder to compete.

Who sets the standards and defines the indicators—and how? This is crucial to the future of such "bottom-up" approaches to regulation. Already there are disputes about how strictly to set standards for certification. Overly lax standards could defeat the purpose of certification. But so too could overly strict standards, if they are too expensive for firms to adopt and for outsiders to monitor. In logging regulation, overly strict standards can impose high costs on loggers without yielding environmental benefits.[18] This tradeoff is of crucial interest in trade negotiations, especially where developing countries fear that onerous standards would freeze them out of export markets. It is worth considering whether global environmental assessment institutions could serve a role in evaluating potential standards.

Standards and indicators are also being applied to governments. TI assesses corruption in national governments, with ratings that catalyze domestic political pressure for reform and affect private sector investment decisions. It has been credited with helping to spur international efforts to reduce corruption (see chapter 7, box 7.3).[19] The International Monetary Fund (IMF) has recently been promoting standards for reporting basic economic data, such as GDP, inflation, employment, and balance of payments. It has also prepared Codes of Good Practice on Fiscal, Monetary, and Financial Transparency, with the explicit aim of promoting good governance. Countries naturally have different capacities to comply with the standards, and the IMF gives them assistance to upgrade their capabilities. Ultimately, though, markets and the global community may look at progress toward compliance as one indicator of a country's commitment to good governance.

Conserving biodiversity: Maintaining current services and future options

In a remote corner of Ethiopia a farmer clears woodland for planting. In the process he eliminates one of the few remaining stands of the wild coffee from which all commercial coffee is descended—and which contains genes that protect against leaf rust, a peril to worldwide coffee production. In the Atlantic Forest of Brazil a prosperous cocoa grower chops down the forest trees that shaded his now-diseased cacao plants, but which also provided habitat for the golden-headed lion tamarin, an endangered species that could be the prime attraction in a future eco-tourism industry. In the lowlands of Sumatra large companies convert forests of rich biodiversity to oil palm plantations.

In all these cases, actors pursuing private profit not only threaten biodiversity of global interest—they also damage resources valuable to their neighbors and country. The damage may be immediate and palpable, but sometimes it is hard to measure in financial terms and its full impact may be deferred, since doomed ecosystems can take decades to unravel. That makes it hard to pick up signals of biodiversity damage, difficult to balance diffuse nonmonetary interests against focused profit-driven ones, and challenging to implement policies that shift incentives from degradation toward sustainable use. The complexity of the problem, along with the possibility of irreversible losses, motivates the attention to biodiversity in this chapter.

The message here is that maintaining biodiversity and ecosystem functions is not an agenda solely of wealthy countries, as some hold. To the contrary: biodiversity has a local constituency that values it for economic and noneconomic reasons. But where biodiversity's services do not yield revenues, it can be difficult for those constituencies to protect their environmental assets against liquidation. Poor societies may be unable, by themselves, to finance the option values of ecosystem conservation. The challenge then is to find ways to ally domestic and global interests that support conservation and sustainable use.

The scale of the problem

Ecosystems are being disrupted on a large scale:

- A global satellite survey estimated a pantropical gross deforestation rate of 0.52 percent annually over 1990–2000, or 9.2 million hectares a year, an area the size of Portugal.[20]
- Coral reefs are being lost to bleaching,[21] pollution, and destructive fishing. A worldwide bleaching event in 1998, associated with El Niño, harmed 16 percent of the world's coral reefs, with possibly half damaged irreversibly. Another 32 percent are thought to be threatened over the next 30 years, and 11 percent have already been lost.[22]
- Three-quarters of all fish stocks are being exploited at or above their sustainable limits. Total harvests from capture fisheries have leveled off or declined. Some fisheries, such as the Northwest Atlantic cod, have completely collapsed.[23] In others, depletion of prized predatory fish have led to shifts in ecosystem structure. Almost 15 million square kilometers of ocean bottom have been scraped by ocean trawlers, possibly causing long-lasting damage to bottom-dwelling species.

What drives ecosystem degradation?

People deliberately degrade ecosystems for profit. To reach any kind of social consensus on policies to reduce ecosystem degradation, it is essential to understand the actors involved, and the incentives that drive them. Forest loss, for instance, results largely from conversion to agriculture by small, medium, and large farmers, though logging often plays a crucial catalytic role in providing access and financing for conversion. Until recently, impoverished shifting cultivators were thought to cause much tropical deforestation. While there are localized, poignant examples of poverty-driven deforestation of this type—for instance, in Madagascar (box 8.3)—shifting cultivation appears to account for only a small proportion of the degradation of closed-canopy tropical forests (figure 8.1).[24] Other small and medium farmers account for much of African deforestation, and a small proportion but significant quantity of deforestation in closed forests elsewhere. This is a diverse group, including some subsistence farmers but many commercially oriented and prosperous operators. And large-scale agriculture, including ranches and plantations, accounts for most deforestation in Latin America and Asia. Poverty, therefore, is not the immediate driver of most tropical deforestation, but tropical deforestation can exacerbate the poverty of communities dependent on the forest for their livelihood.

Returns to forest conversion by smallholders are variable but often modest. Often the returns are lower than the option value of the forests (see section titled "Act now to reduce today's emissions") for carbon sequestration alone. Farmers' conversion of Ecuadorian forest has been estimated to yield a present value of $376 to $1,721 a hectare,[25] depending on the proximity to roads and access to credit.[26] In Sumatra, con-

Box 8.3
Poverty and biodiversity in Madagascar

Madagascar's biodiversity is among the richest and most unusual in the world, an asset difficult to value in monetary terms but with great potential to support ecotourism and perhaps bioprospecting industries. Of its 12,000 plant species, 85 percent are found only on Madagascar. Its 32 endemic lemur species are an attraction for ecotourists. Alkaloids extracted from its rosy periwinkle plant form the basis for some of the most effective cancer treatment drugs, achieving a 90 percent remission rate against childhood leukemia. Yet over the past 40 years, Madagascar has liquidated about half its forests, which contain the overwhelming majority of its biodiversity assets, without realizing offsetting gains in other assets. The country has fallen deeper into poverty, with its GDP per capita falling from $383 (in 1995 dollars) in 1960 to $246 today. In 1997, 16 percent of children died before age five.

What happened? Agricultural productivity stagnated while population tripled. Madagascar's people depend heavily on rice and a few other staple crops. In 1960 average rice productivity was 1.8 tons a hectare—about the same as Indonesia, and much more than the 1 ton a hectare average in Mali. By 2000 productivity had doubled in Mali and more than doubled in Indonesia, but it was almost unchanged in Madagascar. Static productivity—despite a substantial increase in irrigated rice area—reflects in part the implosion of the nation's road network, which fell from 55,000 kilometers in 1960 to 33,000 in 2000. It reflects also a low and declining rate of fertilizer use: only 4 kilograms per hectare, against a Sub-Saharan average of 12 and a developing country average of 96.* Meanwhile, population grew from 5.4 million to 15.5 million.

The combination of an expanding population and stagnant productivity generated pressures for agricultural expansion through forest conversion. Small farmers expanded slash-and-burn cultivation of rice into forest lands officially belonging to the state. The practice is attractive to farmers because of its low labor and input requirements and relatively attractive yields in the first two years. But yields rapidly decline to less than half

a ton per hectare after a year or two. Subsequently, the land is used for even lower productivity uses, such as cattle, or it is abandoned. In drier parts of the country, grazing and fuelwood extraction spur forest degradation. So, while 115,000 square kilometers of forest have been lost since 1960, the area under cultivation for staple crops has expanded by only 15,000 square kilometers.

Forest destruction has not only failed to yield new productive land; it has degraded the productivity of existing farmlands and infrastructure. Denuded hillsides are easily eroded: 130,000 hectares of irrigated land have sustained damage or are threatened by sediment. Sediment also clogs hydropower facilities and threatens freshwater and marine ecosystems.

Madagascar hopes to alleviate poverty and reduce pressure on its biodiversity by boosting agricultural productivity. Improving roads in agriculturally productive areas may increase farmer revenues, reduce fertilizer prices, promote intensification, and absorb labor—reducing incentives for farmers to migrate to the forest frontier. In addition, transferring property and management rights of natural resources to local communities is generating incentives for more sustainable use and conservation of these resources. The country also aims to scale up promising sustainable agricultural technologies, such as conservation tillage, that better protect natural resources and that have the capacity to improve profitability. Expansion of the tiny industrial sector may also relieve pressure on the land.

In the medium to long run, Madagascar's unique natural assets may provide the basis for a lucrative tourist industry based on ecotourism and resorts. The country may also be able to benefit from global markets for biodiversity and carbon sequestration services—if these markets develop on a large scale.

* WRI 2000.
Source: World Bank staff. Forest area, cultivated area, and yields from FAOSTAT database; child mortality from Gwatkin (2000).

---

versions of forest to cassava, upland rice, or rubber agroforest yield negligible returns to land (that is, after the cost of labor is deducted).[27] In Cameroon long and short fallow cultivation of food crops yield present values of, respectively, $288 and $644 per hectare. Intensive cultivation of cocoa offers returns of $785 to $1,236 per hectare, depending on assumptions about cocoa prices; interplanting with fruit boosts returns further.[28] In the Atlantic Forest of Bahia, a highly fragmented long-occupied ecosystem, mean land values are only about $275 a hectare—and remaining forested land is worth (per hectare) 30 percent of equivalent land under agriculture.[29]

Large-scale conversion also yields varying returns. The returns to large-scale monoculture oil palm in Sumatra are estimated at $617 a hectare, not including the $876 that might be realized from sale of timber.[30] But large-scale conversion sometimes yields only modest private and social returns. In the Brazilian Amazon, almost 90 percent of cleared farm property is in extensive pasture or abandoned. Although some ranching may be sustainable, average stocking rates are very low: 40 percent of active pasture has less than 0.5 cattle per hectare. And more than half the converted land is in the 1 percent of properties larger than 2,000 hectares.[31]

Similar variation in actors and profits is found in marine ecosystem degradation. Poor fishers in Southeast Asia practice cyanide fishing to gain a mere $50 a month, threatening reef ecosystems in the process.[32] But highly capitalized and industrial vessels, often subsidized, deplete large fisheries.

Figure 8.1
Current land use in closed canopy forest deforested in 1990–2000

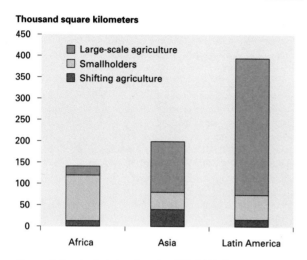

Thousand square kilometers

Legend:
- Large-scale agriculture
- Smallholders
- Shifting agriculture

Source: Authors' calculations based on FAO (2000) Table 46-3.

Sometimes ecosystem degradation is an unintended consequence of other activities. Irrigation and flood control, for instance, have altered many ecosystems. And there are growing threats to coastal ecosystems as, worldwide, coastal cities grow, stimulated by booming transocean trade. Already, 20 percent of the world's people live within 25 kilometers of the coast, 39 percent within 100 kilometers.[33] As urban populations grow along the coasts and major rivers, waste streams grow too. The combination of human waste, animal waste, fertilizer runoff, and nitrous oxide emissions generates massive flows of nitrogen into coastal waters. Nitrogen contributes to eutrophication, a major problem in coastal waters, and to the related phenomenon of hypoxia: oxygen-starved "dead zones."[34] It may also be associated with algal blooms, some of which are harmful to people. Concentrated human populations also load coastal waters with sediments, pathogens, and toxic chemicals. And coastal population growth leads to destruction of mangroves and other habitats that nurture biological resources, including the more than 90 percent of the world's marine fish harvest that comes from coastal waters.[35]

Who has an interest in maintaining ecosystems?
While some people gain from ecosystem damage, others suffer, both locally and globally. Some of the local damage affects lives and livelihoods directly and immediately:

- Run-downs of renewable stocks of fish, timber, or wildlife
- Decreased flood buffering and nutrient filtering due to the loss of wetlands
- Increased flooding and sedimentation in small, steep watersheds due to upland land-use change
- Loss of water yield from cloud forests
- Degraded drinking water quality
- Health and other impacts of air pollution from forest and land fires.

These damages can be large. The Indonesian forest fires of 1997–98 caused an estimated $7.9 billion in domestic damages.[36]

Other keenly felt local ecosystem values are difficult to assign a dollar value. Their constituencies may therefore find it hard to counterbalance the more focused interests that derive benefits from ecosystem degradation. For instance, natural habitats may be locally valued for recreational, spiritual, and aesthetic reasons. In a world where incomes are rising and transport costs are dropping, rare ecosystems may have an option value as the basis for a future ecotourism industry. And more speculatively, the genetic, biophysical, and ecological information embodied in biodiversity may be valuable to future agricultural, pharmaceutical, chemical, materials, and information industries.[37] For instance, gene bank collections currently hold 15 percent or less of the genetic diversity of wild relatives of important crop species, including maize, rice, sorghum, millets, and peas.[38] Loss of some of the remaining 85 percent might constrain development of improved varieties of these crops.

Biodiversity as a global public good
The purely global interest in biodiversity focuses on two aspects: diversity itself and the maintenance of global processes. The term *biodiversity* is often used loosely to refer to biological resources. But those who see biodiversity as a truly global public good see a problem akin to Noah's: making sure that a representative selection of the diverse range of genes, organisms, and ecosystems survives the current onslaught of habitat loss, invasions of alien species, overexploitation, pollution, and climate change. The Noah's Ark strategy reflects people's desires, grounded in

ethics and aesthetics as well as economics, to ensure that future generations can benefit from biodiversity. This is not just a concern of the wealthiest nations. A 1992 survey found that world species loss was considered a "very serious" problem by a larger proportion of people in Brazil, Chile, Mexico, and Poland than in Germany, Norway, Switzerland, or the United Kingdom.[39]

Maintaining global biodiversity requires global cooperation. Think about Noah's problem: how do we maintain a representative set of the world's biodiversity? Conservationists have attempted to identify sets of ecosystems, which taken together contain much of the world's biological variety. One such exercise identified a priority set of 233 terrestrial, freshwater, and marine ecoregions based on distinctiveness of species and ecological processes.[40] More than half cross national boundaries, and so would require some kind of coordination for conservation and sustainable use. And as the Convention on International Trade in Endangered Species demonstrates, international cooperation in trade can help to reshape local incentives driving ecosystem degradation.

In addition to considerations of pure diversity, biodiversity is of global interest because the loss of key species or ecosystems could have transborder or global impacts. This is particularly the case for marine ecosystems, where the loss of one species can fray the food web half an ocean away, and for migratory bird species. Large-scale changes in land cover can contribute to regional climate change. There is evidence that a loss of vegetation in West Africa and in the Eastern Amazon can start a self-reinforcing cycle of reduced rainfall and further vegetation die-offs.[41] Deforestation is a major contributor to global climate change. And there is reason to apply the precautionary principle: the global consequences of massive biodiversity loss are unknown.

Landscape approaches to biodiversity conservation: Ecosystems meet social systems

Balancing interests in biodiversity for the public good is going to require a new breed of ecosystem management institutions. For the most part, problems of biodiversity loss cannot be solved at the farmer's plot or fisherman's territory. Solutions need to consider entire ecosystems and social systems for several reasons. First, the incentives driving biodiversity loss must often be addressed at the market

level—or the political level that governs access to land and water. Second, actions in one part of an ecosystem can affect a distant part, as when water pollution harms a distant reef. Third, to reduce potential conflict, efficiency is necessary—through incentives that keep agriculture on land with high economic value and low ecological value.

Ecosystem management institutions will take quite different forms, depending on the biodiversity involved and the prevailing systems of tenure and governance. Consider a stylized typology of situations (actual situations will often have aspects of more than one type):

- *Aquatic ecosystems,* marine and freshwater, are far ranging, involve many types of actors, and often spill over national boundaries.
- *Frontier forests* are sparsely settled sites of conflict and exploitation as both corporate and popular interests rush to seize rents and claim property. Biodiversity conservation here is an outgrowth of the more fundamental need to establish governance and rationalize land use. These important issues are discussed at length in chapter 5 and so are not treated here.
- *Commons in transition* are areas, often with fairly high population densities, where management of forests, rangelands, or fisheries has broken down, caused often by government appropriation and mismanagement of commons, in some cases exacerbated by population growth. Sustainable use of biodiversity depends on resolving disputes among communities, and clarifying community and government rights and responsibilities.
- *Fragmented habitats with less-disputed tenure* pose difficult policy questions. They tend to be mosaics of agriculture and natural habitat, where both the private opportunity cost and social benefits of sustainable use are high. They include some of the "hotspot" areas where the risk of losing an entire ecosystem is highest.

To give some flavor of how these stylized types differ, consider the global map of population density in forests (see figure 7 in the roadmap). The great, relatively unbroken, sparsely populated forests of Amazonia, the Congo Basin, and Siberia exemplify frontier forests. The densely populated strands of forest in India and Nepal include commons areas under transition from government to community administration. And the populated forests of Central America, coastal Brazil, and Madagascar are examples of biodiversity-rich fragmented habitats.

Described here are some of the institutional challenges in addressing the maintenance of these ecosystems. The point emphasized is that to a large extent these are challenges for local management. The global interest is in supporting these local institutions in maintaining assets of global significance and in coordinating action where management issues cross national boundaries.

Aquatic ecosystem management

The need for an ecosystem-wide approach to fisheries has long been obvious, underlined by the recent disastrous crash of some fisheries. The advent of the 200-mile exclusive economic zone places most (but not all) fish stocks under predominantly national control—and that puts nations in a position to regulate these resources for sustainability. (Chapter 7 discusses some of the factors that determine nations' success in doing so.)

But some fisheries require international management. The Convention on the Conservation of Antarctic Marine Living Resources (CCAMLR) represents an international effort at sustainable ecosystem management—in this case, the 35 million square kilometers of the circumpolar Southern Ocean. The Convention's goal is to manage this area with attention not just to economically exploitable species, such as krill, but to the ecosystem as a whole, encompassing other species of concern, such as penguins and seals.

Similar to the CLRTAP, CCAMLR aims to be an adaptive, learning system. Two working groups, under the supervision of a scientific committee, monitor ecosystem and fishery data. The data help to calibrate ecosystem models and guide decisions by CCAMLR on conservation measures, operationalizing the precautionary principle to ensure that fish stocks do not crash. The Convention faces particular challenges in deterring illegal, unreported, and unregulated capture of Patagonian toothfish (Chilean sea bass), a valuable but very slow-reproducing species. But innovations in monitoring and reporting—including requirements for vessel monitoring systems that permit satellite tracking and implementation of a catch documentation scheme for landings and transshipments of fish—are changing incentives and improving information for management.[42]

Many coastal and marine ecosystems cross national boundaries and demand coordinated transnational action, particularly for enclosed seas and international lakes. The GEF, operating under various mandates to support 45 international waters projects by 2000, has pioneered transboundary diagnostic analysis to identify problems and balance interests across stakeholders. The science-based analysis provides a way of objectively assessing the nature of the problem and engaging stakeholders. It then serves as the basis for agreeing on a Strategic Action Plan. A GEF study found that the analysis and planning, when completed, substantially improved priority setting and consensus forging.[43]

Integrated coastal management is an approach that systematically engages stakeholders in the diagnosis and solution of coastal problems. A recent count found 621 national and subnational examples of integrated coastal management worldwide, with 284 in 99 developing and transition economies.[44] But many of these efforts exist only on paper. Excluding the 110 integrated coastal management efforts in the United States (where the track record is generally longer), only 45 percent are in implementation, and data are lacking on their effectiveness. While integrated coastal management exemplifies the institutional approach to collective action problems championed by this Report, it has not yet fully demonstrated its potential.

Sixty percent of the earth's freshwater resources are found in international river basins, within the borders of more than one state.[45] Forty percent of the world's people live in those shared basins, all with expectations of using the rivers' resources. Historically, competing demands for shared waters have led to tensions and conflict. As populations grow and economies develop, more pressure will be brought to bear on these shared resources. To promote peace, to sustain river basin ecosystems, and to meet the development needs of all those who depend upon shared water resources, it will become imperative that countries cooperatively sustain, manage, and develop international river basins. The Nile Basin Initiative responds to this challenge (box 8.4).

Commons in transition

In South Asia, much of Africa, and parts of Southeast Asia there are regions where people have used forests and woodlands for generations. Historically, some of these common property resources were well managed

Box 8.4
The Nile Basin Initiative

An extraordinary example of cooperation in the management of international river basins is evolving in the Nile River Basin. The Nile, at almost 7,000 kilometers, is the world's longest river. The basin covers 3 million square kilometers and is shared by 10 countries: Burundi, the Democratic Republic of Congo, the Arab Republic of Egypt, Eritrea, Ethiopia, Kenya, Rwanda, Sudan, Tanzania, and Uganda. Tensions, some ancient, arise because all riparians rely to a greater or lesser extent on the waters of the Nile for their basic needs and economic growth. For some, the waters of the Nile are perceived as central to their survival.

The countries of the basin are characterized by extreme poverty, widespread conflict, and increasing water scarcity in the face of growing water demands. This instability compounds the challenges of economic growth in the region, as does a growing scarcity of water relative to the basin's burgeoning population. About 150 million people live in the basin today, with growing water demand per capita. More than 300 million people are projected to be living in the basin in 25 years. The pressures on scarce water resources will be very great.

The countries of the Nile have made a conscious decision to use the river as a force to unify and integrate—rather than divide and fragment—the region, committing themselves to cooperation. Together they have launched the Nile Basin Initiative, led by a Council of Ministers of Water Affairs of the Nile Basin, with the support of a Technical Advisory Committee, and a Secretariat in Entebbe, Uganda. The initiative is a regional partnership within which the countries of the Nile Basin have united in common pursuit of the sustainable development and management of Nile waters. Its Strategic Action Program is guided by a shared vision "to achieve sustainable socio-economic development through the equitable utilization of, and benefit from, the common Nile Basin water resources." The program includes basinwide projects to lay the foundation for joint action, and two subbasin programs of cooperative investments that will promote poverty alleviation, growth, and better environmental management. The initiative enjoys the strong support of many donor partners through an International Consortium for Cooperation on the Nile, chaired by the World Bank.

The Nile waters embody both potential for conflict and potential for mutual gain. Unilateral water development strategies in the basin could lead to serious degradation of the river system and greatly increase tensions among riparians. But cooperative development and management of Nile waters in sustainable ways could increase total river flows and economic benefits, generating opportunities for "win-win" gains that can be shared among the riparians. The Initiative provides an institutional framework to promote this cooperation, built on strong riparian ownership and shared purpose and supported by the international community. Cooperative water resources management might also serve as a catalyst for greater regional integration beyond the river, with benefits far exceeding those from the river itself.

Source: World Bank staff.

---

by community institutions. Elsewhere the resources were so abundant that there was no need for elaborate management. In both cases, many of these woodlands were appropriated by colonial governments, often eager for timber revenues. The problem was that these governments and their independent successors often lacked the ability to manage and protect these resources—and the interest in involving the communities that used them. As population and economic pressures increased, these woodlands have become degraded through conversion and overexploitation.

Since 1985 many countries have begun to transfer control of woodlands back to local communities. Bolivia, Colombia, and Peru transferred almost 50 million hectares to community ownership; Bolivia, Brazil, India, and Peru set up community management over 111.1 million hectares. Indonesia, Nepal, Sudan, Tanzania, and a number of other countries have undertaken similar programs.[46]

Projects in these countries seek to foster community institutions for forest management, as well as formally transfer authority. Doing so often requires changing the national policies and laws for forests and land tenure—and changing the incentives and organizational culture of the national forestry or land management authority. It also requires negotiating rights among traditional users of common property resources—and building social capital and management capacity in local communities. These are formidable challenges, but a decade of effort has yielded some encouraging results—as well as cautionary lessons. Projects in India and Nepal show that communities can realize greater income and environmental gains through management and recuperation of highly degraded forest areas. But there has sometimes been less willingness of government to relinquish areas that still contain valuable timber resources.[47]

Fragmented habitats with less-disputed tenure
The tradeoff between biodiversity goals and private profits is most problematic in more extensively modified areas where most of the original habitat has been lost. These lands, attractive to settlement, retain less-disturbed natural habitat patches within mosaics of agricultural land. One study identified a

set of such areas, the hotspots that have lost more than 70 percent of their original area and now hold about one-third of the world's terrestrial biodiversity on just 1.4 percent of the Earth's surface.[48]

Fragmentation raises the risk of extinction. Smaller fragments support fewer species. Species caught in shrinking fragments may vanish locally; if they are unlucky enough to be restricted to just a few fragments, they risk extinction. It takes time, though, for species to vanish in a newly isolated fragment, as their populations dwindle slowly. In a 10 square kilometers fragment, half the threatened species—those unsupportable by the smaller fragment—are lost in 50 years;[49] in a 1 square kilometer fragment the half life is just 10 years.[50] So over the coming decades there is the risk of an avalanche of extinctions—and the consequent loss of entire ecosystems—if habitat loss and fragmentation continue. But there is also the possibility of reversing the decline if action is swift enough now.

Because these areas have been settled longer, parts of them may exhibit reasonably well-defined land tenure for individuals or groups—though rarely without some degree of dispute. And tenure generally carries with it some measure of legal or traditional rights to modify land cover. So the problem of establishing governance is less pressing than in frontier forests (though rarely absent), and attention focuses on reconciling the interests of landholders with those of the wider community.

The proximity of people and habitats increases the value of environmental services, such as flood prevention and recreation. But favorable agroclimatic conditions and dense populations motivate landholders to drain wetlands, to appropriate stream flows, to "mine" forests, and to expand their towns, croplands, and pastures. These areas thus have high conservation values for the local and global community—and often high exploitation values for the landholder. How can these values be reconciled?

The general approach is to use markets, regulations, or inducements to change the landholder's incentives. It helps to distinguish between incentives that are self-enforcing and those that require external monitoring and enforcement.

Much project-oriented work in promoting biodiversity (apart from establishing protected areas) has been aimed at setting up self-enforcing incentives through new technologies or through new markets. The dream is that a one-time intervention would be sufficient to create a sustainable source of value in biodiversity, one that the landholder would then be motivated to maintain rather than mine. An elegant pilot project in Peru illustrates the principle. There, villagers will "ranch" valuable poison dart frogs in the forest, using a technique that hatches and harvests in a sustainable manner more juveniles than would normally grow. Only juveniles will be exported; since they are impossible to catch in the wild, the scheme will not induce poaching if properly enforced. The frogs fetch high prices, so there is a strong incentive to keep the forest in place.

But there is a growing consensus that this kind of fully self-reinforcing approach, while locally important and worth pursuing where possible, may have limited scope. Few wild biological resources are extremely profitable, resistant to domestication, and more attractive for a landowner to maintain than to liquidate. Large trees, for instance, grow more slowly than money in the bank, so they are always tempting to liquidate in the absence of regulation or strongly felt nonmarket values. Ecotourism today rarely confers substantial per hectare returns, though there are some examples of success (often partially subsidized by donors) in community wildlife management in Africa.[51] Integrated conservation-development projects, premised on the idea that improved local livelihoods would reduce pressure on habitats, have also been disappointing. In some cases local agents were not responsible for habitat degradation; in others unconditional provision of additional income did nothing to diminish the attractiveness of overexploiting natural resources.

A more promising approach to self-reinforcing incentives seeks to shift farmers to more biodiversity-friendly forms of land management.[52] This includes promoting agroforestry systems that mimic and complement the biodiversity and hydrological functions of the original ecosystem while providing more income and employment than annual crops. In Sumatra, smallholder rubber agroforests improved planting stock may be able to maintain half the species richness and carbon levels of primary forest, while offering profits and employment generation superior to that of biodiversity-poor oil palm plantations.[53] Such systems may help to restore biodiversity in degraded ecosystems dominated by agricultural production, to reduce habitat damage downstream from intensive agricultural areas, and to enhance the conservation effectiveness in protected areas by enhancing the habitat quality of surrounding land uses.

But those introducing ecofriendly farming approaches walk a knife-edge. Not profitable enough, and the approach will be shunned. Too profitable, and it could displace the habitats it is supposed to save. So agroforests and similar approaches can complement but not substitute for the maintenance of some areas of natural habitat, and may not always be self-enforcing.

Equity and efficiency in blending development and conservation

Disillusionment with the self-enforcing approach has prompted interest in an alternative that compensates landholders for agreeing to externally verified restrictions on land use.[54] Payments may be ongoing, or where legal institutions are strong, landholders may agree to permanent conservation easements on their property in return for a one-time payment. Payments may be directly financed by the state on behalf of the beneficiaries of environmental services. Or the state may create a market for these services by imposing regulatory requirements on environmental service users.

A well-known example is the U.S. Conservation Reserve Program, which spends about $1.5 billion a year in incentives for landholders to remove environmentally sensitive land from production and establish vegetation that prevents erosion. Funding is based on a scoring system that considers a range of environmental benefits as well as the farmer's asking price, resulting in a cost-effective award system. Europe spends a comparable amount for conservation set-asides.[55]

In the developing world, Latin American countries are leading the way. Costa Rica's Payment for Environmental Services Program (box 8.5) aggregates financing for forest conservation from a variety of dispersed beneficiaries:

- Urban water users (who pay for sediment reduction).
- Run-of-river hydropower facilities (which care about regulation of water flow).
- Domestic taxpayers (concerned with biodiversity and scenic beauty, for their own enjoyment and as a source of tourism and bioprospecting revenue).
- Foreigners (seeking carbon sequestration credits to comply with voluntary or regulatory limits on net CO_2 emissions).

Funds are then used to purchase five-year renewable conservation easements on forested property.

Brazilian states have recently introduced two extremely innovative financing mechanisms. One, the ICMS Ecológico (box 8.6), modifies state revenue-sharing rules to reward municipios (districts) that create public or private protected areas, or protect watersheds. The other (box 8.7) introduces tradability of a long-standing obligation of landholders to maintain a set proportion of each property as a forest reserve. With tradability, farms that are out of compliance can potentially pay others to maintain and expand high-quality forest of biodiversity value, rather than uproot profitable, employment-generating crops in a vain and expensive attempt to recreate a vanished forest. This reduces compliance costs by creating a market for conservation services. Paraná state has recently used tradability as a means of securing stakeholder support for a new law that seeks to secure universal enforcement of the forest reserve obligation.

These examples point the way toward ecosystem management institutions with three important features aimed at balancing interests and forging long-term commitments. First, they would foster a participatory formulation of a vision and specific goals for regional development and landscape management. Environmental goals might well include maintenance of representative ecosystems over areas large enough to ensure their long-term viability. Second, they would allow for flexibility in achieving those goals, reducing the scope for conflict among stakeholders and reducing social and private costs of outcomes that are valued but hard to measure in financial terms. Third, they would set up incentives for landholders to realize the regional vision.

International contributions of funds to such domestic landscape management institutions might be one way to meet both international and domestic goals, while keeping land ownership and management firmly in domestic hands. The domestic institution would assess local goals and priorities, set up transparent rules for providing and distributing incentives, establish compliance and enforcement mechanisms, and receive domestic and international financing, both public and private. It might well be integrated with regional development authorities and use funding to address poverty alleviation needs that are only indirectly tied to land use but are per-

Box 8.5
Costa Rica's program of payment for environmental services

Costa Rica has pioneered a program that allows those who benefit from the environmental services of forests to compensate those who bear the burden of maintaining those forests. The Payments for Environmental Services Program is an outgrowth of a landmark 1996 Forestry Law, which recognizes four environmental services provided by forest ecosystems: mitigation of GHG emissions; hydrological services, including water for human consumption, irrigation, and energy production; biodiversity conservation; and scenic beauty for recreation and ecotourism. Under the program, users of these services finance a national forestry fund (FONAFIFO), which in turn contracts with private landholders for forest conservation and application of sustainable management practices.

The program arose from a growing awareness of forests' importance against a backdrop of rapid deforestation. In 1950 forests covered approximately half of Costa Rica. But in the 1970s and 1980s, the country's deforestation rate was among the highest in the world. Appreciation of the importance of Costa Rica's biodiversity—both as an element of the national patrimony and as a source of revenue through ecotourism—prompted the creation of an extensive national park system. Even so, much of the nation's forest remained in private hands. And from a landholder's viewpoint, extraction of all salable timber and conversion to pasture was more profitable than sustainable forestry, and certainly more profitable than strict forest conservation. By 1995 forest cover had fallen to just one-quarter of Costa Rica's territory. But from the early 1990s there had been increasing attention by NGOs and government agencies to the environmental services of forests, catalyzed in part by a World Bank study that tried for the first time to place economic values on forest environmental services. These discussions culminated in the new forestry law.

The national forestry fund contracts with individuals (for up to 300 hectares of primary and mature secondary forest), with indigenous reserves, and with NGO groups representing smallholders. There are three types of contracts: for conservation of existing forests, for sustainable forest management, and for reforestation. In all cases, participants must present a forest management plan, certified by a licensed forester, that describes the biophysical condition of the land, sets up a monitoring schedule, and specifies actions for the prevention of forest fires, illegal hunting, and illegal harvesting. The landholders cede rights to environmental services (such as sequestered carbon) to FONAFIFO. Payments differ by contract type. Forest conservation contracts, which constitute 85 percent of the contracted area, pay $42 per hectare a year for five years against the completion of specified tasks. By the end of 2001, 4,461 contracts covered 283,384 hectares, with 14 percent of the area belonging to indigenous groups.

The fund finances the program in part through the sale of these services. Hydropower producers, including both small private facilities and the state-owned Compañía Nacional de Fuerza y Luz, are interested in purchasing environmental services such as stream-flow regulation, sediment retention, and erosion control. These private and public sector companies have signed multiyear contracts totaling more than $5.5 million. International sales of carbon offsets (carbon sequestration services) have netted $2 million. The GEF, through the World Bank, recently provided $5 million to support forestry conservation contracts in priority areas of the Mesoamerican Biological Corridor as well as an additional $3 million to strengthen program implementation. This is supplemented by a $32 million World Bank loan to support the program while long-term financing mechanisms are developed and institutionalized. So far, the bulk of the $57 million expended has come from a nationwide fuel tax.

As a pioneering effort, the program faces a variety of challenges—among them, reducing the costs of monitoring and enforcing thousands of small contracts, optimizing the Program's impact on environmental quality, and securing long-term sustainable sources of finance.

Source: Ortiz Malavasi and Kellenberg, background note for *WDR 2003*.

ceived as being part of a comprehensive vision of sustainable local development. Having such an institution in place as a precondition for international conservation finance would allay international fears that the promise of funding would perversely induce greater habitat destruction. It would also allay domestic fears of foreign control of land and threats to sovereignty.

Mitigating and adapting to risks of climate change

People are changing the planet's climate. Burning fossil fuels—and to a lesser but important extent, deforestation and other land use practices—releases CO_2 and other greenhouse gases (GHGs). Accumu-

lating more rapidly in the atmosphere than can be removed by natural sinks, these gases trap heat, changing climate in complex ways, with widespread impacts. This is quintessentially a global problem because GHGs mix rapidly in the atmosphere and have the same impact on climate change regardless of where they are emitted. And it is a long-term problem because the great inertia in social, economic, and physical systems means that it would take decades to moderate the rate of change substantially.

Because of its characteristics, climate change has been a particularly difficult problem to solve. It has been difficult for society to pick up signals—to understand the causes, magnitude, and consequences of climate change. Atmospheric CO_2 has been increas-

Box 8.6
Municipal incentives for conservation

A major source of state finance in Brazil is a value added tax, the ICMS. One-quarter of the tax is rebated by states to municipalities. Of this payment, three-quarters must be proportional to the municipality's contribution; the rest may be distributed according to criteria set by the state. Four states—Paraná, São Paulo, Minas Gerais, and Rondônia—now use the area under protection as one criterion for redistribution.

The ICMS Ecológico is a unique Brazilian mechanism that uses state-to-municipality (including rural districts) transfers to reward the creation and maintenance of protected areas for biodiversity conservation and watershed protection. The intent is to counteract local perceptions that maintenance of protected areas reduces municipal revenue. This provides an incentive for local authorities and communities to support the establishment of protected areas rather than permit, say, the expansion of extensive cattle ranching. But the revenue transfers are untied and need not be devoted to park management.

The proportion devoted to protected area incentives varies from 0.5 percent in Minas Gerais to 5 percent in Paraná and Rondônia. In Minas Gerais much of the redistributive portion of the ICMS is used to support social objectives other than environment.

While the ICMS Ecológico represents only a small proportion of total ICMS disbursements, it constitutes a relatively large incentive by the standards of conservation programs. Annual budgets have been about R$50 million in Paraná and R$15 million in Minas Gerais. (Until 1999, the Brazilian real and U.S. dollar were roughly equivalent.)

Since the programs were adopted, about 1 million hectares have been placed under environmental zoning restrictions in Paraná, and about 800,000 in Minas Gerais. Field interviews suggest that municipal authorities deploy local incentives to induce landholders to undertake these restrictions, in order to attract state funding. The ICMS Ecológico is thus an interesting mechanism because it affects landholder incentives without incurring the large transactions costs associated with payments directly to landholders. Its effectiveness, however, depends on the ability of the state to monitor and enforce landholders' compliance with conservation commitments.

Source: May and others (forthcoming). See also Bernardes (1999); Grieg-Gran (2000).

Box 8.7
Tradable forest obligations efficiently meeting conservation goals

The Brazilian state of Paraná has created a market for conservation by allowing trade in landholder obligations to maintain forests. A long-standing Brazilian law has required that property owners maintain 20 percent of each property under native vegetation (50 percent to 80 percent in the Amazon region). But noncompliance was common.

Paraná's new law allows landowners to satisfy their forest reserve requirements off site, on areas of greater ecological significance but lower opportunity cost. "Trading" of forest reserve is allowed only within biome–river basin combinations in order to ensure full representation of the state's biodiversity. As an incentive for compliance, landholders must prove that they are registered with SISLEG to carry out any legal transaction related to their land, such as sales.

A preliminary analysis of a hypothetical similar program for the nearby state of Minas Gerais illustrates how efficiency-enhancing programs such as this might increase biodiversity conservation and economic output. In a scenario in which for-

est reserve requirements are enforced property-by-property, landholders with less than 20 percent forest cover achieve compliance by abandoning their land to spontaneous regrowth. Because this land is heavily worked and has sparse seed sources, this regrowth is likely to be of low quality, with little real environmental benefit. The private costs of compliance are estimated at about R$1.5 billion. In the trading scenarios, landholders may achieve compliance in part by purchasing forest protection or regeneration from others who have more than 20 percent forest cover. Because of the proximity of forest remnants, regeneration from this source is likely to be more vigorous and of substantially greater ecological value. When landholders are free to trade within the same biome, compliance costs drop by almost three-quarters, while the proportion of higher-ecological-quality forest reserve increases to 72 percent.

Source: Chomitz, Thomas, and Salazar Brandão (forthcoming).

ing since 1750. Svante Arrhenius surmised in 1896 that this might affect global climate, but emerging consensus on aspects of the problem has been achieved only a century later with the IPCC (described earlier). Dispersion of interests in mitigating climate change has been a barrier to achieving agreement on actions. Many of the people most vulnerable

to climate change are poor, live in remote regions—or have not even been born. Even the vulnerable wealthy—owners of oceanfront property, for instance—may not yet rank climate change among their greatest current concerns. The voice of these numerous but diffuse interests is weaker than that of industries and consumers, especially wealthy ones, that are heavily reliant on fossil fuels and would bear the burden of control costs. Finally, climate change is an extreme example of the commitment problem described in chapter 3. Mitigation of climate change will require a concerted, decades-long effort.

With these barriers in mind this section starts by reviewing the consequences and sources of climate change. Using this information, it assesses institutional aspects of undertaking the long-run mitigation of climate change. Then, it examines issues related to adapting to the climate change that past actions have already made inevitable—and that lack of progress in mitigation will exacerbate.

Consequences and causes of climate change

Climate change is already here.[56] Over the past century, mean global surface temperature has increased by 0.4° to 0.8° Celsius (C). According to the IPCC, GHGs released by human action are likely to have been responsible for most of the warming of the past 50 years. Other observed changes are consistent with this warming. Sea levels rose 10 to 20 centimeters over the past century. Over the past 50 years, the summer extent of arctic sea-ice has shrunk by 10 percent or more, and its thickness by 40 percent. Outside the polar regions, glaciers are retreating, affecting mountain ecosystems and water flows. Droughts have become more frequent and intense in Asia and Africa. Many of the world's coral reefs have been damaged by bleaching (see note 21), associated with higher sea temperatures. Animals and plants have shifted their geographic ranges and behavior. Extreme weather events may have increased.

Unchecked, these impacts are predicted to intensify, posing risks of varying kinds for different countries. Impacts will fall heavily on many developing countries, including those that have not contributed to climate change. They are physically vulnerable. Climate-sensitive agriculture bulks large in their economies. And they have less institutional capacity to adapt to change.

Low-lying islands and coastal areas everywhere will be exposed to flooding and storm damage. Bangladesh, for instance, may be severely hit. A recent study predicts that by 2030 an additional 14 percent of the country would become extremely vulnerable to floods caused by increased rainfall.[57] A 10-centimeter increase in sea level would permanently inundate 2 percent of the country, with the additional effect of making floods more severe and

longer lasting. Saltwater intrusions, and more severe dry seasons, will reduce fresh water availability in coastal areas. As coastal populations swell worldwide, a 40-centimeter rise in the sea level would increase the number of coastal dwellers at risk of annual flooding by 75 to 206 million—90 percent of them in Africa and Asia.[58] The starkest local impacts are faced by the low islands of the Pacific, some of which could lose their freshwater and be largely inundated during storm surges if sea levels rise.

Climate change could damage developing-country agriculture. Even taking into account crop substitution possibilities, one study finds that a 2° C temperature increase decreases the value of Indian agricultural land by 36 percent.[59] Arid and semi-arid areas in Africa and Asia will probably face higher temperatures. Feedback between vegetation loss and reduced rainfall could result in faster desertification.[60]

Impacts on industrial countries are thought to be mixed, but may be generally negative.[61] Agricultural productivity will likely improve, in the medium term, in some northern areas. But southern Europe will likely suffer drier summers; much of Europe could experience river flooding. The Atlantic coast of the United States will be vulnerable to rising sea levels, and Australia will likely be more subject to drought.

Current understanding also depicts the global climate as a finely balanced mechanism that goes awry when stressed, with prehistoric instances of 10° C global temperature changes occurring within the span of a decade.[62] There is a risk of catastrophic consequences of climate change that could be irreversibly set in motion during this century. There could, for instance, be an abrupt failure of the great ocean "conveyor belt" currents that warm the North Atlantic and mix deep with surface waters. Biodiversity losses could be massive as habitat fragmentation makes it impossible for plants and animals to migrate in response to rapidly changing temperatures. The risks are difficult to evaluate, but they affect industrial as well as developing countries and are credible enough to demand attention. At the very least they put a premium, or option value, on maintaining lower levels of atmospheric GHGs while the world more carefully examines the consequences and develops options for mitigation.

What drives climate change? GHGs have built up in the atmosphere as a consequence of 250 years of emissions from burning fossil fuel, deforestation, and other sources. Currently, about 40 percent of the human-induced heating effect[63] is from increased atmospheric concentrations of methane (from landfills, rice paddies, and cows), nitrous oxide (from industry and agriculture), and halocarbons such as CFCs. The remaining 60 percent is CO_2. Of the approximately 28.2 billion tons of annual CO_2 emissions, 23.1 billion are from energy and other industrial sources. This component is closely linked to income, across countries, though there is considerable variation in emissions per dollar of GDP and emissions per capita among the wealthier countries. The remaining 5.1 billion tons come from tropical deforestation.

A look at two scenarios[64] for future CO_2 emissions will help provide background for understanding the challenge of mitigating climate change (figure 8.2).

Figure 8.2

Fossil fuel–intensive and climate-friendly scenarios 1990–2100

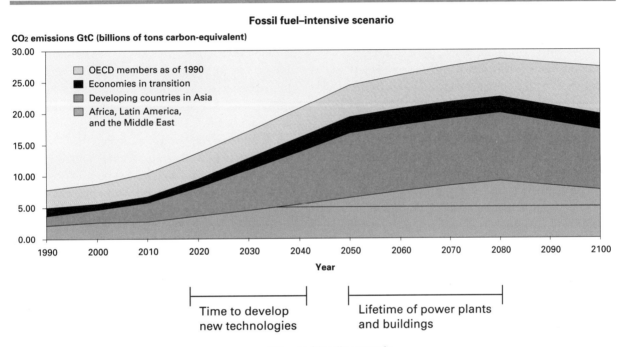

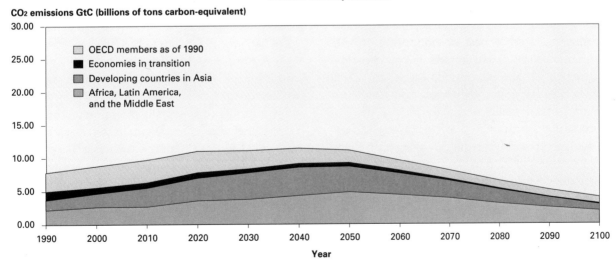

Fossil scenario: +3° to 6.9° C temperature increase by 2100. Climate-friendly scenario: +1.2° to 3.3° C temperature increase by 2100.
Source: Emissions scenarios A1FI and B1 from Nakicenovic and Swart (2000); temperature predictions from Stott and Kettleborough (2002).

Both scenarios start in 1990, with emissions per capita in OECD countries six times the level in Asia (excluding Japan), and with total emissions about equally divided between the developing and developed world. Both scenarios posit rapid economic growth—and substantial convergence of per capita GDP between developed and developing countries. The top panel scenario is not a static extrapolation of current technologies. It already incorporates rapid technological progress, with a 75 percent reduction in energy use per dollar of GDP, and increased use of renewables (up to 17 percent from 5 percent in 1999).

Nonetheless, emissions increase radically over the century, and industrial country emissions in 2100 are far above world emissions in 1990. By 2100 the implied mean increase in global temperature is 3.0° to 6.9° C.[65] The bottom panel scenario posits more vigorous technological change, with a much less energy-intensive economy and a 52 percent share of renewable energy. This holds the temperature increase to the range 1.2° to 3.3° C.[66] In both scenarios, OECD emissions per capita are still twice the level of the developing countries at the end of the century.

These scenarios are illustrative rather than predictive. But they convey three points that are essential to understanding the problems of balancing interests and executing agreements. First, emissions per capita in industrial countries are much higher than in developing countries and are likely to remain higher for some time. In response to this imbalance—richer countries imposing higher per capita externalities—the U.N. Framework Commission on Climate Change (UNFCCC) established differentiated responsibilities for developed countries, requiring them to take the lead in addressing climate change and providing needed technology to the developing world. Second, developing countries will nonetheless emit substantially more than developed countries in the future and therefore must be involved in implementation. Third, pursuing the more climate-friendly scenario requires starting now. Much capital stock—such as power plants and buildings—has a working life of 50 years or more. And many of the renewable and low-carbon energy technologies required for the favorable scenario will require 10–20 years of research and development to bring to market. To have high-efficiency, low-carbon capital in place in the latter half of this century, the process of research, development, and deployment of human-made capital—incorporating greater energy efficiency and increased use of renewables—has to begin now.

In sum, those whose actions cause climate change, and those who bear its risks, form two diverse and only partially overlapping sets of actors. This diversity raises issues of equity and efficiency in seeking options for climate change mitigation—and financing for both mitigation and adaptation.

Mitigating climate change

Concerned about climatic risks, most of the world's nations agreed in 1992 to the UNFCCC. The convention's objective is defined as the "stabilization of greenhouse gas concentrations in the atmosphere at a level that would prevent dangerous anthropogenic interference with the climate system." But the Convention itself did not quantify this level or specify how to achieve it.

As a first step the Kyoto Protocol to the UNFCCC was negotiated in 1997. This agreement would require industrial nations and economies in transition—the Annex B countries—to accept specified limits on emissions of GHGs for 2008–12. The Protocol would decrease compliance costs by allowing Annex B countries to trade their emissions allowances. It would also allow these countries to purchase emissions reductions from developing countries, the reductions being reckoned against assumed "business as usual" levels, since the developing countries' emissions were not capped. The subsequent Marrakech Accords of 2001 allowed for developing countries to generate emissions reductions from forestry projects in only a limited way. At this writing, the Kyoto Protocol has not entered into force.

It is important to recognize that the Protocol's commitments for 2008–12, even if observed by all major emitters, would be only a first step toward the UNFCCC goal. Keeping this in mind, this chapter outlines some strategic considerations in pursuing that long-run goal, a cornerstone of global sustainability.

If the world is to stabilize atmospheric concentrations and provide good living standards to all its citizens, it must switch in the long run to energy technologies (such as wind, solar power, and hydrogen, among others) that emit near-zero net amounts of CO_2. Simple arithmetic shows why. The world's population is now expected to stabilize at about 9 billion around mid-century. Suppose that people then aspire to the current lifestyle of a prosperous country. Among the prosperous countries, Norway has one of the lowest ratios of CO_2 emissions per capita from energy, owing in part to ample use of hydropower. Yet if the global population of 2050 emitted CO_2 on average at this rate, the total would be about 2.5 times current global emissions,[67] which would greatly exceed the planetary absorptive capacity.

Between now and the time the world switches entirely to near-zero-emissions technologies, GHGs will accumulate in the atmosphere. The amount of damage, and the risk of catastrophic changes, will be related to the cumulative amount. To reduce the damage, the world needs to accelerate the shift to lower-emissions energy technologies, increase the efficiency of energy use, and reduce the emissions of GHGs.

Although these actions provide some immediate side benefits in addition to their cumulative effect on reducing climate damages, they involve costs. Because emissions reductions represent a global public good, burden sharing is inevitably contentious. To facilitate global coordination in this effort, a strategy has to reduce the overall cost of mitigating emissions and seek to align local and global interests as far as possible. It also has to avoid free-rider problems. This requires further institutional innovation at both national and global levels.

An adaptive strategy for mitigating climate change provides incentives for taking action now to reduce GHG emissions over three time horizons: near term (5–10 years), medium term (10–20 years), and long term (20–50 years). The global climate change strategy has to be adaptive because climate change mitigation will take most of this century to accomplish. Economic, environmental, and political conditions—and our understanding of climate change—will certainly change markedly over this period. Some actions need to be undertaken now—the impact of those actions will play out over these three time horizons:

■ Vigorously pursue current options to cheaply abate GHG emissions, thus reducing the possibility of triggering catastrophic climate changes and buying time for longer-term, more fundamental actions to take hold.

■ Set up incentives to ensure that the next generation of long-lived capital stock—transport, gen-

erators, and buildings—is energy efficient, to encourage agricultural intensification and maintenance of carbon stocks in forests, and to shift urban structures toward lower energy use.

■ Start now on research and development to ensure that zero-emission energy technologies can be developed and widely deployed by mid-century.

■ Building on current efforts, create adaptive international institutions for fostering cooperation and burden sharing.

Act now to reduce today's emissions

Although non-OECD countries use only about 20 percent as much energy per capita as OECD countries, they use 3.8 times as much energy per dollar of GDP.[68] This disparity suggests looking for ways that developing and transition countries can increase efficiency and reduce fuel costs—with reduced GHG emissions as a welcome side-benefit. Why are these apparent "win-win" opportunities so elusive? Two types of institutional failures get in the way. First, distortions in energy policy may disadvantage society at large, but benefit special interests. Second, firms and households neglect profitable ways of saving energy because it is simply too much trouble to pursue them. Fortunately, there are institutional solutions to both of these problems—though neither is easy to solve.

Many energy-rich countries subsidize energy consumers or producers, resulting in inefficient fuel use, an inappropriate fuel mix, and needless CO_2 emissions. Box 7.6 discussed Iran, which spends 18 percent of its GDP on petroleum product subsidies. Coal subsidies in OECD countries were $8 billion in 1997.[69]

Dismantling subsidies to energy—or to inefficient energy-using industries—is no easy task, for reasons that this report has discussed at length. But it is possible. China reduced CO_2 emissions by 7.3 percent over 1996–2000, largely through industrial restructuring and fuel improvements, while increasing its GDP by 36 percent.[70] These reductions were accompanied by a 32 percent reduction in particulates, which have severe health effects and contribute to global warming.[71]

In both industrial and developing countries households and firms pass up energy-saving investments with extraordinarily high financial rates of return—on paper. Investments such as efficient electric motors, compact fluorescent lights, improved boilers, and insulation can often pay for themselves in a year or two, in the process yielding reductions of both GHGs and local air pollutants. But it takes effort and attention to discover these opportunities, which may appear burdensome and risky to pursue. Consumers may legitimately wonder if an expensive light bulb is really going to last long enough to produce the advertised savings, or if the spectrum of the illumination will be unpleasant. They may not know or much care that some appliances draw a couple of watts of stand-by power, though on a national scale those watts add up to entire generating stations. Corporate executives or government facility managers may not have the information or incentive to find opportunities for reducing heating bills.

New sets of institutions are making it easier for consumers, business, and governments to take advantage of energy efficiency opportunities. These include government initiatives to set standards and disseminate information about efficiency. These initiatives, pioneered in industrial countries, are now being extended to developing and transition economies. Thailand introduced a $189 million demand-side management program in 1993.[72] The program first targeted lighting, which accounts for 20 percent of Thai electricity consumption. The program persuaded Thai manufacturers of fluorescent lights to switch to a new design that consumed 10 percent less energy. The program eased consumer acceptance through a combination of advertising and imposition of standards for light quality and durability. Within a year the new lighting commanded 100 percent of the market. Estimated benefit-cost ratios were 54.6 for consumers and 13.8 for society as a whole, taking account of the program costs.

There appear to be many opportunities for developing countries to reduce GHG emissions at a cost just high enough to be a local deterrent, but quite low for the world. The capture of methane from landfills is an example with global applicability (box 8.8). Examples such as these motivate the "carbon market," which mobilizes funds from the industrial world to tip the balance toward clean energy in the developing and transition economies.

Agricultural intensification, combined with protection of forests from wasteful destruction, has the potential to dramatically reduce CO_2 emissions while

---

Box 8.8
The Prototype Carbon Fund and the carbon market

The Prototype Carbon Fund is a pilot effort to "show how project-based greenhouse gas emissions reduction transactions can promote and contribute to sustainable development and lower the cost of compliance with the Kyoto Protocol." The Protocol, if it comes into force, sets up opportunities for developing countries and economies in transition to adopt cleaner technologies and sell the resulting reductions in GHG emissions to industrial countries that have committed to limits on their own net emissions. (Indeed such a market may come into being even if the Kyoto Protocol fails, arising from national-level policies and voluntary markets for emission reductions.) The carbon market offers tremendous potential. It could reduce the cost to industrial countries of achieving any agreed goal for emissions reductions. It could stimulate the development of renewable energy technologies. And it could provide technology, environmental benefits, and export revenues to the developing and transition world.

Achieving this potential, however, requires resolving a host of technical and institutional problems. Can emission reductions be produced at reasonable cost? How do you credibly measure them? How do you contract for them? Do they really contribute to sustainable development? Answering these questions is important not only for the implementation of carbon markets, but for fostering consensus on their feasibility.

The Prototype Carbon Fund is a learning-by-doing enterprise to help answer these questions. With $145 million contributed by six national governments and 17 private firms, it seeks to purchase emission reductions from 25–30 projects. Its first project finances methane capture and electricity generation at a municipal landfill in Latvia. Without this financing the city of Liepaja would not have found it attractive to capture the methane that landfills emit. The capital costs are high relative to the value of electricity; the economic rate of return would have been only 2.6 percent. A combination of carbon and grant financing for the initial investment boosts the city's return to 22 percent. It will also result in an estimated reduction of 681,000 tons (CO_2 equivalent) of GHG emission, because methane is a powerful heat-trapping gas; using it for electricity not only directly reduces emissions, but also reduces combustion of fossil fuels. The project also provides the city with a landfill built to higher environmental standards.

In undertaking this transaction, the Prototype Carbon Fund pioneered the development of institutional tools for contracting, monitoring, and verifying emission reductions. This information has been widely disseminated as a global public good, reducing transactions costs for future methane-capture projects.

Source: World Bank (2002h).

reducing rural poverty, protecting biodiversity, and providing local environmental services. As mentioned earlier, land-use change contributes 5.1 billion tons per year of CO_2 to the atmosphere, plus or minus 50 percent—that is, 10 percent to 30 percent of total human emissions.[73] Most of the land-use emissions result from the conversion of tropical forests. A substantial portion of this conversion yields pasture or croplands with modest returns. The agricultural intensification strategy described in chapter 5 keeps these forests in place, for future sustainable use, and promotes labor-intensive cropping in more suitable lands. Improved soils and denser crops also serve to absorb CO_2, which increases the land's productivity and resilience. Timber plantations, agroforestry, and biomass plantations could add substantially to sequestration while improving rural livelihoods.

Incentives for forest conservation and soil carbon present implementation problems but offer a vast payoff. Throughout the tropical world farmers may burn a hectare of rainforest to get a one-off gain of a few hundred dollars—while releasing hundreds of tons of CO_2 and destroying priceless biodiversity. Each year, according to FAO data, deforestation claims 3.8 million hectares of tropical forest with biomass greater than 200 tons per hectare, equivalent to about 370 tons per hectare of CO_2 emissions if fully cleared. This implies an abatement cost of only a dollar or two per ton.[74]

Meanwhile, energy users in industrial countries who desire to abate the same amount of CO_2 at home—for voluntary reasons, or to meet a regulatory requirement—may end up spending considerably more. In today's nascent carbon market, buyers are paying $4.40 to $8 per ton to comply with national regulations, and some scenarios for a global carbon market predict substantially higher prices. The potential gains from trade appear to be large. By splitting the difference, energy users in the developed world could, in principle, save money in meeting their CO_2 reduction obligation, help maintain the many services and values of the tropical forest, and invest in a superior livelihood for the tropical farmer. As part of that livelihood improved soils and plantings would sequester even more CO_2.

There are many practical problems in realizing this vision, not least the danger that any particular plot of forest may eventually get burned or cut. But there are practical approaches to addressing these problems.[75] Most important, a global decision to invest in a portfolio of forest and agriculture carbon sinks diversifies this risk. Running these investments through locally controlled landscape management institutions ensures that the arrangements are acceptable. And it also helps shape the long-term incentives for agricultural intensification that averts the long-term pressure for deforestation.

Act now to reduce emissions over the medium and long terms

Actions now to affect the evolution of the capital stock—vehicles, buildings, and generators—can yield huge and long-lasting reductions in GHG emissions and improvements in economic efficiency. Producing this equipment generates vast amounts of emissions. And once in place the equipment drives emissions for decades. Turnover times are about 10 years for vehicles, 30–50 years for power plants, and 80 years for residential buildings. This means great opportunities for reducing long-term emissions and fuel costs by using energy efficient technologies to expand the capital stock, or to replace equipment that is being retired.

The opportunities are particularly great for developing countries, which will be investing massively in long-lived infrastructure as a keystone of development. Between 1997 and 2020 developing countries are expected to expand their electricity-generating capacity by a factor of 2.5, investing $1.7 trillion in new plants and perhaps more in transmission and distribution.[76] Of China's building stock in 2015, half is expected to be built between now and then.[77] Once erected, those buildings are likely to be in place for half a century or more. But current building practices use antiquated technologies that leak heat, do not allow users to adjust heat levels, and consume 50–100 percent more energy than buildings in similar climes elsewhere. The coal to heat these buildings already generates 350 million tons of CO_2 a year and much of northern China's unhealthful levels of sulfur dioxide (SO_2) and particulates. Clearly, a vigorous shift in building practices could have tremendous long-term benefits both for China and for the world's climate. According to a World Bank study, such a shift will take substantial reforms in energy policies so that consumers have an incentive to conserve energy, but in a way to protect the poorest. It will simultaneously require research, development, and dissemination of improved building designs appropriate to local conditions.

Actions now can determine whether development paths "lock in" to high- or low-energy regimes, with self-reinforcing patterns of policy, infrastructure, capital, and lifestyle. Land-rich countries including Australia, Canada, and the United States have evolved energy-intensive lifestyles featuring low fuel prices and heavy reliance on automobiles.[78] Social norms, infrastructure placement, and relative prices discourage individuals from opting for lifestyles that consume fewer resources. And because individuals are locked in to high energy consumption, there is likely to be little political support for increasing energy prices to levels that reflect environmental impacts. Once this lock-in occurs, it may take a generation or more to change. Lock-in is prevalent in the energy supply sector as well. Coal dependence, for instance, creates infrastructure, communities, and powerful political constituencies, making it difficult to shift to less carbon-intensive fuel sources.

Over the longer term the atmosphere's level of greenhouse gases can be stabilized only by switching the world to zero-emission energy sources: wind power, solar power, renewable biomass, fusion, and fossil fuel (with equivalent physical sequestration of CO_2). A few, such as wind power in favorable locations, have good short-term prospects. But most of these technologies are thought to be decades from large-scale commercial realization—and then only if basic and applied research are more vigorously pursued. Historically, new energy technologies have taken half a century or more to displace earlier ones. Accelerated development and deployment of new technologies are therefore essential for substantial reductions of emissions in this century.

There is an urgent need to boost basic research in energy technologies. The lag times between basic research and large-scale commercial deployment are sobering. Private industry is not willing to undertake the necessary basic research in areas such as fusion, geological carbon sequestration, high-efficiency coal combustion, or high-efficiency building technologies for tropical climates. Moreover, there is at least anecdotal evidence of high returns to government funding even in relatively applied research. For instance, a $3 million public investment in technologies for efficient windows is projected to yield $15 billion in energy savings through 2015 in the United States alone.[79] Yet public funding for basic energy

research has declined in Europe and the United States.[80] Only 21.8 percent of the energy research budgets of countries belonging to the International Energy Association is devoted to renewable energy and conservation.[81]

Increased funding for research could substantially advance the time at which low-emissions energy technologies are deployed and thereby reduce the burden of GHG emissions controls. This in turn could facilitate international agreements on such controls. New technologies could also provide a wide range of environmental benefits. Most important, new technologies—especially those related to energy use and efficiency—may be able to reduce the energy bill of the developing world. This provides a powerful rationale for collaborative global research on energy, involving scientists and engineers from both the developing and developed world. It also suggests efforts to ensure that technologies derived from this research are available on favorable terms to all.

International cooperation to reduce emissions

Short horizon or long, these agendas require complementary actions now. Taxes and carbon markets have a number of advantages. They can provide price signals that spur cost-efficient energy conservation and forest conservation. These signals may provide the demand stimulus that drives renewable technologies such as wind power and solar power down the learning curve, making them competitive with fossil fuels in some areas. This mechanism can therefore support the development and transfer of technology adapted to developing countries. Properly set up, carbon markets (such as those envisioned under the Kyoto Protocol) can result in the decentralized transfer of resources and technology to sustainable development projects in developing and transition economies.

Initiatives to encourage the adoption of low-emission capital equipment, and development of low-emissions or efficient technologies, can complement carbon markets and carbon taxes. Imposing energy standards (for instance, on cars or buildings) could be economically inefficient, but such regulations might have advantages. They might fight market failures for which price remedies are not apt, such as a tendency for building developers to shift recurrent energy costs to ill-informed renters or buyers. Or they might prove to be more politically acceptable, and more amenable, to a long-term commitment than taxes. And as more people switch to efficient equipment, it becomes easier to support tighter limits on emissions associated with carbon markets. Similarly, accelerating research on new technologies can nicely complement price policies and other policies that encourage rapid development, dissemination, and uptake of those technologies.

How can emissions reductions—beyond those that pay for themselves—be financed? This remains the most contentious issue in climate change mitigation. In carbon markets, for instance, the allocation of emission allowances determines who pays for reductions. In the view of many, equal per capita allocation of allowances across the world—perhaps entailing transfers from rich emitters to poor countries—would constitute an equitable allocation. But such an allocation rule, if imposed abruptly, might disrupt the rich emitters' economies and thus would not secure their participation in the scheme. On the other hand, a strong link between past emissions and current allowances, applied globally, would hurt the development prospects of poor nations and thus be unacceptable. Hybrid allocation schemes that blend per capita and "grandfathered" allocations and shift toward the former over time have been proposed as a compromise. Other alternatives include coordinated national carbon taxes, whereby each country retains the tax revenue and combinations of allowances and taxes, and the taxes serve as a "safety valve," limiting compliance costs if allowance prices rise too high. Agreements on burden sharing are stymied in part by uncertainty about the actual economic burden that any of these systems would entail.

The experience of the CLRTAP suggests that it may not be necessary to work out long-run burden-sharing formulas in great detail in advance. A practical alternative is to engage all parties by starting with confidence-building steps, while maintaining momentum to tackle progressively more ambitious goals, more difficult decisions, and longer-term commitments as options are better understood. It is urgent, however, to develop a framework that does not penalize nations or other actors that voluntarily reduce their emissions in advance of commitments.

Adapting to climate change

The climate system has considerable inertia. Even if GHG emissions were magically halted today, the effect of past emissions would continue to raise temperatures and sea levels for centuries to come. It follows, then, that adaptation efforts are necessary—but the adaptation agenda has only begun to be addressed.

Some impacts of climate change are relatively predictable and will play out inexorably over coming decades. Dealing with them will require foresight, commitment, and resources. For instance, an obvious way to reduce vulnerability to a rise in the sea level is to avoid the emergence of large settlements in low-lying areas. However, it is generally difficult to exclude urban settlers from areas attractive to them. Adaptation considerations may therefore require larger current investments in developing settlement alternatives, as a complement to the protection of areas that are at increasing risk. Other long-horizon issues include advance planning to replace threatened water supplies, developing drought-resistant crop varieties, and maintaining biodiversity corridors so that wildlife can migrate in response to changing temperature.

An immediate and enduring effect of climate change is to increase climate-related risks, such as droughts, floods, and storms. This occurs both because the climate itself becomes more volatile and because the past becomes an ever less reliable guide to the future, especially for infrequent catastrophic events. A recent study found that large floods are becoming more frequent, as climate change models would predict.[82] This suggests that the cost of building (or insuring) infrastructure to a given risk standard (say, to withstand a once-in-100-years flood) is rising even now.

There is growing appreciation that developing countries, especially, are not dealing optimally with current weather-related risks, let alone future ones. So efforts to reduce current vulnerabilities will not only have immediate payoffs—they will increase the countries' capacity to deal with increasing vulnerabilities to climate change.

One emerging set of innovative coping mechanisms involves the use of long-term weather forecasting and insurance markets to mitigate the risks of extreme weather events. These events can be particularly devastating to poor rural dwellers, whose entire network of mutual support can be disabled by droughts, floods, and storms. An interesting byproduct of global climate research has been the increasing ability to forecast seasonal climate patterns months in advance. For instance, sea temperatures in the eastern Pacific can be used to predict season-ahead climate in Zimbabwe and thus potentially to help poor farmers optimize their planting decisions.[83] These predictions could also help marketing agents prepare for droughts, significantly reducing the impacts on household welfare.[84]

There is also more interest in using insurance markets to help poor farmers cope with weather risks—a role that traditional crop insurance has never been able to play well because of the costs of enrolling small farmers, measuring damages and processing claims, and avoiding moral hazard and adverse selection.[85] Weather insurance, in contrast, depends on easily measurable temperature and precipitation data—and facilitates reinsurance. A current International Finance Corporation pilot project is exploring the potential for this kind of insurance in the developing world. These initiatives underline the value of weather data as both local and global public goods.

Management of large-scale climate risks will become more important at the subnational and national scale. Indeed, the financial damages from weather-related catastrophes are increasing rapidly, though it is difficult to separate greater exposure from the higher frequency of extreme events. There is a strong role for individual nations, and the world at large, to insure poor vulnerable regions against these catastrophes, a role already filled (on an ad hoc and sometimes inadequate basis) through a patchwork of disaster relief responses. A key commitment problem in designing a more comprehensive system is providing adequate insurance without encouraging risk-seeking or environmentally damaging behavior, such as settlements in areas that are at risk of landslides, or agriculture in fragile areas.[86]

The most general and effective way to help vulnerable poor countries adapt to climate change is to promote rapid and sustainable development. Over the coming decades more vigorous growth rates and accelerated investments in human capital will shift these countries out of climate-sensitive sectors and improve their capacity to cope with climate-related risks.

Conclusion

The distinctive feature of global problems is the lack of a central authority for coordination and enforcement. Despite this obstacle, there are encouraging examples of successful transnational institution building to tackle transborder environmental problems. Success has been greatest in cases such as stratospheric ozone and acid rain, where the problem can be made operational in precise technical terms; where international action can therefore focus on tightly defined interventions; and where the perceived benefits of collective action have been high, for key actors, relative to the cost. It will be more difficult for other environmental and social problems—where the relationship between action and impact is less well understood, and where the costs and benefits of action do not coincide. Yet an adaptive strategy of the type described in this chapter has much to recommend itself because the frequency and urgency of such problems is bound to increase as globalization progresses along many dimensions. The next chapter illustrates some ways of approaching the linkages among social, economic, and environmental issues within and between countries in a shrinking world.

CHAPTER 9

Pathways to a Sustainable Future

Accelerated growth in productivity and income can eliminate poverty and enhance prosperity in developing countries. This growth needs to be achieved at the same time critical ecosystem services are improved and the social fabric that underpins development is strengthened. A close look at what is happening on the ground (chapters 4–8) reveals both cause for concern and cause for hope.

Concern stems from evidence that getting the world on a sustainable path is problematic:

- In many developing countries, productivity is low, growth is stagnant, and unemployment is high.
- The number of people living on less than $1 a day (1.2 billion) is dropping but it is still a challenge, and more people are living on fragile lands.
- Income inequality is rising. Average income in the wealthiest 20 countries is 37 times that in the poorest 20 countries—twice the ratio in 1970.
- Many of the poorest countries are wracked by civil conflict, with animosities deep and prolonged.
- Stress on the environment is increasing. Fisheries are being overexploited, soils degraded, coral reefs destroyed, tropical forests lost, air and water polluted.
- The financial transfers to address these issues are far from adequate, even though the resources are available.

Hope springs from the genuine progress made already in boosting average per-capita incomes in developing countries and reducing infant mortality and illiteracy rates—and from the greater awareness of the problems that remain. Disparate groups now agree that the current development path, though possible for a while, is not sustainable. Science and technology are providing some answers, but they will not be sufficient without complementary changes in institutions. The world community, in confronting some of the challenges, is grappling with new strategies and goals:

- Development agencies are shifting to more participatory and holistic approaches with a medium-term perspective, through the Comprehensive Development Framework (CDF) and focused poverty reduction strategies, backed by actions on the ground through partnerships, broader inclusion in the preparation of assistance strategies, and some shifts in lending and grant aid.
- The private sector is more committed to sustainable development, with greater use of triple-bottom-line accounting by firms and greater use of environmental and social criteria by investors.
- Governments and civil society are supporting the Convention on Biodiversity, the Convention to Combat Desertification, the Convention on Climate Change, and the Millennium Development Goals. And civil society is demanding more public and private accountability.

Although encouraging, these advances are small relative to the many challenges of sustainable development. Sustainability requires thinking long term, but acting now—it also requires coordination. This Report recognizes the importance of economic incentives and policies in changing behavior, but it does not focus on specific policies or organizational designs. (Nor does it evaluate projections based on different policy or organizational scenarios.) Instead it argues that well known and appropriate policies have not been adopted or implemented because of distributional problems and institutional weaknesses, and that sustainable development with faster growth and higher productivity, capable of eliminating poverty and achieving a more just and sustainable development path, requires much stronger institutions. To support improvements in well-being, these institutions would need to manage a broader portfolio of assets and adapt to new problems and opportunities. Technologies and preferences will change, and resource allocation and distribution issues cannot be neatly separated.

Managing risk is important. Not all risks are insurable. Not all irreversible changes are bad, but some are. For the assets most at risk—the natural and social—markets cannot provide the basic coordinating functions of sensing problems, balancing interests, and executing policies and solutions. These types of assets have impacts, good and bad, that extend beyond individual transactions and thus require coordination to promote good spillovers and minimize the bad. This coordination reveals the need for institutions that are capable of organizing dispersed interests, confronting vested interests, and ensuring credible commitments in execution.

This Report shows that rising income can facilitate but not guarantee better environmental and social outcomes by permitting countries to simply "grow out of" pollution or civil conflict. It also shows that low income does not condemn people to a deteriorating environment or social climate. What makes the difference? Public action, through competent institutions.

Mobilizing institutional responses is more difficult for some problems than others. Problems with impacts and risks that are diffuse and long term (such as climate change and biodiversity loss) are less readily perceived and appreciated than those immediately felt and measured (i.e., some forms of local air and water pollution and deforestation). Assets that are public goods or common property goods—such as clean air, forests, fisheries, and water—are a challenge to manage sustainably. The reason is that private property rights are difficult to assign or enforce, or if improperly designed they fragment and undermine the underlying joint functions of an asset—say, an interconnected ecosystem. In addition, the concerns of the poor and powerless are less likely to attract the attention of society's many institutions than those of strong and vested interest groups. That is why greater equality in access to assets and voice makes a difference in the kinds of environmental and social concerns that society addresses.

This Report argues that, for countries and local communities, extreme inequalities in assets, power, and voice are corrosive, linked, and self-perpetuating. When the poor lack voice and a stake in society, social assets (such as trust) and environmental assets (on which the poor depend) are eroded, stability is undermined, and the ability to solve economic, social, and environmental problems (that require collective action) dissipates.

As the world comes to resemble a single community, these lessons may apply even at the global level. At the very least, inequality and the lack of hope for the poorest countries will inhibit attempts at solving global problems—not just the current preoccupations with cross-border spillovers of conflict and terrorism, but also the currently unimagined problems that will require global cooperation 20 or 50 years hence. That is why ending global poverty is much more than a moral imperative—it is the cornerstone of a sustainable world.[1]

The next 20 to 50 years are a demographic window of opportunity, created by the deceleration of population growth rates and the decline in dependency ratios. This period will also witness completion of the urban transition in most countries. The demographic transition will permit greater savings if the working age population has jobs and investment opportunities. The urban transition will facilitate income generation, but over the next 50 years it will also require massive investments. Many of these investments are likely to be long-lived—so getting them right by incorporating environmental and social concerns in their design now is critical.

Even the next 15 years (2003–2018) could bring a record period of economic growth in developing countries. Driven by growth in China and India, income in the low- and middle-income countries will almost double—accounting for more than a third of the 60 percent increase in world output.[2] This period offers the opportunity to lay the foundation for inclusive growth—which will require confronting barriers to change. Institutions that can manage the social and economic transitions, by partially compensating losing interests, are much easier to create in rapidly growing economies than in economies where inclusion requires a battle over stagnant shares.[3] For many countries whether the opportunities generated by new growth are inclusive, or whether they lock in vested interests and exclusive institutions, will depend on decisions taken in the next few years.

Acting today

This Report outlines actions that can be taken now to improve the ability of institutions to identify, adopt, and implement policies that facilitate growth while addressing critical environmental and social issues.

Institutional and sectoral approaches are complementary

Sustainable development requires action across many sectors and disciplines, including water, energy, health, agriculture, biodiversity, and others. In a companion document, the World Bank sets forth some recommendations and action plans to advance sectoral goals.[4]

This Report takes a different approach—but one intended to complement and support the sectoral perspectives. Its message is that proposing and endorsing a set of action plans are important first step, but realizing them requires an institutional apparatus that cuts across sectors. Achieving all the broad sectoral goals will involve problem diagnosis, decisions with distributional consequences, and coordinated and sustained commitments to action. These functional capabilities require general improvement in coordinating institutions within and across countries.

Making progress on the sectoral issues, for example, requires first a better understanding of local conditions and a better ability to diagnose local problems. Domestic and international institutions will be required to fund and implement R&D where local capacities are deficient. Second, some difficult distributional issues must be resolved: How to divide the water among claimants? How to allocate health resources among preventive, primary, and secondary care? What sort of land uses to permit, for whom, if environmental processes are to be maintained? Without institutions that represent fairly the interests of dispersed and (usually) voiceless interests, institutions affecting these sectors are prone to capture by vested interests, and they are unlikely to implement efficient or equitable solutions. Third, commitment problems loom large. Health and water services often dete-

riorate after costly initial investments for lack of routine funding and maintenance. This speaks to the challenge of organizing beneficiaries for sustained commitments.

This Report shows that even with imperfect institutions it is possible—indeed imperative—to build now on the many institutional innovations already out there that show the way forward.

Many, if not all, of the institutional innovations cited in this Report already show signs of being replicable and capable of being scaled up to meet the challenges ahead. For example, the pilot experience with security of tenure in *favelas* in Brazil is being extended to hundreds of thousands of households. The multistakeholder pilot pollution disclosure programs in China have moved from 2 pilot municipalities to 13; countrywide implementation is currently under discussion. The village initiative in Morocco is being replicated in a dozen other villages. The forest concession program in Cameroon has created a constituency for expanding it to other sectors. There is much creativity under way with initiatives emerging from the public sector, the private sector, and civil society. An enabling environment is needed to encourage such initiatives, to facilitate partnerships, and to help mobilize the resources needed to scale up promising activities within countries, and across countries.

Picking up signals early

Being sensitive to early signs of problems, especially from the fringes, is important if society is to avoid costly crises later. HIV/AIDS is a case in point. In the early stages of the epidemic, HIV/AIDS received little attention since no one knew how contagious it was or the trajectory of future costs. By now, with the evidence available, all countries should have programs to identify the problem early and to stay ahead of the epidemic. The same is true for environmental issues—the status of biodiversity, air pollution, lead in gasoline, or the drawdown of acquifers in arid regions.

Creating information for constituencies and constituencies for information. There is a need for significant investment in information and indicators at global and local levels, where this information would find users and audiences. The initiative must go well beyond current attempts to devise indicators of sustainable development, including summary indexes that try to capture sustainable development in a sin-

Box 9.1
Think spatially

The usefulness of the spatial approach adopted in this Report is evident from the map below. The problem, in this case, is the incidence of poverty in Ecuador at varying scales. Pockets of poverty at the canton level are obscured by aggregation, potentially undermining national level responses.

Spatial disaggregation of poverty

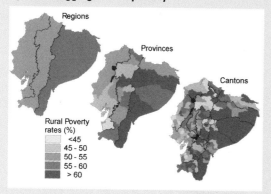

Source: Elbers, C., Lanjouw, J. and Lanjouw, P. Forthcoming. 'Micro-Level Estimation of Poverty and Inequality', *Econometrica,* and Demombynes, G., C. Elbers, J.O. Lanjouw, P. Lanjouw, J. Mistiaen and B. Ozler (2002), Producing an improved geographic profile of poverty. Methodology and evidence from three developing countries, WIDER Discussion paper No. 2002/39, United Nations University, Helsinki.

gle headline number. If society is to sustain development, it needs good indicators, but it also needs individuals and groups who demand and use detailed, and quality information to solve problems, and others who produce information to meet that demand. Summary indicators should rest on a solid foundation of supporting data.

Environmental and social problems are easy to misdiagnose when there is a lack of reliable, current, and geographically disaggregated information. For many important aspects of the environment, global conditions or trends are worrisome, but society lacks the detailed data to monitor, diagnose, and manage the problems at local, national, and global levels. Data for the social sphere are similarly limited. For most countries, reliable, up-to-date, spatially disaggregated information is lacking on poverty and many other social concerns (health, education, crime).

These data gaps inhibit understanding of—and consensus on—the impacts of policy reforms, national and international, on poverty in the develop-

ing world. They also impede the formulation and execution of strategies to combat desertification, other forms of ecosystem degradation, and biodiversity loss. And they muddy the discussion of the nature and impacts of global inequality. Fortunately, rapid changes in communication and information technology make it more feasible to gather this information through a combination of surveys, reports from ground observers, and information from satellites and other sensors. As information costs continue to plummet, the scope for expanding the collection of this kind of information is immense. Innovative information systems can track and deter industrial polluters (as in Indonesia's PROPER system) and illegal deforestation and forest fires (as in Mato Grosso's environmental control system).

Although information provision can sometimes be a catalyst for change, the most effective systems are those that create constituencies for information. The constituencies may be public agencies that use the information to plan and assess strategies for pollution control, crime prevention, or public health delivery. Or they may be civil society organizations that use information to mobilize dispersed interests. It is demand by users that stimulates and maintains the production of relevant, reliable information.

This Report proposes an intensive global effort to develop and fund a program to fill data gaps, which would include:

- More local poverty, health, and education data linked to national totals
- More spatially disaggregated data on economic and environmental health conditions for the analysis of local problems and impacts
- More coupling of satellite-based remote sensing data with local "ground-truthing" information, to measure the extent and quality of land under different types of habitat or land cover
- More monitoring of soil degradation, its causes and impacts
- More effort at measuring hydrological conditions.
- More investments in geospatial information, such as the availability of infrastructure services, and accurate current maps of road networks
- More coordination and augmentation of national efforts to monitor the Millennium Development Goals, to increase comparability, and to provide desirable levels of frequency and geographic detail.

Balancing interests

To equitably and efficiently balance interests within a society, two elements are necessary: first, getting everyone fairly represented at the bargaining table; second, facilitating negotiation once everyone is there. For many problems at the level of the community or nation—especially those relating to environmental and social issues—the responsibility lies with the government. But governments vary in their capacity to undertake these tasks. An expanding set of institutional tools can assist or complement governments in balancing interests, and they can assist citizens in ensuring that their governments are fair and responsive in doing so. These tools become even more important at the international level, where they must substitute for government. It is fundamentally difficult to balance interests in heterogeneous societies. But taken together, in a context of increasingly democratic institutions and decreasing costs of information and communication, these tools give some hope.

Transparency, performance reporting, and accountability. Often the biggest barrier to balancing interests is an imbalance in the power or influence of parties. Devices for accountability—including transparency and performance reporting—are useful tools for countering the tendency of entrenched interests to capture institutions or to be unresponsive to dispersed or less powerful interests. Providing this kind of information helps level the playing field for negotiation, since less powerful interests will typically have poorer access to information. Performance reporting can also help governments, companies, and other organizations understand the effectiveness and impacts of their own actions, for instance

- *National reporting*—transparency in fiscal affairs, reliability of legal institutions, and adequacy of environmental impact reviews—can all provide the information and incentives necessary to improve governance and the balancing of interests. Examples include the recent International Monetary Fund Codes of Good Practice on transparency in fiscal, monetary, and financial policies, and WTO requirements on subsidy reporting. Another example is the Aarhus Convention—a voluntary commitment to environmental transparency. National reporting requirements under the WTO, multinational environmental agreements, and other international treaties can help nations track and man-

age their own compliance processes and help build confidence among parties to forge agreements.

- *Independent audits of public programs*—especially programs related to the management of public assets, such as land, water, forests, minerals, and fisheries and the regulation of pollution—can deter corruption and promote better management of environmental resources. Regular audits of national environmental assets can be useful in detecting and diagnosing problems. Public ratings of governments' transparency and corruption can affect investment and provide a check on government capture by vested interests. Assessment of the distributional impact of government expenditures provides an essential basis for renegotiating them.
- *Performance reporting for cities and local governments* provides a tool for citizens to ensure that governments are responsive to public needs and are equitably and efficiently implementing agreed-on programs in health, sanitation, water supply, public safety, and other areas of public concern.
- *Performance reporting by private firms*—financial, environmental, and social—helps society to identify actors with disproportionately large impacts, both good and bad, and to understand trade-offs and complementarities between economic performance, and economic, environmental, and social performance.

Forums and networks for negotiation. Governments and civil society can seek ways to facilitate negotiation between affected parties. For instance, Colombia's regional environmental authorities have set up structured negotiations between water polluters and water users to help determine tolerable levels of pollution. Participatory budgeting has transformed the budgetary process in more than 80 Brazilian cities. At the international level, the Convention on Long-Range Transboundary Air Pollution forums on air pollution and the Global Environment Facility-sponsored transboundary diagnostic assessments for international waters provide structured means of assessing options. These forums become more effective when they build up social capital through dense networks of trust and information linking technical experts, government officials and legislators, civil society, and special interests.

Compensation and incentives. Even win-win outcomes usually have a loser—a party whose losses are outbalanced by social gains. Basic principles for balancing interests therefore include minimizing the losses, compensating losers, or providing incentives that reconcile private and social objectives.

One way to do this in the environmental sphere is through market-based permits. Where actors have different costs of complying with social objectives, trading rights or obligations can substantially reduce compliance costs for individuals and for society as a whole (see box 8.7). Assignment of valuable permit rights (pollution permits, fishery quotas) is also a means of compensating potential losers and ensuring participation in a reformed system. When the potential losers are wealthy interests, however, there may be an unavoidable trade-off between equity and cooperation.

Certification systems are another means of aligning private and social incentives. Certification of firms helps investors identify companies with better environmental and social performance, thus promoting incentives for more socially responsible behavior. Certification of financial institutions (including private banks, bilateral export-import banks, and multilateral development banks) can promote standards for assessing the environmental and social impacts of investment projects. Certification of products (wood, coffee, fish, beach resorts, garments) can allow consumers and investors to reward firms that employ environmentally and socially sustainable production processes. Certification of diamonds and other lootable commodities can be part of a strategy to avert civil conflict over point-source wealth. Even governments may find it advantageous to participate in voluntary certification schemes. For instance, the Alaska state government applied for, and received, certification by the Marine Stewardship Council for management of its salmon fishery (see box 7.9).

The success of these efforts depends on how they influence producer, consumer, and investor behavior. And that depends on the costs of certification, the proportion of the industry that is sensitive to certification, and the legitimacy, integrity, and reliability of the certification criteria and process.

To become more widespread and effective, certification systems require coordinated international attention on several grounds. First, there are important links to the world trade system and a need for coordination with WTO activities—to ensure that standards are not used to disguise protectionism.

Second, careful attention is needed to monitor the possibility that complying with certification procedures may be too burdensome for small firms. Third, and probably most important, there is a need to ensure the integrity of the evolving certification systems. For these systems to work on a large scale, they will probably require a massive expansion of "markets for honesty." These are the networks of private auditors and certifiers, and their accreditation agencies, that provide ISO certification, shipping certification, and audits of corporate earnings.

Implementing

Implementing and executing policies and programs requires appropriate institutional capacity. Mention of capacity-building evokes respect and approval—but not always excitement or enthusiasm. It has usually been seen as an add-on to projects and programs with other, more important purposes. It is often identified with failed technical assistance projects that relied heavily on the ephemeral input of foreign consultants. The same is true of monitoring and evaluation, another project add-on that often fails to be executed with rigor or to provide much insight. Yet institutional competence, especially the ability to learn, is crucial to efficient use of development investments and to solving the coordination problems described in this Report.

Promoting capacity-building and problem-solving in the developing world. The need to emphasize long-term capacity-building has been recognized for more than a decade.[5] Yet, despite technical cooperation grants of $201.3 billion over 1990–2001,[6] progress in institution-building in developing countries has been disappointing. Most of those funds, to be sure, have been devoted to project preparation. Such investments may have been effective in achieving project goals through reliance on expatriate inputs, but at the cost of forgone opportunities to bolster local capacity. There are failures, too, in the demand for institution-building. Often, lack of ownership, lack of government interest in bolstering capacity, and pressures for rent-seeking have kept competent institutions from taking root.[7]

Several new approaches could help place learning and institutional development at the core of sustainable development efforts—that is, projects and programs designed around institutional development, rather than vice versa. These approaches recognize that capacity-building is not accomplished in a few years and thus is not well suited to lending for individual projects or adjustment programs. These approaches also recognize that capacity has a strong social capital component, involving not just people but enduring networks that link policymakers, experts, civil society, and the private sector. And these approaches generate virtuous circles when information and indicators are made available to groups that demand and act on that information.

The new approaches use a variety of new types of learning organizations to stimulate both the demand for and supply of institutional skills; they include:

- *Think-and-do tanks,* policy analytic and action-oriented organizations that build links (twinning) to universities and think tanks in other developing countries and in the developed world, to government line agencies in their own countries, and to local governments and community organizations working on the ground (box 9.2).
- *Scientific research organizations,* based in the developing world, that combine local and global expertise and help to nurture "policy entrepreneurs" at home in both scientific and policy worlds.
- *Learning networks* for sharing knowledge, such as the Union of Capital Cities of Ibero-America—real-time, demand-driven learning networks run by national and international associations of mayors, local government officials, and city practitioners share experiences among their members and other cities through the Internet and workshops.
- *CSOs for monitoring and evaluating government and corporate performance.* These groups that in-

Box 9.2
Problem solving by think-and-do tanks

Think-and-do tanks fill the knowledge management need for policy innovation by promoting open interaction between academia, government, business and civil society.* They combine rigorous analytical research with practical policy-oriented analysis. Although new research institutes have spread in developing countries, few have the quality, funding, and prestige to influence development priorities and policy choices. The best ones use their capabilities to innovate and solve problems unique to their country.

- Singapore's Institute for South East Asian Studies, established in 1968, describes its philosophy as, "linking people, ideas and capital for the purpose of bringing about widespread prosperity."
- Malaysia's Institute of Strategic and International Studies, established in 1986, sees its role in a development context, "a country bent on reform and achieving high economic growth needs ideas. Some of the best ideas come from the economically successful countries, and we need to organize ourselves to learn from these experiences."
- Korean Development Institute, an autonomous institute set up in 1971 with government funding through a $15 million grant from USAID, reports directly to the president and provides independent advice on long and short-term domestic economic policies, and more recently social development.
- Demos, the United Kingdom's independent, nonprofit institute established in 1993 to "solve people's problems," has an advisory board of successful and innovative business leaders, university professors, notable members of civil society, and a range of former elected officials. Its strong technical reputation gives it good contacts with senior levels of government.

- Brazil's IMAZON, Amazon Institute of People and the Environment, founded in 1990, a nonprofit research institution, in the Eastern Amazonian city of Belem, is based on the idea that the power of scientists to influence patterns of land use lies in the appropriateness and quality of the information produced and in their ability to make that information accessible to those working on sustainable resource use at regional, municipal, and community levels.

Funding and support

The prerequisites for establishing quality institutions are recognition of need, a strong champion in government, availability of core funding, and an independent legal status. Governments dedicated to dynamic development and facilitating the transformation of society recognize the need and rely heavily on problem-solving institutes. Funding of sufficient scale and duration determines the ability of an institute to consolidate analytical strength, maintain autonomy, and achieve a reputation for quality advice. Funding includes public and private seed money, often in the form of endowments supplemented by additional grants from individuals, corporations, philanthropic organizations, donor agencies, and government for particular studies. Institutes that receive all their funding from government must be assured of an independent legal status, reporting to the head of government. Independence is reinforced through the quality of the work, which should be open to scrutiny by the public. The Global Development Network, founded in 1999, provides funding and other support for policy research institutions in seven regional networks spanning the developing world.[†] It helps build capacity and research expertise by linking these networks of researchers to their counterparts in Europe, North America, and Japan. The

(Box continues on next page).

Box 9.2   *(continued)*

Euro-Mediterranean Network also promotes peer reviewed professionalism. Set up in 2000 with EU funding,[‡] it groups 97 economic institutes from 27 countries around the Mediterranean. These networks promote professionalism through funding and peer review of research.

Other ingredients for success
A variety of features are important in ensuring that an institute produces good analysis, valued by decisionmakers. Some advice from the institute directors:

- Combine a strong analytical base with a good understanding of on-the-ground realities. Learn by listening to the people the authorities are not listening to (the fringes of society) and by remaining close to the realities of your country. This promotes creativity and relevant policy solutions.
- Attract the best and brightest nationals back to your country to take advantage of the knowledge they gained abroad and their understanding of local culture and traditions to function as cultural translators. Recruit a good mix of people to bring the necessary breadth of knowledge to solve complex problems.

- Open access to senior policymakers is critical, but maintain independence. With autonomy comes responsibility. Make policy recommendations constructive. Garner high-level national support based on the quality and creativity of the work. Seek peer review by publishing articles in professional journals as a means of reinforcing quality.
- Stimulate healthy debate of complex issues by being informative, bringing out the substance behind political programs, evaluating the costs, benefits, options and choices.
- Create a team-based approach—no hierarchy—where experts coach, coordinate the work of others, and the director ensures ultimate quality control.
- Oversee the implementation of your institute's recommendations. This provides valuable lessons and continuously improves your policymaking capabilities.

* Unpublished background note, "Management knowledge and Innovation & the Role of 'Idea Institutes,'" January 2001, World Bank and Al Akhawayn University, Ifrane Morocco; Grindle (1997).
† http://www.gdnet.org/
‡ http://www.femise.org/Presentation/presentation.htm

dependently monitor and report on government and corporate expenditures and activities have proliferated recently.[8] They can help improve government and corporate accountability, create incentives for monitoring and evaluation within government and corporations, and mobilize public demand for institutional improvements.

- *Mainstreaming monitoring and evaluation functions inside government agencies.* Responding to both internal and public demand for increased efficiency and accountability, some governments are improving internal capabilities for monitoring and evaluating programs and projects.[9]

Donors and multilateral development banks can support the evolution of this intellectual ecosystem of organizations that learn—and apply that learning to improving policies and projects. Donors can support these organizations, through direct funding and twinning arrangements on a large scale. These are long-term efforts that bear fruit over a decade or two as the institutions train people, enhance the prestige of necessary but neglected professions, such as policy analysis, and build dense networks of trust and knowledge. Funding must be committed over periods much longer than traditional projects, and funders must accept that the impacts of these investments, though potentially enormous, will be deferred and difficult to quantify. Donors can also

design projects with learning as a central output, providing hands-on monitoring, evaluation, and implementation experience to learning organizations.

Expanding the scope of global assessment institutions to address emerging issues. At the transnational and global level, assessment institutions such as the IPCC have shown their value in forging consensus on the problems and the options for addressing them.[10] More institutions like the IPCC are needed to address the new global problems that continue to emerge all the time. For instance, questions at the intersection of trade and environment are sure to proliferate, as the discussion of product certification illustrates. Trade policy is an area where more systematic analysis of options might help in forging agreements. Deepening scientific knowledge exposes overlooked transnational environmental processes. For instance, there is increasing attention to the global nitrogen cycle and its effect on marine ecosystems. Technical change, too, brings new problems and risks as well as opportunities. Balancing the environmental risks and benefits of genetically modified organisms is a clear example. And social changes require ongoing and forward-looking attention. For instance, intensifying pressures for international migration have far-reaching ramifications. In all of these areas, there is a strong argument for concerted international attention—and for achieving some consensus on the relevant issues.

Ensuring greater inclusion
*Increased voice and major increases in substantive de-
mocratization.* Inclusiveness can be expanded through
significant changes in governance that increase representation and accountability, such as empowering
local government through well-designed decentralization reforms; electing rather than appointing mayors (Mexico City); replacing military with elected
regimes (Cubatão), or empowering groups excluded
from decisionmaking—women, indigenous people,
and other disadvantaged groups, who may be in the
majority (see boxes 3.8 and 7.10).

Better distribution of access to assets. Dynamic
growth and development processes create more assets
and new types of assets. It will be much easier to increase inclusiveness by ensuring that the poor and disenfranchised, as well as the middle class, have greater
access to these newly created assets. How? By increasing access to education, which build human capital;
by expanding market-based rural land reforms to increase smallholders' access to agricultural land and
complementary assets (water, roads, and knowhow);
by expanding the provision of secure tenure (protection from arbitrary eviction) in urban slums or other
informal urban settlements; by increasing access to
knowledge (the new asset frontier). Any remaining
need to improve access to assets by redistributing existing assets must be based on carefully designed measures that balance interests so that good institutions
that enable people and assets to thrive can emerge.

Ongoing dialogue: a global vision and accord
To overcome the barriers to solving collective problems more rapidly and systematically requires mutual commitments by developing and developed
countries to a bold global vision and accord. This vision requires a massive and steady effort to eliminate
poverty and to protect and manage a broader portfolio of assets that will ensure the well-being of future generations.

A global vision
Today the lessons of history are clearer than ever, for
instance:

■ Prosperity and well-being, like peace, are indivisi-
ble and must be shared if they are to be maintained.
■ Two generations—fifty years—are enough to eliminate poverty and to move to a more sustainable development path.

But negotiating this great transformation in the
next 20 to 50 years requires a renewed commitment
by all countries—developed and developing—to this
overarching common vision. The vision is ambitious, but achievable. Many small, poor countries—
Denmark, Ireland, Japan, Malaysia, Norway, and the
Republic of Korea—have made the leap at different
times from illiteracy and mass poverty to literacy and
affluence within two generations. They were late
industrializers in a global economy already dominated by giants. The European Union shows how
the prospect of mutually beneficial integration can
induce poorer countries to adopt higher standards
of environmental and economic management while
the richer ones provide resources and help to boost
capacity. The experience of the Dust Bowl in the
United States shows how small, individual states
could not solve their problems without the migration opportunities offered by other states, or the
channeling of knowledge and financial resources
from other states that helped to restore economic
health over many decades.

The European Recovery Program (the Marshall
Plan) after World War II showed how mobilizing
resources on a grand scale can build economies and
transform enmity into partnership. The architects of
the Marshall Plan accepted the challenge of tackling
"hunger, poverty, desperation, and chaos" by rebuild-
ing a continent in the interest of political stability,
social development, and a healthy world economy.
They had learned the hard lessons of history: the
Treaty of Versailles ending the First World War in
1919 had imposed unilateral conditions and enforced
severe reparations on the vanquished, paving the way
for political extremism. The designers of the Marshall
Plan avoided these mistakes and paved the way for
peace. The Treaty of Versailles courted conflict. The
Marshall Plan broke a vicious cycle of poverty and re-
gret; it supported economic reconstruction and social order; and it injected money and ideas to rebuild
Europe and herald more than 50 years of unprecedented peace, prosperity, and partnership.

Balancing interests and forging credible commitments for the long haul is difficult at the national
level but even more so at the global level. Yet it is increasingly necessary because national action is insufficient to deal with the scale of spillovers (box 9.3)
generated by a more interconnected world and global
economy. So increased global coordination is necessary to expand the capacity and opportunities of the

Box 9.3
A big push—to address spillovers and seize opportunities

The many global challenges are deeply linked—to each other and to local concerns. So are their solutions. Managing global spillovers, both environmental and social, and taking advantage of a window of opportunity over the next 20–50 years, will require a big push by global institutions—and by national and local institutions.

There are important biophysical links among the spillovers.

- Deforestation, an important cause of biodiversity loss, contributes to climate change. Climate change, in turn, puts stress on ecosystem resources, including grazing lands, water resources, and coral reef fisheries that nourish some of the world's poorest people. It transforms grazing lands to desert. And it threatens cities and coastal populations with more storms and flooding.
- Poverty alleviation and global growth are linked to biodiversity conservation. In the poorest countries, good governance is necessary to protect renewable resources and the people who depend on them—and it is a prerequisite for the ecosystem management organizations advocated here. Furthermore, vigorous local and global development may pull farm populations away from forest lands that are marginal for agriculture but valuable for environmental services. So faster development and the creation of better institutions may avert the sacrifice of valuable ecosystems for ephemeral gain.
- Atmospheric greenhouse gas concentrations cannot be stabilized if the poor countries follow the same emissions path as the developed countries—even if the developed countries were to cut their emissions to zero. Global sustainability requires that all countries work together to pursue long-term paths to low emissions. But equity, and international cooperation, require that greenhouse gases be stabilized without jeopardizing the development aspirations of poor countries.
- Trade and other internationally negotiated policies can affect poverty, biodiversity loss, greenhouse gas emissions, and other global environmental spillovers such as nitrogen emis-

sions and toxins. Coordination at the international level and actions at the national level are important to pursue synergies among goals and avoid unintended consequences. Social spillovers, from institutional and environmental weakness, also tightly bind the interests of rich and poor nations and motivate common interests in sustainable development.

- Infectious diseases are a global concern. Urbanization and faster travel speed the transmission of disease, increasing the chances of epidemics. The misuse of antibiotics—overuse in wealthy countries and underuse in poor ones—stimulates faster evolution of microbes, against which there is a diminishing supply of fall-back drugs.* And human populations—particularly the poor, displaced to fragile lands—are in closer contact with disease reservoirs in forests and wetlands and among domestic animals.
- Poverty contributes to civil conflict and the potential collapse of the state, with transnational impacts. Poverty and the failure of governance are strong risk factors for civil conflict. Nations that experience conflict are at great risk of relapse. Domestic conflicts often have international repercussions, as refugees and violence spill across borders. And terrorism and crime take root in a state vacuum.
- Income disparities create strong pressures for migration, and when these pressures meet closed borders, tensions arise. One study estimates that each 10 percent increase in the foreign-to-local wage difference increases emigration by 1 per thousand population in African countries.† Historically, such labor movements have been powerful avenues of poverty alleviation (chapter 4). But strong migration pressures, combined with a growing population and blocked outlets, lead to tensions and fuel the illegal market in smuggling people, estimated at $7 billion a year.‡

* WHO (2001).
† Hatton and Williamson (2001).
‡ NIC (2000).

---

weaker segments of the global community. A self-enforcing global accord may be required to get the commitment to finance such a scaled-up effort, to build capacity to use the funds wisely, and to take on difficult reforms in developing as well as industrial countries.

A global accord

There is growing recognition of the need for mutual commitments and for accelerated improvements in key development indicators. Support for the Millennium Development Goals, which propose to cut the proportion of people in extreme poverty by half by 2015 is now widespread. The goals set ambitious quantitative targets for reducing hunger, increasing primary schooling, improving health, promoting

gender equity, and ensuring environmental sustainability (box 9.4). One calculation puts the cost of meeting just the nonenvironmental targets at $40 to $70 billion a year above the current $50 billion in development assistance. Another estimate puts the cost of reaching the environmental goals over a longer period at $25 billion per year.[11]

The recent International Conference on Financing for Development in Monterrey also confirmed the need for more aid, trade, and debt forgiveness by industrial countries, in tandem with domestic reforms in developing countries to increase domestic resource mobilization and facilitate foreign direct investment (box 9.5).

The recent proposal for the New Partnership for Africa's Development (NEPAD) is also based on an

Box 9.4
Millennium Development Goals (1990–2015)

1. Eradicate extreme poverty and hunger
   - Halve the proportion of people with less than $1 a day.
   - Halve the proportion of people who suffer from hunger.
2. Achieve universal primary education
   - Ensure that boys and girls alike complete primary schooling.
3. Promote gender equality and empower women
   - Eliminate gender disparity at all levels of education.
4. Reduce child mortality
   - Reduce by two-thirds the under-five mortality rate.
5. Improve maternal health
   - Reduce by three-quarters the maternal mortality ratio.
6. Combat HIV/AIDS, malaria and other diseases
   - Reverse the spread of HIV/AIDS
7. Ensure environmental sustainability
   - Integrate sustainable development into country policies and reverse loss of environmental resources.
   - Halve the proportion of people without access to potable water.
   - Significantly improve the lives of at least 100 million slum dwellers.
8. Develop a global partnership for development
   - Raise official development assistance.
   - Expand market access.
   - Encourage debt sustainability.

Source: www.developmentgoals.org

Box 9.5
Outcome of the International Conference on Financing for Development, Monterrey, Mexico

- Mobilize domestic financial resources for development—by improving governance, macroeconomic policies, and social safety nets.
- Mobilize foreign direct investment and other private flows—by improving the climate for business.
- Make international trade an engine for growth and development—by engaging in a true development round.
- Increase international financial cooperation for development—by doubling official development assistance and focusing it effectively in the most needy.
- Provide sustainable debt financing and external debt relief—by matching financing needs and repayment capacities.
- Address systematic issues—by enhancing the coherence and consistency of the international monetary, financial, and trading systems.

Source: International Conference on Financing for Development, Monterrey, Mexico, (March 2002).

arrangement in which developing countries take responsibility for improved governance, and industrial countries help through more aid, debt forgiveness, and market access. The Council of the European Union's proposed Global Deal has many of the same elements.[12]

In the spirit of these initiatives and to maintain the momentum of the Millennium Development Goals beyond 2015, this Report calls for extending the following goals:

- To fully eliminate global poverty, and
- To put the global economy on a more sustainable development path by the middle of this century.

The two features added to existing initiatives are a deeper target over a longer time horizon, and a greater focus on institutional development. It will require 10 or 20 years—starting now—to build up the institutions that can help shift trajectories from

unsustainable to sustainable paths over the next 50 years. Many of these long-horizon initiatives will yield benefits in the medium term in support of the Millennium Development Goals. But because many future problems cannot be foreseen, it is important that institutional foundations be strong and that a process and a framework be developed that are robust in picking up new signals, balancing a broader range of interests, and maintaining commitments to the global vision.

As noted in chapter 1, at a modest 3 percent annual rate of growth, the global economy in 50 years will be four times the size it is now. Will that larger economy generate less environmental and social stress than the much smaller economy does today? Most of the physical capital required for the economy 50 years hence has not yet been created. This provides an opportunity to incorporate inclusiveness and sustainability criteria in new investments now. The potential is there to shift development paths, provided institutions that adapt and implement better policies can be put in place.

For development strategies and development assistance, this means placing a greater emphasis on:

- Identifying vicious circles that keep the pace of growth low and the distribution of assets unequal—and developing strategic interventions to break these vicious circles.

■ Investing in projects, programs, and initiatives that bring about better, more inclusive institutions and ensure systematic learning.

Greater inclusion, better information flows, more transparency, and wider forums for balancing interests will help to improve the functioning of global and local institutions to fight poverty and promote sustainability. Investments in global poverty reduction and in greater inclusiveness will help ensure the representation of all interests in the design of the new and improved institutions.

There is no understating the difficulty of these challenges. Nor is there an easy solution. Social inertia is great, and institutional change can take decades. Overcoming the inertia to tackle these difficult problems—the fears and risks of unilateral action—requires coordination. The Report suggests mutually reinforcing ways to catalyze institutional change, to mobilize dispersed constituencies, and to support capacity development. The core components of a global accord include:

■ *Building capacity to use resources wisely.* It is now well established that the effectiveness of development assistance—indeed, of all investment—depends greatly on the quality of economic policies and the reliability and capability of market and nonmarket institutions.[13] But there is a lot more to building capacity than technical assistance, as discussed in this chapter's earlier section titled "Implementing."
■ *Providing the necessary funding.* Capital markets (foreign direct investment and private financing) can cover much of the funding required to shift to a more sustainable path if appropriate policies are in place. For example, they can cover investment in new and replacement capital (buildings and equipment) to improve energy efficiency and meet the demands of an urban population that will double. But expanded domestic resources and development assistance will be needed to cover the part of these costs that involve the provision of local, national, and global public goods. Institution building is one of these public goods. The estimated funding requirements for the Millennium Development Goals, would not be enough to support a broader and deeper agenda of institution-building. There are some rough estimates[14] of the

resources that can to be freed up say, by eliminating perverse subsidies in industrialized and developing countries and redirecting them to support institutional building and the investment requirements of a shift to a more sustainable path. However, a serious data and analytic effort is needed to confirm this information at greater levels of detail, country by country.
■ *Undertaking difficult reforms* for both the developed and the developing world.

Main responsibilities of developing countries
A development strategy that emphasizes inclusiveness, shared growth, and better governance places large demands on leaders in developing countries. They must commit to better economic, social, and environmental management—and thus to better governance. To manage their resources, and what they receive from outside, they need to:

■ *Strengthen institutions.* The rule of law and good governance allow families and firms to have confidence—in other words, to save and invest.
■ *Broaden inclusiveness in the access to assets.* Schooling, health care, and provision of environmental assets that protect health, market-based rural land reform, and regularization of urban tenure (providing protection from eviction without due legal process) all promote asset generation for the poor.
■ *Increase transparency.* An open and verifiable flow of information is important to tighten accountability in government and the private sector through such steps as opening procedures for bidding, strengthening meritocracy in the civil service, and making sure that public and corporate budgeting and resource management are governed by law, open to the public, and under proper oversight institutions.

The success of the reforms would be long term; they would secure opportunities and voice for families and their children so they can save, invest, and engage in their communities. But good policies, to be sustained, will require committed support and the legacy of reversals and stalemates is stunning. Research on aid and policy shows that aid is not worth much without good policies and institutions; in fact, it can even be harmful. Research also shows that good policies and institutions are essential to growth and development. This Report has argued that often but not always good policies presuppose good institutions, and these take time to evolve. Funds and assistance will not be available without the conviction that there is capacity to use them effectively. But capacity-building requires patient investment to remove critical barriers because its payoffs are large but take time to be realized. Fundamental reforms require better institutions, which evolve slowly. These requirements are interlinked. So developing country leaders need to know that they will have long-term, reliable support from the larger development community. Without such support—and the quid pro quo on reform to support it—many developing countries will remain in cycles of promise and disappointment. With support, these cycles can be broken.

Main responsibilities of developed countries

Enabling developing countries to develop more rapidly through increased aid, trade, migration, and access to knowledge and technology will place big demands on leaders and voters in developed countries. The actions required of them include:

- *Increase aid and make it more effective.* Developed countries should strengthen the ability of developing countries to pursue sustainable development by providing development assistance that supports public goods and attracts private investment.[15]
- *Reduce debt.* This has started under the Heavily Indebted Poor Countries Debt (HIPC) Initiative, and it is essential to go farther for all developing countries by agreeing on poverty reduction strategies and improving accountability.
- *Open agricultural, industrial, and labor markets.* Developed country trade barriers impede exports from developing countries and undermine the livelihoods of the poor. Unrestricted access to developed country markets in textiles and clothing could yield $9 billion a year, and access to agricultural markets $11.6 billion a year.[16]
- *Improve developing country access to technology and knowledge.* Implement incentives to promote the transfer and dissemination of technologies to developing countries—including those for climate mitigation, disease prevention, and agricultural development. Support more research on crops,

vaccines, and adaptation strategies that would improve the livelihood for poor people.

Joint responsibilities of developing and developed countries

Together the developed and developing countries must address the most urgent problems facing humanity. Their joint responsibility is to *establish a global partnership to set the rules for making rules and the modalities of burden sharing.* As the world becomes more interconnected—environmentally, economically, socially—new institutions and rules must be agreed on and implemented. These will include rules for international trade; rules to avert conflict; rules on migration; rules governing the use of the biosphere; and rules affecting property rights in ideas, technological processes, and genetic information. The consequences will be enduring. If these institutions are to be effective, the rules for making rules have to be fair—in process and in outcome.

There is a role for all actors in the global system: Governments of developing, transition, and developed nations; provinces, cities, and local communities; civil society organizations; private firms; individuals.

- All governments can improve the accountability of public agencies and the provision of information about social and environmental conditions—to improve the ability of the general public and civic groups to identify problems, balance interests fairly, and come up with solutions.
- Civil society organizations can help to aggregate the voices of dispersed interests and provide independent verification of public, private, and nongovernmental performance. Academia needs to be recognized as a key actor in learning, monitoring, and evaluating.
- The private sector can advance economic, social and environmental objectives by helping to construct a framework that provides appropriate incentives for firms to be accountable in all three dimensions.

If the global community sees merit in such an accord, the accord's elements will need more careful work over the next few years to develop an implementable program that can adjust to contingencies without undermining the promise of the accord.

Ongoing dialogue: some open questions

To make more headway on the accord and to define a process and framework that is "fair" will require dealing with some global issues of sustainable development that remain the subject of heated debate. Mentioned here are four important and controversial topics whose resolution has important policy and institutional implications, requiring credible global assessments.

When is consumption overconsumption?

Concern is often expressed about "overconsumption" in wealthy countries and about the threats to sustainability of increasing levels of global consumption. But what kind of consumption qualifies as overconsumption, why is it harmful, and what should be done about it? Does overconsumption imply that there should be a limit on total global consumption (and that as a result, the already high levels of consumption in developed countries need to be reduced to enable increased consumption in poor countries)? On these questions there is little clarity.

One interpretation of overconsumption is that it refers to the environmental externalities associated with consumption at higher levels of per capita income. For example, carbon dioxide emissions, and their contribution to climate change, are highly correlated with consumption of electricity, home heating, transport services, and energy-intensive manufactured goods—all of which tend to increase strongly with income. In these cases, the *over* prefix is justified, since the externalities are by definition inefficient (there is no balancing of costs against benefits) and usually inequitable (wealthier people impose the damages upon poorer people). But the overall level of consumption is not the source of the problem. It is the combination of the specific consumption mix and the production processes that generates the externality. And for these there are well-established policy prescriptions from public finance.

Another interpretation of overconsumption, much more difficult to document, has to do with social externalities. People judge the adequacy of their consumption—clothing, automobiles, housing—in part against norms set by others. If this is true, consumption takes on some of the aspects of an arms race. What are the policy implications? Mutual restraint is needed (a coordination problem par excellence) to shift resources from competitive individual consumption to consumption of public goods. But these externalities need to be much better understood before there can be any agreement on the actions to address them.

What is the future of agriculture and genetically modified organisms?

Despite great promise for improving the agriculture of the poor, biotechnology in general and transgenics research in particular have barely begun to address the problems of the poor. Some applications generate little controversy, such as marker-assisted genetic selection. Others, such as the creation of transgenic organisms, have generated much concern about food safety and potential environmental impacts.

Comfort with the new technology is determined in large measure by societies' comfort with their scientific and food safety institutions and their feelings about emerging concentrations of economic power in multinational "life-sciences" corporations. Solutions to these complex issues are all playing out against a backdrop of globalization-related uncertainty, which has left many people unsettled over their capacity to control their lives and their environment. It is the rural poor in developing countries who most need access to these new agricultural technologies. The precautionary principle tells us that we should err on the side of caution, look at alternatives, and ensure a fully transparent and democratic process. This requires more clearly sorting what is known from current science from what is not, so that the political process can act more effectively.

How to balance interests and avoid the race for property rights at the intellectual frontier?

Intellectual property rights (IPRs) is the next generation of assets that can increase or decrease inclusiveness with consequences for the evolution of quality institutions. IPRs represent a compromise between the interests of users, owners, and creators. It often costs very little to duplicate a seed, a computer program, a song, a drug, a blueprint for a printed circuit or a meteorological database. Once these products have been created, their widespread dissemination would bring great consumer benefits. So why not make them available for only the cost of reproduction? Because there would then be no incentive for private actors to create the information and innovation behind these products. Intellectual property rights such as patents and copyrights, balance these static and dynamic aspects of efficiency.

The Trade-Related Aspects of Intellectual Property Rights (TRIPS) agreement under the WTO represents a global strengthening of the rights of producers in terms of users. Its immediate effect will be to increase royalty payments to intellectual property rights holders, who are overwhelmingly in the developed world. One estimate found that full application of TRIPS would increase annual net patent rents to the United States, Germany, and Japan alone by $31 billion.[17]

Will the emerging intellectual property rights regime be detrimental to the long-run interests of developing countries? The issue is hotly debated. In principle, TRIPS provides a wide latitude for a developing country to fine-tune an intellectual property rights system appropriate to its needs.[18] In practice, developing countries' ability to maneuver may be more limited, and the potential for unequal outcomes is worrisome. While the outlines of the global intellectual property rights regime are clear, many crucial details may not yet be established. Global discussions might address ways for developing countries to strengthen (a) collaborative efforts at patent examination, (b) standards for the breadth and novelty of patent claims, (c) protection of rights to genetic resources and traditional knowledge, (d) global competition policy, and (e) the rationale for public funding and dissemination of census data, environmental and meteorological data, and genetic data. Strengthening the capacity of developing countries to participate in these discussions might also lead to more equitable outcomes.

What are the prospects for global migration?
Global inequality, combined with global demographic trends, will create more pressure for migration. An extensive literature shows that wage differentials drive migration. Fertility rates are highest in places that have the least capacity for absorbing labor. Meanwhile, aging in the developed world will drastically reduce the size of the labor force and increase the demand for low-skilled labor for tasks resistant to automation, such as care of the elderly. At the same time, costs of migration will decline—especially information costs, but also transport. In sum, there's likely to be a drastically greater supply of, and demand for, international migrants over the next half century.

Dealing with this pressure is a global challenge. There are collective decisions to be made, and every option has costs and benefits. There are many reasons to support both more long-term as well as circular migration (the latter can help speed up learning in lagging regions), but migration remains a politically sensitive issue in receiving countries. There are issues related to assimilation of newcomers—as well as exaggerated fears and misconceptions. The decision of one potential receiving country to restrict immigration has implications for other receiving countries, and for the sending countries. Stresses associated with immigration may be related more to the rate of change than to the level of change. Assimilation processes for immigrants are best measured in decades rather than years. Advance preparation in both sending and receiving societies over the next generation could yield a much preferred world in 2050 compared with one in which no foresight is exercised.

* * *

This Report argues that the lack of assets, opportunity, and effective voice for large segments of the population blocks the emergence of general welfare-enhancing policies, impedes growth, and undermines the potential for positive change. At the national level, it robs us of the talents of those left out in society. And at the international level, it deprives us of the contribution poor countries can make to a more just and sustainable future. A more sustainable development path is more socially inclusive; it enables societies to transform and solve collective action problems. The challenge, now and in the future, is to develop the courage and commitment to manage the processes that underpin human life and well-being and to bring about a transformation that improves the quality of the environment, strengthens our social fabric, and enhances the quality of people's lives. The more people heard, the less assets wasted.

Bibliographic note

This Report draws on a wide range of World Bank documents and on numerous outside sources. Background papers and notes were prepared by Sherburne Abbott, G. Acharya, Alain Bertaud, José Brakarz, Kjell Arne Brekke, Tim Campbell, Roberto Chavez, Monica das Gupta, John Dixon, Scott Gates, Nils Petter Gleditsch, Rognvaldur Hannesson, Karla Hoff, Pernille Holtedahl, Eckard Janeba, John Kellenberg, Stein Kuhnle, Huck-ju Kwon, Desmond McNeill, Edgar Ortiz Mtialavasi, S. Mansoob Murshed, Eric Neumayer, Jelena Pantelic, Sanjeev Prakash, Jane Pratt, Per Selle, Guttorm Schjeldrup, Haakon Vennemo, Nicolas Sambanis, Paul Steinberg, Arne Tesli, and Ahmed Zainabi.

Background papers for the report are available either on the World Wide Web http://econ.worldbank.org/wdr/wdr2003/ or through the World Development Report office. The views expressed in these papers are not necessarily those of the World Bank or of this Report.

Many people, both inside and outside the World Bank, gave comments to the team. Valuable comments and contributions were provided by Herbert Acquay, Sadiq Ahmed, Eleodoro O. Mayorga Alba, Mir A. Altaf, Ali Amahan, Ivar Andersen, Jock Anderson, Shlomo Angel, William Ascher, Robert Bacon, Deniz Baharoglu, Tulio Barbosa, Scott Barrett, Carl Bartone, Richard Barrows, Tamsyn Barton, Esra Bennathan, Alain Bertaud, Derek Beyerlee, Anthony Bigio, Hans Binswanger, Slyvain Bisarre, James Bond, Maria Borda, Milan Brahmbhatt, José Brakarz, Marjory-Anne Bromhead, Dan Bromley, Lester Brown, Piet Buys, Tim Campbell, Franklin Cardy, David S. Cassells, Christophe Chamley, Nadereh Chamlou, Roberto Chavez, Ajay Chhibber, Tanzib Chowdhury, Hoon Mok Chung, Dean Cira, Kevin Cleaver, Robert Clement-Jones, William Cobbett, Paul Collier, Maureen Cropper, Csabi Csabi, Partha Dasgupta, Laura De Brular, Klaus Deininger, Shanta Devarajan, Simeon Djankov, David Dollar, Ahmed Eiweida, Enos Esikuri, David Ellerman, Antonio Estache, Ke Fang, Marianne Fay, Peter Fallon, Shahrokh Fardoust, Catherine Farvacque, John Flora, David Freestone, Maria Emilia Freire, Alan Gelb, Alan Gilbert, Gershon Feder, Robert Frank, Scott Gates, Hafez Ghanem, Indermit Gill, Sumila Gulyani, Kenneth Gwilliam, Agi Kiss, Kirk Hamilton, Jeff Hammer, David Hanrahan, Rognvaldur Hamnesson, Jarle Harstad, Marea Eleni Hatziolos, John Henderson, Jesko Hentschel, Vernon Henderson, Mark Hildebrand, Rafik Fatehali Hirji, Daniel Hoornweg, J. C. Hourcade, Sarwat Hussain, Gregory Ingram, William Jaeger, Vijay Jagannathan, Emmanuel Jimenez, Todd M. Johnson, Olga Jonas, Steen Lau Jorgensen, David Kaimowitz, Hirochi Kawashima, Phil Keefer, Charles Kenny, Homi Kharas, John Kellenberg, Elizabeth King, Kenneth King, Nalin Kishor, Agi Kiss, Stephen Knack, Somik Lall, Manuel Lantin, Frannie Leautier, Franck Michel Lecocq, Johannes Linn, Josef Lloyd Leitmann, Andres Liebenthal, Stephen Malpezzi, Robin Mearns, Gerhard Menkhoff, Fatema Mernissi, Alan Miller, Pradeep Mitra, Augusta Molnar, Caroline Moser, Desmond McNeill, Mohan Munasinghe, Mustapha Kamel Nabli, Aksel Naerstad, Andrew Nelson, Martien van Nieuwkoop, Letitia Obeng, Alexandra Ortiz, Edgar Ortiz, Amy Nolan Osborn, Elinor Ostrom, Mead Over, Stefan P. Pagiola, Guillermo Perry, Guy Pfefferman, Robert Picciotto, Robert Prescott-Allen, Lant Pritchett, Felicity Proctor, C. Sanjivi Rajasingham, Vijayendra Rao, John Redwood, Francisco Reifschneider, Ritva Reinikka, Felix Remy, Jozef Ritzen, F. Halsey Rogers, David Rosenblatt, Michael L. Ross, Ina-Marlene Ruthenberg, Maria Sarraf, David Satterthwaite, Sara J. Scherr, Richard Scurfield, Louis Scura, Luis Serven, Cosma Shalizi, Priya Shyamsundar, David Simpson, Anil Sood, Lyn Squire, Andrew Steer, Vivek Suri, Lee Summer Travers, Timothy S. Thomas, Tom Tietenberg, Jane Toll, Thomas Tomich, John Underwood, Keshav Varma, Haakon Vennemo, David G. Victor, Jeffrey Vincent, Tara Vishwanath, Joachim von Amsberg, Michael Walton, Hua Wang, Robert Watson, Jaime Webbe, Monika Weber-Fahr, Anna Wellenstein, David Wheeler, Anthony J. Whitten, Jeff Williamson, Roland White, Julie Viloria-Williams, Michael Woolcock, Sven Wunder, and Hania Zlotnik.

Other valuable assistance was provided by Trinidad Angeles, Carey Ann Cadman, Meta de Coquereaumont, Jean-Pierre S. Djomalieu, Kristyn Ebro, Ines Garcia-Thoumi, John Garrison, Anita Gordon, Rita Hilton, Sergio Jellinek, Lawrence MacDonald, Nacer Mohamed Megherbi, Joyce Msuya, Jean Gray Ponchamni, William Reuben, Carolyn Reynolds, Roula Yazigi.

The team wishes to thank individuals who participated in the following events during the planning and drafting stages of this Report. The participants in these workshops and video conferences are listed in the Web Page. *Berlin, Brussels, China, Costa Rica, London, New York, Nigeria, Oslo, Paris, South Africa, Vietnam*, and *Washington.*

Despite efforts to compile a comprehensive list, some who contributed may have been inadvertently omitted. The team apologizes for any oversights and reiterates its gratitude to all who contributed to this Report.

Endnotes

Chapter 1

1. World Bank 2001h CD Rom (SIMA 349).
2. Chen and Ravallion (2000).
3. World Bank 2001h CD Rom (SIMA 349).
4. World Bank 2001h CD Rom (SIMA 349).
5. World Bank 2001h CD Rom (SIMA 349).
6. The quality and coverage of the household survey data used to measure poverty have improved dramatically in the past 10 to 15 years, and the World Bank has played an important role in facilitating this improvement. Since 1990, the Bank's $1 per day poverty estimates have drawn fully on these new data. However, the paucity of adequate survey data for the past naturally makes estimation over longer periods more hazardous. In *Globalization, Growth and Poverty* (World Bank 2002g), it was estimated that the number of people living below $1 per day had fallen by 200 million between 1980 and 1998. As noted in the Report, that estimate had to draw on two different sources that used different methods. Further checks using more consistent methods corroborate the earlier estimate. These estimates also suggest that if China were excluded, there would have been little or no net decline in the total number of poor people.
7. In 1978 China abandoned its reliance on collective agriculture, sharply increased the prices paid for agricultural goods, and dramatically increased the role of market signals and foreign investment.
8. Brown and others (2001). World Watch Institute's estimates based on national-level surveys of body weight by the United Nations (U.N.) and the World Health Organization (WHO).
9. World Bank 2001i.
10. World Bank 2001h; Sambanis (2000, p. 13).
11. UNDP, UNEP, and others (1999).
12. UNDP, UNEP, and others (1999).
13. UNDP, UNEP, and others (1999).
14. Available at World Bank Group, "Access to Safe Water," <http://www.worldbank.org/depweb/english/modules/environm/water/> (2000).
15. UNEP (1997b); Scherr (1999); Scherr and Yadav (1996); White, Murray and others (2002); Cosgrove and Rijsberman (2000).
16. World Bank (2001c).
17. UNDP, UNEP, and others (1999).
18. Myers, Mittermeier, and others (2000).
19. UNDP, UNEP, and others (1999).
20. UNDP, UNEP, and others (1999).
21. World Bank (2001c).
22. Social change and cultural evolution have also been speeding up, but not uniformly within or across societies. Some cultures are less able to adapt to speed of change even if they wanted to, while others may not even want to.
23. Inconsistencies between human and natural processes manifest themselves spatially (location-specific sources and sinks) and at different scales.

24. Until recently, the carbon emissions generated by energy-intensive activities (that rely on fossil fuels, such as coal) did not affect global temperatures because they had not exceeded the biosphere's absorptive capacity. Now more expensive alternatives are needed to avoid further damage.
25. Dasgupta (2002).
26. Yi (2002).
27. Bloom and Williamson (1997).
28. Much like the dynamics by which teams become more creative, populations moving to cities go through stages of forming, storming, norming, and performing. *Forming* occurs when individuals with different backgrounds come together; *storming,* when their different perspectives clash; *norming,* when more inclusive norms evolve; and *performing,* when constructive behavior replaces destructive behavior. The result is that cities, in the best cases, become centers where different cultural values come together and jointly develop more inclusive values to accommodate different perspectives and provide space for different subgroups to specialize and innovate.
29. The complete series for developing and for high-income countries for 1950–2050 were created using various interpolations and extrapolations of existing data while maintaining consistency with available World Bank and U.N. control totals. Estimates for size classes of 100,000 population and more were made using the following sources: U.N. and World Bank control totals for urban population in developing and high-income countries; U.N., *World Urbanization Prospects, 1999 Revision,* digital files from the U.N. Population Division; and the database of cities above 100,000 population compiled for the U.N.-HABITAT Successful Cities project. (World Bank projections for urban population are lower than those of the U.N. and closer to those of the International Institute for Applied Systems Analysis, as they assume a slower growth rate for most countries.) The populations of smaller towns (those with populations of less than 100,000) were calculated as the residual of total urban population as indicated by U.N. and World Bank sources minus the total estimated population of cities larger than 100,000.
30. Krugman (1998); Gallup and Sachs (1998).
31. Henderson, Shalizi, and Venables (2001).
32. Meaningfully evaluating the consequences or probabilities of outcomes, tradeoffs, and priorities becomes difficult, if not impossible, without the appropriate data and information. For environmental and social variables, there may be some time-series data at the local level, but there are rarely equivalent disaggregated data for GDP variables. At the national level, the situation is often reversed. This obstructs any attempt to quantitatively model or assess changes over time or their determinants. This Report relies heavily on case studies that are thought to be representative.

Chapter 2

1. *Utility* or *well-being* has always been an inherently unmeasurable concept. Despite the limitations, measures of self-reported happiness or overall satisfaction with life have sometimes been used as a proxy. See Oswald (1997).

2. The importance of social participation to human well-being is reflected, for instance, in the negative correlation between people's self-reported happiness and unemployment, controlling for income (Blanchflower and Oswald 2000). Consistent with the happiness data, suicidal behavior is also more prevalent among the unemployed (Oswald 1997). The importance of the environment is reflected, for example, in the results of a survey of over 35,000 people in the G-20 countries, in which about one in four citizens spontaneously mentions environmental issues as a major concern facing his or her country. Although the focus of the environmental concern varies, in part by the country's level of development (in Asia, for example, people are more concerned about the effect of pollution on human health, whereas elsewhere people in the G-20 seem equally concerned about the effect of pollution on human health and the loss of natural resources), the percentage of people citing water pollution, air pollution, and loss of natural areas and species was high—ranging from 63 percent (for species loss) to 71 percent (for water pollution). *See:* Environics International. (see International Environmental Monitor Survey Oct–Dec 2001 on line at www.environicsinternational.com).

3. Dasgupta (2001a) has shown that along any arbitrary consumption path, the aggregate present value (discounted integral) of utility increases during a short interval of time if and only if wealth (estimated at shadow prices defined along the consumption path) increases during the interval, at constant shadow prices. See also Hamilton (2000).

4. Adjusted net savings are also referred to as genuine savings in the literature.

5. Whether social assets should be included in a measure of net wealth and savings is still an issue of debate. See note 14.

6. The adjustment for CO_2 emissions reflects the damage to global assets associated with economic activity in a given country. If we assume certain property rights, in particular that each country has the right not to be damaged by CO_2 emissions from its neighbors, then the estimate of global damage represents the sum of a) the damage a country's CO_2 emissions does to its own assets over time and b) the notional damage payments owing to all other countries affected by these emissions.

7. The effects of improved life expectancy, which have a direct bearing on human assets, are also not included.

8. After accounting for population growth Dasgupta (2001b) finds that changes in wealth (adjusted net savings per capita) are negative in the Indian subcontinent and Africa but positive in China.

9. Some NGOs have begun experimenting with Internet-based information provision as a way of stimulating debate about public policy; increasing the transparency of the actions of private corporations, public agencies, and legislators; and facilitating feedback from civil society to elected officials.

10. Assets can be classified in many different ways depending on the analytic purposes at hand, and the list presented in this chapter is by no means an exhaustive one. For instance, cultural assets can also be important in affecting human well-being. It may also be appropriate, depending on the nature of the analysis, to draw finer distinctions within the categories mentioned here—for instance, between physical and financial assets within human-made assets.

11. The waste from other species is usually more easily biodegradable in natural processes.

12. Trust is usually accumulated through repeated interactions.

13. Interpersonal networks can be thought of as assets, but networks that fail to give rise to mutual beliefs that sustain good outcomes are not socially productive.

14. Although there is still a great deal of debate concerning social capital (centering on what constitutes social capital, whether the word *capital* should be used in this context at all, and on how to analyze and measure the effects of social capital), there is a growing body of evidence that shared values, informal ties, and interpersonal networks can have an important impact on outcomes—notwithstanding some of the difficulties in measuring social capital. See Grootaert and van Bastelaer (2001) for different definitions of what constitutes social capital; Solow (2000) and Bowles and Gintis 1999) for examples of objections to the use of the term "capital"; and Stone (2001) on measurement problems in empirical work. In the social capital literature, institutions and organizations are included under the concept of *structural social capital*, while another set of elements (trust, shared values, norms) are included as *cognitive social capital*. This Report reserves the term *social capital* for interpersonal networks and the trust and shared values they generate, but excludes norms, which function as informal rules. Instead, as in the institutional economics literature, we separate the term "institutions" from social capital and use *institutions* for the mechanisms or rules of the game (both formal and informal) that determine how individuals and groups interact, coordinate, and allocate resources. (Although as chapter 3 shows, *social capital* narrowly defined as cognitive social capital and *institutions* broadly defined to include embedded organizations share critical asset-like characteristics that underpin a society's ability to put other assets to good use.) This report also includes embedded organizations as institutions (but not organizations as agencies).

15. Natural assets can also have "intrinsic" values. Ecosystems preceded the evolution of humans and can function without humans, but humans cannot survive without ecosystems. However, in that humans are increasingly acquiring the knowledge and technology to preserve or destroy ecosystems, the report focuses on instrumental values.

16. In the more narrow economic definition, two inputs in the production function are gross complements if their cross-price elasticity of demand (the extent to which the demand for one input rises when the price of the other input increases) is positive. Where markets do not exist, the price elasticity of demand cannot be determined, even though technically the assets are complementary. We use this broader concept throughout.

17. The examples given in the text are at a micro level. A more macro-level example is one by Knack and Keefer (1997), which considers the role of social capital using mea-

sures of trust and civic norms and shows a positive association with growth.

18. Both social capital and informal and formal institutions can lower transaction costs and increase efficiency. In facilitating innovation, they can also increase productivity growth. Hence good social capital and institutions are crucial to economic growth.

19. Krishna and Uphoff (1999).

20. Reid and Salmen (2000).

21. Galor and Zeira (1993).

22. Uzzi (1997).

23. Yli-Renko (1999).

24. See Suvanto (2000) for a discussion of how social capital enhances innovation and accelerates product development in firms.

25. Zaheer, McEvily, and Perrone (1998).

26. A measure that captures both the shortening of life and the amount of time lived in varying degrees of dysfunction because of illness is the disability adjusted life year (DALY). Estimates (Murray and Lopez 1996) suggest that environmental "bads" account for a significant proportion—ranging from 10–20 percent of total DALYs—of the total burden of disease across developing country regions.

27. Clark (1898).

28. Even in the most advanced industrial countries, however, physical assets account for only a small proportion of total assets; human, social, and environmental assets account for the bulk.

29. World Bank (2000f).

30. World Bank (2000f).

31. World Bank (2000f).

32. Meaning that there is evidence of embodied technical progress.

33. In addition to collecting water, watersheds perform two other big roles: cleaning water and stabilizing its flow. Stabilization is valuable because rainfall is generally very uneven. The watershed automatically compensates for the mismatch between the supply of rainfall and the flow downstream because the soil in the watershed is absorbent and releases water gradually. Trees play a central role in this system by holding the soil in place (important for water stabilization and cleansing, because the soil acts as a filter), and by interacting with the fungi and micro-organisms in the soil to break down pollutants and purify water. While there may be substitutes for the cleansing function of watersheds, there are few substitutes for their flow control function, even in industrial communities (Heal 2000).

34. In 1993 more than 600,000 metric tons of shrimp were harvested from 960,000 hectares of ponds worldwide. About 80 percent of the total production came from Asia, and the rest from Latin America. The availability of shrimp larvae—as commercial hatcheries were established through the Asia Pacific region during the 1970s and 1980s—the marketing of formulated feeds, and active support of the government, set the stage for the industry's takeoff in the 1980s (Primavera 1994).

35. Farming systems fall into four broad categories—traditional, extensive, semi-intensive, and intensive—character-

ized by increased stocking rates and requiring corresponding feed and water management inputs.

36. Primavera (1994).

37. Note that the economic losses associated with the mangrove destruction that often accompanies shrimp farming is not considered here.

38. When the industry is highly developed, specialization includes producers of farm equipment, algal feeds, formulated feeds, spanners, and services. Hence, it can involve many jobs and large amounts of capital equipment. For example, the Ecuadorian shrimp industry in 1990 had a total capitalization of $1.66 million and employed around 100,000 people. Similarly, in Thailand around 114,000 people were employed in 19,000 shrimp farms in 1991, and in India shrimp processing plans employed some 500,000 people (Primavera 1994).

39. See Dasgupta (2000).

40. Because ecosystems are integrated systems, parceling an ecosystem into different parts that are then privatized can create problems since each individual owner may allocate his land to a different use without regard to the needs of the ecosystem as a whole, resulting in a loss of biodiversity and ultimately the resilience of the ecosystem itself.

41. See Dorsey (1998).

42. Reduction in the ozone layer results in an increase in the ultraviolet radiation reaching the earth's surface. Exposure to more solar ultraviolet radiation can lead to a very large increase in skin cancer rates and deaths.

43. The exercise does not look at the effects of environmental assets. Physical capital is proxied by investment as a share of GDP. Social assets are measured by the lack of racial and nationality tensions. Political terrorism is measured using International Country Risk Guide (ICRG) indexes. The distribution of human capital is proxied by average years of schooling. The distribution of education, measured by the Gini coefficient, is taken from Thomas, Wang, and Fan (2001). Why does the distribution of education matter? In countries with a very skewed distribution of education, education may not match the level of dispersion of ability. If the dispersion of education is lower than the dispersion of ability in society, then widening the dispersion of education can increase per capita income.

44. The minimum threshold level of the (principal component) of the International Country Risk Guide (ICRG) index of racial and nationality tensions and political terrorism was −0.23.

45. This focus on assets is not to detract from the importance of total factor productivity (TFP) growth in sustaining growth. In cross-country regressions much of the differences in growth performance across countries are accounted for by differences in TFP growth. It should be noted, however, that some of the observed differences could actually reflect mismeasurement and omitted variables rather than true differences in TFP growth, and part of TFP growth itself could ultimately be due to asset accumulation. Indeed a main vehicle for TFP growth is new technology introduced through imported capital and new intermediate goods (embodied technical progress). It should also be noted that, in looking

at the determinants of growth over time within a country (rather than at differences in growth performances across countries), asset accumulation is found to account for the bulk of GDP growth.

46. For example, Collier (1999) finds that during civil wars GDP per capita declines at 2 percent a year owing partly to a direct reduction in production and partly to a gradual loss of capital stock through destruction, dissaving, and the portfolio substitution of capital abroad.

47. Once such low levels of social assets are reached, there can be a downward spiral in which violence promotes the emergence of perverse social assets—those based on crime and violence, which benefit a few members of the group but harm the community at large (Moser and McIlwaine 2001).

48. As mentioned earlier (see note 2), surveys indicate that people value the environment. Research also shows that people's health is positively affected by exposure to, and interaction with, the natural world. For instance, in an article in the *American Journal of Health Promotion*, Dr. Frumkin (2001) examined a series of studies looking at human health and animals, plants, landscapes, and wilderness. Within each of these domains he found a wide body of evidence linking the domain with human health. For example, one study found that pet owners had significantly lower blood pressure and cholesterol levels and fewer minor health problems than people who did not own pets. Honeyman (1990) has found that people who are shown urban scenes with vegetation recover from stress more quickly than people who are shown urban scenes without vegetation. In fact, there is a theory—expanded by Wilson and Kellert (1994)—which asserts that human evolutionary history has made a human connection with nature a necessity, not a luxury.

49. The poor can be affected by adverse environmental outcomes in three broad ways: natural resource degradation can affect their livelihoods; environmental degradation can affect their health; and ecological fragility and the likelihood of disasters can affect the poor more than others because of their greater vulnerability (effects of climate change on poor nations). See Department for International Development and others (2002). See also Cavendish (1999) who documents empirically how environmental resources make a significant contribution to average rural incomes in Zimbabwe.

50. The agricultural sector in Madagascar suffered from discriminatory policies in the past (with negative rates of protection for rice, for example, of up to 43 percent, and with only irrigated wheat and sugar enjoying protection). While the reforms of the mid-1990s (devaluation of the exchange rate, reduction in import barriers, liberalization of markets, privatization of most state enterprises) contributed to a more balanced incentive structure, productivity continues to be hampered by a lack of fertilizer, inadequate road infrastructure, and segregated markets (Paternostro, Razafindravonona, and Stifel 2001). See also box 8.3.

51. Cole, Rayner, and Bates (1997).

52. Easterly (1999).

53. See Borghesi (1999) and Shalizi and Kraus (2001).

54. See Dasgupta and others (2002). The theoretical literature has identified several factors that could give rise to a

Kuznets curve relationship: if structural changes inherent in the development process lead to cleaner industries (Syrquin 1989); if abatement technologies exhibit increasing returns to scale (Andreoni and Levinson 1998); if development is accompanied by demand for a better environment to which policies and institutions respond (Grossman 1995); and if the stock of environmental assets declines over time while demand rises.

55. Based on Sebastian, Lvovsky, and de Koning (1999), Murray and Lopez (1996), Smith (1998), and World Bank estimates, 9 percent of DALYs in developing countries are accounted for by water supply and sanitation and urban air pollution. Indoor air pollution accounts for an additional 2 percent of DALYs. While not an externality, indoor air pollution justifies public funding from a poverty reduction perspective.

56. And the costs of delay in addressing pollution problems can sometimes be very high. The experience of industrial countries with pollution remediation to reduce harmful health effects is illustrative. For the cases of Itai-itai disease (from cadmium poisoning), the Yokkaichi asthma (from sulfur emissions), and the Minamata disease (mercury poisoning) in Japan, the costs of cleanup and compensation to victims are estimated at 1.4 to 102 times the costs of prevention. More important, the costs of prevention were affordable at the time, given Japan's per capita income and fiscal resources. The problems were lack of knowledge of the consequences of neglect, and different priorities. Moreover, there can be costs associated with "lock-in": delays in implementing changes in incentives to address pollution problems can lead to investments and technological lock-ins that cumulatively increase the costs of reversing the environment-unfriendly policies later on.

57. For instance, a study on China—notable for its analysis of both the costs and the benefits of addressing air pollution based on firm-level data—shows that a "statistical life" can be saved by removing 100 tons of sulfur dioxide annually from Beijing's atmosphere. Estimates of abatement costs for large plants were $3 a ton, when 10 percent of the emissions are controlled. So abating 100 tons—at a cost of $300—would save one life. (The abatement costs for small plants were considerably higher, but large plants are a much larger source of air pollution in Beijing.) (World Bank 2000d).

58. However, costs of abatement can be disproportionately greater for small- and medium-size firms. It may still be the case, however, that policy and regulatory levels are not high enough to affect economic growth, because industry within individual countries may be resisting greater regulation for fear of becoming uncompetitive—with the result that pollution levels are also suboptimal.

59. Dasgupta and others (2002).

60. The U.S. Superfund, for example, shows how high the costs of cleaning up severely polluted areas after the fact can be: the program has allocated more than $100 billion. Part of the problem is that the consequences of the pollution were not known at the time—many of the sites were polluted long ago.

61. See Pagiola and Rothenberg (2002) which provides a good compilation of case studies analyzing different market-based approaches to forest conservation.

62. Heal (2000).

63. Classic examples of fish population collapse where overfishing may have played a role include the sardine stocks of California and Japan in the late 1940s and the anchovy stocks of Peru and Chile in 1972. More recent examples of overfishing include the collapse of the Canadian cod fishery and several New England groundfish stocks. Groundfish are marine fish that live and feed on or near the bottom of the ocean. Their now-reduced numbers include edible species that New Englanders have relied on for generations. The most important are haddock, cod, and yellowtail flounder (Botsford, Castilla, and Peterson 1997).

64. Coase (1960).

65. Myers and Kent (2001).

66. The term *energy subsidies* can refer to transfers to consumers through underpricing or transfers to producers through overpricing.

67. Some 85 percent of total primary energy supply is from fossil fuels and 7 percent from nuclear energy.

68. Fossil fuels cause many environmental problems apart from the better-known ones of oil spills and mining tailings. They cause pollution (sulfur dioxide, nitrogen oxide particulates, and carbon dioxide). They harm health and affect production both directly and through acid rain (which in turn damages forests and water bodies). They are also the largest contributor to global warming.

69. Myers and Kent (2001).

70. OECD (2001c).

71. R&D for renewables is also subsidized, but the net subsidy (in terms of the relative price effect) is biased toward fossil fuels, and the total budget drain is higher than if fossil fuels were not subsidized at all.

72. Data Resources Inc. (1997) estimates that there would be a loss of 104,000 mining jobs in Europe and Japan (OECD 2001c).

73. Eskeland and Devarajan (1996).

74. There are two reasons why a small additional amount of consumption to be made available at some future year could be socially less valuable than that same additional amount made available today (why the consumption rate of interest could be positive). One is impatience, and the possibility of no tomorrow. Another is the expectation that consumption will be greater in the future than it is today, which means that the benefit from additional future consumption will be less. Thus the consumption rate of interest is equal to the pure rate of time preference (reflecting the first consideration) plus the product of the percentage increase in marginal well-being consequent on a percentage increase in consumption (called the elasticity of marginal well-being) and the percentage rate of change of consumption (reflecting the second consideration) (Dasgupta (2001a)).

75. Since the consumption rate of interest is made up of two components (see note 74), there is no reason to believe that rates should remain constant over time.

76. Newell and Pizer (2001). Example: Suppose the current consumption rate of interest is 4 percent, and you know that over the next 100 years the rate could either rise to 7 percent or fall to 1 percent. And suppose your project were to yield a benefit of $100 a hundred years from now. The lower rate path would value the $100 dollars at $20.28 today; the higher at only $0.20 today. If you recognize the uncertainty in future interest rates, and place equal weight on these two outcomes, the expected value of $100 in 2102 would be $10.24. Now suppose we evaluated the expected value one year into the future, in 2103. Based on the lower rate of 1 percent in 2102, the same $20.28 is worth $20.08 ($20.28/1.01 = $20.08), and the $0.20 is worth $0.19. Averaging these, the expected value of $100 delivered in the year 2103 would be $10.13. This is very close to the value of the lower rate of 1 percent $20.28 multiplied by the probability of that outcome, 50 percent ($10.14). In this way, the change in value between periods comes to depend solely on the lower rate. Why? Intuitively, discounting benefits 100 years hence depends only on the lower rate because the higher rate discounts future benefits to such an extent that it adds very little to the expected value. See also Weitzman (1998).

77. As discussed in the following chapter, both informal and formal mechanisms shape the incentive structure facing individuals and hence affect environmental outcomes.

78. The broad range of economic instruments includes taxes and charges, tradable quotas, tradable emission permits, environmental subsidies, deposit-refund systems, performance bonds, noncompliance fees, resource pricing, and resource royalties (OECD 1988; OECD 2001c).

79. German Advisory Council on Global Change (2002a).

80. Fossil fuel combustion is the largest source of human-caused greenhouse gas emissions—so there are both present and future costs to society.

81. World Bank (2000d), and www.worldbank.org/nipr.

82. OECD (2001c).

83. World Bank (2000c).

84. OECD (1999, 2001c).

85. Acharya and Dixon, background paper for *WDR 2003*.

Chapter 3

1. Sen (1999).

2. See *WDR 1992* for policies specifically addressing environmental assets.

3. Analysts such as Ronald Coase, Avner Greiff, Douglass North, Mancur Olson, and Robert Fogel have greatly contributed to the development of ideas presented in this chapter, even though they are not directly cited (and bear no responsibility for the content here).

4. Ihrig and Moe (2000).

5. de Soto (2000).

6. Besley and Burgess (2001).

7. Steinberg (2001).

8. Farrington and Bebbington (1993, p. 106).

9. Farrington and Bebbington (1993, p. 73).

10. Rose-Ackerman (1999).

11. Steinberg (2001).

12. Dunlap, Gallup, and Gallup (1993); Dunlap and Mertig (1995); Brechin and Kempton (1994); Kidd and Lee (1997); Steinberg (2001, pp. 27–45).

13. Baland and Platteau (1996); Ostrom and Gardner (1993).

14. Kaufmann, Kraay, and Zoido-Lobatón (1999).

15. Sachs and Warner (1995).

16. Svensson (1998).

17. The threat of invasions, in turn, provides an interpretation of why a system of feudal lords or states emerge. See Grossman and Kim (1995); Skaperdas (1992); and Hirshleifer (1996) for an analysis of emerging institutions.

18. This section draws heavily on Hannesson (background paper for WDR 2003).

19. Botsford, Castilla, and Peterson (1997).

20. In some instances the stock collapses and is gone for many years. See box 3.4.

21. World Bank (2000d); Dasgupta, Laplante, and Mamingi (2001); Dasgupta and Wheeler (1997).

22. See Ter-Minassian (1997); Eskeland, Litvack, and Rodden (2002); Bardhan and Mookherjee (2000).

23. World Bank (2000d).

24. Bolt and others (forthcoming). The model uses monitored concentrations of TSP and PM10 (small dust), city and county information to estimate determinants of dust and small dust particles, and then uses this to project pollution levels for a larger number of cities. The results yield good estimates, but are not accurate at the city level.

25. World Bank (2000d).

26. Holtedahl and Vennemo (Background paper for the WDR 2003); Dasgupta and Wheeler (1997).

27. World Bank (1998a).

28. King and Özler (1998); Jimenez and Sawada (1999); Eskeland and Filmer (2002).

29. Ostrom and Gardner (1993); Baland and Platteau (1996).

30. This is one of the reasons regulations focus on installations and procedures, not only on results.

31. Conroy (2001).

32. Alston, Libecap, and Schneider (1996); Anderson and Hill (1990).

33. The logic in this section is inspired by the works of Grossman and Kim (1995); Skaperdas (1992); Sugden (1986); Posner (1981); who all deserve credit.

34. Events of hyperinflation and arrests in savings are of course spectacularly brutal—but poor people and the middle class often are hurt through their savings under inflation and fiscal repression (Easterly and Fischer 2001). Formal institutions often fail to protect and support the savings of the poor. Rutherford (2000) documents how the poor pay dearly to find adequate outlets for their savings. de Soto (2000) documents how the poor are harmed when formal institutions fail to welcome and support their assets and activities.

35. See Moser and Grant (2000); Fajnzylber, Lederman, and Loayza and Fruhling (forthcoming); Tulchin, and Golding (forthcoming).

36. Aghion, Caroli, and Garcia-Peñalosa (1999) review models of the microlevel links; Rodrik (1996) and Nelson and Morrisey (1998) emphasize the links through political support, and negotiating change.

37. See de Janvry and others (2001) for a review.

38. Deininger and Squire (1998).

39. Easterly (2002).

40. Acemoglu, Johnson, and Robinson (2001).

41. Banerjee and Iyer (2002)

42. Banerjee, Gertler, and Ghatak (2001).

43. Findlay and Lundahl (1994).

44. Hoff and Sen (2001).

45. "Our perspective suggests that, as in Bates' (1981) analysis of the political economy of Africa, bad economic policies should be understood as part of a package of often inefficient redistributive tools" (Acemoglu and others 2002). "Institutions that provide dependable property rights, manage conflict, maintain law and order, and align economic incentives with social costs and benefits are the foundation of long term growth . . . China, Botswana, Mauritius and Australia—four cases of success in our sample—all owe their performance to the presence (or creation) of institutions that have generated market-oriented incentives, protected property rights . . . and enabled social and political stability" (Rodrik 2002); Acemoglu and others (forthcoming).

46. McGuire and Olson (1996); Clague and others (1999).

47. Buchanan (2001).

48. Boyce (2002).

49. Abramson and Inglehart (1995).

50. World Bank (2000d).

51. Yes, markets can help in this. Indeed, they are central. But when markets fail, policies are needed to correct those failures. However, policies also fail. So institutions are needed that learn and adapt to support better policies.

Chapter 4

1. Drylands are classified as arid and dry semi-arid land without access to irrigation. Aridity is defined according to an aridity index that is the ratio of precipitation and potential evapo-transpiration (UNEP World Atlas of Desertification, 1992 and 1997). Terrain constraints are purely based on steepness of slope (8 percent or more and would not include people on mountain plateaus or valley floors). Poor soils are identified by the United Nations' Food and Agriculture Organization (FAO) as unsuitable for rainfed agriculture. (For details on soil constraints, see http://www.fao.org/ag/AGL/agll/gaez, *Plate 27.*) Forests are defined according to LandScan data and include deciduous broadleaf, deciduous needle leaf, evergreen broadleaf, evergreen needle forest, and mixed forest of the U.S. Geological Survey Global Land Cover Characterization classification.

The definition of fragile lands does not include weather related fragility factors (areas prone to floods, storms and cold temperatures) which would significantly increase the estimated population on fragile land. Fragile and marginal agricultural lands are used interchangeably, as distinct from people or groups marginalized in society, although often the people living on fragile land are among the most marginalized groups in society.

Population estimates combine digital maps on population distribution with maps of the geophysical characteristics (aridity, slope, soils, and forests). Estimates of rural population distribution are based on two global population datasets. The Center for International Earth Science Information Network (CIESIN) Gridded Population of the World (GPW v2) is based on total population estimates for 120,000 administrative reporting units (districts or counties)—see http://sedac.ciesin.org/plue/gpw/index.html. Population distribution within each unit is assumed to be constant. The Oakridge National Lab (ORNL) LandScan dataset uses larger administrative units and adjusts population distribution based on proximity to roads and settlements, steepness of slope, nighttime lights from satellite data, and land cover (see http://www.ornl.gov/gist/projects/LandScan/SIMPLE/smaps.htm). For each population dataset urban areas are masked out using a global map of nighttime city lights from the U.S. National Oceanic and Atmospheric Administration (NOAA). GPW (CIESIN) tends to yield roughly 10 percent higher estimates for fragile lands than LandScan, which already reduced population numbers in areas of steep slopes and unsuitable land cover categories. For some countries, the proportion was even higher. This Report uses an average of the two results as a best estimate of the true population distribution. Population was uniformly adjusted for each country to match the World Bank's rural population estimates for the corresponding year.

Forest data source: Global Land Cover Characterization, U.S. Geological Survey (USGS) Earth Resources Observation System (EROS) Data Center, University of Nebraska-Lincoln (UNL), and Joint Research Centre of the European Commission, 30 arc seconds resolution (approx. 1km), http://edcdaac.usgs.gov/glcc/glcc.html.

2. Pratt and Shilling (background paper for WDR 2003).

3. Our analysis suggests that 1.4 billion people worldwide inhabit fragile lands, of whom 1.3 billion are in developing countries. This includes an estimated 130 million people living in forests with no other geophysical constraints. Many of these forests are in fragile ecosystems in remote tropical areas of the Amazon and Central Africa or the boreal forests of Asia. Forest conversion to agriculture may be possible, but with short-lived benefits and unsustainable yields in many places. Moreover, conversion to agricultural or other commercial uses may ignore important public goods benefits (such as the livelihoods of local people who depend in part on forest products, watershed and ecosystem management, soil maintenance, biodiversity, or aesthetic values—see also chapters 5 and 8 for further discussion of forest conversions).

The estimates of people living on fragile land may be on the conservative side. A 1997 CGIAR study on the priorities for marginal lands estimated that 1.7 billion people inhabit marginal lands (CGIAR 1997). According to this work, roughly 70–75 percent of the rural populations in Sub-Saharan Africa and North Africa and the Middle East and 65 percent in Asia and Central and South America live on fragile lands. A 1995 study using FAO land classifications

and World Bank population data estimated that about 2 billion rural people are on marginal lands with little or no access to technology, and are remote from services (Pretty 1995).

The lower estimates in this report are due to a more narrow definition of arid lands, terrain constraints and forests (see note 1). The difference may also be due to the higher resolution population grids selected and the fact that geographic information system (GIS) datasets are available now that were not available in 1995 and 1997. The World Bank's estimate of 1.3 billion people is intended to focus on the poorest rural groups and indicates a large population for whom appropriate services and creative solutions have been lacking.

4. See Cardy (2002). There were an estimated 25 million environmental refugees in 1995 (excluding temporary refugees from flooding, who return to their land). The United States Committee on Refugees available on line at www.refugees.com estimates that 14.1 million refugees officially crossed a border in 1999 and another 21 million are internally displaced people.

5. See Davis (1993) and World Bank Operational Directive 4.2 on "Indigenous Peoples." The 250 million estimate of indigenous people is a conservative estimate. Precision is difficult, since such data are not systematically collected in many countries. This chapter looks at a broader population in the rural periphery, which would include some indigenous groups. It does not focus on the problems of indigenous groups, but recognizes their disproportionate level of poverty and their stores of local knowledge, traditions, and links with natural environments.

6. See Bonkoungou (2001); UNDP/UNSO, Office to Combat Desertification and Drought.

7. See UNEP (1992, 1997). The authors estimate that slightly more than 1 billion people are dependent on agriculture for their livelihoods and live on drylands. UNEP's estimate includes subhumid and arid or semi-arid irrigated areas (which we have omitted).

8. See http://www.ifpri.cgiar.org/pubs/fps/fps36.htm and Bank staff estimates of R&D funding for fragile lands.

9. See Doble (2001); UNDP/UNSO, Office to Combat Desertification and Drought.

10. See Swearingen and Bencherifa (1996); McNeill (2000); Leach and Mearns (1996).

11. Okoth-Ogendo, H.W.O. (2001); Gibson, McKean, Ostrom (2000).

12. See Williams (2001). See http://ag.arizona.edu/OALS/ALN/aln49/Williams.html.

13. See International Panel on Climate Change (2002), pages 44–46 of the Technical Summary.

14. See FAO, UNEP, and UNDP (1994); ESCAP (1993); (UNEP/ISRIC 1990).

15. See Ojima (2001). Available from START Secretariat, Washington, D.C.

16. See Ojima (2001); UNDP and others (2000); World Resources Institute (2000); Mearns (2001) and (2002).

17. Mearns (2001); Mearns (2002).

18. See Munn, Whyte, and Timmerman (2000). Desertification is defined as land degradation in arid, semi-arid, and dry subhumid areas resulting from various factors, including climate variations and human activities.

19. National Research Council (1999).

20. UNDP (1997).

21. Hazell (1998); Hazell and Fan (2000); Fan, Hazell, and Thorat (2000); Wood and others (1999), variously cited in recent overviews by several international organizations, such as Dixon, Gulliver, and Gibbon (2001); World Bank (2002k); and IFAD (2001).

22. http://www.cimmyt.cgiar.org/Research/Maize/map/developing_world/nmaize/new_maize.htm.

23. See Pagiola (1999) and Hassan and Dregne (1997).

24. Pratt and Shilling, Background paper for the WDR 2003.

25. Scherr, Sara J., A. White, and D. Kaimowitz. 2002.

26. Pratt and Shilling, Background paper for the WDR 2003.

27. Pratt and Shilling, Background paper for the WDR 2003.

28. Reinikka and Svensson (2001 and 2002).

29. See World Bank (2001b).

30. Hemmati and Gardiner (2002); and Lubbock and Bourqia (1998).

31. See Abraham and Platteau (forthcoming).

32. Zainabi, *World Development Report 2003* background paper.

33. See Donnely-Roark, Ouedraogo, and Ye (2001); Kim, Alderman, and Orazem (1998); de Umanzor and others (1997); Fuller and Rivarola (1998).

34. See Harper (2000).

35. See Rao (2002).

36. See de Ferranti and others (2002); McMahon and Felix (2001); World Bank and International Financing Corporation (2002); Sachs and Warner (1995).

37. Chapter 6, McMahon and Felix (2001).

38. World Bank and International Financing Corporation (2002); McMahon and Felix (2001); Davis and others (2001); Heilburnn (2002).

Chapter 5

1. Pinstrup-Andersen, Panya-Lorch, and Rosegrant (1999).

2. Meyer and others (2000).

3. Readers seeking a comprehensive treatment of issues related to rural development, water resources, and agricultural research are invited to read the World Bank's recently completed publications: World Bank (2001a, 2002a, and 2002b). We would also like to recommend IFAD (2001), Eicher and Statz (1998), and Alexandratos (1995) for comprehensive, authoritative, and balanced treatments of rural development issues in a forward-looking context.

4. Crosson and Anderson (2002) show that in developing countries yield trends for rice, wheat, and coarse grains were linear over the 39 years from 1960 through 1998. For the decade 1988 to 1998 rice yields were above the trend for 9 of the 11 years, below for 8 of 11 years for wheat, and 8 of 11 years for coarse grains. In an environment of record low

commodity prices these yield averages have been influenced by relatively poor land going out of production (increases average yields) and lower fertilizer use (lowers average yields).

5. Alexandratos (1995).

6. Rosegrant and others (2001).

7. Of the 1 billion poor people identified in 58 poverty profiles completed by the World Bank, 75 percent live in rural areas.

8. Crosson (1995).

9. Crosson (1995); Lindert (2000).

10. Lindert (2000).

11. Murgai, Mubarik, and Byerlee (2001).

12. Sanchez (forthcoming).

13. Pinstrup-Andersen, Panya-Lorch, and Rosegrant (1999).

14. Low external input systems have a role to play, especially in remote, poor areas. Phosphorous inputs, in addition to that made available by green manuring, is inevitably necessary on phosphorous-poor soils, however, because green manure from phosphorus-poor soils is also poor in phosphorous (Alexandratos 1995). Green manuring competes with land for food and often has high labor cost during periods of peak labor demand. See Hazell (2001); Reardon and others 1999; Ruttan (1990). Ruttan estimates that low external input systems have the potential to increase food output by only about 1 percent a year in Africa, roughly the same rate observed over the past 20 years, and well short of the expected 3–3.5 percent annual growth in Africa's food demand.

15. African farmers pay three to five times the world market price for fertilizer and receive only 30 to 60 percent of the market value for their products (Hazell 2001). This is due in part to high African transport costs (owing to many landlocked countries and poor quality of infrastructure) (Limao and Venables 2001) and in part to well-documented policy distortions, related to pro-urban bias and implicit taxation of agriculture (Lipton 1977; Berg 1981). Under such conditions it usually does not pay for an African farmer to apply fertilizer.

16. Sanchez (forthcoming).

17. Rosegrant and others (2001).

18. World Water Council (2000).

19. This section is based on IBSRAM (2001).

20. Note that these estimates of land lost through degradation suffer from the estimation problem discussed in the previous section. Lindert's (2000) results suggest strongly that they are upwardly biased.

21. This section is based on International Water Management Institute (IWMI 2001).

22. FAO (1997).

23. IWMI (2001).

24. Ravallion and Datt (1996).

25. Timmer (1997); Deininger and Squire (1998).

26. Ravallion and Datt (1996); Lanjouw and Lanjouw (2001).

27. Mellor (2000).

28. See Rodrik (1999).

29. See for example, Alesina and Rodrik (1994); Persson and Tabellini (1994); and Deininger and Squire (1998).

30. Engerman and Sokoloff (1997).

31. See Tomich, Kilby, and Johnson (1995) for a thorough treatment of these issues.

32. IFAD (2000).

33. IFAD (2000).

34. Sanchez (forthcoming).

35. Salamini (1999).

36. Paarlberg (2001).

37. See Gaskell and others (1999); Wambugu (1999).

38. See Paarlberg (2001) for a discussion of the political economics of countries' positions on biotechnology.

39. Paarlberg (2001).

40. See Byerlee and Fischer (2000) for an excellent review of these institutional models.

41. Siamond vs. Chakrabarty, 447 U.S. 303, 206 U.S.P.Q. 193 (1980).

42. See, for example, IFAD (2001), chapter 4; Alexandratos (1995), chapter 12; IFPRI (1999); Lele, Lesser, and Horstkotte-Wesseler (1999); Foundation News (1999).

43. See Paarlberg (2001); also Moore (2001).

44. Available on-line at http://europa.eu.int/comm/research/press/2001/pr2312en.html.

45. Paarlberg (2001).

46. That Thalidomide was not marketed in the United States had nothing to do with suspected teratogenic effects. The delay in the approval process stemmed from other concerns about the drug. Thalidomide was still in the approval process in the U.S. FDA when it was discovered in Europe that it caused birth defects.

47. See, for example, http://www.house.gov/waxman/FDA/FDAMA/fdama.html.

48. Seventy-four percent of European citizens hold the agri-food industry responsible for the BSE problem. Sixty-nine percent hold politicians responsible as well. Respondents showed high regard for European scientists but wished that scientists would keep them better informed (http://europa.eu.int/comm/research/press/2001/pr2312en.html).

49. House of Lords (2000).

50. See Echikson (1999).

51. Wambugu (1999).

52. IFAD (2001, p. 138).

53. See Paarlberg (2001).

54. This section borrows heavily from Deininger and Feder (1998).

55. For a good review of these issues, see Lele, Lesser, and Horstkotte-Wesseler (1999).

56. Lele, Lesser, and Horstkotte-Wesseler (1999).

57. See World Bank (2001b).

58. Losey, Rayor, and Carter, (1999).

59. See *Nature Science Update,* "Monarchs safe from BT." Available on-line at: http://www.nature.com/nsu/010913/010913-12.html.

60. Statement by European Commissioner for Health and Consumer Protection David Byrne (Birchard 2000, p. 321, cited in Paarlberg 2001).

61. Applying these standards requires that new generally modified food products be assessed for unexpected genetic effects that might mislead consumers relative to the non-genetically modified food equivalent. These include comparing toxin levels, nutrient composition, potential introduced allergens, new composition, marker genes that could transfer antibiotic resistance to clinically significant organisms, plants not originally developed as food products, and nutrients or toxins making the product unacceptable for animal feed (ESCOP 2000, cited in Paarlberg 2001).

62. See Byerlee and Fischer (2000) for an excellent review of institutional models for public-private cooperation.

63. Personal communication with Richard Barrows.

64. Personal communication with Richard Barrows.

65. This tax would be an annual tax calculated on either a market ad valorem or per hectare basis, but invariant with the use of the land.

66. De Janvry and others eds. (2001). (2002).

67. Of course, it is also necessary to have prices that make the venture profitable, transportation and marketing systems that allow the product to move into urban markets, and credit that encourages commercial activity, among other conditions.

68. Deininger and Binswanger (2001).

69. For example, whether a city can divert water from a small farmer irrigator without compensation will depend on how property rights are allocated.

70. Personal communication with John Briscoe.

71. Personal communication with John Briscoe.

72. Ostrom and Gardner (1993).

73. OECD (1998).

74. The evolution of informal markets has been documented in the state of Gujarat, India. See Shah (1993).

75. The process is partially political because the political process will determine the standards of environmental quality that society will demand. In several basins with functioning water markets in the United States environmental groups and even the U.S. EPA purchased water to augment flow for environmental purposes.

76. Schneider (1995).

77. For the Philippines see Coxhead, Rola, and Kim (2001); for Philippines and Thailand see Uhilg (1988).

78. White and Martin (2002).

79. Scherr, White, and Kaimowitz (2002).

80. Wells and others (1999).

81. See an extensive discussion with case studies in Ascher (1999).

82. Cochrane and others (1999).

83. World Bank (2001e).

84. Carter and Zimmerman (2000).

85. Scholz (1985).

86. For example, for Amazon see Alston, Libecap, and Schneider (1995) and Schneider (1995); for Thailand see Uhilg (1988).

87. Iremonger, Ravilious, and Quinton (1997).

88. Bruner and others (2001).

89. Bruner and others (2001); Mahar and Ducrot (1998).

90. Available on line at: http://www/worldwildlife.org/forests/forest.cfm?sectionid=181&newspaperid=17.

91. "Carrasco da Mata—o massacre de Motoserra." *Veja,* April 17, 1999. English language version available on line at

http://www.iucn.org/reuters/1999/articles/winningbrasil.htm

92. Rosegrant and others (2001), p. 6.

93. Henderson, Shalizi, and Venables (2001).

Chapter 6

1. For ease of reference the terms "urban" and "city" are used interchangeably here. A "town" can be considered the smallest class of urban area, having a less diverse economy than the next city-size category and minimal administrative or fiscal autonomy. This chapter also uses the terms "local government" or "local authority" mainly in reference to a "municipality," understood here as the lowest organized unit within the administrative apparatus of the state. Many large urban areas, often called "metropolises," span more than one municipality.

2. This trend appeared earliest and has been documented most extensively for Latin America and the Caribbean: Campbell (1997, background note for WDR 2003); Reilly (1995); for a global review, see World Bank (2000b).

3. At the same time, certain conservative cultural and religious norms may be more strictly enforced by people who feel these values to be challenged by contact with urban society.

4. Holtedahl and Vennemo, background note for WDR 2003.

5. Wells and others 1999.

6. Sassen (2001); Wheeler, Aoyama, and Wolf (2000).

7. Glaeser (1998).

8. Lall and Ghosh (2002).

9. Glaeser and others (1992).

10. Quigley (1998); Mills (2000); Ciccone and Hall (1996); Prud'homme (1994).

11. Urban areas can provide more options to use competition for service provision, as in Colombia's national school voucher program which enabled municipalities to help low-income households obtain places in private schools (Angrist and others forthcoming).

12. Hardoy, Mitlin, and Satterthwaite (2001), box 1.4.

13. Urbanization, beyond its positive impact on income, is an important determinant of nonmonetary indicators of well-being at the national level, including education (literacy, school enrollment), health (infant and child mortality, life expectancy, malnutrition), and access to basic infrastructure (water, sanitation, electricity, telecommunications). Urbanization can have a larger impact than economic growth on these social indicators (Ryan and Wodon 2001).

14. The effect of urbanization on education outcomes is also greater than the effects of measures of bureaucratic efficiency and of corruption (Jayasuriya and Wodon, background paper for the WDR 2003).

15. Williamson (1988).

16. Mazumdar (1987); Wodon and Konig (2001).

17. Lucas (1998).

18. Wodon and others (2001).

19. Oberai and Manmohan Singh (1984). Williamson (1988) cites further evidence in concurrence.

20. De Haan (1999, 2000).

21. A study in Kenya found that remittances from rural-urban migrants, measured by the urban-based nonfarm income component of smallholder household income, were the most important determinant of innovation by smallholders and of rates of smallholder poverty. Probability of migration, in turn, was determined by access to primary education in rural areas (Collier and Lal 1980).

22. McGranahan and Satterhwaite (2000); Pugh (1996); Bartone and others (1994).

23. With increasing economic development and urban growth, industrial activities become a major source of nonorganic pollutants. However, not all of the accompanying structural changes are unfavorable to the environment—shifting production from raw materials processing to assembly and services generates less water pollution (World Bank 2000a).

24. Yusuf (2001).

25. Aggregate, comparable cross-country data are lacking on the urban incidence of income poverty. The U.N.-Habitat Urban Indicators database for over 200 cities (nonrandom sample) indicates income poverty rates averaging about 15 percent in the Asian and Middle Eastern cities to over 40 percent in Sub-Saharan Africa; however, the population living in precarious conditions, subject to environmental hazards and vulnerable to both economic and physical risks (as in informal slum settlements) is estimated to be higher than income poverty rates, ranging from 30 percent to more than 60 percent of residents in many cities (U.N.-Habitat 1996).

26. McGranahan and others (2001); World Bank (2000a).

27. "Ecological footprint" refers to the estimated land and forest area-equivalent required to meet the needs of cities for energy and waste disposal. Rees (1997) argues that the concentration of urban populations permits influencing this footprint through changes in consumption choices.

28. Kojima and Lovei (2001); Lvovsky (2001).

29. For the poorest cities and their poorest residents, indoor pollution from burning biomass and low-quality coal for cooking and heating remains a major health issue as well.

30. Lvovsky and others (2000).

31. World Bank (2000a).

32. Depending on the country, stationary sources (such as coal combustion) may be mainly responsible for local pollutants such as nitrogen oxides, sulfur dioxide, and suspended particulate matter, as in China, but in other countries motor vehicles account for most nitrogen oxide and particulates. Generally, motor vehicles also cause most of the emissions of carbon monoxide, ground-level ozone, and carbon dioxide.

33. Holtedahl and Vennemo, background paper for the WDR 2003.

34. World Bank (2002a), chapter 4.

35. Improving traffic flow reduces fuel consumption per kilometer.

36. Kojima and Lovei (2001).

37. Gambrill, Foster, and Katakura (2001).

38. Black-Arveláez (2001).

39. Pantelic (background note for the WDR 2003).

40. Intergovernmental Panel on Climate Change (IPCC) forecasts.

41. United Nations (1999), 1999 revisions.

42. In most small island states the bulk of population and infrastructure is located in coastal plains (IPCC 2001).

43. As quoted in the International Federation of Red Cross and Red Crescent Societies (1999).

44. Federal Emergency Management Agency (FEMA 1998).

45. Anderson (2000).

46. Badly designed insurance schemes create perverse incentives—for example, in Florida the creation of a public underwriting agency by the state government to cover private insurers for hurricane losses encouraged property development in hazardous zones, because risks were shared with taxpayers and property owners were given a false sense of security (Dunn and Flavin 1999).

47. Bigio (forthcoming).

48. Strictly speaking, a solid waste disposal facility and a mass transport system (bus or metro) are not fully public goods because they can become congested (reducing available use) and access can be restricted; such goods would technically be considered club goods. However, the main interest here is in activities that affect urban public goods—in this case, an environment free of solid waste and a highly accessible city.

49. Serageldin, Shluger, and Martin-Brown (2001).

50. Fang (2000).

51. Peñalosa (2001) (updated April 2002).

52. OECD, Territorial Development, *Urban Brownfields* (http://www.oecd.org/tds/bis/brownfields-chap3.htm).

53. Interview (January 29, 2002) with Dr. Ahmet Samsunlu, Technical University of Istanbul, and former minister of housing, city planning, resettlement and the environment; Hacaoglu (2001); Yildizcan (2002).

54. This section draws heavily on World Bank (2002a).

55. Typically, they have average population densities of well over 30 residents per hectare, considered the minimum needed to sustain a public transport system.

56. Koster and de Languen (1998).

57. See chapter 4, "Social Sustainability," in World Bank (1996a).

58. Willoughby (2000).

59. International Council for Local Environmental Initiatives (ICLEI 1991); Kamel (2000).

60. Bartone (2002); see also Wilson, Whiteman, and Tormin (2001).

61. Linz (2002).

62. Bartone (2002).

63. Rosenweig and Solecki (2000).

64. Hentschel (2001).

65. Numerous country poverty assessments (based on national survey data) reveal relatively high intraurban inequality in income and access to services—often greater than inequality within rural areas. See Hentschel and Bump (1999); Eastwood and Lipton (2000), table II.2.

66. McGranahan and others (2001), table 4.3.

67. U.N.-Habitat, Urban Indicators Program database (1998 data).

68. Such disparities are also evident between lower- and higher-income neighborhoods (Hardoy, Mitlin, and Satterthwaite 2001, box 4.1).

69. Stephens and others (1997).

70. Rualdo Menegat, *Atlas Ambiental de Porto Alegre*, 1998. Cited with other examples in Hardoy, Mitlin, and Satterthwaite (2001).

71. Slum population measured by a composite index of housing condition, legal compliance of structure, and access to basic services (water and sewerage). UN-Habitat, "Millenium Development Goal 7, Target 11, Indicator 31: Proportion of Population with Secure Tenure," April 2002 estimates.

72. Perceived stigma and/or job discrimination on the basis of residence is reported by slumdwellers in many studies; for Perlman (2002) see Rio de Janeiro; for Baker (2001) see Montevideo, Uruguay; and for Jamaica, see Moser and Holland (1995).

73. McIlwaine and Moser (2001).

74. Rolnik (1999).

75. FYR Macedonia, "Poverty Reduction Strategy Paper: Urban Poverty Chapter," January 2002 draft.

76. U.N.-Habitat *Global Campaign for Secure Tenure* (Nairobi, 1999). See www.urbanobservatory.org.

77. Estimates of "squatters and others" (a residual excluding formal owner-occupants and tenants) average around 15 percent of residents of low- and middle-income cities (300 million people), according to the U.N.-Habitat's Urban Indicators Database (1998 data). Documented cases of actual or threatened forced eviction affected almost 8 million people over 1998–2000 worldwide. See Centre on Housing Rights and Evictions (COHRE 2001).

78. Analysts have identified a continuum of at least 10 categories of tenure in cities of developing countries. De facto tenure security may include customary rights and occupancy rights (important particularly in African cities), which are based on duration of use and recognition by the community. Governments often regularize tenure status by acknowledging these informal rights, thereby granting de facto tenure security (Payne 2001; Payne and Fernandes 2001); Durand-Lasserve, and Royston (2002).

79. The probability of households' demanding garbage collection increased by 32 percent in going from squatter to moderate security status and by 44 percent when the squatters were compared with the high-security (legal certification) case (Hoy and Jimenez 1998).

80. Lall, Deichmann, and Lundberg (2002).

81. Fernandes (forthcoming).

82. Jimenez (1985).

83. Appadurai (2001).

84. Payne (2001); Gilbert (2002).

85. de Soto (2000).

86. Gilbert (2002); Calderon Cockburn (2002).

87. Struyk (1997); Grover, Munro-Faure, and Solovier (chapter 3 in Payne 2002).

88. Ward (1998); Payne 2002 (chapter 1 and conclusion).

89. Mutual protection within the community can be sufficient to fend off property challenges from other individuals. But female-headed households are least able to assert their rights and may benefit more from the greater security of formal titles (Lanjouw and Levy 1998).

90. Payne (2001).

91. Addressing is not a substitute for formal land registry but is fully complementary and upgradeable. (See http://web.mit.edu/urbanupgrading/upgrading/issues-tools/tools/street-addressing.html.)

92. World Bank (2000b).

93. Burra (2001b), and local press reports in Pune.

94. World Bank (2002c).

95. Readers interested in urban policy more broadly may consult the urban development Web site of the World Bank (www.worldbank.org/html/fpd/urban), or U.N.-Habitat (www.unchs.org). See also chapters 6 and 7 of World Bank (2000b) and annex E of World Bank (2001f).

96. See also World Bank (2000b), which discusses decentralization.

97 Holtedahl and Vennemo, background paper for WDR 2003.

98. This shift is characterized as moving from "expose-oppose" to "expose-oppose-propose," in Devas and others (2001).

99. This section refers to the Orangi Pilot Project's work on sanitation in Karachi and the many successful community organization–municipal partnerships in Thailand, supported by what is currently part of the Community Organizations Development Institute (Hardoy, Mitlin, and Satterthwaite 2001). The Philippines example is from Viloria-Williams (2002) background note for the WDR 2003.

100. Durban Metro, *Safer City Project,* May 2000; January 2002 interview with Richard Dobson, Programme Leader, Inner Thekwini Renewal and Urban Management Program, Durban.

101. See the city's Web site (www.obninsk.ru) for details (Gonzales de Asis and Acuña-Alfaro 2002).

102. Katz and Campbell (1996).

103. Souza (2001); Municipality of Porto Alegre, "Porto Alegre Participatory Budget," September 2000. U.N.—Habitat and The Together Foundation, Best Practices for Human Settlements Database (www.bestpractices. org).

104. World Bank–supported Urban Development and Decentralization Program Project in Senegal (ID P002365, approved in 1997); Guinea *Third Urban Development Project* (ID P001974, approved in 1999).

105. Campbell background paper for the WDR 2003.

106. Stephens and Wikstrom (2000).

107. ICLEI Initiatives (2002).

108. Velasquez (1998).

109. Other terms may be used for city strategic planning efforts, which have many antecedents and sources of support in both industrial and developing countries, such as the U.N. Urban Management Program's Sustainable Cities Program (www.unhabitat.org/ump/cityconsultation.htm). The term city development strategy is used here since it was adopted as one of the main activities supported by an international coalition of cities and donors—the Cities Alliance—created in 1999 to fund poverty-focused city development strategies and scaled-up slum upgrading in cities of developing and transition economies. (www.citiesalliance.org).

110. UN-Habitat and Urban Management Program (2001).

111. Andres Escobar, General Manager, Metro Vivienda, Bogotá, Colombia, December 2001 communication.

112. Sevilla (2000).

113. Figures for years in the 1990s. Bertaud background paper for the WDR 2003.

114. Bertaud (1999).

115. Bertaud (2000).

116. World Bank (2002b).

117. Land-use regulations and growth controls that restrict the supply of developed land are a major contributor to higher prices of serviced land and housing (Shlomo 2000).

118. The largest are the International Union of Local Authorities, Metropolis, World Federation of United Cities, and World Associations of Cities and Local Authorities Coordination.

119. See UCCI Web site at www.ayudaurbana.com.

120. City networks in East Asia, such as that of the Chinese mayors association (http://en.townsfuture.com) and Philippine city league (ww.cdsea.org) are linking in a regional Web site (www.infocity.org).

121. For example, the city of Detroit, Michigan, after receiving a poor ranking in a national rating of U.S. cities, created its own "Comeback Index," monitored by an independent institution, to track its improved performance.

Chapter 7

1. Olson (1996, p. 22).
2. Filmer (2000).
3. Sen (1983).
4. Besley and Burgess (2000).
5. Sen (1983).
6. See "Examples of Good Practice in Bank Projects Focused in Primary Education: El Salvador EDUCO Basic Education Modernization Project" available at: www.worldbank.org/oed/oeddoclib.
7. King, Orazem, and Wohlgemuth (1999); Angrist and others (forthcoming).
8. Eskeland and Filmer (2002).
9. Eigen-Zucchi (2001).
10. Eigen-Zucchi (2001).
11. Calvo (2000).
12. Rodden, Eskeland and Litvack, forthcoming.
13. World Bank (2002n, p. 113, box 5.7).
14. See the homepage of the World Bank's Small & Medium Enterprise Department, at: http://www.ifc.org/sme/index.html.
15. de Soto (2000, p. 20).
16. Djankov and others (2002).
17. Djankov and others (2002); Glaeser and Schleifer (2001).
18. *World Development Report 1997,* p. 6.
19. de Soto (2000, p. 21).

20. See, for example, Huther and Shah (2000); Transparency International (2000).

21. Ciccone and Hall (1996).

22. Henderson and others (2001).

23. Henderson (2000); Lall, Shalizi, and Deichmann (forthcoming). See also World Bank (2000b, chapter 6).

24. Canning (1999); Canning and Bennathan (2000).

25. World Bank (1994), and a World Bank Policy Research Report that is forthcoming on regulatory reforms in infrastructure.

26. Borghesi (1999), Shalizi and Kraus (2001), and World Bank (2000a).

27. Easterly (1999).

28. Myers and Kent (2001), p. 22.

29. World Bank (1992b).

30. Tullock (1975).

31. OECD (2001a), and World Bank (2002d).

32. Moore (2002).

33. World Bank (2001d).

34. OECD (2001a, p. 153).

35. FAO (2000).

36. World Bank (2001e).

37. World Bank (2001e), p. 2.

38. World Bank (2001e), p. 2.

39. World Bank (2000c).

40. Myers and Kent (2001, p. 149).

41. Myers and Kent (2001, p. 153).

42. Myers and Kent (2001, p. 152).

43. See the FAO Fishery Statistics Web page at: http://www.fao.org/fi/statist/nature_china/30jan02.asp.

44. FAO, 2002b, p. 11.

45. Willmann, Boonchuwong, and Piumsombun (2002, p. 187).

46. Willmann, Boonchuwong, and Piumsombun (2002, p. 191).

47. Willmann, Boonchuwong, and Piumsombun, (2002, p. 191).

48. Hannesson (background paper for the WDR 2003, p. 13).

49. Hannesson (background paper for the WDR 2003, p. 6 and 7).

50. FAO (2002b, p. 19).

51. FAO (2002b, p. 20).

52. FAO (2002b, p. 22).

53. Holtedahl and Vennemo, background paper for WDR 2003. See also World Bank (2001a).

54. Kojima and Lovei (2001, p. 1).

55. Dasgupta and others (2002).

56. This section draws on Lovei (1999); Rosner and Markowitz (1985); and Holtedahl Vennemo, background paper for WDR 2003.

57. Lovei, 1999, p. 11.

58. This section draws heavily on World Bank (2002c).

59. Wang and others (2002, p. 3).

60. World Bank (2001a, p. xx).

61. Holtedahl and Vennemo, background paper for WDR 2003 report that this statement is well known among environmental authorities, but it is not by itself sufficient to release detailed environmental data in all the provinces. Air quality information in 41 large cities is the exception: progress in other areas is still pending.

62. Wang and others (forthcoming, p. 2).

63. Communication with Hua Wang. See the World Bank's website on New Ideas in Pollution Regulation at: http://www.worldbank.org/nipr/index.htm for additional information on the approach of combining traditional enforcement measures with information and disclosure to improve incentives and reduce air poluution.

64. Wang and others (forthcoming, p. 6).

65. World Bank (2000d, p. 57).

66. World Bank (2000d, p. 63).

67. See Weber-Fahr (2002) for a discussion of both perspectives with regard to mining.

68. de Ferranti, Perry, Lederman and Maloney (2002, p. 4).

69. See Murshed (2002a); Auty (1997); Auty and Gelb (2001); Isham and others (2002); Sachs and Warner (1995); Auty (2002).

70. Ross (2001a).

71. Auty (2001); Isham and others (2002).

72. Isham and others (2002). Revenue flows from other types of resources such as agriculture are more diffused throughout the economy (diffuse-source economies) and do not present as many challenges to the emergence of inclusive and accountable institutions.

73. Auty and Kiiski (2001, p. 3). Although causality may be unclear if natural resource sector is the only activity able to continue in weak institutional environments, empirical studies using lagged variables for the natural resource dependency criterion suggest that causality runs from resource factors to institutions to economic performance. See for example, Isham and others (2002).

74. Murshed (2002b, p. 1).

75. Former socialist countries in Europe, Asia, and Africa are excluded owing to incomplete data.

76. Isham and others (2002 p. 5).

77. See, for example, Auty (1997); Auty and Gelb (2001); Isham and others (2002); Murshed and Perälä (2001); Rodriguez and Sachs (1999); Sachs and Warner (1999a, 1999b).

78. McGuire and Olson (1996).

79. Addison, Le Billon, and Murshed (2000).

80. Auty and Kiiski (2001, p. 25).

81. Heilbrunn (2002).

82. Malaysia's natural resources may be considered diffuse, but had many point-source features at the time of independence. For a study on Botswana, see Sarraf and Jiwanji (2001).

83. Rodrik (1999).

84. See Kremer and Jayachandran (2002).

85. World Bank (1998b).

86. The fungibility effect, explored by Devarajan and Swaroop (1998), does not depend on fraud. An inflow—even in kind, such as for a school project—has a substitution effect and an income effect. The income effect boosts expenditure on all normal goods, including schools and planes,

while the substitution effect of a school project—which can boost school expenditures beyond the income effect—exists only if the donor succeeds in reducing the marginal cost of schools to the recipient government. The illustrative use, here, of planes, is not accidental: See Devarajan and Haque (2002) for an example.

87. Alesina and Weder (forthcoming); Knack (2001).

88. Alesina (1998); Burnside and Dollar (1998); World Bank (2002g).

89. World Bank (2000d, p. 3).

90. World Bank (1998c); Sambanis (2000).

91. World Bank (1998c, p. v).

92. Sambanis, background paper for *WDR 2003*.

93. See Fajnzylber, Lederman, and Loayza (2000); Collier and Hoeffler (2000); Sambanis, Nicolas, background paper for *WDR 2003*.

94. Fajnzylber, Lederman, and Loayza (1998); Demombynes and Özler (2002).

95. Collier and Hoeffler (2001), abstract.

96. See for example Collier and Hoeffler (2000, 2001).

97. Collier and Hoeffler (2000); Ross (2001b).

98. See Isham and others (2002).

99. Ross (2001a, p. 9).

100. Ross (2001a).

101. Addison and Murshed (2002) argue that the failure to credibly commit to peace is partly a consequence of the impatience to consume resource rents.

102. Ross (2001a) chose the 13 conflicts from a larger set of 21 recent conflicts where scholars and journalists indicated that natural resources played an important role, including Afghanistan, Angola, Angola-Cabinda, Cambodia, the Democratic Republic of Congo (the 1996–97 and 1998–2001 conflicts), Indonesia-Aceh, Indonesia–West Papua, Liberia, Papua New Guinea, the Republic of Congo, Sierra Leone, and Sudan.

103. Ross (2001b).

104. Fearon (2001).

105. Collier and Hoeffler (2000).

106. Murshed (2002a, p. 3).

107. North and Weingast (1989).

108. Acemoglu and Robinson (2000a, 2000b). Stewart, 2000, also emphasizes the importance of addressing intergroup or horizontal inequality for conflict prevention.

109. Sambanis, Nicolas, background paper for *WDR 2003*.

Chapter 8

1. This account draws on National Academy of Sciences (NAS 1996); UNEP (1999); and Jager and others (2001). The quote is from NAS (1996).

2. Munton and others (1999); Jager and others (2001).

3. Clark and Dickson (1999); the framework in this chapter has benefited greatly from this study of global problem solving institutions, however, it should not be considered representative of the Social Learning Group's views.

4. Dubash and others (2001).

5. Victor, Raustiala, and Skolnikoff (1998).

6. Victor, Raustiala, and Skolnikoff (1998).

7. Data for COP-6B of the Kyoto Protocol.

8. GEF (1999, p. 7).

9. Chayes and Chayes (1995).

10. Hunter, Salzman, and Zaelke (2001).

11. Mitchell (1995); a background paper for *WDR 2003*.

12. See an extensive discussion in *Greening Industry*.

13. Sustain Ability Ltd. and UNEP (2001).

14. Dowell, Hart, and Yeung (2000)

15. King and Lennox (forthcoming).

16. Gereffi, Garcia-Johnson, and Sasser (2001).

17. Social Investment Forum (2001).

18. Boscolo and Vincent (2000).

19. Richardson (2001).

20. FAO (2000, p. 312). This Forest Resources Assessment (FRA) remote-sensing survey is based on random sampling of 10 percent of the pantropical forest area. It is distinct from the better-known FRA country-based deforestation estimates, which rely on national reports of varying consistency, periodicity, and accuracy.

21. Bleaching events—loss of coral's symbiotic algae, often leading to death of the coral—are associated with temporary spikes in sea temperature comparable to the permanent rises expected from global warming, and are probably exacerbated by other stresses.

22. Wilkinson, ed. (2000).

23. Rannesson, background paper for *WDR 2003*.

24. These categorizations are based on a global sample of satellite images that recognizes 9 classes of land cover. Following FAO (2000, pp. 313–14), deforestation of closed canopy forest has been categorized as shifting agriculture if it resulted in open forest or long fallow; smallholder agriculture if it resulted in fragmented forest, shrubs, or short fallow; and large-scale agriculture if it resulted in plantations, other land cover, or water bodies.

25. These figures represent the total net present value of returns over time.

26. Wunder (2000, p. 210).

27. Tomich and others (1998).

28. Kotto-Same and others (2000, p. 35).

29. Chomitz and others, forthcoming.

30. Tomich and others (1998).

31. Chomitz and Thomas (2001).

32. Burke, Selig, and Spalding (2002, p. 30).

33. Burke and others (2001, p. 23).

34. Tilman and others (2001).

35. Burke and others (2001, p. 51).

36. World Bank (2001e).

37. As Simpson, Sedjo, and Reid (1996) elegantly demonstrate, bioprospecting as currently practiced is unlikely to yield significant per hectare rents, because genetic information in one hectare is likely to be duplicated in another part of the same habitat. But the loss of an entire, distinctive ecosystem might carry with it significant aggregate losses of biological information.

38. Wood, Sebastian, and Scherr (2000) p. 71.

39. Steinberg (2001, p. 39).

40. Olson and Dinerstein (1998).

41. Zheng and Eltahir (1997).

42. Lant and Sant (2001).

43. Bewers and Uitto (2001).

44. Sorensen (2002, p. 9).

45. Postel and Wolf (2001).

46. White and Martin (2002); Wily and Dewees (2001).

47. OED (2002); Ross (2001b).

48. Myers and others (2000).

49. Brooks, Pimm, and Oyugi (1999).

50. Ferraz and others (2002).

51. Roe and others (2000).

52. For a review, see McNeely and Scherr (2001).

53. Tomich and others (1998).

54. Ferraro (2002).

55. OECD (1997).

56. IPCC, 2001.

57. World Bank (2000a).

58. Nicholls, Hoozemans, and Marchand (1999). Cited in McCarthy and others (2001, p. 396).

59. Such predictions should be taken only as indicative, given the uncertainty about many dimensions of climate change. Higher mean precipitation would ameliorate the impacts, according to the study. Increased summer monsoon variability, not accounted for in the model, would have the opposite effect.

60. McCarthy and others (2001, p. 517).

61. Watson and others (2000); IPPC (2002).

62. A recent authoritative review is National Research Council (2001).

63. To be precise, 40 percent of the radiative forcing from well-mixed greenhouse gases in 2000 as compared with 1750 (Houghton and others (2001, p. 351).

64. These are IPCC scenarios A1FI and B1 from Naki-cenovic and Swart (2000). Underlying data are available at sres.ciesin.org. Emissions include gases other than CO_2, and emissions from land use. The ratio in 2100 of per capita GDP in the non-OECD (membership as of 1990) to OECD countries is 57 percent in A1FI and 51 percent in B1. In A1FI, the 2100 share in primary energy of renewables is 17 percent; for B1, the share, including 'nonfossil electric' is 53 percent. The actual 1999 share was about 5 percent (IEA 2001, p. 312).

65. Stott and Kettleborough (2002).

66. Stott and Kettleborough (2002).

67. Basis of calculation: 1999 Norway emissions, 34.3 million tons CO_2. Population: 4 million. Global emissions: 6.3 billion tons per year; carbon equivalent from fossil fuels and cement, 1.7 billion tons per year; carbon equivalent from land-use change; 3.66 tons CO_2 per ton.

68. IEA (2001).

69. OECD (2001b, p. 153).

70. Streets and others (2001).

71. However, a concomitant 21 percent reduction in SO_2 emissions yielded health benefits but contributed to global warming because SO_2 aerosols have a cooling effect.

72. The description of the Thai program is based on Singh and Mulholland (2000).

73. Houghton and others (2001, p. 39).

74. Author's calculation based on data on biomass density and deforestation from FAO 2000. Carbon-to-biomass ratio assumed to be 0.5.

75. Chomitz (2002).

76. International Energy Agency (1999b, pp. 99, 105).

77. This example is based on World Bank (2002b).

77. Schipper, Murtishaw, and Unander (2001).

79. President's Committee of Advisors on Science and Technology (1997).

80. President's Committee of Advisors on Science and Technology (1997).

81. OECD (2001b, p. 153).

82. Milley and others (2002).

83. Dilley (2000).

84. Arndt and Bacou (2002).

85. Skees and others (2002).

86. Skees and others (2002).

Chapter 9

1. World Bank (2002b).

2. World Bank (2000a), p. 29

3. Rodrik (2002).

4. World Bank (2002g, 2001f, forthcoming) and DFID (2002).

5. World Bank (1996b).

6. World Bank (2002a), page 93.

7. World Bank (2002c).

8. Mackay (2000), pp. 43–56; Sustainability Ltd, and UNEP (2001); Dowell, Hart, and Yeung (2000).

9. Guerrero O. (1999).

10. These institutions have sometimes become fully integrated with operational international efforts to negotiate and implement agreements, as in the case of CLRTAP and with transboundary assessments of international waters management.

11. Devarajan, Miller, and Swanson (2002).

12. Council of the European Union (2002).

13. World Bank (2000b); World Bank (2002d, p. 98.

14. Myers and Kent (2001); Fischer and Toman (1998); Ascher (1999).

15. See World Bank (2002a), chapter 4.

16. World Bank (2002b), p. 58–9.

17. World Bank (2002ee), p. 133.

18. World Bank (2002ee), pp. 141–142.

References

Abraham, Anita, and Platteau, Jean-Philippe. Forthcoming. "Participatory Development: Where Culture Creeps In." In Vijayendra Rao and Michael Walton, eds. *Culture and Public Action*. Stanford, Calif.: Stanford University Press.

Abramson, Paul R., and Ronald Inglehart. 1995. *Value Change in Global Perspective*. Ann Arbor: University of Michigan Press.

Acemoglu, Daron, Simon Johnson, and James A. Robinson. 2001. "Reversal of Fortune: Geography and Institutions in the Making of the Modern World Income Distribution." National Bureau of Economic Research Working Paper 8460. Cambridge, Mass.

Acemoglu, Daron, Simon Johnson, James Robinson, and Yunyong Thaicharoen. Forthcoming. "Institutional Causes, Macroeconomic Symptoms: Volatility, Crisis and Growth." *Journal of Monetary Economics*.

Acemoglu, Daron, and James A. Robinson. 2000a. "Inequality, Growth and Development: Democratization or Repression?" *European Economic Review* 44:683–93.

———. 2000b. "Why Did the West Extend the Franchise? Democracy, Inequality and Growth in Historical Perspective." *Quarterly Journal of Economics* 115(4): 1167–99.

Adams, James D. 2001. "Comparative Localization of Academic and Industrial Spillovers." National Bureau of Economic Research Working Paper 8292. Cambridge, Mass.

Addison, Tony, Philippe Le Billon, and S. Mansoob Murshed. 2000. "On the Economic Motivation for Conflict in Africa." Paper presented at World Bank ABCDE–Europe Conference, Paris, June 2000.

Addison, Tony and Mansoob Murshed. 2002. "Credibility and Reputation in Peacemaking." Forthcoming in the *Journal of Peace Research* July.

Aghion, Philippe, Eve Caroli, and Cecilia Garcia–Peñalosa. 1999. "Inequality and Economic Growth: The Perspective of the New Growth Theories." *Journal of Economic Literature* 37(4):1615–60.

Alesina, Alberto. 1998. "The Political Economy of Macroeconomic Stabilizations and Income Inequality: Myths and Reality." In V. Tanzi and Ke–young Chu, eds., *Income Distribution and High Quality Growth*. Cambridge, Mass.: MIT Press.

Alesina, Alberto, and Dani Rodrik. 1994. "Distributive Policies and Economic Growth." *Quarterly Journal of Economics* 109(2):465–90.

Alesina, Alberto, and Beatrice Weder. Forthcoming. "Do Corrupt Governments Receive Less Foreign Aid?" *American Economic Review*.

Alexandratos, Nikos, ed. 1995. *World Agriculture: Toward 2010, A FAO Study*. Rome: Food and Agriculture Organization of the United Nations; and John Wiley and Sons, Ltd.

Alston, Lee, Gary D. Libecap, and Robert Schneider. 1995. "Property Rights and the Preconditions for Markets: The Case of the Amazon Frontier." *Journal of Institutional and Theoretical Economics* 151(1):89–107.

———. 1996. "The Determinants and Impact of Property Rights: Land Titles on the Brazilian Frontier." *The Journal of Law, Economics and Organization* 12(1):25–61.

Amahan, Ali. 1998. *Mutations sociales dans le Haut Atlas: Les Ghoujdama*. Paris, Rabat: Maison des Sciences de l'Homme, Paris, and Editions La Porte, Rabat.

Anbarasan, Ethirajan, and Choi Yul. 2001. "The Greening of Korea." *UNESCO Courier* 54(2):47–51.

Andean Center for Economics in the Environment. 2001. "Economic Instruments and Environment: Can Economic Instruments Work in Developing Countries?" Available on line at www.andeancenter.com.

Anderson, Mary B. 2000. "The Impacts of Natural Disasters on the Poor: A Background Note." World Bank, Washington, D.C. Processed.

Anderson, Terry. 1996. "Conservation—Native American Style: A Summary." Political Economy Research Center Policy Series PS–6. Bozeman, Montana. Available online at http://www.perc.org/publications/policyseries/conservation_full.html.

Anderson, Terry L., and Peter J. Hill. 1990. "The Race for Property Rights." *Journal of Law and Economics* 33: 177–97.

Andreoni, J., and A. Levinson. 1998. "The Simple Analytics of the Environmental Kuznets Curve." National Bureau of Economic Research Working Paper 6739. Cambridge, Mass.

Angrist, Joshua D., Eric Bettinger, Erik Bloom, Elizabeth King, and Michael Kremer. Forthcoming. "Vouchers for Private Schooling in Colombia: Evidence from a Randomized Natural Experiment." *American Economic Review*.

Appadurai, Arjun. 2001. "Deep Democracy: Urban Governmentality and the Horizon of Politics." *Environment and Urbanization* 13(2):23–43.

Araujo, J., and M. Neto Costa. 1999. "The Impact of Civil Conflict on Long-Term Performance in the Height of the Angolan Experience." World Bank Institute, World Bank, Washington, D.C. Processed.

Arndt, C., and M. Bacou. 2002. "Economy–Wide Effects of Climate Variability and Climate Prediction in Mozambique." *American Journal of Agricultural Economics* 82(3): 750–754.

Ascher, William. 1999. *Why Governments Waste Natural Resources: Policy Failures in Developing Countries*. Baltimore, Md.: Johns Hopkins University Press.

Auty, Richard M., ed. 2001. *Resource Abundance and Economic Development*. Oxford: Oxford University Press.

———. 2002. "Best Practice for Economic Diversification in Mineral Economies." Paper presented at the Managing Volatility Workshop. World Bank, Washington, D.C.

Auty, Richard M., and Alan H. Gelb. 2001. "Political Economy of Resource–Abundant States." In R. M. Auty, ed., *Resource Abundance and Economic Development*. New York: Oxford University Press.

Auty, R. M., and Sampsa Kiiski. 2001. "Natural Resources, Capital Accumulation, Structural Change, and Welfare." In R. M. Auty, ed., *Resource Abundance and Economic Development*. New York: Oxford University Press.

Baker, Judy L. 2001. "Social Exclusion in Urban Uruguay." Latin America and the Caribbean Region, World Bank, Washington, D.C. Processed.

Baland, Jean-Marie, and Jean-Philippe Platteau. 1996. *Halting Degradation of Natural Resources*. Food and Agriculture Organization of the United Nations, Oxford: Clarendon Press. Available online at www.fao.org.

Banerjee, Abhiji, Paul J. Gertler, and Maitreesh Ghatak. 2001. "Empowerment and Efficiency: Tenancy Reform in West Bengal." Department of Economics, University of Chicago. Processed.

Banerjee, Abhijit, and Lakshmi Iyer. 2002. "History, Institutions and Economic Performance: The Legacy of Colonial Land Tenure Systems in India." Cambridge, Mass.: MIT.

Banerjee, Abhiji, Dilip Mookherjee, Kaivan Munshi, and Debraj Ray. 1997. "Inequality, Control Rights and Rent Seeking—A Theoretical and Empirical Analysis of Sugar Cooperatives in Maharashtra." Boston University, Institute for Economic Development 80.

Bardham, Pranab K., and Dilip Mookherjee. 2000. "Capture and Governance at Local and National Levels." *American Economic Review* 90(2):135–39.

Bartone, Carl. 2002. "Institutional Arrangements for Solid Waste Management in Metropolitan Areas." Presentation in Metropolitan Governance Seminar Series, World Bank Institute, March 6, Washington, D.C. Processed.

Bartone, Carl, Janis Bernstein, Josef Leitmann, and Jochen Eigen. 1994. "Toward Environmental Strategies for Cities." United Nations Development Programme/ United Nations Commission on Human Settlements/ World Bank Urban Management Program 18. Washington, D.C.

Behnke, R. H., Jr., I. Scoones, and C. Kerven, eds. 1993. *Range Ecology at Disequilibrium: New Models of Natural Variability and Pastoral Adaptation in African Savannas.* London: Overseas Development Institute.

Berg, Elliot. 1981. "Accelerated Development in Sub-Saharan Africa." World Bank, Washington, D.C.

Bernardes, Aline Tristao. 1999. "Some Mechanisms for Biodiversity Protection in Brazil, with Emphasis on Their Application in the State of Minas Gerais." World Bank: Washington, D.C. Processed.

Bertaud, Alain. 1999. "Cracow in the Twenty-First Century: Princes or Merchants? A city's structure under the conflicting influences of land markets, zoning regulations, and a socialist past." Europe and Central Asia Region, Infrastructure Department Working Paper 8. World Bank, Washington, D.C.

———. 2000. "The Costs of Utopia: Brasilia, Johannesburg and Moscow." City of Helsinki Web site, Gavle. Available online at http://www.hel.fi/english/index.html. Processed.

Besley, Timothy, and Robin Burgess. 2000. "Land Reform, Poverty Reduction and Growth: Evidence from India." *Quarterly Journal of Economics* 115(2):389–430.

———. 2001. "Political Agency, Government Responsiveness and the Role of the Media." *European Economic Review* 45(4–6):629–40.

Bewers, J. Michael, and Juha I. Uitto. 2001. "International Waters Program Study." Global Environment Facility, Washington, D.C.

Bigio, Anthony G. Forthcoming. "Cities and Climate Change." In *Building Resilience in Metropolitan Areas.* Washington, D.C.: World Bank.

Binswanger, Hans P., and Klaus Deininger. 1997. "Explaining Agricultural and Agrarian Policies in Developing Countries." *Journal of Economic Literature* 35(4): 1958– 2005.

Black-Arveláez. 2001. "Economic Instruments and the Environment." *Andean Center for Economics and the Environment Bulletin* 4(1):1.

Blanchflower, David G., and Andrew J. Oswald. 2000. "Well-Being over Time in Britain and the USA." National Bureau of Economic Research Working Paper 7487. Cambridge, Mass.

Bloom, D. E., and J. G. Williamson. 1997. "Demographic Transition and Economic Miracles in Emerging Asia." National Bureau of Economic Research Working Paper 6268. Cambridge, Mass.

Bolt, K., U. Deichmann, K. Hamilton, B. Ostro, K. Pandy, and D. Wheeler. Forthcoming. "The Human Cost of Air Pollution: New Estimates for Developing Countries." World Bank Policy Research and Environment Department Working Paper, Washington, D.C.

Bohn, Henning, and Robert T. Deacon. 2000. "Ownership Risk, Investment, and the Use of Natural Resources." *American Economic Review* 90(3):526–49.

Bonkoungou, Eduoard. 2001. "Biodiversity in Drylands: Challenges and Opportunities for Conservation and Sustainable Land Use." United Nations Development Programme, Nairobi.

Boonchuwong, P., W. Dechboon, and M. Ahmed. 2002. "Bioeconomic modeling of the fisheries in the Gulf of Thailand." PRIAP Working Paper 8. Policy Research and Impact Assessment Program. International Center for Living Aquatic Resources Management: The World Fish Center, Penang, Malaysia.

Borghesi, Simone. 1999. "The Environmental Kuznets Curve: A Survey of the Literature." European University Institute, Florence. Available online at http://www.feem. it/web/activ/wp/abs99/85–99.pdf. Processed.

Boscolo, Marco, and Jeffrey R. Vincent. 2000. "Promoting Better Logging Practices in Tropical Forests: A Simulation Analysis of Alternative Regulations." *Land Economics* 76(1): 1–14.

Botsford, L. D., J. C.Castilla, and C. H. Peterson. 1997. "The Management of Fisheries and Marine Ecosystems." *Science* 277: 509–15.

Bowles, Samuel, and Herbert Gintis. 1999. " 'Social Capital' and Community Governance." University of Massachusetts, Amherst. Available online at http://www-unix.oit. umass.edu/~bowles/papers/Socap.PDF. Processed.

Boyce, James K. 2002. *The Political Economy of the Environment.* Cheltenham, U.K.: Edward Elgar.

Brakarz, José, with Margarita Greene and Eduardo Rojas. 2002. *Ciudades para todos: La experiencia reciente en programa de majoramiento de barrios.* Washington, D.C.: Inter-American Development Bank.

Brechin, Steven R., and Willett Kempton. 1994. "Global Environmentalism: A Challenge to the Postmaterialism Thesis?" *Social Science Quarterly* 75(2):245–69.

Breman, H., and C. T. Wit. 1983. "Rangeland Productivity and Exploitation in the Sahel." *Science* 221(4618): 1341–46.

Brockerhoff, Martin, and Ellen Brennan. 1998. "The Poverty of Cities in Developing Regions." *Population and Development Review* 24(1):1–40.

Brooks, Thomas M., Stuart L. Pimm, and Joseph O. Oyugi. 1999. "Time Lag between Deforestation and Bird Extinction in Tropical Forest Fragments." *Conservation Biology* 13(5):1140–50.

Brown, Lester R., Flavin Christopher, and Hilary French. 2001. *State of the World 2001.* New York: W. M. Norton.

Brundtland Commission. 1987. "Our Common Future." The World Commission on Environment and Development, Geneva. Available online at http://geneva-international.org/GVA/WelcomeKit/Environnement/chap_5.E.html.

Bruner, Aaron G., Raymond E. Gullison, Richard E. Rice, and Gustavo A. B. de Fonseca. 2001. "Effectiveness of Parks in Protecting Tropical Biodiversity." *Science* 291: 125–8.

Brunner, Jake, and Francois Ekoko. 2000. "Cameroon." In Frances J. Seymour and Navroz K. Dubash, eds. *The Right Conditions: The World Bank, Structural Adjustment, and Forest Policy Reform.* Washington, D.C.: World Resources Institute.

Buchanan, James M. 2001. "The Constitutional Way of Thinking." George Mason University. Processed.

Burke, Lauretta, Yumiko Kura, Ken Kassem, Carmen Revenga, Mark Spalding, and Don McAllister. 2001. *Pilot Analysis of Global Ecosystems: Coastal Ecosystems.* Washington, D.C.: World Resources Institute. Available online at http://www.wri.org/wr2000/coast_page.html.

Burke, Lauretta, Elizabeth Selig, and Mark Spalding. 2002. *Reefs at Risk in Southeast Asia.* Washington, D.C.: World Resources Institute.

Burnside, Craig, and David Dollar. 1998. "Aid, the Incentive Regime, and Poverty Reduction." World Bank Policy Research Department Working Paper No. 1937. June. Washington, D.C.

Burra, Sundar. 2001a. "Resettlement and Rehabilitation of the Urban Poor: The Mumbai Urban Transport." Society for Promotion of Area Resource Centers, Mumbai. Processed.

———. 2001b. "Slum Sanitation in Pune: A Case Study." Society for Promotion of Area Resource Centres, Mumbai. Available online at www.sparcindia.org. Processed.

Byerlee, Derek, and Ken Fischer. 2000. "Accessing Modern Science: Policy and Institutional Options for Agricultural Biothechnology in Developing Countries." World Bank, Washington, D.C. Processed.

Calvo, Guillermo A. 2000. "The Case for Hard Pegs in the Brave New World of Global Finance." Paper presented at ABCDE Europe, Paris, June 26.

Calderon Cockburn, Julio. 2002. "The Mystery of Credit." Lincoln Institute of Land Policy, Cambridge. Processed.

Campbell, Tim. 1997. "Innovations and Risk Taking: The Engine of Reform in Local Governments in Latin America and the Caribbean." World Bank Discussion Paper 357. Washington, D.C.

———. Forthcoming. *The Quiet Revolution: The Rise of Political Participation and Local Government in Latin America and the Caribbean.* Washington, D.C: World Bank.

Canning, David. 1999. "Infrastructure's Contribution to Aggregate Output." World Bank Policy Research Working Paper 2246. Washington, D.C.

Canning, David, and Esra Bennathan. 2000. "The Social Rate of Return on Infrastructure Investment." World Bank Policy Research Working Paper 2390. Washington, D.C.

Cardy, W. Franklin. 2002. "Environment and Forced Migration: A Review." In Michael B. K. Darkosh and Apollo Rwonmire, eds., *Human Impact on Environmental and Sustainable Development in Africa.* Oxford: Ashgate Publishing.

Carlin, Elaine. 2002. "Oil Pollution from Ships at Sea: The Ability of Nations to Protect a Blue Planet." In Edward Miles, Arild Underdal, Steinar Andresen, Jorgen Wettestad, Jon Birger Skjaerseth, and Elaine M. Carlin, eds., *Environmental Regime Effectiveness: Confronting Theory with Evidence.* Cambridge, Mass.: MIT Press.

Carson, R. 1962. *Silent Spring.* Boston: Houghton Mifflin.

Carter, Michael R., and Frederick J. Zimmerman. 2000. "The Dynamic Cost and Persistence of Asset Inequality in an Agrarian Economy." *Journal of Development Economics* 63(2): 265–302.

Cavendish, William. 1999. "Poverty, Inequality and Environmental Resources: Quantitative Analysis of Rural Households." T. H. Huxley School, Imperial College of Science, Technology and Medicine Working Paper Series 99–9. London.

CGIAR (Consultative Group on International Agricultural Research). 1997. "Report of the Study on CGIAR Research Priorities for Marginal Lands." Technical Advisory Committee Working Document. Food and Agriculture Organization of the United Nations, Rome.

Chayes, Abraham, and Antonia Handler Chayes. 1995. *The New Sovereignty: Compliance with International Regulatory Agreements.* Cambridge, Mass.: Harvard University Press.

Chéret, Ivan. 1993. "Managing Water: The French Model." In Ismael Serageldin and Andrew Steer, eds., *Valuing the Environment.* Washington, D.C.: World Bank.

Chen, Shoahua, and Martin Ravallion. 2000. "How Did the World's Poorest Fare in the 1990s?" World Bank Policy Research Working Paper 2409. World Bank, Policy Research Department, Washington, D.C.

Chomitz, Kenneth. 2002. "Baseline, Leakage and Measurement Issues: How Do Forestry and Energy Projects Compare?" *Climate Policy* 2(1):35–49.

Chomitz, Kenneth M., Keith Alger, Timothy S. Thomas, Heloisa Orlando, and Paulo Vila Nova. Forthcoming. "Opportunity Costs of Conservation in a Biodiversity Hotspot: The Case of Bahia." World Bank, Washington, D.C.

Chomitz, Kenneth, and T. Thomas. 2001. "Geographic Patterns of Land Use and Land Intensity in the Brazilian Amazon." World Bank Policy Research Working Paper 2687. Washington, D.C.

Ciccone, Antonio, and Robert E. Hall. 1996. "Productivity and the Density of Economic Activity." *American Economic Review* 86(1):54–70.

Clague, Christopher, Philip Keefer, Stephen Knack, and Mancur Olson. 1999. "Contract-Intensive Money: Contract Enforcement, Property Rights, and Economic Performance." *Journal of Economic Growth* 4:185–209.

Clark, J. B. 1898. "The Future of Economic Theory." *Quarterly Journal of Economics* 13(2):1–14.

Clark, William, and Nancy Dickson. 1999. "The Global Environmental Assessment Project: Learning from Efforts to Link Science and Policy in an Interdependent World." *Acclimations* 8:6–7.

Coase, Ronald. 1960. "The Problem of Social Cost." *Journal of Law and Economics* 3:1–44.

Cochrane, Mark, Ane Alencar, Mark D. Schulze, Carlos M. Souza, Daniel C. Nepstad, Paul Lefebvre, and Eric A. Davidson. 1999. "Positive Feedbacks in the Fire Dynamic in Closed Canopy Tropical Forests." *Science* 284: 1832–35.

COHRE (Centre on Housing Rights and Evictions). 2001. "Forced Evictions: Violations of Human Rights." Global Survey on Forced Evictions 8. Geneva.

Cole, M. A., A. J. Rayner, and J. M. Bates. 1997. "The Environmental Kuznets Curve: An Empirical Analysis." *Environment and Development Economics* 2(4):401–16.

Collier, Paul. 1999. "On the Economic Causes of Civil War." *Oxford Economic Papers* 51(1):168–83.

Collier, Paul, and Anke Hoeffler. 2000. "On the Incidence of Civil War in Africa." World Bank, Washington, D.C. Available online at http://www.worldbank.org/research/conflict/papers.htm. Processed.

———. 2001. "Greed and Grievance in Civil War." World Bank, Washington, D.C. Processed.

Collier, Paul, and Deepak Lal. 1980. "Poverty and Growth in Kenya." World Bank Staff Working Paper 389. Washington, D.C.

Collomb, Jean-Gael, and Heriette Bikié. 2001. "1999–2000 Allocation of Logging Permits in Cameroon: Fine-Tuning Central Africa's First Auction System." Global Forest Watch, Cameroon. Available online at www.globalforestwatch.org.

Conroy, Mike. 2001. "Yellowstone Honors Army for Saving Park." U.S. Army Environment Center. Available online at http://www.dtic.mil/armylink/news/Oct2000/a20001004 yellowstone2.html.

Cosgrove, W. J., and F. R. Rijsberman. 2000. *World Water Vision: Making Water Everybody's Business.* London: Earthscan for the World Water Council.

Council of the European Union. 2002. "Towards a Global Partnership for Sustainable Development." Communication from the Commission to the European Parliament, the Council, the Economic and Social Committee, and the Committee of the Regions, February 25. Brussels.

Coxhead, Ian, Agnes Rola, and Kwansoo Kim. 2001. "How Do National Markets and Price Policies Affect Land Use at the Forest Margin? Evidence from the Philippines." *Land Economics* 77(2):250–67.

Crosson, Pierre. 1995. "Soil Erosion and Its On-Farm Productivity Consequences: What Do We Know?" RFF Discussion Paper 95–29. Resources for the Future, Washington, D.C.

Crosson, Pierre, and Jock R. Anderson. 2002. "Technologies for Meeting Future Global Demands for Food." RFF Discussion Paper 02–02. Resources for the Future, Washington, D.C.

Dasgupta, Partha. 2000. "Valuing Biodiversity." In Simon Levin, ed., *Encyclopedia of Biodiversity.* New York: Academic Press. Forthcoming.

Dasgupta, Partha. 2001a. *Human Well-Being and the Natural Environment.* Oxford: Oxford University Press.

———. 2001b. "Valuing Objects and Evaluating Policies in Imperfect Economies." *Economic Journal* 111(471): C1–29.

———. 2002. "Population and Resources: An Exploration of Reproductive and Environmental Externalities." *Population and Development Review* 26(4):643–89.

Dasgupta, S., B. Laplante, and N. Mamingi. 2001. "Pollution and Capital Markets in Developing Countries." *Journal of Environmental Economics and Management* 42(3).

Dasgupta, Susmita, Benoit Laplante, Hua Wang, and David Wheeler. 2002. "Confronting the Environmental Kuznets Curve." *Journal of Economic Perspectives* 16(1):147–68.

Dasgupta, Susmita, and David Wheeler. 1997. "Citizen Complaints as Environmental Indicators: Evidence from China." World Bank Policy Research Working Paper 1704. Washington, D.C.

Davis, Jeffrey, Rolando Ossowski, James Daniel, and Steven Barnett. 2001. "Stabilization and Savings Fund for Nonrenewable Resources: Experience and Fiscal Policy Implica-

tions." IMF Occasional Paper 205. International Monetary Fund, Washington, D.C.

Davis, Shelton. 1993. "Indigenous Views of Land and the Environment." World Bank Discussion Paper 188. Washington, D.C.

de Ferranti, David, Guillermo E. Perry, Daniel Lederman, and William F. Maloney. 2002. "From Natural Resources to the Knowledge Economy: Trade and Job Quality." World Bank, Washington, D.C. Available online at http://..1nweb18.worldbank.org/External/laconst.

De Haan, Arjan. 1999. "Livelihoods and Poverty: The Role of Migration—A Critical Review of the Migration Literature." *Journal of Development Studies* 36(2):1–47.

———. 2000. "Migrants, Livelihoods, and Rights: The Relevance of Migration in Development Policies." World Bank Social Development Working Paper 4. Washington, D.C.

de Janvry, Alain, Gustavo Gordillo , Jean-Philippe Platteau, and Elisabeth Sadoulet, eds. 2001. *Access to Land, Rural Poverty and Public Action.* New York: Oxford University Press.

de Mello Lemos, Maria Carmen. 1998. "The Politics of Pollution Control in Brazil: State Actors and Social Movements Cleaning up Cubatão." *World Development* 26(1): 75–87.

de Soto, Hernando. 2000. *The Mystery of Capital: Why Capitalism Triumphs in the West and Fails Everywhere Else.* New York: Perseus Book Group.

de Umanzor, Sandra, Isis Soriano, Marta Rosa Vega, Emmanuel Jimenez, Laura Rawlings, and Diana Steele. 1997. "El Salvador's EDUCO Program: A First Report on Parent's Participation in School-Based Management." World Bank Working Paper Series on Impact Evaluation of Education Reforms 4. Washington, D.C.

Di Primio, Juan Carlos. 1998. "Data Quality and Compliance Control in the European Air Quality Regime." In David G. Victor, Kal Raustiala, and Eugene B. Skolnikoff, eds., *The Implementation and Effectiveness of International Environmental Commitments: Theory and Practice.* Cambridge, Mass.: MIT Press.

Deininger, Klaus, and Hans Binswanger. 2001. "The Evolution of the World Bank's Land Policy." In Alain de Janvry, Gustavo Gordillo, Jean-Philippe Platteau, and Elisabeth Sadoulet, eds., *Access to Land, Rural Poverty, and Public Action.* New York: Oxford University Press.

Deininger, Klaus, and Gershon Feder. 1998. "Land Institutions and Land Markets." World Bank Policy Research Working Paper 2014. Washington, D.C.

Deininger, K., and Lyn Squire. 1998. "New Ways of Looking at Old Issues: Inequality and Growth." *Journal of Development Economics* 57(2):259–87.

Demombynes, Gabriel, and Berk Özler. 2002. "Inequality, Property Crime, and Violent Conflict in South Africa." World Bank, Washington, D.C. Processed.

Devarajan, Shantayanan, and Trina Haque. 2002. "Human Development Policy Note." World Bank, Washington, D.C. Processed.

Devarajan, Shantayanan, Margaret J. Miller, and Eric V. Swanson. 2002. "Goals for Development: History, Prospects and Costs." World Bank, Washington, D.C. Processed.

Devarajan, Shantayanan, and Vinaya Swaroop. 1998. "The Implications of Foreign Aid Fungibility for Development Assistance." World Bank Policy Research Working Paper 2022. Washington, D.C.

Devas, Nick, Philip Amis, Richard Batley, Ursula Grant, Fiona Nunan, and Elyzabeth Vidler. 2001. "Urban Governance, Partnership and Poverty: ESCOR–Funded Research in Ten Cities: 1998–2001." University of Birmingham, U.K. Available online at http://www.bham.ac. uk/IDD/activities/urban/urbgov.htm.

DfID (Department for International Development, United Kingdom), European Commission Directorate General for Development, UNDP (United Nations Development Program), and World Bank. 2002. "Linking Poverty Reduction and Economic Management: Policy Challenges and Opportunities." Washington, D.C. Processed.

Diamond, Jared. 1997. *Guns, Germs and Steel: The Fate of Human Societies.* New York: W. W. Norton.

Diener, E. 1984. "Subjective Well-Being." *Psychological Bulletin* 95:542–75.

Dilley, Maxx. 2000. "Reducing Vulnerability to Climate Variability in Southern Africa: The Growing Role of Climate Information." *Climatic Change* 45: 63–73.

Dixon, John, Aidan Gulliver, and David Gibbon. 2001. "Global Farming Systems Study: Challenges and Priorities to 2030." Rome. Food and Agriculture Organization of the United Nations.

Djankov, Simeon, Rafael La Porta, Rafael Lopez-de-Silanes, and Andrei Schleifer. 2002. "The Regulation of Entry." *The Quarterly Journal of Economics* 117(1): 1–37.

Doble, Philip. 2001. "Poverty and the Drylands." United Nations, Nairobi.

Donnely-Roark, Paula, K. Ouedraogo, and X. Ye. 2001. "Can Local Institutions Reduce Poverty? Rural Decentralization in Burkina Faso." World Bank Policy Research Working Paper 2677. Washington, D.C.

Dorsey, Eleanor. 1998. *The Road to Groundfish Collapse and Turning the Corner to Recovery: A Brief History of the New England Fisheries Crisis.* Boston, Mass.; Rockland, Me.; Concord, N.H.; Providence, R.I.; Montpelier, Vt.: Conservation Law Foundation.

Dowell, Glen, Stuart Hart, and Bernard Yeung. 2000. "Do Corporate Global Environmental Standards Create or Destroy Market Value?" *Management Science* 46(8): 1059–74.

DRI (Data Resources Inc.) 1997. "Effects of Phasing Out Coal Subsidies in OECD Countries." In OECD, eds., *Environmental Taxes and Green Reforms.* Paris: DRI/McGraw-Hill.

Dubash, Navroz, Mairi Dupar, Smitu Kothari, and Tundu Lissu. 2001. "A Watershed in Global Governance? An Independent Assessment of the World Commission on Dams." World Resources Institute, Washington, D.C. Available online at http://www.wri.org/wri/pdf/wcd_full.pdf.

Dunlap, Riley E., and Angela G. Mertig. 1995. "Global Concern for the Environment: Is Affluence a Prerequisite?" *Journal of Social Issues* 51(4):121–37.

Dunlap, Riley E., George H. Gallup, Jr., and Alec M. Gallup. 1993. *Health of the Planet: Results of a 1992 International Environmental Opinion Survey of Citizens in 24 Nations.* Princeton, N.J.: The George H. Gallup International Institute.

Dunn, Seth, and Christopher Flavin. 1999. "Destructive Storms Drive Insurance Losses Up—Will Taxpayers Have to Bail Out Insurance Industry?" *Worldwatch Institute, Worldwatch News Brief* 99–3: Washington, D.C.

Durand-Lasserve, Alain, and Lauren Royston, eds. 2002. *Holding Their Ground: Secure Land Tenure for the Urban Poor in Developing Countries.* London: Earthscan.

Durban Metro. 2000. Safer City Project. Available online at SaferCities@durban.gov.za.

Easterly, William. 1999. "Life during Growth." *Journal of Economic Growth* 4(3):239–75.

———.2002. "Inequality Does Cause Underdevelopment: New Evidence." Center for Global Development Working Paper 1. Washington, D.C.

———. Forthcoming. "Can Institutions Resolve Ethnic Conflict?" *Economic Development and Cultural Change.*

Easterly, William, and Stanley Fischer. 2001. "Inflation and the Poor." *Journal of Money, Credit and Banking* 33(2): 160–78.

Eastwood, Robert, and Michael Lipton. 2000. "Rural-Urban Dimensions of Inequality Change." World Institute for Development Economics Research Working Paper 2003. Helsinki.

EBRD (European Bank for Reconstruction and Development). 2002. *Transition Report 2000.* London.

Echikson, William. 1999. "Food Scares Whet Europe Appetite for U.S.-Type Oversight." *Christian Science Monitor* 28 July. Available online at http://www.csmonitor. com/durable/1999/07/28/fp7s1-csm.shtml.

Economist. 2001. "The Future of Farming in the Great American Desert." *The Economist* (December 15): 26–7.

Ehrlich P., and Ehrlich A. 1981. *Extinction: The Causes and Consequences of the Disappearance of Species.* New York: Random House.

Eicher, Cark K., and John M. Staatz. 1998. *International Agricultural Development.* Baltimore, Md.: Johns Hopkins University Press.

Eigen, Peter, and Christian Eigen-Zucchi. 2002. "Corruption and Global Public Goods." In Kaul, Inge, eds., *Providing Global Public Goods: Managing Globalization.* New York: Oxford University Press.

Eigen-Zucchi, Christian. 2001. *The Measurement of Transactions Costs,* Fairfax, Virginia, George Mason University. Ph.D. Dissertation. Available online at http://eigen1.tripod. com/tpi. pdf.

Engerman, Stanley L., Stephen H. Haber, and Kenneth L. Sokoloff. 2000. "Inequality, Institutions, and Differential Paths of Growth among New World Economies." In Claude Menard, ed., *Institutions, Contracts, and Organizations: Perspectives from New Institutional Economics.* London: Edward Elgar.

Engerman, Stanley L., and Kenneth L. Sokoloff. 1997. "Factor Endowments: Institutions, and Differential Paths of Growth Among New World Economies: A View from Economic Historians of the United States." In Stephen H. Haber, ed., *How Latin America Fell Behind: Essays in the Economic Histories of Brazil and Mexico, 1800–1914.* Stanford, Calif.: Stanford University Press.

———. 2001. "The Evolution of Suffrage Institutions in the New World." National Bureau of Economic Research Working Paper 8512. Cambridge, Mass.

ESCAP. 1993. "State of Urbanization in Asia and the Pacific." United Nations, New York.

Eskeland, Gunnar S., and Shantayanan Devarajan. 1996. *Taxing Bads by Taxing Goods: Pollution Control with Presumptive Charges.* Washington, D.C.: World Bank.

Eskeland, Gunnar S., and Deon Filmer. 2002. "Autonomy, Participation, and Learning in Argentine Schools." World Bank Policy Research Working Paper 2766. Washington, D.C.

Eskeland, Gunnar S., Jennie Litvack, and Jonathan Rodden. 2002. *Decentralization and the Challenge of Hard Budget Constraints.* Boston: MIT Press.

Essama-Nssah, B., and James Gockowski. 2000. "Cameroon: Forest Sector Development in a Difficult Political Economy." Evaluation Country Case Study Series. World Bank, Washington, D.C.

Fajnzylber, Pablo, Daniel Lederman, and Norman Loayza. 1998. "Determinants of Crime Rates in Latin America and the World." World Bank, Latin America and Caribbean Studies Viewpoints. Washington, D.C.

———. 2000. "Crime and Victimization: An Economic Perspective." *Economía* 1(1):219–302.

———. Forthcoming. "Inequality and Violent Crime." *Journal of Law and Economics.*

Fan, Shenggen, Peter Hazell, and Sukhadeo Thorat. 2000. "Government Spending, Agricultural Growth and Poverty in Rural India." *American Journal of Agricultural Economics* 82(4):1038–51.

Fang, Ke. 2000. *Redevelopment in the Inner City of Contemporary Beijing: Survey, Analysis and Investigation.* Beijing: China Architectural Industry Press.

FAO (Food and Agriculture Organization of the United Nations). 1997. "Irrigation Potential in Africa: A Basin Approach." Rome.

———. 2000. "Global Forest Resources Assessment 2000." Rome. Available on line at http://www.fao.org/forestry/fo/fra/main/index.jsp.

——- 2002a. "FAO Fishery Statistics." Available online at http://www.fao.org/WAICENT/FAOINFO/FISHERY/statist/statist.asp.

——— 2002b. "The State of World Fisheries and Aquaculture." Available online at http://www.fao.org/sof/sofia/index_en.htm.

FAO, UNEP, and UNDP (Food and Agriculture Organization of the United Nations, United Nations Environment Programme, and United Nations Development Programme). 1994. "Land Degradation in South Asia: Its Severity, Causes and Effects upon the People." World Soil Resources Report Rome. Available online at http://www.fao.org/docrep/V4360E/V4360E00. htm.

Farrington, John, and Anthony Bebbington, eds. 1993. *Reluctant Partners? Non-governmental Organizations, the State and Sustainable Agricultural Development.* New York: Routledge.

Fearon, James. 2001. "Why Do Some Civil Wars Last So Much Longer than Others?" World Bank–University of California, Irvine, Conference. Processed.

FEMA (Federal Emergency Management Agency). 1998. "Report on Costs and Benefits of Natural Hazard Mitigation." Washington, D.C.

Fernandes, Edesio. Forthcoming. "Combining Tenure Policies, Urban Planning and City Management in Brazil." In Payne, Geoffrey, ed., *Land, Rights and Innovations.* London: Intermediate Technology Development Group.

Ferraro, Paul J. 2002. "Global Habitat Protection: Limitations of Development Approaches and a Role for Conservation Performance Payments." *Conservation Biology* 15(4):990–1000.

Ferraz, Goncalo, Gareth J. Russell, Philip C. Stouffer, Richard O. Bierregaard, Stuart L. Pimm, and Thomas E. Lovejoy. 2002. "Rate of Species Loss from Amazonian Forest Fragments." Wooster College, Wooster. Processed.

Filmer, Deon. 2000. "The Structure of Social Disparities in Education: Gender and Wealth." World Bank Policy Research Working Paper 2268. Washington, D.C.

Findlay, Ronald, and Mats Lundahl. 1994. "Natural Resources, 'Vent-for-Surplus' and the Staples Theory." In Gerald M. Meir, ed. *From Classical Economics to Development Economics.* New York: St. Martin's Press.

Fischer, Carolyn, and Michael Toman. 1998. "Environmentally and Economically Damaging Subsidies: Concepts and Illustrations." Resources for the Future: Climate Issue Brief 14. Washington, D.C.

Foundation News. 1999. "The Rockefeller Foundation and Plant Biotechnology." June 24.

Frank, Robert H. 1985. *Choosing the Right Pond: Human Behavior and the Quest for Status.* New York: Oxford University Press.

Frank, Robert H., and Philip J. Cook. 1995. *The Winner-Take-All Society : Why the Few at the Top Get So Much More than the Rest of Us.* New York: The Free Press.

Freeman, Richard B., and Remco H. Oostendorp. 2000. "Wages around the World: Pay across Occupations and Countries." National Bureau of Economic Research Working Paper 8058. Cambridge, Mass.

Fruhling, Hugo, Joseph S. Tulchin, and Heather A. Golding. Forthcoming. *Crime and Violence in Latin America: Citizen Security, Democracy, and the State.* Washington, D.C.: Woodrow Wilson Center Press.

Frumkin, Howard. 2001. "Beyond Toxicity: Human Health and the Natural Environment." *American Journal of Preventive Medicine* 20(3):234–40.

Fuller, Bruce, and Magdalena Rivarola. 1998. "Nicaragua's Experiment to Decentralize Schools: Views of Parents, Teachers and Directors." World Bank Working Paper Series on Impact Evaluation of Education Reforms 5. Washington, D.C.

Gallup, John, and Jeffrey Sachs. 1998. "Geography and Economic Growth." Paper presented at World Bank Annual Conference on Economic Development. Washington, D.C., April 20–21. Available online at http://www. worldbank.org/html/rad/abcde/html/sachs.htm.

Galor, Oded, and Joseph Zeira. 1993. "Income Distribution and Macroeconomics." *Review of Economic Studies* 60(1): 35–52.

Galtung, Fredrik. 2000. "A Global Network to Curb Corruption: The Experience of Transparency International." In Ann M. Florini, ed., *The Third Force: The Rise of Transnational Civil Society.* Washington, D.C.: Carnegie Endowment for International Peace.

Gambrill, Martin, Vivien Foster, and Yoko Katakura. 2001. "Lessons of Experience with Condominial Water and Sewerage Programs in Brazil and Bolivia." World Bank, Washington, D.C. Processed.

Garreau, Joel. 2001. "Flocking Together to the Web." *The Washington Post* May 9:C1.

Gaskell, George, Martin W. Bauer, John Durant, and Nicholas C. Allum. 1999. "Worlds Apart? The Reception of Genetically Modified Foods in Europe and the U.S." *Science,* 285–384.

GEF (Global Environment Facility). 1999. "An Interim Assessment of Biodiversity Enabling Activities: National Biodiversity Strategies and Action Plans." Washington, D.C.

Gereffi, Gary, Ronie Garcia-Johnson, and Erika Sasser. 2001. "The NGO-Industrial Complex." *Foreign Policy* July/August:56–65.

German Advisory Council on Global Change. 2002a. "Charging the Use of Global Commons." German Advisory Council on Global Change Policy Paper 2. Berlin.

———. 2002b. "Charging the Use of Global Commons, Special Report." German Advisory Council on Global Change Secretariat. Berlin.

Gibson, Clark C., Margaret A. McKean, and Elinor Ostrom, eds. 2000. *People and Forests: Communities, Institutions and Governance.* Cambridge, Mass.: MIT Press.

Gilbert, Alan. 2002. "On the Mystery of Capital and the Myths of Hernando de Soto: What Difference Does Legal Title Make?" *International Development Planning Review* 24:1–20.

Glaeser, Edward L. 1998. "Are Cities Dying?" *Journal of Economic Perspectives* 12(2):139–60.

Glaeser, Edward L., and Andrei Schleifer. 2001. "The Rise of the Regulatory State." National Bureau of Economic Research Working Paper 8650. Cambridge, Mass.

Glaeser, Edward L., Hedi D. Kallal, José A. Scheinkman, and Andrei Shleifer. 1992. "Growth in Cities." *Journal of Political Economy* 100(6):1126–52.

Gonzales de Asis, Maria, and Jairo Acuña-Alfaro. 2002. "Civic Participation in Local Governance." Governance Training Module, World Bank Institute, Washington, D.C. Available online at http://www.worldbank.org/ wbi/governance/pdf/ fy02brief/civic_local_annex.pdf. Processed.

Grieg-Gran, Maryanne. 2000. "Fiscal Incentives for Biodiversity Conservation: The ICMS Ecológico in Brazil." International Institute for Environment and Development Discussion Paper 00–01. London.

Grindle, Merilee S., ed. 1997. *Getting Good Government: Capacity Building in the Public Sectors of Developing Countries.* Cambridge, Mass.: Harvard University Press.

———. 2000. *Audacious Reforms: Institutional Invention and Democracy in Latin America.* Baltimore: Johns Hopkins University Press.

Grootaert, Christian, and Thierry van Bastelaer. 2001. "Understanding and Measuring Social Capital: A Synthesis of Findings and Recommendations from the Social Capital Initiative." World Bank Social Capital Initiative Working Paper 24. Washington, D.C.

Grossman, Gene. 1995. "Pollution and Growth: What Do We Know?" In I. Goldin and L. Alan Winters, eds., *Economics of Sustainable Development.* Cambridge: Cambridge University Press.

Grossman, Herschel I., and Minseong Kim. 1995. "Swords or Plowshares? A Theory of the Security of Claims to Property." *Journal of Political Economy* 103(6):1275–88.

Guerrero, O., and R. Pablo. 1999. "Comparative Insights from Colombia, China, and Indonesia." World Bank Operations Evaluation Department 5. Washington, D.C.

Gwatkin, Davidson. 2000. "Socio-Economic Differences in Health, Education, and Nutrition in Madagascar." World Bank, Washington, D.C. Processed.

Hacaoglu, Selcan. 2001. "Turkey's Bay of the Ottoman Sultans Recovers from Industrial Filth." *Associated Press* November 27.

Hall, Robert E., and Charles I. Jones. 1999. "Why Do Some Countries Produce So Much More Output per Worker than Others?" *Quarterly Journal of Economics* 114(1): 83–116.

Hamilton, Kirk. 2000. "Genuine Saving as a Sustainability Indicator." World Bank Environmental Economics Series 77. Washington, D.C.

Hardoy, Jorge E., Diana Mitlin, and David Satterthwaite. 2001. *Environmental Problems in an Urbanizing World.* London: Earthscan.

Harper, Malcolm. 2000. *Public Services through Private Enterprises: Micro Privatization for Improved Delivery.* New Delhi: Chapman Enterprises.

Hassan, Hassan, and H. E. Dregne. 1997. "Natural Habitats and Ecosystems Management in Drylands." World Bank Environment Department Paper 51. Washington, D.C.

Hatton, Timothy J., and Jeffrey Williamson. 1998. *The Age of Mass Migration: Causes and Economic Impact.* New York and Oxford: Oxford University Press.

———. 2001. "Demographic and Economic Pressures on Emigration out of Africa." National Bureau of Economic Research Working Paper 8124. Cambridge, Mass.

Hayek, Friedrich A. 1945. "The Use of Knowledge in Society." *American Economic Review* 35(4):519–30.

Hazell, Peter. 1998. "Why Invest More in the Sustainable Development of Less-Favored Lands?" International Food Policy Research Institute Report No. 20. Washington, D.C. Available online at http://www. ifpri.cgiar.org/reports/ 0798rpt.htm.

———. 2001. "Shaping Globalization for Poverty Alleviation and Food Security: Technology Change." 2020 Vision for Food, Agriculture, and the Environment No. Focus 8, Policy Brief 8 of 13. International Food Policy Research Institute, Washington, D.C. Available online at http://www. ifpri.cgiar.org/ 2020/focus/focus08.htm.

Hazell, Peter, and Fan Shenggen. 2000. "Should Developing Countries Invest More in Less-Favored Areas?: An Empirical Analysis of Rural India." *Economic and Political Weekly* 35(17):

Heal, G. 2000. *Nature and the Market Place: Capturing the Value of Ecosystem Services.* Washington, D.C.: Island Press.

Heilburnn, John R. 2002. "Governance and Oil Funds." Colorado School of Mines, Golden, Colo. Processed.

Hellman, Joel S., Geraint Jones, and Daniel Kaufmann. 2000. " 'Seize the State, Seize the Day': State Capture, Corruption, and Influence in Transition." World Bank Policy Research Working Paper 2444. Washington, D.C.

Hemmati, Minu, and Rosalie Gardiner. 2002. "Gender Equity and Sustainable Development: Towards Earth Summit 2002." Social Briefing 2. Available online at http:// www.earthsummit2002.org/es/issues/ gender/gender.PDF.

Henderson, Vernon. 2000. "How Urban Concentration Affects Economic Growth." World Bank Policy Research Working Paper 2326. Washington, D.C.

Henderson, J. Vernon, Zmarak Shalizi, and Anthony J. Venables. 2001. "Geography and Development." *Journal of Economic Geography* 1:81–105.

Hentschel, Jesko. 2001. "Poverty in Cali, Colombia." World Bank, Washington, D.C. Processed.

Hentschel, Jesko, and Jesse Bump. 1999. "Urban Poverty Dimensions: Some Cross-Country Comparisons." World Bank, Washington, D.C. Processed.

Hirsch, Fred. 1978. *Social Limits to Growth*. London, New York: Routledge.

Hirshleifer, Jack. 1996. "Anarchy and its Breakdown." In Michelle R. Garfinkel and Stergios Skaperdas, eds., *The Political Economy of Conflict and Appropriation*. Cambridge: Cambridge University Press.

Hochstetler, Kathryn. 1997. "The Evolution of the Brazilian Environmental Movement and Its Political Roles." In Douglas A. Chambers and others, eds. *The New Politics of Inequality in Latin America: Rethinking Participation and Representation*. New York: Oxford University Press.

Hoff, Karla, and Arijit Sen. 2001. "Empowerment and Home-Ownership." World Bank, Washington, D.C. Processed.

Hoff, Karla, and Joseph Stiglitz. 2002. "After the Big Bang? Obstacles to the Emergence of the Rule of Law in Post-Communist Societies." World Bank, Washington, D.C. Processed.

Honeyman, M. 1990. "Vegetation and Stress: A Comparison Study of Varying Amounts of Vegetation in Countryside and Urban Scenes." In D. Relf, ed., *The Role of Horticulture in Human Well-Being and Social Development: A National Symposium*. 1992 Timber Press, 143–145.

Hoogeveen, Hans. 2001. "Assessing Uganda's Decentralization." World Bank, Washington, D.C. Processed.

Houghton, John, Ding Yihui, David J. Griggs, Maria Noguer, Paul J. van der Linden, and Xiaosu Dai, eds. 2001. *Climate Change 2001: The Scientific Basis*. Cambridge, Mass.: Cambridge University Press.

House of Lords, Select Committee on Science and Technology. 2000. "Science and Society." London. Available online at http://www.parliament.the-stationery-office.co. uk/pa/ ld199900/ldselect/ldsctech/38/3801.htm.

Hoy, Michael, and Emmanuel Jimenez. 1998. "The Impact on the Urban Environment of Incomplete Property Rights." World Bank, Washington, D.C. Processed.

Hunter, David, James Salzman, and Durwood Zaelke, eds. 2001. *International Environmental Law and Policy*. New York: Foundation Press. Available online at http://www. wcl.american.edu/environment/iel/.

Huther, Jeff, and Anwar Shah. 2000. "Anti-Corruption Policies and Programs: A Framework for Evaluation." World Bank Policy Research Working Paper Series 2501. Washington, D.C.

IADB (Inter-American Development Bank). 1997. *Economic and Social Progress in Latin America: Latin America after a Decade of Reforms*. Baltimore and London: Johns Hopkins University Press. Available online at http:// www.iadb.org/ oce/ipes/.

IBSRAM (International Board for Soil Research and Management). 2001. "Background Study on Land Degradation in Selected Regions and Some Consequences for Rural Development." World Bank, Washington, D.C. Available online at http://wbln0018.worldbank.org/essd/rdv/vta.nsf/Gweb/ Studies. Processed.

ICLEI (International Council for Local Environmental Initiatives). 1991. "Solid Waste Management: Bandung, Indonesia." ICLEI Case Study 3. Toronto.

———. 2002. "Second Local Agenda 21 Survey." Background Paper No. 15. Paper presented at the Commission on Sustainable Development, Second Preparatory Session (28 Jan–8 Feb, 2002). New York: United Nations, Department of Economic and Social Affairs. Also available online at www.iclei.org.

IFAD (International Fund for Agricultural Development). 1999. "Improving Tassa Planting Pits—Using Indigenous Soil and Water Conservation Techniques to Rehabilitate Degraded Plateaus in the Tahoua Region of Niger." MOST/CIRAN Best Practices on Indigenous Knowledge. Available online at http://www.unesco.org/ most/bpik10. htm.

———. 2000. *Rural Poverty Report 2000*. Oxford University Press.

———. 2001. *"Rural Poverty Report 2001: The Challenge of Ending Rural Poverty."* Available online at http://www. ifad.org/poverty/.

IFPRI (International Food Policy Research Institute). 1999. "Biotechnology for Developing-Country Agriculture: Problems and Opportunities." 2020 Focus 2. Washington, D.C.

Ihrig, Jane, and Karine Moe. 2000. "The Dynamics of Informal Employment." Federal Reserve Board, International Finance Discussion Paper 664. Washington, D.C. Available online at http://www.federalreserve.gov/pubs/ ifdp/2000/664/default.htm.

International Council for Local Environmental Issues. 2002. "Second Local Agenda 21 Survey." Paper presented at the Commission on Sustainable Development, Second Preparatory Session, available on line at www.iclei.org.

IEA (International Energy Agency). 1999a. *World Energy Outlook—1999 Insights. Looking at Energy Subsidies: Getting the Price Right*. London: IEA Publications.

———. 1999b. *World Energy Outlook 2000*. London: IEA Publications.

International Federation of Red Cross and Red Crescent Societies. 1999. *World Disasters Report 1999*. Geneva.

IPCC (Intergovernmetal Panel on Climate Change). 2001. "Human Settlements, Energy and Industry." In IPCC, ed., *Third Assessment Report, 2001*. Cambridge: Cambridge University Press.

———. 2002. "Climate Change 2001: Impacts, Adaptation, and Vulnerability." In James J. McCarthy, Osvaldo F. Canziani, Neil A. Leary, David J. Dokken, and Kasey S. White, eds., Cambridge: Cambridge University Press.

Iremonger, S., C. Ravilious, and T. Quinton. 1997. "A Statistical Analysis of Global Forest Conservation." In S. Iremonger, C. Ravilious, and T. Quinton, eds., *A Global Overview of Forest Conservation*. Cambridge: Center for International Forestry Research and WCMC.

Isham, Jonathan, Michael Woolcock, Lant Pritchett, and Gwen Busby. 2002. "The Varieties of Rentier Experience: How Natural Resource Endowments Affect the Political Economy of Economic Growth." Middlebury College, Middlebury, Vt., World Bank, Washington, D.C., Harvard University, Cambidge, Mass., and Yale University, New Haven, Conn. Processed.

Iskandar Kamel, Laila. 2000. "Urban Governance: The Informal Sector and Municipal Solid Waste in Cairo." Available online at http://www.archis.org/english/ archis_ art_e_2000/ archis_art_0012b_e.html.

IWMI (International Water Management Institute). 2001. "Water for Rural Development." Background paper prepared for the World Bank Agricultural Strategy Paper. Colombo, Sri Lanka. Processed.

Jacobs, Goff, Amy Aeron-Thomas, and A. Astrop. 2000. "Estimating Global Road Fatalities." Transport Research Laboratory Report 445. Berkshire, U.K. Available online at http://www.grsproadsafety.org/activities/campaigns/ 5/10.pdf.

Jäger, Jill, Nancy M. Dickson, Adam Fenech, Peter M. Haas, Edward A. Parson, Vassily Sokolov, Ferenc L. Tóth, Jeroen van der Sluis, and Claire Waterton. 2001. "Monitoring in the Management of Global Environmental Risk." In William C. Clark, Jill Jäger, Josee van Eijndhoven, and Nancy M. Dickson, eds., *Learning to Manage Global Environmental Risks Vol. II.* Cambridge, Mass. and London: MIT Press.

Jäger, Jill, Josee van Eijndhoven, and William C. Clark. 2001. "Knowledge and Action: An Analysis of Linkages among Management Functions for Global Environmental Risks." In William C. Clark, Jill Jäger, Josee van Eijndhoven, and Nancy M. Sdickson, eds., *Learning to Manage Global Environmental Risks Vol. II.* Cambridge, Mass., and London: MIT Press.

Jensen, Jesper, and David Tarr. 2002. "Trade, Foreign Exchange, and Energy Policies in the Islamic Republic of Iran: Reform Agenda, Economic Implications, and Impact on the Poor." World Bank Policy Research Working Paper 2768. Washington, D.C.

Jimenez, Emmanuel. 1985. "Urban Squatting and Community Organization in Developing Countries." *Journal of Public Economics* 27(1):69–92.

Jimenez, Emmanuel, and Yasuyuki Sawada. 1999. "Do Community-Managed Schools Work? An Evaluation of El Salvador's EDUCO Program." *World Bank Economic Review* 13(3):415–41.

Kamel, Laila Iskandar. 2000. "Urban Governance: The Informal Sector and Municipal Solid Waste in Cairo." *ARCHIS* December. Available online at www.archis.org.

Katz, Travis, and Tim Campbell. 1996. "Manos a la obra." World Bank, Latin America and the Caribbean Technical Department, Washington, D.C. Processed.

Kaufmann, Daniel, Aart Kraay, and Pablo Zoido-Lobatón. 1999. "Governance Matters." World Bank Policy Research Working Paper 2196. Washington, D.C.

Kidd, Quentin, and Aie-Rie Lee. 1997. "Postmaterial Values and the Environment: A Critique and Reappraisal." *Social Science Quarterly* 78(1):1–15.

Kim, Jooseop, Harold Alderman, and Peter Orazem. 1998. "Can Cultural Barriers Be Overcome in Girls' Schooling? The Community Support Program in Rural Balochistan." World Bank Working Paper Series on Impact Evaluation of Education Reforms 10. Washington, D.C.

King, Andrew, and Michael Lennox. Forthcoming. "Exploring the Locus of Profitable Pollution Reduction." *Management Science.*

King, Elyzabeth, Peter Orazem, and Darin Wohlgemuth. 1999. "Central Mandates and Local Incentives: The Colombia Education Voucher Program." *World Bank Economic Review* 13(3):467–91.

King, Elyzabeth, and Berk Özler. 1998. "What's Decentralization Got to Do With Learning?" World Bank Working Paper Series on Impact Evaluation of Education Reforms 9. Washington, D.C.

Klenow, Peter J., and Andrés Rodriguez-Clare. 1997. "The Neoclassical Revival in Growth Economics: Has It Gone Too Far?" In Ben S. Bernanke and Julio S. Rotemberg, eds., *NBER Macroeconomics Annual.* Cambridge and London: MIT Press.

Knack, Stephen. 2001. "Aid Dependence and the Quality of Governance: Cross-Country Empirical Tests." *Southern Economic Journal* 68(2):310–29.

Knack, Stephen, and Philip Keefer. 1997. "Does Social Capital Have an Economic Payoff? A Cross-Country Investigation." *Quarterly Journal of Economics* 112(4):1251–88.

Kojima, Masami, and Magda Lovei. 2001. "Urban Air Quality Management: Coordinating Transport, Environment and Energy Policies in Developing Countries." World Bank Technical Paper, Pollution Management Series 508. Washington, D.C.

Koster, J. H., and M. de Languen. 1998. "Preventive Transport Strategies for Secondary Cities". In P. Freman and C. Jamet, eds., *Urban Transport Policy: A Sustainable Development Tool.* Rotterdam: Balkema.

Kotto-Same, J., A. Moukam, R. Njomgang, T. Tiki-Manga, J. Tonye, C. Diaw, J. Gockowsky, S. Hauser, S. Weise, D. Nwaga, L. Zapfack, C. Palm, P. Woomer, A. Gillison, D. Bignell, and J. Tondoh. 2000. "Alternatives to Slash-and-Burn: Summary Report and Synthesis of Phase II in Cameroon." Consultative Group on International Agricultural Research, Nairobi.

Kremer, Michael. 2000. "Creating Markets for New Vaccines." National Bureau of Economic Research Working Paper 7716. Cambridge, Mass.

Kremer, Michael, and Seema Jayachandran. 2002. "Odious Debt." Paper presented at the Conference on Macroeconomic Policies and Poverty Reduction. Washington, D.C. Available online at http://www.imf.org/external/ NP/Res/seminars/2002/poverty/.

Krishna, Anirudh, and Norman Uphoff. 1999. "Mapping and Measuring Social Capital: A Conceptual and Empirical Study of Collective Action for Conserving and Developing Watersheds in Rajasthan, India." World Bank Social Capital Initiative Working Paper 13. Washington, D.C.

Krueger, Anne. 1974. "The Political Economy of the Rent-Seeking Society." *American Economic Review* 64(3): 291–303.

———. 1996. "The Political Economy of Controls: American Sugar." In Lee J. Alston, Thrainn Eggertsson, and North Douglass, eds., *Empirical Issues in Institutional Change.* Cambridge, New York, and Melbourne: Cambridge University Press.

Krugman, Paul. 1998. "The Role of Geography in Development." Paper presented at the Annual World Bank Conference in Development Economics, Washington, D.C.

Kudat, A., and B. Ozbilgin. 1996. "Uzbekistan Water Supply, Sanitation and Health Project: Salinity Taste Tolerance Assessment." World Bank, Washington, D.C.

Kudat, A., B. Ozbilgin, and V. Borisov. 1997. "Reconstructing Russia's Coal Sector." In Michael M. Cernea and Ayse Kudat, eds., *Social Assessments for Better Development: Case Studies in Russia and Central Asia.* Washington, D.C.: World Bank.

Lacey, Robert. 1986. *Ford: the Man and the Machine.* Boston: Little, Brown.

Lall, Somik, Uwe Deichmann, and Mattias Lundberg. 2002. "Tenure, Diversity and Commitment: Community Participation for Urban Service Provision." World Bank, Washington, D.C. Processed.

Lall, Somik, and Sudeshna Ghosh. 2002. "Learning by Dining: Informal Networks and Productivity in Mexican Industry." World Bank Policy Research Paper 2789. Washington, D.C.

Lall, Somik, Zmarak Shalizi, and Uwe Deichmann. Forthcoming. "Agglomeration Economies and Productivity in Indian Industry." *Journal of Economic Literature.*

Lambsdorff, Johann Graf. 1999. "Corruption in Empirical Research—A Review." Transparency International Working Paper. Berlin. Available online at www.transparency. org.

Lanjouw, Jean A., and Peter Lanjouw. 2001. "The Rural Non-Farm Sector: Issues and Evidence from Developing Countries." *Agricultural Economics* 26:1–23.

Lanjouw, Jean A., and Philip I. Levy. 1998. "Untitled: A Study of Formal and Informal Property Rights in Urban Ecuador." Economic Growth Center, Center Discussion Paper 788. Yale University, New Haven, Conn. Available online at http://www.library.yale.edu/socsci/egcdp788. pdf.

Lant, M., and G. Sant. 2001. "Patagonian Toothfish: Are Conservation and Trade Measures Working?" *Traffic Bulletin* 19(1):1–18.

Leach, Melissa, and Robin Mearns. 1996. *The Lie of the Land, Challenging Received Wisdom in African Environmental Change and Policy.* Oxford: James Currey Publishers Ltd. and Heinemann.

Lee, Su-Hoon, Michael Hsin-Huang Hsiao, Hwa-Jen Liu, On-Kwok Lai, Francisco Magno, and Alvin Y. So. 1999. "The Impact of Democratization on Environmental Movements." In Su-Hoon Lee and Alvin Y. So, eds., *Asia's Environmental Movements: Comparative Perspectives.* M.E. Sharpe.

Leitmann, Joseph. 2001. *Sustaining Cities: Environmental Planning and Management in Urban Design.* New York: McGraw-Hill.

Lele, Uma, William Lesser, and Gesa Horstkotte-Wesseler, eds. 1999. *Intellectual Property Rights in Agriculture: The World Bank's Role in Assisting Borrower and Member Countries.* Washington, D.C.: World Bank.

Limão, Nuno, and Anthony J. Venables. 2001. "Infrastructure, Geographical Disadvantage, Transport Costs, and Trade." *The World Bank Economic Review* 15(3):451–79.

Lindert, Peter H. 2000. *Shifting Ground: The Changing Agricultural Soils of China and Indonesia.* Cambridge, Mass.: MIT Press.

Linz, Austria. 2002. "Citizens Participation in the Siting of Waste Facilities." Case Study 15.

Lipton, Michael. 1977. *Why Poor People Stay Poor: A Study of Urban Bias in World Development.* Canberra: Australian National University Press.

Losey J.E., L.S. Rayor, and M.E. Carter. 1999. "Transgenic Pollen Harms Monarch Larvae." *Nature* 399:214.

Loureiro, Wilson. 1998. "Uma Experiencia Brasileira exitosa no incentivo economico para a conservacao da biodiversidade." *Cadernos de Biodiversidade* 1(2):25–47.

Lovei, Magda. 1999. "Eliminating a Silent Threat: World Bank Support for the Global Phaseout of Lead from Gasoline." World Bank, Washington, D.C.

Lubbock, A., and Rahman Bourqia. 1998. "Gender and Household Food Security, Survival, Change and Decision- Making in Rural Households: Three Village Case Studies from Eastern Morocco." International Fund for Agricultural Research, Rome. Available on line at http://www.ifad.org/gender/thematic/morocco/mo_ toc.htm.

Lucas, Robert E. B. 1998. "Internal Migration and Urbanization: Recent Contributions and New Evidence." World Bank, Washington, D.C. Processed.

Lvovsky, Kseniya. 2001. "Health and Environment." World Bank Environment Strategy Papers 1. Washington, D.C.

Lvovsky, K., G. Hughes, D. Maddison, B. Ostro, and D. Pearce. 2000. "Environmental Costs for Fossil Fuels: A Rapid Assessment Method with Application to Six Cities." World Bank Environment Department Paper 78. Washington, D.C.

Mackay, Keith. 2000. "New Evaluation Trends in Public Policy Reform and Governance." Paper presented at a seminar and workshop organized by the Development Bank of South Africa, the African Development Bank, and the World Bank, Johannesburg.

Mahar, Dennis J., and Cecile E. H. Ducrot. 1998. "Land-Use Zoning on Tropical Frontiers: Emerging Lessons from the Brazilian Amazon." World Bank Institute EDI Case Study 19674. Washington, D.C.

Mason, Edward S., Mahn Je Kim, Dwight H. Perkins, Kwang Suk Kim, and David C. Cole. 1980. *The Economic and Social Modernization of the Republic of Korea.* Cambridge, Mass., and London: Harvard University Press.

May, Peter H., Fernando Veiga Neto, Valdir Denardin, and Wilson Loureiro. Forthcoming. "The 'Ecological' Value-Added Tax: Municipal Responses in Paraná and Minas Gerais, Brazil." In Stephano Pagiola, Joshua Bishop, and Natasha Landell Mill, eds., *Selling Forest Environmental Services: Market-Based Mechanisms for Conservation.*

Mazumdar, Dipak. 1987. "Rural-Urban Migration in Developing Countries." In Peter Nijkamp, ed., *Handbook of Regional and Urban Economics Vol. II.* Amsterdam: Elsevier Science Publishers.

McCarthy, James J., Osvaldo F. Canziani, Neil A. Leary, David J. Dokken, and Kasey S. White. 2001. "Climate Change 2001: Impacts, Adaptation, and Vulnerability." Cambridge: Cambridge University Press.

McGranahan, Gordon, Pedro Jacobi, Jacob Songsore, Charles Surjadi, and Marianne Kjellén. 2001. *The Citizens at Risk: From Urban Sanitation to Sustainable Cities.* London: Earthscan.

McGranahan, G., and D. Satterthwaite. 2000. "Environmental Health or Ecological Sustainability? Reconciling the Brown and Green Agendas in Urban Development." In Cedric Pugh, ed., *Sustainable Cities in Developing Countries.* London: Earthscan.

McGuire, M., and Mancur Olson. 1996. "The Economics of Autocracy and Majority Rule." *Journal of Economic Literature* 34(1):72–96.

McIlwaine, Cathy, and Caroline O. N. Moser. 2001. "Violence and Social Capital in Urban Poor Communities: Perspectives from Colombia and Guatemala." *Journal of International Development* 13(7):965–84.

McMahon, Gary, and Remy Felix, eds. 2001. *Large Mines and the Community: Socioeconomic and Environmental Effects in*

Latin America, Canada, and Spain. Washington, D.C.: World Bank and International Development Research Center.

McNeely, Jeffrey R., and Sara J. Scherr. 2001. "Common Ground: How Ecoagriculture Can Help Feed the World and Save Wild Biodiversity." International Union for the Conservation of Nature and Natural Resources—The World Conservation Union Report 5/01. Available online at http://www.futureharvest.org/earth/common_ground_bio. shtml.

McNeill, J. R. 2000. *Something New under the Sun: An Environmental History of the Twentieth-Century World.* New York: W. W. Norton.

Mearns, Robin. 2001. "Contextual Factors in the Management of Common Grazing Lands: Lessons from Mongolia and Northwestern China." Proceedings of the XIX International Grassland Congress.

———. 2002. "Taking Stock: Policy, Practice, and Professionalism in Rangeland Development." Symposium on Rangelands Professionals and Policy. Kansas City, Missouri, February 2002.

Meitzner, Laura S., and Martin L. Price. 1996. *Ideas for Growing Food Under Difficult Conditions.* North Fort Myers, Fla.: ECHO.

Mellor, John. 2000. "Faster More Equitable Growth: The Relation between Growth in Agriculture and Poverty Reduction." Harvard University Consulting Assistance on Economic Reform II Discussion Paper 70. Cambridge, Mass. Available online at http://www. cid.harvard.edu/ caer2.

Mernissi, Fatema. 1997. *Les Ait Debrouille Haut-Atlas.* Rabat: Editions Le Fennec.

Millar, David. 1999. "Farmer's Path of Experimentation: The PTD Process in Northern Ghana." *ILEIA Newsletter* September: 43–6.

Milley, P. C. D., R. T. Wetherald, K. A. Dunne, and T. L. Delworth. 2002. "Increasing Risk of Great Floods in a Changing Climate." *Nature* 415:514–17.

Mills, Edwin S. 2000. "The Importance of Large Urban Areas and Governments' Roles in Fostering Them." In Shahid Yusuf, Weiping Wu, and Simon Evenett, eds., *Local Dynamics in an Era of Globalization.* Washington, D.C.: World Bank.

Mirovitskaya, Natalia. 1998. "The Environmental Movement in the Former Soviet Union." In Andrew Tickle and Ian Welsh, eds., *Environment and Society in Eastern Europe.* New York: Addison Wesley Longman.

Mitchell, Ronald B. 1995. "Compliance with International Treaties: Lessons from Intentional Oil Pollution." Environment 37:10–12, 36–41.

Moore, Julia A. 2001. "Frankenfood or Doubly Green Revolution: Europe vs. America on the GMO Debate." In Albert H. Teich, Stephen D. Nelson, Ceilia McEnaney, and Stephen J. Lita, eds., *AAAS Science and Technology Policy Yearbook 2001.* Washington, D.C.: American Association for the Advancement of Science.

Moore, Mike. 2002. "Trade Gains Are What the Poor Need." *International Herald Tribune* March 14.

Moser, Caroline, and Emma Grant. 2000. "Violence and Security in Urban Areas: Their Implications for Governance, Health and Labor Markets." National Academy of Sciences Panel on Urban Population Dynamics. Processed.

Moser, Caroline, and Cathy McIlwaine. 2001. *Violence in a Post-Conflict Context: Urban Poor Perceptions from Guatemala.* Washington, D.C.: World Bank.

Moser, Caroline O. N., and Jeremy Holland. 1995. "A Participatory Study of Urban Poverty and Violence in Jamaica." World Bank Transportation, Water and Urban Development Department, Washington, D.C.

Munn, R. E., A. Whyte, and P. Timmerman, eds. 2000. *Emerging Issues for the 21st Century: A Study for GEO–2000.* Nairobi: United Nations Environment Programme, Division of Environmental Information, Assessment and Early Warning.

Munton, Don, Marvin Soroos, Elena Nikitina, and Mark A. Levy. 1999. "Acid Rain in Europe and North America." In Oran Young, ed., *The Effectiveness of International Enviromental Regimes: Causal Connections and Behavioral Mechanisms.* Cambridge, Mass.: MIT Press.

Murgai, Rinku, Ali Mubarik, and Derek Byerlee. 2001. "Productivity Growth and Sustainability in Post-Green Revolution Agriculture: The Case of the Indian and Pakistan Punjabs." *World Bank Research Observer* 16(2): 199–218.

Murray, C. J., and A. D. Lopez. 1996. *The Global Burden of Disease.* Cambridge, Mass.: Harvard University Press.

Murshed, S. Mansoob. 2002. "Conflict, Civil War and Underdevelopment." Institute of Social Studies. Available online at http://www.wider.unu.edu/whoswho/murshedpapers.htm. Processed.

Murshed, S. Mansoob, and Maiju Perälä. 2001. "Does the Type of Natural Resource Endowment Influence Growth?" UNU/WIDER, Helsinki. Available online at http://www. wider.unu.edu/whoswho/murshedpapers.htm. Processed.

Myers, Norman, and Jennifer Kent. 2001. *Perverse Subsidies: How Misused Tax Dollars Harm the Environment and the Economy.* Washington, D.C., Covelo, London: Island Press for International Institute for Sustainable Development.

Myers, Norman, Russell A. Mittermeier, Cristina G. Mittermeier, Gustavo A. B. Fonseca, and Jennifer Kent. 2000. "Biodiversity Hotspots for Conservation Priorities." *Nature* 403:853–58.

Nakicenovic, N., and R. Swart, eds. 2000. *Special Report of the Intergovernmental Panel on Climate Change on Emission Scenarios.* Cambridge: Cambridge University Press.

NAS (National Academy of Sciences). 1996. "The Ozone Depletion Phenomenon." Washington, D.C. Available online at http://www. beyonddiscovery.org/.

National Intelligence Council. 2000. "Global Trends 2015: A Dialogue about the Future with Nongovernment Experts. NIC 2000–02. Washington, D.C.

National Research Council. 1999. *Our Common Journey: A Transition toward Sustainability.* Washington, D.C.: National Academy Press.

———. 2001. *Abrupt Climate Change: Inevitable Surprises.* Washington, D.C.: National Academy Press.

Nelson, Douglas R., and Oliver Morrisey. 1998. "East Asian Economics Performance: Miracle or Just a Pleasant Surprise?" *World Economy* 21(7):855–79.

Newell, Richard, and William Pizer. 2001. "Discounting the Benefits of Climate Change Mitigation." Pew Center on Global Climate Change, Arlington, Va. Available online at http://www.pewclimate.org/projects/econ_discounting.cfm.

Newsletter. 1998. "Stories from the Cities 1997–98: Durban-Diakonia Council of Churches." Newsletter July/August Article 3.

Niamir-Fuller, Maryam. 1998. "The Resilience of Pastoral Herding in Sahelian Africa." In Fikret Berkes and Carl Folke, eds., *Linking Social and Ecological Systems*. Cambridge: Cambridge University Press.

Nicholls, J. R., F. M. J. Hoozemans, and M. Marchand. 1999. "Increasing Flood Risk and Wetland Losses Due to Global Sea-Level Rise: Regional and Global Analyses." *Global Environmental Change* 9:S69–87.

North, Douglas, and Barry Weingast. 1989. "Constitutions and Commitment: The Evolution of Institutions Governing Public Choice in the Seventeenth-Century England." *Journal of Economic History* 49(4):803–32.

Oberai, A. S., and H. K. Manmohan Singh. 1984. "Migration, Employment and the Urban Labor Market: A Study of the Indian Punjab." *International Labor Review* 123(4): 507–23.

OECD (Organisation for Economic Co-operation and Development). 1988. "Economic Instruments for Pollution Control and Natural Resources Management." *OECD Countries: A Survey*. Document ENV/EPOC/GEEI (98)35/REV1/FINAL.

———. 1997. "The Environmental Effects of Agricultural Land Diversion Schemes." Paris.

———. 1998. "Water Management: Performance and Challenges in OECD Countries."

———. 1999. *Voluntary Approaches for Environmental Policy—Assessment*. Paris.

———. 2001a. *Agricultural Policies in OECD Countries: Monitoring and Evaluation*. Paris.

———. 2001b. "OECD Environmental Outlook." Paris.

———. 2001c. *Sustainable Development: Critical Issues*. Paris.

OED (Operations Evaluation Department). "Community Forestry in Nepal." Précis. World Bank, Washington, D.C.

Ojima, Dennis. 2001. "Critical Drivers of Global Environmental and Land Use Changes in Temperate Asia." Paper presented at the Open Symposium on Change and Sustainability of Pastoral Land Use Systems in Temperate and Central Asia. Ulaanbaatar, Mongolia.

Olson, David M., and Eric Dinerstein. 1998. "The Global 200: A Representation Approach to the Conserving the Earth's Distinctive Ecoregions." Conservation Science Program, World Wildlife Fund–U.S., Washington, D.C. Processed.

Olson, Mancur. 1996. "Distinguished Lecture on Economics in Government. Big Bills left on the Sidewalk: Why Some Nations are Rich and Others Poor." *Journal of Economic Perspectives* 10(2):3–24.

O'Rourke, Kevin, and Jeffrey Williamson. 1995. "Around the European Periphery: 1870 to 1910." National Bureau of Economic Research Working Paper 5392. Cambridge, Mass.

Oshima, Harry T. 1987. *Economic Growth in Monsoon Asia: A Comparative Survey*. Tokyo: University of Tokyo Press.

Ostrom, Elinor, and Roy Gardner. 1993. "Coping with Asymmetries in the Commons: Self-Governing Irrigation Systems Can Work." *Journal of Economic Perspectives* 7(4):93–112.

Oswald, A. J. 1997. "Happiness and Economic Performance." *Economic Journal* 107(445):1815–31.

Paarlberg, Robert L. 2001. *The Politics of Precaution: Genetically Modified Crops in Developing Countries*. Baltimore: Johns Hopkins University Press.

Pagiola, Stefano. 1999. "Global Environmental Benefits of Land Degradation Control on Agricultural Land." World Bank Environment Paper 16. World Bank, Washington, D.C.

Pagiola, Stefano, and Ina-Marlene Ruthenberg. 2002. "Selling Biodiversity in a Coffee Cup: Shade-grown coffee and Conservation in Mesoamerica." In Stefano Pagiola, Joshua Bishop, and Natasha Landell-Mills, eds., *Selling Forest Environmental Services: Market-Based Mechanisms for Conservation and Development*. London: Earthscan.

Pardey, Philip G., and Nienke M. Beintema. 2001. "Slow Magic: Agricultural R&D a Century After Mendel." International Food Policy Research Institute, Washington, D.C.

Paternostro, Stefano, Jean Razafindravonona, and David Stifel. 2001. "Madagascar. Poverty and Socio Economic Developments: 1993–1999." World Bank, Africa Region Working Paper Series 19. Washington, D.C.

Pavot, W. 1991. "Further Validation with the Satisfaction of Life Scale: Evidence for the Cross-Method Convergence of Well-Being Measures." *Journal of Personality* 57(1):149–61.

Payne, Geoffrey. 2001. "Urban Land Tenure Policy Options: Titles or Rights?" *Habitat International* 25(3):415–29.

Payne, Geoffrey, ed. 2002. *Land, Rights and Innovations: Improving Tenure Security for the Urban Poor*. London: ITDG Publishing.

Payne, Geoffrey, and Edesio Fernandes. 2001. "Legality and Legitimacy in Urban Tenure Issues." Lincoln Institute of Land Policy Working Paper WP01GP1.

Peñalosa, Enrique. 2001. "The Livable City: Experiences in Bogota, Colombia." Paper presented at a seminar on Empowerment, Culture and Civic Engagement, July 24–25. World Bank, Washington, D.C. Unpublished proceedings.

Pender, John, and Peter Hazell. 2000. "Promoting Sustainable Development in Less-Favored Lands." Focus 4: (brief 9 of 9).

Perlman, Janice. 2002. "The Metamorphosis of Marginality: Rio's *Favelas* 1969–2002." The Mega-Cities Project and Trinity College. Presentation at the World Bank, May 7. Washington, D.C.

Persson, Torstein, and Guido Tabellini. 1994. "Representative Democracy and Capital Taxation." *Journal of Public Economics* 55(1):53–70.

Pezzey, J. 1989. "Economic Analysis of Sustainable Growth and Sustainable Development." World Bank Environment Department Working Paper 15. Washington, D.C.

Pinstrup-Andersen, Per, Rajul Panya-Lorch, and Mark W. Rosegrant. 1999. "World Food Prospects: Critical Issues for the Early Twenty-First Century." International Food Policy Research Institute, Washington, D.C.

Pollard, Sidney. 1997. *Marginal Europe: The Contribution of the Marginal Lands since the Middle Ages*. Oxford: Clarendon Press.

Posner, Richard A. 1981. *The Economics of Justice*. Cambridge, Mass., and London: Harvard University Press.

Postel, Sandra L., and Aaron T. Wolf. 2001. "Dehydrating Conflict." *Foreign Policy* (September/October):2–9.

President's Committee of Advisors on Science and Technology. 1997. "Report to the President on Federal Energy Research and Development for the Challenges of the Twenty-First Century." Washington, D.C.

Pretty, Jules N. 1995. *Regenerating Agriculture: Policies and Practice for Sustainability and Self-Reliance.* Washington, D.C.: Joseph Henry Press.

Primavera, J. Honculada. 1994. "Shrimp Farming in the Asia-Pacific: Environmental and Trade Issues and Regional Cooperation." Nautilus Institute Workshop on Trade and Environment in Asia-Pacific: Prospects for Regional Cooperation, September 23–5. Berkeley, Calif. Available online at http://www.nautilus.org/ papers/enviro/trade/shrimp.html. Processed.

Prud'homme, Remy. 1994. "On the Economic Role of Cities." Paper presented at Cities and the New Global Economy, in Melbourne Nov. 20–23. The Centre for Developing Cities, University of Canberra and Organisation for Economic Co-operation and Development (endnote 4); available online at http://cities/publications/ OECDpaper/endnotes.htm

Pugh, Cedric, ed. 1996. *Sustainability, the Environment, and Urbanization.* London: Earthscan.

Quigley, John M. 1998. "Urban Diversity and Economic Growth." *Journal of Economic Perspectives* 12(2):127–138.

Raff, Daniel M. G., and Lawrence Summers. 1986. "Did Henry Ford Pay Efficiency Wages?" Working Paper Series 2101. National Bureau of Economic Research, Cambridge, Mass.

Rao, Vijayendra. 2002. "Community Driven Development: A Brief Review of the Research." World Bank, Washington, D.C. Processed.

Rao, Vijayendra, and Michael Woolcock. 2001. "Social Networks and Risk Management Strategies in Poor Urban Communities: What Do We Know?" World Bank, Washington, D.C. Processed.

———. 2002. "Networks, Mobility and Survival in Delhi Slums: A Mixed-Method Analysis." World Bank, Washington, D.C. Processed.

Ravallion, Martin, and Gaurav Datt. 1996. "How Important to India's Poor Is the Sectoral Composition of Economic Growth?" *The World Bank Economic Review* 10(1):1–26.

Reardon, Thomas, Christopher Barrett, Valerie Kelly, and Kimseyinga Savadogo. "Policy Reforms and Sustainable, Agricultural Intensification in Africa." *Development Policy Review (U.K.)* 17(4):375–95.

Rees, Williams. 1997. "Is Sustainable City an Oxymoron?" *Local Environment* 2(3):303–10.

Reid, Catherine, and Lawrence Salmen. 2000. "Understanding Social Capital. Agricultural Extension in Mali: Trust and Social Cohesion." World Bank Social Capital Initiative Working Paper 22. Washington, D.C.

Reij, Chris P., I. Scoones, and C. Toulmin. 1996. *Sustaining the Soil; Indigenous Soil and Water Conservation in Africa.* London: Earthscan.

Reilly, Charles A., eds. 1995. *New Paths to Democratic Development in Latin America: The Rise of NGO-Municipal Collaboration.* Boulder, Colo.: Lynne Rienner Publishers.

Reinikka, Ritva, and Jakob Svensson. 2002. "Explaining Leakage of Public Funds." Centre for Economic Policy Research Discussion Paper Series 3227:1–45. United Kingdom.

Richardson, Peter. 2001. "Corruption." In P. J. Simmons and Chantal De Jonge Oudraat, eds., *Managing Global Issues: Lessons Learned.* Washington, D.C.: Carnegie Endowment for International Peace.

Rodden, Jonathan, Gunnar S. Eskeland and Jennie Litvack. Forthcoming. *Fiscal Decentralization and the Challenge of Hard Budget Constraints.* Cambridge, Mass.: MIT Press.

Rodriguez, Francisco, and Jeffrey D. Sachs. 1999. "Why Do Resource Abundant Economies Grow More Slowly? A New Explanation and an Application to Venezuela." *Journal of Economic Growth* 4(3):277–303.

Rodrik, Dani. 1996. "Understanding Economic Policy Reform." *Journal of Economic Literature* 34(1):9–41.

———. 1999. "Where Did All the Growth Go? External Shocks, Social Conflict, and Growth Collapses." *Journal of Economic Growth* 4(4):385–412.

———. 2002. "Institutions, Integration, and Geography: In Search of Deep Determinants of Economic Growth." John F. Kennedy School of Government, Harvard University, Boston, Mass. Available online at http://ksghome.harvard.edu/~.drodrik.academic.ksg/papers.html. Processed.

———, ed. Forthcoming. *In Search of Prosperity: Analytic Narratives on Economic Growth.* Princeton, N.J.: Princeton University Press.

Roe, Dilys, James Mayers, Maryanne Grieg-Gran, Ashish Kothari, Christo Fabricius, and Ross Hughes. 2000. *Evaluating Eden: Exploring the Myths and Realities of Community Based Wildlife Management.* London: International Institute for Environment and Development.

Rolnik, Raquel. 1999. "Territorial Exclusion and Violence: The Case of São Paulo, Brazil." Comparative Urban Studies Occasional Papers 26. Woodrow Wilson International Center for Scholars.

Rose-Ackerman, Susan. 1999. *Corruption and Government: Causes, Consequences, and Reform.* New York: Cambridge University Press.

Rosegrant, Mark W., Michael S. Paisner, Meijer Siet, and Julie Witcover. 2001. "2020 Global Food Outlook: Trends, Alternatives, and Choices." International Food Policy Research Institute, Washington, D.C.

Rosenweig, C., and W. D. Solecki, eds. 2000. *Climate Change and Global City: Two Metropolitan East Coast Regional Assesments.* New York: Columbia Earth Institute.

Rosner, D., and G. Markowitz. 1985. "The Public Health Controversy over Leaded Gasoline during the 1920s." *American Journal of Public Health* 75:344–52.

Ross, Michael. 2001a. "How Does Natural Resource Wealth Influence Civil War?" University of California at Los Angeles Political Science Department, Los Angeles. Available online at: http://www.eireview.org/. Processed.

Ross, Michael. 2001b. *Timber Booms and Institutional Breakdown in Southeast Asia.* Cambridge: Cambridge University Press.

Ross-Larson, Bruce. 1980. "Social and Political Setting." In Kevin Young, Willen C. M. Bussink, and Parvez Hasan, eds., *Malaysia: Growth and Equity in a Multiracial Society.* Washington, D.C.: International Bank for Reconstruction and Development.

Rutherford, Stuart. 2000. *The Poor and Their Money.* New Delhi: Oxford University Press.

Ruttan, V. 1990. "Models of Agricultural Development." In C. and J. Staatz Eicher, eds., *Agricultural Development in the Third World.* Baltimore: Johns Hopkins University Press.

Ryan, B., and Quentin Wodon. 2001. "Assessing the Realism of International Development Goals." World Bank, Washington, D.C. Processed.

Sachs, Jeffrey D., and Andrew M. Warner. 1995. "Economic Convergence and Economic Policies." National Bureau of Economic Research Working Paper 5039. Cambridge, Mass.

———. 1999a. "Natural Resource Intensity and Economic Growth." In Jörg Mayer, Brian Chambers, and Ayisha Farooq, eds., *Development Policies in Natural Resources Economies.* Cheltenham, U.K.: Edward Elgar.

———. 1999b. "The Big Push, Natural Resource Booms and Growth." *Journal of Development Economics* 59(1): 43–76.

Salamini, Francesco. 1999. "North-South Innovation Transfer." *Nature Biotechnology* 17 (Supplement) 11–12.

Sambanis, Nicolas. 2000. "Partition as a Solution to Ethnic War: An Empirical Critique of the Theoretical Literature." *World Politics* 52:437–483.

Sanchez, Pedro. 2002. "Soil Fertility and Hunger in Africa." *Science* 295(5562): 2019–20.

Sanchez, P. A., Bashir Jama, Amadou I. Niang, and Cheryl A. Palm. 2001. "Soil Fertility, Small-farm Intensification and the Environment in Africa." In D. R. Lee and C. B. Barret, eds., *Tradeoffs or Synergies? Agricultural Intensification, Economic Development and the Environment.* New York: CABI Publishing.

Sarraf, Maria, and Moortaza Jiwanji. 2001. "Beating the Resource Curse: The Case of Botswana." World Bank Environment Department Papers 83. Washington, D.C.

Sassen, Saskia. 2001. *The Global City: New York, London, Tokyo.* Princeton, N.J.: Princeton University Press.

Scheffer, Marten, Steve Carpenter, Jonathan A. Foley, Carl Folke, and Brian Walker. 2001. "Catastrophic Shifts in Ecosystems." *Nature* 413: 591–596.

Scherr, Sara. 1999. "Soil Degradation—A Threat to Developing Country Food Security by 2020?" Food, Agriculture, and the Environment Discussion 27. International Food Policy Research Institute, Washington, D.C.

Scherr, Sara J., A. White, and D. Kaimowitz. 2002. "Strategies to Improve Rural Livelihoods through Markets for Forest Products and Services." Forest Trends and Center for International Forestry Research, Washington, D.C.

Scherr, Sara, and S. Yadav. 1996. "Land Degradation in the Developing World: Implications for Food, Agriculture, and the Environment to 2020." International Food Policy Research Institute Discussion Paper 14. Washington, D.C.

Schipper, Lee, Scott Murtishaw, and Fridtjof Unander. 2001. "International Comparisons of Sectoral Carbon Dioxide Emissions Using a Cross-Country Decomposition Technique." *Energy Journal* 22(2):35–75.

Schneider, Robert R. 1995. "Government and Economy on the Amazon Frontier." World Bank Environment Working Paper 11. Washington, D.C.

Scholz, Ulrich. 1985. "Types of Spontaneous Settlement in Thailand." In Walther Manshard and William B. Morgan, eds., *Agricultural Expansion and Pioneer Settlements in the Humid Tropics.* Tokyo: United Nations University Press.

Scoones, Ian, eds. 1994. *Living with Uncertainty: New Directions in Pastoral Development in Africa.* London: Intermediate Technology Development Group Publishing.

Sebastian, Iona, Kseniya Lvovsky, and de Henk Koning. 1999. "Decision Support System for Integrated Pollution Control: Software for Education and Analysis of Pollution Management. User Guide." World Bank, Washington, D.C.

Sen, Amartya. 1983. "Development: Which Way Now?" *Economic Journal* 93(372):742–62.

———. 1999. *Development as Freedom.* New York: Anchor Books.

Serageldin, Ismael, Ephim Shluger, and Joan Martin-Brown. 2001. *Historic Cities and Sacred Sites: Cultural Roots for Urban Futures.* Washington, D.C.: World Bank.

Sevilla, Manuel. 2000. "Participación privada en el mejoramiento urbano: Sondeo de cuatro casos en El Salvador." SACDEL, San Salvador.

Shah, Tushaar. 1993. *Groundwater Markets and Irrigation Development.* Mumbai: Oxford University Press.

Shalizi, Zmarak, and Christine Kraus. 2001. "Globalization, Openness and the Environment." World Bank, Washington, D.C. Processed.

Shlomo, Angel. 2000. *Housing Policy Matters.* Oxford: Oxford University Press.

Simpson, R. David, Roger A. Sedjo, and John W. Reid. 1996. "Valuing Biodiversity for Use in Pharmaceutical Research." *Journal of Political Economy* 104(1):163–185.

Singh, Jas, and Carol Mulholland. 2000. "DSM in Thailand: a Case Study." World Bank Energy Sector Management Assistance Programme Technical Series 008. Washington, D.C.

Skaperdas, Stergios. 1992. "Cooperation, Conflict, and Power in the Absence of Property Rights." *American Economic Review* 82(4):720–739.

Skees, Jarry, Panos Varangis, Donald Larson, and Paul Siegel. 2002. "Can Financial Markets Be Tapped to Help Poor People Cope with Weather Risks?" World Bank Policy Research Working Paper 2812. Washington, D.C.

Smith, Adam. 1776/1981. *An Inquiry into the Nature and Causes of the Wealth of Nations.* R. H. Campbell and A. S. Skinner, eds. Indianapolis: Liberty Classics.

Smith, Kirk R. 1998. "Indoor Air Pollution in India: National Health Impacts and the Cost-Effectiveness of Intervention." Goregaon, Mumbai.

Social Investment Forum. 2001. "2001 Report on Socially Responsible Investing Trends in the United States." Social Investment Forum. Washington, D.C. Available online at www.socialinvest.org.

Sokoloff, Kenneth L., and Stanley L. Engerman. 2000. "History Lessons: Institutions, Factor Endowments, and Paths of Development in the New World." *Journal of Economic Perspectives* 14(3):217–232.

Solow, Robert. 2000. "Notes on Social Capital and Economic Performance." In Partha Dasgupta and Ismail Serageldin, eds., *Social Capital: A Multifaceted Perspective.* Washington, D.C.: World Bank.

Sorensen, Jens. 2002. "Baseline 2000 Background Report: The Status of Integrated Coastal Management as an International Practice." Harbor and Coastal Center, University of Massachusetts, Boston. Available online at http://www. uhi.umb. edu/b2k/baseline 2000.pdf.

Souza, Celina. 2001. "Participatory Budgeting in Brazilian Cities: Limits and Possibilities in Building Democratic Institutions." *Environment and Urbanization* 13(1): 159–184.

Sparks, Allistar. 1996. *Tomorrow Is Another Country: The Inside Story of South Africa's Road to Change.* Chicago: University of Chicago Press.

State Environmental Protection Agency (China). 2001. "New Countermeasures for Air Pollution Control in China, Final Report." Beijing.

Steinberg, David Joel, ed. 1987. *In Search of Southeast Asia: A Modern History.* Honolulu: University of Hawaii Press.

Steinberg, Paul F. 2001. *Environmental Leadership in Developing Countries: Transnational Relations and Biodiversity Policy in Costa Rica and Bolivia.* Cambridge, Mass.: MIT Press.

Stephens, C., M. Akerman, S. Avle, P. B. Maia, P. Campanario, B. Doe, and D. Tetteh. 1997. "Urban Equity and Urban Health: Using Existing Data to Understand Inequalities in Health and Environment in Accra, Ghana and São Paulo, Brazil." *Environment and Urbanization* 9(1):181–202.

Stephens, G. Ross, and Nelson Wikstrom. 2000. *Metropolitan Government and Governance: Theoretical Perspectives, Empirical Analysis, and the Future.* New York: Oxford University Press.

Stewart, Frances. 2000. "Crisis Prevention: Tackling Horizontal Inequalities." Oxford Development Studies 28(3): 245–62.

Stone, Wendy. 2001. "Measuring Social Capital: Towards a Theoretically Informed Measurement Framework for Researching Social Capital in Family and Community Life." Australian Institute of Family Studies Research Paper 24. Melbourne, Australia.

Stott, Peter, and J. A. Kettleborough, 2002. "Origins and Estimates of Uncertainty in Predictions of Twenty-First Century Temperature Rise." *Science* 416:723–725.

Streets, David G., Kejun Jiang, Xiulian Hu, Jonathan E. Sinton, Xiao-Quan Zhang, Deying Xu, Mark Z. Jacobson, and James E. Hansen. 2001. "Recent Reductions in China's Greenhouse Gas Emissions." *Science* 294:1835–1837.

Struyk, Raymond J. 1997. *Restructuring Russia's Housing Sector: 1991–1997.* Washington, D.C.: The Urban Institute.

Sugden, Robert. 1986. *The Economics of Rights, Cooperation, and Welfare.* Oxford and New York: Basil Blackwell.

Summers, Robert, and Alan Heston. 1991. "Penn World Tables (Mark 5): An Expanded Set of International Comparisons, 1950–1988." *Quarterly Journal of Economics* 106(2): 327–368.

SustainAbility Ltd., and United Nations Environment Programme. 2001. *Buried Treasure: Uncovering the Business Case for Corporate Sustainability.* London: SustainAbility.

Suvanto, Tina. 2000. "Social Capital and Value Creation: A Theoretical Approach." 47891N. Helsinki.

Svensson, Jakob. 1998. "Investment, Property Rights and Political Instability: Theory and Evidence." *European Economic Review* 42(7):1317–1341.

Swearingen, Will D., and Abdellatif Bencherifa, eds. 1996. *North African Environment at Risk: State, Culture and Society in Arab North Africa.* Boulder, Colo.: Westview Press.

Syrquin, Moshe. 1989. "Patterns of Structural Change." In H. Chenery and T. N. Srinivasan, eds., *Handbook of Development Economics Vol. I.* Amsterdam: North Holland.

Tendler, Judith. 1997. *Good Governments in the Tropics.* Baltimore: Johns Hopkins University Press.

Ter-Minassian, Teresa, ed. 1997. *Fiscal Federalism in Theory and Practice.* Washington, D.C: International Monetary Fund.

Tilman, D., J. Fargione, B. Wolff, C. D'Antonio, A. Dobson, R. Howarth, D. Schindler, W. H. Shlesinger, D. Simberloff, and D. Swackhamer. 2001. "Forecasting Agriculturally Driven Global Environmental Change." *Science* 292:281–284.

Timmer, C. Peter. 1997. "How Well Do the Poor Connect to the Growth Process?" Harvard University Consulting Assistance on Economic Reform II Discussion Paper 17. Cambridge, Mass. Available online at http://www.cid.harvard.edu/caer2.

Tomich, Thomas P., Peter Kilby, and Bruce F. Johnson. 1995. *Transforming Agrarian Economies: Opportunities Seized, Opportunities Missed.* Ithaca, N.Y. and London: Cornell University Press.

Tomich, Thomas P., M. van Noordwijk, S. Budidarsono, A. Gillion, T. Kusumanto, M. Murdiyarso, F. Stolle, and A. M. Fagi. 1998. "Alternatives to Slash-and-Burn in Indonesia: Summary Report and Sysnthesis of Phase II." Alternatives to Slash-and-Burn Programme Indonesia Report 8. CGIAR, Bogor. Available online at http://www. asb.cgiar.org/CR_Indonesia.shtm.

TI (Transparency International). 2000. *Confronting Corruption: The Elements of a National Integrity System.* Berlin.

Tullock, Gordon. 1975. "The Transitional Gains Trap." *Bell Journal of Economics* 6(2):671–78.

Turner, John F. C., and Robert Fichter, eds. 1972. *Freedom to Build.* New York: Macmillan.

Uhlig, Harald. 1988. "Spontaneous and Planned Settlement in South East Asia." In Walther Manshard and William B. Morgan, eds., *Agricultural Expansion and Pioneer Settlements in the Humid Tropics.* Tokyo: United Nations University Press.

United Nations. 1999. "World Urbanization Prospects: The 1999 Revision. Part 2: Urban Agglomerations." New York.

United Nations–Habitat, eds. 1996. *An Urbanizing World: Global Report on Human Settlements.* New York: United Nations Center for Human Settlements (Habitat), and Oxford University Press.

———. 1998. "Global Urban Indicators Database." Nairobi.

———. 1999. "Global Campaign for Secure Tenure." Nairobi. Pamplet.

United Nations–Habitat and Urban Management Programme. 2001. "City Development Strategy: Consolidation of Lessons from UMP/UNCHS Experience." Paper presented at Cities Alliance Public Policy Forum, Kolkuta. December 9–12.

UNDP (United Nations Development Programme). 1997. "Aridity Zones and Dryland Populations: An Assessment of Population Levels in the World's Drylands." UNDP and United Nations Office to Combat Desertification and Drought, Nairobi.

UNDP (United Nations Development Programme), UNEP (United Nations Environment Programme), World Bank, and WRI (World Resources Institute). 1999. "World Resources 1998–99: A Guide to the Global Environment."

———. 2000. *World Resources 2000–2001: People and Ecosystems, the Fraying Way of Life.* Oxford: Elsevier Science Ltd.

UNEP (United Nations Environment Programme). 1992. *World Atlas of Desertification.* New York: Oxford University Press.

———. 1997. *World Atlas of Desertification.* New York: Oxford University Press.

———. 1999. "Synthesis of the Reports of the Scientific, Environmental Effects, and Technology and Economic Assessment Panels of the Montreal Protocol: A Decade of Assessment for Decision Makers Regarding the Protection of the Ozone Layer: 1998–1999." Nairobi.

UNEP (United Nations Environment Programme) and GRID (Global Resource Information Database)–Arendal. 1997. *Assessment of Human Induced Soil Degradation (GLASOD) Extract of West Africa Dataset.* GRID-Arendal online GIS and Maps database. Available online at www.grida.no.

USDA (U.S. Department of Agriculture). 2001. *Food and Agricultural Policy: Taking Stock for the New Century.* Washington, D.C. Available online at http://www.usda. gov.

U.S. Embassy in China. 1998. "The Fading of Chinese Environmental Secrecy." U.S. Embassy in China, Beijing.

Uzzi, B. 1997. "Social Structure and Competition in Interfirm Networks: The Paradox of Embeddedness." *Administrative Science Quarterly* 29(4):598–621.

Velásquez, Luz Stella. 1998. "Agenda 21: A Form of Joint Environmental Management in Manizales, Colombia." *Environment and Urbanization* 10(2):9–36.

Veríssimo, C. Souza Jr., R. Salomão, and R. Barreto. 2000. "Identificação de areas com potencial para a criação de florestas públicas de produção na Amazônia legal." Food and Agriculture Organization of the United Nations. Processed.

Victor, David G., Kal Raustiala, and Eugene B. Skolnikoff. 1998. *The Implementation and Effectiveness of International Environmental Commitments: Theory and Practice.* Cambridge, Mass.: MIT Press.

Wambugu, Florence. 1999. "Why Africa Needs Agricultural Biotech." *Nature* 400:15–16.

Wang, Hua, Jinnan Wang, Genfa Lu, David Wheeler, and Jun Bi. Forthcoming. "Public Ratings of Industry's Environmental Performance: China's Greenwatch Program." World Bank Policy Research Working Paper series. Washington, D.C.

Ward, Peter M. 1998. "International Forum on Regularization and Land Markets." *Land Lines* July. Available online at www.lincolninst.com.

Watson, D., and L. A. Clark. 1991. "Self Versus Peer Ratings of Specific Emotional Traits: Evidence of Convergent and Discriminant Validity." *Journal of Personality and Social Psychology* 60(6):927–940.

Watson, Robert T., Ian R. Noble, Bert Bolin, N. H. Ravindranath, David J. Verardo, and David J. Dokken, eds. 2000. *Land Use, Land-Use Change, and Forestry: A Special Report of the IPCC.* Cambridge: Cambridge University Press. Available online at http://www.grida.no/climate/ipcc/land_use/.

Weber-Fahr, Monika. 2002. "Treasure or Trouble? Mining in Developing Countries." World Bank and the International Finance Corporation. Available online at http:// www.eireview.org/eir/eirhome.nsf

Weitzman, Martin L. 1998. "Why the Far-Distant Future Should Be Discounted at Its Lowest Possible Rate." *Journal of Environmental Economics and Management* 36(3): 201–8.

Wells, Michael, Scott Guggenheim, Asmeen Khan, Wahjudi Wardojo, and Paul Jepson. 1999. "Investing in Biodiversity: A Review of Indonesia's Integrated Conservation and Development Projects." World Bank, Washington, D.C.

Wheeler, James O., Yuko Aoyama, and Barney Wolf, eds. 2000. *Cities in the Telecommunications Age: The Fracturing of Geography.* New York: Routledge.

White, Andy, and Alejandra Martin. 2002. "Who Owns the World's Forests? Forest Tenure and Public Forests in Transition." Forest Trends, Washington, D.C. Processed.

White, Robin, Siobhan Murray, and Mark Rohweder. 2002. "Pilot Analysis of Global Ecosystems (PAGE): Grasslands Ecosystems." World Resources Institute, Washington, D.C. Available online at http://www.wri.org/wr2000/grasslands_page.html.

Wilkinson, Clive R., ed. 2000. *Status of Coral Reefs of the World.* Queensland, Australia: Coral Reef Monitoring Center.

Williams, Martin A. J. 2001. "Interactions of Desertification and Climate: Present Understanding and Future Research Imperatives." *Arid Lands Newsletter* 49 (May– June).

Williamson, Jeffrey. 1988. "Migration and Urbanization." In Hollis Chenery and T. N. Srinivasan, eds., *Handbook of Development Economics Vol. II.* Amsterdam: Elsevier Science Publishers.

———. 1997. "Growth, Distribution and Demography: Some Lessons From History." National Bureau of Economic Research Working Paper 6244. Cambridge, Mass.

Williamson, Oliver E. 2000. "The New Institutional Economics: Taking Stock, Looking Ahead." *Journal of Economic Literature* 38(3):595–613.

Willmann, Rolf, Pongpat Boonchuwong, and Somying Piumsombun. 2002. "Fisheries Management Costs in Thai Marine Fisheries." Food and Agriculture Organization of the United Nations and Kasetsart University Campus, Bangkok. Processed.

Willoughby, Christopher. 2000. "Singapore's Experience in Managing Motorization, and Its Relevance to Other Countries." World Bank, Transportation, Water, and Urban Development Discussion Paper 43. Washington, D.C.

Wilson, David, Andrew Whiteman, and Angela Tormin. 2001. "Strategic Planning Guide for Municipal Solid Waste Management." World Bank, Washington D.C.

Wilson, Edward, and Stephen Kellert, eds. 1994. *The Biophilia Hypothesis.* Washington, D.C.: Island Press.

Wily, Liz, and Peter A. Dewees. 2001. "From Users to Custodians: Changing Relations between People and the State in Forest Management in Tunisia." World Bank Policy Research Working Paper 2569. Washington, D.C.

Wodon, Quentin, Rodrigo Castro, Kihoon Lee, Gladys Lopez-Acevedo, Corinne Siaens, Carlos Sobrado, and Jean-Philippe Tre. 2001. "Poverty in Latin America: Trends (1986–1998) and Determinants." *Cuadernos de Economía* 114:127–153.

Wodon, Quentin, and Gonzalez G. Konig. 2001. "The Impact of Remittances on Income Distribution." World Bank, Latin America and Caribbean Region, Washington, D.C. Processed.

Wood, Stanley, Freddy Nachtergaele, Daniel Nielsen, and Aiguo Dai. 1999. "Spatial Aspects of the Design and Targeting of Agricultural Development Strategies." International Food Policy Research Institute Discussion Paper 44. Washington, D.C. Available online at http://www. ifpri.org/.

Wood, Stanley, Kate Sebastian, and Sara J. Scherr. 2000. "Pilot Analysis of Global Ecosystems: Agroecosystems." Washington D.C.: International Food Policy Research Institute and World Resources Institute.

Woolcock, Michael, Lant Pritchett, and Jonathan Isham. 2001. "The Social Foundations of Poor Economic Growth in Resource-Rich Countries." In R. M. Auty, eds., *Resource Abun-*

dance and Economic Development. New York: Oxford University Press.

World Bank. 1991. "Growth, Poverty Alleviation, and Improved Income Distribution in Malaysia: Changing Focus of Government Policy Intervention." Report 8667–MA. Washington, D.C.

———. 1992a. "Malaysia: Fiscal Reform for Stable Growth." Report 10120–MA. Washington, DC.

———. 1992b. World Development Report 1992: Development and the Environment. New York: Oxford University Press.

———. 1993. "Indigenous Peoples." Operational Directive 4.2.

———. 1994. World Development Report 1994: Infrastructure for Development. New York: Oxford University Press.

———. 1996a. "Sustainable Transport: Priorities for Policy Reform." Development in Practice Series. Washington, D.C.

———. 1996b. "Technical Assistance." Operations and Evaluation Department Lessons and Practices No. 7. Washington, D.C.

———. 1997a. "Five Years after Rio: Innovations in Environmental Policy." Environmentally Sustainable Development Studies and Monographs Series 18. Washington, D.C.

———. 1997b. World Development Report 1997: The State in a Changing World. New York: Oxford University Press.

———. 1998a. "Aral Sea Basin Program (Kazakhstan, Kyrgyz Republic, Turkmenistan, and Uzbekistan): Water and Environmental Management Project Document. Washington, D.C.

———. 1998b. Assessing Aid: What Works, What Doesn't and Why. New York: Oxford University Press.

———. 1998c. "Post-Conflict Reconstruction." Washington, D.C.

———. 1999. World Development Report 1998/1999: Knowledge for Development. New York: Oxford University Press.

———. 2000a. "Bangladesh: Climate Change and Sustainable Development." Report 21104–BD." Washington, D.C.

———. 2000b. "Global Economic Prospects 2000." Washington, D.C.

———. 2000c. Global Development Finance. Washington, D.C.

———. 2000d. Greening Industry: New Roles for Communities, Markets, and Governments. New York: Oxford University Press.

———. 2000e. India: Reducing Poverty, Accelerating Development. New Delhi: Oxford University Press and World Bank.

———. 2000f. "Partners in Transforming Development: New Approaches to Developing Country-Owned Poverty Reduction Strategies." Available online at http://www.poverty/strategies/prspbroc.pdf.

———. 2000g. The Quality of Growth. New York: Oxford University Press.

———. 2000h. World Development Report 1999/2000: Entering the 21st Century. New York: Oxford University Press.

———. 2001a. "China: Air, Land and Water—Environmental Priorities for a New Millennium." Washington, D.C.

———. 2001b. Engendering Development through Gender Equality in Rights, Resources, and Voice. New York: Oxford University Press.

———2001c. "Environment Strategy Paper: Making Sustainable Commitments (Revised Draft)." Washington, D.C. Processed.

———. 2001d. "Implementation Completion Report No. 22390–TUN: North West Mountainous Areas Development Project." Washington, D.C. Processed.

———. 2001e. "Indonesia: Environment and Natural Resource Management in a Time of Transition." Environment and Social Development Unit Report. Washington, D.C.

———. 2001f. Making Sustainable Commitments: An Environment Strategy for the World Bank. Washington, D.C: World Bank.

———. 2001g. "Trade and Foreign Exchange Policies in Iran: Reform Agenda, Economic Implications and Impact on the Poor." Processed.

———. 2001h. World Development Indicators. Washington, D.C., and London: World Bank.

———. 2001i. World Development Report 2000/2001: Attacking Poverty. New York: Oxford University Press.

———. 2002a. "A Revised Forest Strategy for the World Bank Group." Washington, D.C.

——— 2002b. A Case for Aid: Building Consensus for Development Assistance. Washington, D.C.

———. 2002c. "China: Opportunities to Improve Energy Efficiency in Buildings." World Bank Discussion Paper, Washington, D.C.

———. 2002d. "Cities on the Move: A World Bank Urban Transport Strategy Review." Washington, D.C. Processed.

———. 2002e. "Global Development Finance: Financing the Poorest Countries 2002." Washington, D.C.

World Bank. 2002ee. Global Economic Prospects. Washington, D.C.

———. 2002f. "Global Poverty Monitoring Website." Washington, D.C., World Bank. Available online at http://www.worldbank.org/research/povmonitor/index.htm.

———. 2002g. Globalization, Growth, and Poverty: Building an Inclusive World Economy. New York: Oxford University Press.

———. 2002h. "Mexico Low-Income Housing: Issues and Options." Report 22534–ME. Washington, D.C. Processed.

———. 2002i. "Prototype Carbon Fund, First Annual Report and Project Concept Note, Liepaja Region Solid Waste Management Project." Washington, D.C. Processed.

———. 2002j. "Public Expenditure and Institutional Review of the Dominican Republic." Washington, D.C. Processed.

———. 2002k. "Reaching the Rural Poor: An Updated Strategy for Rural Development." Washington, D.C. Processed.

———. 2002l. Rural Development Strategy. Washington, D.C.

———. 2002m. "The World Bank's Experience with Institutional Development." Operations and Evaluation Department, Lessons and Practices 14. Washington, D.C.

———. 2002n. "Water Resources Sector Strategy: Strategic Directions for World Bank Engagement." Washington, D.C. Processed.

———. 2002o. World Development Report 2002: Building Institutions for Markets. New York: Oxford University Press.

———. Forthcoming. "Johannesburg and Beyond: An Agenda for Action." Paper to be presented by Environmentally and Socially Sustainable Development in run-up to World Summit on Sustainable Development, August 2002.

World Bank and International Finance Corporation. 2002. "Treasure or Trouble? Mining in Developing Countries." Washington, D.C.

WHO (World Health Organization), Department of Communicable Disease Surveillance and Response. 2001. "WHO Global Strategy for Containment of Antimicrobial Resistance." Washington, D.C.

World Values Surveys and European Values 1981–4, 1990–3, 1995–7. ICPSR 2790. Available from Inter-university Consortium for Political and Social Research at http://www.icpsr.umich.edu/.

World Water Council. 2000. "A Water Secure World: Vision for Water, Life, and the Environment." Commission Report. Marseille.

Worster, Donald. 1979. *Dust Bowl: The Southern Plains in the 1930s.* New York: Oxford University Press.

WRI (World Resources Institute). 2000. *World Resources 2000–01 People and Ecosystems: The Fraying Web of Life.* Washington, D.C.

Wunder, Sven. 2000. *The Economics of Deforestation: The Example of Ecuador.* New York: St. Martin's Press.

Yi, Zeng. 2002. "Old-Age Insurance and Sustainable Development in Rural China." In Kochendörfer-Lucius and Pleskovic, eds., *Villa Borsig Workshop Series 2001.* Berlin.

Yildizcan, Guzin. 2002. "Drive to Resuscitate the Golden Horn." World Bank, Operations and Evaluation Department Précis 34. Washington, D.C.

Yli-Renko, H. 1999. "Dependence, Social Capital, and Learning in Key Customer Relationships: Effects of the Performance of Technology-Based New Firms." Master's thesis. Helsinki University of Technology.

Yusuf, Shahid. 2001. "East Asia's Urban Regions: A Strategy for the Coming Decade." World Bank, Washington, D.C. Processed.

Zaheer, A., B. McEvily, and V. Perrone. 1998. "Does Trust Matter? Exploring the Effects of Interorganizational and Interpersonal Trust on Performance." *Organisation Science* 9(2):141–159.

Zheng, X., and E. A. B. Eltahir. 1997. "The Response to Deforestation and Desertification in a Model of West African Monsoons." *Geophysical Research Letters* 24(2): 155–158.

Background papers for WDR 2003

Acharya, G., and John Dixon. "No one Said it was Going to be Easy: An Analysis of the Recommendations made by the 1992 World Development Report and the Experience in the Last Decade."

Bertaud, Alain. "The Spatial Organization of Cities: Deliberate Outcome or Unforeseen Consequence?"

———. Metropolitan Structure, Densities and Livability."

Brekke, Kjell Arne, and Desmond McNeill. "Identity Signaling in Consumption: A Case for Provision of More Public Goods."

Campbell, Tim. "The Evolution of Governance in Metropolitan Areas."

Chavez, Roberto. "Supported Peru Sites and Services Development Projects."

Das Gupta, Monica. "Population and Sustainable Development."

Gates, Scott, Nils Petter Gleditsch, and Eric Neumayer. "Environmental Commitment, Democracy and Inequality."

Hannesson, Rognvaldur. "The Development of Economic Institutions in World Fisheries."

———. "Trends in World Fish Catches. Do We Face a Crisis?"

Hoff, Karla. "Paths of Development and Institutional Barriers to Economic Opportunities."

Holtedahl, Pernille, and Haakon Vennemo. "Environmental Challenges in China: Success, and Failures, Determinants, Driving Forces."

Janeba, Eckard, and Guttorm Schjeldrup. "The Future of Globalization: Tax Competition and Trade Liberalization."

Jayasuriya, Ruwan, and Quentin Wodon. "Measuring and Explaining Country Efficiency in Improving Health and Education Indicators: The Role of Urbanization."

Kuhnle, Stein, Sanjeev Prakash, Huck-ju Kwon, and Per Selle. "Political Institutions, Democracy and Welfare: A Comparative Study of Norway and Korea."

Murshed, Mansoob S. "On Natural Resource Abundance and Underdevelopment."

Pratt, Jane, and John D. Shilling. "High Time for Mountains: A Program for Sustaining Mountain Resources and Livelihoods."

Sambanis, Nicolas. "Preventing Violent Civil Conflict: The Scope and Limits of Government Action."

Steinberg, Paul. "Civic Environmentalism in Developing Countries: Opportunities for Innovation in State-Society Relations."

Tesli, Arne. "The Use of EIA and SEA Relative to the Objective of Sustainable Development."

Zainabi, Ahmed. "Pérennité des actions d'autopromotion communautaire: Cas de la Vallée du Dra Moyen (Province de Zagora)."

Background notes for WDR 2003

Chavez, Roberto. "Revisiting the Peru Sites and Services Development Projects."

Cira, Dean. "Regularizing *Favelas* in Brazil."

Ortiz Malavasi, Edgar, and John Kellenberg. "Program of Payments for Environmental Services in Costa Rica."

Pantelic, Jelena. "Hazard Mitigation Through Collective Action."

Viloria-Williams, J. "Notes on Urban Upgrading (UU) Experiences in Two Countries."

Introduction to Selected World Development Indicators

In this year's edition, development data are presented in four tables presenting comparative socioeconomic data for more than 130 economies for the most recent year for which data are available and, for some indicators, for an earlier year. An additional table presents basic indicators for 75 economies with sparse data or with populations of less than 1.5 million.

The indicators presented here are a selection from more than 800 included in *World Development Indicators 2002*. Published annually, *World Development Indicators* reflects a comprehensive view of the development process. Its opening chapter reports on the Millennium Development Goals which grew out of agreements and resolutions of world conferences organized by the United Nations (UN) in the past decade, and reaffirmed at the Millennium Summit in September 2000 by member countries of the UN. The other five main sections recognize the contribution of a wide range of factors: human capital development, environmental sustainability, macroeconomic performance, private sector development, and the global links that influence the external environment for development. *World Development Indicators* is complemented by a separately published database that gives access to over 1,000 data tables and 500 time-series indicators for 225 economies and regions. This database is available through an electronic subscription (*WDI Online*) or as a CD-ROM.

Data sources and methodology

Socioeconomic and environmental data presented here are drawn from several sources: primary data collected by the World Bank, member country statistical publications, research institutes, and international organizations such as the United Nations and its specialized agencies, the International Monetary Fund (IMF), and the OECD (see the *Data Sources* following the *Technical notes* for a complete listing). Although international standards of coverage, definition, and classification apply to most statistics reported by countries and international agencies, there are inevitably differences in timeliness and reliability arising from differences in the capabilities and resources devoted to basic data collection and compilation. For some topics, competing sources of data require review by World Bank staff to ensure that the most reliable data available are presented. In some instances, where available data are deemed too weak to provide reliable measures of levels and trends or do not adequately adhere to international standards, the data are not shown.

The data presented are generally consistent with those in *World Development Indicators 2002*. However, data have been revised and updated wherever new information has become available. Differences may also reflect revisions to historical series and changes in methodology. Thus data of different vintages may be published in different editions of World Bank publications. Readers are advised not to compile data series from different publications or different editions of the same publication. Consistent time-series data are available on *World Development Indicators 2002* CD-ROM and through *WDI Online*.

All dollar figures are in current U.S. dollars unless otherwise stated. The various methods used to convert from national currency figures are described in the *Technical notes.*

Because the World Bank's primary business is providing lending and policy advice to its low- and middle-income members, the issues covered in these tables focus mainly on these economies. Where available, information on the high-income economies is also provided for comparison. Readers may wish to refer to national statistical publications and publications of the Organisation for Economic Co-operation and Development (OECD) and the European Union for more information on the high-income economies.

Changes in the System of National Accounts

This edition of the Selected World Development Indicators, as in last year's edition, uses terminology in line with the 1993 System of National Accounts (SNA). For example, in the 1993 SNA *gross national income* replaces *gross national product.* See the technical notes for tables 1 and 3.

Most countries continue to compile their national accounts according to the 1968 SNA, but more and more are adopting the 1993 SNA. A few low-income countries still use concepts from older SNA guidelines, including valuations such as factor cost, in describing major economic aggregates.

Classification of economies and summary measures

The summary measures at the bottom of each table include economies classified by income per capita and by region. GNI per capita is used to determine the following income classifications: low-income, $745 or less in 2001; middle-income, $746 to $9,205; and high-income, $9,206 and above. A further division at GNI per capita $2,975 is made between lower-middle-income and upper-middle-income economies. See the table on classification of economies at the end of this volume for a list of economies in each group (including those with populations of less than 1.5 million).

Summary measures are either totals (indicated by **t** if the aggregates include estimates for missing data and nonreporting countries, or by an **s** for simple sums of the data available), weighted averages (**w**), or median values (**m**) calculated for groups of econo-mies. Data for the countries excluded from the main tables (those presented in Table 1a) have been included in the summary measures, where data are available, or by assuming that they follow the trend of reporting countries. This gives a more consistent aggregated measure by standardizing country coverage for each period shown. Where missing information accounts for a third or more of the overall estimate, however, the group measure is reported as not available. The section on *Statistical methods* in the *Technical notes* provides further information on aggregation methods. Weights used to construct the aggregates are listed in the technical notes for each table.

From time to time an economy's classification is revised because of changes in the above cutoff values or in the economy's measured level of GNI per capita. When such changes occur, aggregates based on those classifications are recalculated for the past period so that a consistent time series is maintained.

Terminology and country coverage

The term *country* does not imply political independence but may refer to any territory for which authorities report separate social or economic statistics. Data are shown for economies as they were constituted in 2000, and historical data are revised to reflect current political arrangements. Throughout the tables, exceptions are noted.

Technical notes

Because data quality and intercountry comparisons are often problematic, readers are encouraged to consult the *Technical notes*, the table on Classification of Economies by Income and Region, and the footnotes to the tables. For more extensive documentation see *World Development Indicators 2002.*

Readers may find more information on the WDI 2002, and orders can be made online, by phone, or fax as follows:

For more information and to order online: http://www.worldbank.org/data/wdi2002/index.htm. To order by phone or fax: **1-800-645-7247** or 703-661-1580; Fax 703-661-1501
To order by mail: The World Bank, P.O. Box 960, Herndon, VA 20172-0960, U.S.A.

Table 1. Key indicators of development

	Population			Gross national income (GNI)[a]		PPP gross national income (GNI)[b]		Gross domestic product	Life expectancy at birth	Under-5 mortality rate	Adult illiteracy rate	Carbon dioxide emissions
	Millions 2001	Avg. annual % growth 1990–2001	density people per sq. km 2001	Billions of dollars 2001	per capita dollars 2001	Billions of dollars 2001	per capita dollars 2001	per capita % growth 2000–2001	Years 2000	Per 1,000 2000	% of people 15 and above 2000	Millions of tons 1998
Albania	3.4	0.4	126	4.2	1,230	13	3,880	5.6	74	. .	15	1.6
Algeria	30.9	1.9	13	50.4	1,630	159[c]	5,150[c]	0.3	71	39	33	106.6
Angola	13.5	3.1	11	6.7	500	21[c]	1,550[c]	0.3	47	208	. .	5.9
Argentina	37.5	1.3	14	261.0	6,960	438	11,690	–4.8	74	22	3	136.9
Armenia	3.8	0.7	135	2.1	560	11	2,880	9.4	74	17	2	3.4
Australia	19.4	1.2	3	383.3	19,770	500	25,780	1.3	79	7	. .	331.5
Austria	8.1	0.5	98	194.5	23,940	220	27,080	0.9	78	6	. .	63.9
Azerbaijan	8.1	1.1	94	5.3	650	25	3,020	8.2	72	21	. .	38.8
Bangladesh	133.4	1.8	1,025	49.9	370	224	1,680	3.3	61	83	59	23.4
Belarus	10.0	–0.2	48	11.9	1,190	80	8,030	4.4	68	14	0[d]	60.5
Belgium	10.3	0.3	313	239.8	23,340	290	28,210	0.8	78	7	. .	101.3
Benin	6.4	2.8	58	2.3	360	7	1,030	3.1	53	143	63	0.7
Bolivia	8.5	2.4	8	8.0	940	20	2,380	–1.2	63	79	14	12.1
Botswana	1.6	2.1	3	5.9	3,630	14	8,810	4.8	39	99	23	3.8
Brazil	172.6	1.4	20	528.5	3,060	1,286	7,450	0.2	68	39	15	299.6
Bulgaria	8.1	–0.6	73	12.6	1,560	48	5,950	5.1	72	16	2	47.4
Burkina Faso	11.6	2.4	42	2.4	210	12[c]	1,020[c]	3.2	44	206	76	1.0
Burundi	6.9	2.2	270	0.7	100	4[c]	590[c]	1.3	42	176	52	0.2
Cambodia	12.3	2.7	69	3.3	270	19	1,520	3.2	54	120	32	0.7
Cameroon	15.2	2.4	33	8.7	570	25	1,670	3.1	50	155	24	1.8
Canada	31.0	1.0	3	661.9	21,340	864[c]	27,870[c]	0.6	79	7	. .	467.2
Central African Republic	3.8	2.2	6	1.0	270	4[c]	1,180[c]	0.0	43	152	53	0.2
Chad	7.9	2.9	6	1.6	200	7	930	5.8	48	188	57	0.1
Chile	15.4	1.5	21	66.9	4,350	145	9,420	1.7	76	12	4	60.2
China	1,271.9	1.0	136	1,131.0	890	5,415	4,260	6.5	70	39	16	3,108.0
Hong Kong, China	6.9	1.7	. .	*176.2*	*25,920*	179	26,050	–0.1	80	. .	6	35.8
Colombia	43.0	1.9	41	82.0	1,910	258	5,980	–0.2	72	23	8	67.8
Congo, Dem. Rep.	52.4	3.2	23	. .	. .[e]	. .	. .	. .	46	163	39	2.4
Congo, Rep.	3.1	3.0	9	2.2	700	2	580	0.1	51	106	19	1.8
Costa Rica	3.9	2.2	76	15.3	3,950	31	8,080	–1.0	77	13	4	5.1
Côte d'Ivoire	16.4	3.0	52	10.3	630	24	1,470	–3.3	46	180	53	13.2
Croatia	4.4	–0.8	78	19.9	4,550	37	8,440	4.1	73	9	2	19.8
Czech Republic	10.3	–0.1	133	54.1	5,270	149	14,550	3.6	75	7	. .	118.3
Denmark	5.4	0.4	126	166.3	31,090	150	27,950	0.7	76	6	. .	53.4
Dominican Republic	8.5	1.7	176	19.0	2,230	50	5,870	1.1	67	47	16	20.3
Ecuador	12.9	2.1	47	16.0	1,240	40	3,070	3.3	70	34	8	26.3
Egypt, Arab Rep.	65.2	2.0	65	99.4	1,530	247	3,790	1.4	67	52	45	105.8
El Salvador	6.4	2.0	309	13.1	2,050	29	4,500	0.0	70	35	21	6.1
Eritrea	4.2	2.7	42	0.8	190	4	970	2.5	52	103	44	. .
Estonia	1.4	–1.3	32	5.2	3,810	14	10,020	5.3	71	11	0	17.0
Ethiopia	65.8	2.3	66	6.8	100	47	710	5.4	42	179	61	2.0
Finland	5.2	0.4	17	124.2	23,940	131	25,180	0.5	77	5	. .	53.3
France	59.2	0.4	108	1,377.4[f]	22,690[f]	1,495	25,280	1.6	79	6	. .	369.9
Georgia	5.0	–0.8	72	3.1	620	14	2,860	4.6	73	21	. .	5.2
Germany	82.2	0.3	230	1,948.0	23,700	2,098	25,530	0.5	77	6	. .	825.2
Ghana	19.7	2.4	87	5.7	290	39[c]	1,980[c]	1.9	57	112	28	4.4
Greece	10.6	0.4	82	124.6	11,780	189	17,860	3.9	78	8	3	85.2
Guatemala	11.7	2.6	108	19.6	1,670	45	3,850	–0.6	65	49	31	9.7
Guinea	7.6	2.5	31	3.0	400	15	1,980	0.7	46	161	. .	1.2
Haiti	8.1	2.1	294	3.9	480	12[c]	1,450[c]	–3.5	53	111	50	1.3
Honduras	6.6	2.7	59	5.9	900	16	2,450	0.1	66	44	25	5.1
Hungary	10.2	–0.2	110	48.9	4,800	128	12,570	4.0	71	11	1	58.7
India	1,033.4	1.8	348	474.3	460	2,530	2,450	2.7	63	88	43	1,061.0
Indonesia	213.6	1.6	118	144.7	680	628	2,940	1.8	66	51	13	233.6
Iran, Islamic Rep.	64.7	1.6	40	112.9	1,750	403	6,230	3.0	69	41	24	289.9
Ireland	3.8	0.8	56	88.4	23,060	105	27,460	5.6	76	7	. .	38.3
Israel	6.4	2.8	309	*104.1*	*16,710*	*121*	*19,330*	. .	78	7	5	60.3
Italy	57.7	0.2	196	1,123.5	19,470	1,404	24,340	1.8	79	7	2	414.9
Jamaica	2.7	0.9	246	7.3	2,720	10	3,650	0.4	75	24	13	11.0
Japan	127.1	0.3	349	4,574.2	35,990	3,487	27,430	–0.6	81	5	. .	1,133.5
Jordan	5.0	4.2	57	8.8	1,750	21	4,080	1.2	72	30	10	13.9
Kazakhstan	14.8	–0.8	5	20.1	1,360	94	6,370	13.5	65	28	. .	122.9
Kenya	30.7	2.5	54	10.3	340	31	1,020	–1.0	47	120	18	9.1
Korea, Rep.	47.6	1.0	483	447.7	9,400	863	18,110	2.3	73	10	2	363.7
Kuwait	2.0	–0.4	115	*35.8*	*18,030*	*37*	*18,690*	. .	77	13	18	49.1
Kyrgyz Republic	5.0	1.1	26	1.4	280	13	2,710	4.2	67	35	. .	6.4
Lao PDR	5.4	2.4	23	1.6	310	9[c]	1,610[c]	2.9	54	. .	51	0.4
Latvia	2.3	–1.2	38	7.6	3,260	18	7,870	9.0	70	17	0[d]	7.9
Lebanon	4.4	1.7	429	17.6	4,010	20	4,640	0.0	70	30	14	16.3
Lesotho	2.1	1.9	68	1.1	550	6[c]	2,670[c]	1.7	44	143	17	. .
Lithuania	3.5	–0.5	54	11.4	3,270	27	7,610	4.3	73	11	0[d]	15.6
Macedonia, FYR	2.0	0.6	80	3.4	1,690	10	4,860	–4.7	73	17	. .	12.4
Madagascar	16.0	2.9	27	4.2	260	14	870	3.7	55	144	34	1.3
Malawi	10.5	1.9	112	1.8	170	7	620	0.7	39	193	40	0.7
Malaysia	23.8	2.4	72	86.5	3,640	198	8,340	–1.8	73	11	13	120.5

Note: For data comparability and coverage, see the technical notes. Figures in italics are for years other than those specified.

	Population — Millions 2001	Population — Avg. annual % growth 1990–2001	Population — density people per sq. km 2001	Gross national income (GNI)[a] — Billions of dollars 2001	GNI[a] — per capita dollars 2001	PPP gross national income (GNI)[b] — Billions of dollars 2001	PPP GNI[b] — per capita dollars 2001	Gross domestic product per capita % growth 2000–2001	Life expectancy at birth — Years 2000	Under-5 mortality rate — Per 1,000 2000	Adult illiteracy rate — % of people 15 and above 2000	Carbon dioxide emissions — Millions of tons 1998
Mali	11.1	2.5	9	2.3	210	9	810	−0.9	42	218	59	0.5
Mauritania	2.8	2.9	3	1.0	350	5	1,680	1.4	52	164	60	2.9
Mexico	99.4	1.6	52	550.5	5,540	872	8,770	−1.8	73	36	9	374.0
Moldova	4.3	−0.2	130	1.4	380	10	2,420	6.3	68	22	1	9.7
Mongolia	2.4	1.3	2	1.0	400	4	1,800	0.4	67	71	1	7.7
Morocco	29.2	1.8	65	34.6	1,180	108	3,690	4.8	67	60	51	32.0
Mozambique	18.1	2.2	23	3.7	210	18[c]	1,000[c]	6.7	42	200	56	1.3
Myanmar	48.3	1.6	73	..	..[e]	..	..	..	56	126	15	8.2
Namibia	1.8	2.4	2	3.5	1,960	12[c]	6,700[c]	2.6	47	112	18	0.0
Nepal	23.6	2.4	165	5.9	250	34	1,450	3.4	59	105	58	3.0
Netherlands	16.0	0.6	473	385.4	24,040	424	26,440	0.4	78	7	..	163.8
New Zealand	3.8	1.0	14	47.6	12,380	74	19,130	1.3	78	7	..	30.0
Nicaragua	5.2	2.8	43	..	..[e]	..	..	..	69	41	33	3.4
Niger	11.2	3.4	9	2.0	170	9[c]	770[c]	1.7	46	248	84	1.1
Nigeria	129.9	2.7	143	37.1	290	108	830	1.6	47	153	36	78.5
Norway	4.5	0.6	15	160.6	35,530	138	30,440	0.8	79	5	..	33.6
Pakistan	141.5	2.5	183	59.6	420	271	1,920	0.9	63	110	57	97.1
Panama	2.9	1.7	39	9.5	3,290	17[c]	5,720[c]	−1.3	75	24	8	5.8
Papua New Guinea	5.3	2.5	12	3.0	580	11[c]	2,150[c]	−5.8	59	75	36	2.3
Paraguay	5.6	2.6	14	7.3	1,300	25[c]	4,400[c]	−3.0	70	28	7	4.6
Peru	26.1	1.7	20	52.1	2,000	122	4,680	−1.4	69	41	10	27.9
Philippines	77.0	2.1	258	80.8	1,050	336	4,360	1.5	69	39	5	76.0
Poland	38.7	0.1	127	163.9	4,240	359	9,280	1.2	73	11	0[d]	321.7
Portugal	10.2	0.3	112	109.2	10,670	177	17,270	−0.3	76	8	8	54.6
Romania	22.4	−0.3	97	38.4	1,710	156	6,980	5.5	70	23	2	92.4
Russian Federation	144.8	−0.2	9	253.4	1,750	1,255	8,660	5.5	65	19	0[d]	1,434.6
Rwanda	8.7	2.0	353	1.9	220	9	1,000	4.3	40	203	33	0.5
Saudi Arabia	21.4	2.8	10	149.9	7,230	236	11,390	..	73	23	24	283.0
Senegal	9.8	2.6	51	4.7	480	15	1,560	3.2	52	129	63	3.3
Sierra Leone	5.1	2.3	72	0.7	140	2	480	3.1	39	267	..	0.5
Singapore	4.1	2.7	6,726	99.4	24,740	100	24,910	..	78	6	8	82.3
Slovak Republic	5.4	0.2	112	20.0	3,700	63	11,610	3.2	73	10	..	38.1
Slovenia	2.0	0.0	99	19.4	9,780	36	18,160	2.9	75	7	0[d]	14.6
South Africa	43.2	1.9	35	125.5	2,900	411[c]	9,510[c]	1.2	48	79	15	343.7
Spain	39.5	0.2	79	586.9	14,860	796	20,150	2.7	78	6	2	247.2
Sri Lanka	19.6	1.3	304	16.3	830	70	3,560	1.0	73	18	8	8.1
Sweden	8.9	0.3	22	225.9	25,400	219	24,670	1.0	80	4	..	48.6
Switzerland	7.2	0.6	182	266.5	36,970	226	31,320	0.9	80	6	..	41.8
Syrian Arab Republic	16.6	2.9	90	16.6	1,000	57	3,440	1.0	70	29	26	50.6
Tajikistan	6.2	1.5	44	1.1	170	7	1,150	4.1	69	30	1	5.1
Tanzania	34.5	2.7	39	9.2[g]	270[g]	19[g]	540[g]	2.3	44	149	25	2.2
Thailand	61.2	0.9	120	120.9	1,970	401	6,550	0.9	69	33	5	192.4
Togo	4.7	2.7	86	1.3	270	7	1,420	−0.1	49	142	43	0.9
Tunisia	9.7	1.6	62	20.1	2,070	62	6,450	4.2	72	30	29	22.4
Turkey	66.2	1.5	86	168.3	2,540	440	6,640	−7.8	70	43	15	202.0
Turkmenistan	5.3	3.3	11	5.0	950	24	4,580	18.4	66	43	..	27.9
Uganda	22.8	3.0	116	6.3	280	29[c]	1,250[c]	2.0	42	161	33	1.3
Ukraine	49.1	−0.5	85	35.2	720	204	4,150	10.0	68	16	0[d]	353.6
United Kingdom	59.9	0.4	249	1,451.4	24,230	1,466	24,460	1.9	77	7	..	542.3
United States	284.0	1.2	31	9,900.7	34,870	9,902	34,870	0.3	77	9	..	5,447.6
Uruguay	3.4	0.7	19	19.0	5,670	29	8,710	−3.7	74	17	2	5.8
Uzbekistan	25.1	1.8	61	13.8	550	62	2,470	2.6	70	27	1	109.2
Venezuela, RB	24.6	2.1	28	117.2	4,760	145	5,890	0.7	73	24	7	155.4
Vietnam	79.5	1.7	244	32.6	410	169	2,130	4.7	69	34	7	43.9
Yemen, Rep.	18.0	3.8	34	8.3	460	14	770	−1.0	56	95	54	14.2
Yugoslavia, Fed. Rep.	10.6	0.1	108	..	..[h]	..	..	4.9	72	15	..	..
Zambia	10.3	2.5	14	3.3	320	8	790	3.2	38	186	22	1.6
Zimbabwe	12.8	2.0	33	6.2	480	30	2,340	−9.8	40	116	11	14.1
World	**6,132.8 s**	**1.4 w**	**47 w**	**31,500.0 t**	**5,140 w**	**46,403 t**	**7,570 w**	**0.2 w**	**66 w**	**78 w**	**.. w**	**22,825.0 s**
Low income	2,510.6	2.0	76	1,069.1	430	5,134	2,040	2.4	59	115	37	2,418.7
Middle income	2,667.2	1.2	40	4,922.0	1,850	15,235	5,710	1.7	69	39	14	8,830.1
Lower middle income	2,163.5	1.1	48	2,676.5	1,240	10,867	5,020	3.3	69	42	15	6,660.4
Upper middle income	503.7	1.3	24	2,247.7	4,460	4,397	8,730	−0.5	71	30	10	2,169.6
Low & middle income	5,177.8	1.5	52	5,990.3	1,160	20,338	3,930	1.5	64	85	25	11,248.8
East Asia & Pacific	1,825.2	1.2	115	1,649.4	900	7,383	4,040	4.5	69	45	15	4,021.6
Europe & Central Asia	474.6	0.2	20	930.5	1,960	3,319	6,990	2.4	69	25	3	3,134.8
Latin America & Carib.	523.7	1.6	26	1,861.8	3,560	3,704	7,070	−1.1	70	37	12	1,309.8
Middle East & N. Africa	300.7	2.1	27	601.3	2,000	1,544	5,230	..	68	54	35	1,076.0
South Asia	1,379.8	1.9	289	615.6	450	3,176	2,300	2.5	62	96	45	1,194.4
Sub-Saharan Africa	673.9	2.6	29	317.0	470	1,094	1,620	0.7	47	162	39	512.2
High income	955.0	0.7	31	25,506.4	26,710	26,431	27,680	0.6	78	7	..	11,576.2

a. Preliminary World Bank estimates calculated using the World Bank Atlas method. b. Purchasing power parity; see the Technical Notes. c. The estimate is based on regression; others are extrapolated from the latest International Comparison Programme benchmark estimates. d. Less than 0.5. e. Estimated to be low income ($745 or less). f. GNI and GNI per capita estimates include the French Overseas departments of French Guiana, Guadeloupe, Martinique, and Réunion. g. Data refer to mainland Tanzania only. h. Estimated to be lower middle income ($745 to $2,975).

Table 2. Poverty and income distribution

Economy	Survey year	Population below the poverty line (%)			Survey year	Population below $1 a day %	Poverty gap at $1 a day %	Population below $2 a day %	Poverty gap at $2 a day %	Survey year	Gini index	Lowest 10%	Highest 10%
		Rural	Urban	National									
Albania	1996	..	15	..		..	..	..	..		..	..	..
Algeria	1995	30.3	14.7	22.6	1995	<2	<0.5	15.1	3.6	1995 a,b	35.3	2.8	26.8
Angola		..	..	..		..	..	..	..		..	..	..
Argentina	1993	..	..	17.6		..	..	..	..		..	..	..
Armenia		..	..	..	1996	7.8	1.7	34.0	11.3	1996 a,b	44.4	2.3	35.2
Australia		..	..	..		..	..	..	..	1994 c,d	35.2	2.0	25.4
Austria		..	..	..		..	..	..	..	1995 c,d	31.0	2.5	22.5
Azerbaijan	1995	..	..	68.1	1995	<2	<0.5	9.6	2.3	1995 c,d	36.0	2.8	27.8
Bangladesh	1995–96	39.8	14.3	35.6	1996	29.1	5.9	77.8	31.8	1995–96 a,b	33.6	3.9	28.6
Belarus	2000	..	..	41.9	1998	<2	<0.5	<2	<0.5	1998 a,b	21.7	5.1	20.0
Belgium		..	..	..		..	..	..	..	1996 c,d	28.7	3.2	23.0
Benin	1995	..	..	33.0		..	..	..	..		..	..	..
Bolivia	1995	79.1	..	..	1999	14.4	5.4	34.3	14.9	1999 a,b	44.7	1.3	32.0
Botswana		..	..	..	1985–86	33.3	12.5	61.4	30.7		..	..	..
Brazil	1990	32.6	13.1	17.4	1998	11.6	3.9	26.5	11.6	1998 c,d	60.7	0.7	48.0
Bulgaria		..	..	..	1997	<2	<0.5	21.9	4.2	1997 c,d	26.4	4.5	22.8
Burkina Faso		..	..	..	1994	61.2	25.5	85.8	50.9	1998 a,b	55.1	2.0	46.8
Burundi	1990	..	..	36.2		..	..	..	..	1998 a,b	42.5	1.8	32.9
Cambodia	1997	40.1	21.1	36.1		..	..	..	..	1997 a,b	40.4	2.9	33.8
Cameroon	1984	32.4	44.4	40.0	1996	33.4	11.8	64.4	31.2	1996 a,b	47.7	1.9	36.6
Canada		..	..	..		..	..	..	..	1994 c,d	31.5	2.8	23.8
Central African Republic		..	..	..	1993	66.6	38.1	84.0	58.4	1993 a,b	61.3	0.7	47.7
Chad	1995–96	67.0	63.0	64.0		..	..	..	..		..	..	..
Chile	1998	..	..	21.2	1998	<2	<0.5	8.7	2.3	1998 c,d	56.7	1.3	45.6
China	1998	4.6	<2	4.6	1999	18.8	4.4	52.6	20.9	1998 c,d	40.3	2.4	30.4
Hong Kong, China		..	..	..		..	..	..	..	1996 c,d	52.2	1.8	43.5
Colombia	1992	31.2	8.0	17.7	1998	19.7	10.8	36.0	19.4	1996 c,d	57.1	1.1	46.1
Congo, Dem. Rep.		..	..	..		..	..	..	..		..	..	..
Congo, Rep.		..	..	..		..	..	..	..		..	..	..
Costa Rica	1992	25.5	19.2	22.0	1998	12.6	6.2	26.0	12.8	1997 c,d	45.9	1.7	34.6
Côte d'Ivoire	1995	..	..	36.8	1995	12.3	2.4	49.4	16.8	1995 a,b	36.7	3.1	28.8
Croatia		..	..	..	1998	<2	<0.5	<2	<0.5	1998 c,d	29.0	3.7	23.3
Czech Republic		..	..	..	1996	<2	<0.5	<2	<0.5	1996 c,d	25.4	4.3	22.4
Denmark		..	..	..		..	..	..	..	1992 c,d	24.7	3.6	20.5
Dominican Republic	1992	29.8	10.9	20.6	1996	3.2	0.7	16.0	5.0	1998 c,d	47.4	2.1	37.9
Ecuador	1994	47.0	25.0	35.0	1995	20.2	5.8	52.3	21.2	1995 a,b	43.7	2.2	33.8
Egypt, Arab Rep.	1995–96	23.3	22.5	22.9	1995	3.1	<0.5	52.7	13.9	1995 a,b	28.9	4.4	25.0
El Salvador	1992	55.7	43.1	48.3	1998	21.0	7.8	44.5	20.6	1998 c,d	52.2	1.2	39.5
Eritrea	1993–94	..	..	53.0		..	..	..	..		..	..	..
Estonia	1995	14.7	6.8	8.9	1998	<2	<0.5	5.2	0.8	1998 c,d	37.6	3.0	29.8
Ethiopia		..	..	..	1995	31.3	8.0	76.4	32.9	1995 a,b	40.0	3.0	33.7
Finland		..	..	..		..	..	..	..	1991 c,d	25.6	4.2	21.6
France		..	..	..		..	..	..	..	1995 c,d	32.7	2.8	25.1
Georgia	1997	9.9	12.1	11.1	1996	<2	<0.5	<2	<0.5	1996 c,d	37.1	2.3	27.9
Germany		..	..	..		..	..	..	..	1994 c,d	30.0	3.3	23.7
Ghana	1992	34.3	26.7	31.4	1999	44.8	17.3	78.5	40.8	1999 a,b	40.7	2.2	30.1
Greece		..	..	..		..	..	..	..	1993 c,d	32.7	3.0	25.3
Guatemala	1989	71.9	33.7	57.9	1998	10.0	2.2	33.8	11.8	1998 c,d	55.8	1.6	46.0
Guinea	1994	..	..	40.0		..	..	..	..	1994 a,b	40.3	2.6	32.0
Haiti	1995	66.0	..	..		..	..	..	..		..	..	..
Honduras	1993	51.0	57.0	53.0	1998	24.3	11.9	45.1	23.5	1998 c,d	56.3	0.6	42.7
Hungary	1993	..	..	8.6	1998	<2	<0.5	7.3	1.7	1998 a,b	24.4	4.1	20.5
India	1994	36.7	30.5	35.0	1997	44.2	12.0	86.2	41.4	1997 a,b	37.8	3.5	33.5
Indonesia	1999	..	..	27.1	1999	12.9	1.9	65.5	21.5	1999 a,b	31.7	4.0	26.7
Iran, Islamic Rep.		..	..	..		..	..	..	..		..	..	..
Ireland		..	..	..		..	..	..	..	1987 c,d	35.9	2.5	27.4
Israel		..	..	..		..	..	..	..	1997 c,d	38.1	2.4	28.3
Italy		..	..	..		..	..	..	..	1995 c,d	27.3	3.5	21.8
Jamaica	2000	..	..	18.7	1996	3.2	0.7	25.2	6.9	2000 a,b	37.9	2.7	30.3
Japan		..	..	..		..	..	..	..	1993 c,d	24.9	4.8	21.7
Jordan	1997	..	..	11.7	1997	<2	<0.5	7.4	1.4	1997 a,b	36.4	3.3	29.8
Kazakhstan	1996	39.0	30.0	34.6	1996	<2	<0.5	15.3	3.9	1996 a,b	35.4	2.7	26.3
Kenya	1992	46.4	29.3	42.0	1994	26.5	9.0	62.3	27.5	1997 a,b	44.9	2.4	36.1
Korea, Rep.		..	..	..	1993	<2	<0.5	<2	<0.5	1993 a,b	31.6	2.9	24.3
Kuwait		..	..	..		..	..	..	..		..	..	..
Kyrgyz Republic	1997	64.5	28.5	51.0		..	..	..	..	1999 a,b	34.6	3.2	27.2
Lao PDR	1993	53.0	24.0	46.1	1997	26.3	6.3	73.2	29.6	1997 a,b	37.0	3.2	30.6
Latvia		..	..	..	1998	<2	<0.5	8.3	2.0	1998 c,d	32.4	2.9	25.9
Lebanon		..	..	..		..	..	..	..		..	..	..
Lesotho	1993	53.9	27.8	49.2	1993	43.1	20.3	65.7	38.1	1986–87 a,b	56.0	0.9	43.4
Lithuania		..	..	..	1996	<2	<0.5	7.8	2.0	1996 a,b	32.4	3.1	25.6
Macedonia, FYR		..	..	..		..	..	..	..		..	..	..
Madagascar	1993–94	77.0	47.0	70.0	1999	49.1	18.3	83.3	44.0	1999 a,b	38.1	2.6	28.6
Malawi	1990–91	..	..	54.0		..	..	..	..		..	..	..
Malaysia	1989	..	..	15.5		..	..	..	..	1997 c,d	49.2	1.7	38.4

Note: For data comparability and coverage, see the technical notes.

| | National poverty lines | | | | | International poverty line | | | | | | Percentage share of income or consumption | |
| | Population below the poverty line (%) | | | | | | | | | | | | |
Economy	Survey year	Rural	Urban	National	Survey year	Population below $1 a day %	Poverty gap at $1 a day %	Population below $2 a day %	Poverty gap at $2 a day %	Survey year	Gini index	Lowest 10%	Highest 10%
Mali		..	..	..	1994	72.8	37.4	90.6	60.5	1994 [a,b]	50.5	1.8	40.4
Mauritania	1989–90	..	..	57.0	1995	28.6	9.1	68.7	29.6	1995 [a,b]	37.3	2.5	28.4
Mexico	1988	..	..	10.1	1998	15.9	5.2	37.7	16.0	1998 [c,d]	53.1	1.3	41.7
Moldova	1997	26.7	..	23.3	1997	11.3	3.0	38.4	14.0	1997 [c,d]	40.6	2.2	30.7
Mongolia	1995	33.1	38.5	36.3	1995	13.9	3.1	50.0	17.5	1995 [a,b]	33.2	2.9	24.5
Morocco	1998–99	27.2	12.0	19.0	1990–91	<2	<0.5	7.5	1.3	1998–99 [a,b]	39.5	2.6	30.9
Mozambique		..	..	..	1996	37.9	12.0	78.4	36.8	1996–97 [a,b]	39.6	2.5	31.7
Myanmar		..	..	..									
Namibia		..	..	..	1993	34.9	14.0	55.8	30.4				
Nepal	1995–96	44.0	23.0	42.0	1995	37.7	9.7	82.5	37.5	1995–96 [a,b]	36.7	3.2	29.8
Netherlands		..	..	..		..	..	..	..	1994 [c,d]	32.6	2.8	25.1
New Zealand		..	..	..		..	..	..	..				
Nicaragua	1993	76.1	31.9	50.3						1998 [a,b]	60.3	0.7	48.8
Niger	1989–93	66.0	52.0	63.0	1995	61.4	33.9	85.3	54.8	1995 [a,b]	50.5	0.8	35.4
Nigeria	1992–93	36.4	30.4	34.1	1997	70.2	34.9	90.8	59.0	1996–97 [a,b]	50.6	1.6	40.8
Norway		..	..	..		..	..	..	..	1995 [c,d]	25.8	4.1	21.8
Pakistan	1991	36.9	28.0	34.0	1996	31.0	6.2	84.7	35.0	1996–97 [a,b]	31.2	4.1	27.6
Panama	1997	64.9	15.3	37.3	1998	14.0	5.9	29.0	13.8	1997 [a,b]	48.5	1.2	35.7
Papua New Guinea		..	..	..						1996 [a,b]	50.9	1.7	40.5
Paraguay	1991	28.5	19.7	21.8	1998	19.5	9.8	49.3	26.3	1998 [c,d]	57.7	0.5	43.8
Peru	1997	64.7	40.4	49.0	1996	15.5	5.4	41.4	17.1	1996 [c,d]	46.2	1.6	35.4
Philippines	1997	50.7	21.5	36.8		..	..	..	..	1997 [a,b]	46.2	2.3	36.6
Poland	1993	..	..	23.8	1998	<2	<0.5	<2	<0.5	1998 [a,b]	31.6	3.2	24.7
Portugal		..	..	..	1994	<2	<0.5	<2	<0.5	1994–95 [c,d]	35.6	3.1	28.4
Romania	1994	27.9	20.4	21.5	1994	2.8	0.8	27.5	6.9	1994 [a,b]	31.1	3.2	25.0
Russian Federation	1994	..	..	30.9	1998	7.1	1.4	25.1	8.7	1998 [a,b]	48.7	1.7	38.7
Rwanda	1993	..	..	51.2	1983–85	35.7	7.7	84.6	36.7	1983–85 [a,b]	28.9	4.2	24.2
Saudi Arabia		..	..	..		..	..	..	..				
Senegal	1992	40.4	..	33.4	1995	26.3	7.0	67.8	28.2	1995 [a,b]	41.3	2.6	33.5
Sierra Leone	1989	76.0	53.0	68.0	1989	57.0	39.5	74.5	51.8	1989 [a,b]	62.9	0.5	43.6
Singapore		..	..	..									
Slovak Republic		..	..	..	1992	<2	<0.5	<2	<0.5	1992 [c,d]	19.5	5.1	18.2
Slovenia		..	..	..	1998	<2	<0.5	<2	<0.5	1998 [a,b]	28.4	3.9	23.0
South Africa		..	..	..	1993	11.5	1.8	35.8	13.4	1993–94 [a,b]	59.3	1.1	45.9
Spain		..	..	..		..	..	..	..	1990 [c,d]	32.5	2.8	25.2
Sri Lanka	1995–96	..	..	25.0	1995	6.6	1.0	45.4	13.5	1995 [a,b]	34.4	3.5	28.0
Sweden		..	..	..		..	..	..	..	1992 [c,d]	25.0	3.7	20.1
Switzerland		..	..	..		..	..	..	..	1992 [c,d]	33.1	2.6	25.2
Syrian Arab Republic		..	..	..		..	..	..	..				
Tajikistan		..	..	..		..	..	..	..	1998 [a,b]	34.7	3.2	25.2
Tanzania	1993	49.7	24.4	41.6	1993	19.9	4.8	59.7	23.0	1993 [a,b]	38.2	2.8	30.1
Thailand	1992	15.5	10.2	13.1	1998	<2	<0.5	28.2	7.1	1998 [a,b]	41.4	2.8	32.4
Togo	1987–89	..	..	32.3		..	..	..	..				
Tunisia	1990	21.6	8.9	14.1	1995	<2	<0.5	10.0	2.3	1995 [a,b]	41.7	2.3	31.8
Turkey		..	..	..	1994	2.4	0.5	18.0	5.0	1994 [a,b]	41.5	2.3	32.3
Turkmenistan		..	..	..	1998	12.1	2.6	44.0	15.4	1998 [a,b]	40.8	2.6	31.7
Uganda	1993	..	..	55.0		..	..	..	..	1996 [a,b]	37.4	3.0	29.8
Ukraine	1995	..	..	31.7	1999	2.9	0.6	31.0	8.0	1999 [a,b]	29.0	3.7	23.2
United Kingdom		..	..	..		..	..	..	..	1995 [c,d]	36.8	2.3	27.7
United States		..	..	..		..	..	..	..	1997 [c,d]	40.8	1.8	30.5
Uruguay		..	..	..	1989	<2	<0.5	6.6	1.9	1989 [c,d]	42.3	2.1	32.7
Uzbekistan		..	..	..	1993	3.3	0.5	26.5	7.3	1998 [c,d]	44.7	1.2	32.8
Venezuela, RB	1989	..	..	31.3	1998	23.0	10.8	47.0	23.0	1998 [c,d]	49.5	0.8	36.5
Vietnam	1993	57.2	25.9	50.9		..	..	..	..	1998 [a,b]	36.1	3.6	29.9
Yemen, Rep.	1992	19.2	18.6	19.1	1998	15.7	4.5	45.2	15.0	1998 [a,b]	33.4	3.0	25.9
Yugoslavia, Fed. Rep.		..	..	..		..	..	..	..				
Zambia	1993	..	..	86.0	1998	63.7	32.7	87.4	55.4	1998 [a,b]	52.6	1.1	41.0
Zimbabwe	1990–91	31.0	10.0	25.5	1990–91	36.0	9.6	64.2	29.4	1995 [a,b]	50.1	2.0	40.4

a. Refers to expenditure shares by percentiles of population. b. Ranked by per capita expenditure. c. Refers to income shares by percentiles of population. d. Ranked by per capita income.

Table 3. Economic activity

| | Gross domestic product | | Agricultural productivity Agr. Value added per agricultural worker 1995 dollars | | Value added as % of GDP | | | Household final cons. expenditure % of GDP | General gov't. final cons. expenditure % of GDP | Gross capital formation % of GDP | External balance of goods and services % of GDP | GDP implicit deflator |
	Millions of dollars 2001	Avg. annual % growth 1990–2001	1988–90	1998–2000	Agricultural 2001	Industry 2001	Services 2001	2001	2001	2001	2001	Avg. annual % growth 1990–2001
Albania	4,114	3.7	1,136	1,978	49	27	24	91	13	19	–23	34.4
Algeria	53,009	2.0	1,776	1,962	12	76	12	41	15	28	16	16.9
Angola	9,471	2.0	226	121	8	67	25	54	..a	34	12	658.8
Argentina	268,773	3.7	7,284	10,246	5	28	68	71	14	16	–1	4.2
Armenia	2,012	–0.7	..	5,477	26	34	40	99	9	19	–26	171.5
Australia	368,571	4.0	24,281	33,765	3	26	71	60	19	24	–2	1.6
Austria	188,742	2.1	15,575	28,523	2	33	65	57	20	24	0	1.9
Azerbaijan	5,692	2.7	..	708	20	38	42	59	10	27	4	59.1
Bangladesh	46,652	4.9	251	296	23	25	52	79	5	23	–7	3.9
Belarus	12,070	–0.8	..	1,985	16	42	42	70	14	18	–2	318.1
Belgium	227,618	2.1	29,807	55,874	2	27	72	54	21	22	3	1.9
Benin	2,269	4.8	397	586	38	15	47	80	12	20	–13	7.6
Bolivia	7,960	3.8	956	1,039	22	15	63	74	16	18	–8	7.9
Botswana	5,142	5.2	773	688	4	44	52	58	28	20	–6	8.9
Brazil	502,509	2.8	2,985	4,356	8	36	56	60	20	21	–1	168.1
Bulgaria	12,714	–1.5	3,413	6,252	14	28	58	69	19	17	–5	92.9
Burkina Faso	2,328	4.9	148	180	35	17	47	74	16	29	–18	3.5
Burundi	689	–2.2	183	141	50	19	31	90	14	7	–11	12.6
Cambodia	3,384	4.8	398	403	37	20	42	92	..a	15	–7	21.7
Cameroon	8,591	2.1	842	1,104	46	21	33	69	11	18	2	4.8
Canada	677,178	3.0	25,362	36,597	..	..	..	58	19	20	3	1.4
Central African Republic	978	2.1	381	469	55	21	25	78	11	14	–3	4.3
Chad	1,603	2.5	173	227	39	14	48	91	8	43	–42	6.7
Chile	63,545	6.4	4,853	5,712	11	34	56	63	12	23	1	6.8
China	1,159,017	10.0	227	321	15	52	33	48	12	39	1	6.2
Hong Kong, China	162,642	3.9	..	..	0	14	85	58	10	28	5	3.3
Colombia	83,432	2.7	3,889	3,448	13	30	57	68	19	12	1	20.1
Congo, Dem. Rep.	..	–5.1	248	252	..	..	..	..	..	..	..	1,423.1
Congo, Rep.	2,751	–0.1	489	475	6	67	26	28	12	25	35	10.4
Costa Rica	16,156	5.1	3,721	5,140	9	29	62	70	14	18	–2	16.3
Côte d'Ivoire	10,411	3.1	937	1,097	24	22	54	74	9	10	7	8.4
Croatia	19,821	1.1	..	8,839	8	32	59	60	21	26	–7	72.2
Czech Republic	56,424	1.1	..	5,637	4	41	55	54	20	30	–4	10.6
Denmark	162,817	2.5	29,551	54,090	3	26	71	48	25	22	5	2.3
Dominican Republic	21,211	6.0	2,010	2,769	11	34	55	78	8	24	–10	9.1
Ecuador	17,982	1.7	1,489	1,773	11	33	56	68	10	25	–3	38.5
Egypt, Arab Rep.	97,545	4.6	997	1,240	17	34	49	72	10	23	–5	7.7
El Salvador	13,963	4.5	1,619	1,710	10	30	60	88	10	17	–15	6.9
Eritrea	681	3.1	..	..	17	29	54	146	..a	40	–85	10.4
Estonia	5,281	0.2	..	3,698	6	28	66	55	21	29	–5	45.4
Ethiopia	6,366	4.9	..	138	52	11	37	83	17	17	–16	6.1
Finland	121,987	3.0	23,997	36,557	4	34	62	50	21	20	10	2.0
France	1,302,793	1.8	30,641	53,785	3	26	71	55	23	21	1	1.5
Georgia	3,138	–5.6	..	..	21	23	57	89	9	19	–16	279.0
Germany	1,873,854	1.5	16,878	29,553	1	31	68	58	19	23	0	1.9
Ghana	5,301	4.2	543	558	36	25	39	79	16	24	–18	26.6
Greece	116,347	2.3	10,525	13,400	8	24	68	71	15	22	–8	8.5
Guatemala	20,629	4.1	1,932	2,112	23	20	58	88	5	16	–9	9.9
Guinea	2,885	4.1	249	292	25	38	37	77	6	25	–8	5.0
Haiti	3,771	–0.4	430	334	28	20	51	104	..a	11	–15	19.3
Honduras	6,386	3.1	855	979	18	32	51	66	13	35	–14	18.0
Hungary	52,361	1.9	5,133	5,016	..	..	..	64	10	31	–4	18.3
India	477,555	5.9	343	397	24	27	48	68	11	24	–3	7.7
Indonesia	145,306	3.8	674	734	16	47	37	67	7	17	9	15.8
Iran, Islamic Rep.	118,868	3.6	2,838	3,756	19	26	54	60	15	20	5	25.8
Ireland	101,185	7.6	..	..	4	36	60	49	14	23	14	3.6
Israel	110,386	5.1	..	..	..	..	..	59	29	19	–7	10.0
Italy	1,090,910	1.6	13,916	24,827	3	30	68	60	18	20	1	3.6
Jamaica	7,784	0.6	1,027	1,559	6	31	63	66	16	29	–11	22.0
Japan	4,245,191	1.3	25,293	30,086	1	32	66	56	16	26	2	0.0
Jordan	8,829	4.8	1,810	1,422	2	25	73	80	24	22	–26	2.9
Kazakhstan	22,635	–2.8	..	1,421	9	48	43	70	14	13	3	168.6
Kenya	10,419	2.0	264	225	21	19	60	85	11	13	–9	13.0
Korea, Rep.	422,167	5.7	7,159	12,374	4	41	54	61	10	27	2	4.5
Kuwait	37,783	3.2	..	..	..	..	..	41	22	11	26	3.0
Kyrgyz Republic	1,525	–2.9	..	1,583	38	27	35	65	20	15	0	95.2
Lao PDR	1,712	6.4	457	578	53	23	24	..	..	..	..	28.4
Latvia	7,549	–2.2	..	2,499	5	26	69	59	22	28	–9	42.0
Lebanon	16,709	5.4	..	29,241	12	22	66	94	18	19	–31	15.1
Lesotho	789	3.9	595	540	20	46	34	91	27	33	–52	9.6
Lithuania	11,834	–2.3	..	3,129	8	31	61	68	17	22	–6	63.3
Macedonia, FYR	3,445	–0.2	..	4,095	11	31	58	71	24	19	–14	66.0
Madagascar	4,566	2.4	195	181	25	12	63	83	7	18	–8	17.8
Malawi	1,826	3.7	81	130	37	16	47	86	17	10	–14	33.0
Malaysia	87,540	6.5	5,680	6,519	8	50	42	45	12	24	18	3.6

Note: For data comparability and coverage, see the technical notes. Figures in italics are for years other than those specified.

| | Gross domestic product | | Agricultural productivity Agr. Value added per agricultural worker 1995 dollars | | Value added as % of GDP | | | Household final cons. expenditure % of GDP | General gov't. final cons. expenditure % of GDP | Gross capital formation % of GDP | External balance of goods and services % of GDP | GDP implicit deflator Avg. annual % growth |
	Millions of dollars 2001	Avg. annual % growth 1990–2001	1988–90	1998–2000	Agricultural 2001	Industry 2001	Services 2001	2001	2001	2001	2001	1990–2001
Mali	2,629	4.1	252	285	38	26	36	78	13	20	−10	6.9
Mauritania	1,030	4.2	391	480	21	29	50	68	16	26	−10	6.2
Mexico	617,817	3.1	1,522	1,767	4	27	69	70	12	21	−2	18.2
Moldova	1,478	−8.4	..	1,299	28	21	52	85	15	21	−21	103.1
Mongolia	1,049	1.2	1,125	1,300	30	17	53	67	19	30	−16	51.4
Morocco	33,733	2.5	1,847	1,785	16	32	53	62	18	25	−5	2.6
Mozambique	3,561	7.5	123	134	22	26	52	74	12	31	−18	28.5
Myanmar	..	..	..	..	60	9	31	87	..ᵃ	13	0	25.2
Namibia	3,168	4.1	1,031	1,468	11	28	61	54	29	24	−7	9.4
Nepal	5,525	4.9	188	188	38	23	39	72	10	26	−8	7.8
Netherlands	374,976	2.8	34,080	53,819	3	27	70	50	23	22	5	2.1
New Zealand	48,277	2.9	22,341	27,106	..	..	..	64	16	21	−1	1.5
Nicaragua	..	2.8	1,251	1,813	..	..	..	..	..	..	..	..
Niger	1,939	2.6	204	214	39	18	44	84	13	13	−10	5.8
Nigeria	41,237	2.5	499	672	30	46	25	67	13	23	−4	26.5
Norway	165,458	3.5	21,200	33,305	2	43	55	43	19	22	16	3.2
Pakistan	59,605	3.7	513	630	25	23	51	78	11	15	−4	9.7
Panama	10,170	3.8	2,192	2,632	7	17	77	61	15	30	−6	1.9
Papua New Guinea	2,959	3.6	666	767	26	42	32	64	14	19	3	7.3
Paraguay	6,926	2.0	3,261	3,508	21	27	52	83	10	22	−15	11.8
Peru	54,047	4.3	1,371	1,693	8	27	65	72	11	18	−1	23.3
Philippines	71,438	3.3	1,339	1,328	15	31	54	68	14	17	0	8.2
Poland	174,597	4.5	1,632	1,874	3	32	65	80	..ᵃ	27	−7	21.4
Portugal	108,479	2.7	5,307	7,235	4	31	66	63	20	28	−12	5.1
Romania	39,714	−0.3	2,367	3,592	12	37	51	73	13	19	−5	90.7
Russian Federation	309,951	−3.7	..	2,249	7	37	56	51	14	22	13	139.6
Rwanda	1,703	0.8	295	235	44	22	34	85	14	18	−16	13.1
Saudi Arabia	173,287	1.5	7,060	..	..	..	..	33	27	16	24	2.2
Senegal	4,620	3.9	344	304	18	27	55	78	10	20	−8	4.2
Sierra Leone	749	−2.8	612	336	49	31	21	85	16	9	−9	27.1
Singapore	92,252	7.8	27,176	49,905	0	34	66	40	10	31	18	1.3
Slovak Republic	20,522	2.3	..	..	4	30	66	55	17	35	−7	10.0
Slovenia	18,810	2.9	..	31,539	3	38	58	55	21	28	−4	18.3
South Africa	113,274	2.1	3,586	3,866	3	31	66	63	19	15	3	9.3
Spain	577,539	2.6	16,127	21,824	4	31	66	59	17	26	−2	3.8
Sri Lanka	16,346	5.1	694	753	19	26	55	70	10	26	−7	9.1
Sweden	210,108	2.0	26,070	34,556	..	..	..	50	26	18	5	2.0
Switzerland	247,362	0.9	..	..	..	..	..	61	14	20	5	1.2
Syrian Arab Republic	17,938	5.5	2,056	2,890	24	30	46	63	13	19	5	6.4
Tajikistan	1,058	−8.7	..	1,236	19	26	55	76	8	20	−4	202.3
Tanzaniaᵇ	9,119	3.1	178	189	45	16	39	83	10	19	−11	20.0
Thailand	114,760	3.8	778	909	10	40	50	61	9	24	5	3.9
Togo	1,259	2.2	451	538	39	21	40	87	9	20	−16	6.6
Tunisia	20,035	4.7	2,228	3,083	12	29	59	62	14	28	−4	4.3
Turkey	147,627	3.3	1,847	1,878	15	27	58	69	13	15	2	74.1
Turkmenistan	5,962	−2.8	..	1,229	27	50	23	34	16	40	10	328.0
Uganda	5,707	6.8	298	353	42	19	38	88	12	19	−20	11.3
Ukraine	37,588	−7.9	..	1,345	15	41	45	59	18	19	3	220.9
United Kingdom	1,406,310	2.6	28,660	34,938	1	29	70	65	19	18	−2	2.8
United States	10,171,400	3.5	..	..	..	..	..	68	14	21	−3	2.0
Uruguay	18,429	2.9	6,833	9,100	6	27	67	75	13	14	−1	27.7
Uzbekistan	11,270	0.0	..	1,035	36	21	43	69	18	11	2	211.6
Venezuela, RB	124,948	1.5	4,449	5,143	5	50	45	68	8	19	5	42.8
Vietnam	32,903	7.6	181	240	24	37	39	69	6	27	−2	14.0
Yemen, Rep.	9,098	5.6	333	377	15	42	43	65	14	18	2	21.3
Yugoslavia, Fed. Rep.	10,883	0.7	..	..	..	..	..	81	23	16	−20	54.4
Zambia	3,647	0.8	219	217	22	26	52	85	12	21	−17	48.1
Zimbabwe	9,057	1.8	295	366	18	24	58	72	19	8	1	28.4
World	**31,283,839 t**	**2.7 w**	**.. w**	**887 w**	**5 w**	**31 w**	**64 w**	**61 w**	**17 w**	**22 w**	**1 w**	
Low income	1,083,360	3.4	361	417	23	32	45	70	11	20	−1	
Middle income	5,097,044	3.4	633	802	10	38	52	59	15	25	1	
Lower middle income	2,733,167	3.7	395	543	12	41	46	57	13	27	3	
Upper middle income	2,360,861	3.1	..	3,661	7	35	59	62	17	22	−1	
Low & middle income	6,179,333	3.4	514	620	12	37	51	61	14	24	1	
East Asia & Pacific	1,664,211	7.5	..	..	14	48	37	53	11	31	4	
Europe & Central Asia	986,652	−0.9	..	2,099	10	34	56	60	15	21	4	
Latin America & Carib.	1,943,350	3.1	2,595	3,165	7	34	59	64	17	21	−1	
Middle East & N. Africa	652,277	3.0	..	..	..	..	..	52	18	20	10	
South Asia	615,308	5.5	345	401	24	26	49	70	10	23	−3	
Sub-Saharan Africa	315,269	2.6	386	362	15	29	57	70	16	17	−2	
High income	25,103,679	2.5	..	..	..	..	..	61	17	22	0	

a. Data on general government final consumption expenditure are not available separately; they are included in household final consumption expenditure. b. Data cover mainland Tanzania only.

Table 4.   Trade, aid, and finance

	Merchandise trade		Manufactured exports	High technology exports	Current account balance	Net private capital flows	Foreign direct investment	Official development assistance[a]	External debt		Domestic credit provided by banking sector
	exports	imports	% of total merchandise exports	% of manufactured exports					Total	Present value	
	Millions of dollars 2001	Millions of dollars 2001	2000	2000	Millions of dollars 2001	Millions of dollars 2000	Millions of dollars 2000	Dollars per capita 2000	Millions of dollars 2000	% of GNI 2000	% of GDP 2001
Albania	280	1,210	82	1	−246	142	143	93	784	13	46.5
Algeria	20,050	9,700	2	4	..	−1,212	10	5	25,002	50	30.2
Angola	7,350	3,950	..	..	−414	1,206	1,698	23	10,146	137	−0.5
Argentina	26,655	20,311	32	9	−8,970	16,619	11,665	2	146,172	56	37.1
Armenia	335	890	43	5	−278	159	140	57	898	31	10.0
Australia	63,386	63,886	29	15	−15,330	..	11,527	..	..	..	94.0
Austria	70,293	73,857	83	14	−4,027	..	9,066	..	..	..	125.9
Azerbaijan	2,460	1,725	8	4	−73	175	130	17	1,184	20	5.7
Bangladesh	6,300	8,154	91	0	−1,284	269	280	9	15,609	20	38.7
Belarus	7,470	8,310	67	4	−273	123	90	4	851	8	19.2
Belgium	188,862[b]	181,705[b]	78[b]	10	13,037	..	17,902[b]	..	..	..	121.5
Benin	380	670	3	0	−97	30	30	38	1,598	45c	4.8
Bolivia	1,257	1,673	29	..	−464	923	733	57	5,762	34c	63.0
Botswana	2,310	2,360	..	..	517	27	30	19	413	6	−75.2
Brazil	58,223	58,265	59	19	−23,208	45,672	32,779	2	237,953	39	59.2
Bulgaria	5,125	7,315	57	..	−701	1,114	1,002	38	10,026	82	22.0
Burkina Faso	210	540	..	..	−77	10	10	30	1,332	31c	16.3
Burundi	35	140	0	..	−33	12	12	14	1,100	97	32.7
Cambodia	1,531	1,476	..	..	−19	126	126	33	2,357	62	6.5
Cameroon	1,770	1,500	5	1	−171	−21	31	26	9,241	75	16.4
Canada	262,240	228,250	64	19	18,884	..	62,758	..	..	..	93.2
Central African Republic	150	120	..	..	16	5	5	20	872	57	12.1
Chad	180	360	..	..	−660	14	15	17	1,116	42	12.5
Chile	17,665	17,184	16	3	−1,782	4,833	3,675	3	36,978	51	76.7
China	266,155	243,567	88	19	19,404	58,295	38,399	1	149,800	13	132.7
Hong Kong, China	190,676[d]	202,252	95[d]	23	8,827	..	..	1	..	..	142.0
Colombia	12,414	12,947	34	7	−1,693	3,130	2,376	4	34,081	41	34.3
Congo, Dem. Rep.	420	310	..	..	..	1	1	4	11,645	..	..
Congo, Rep.	2,395	940	..	..	..	14	14	11	4,887	206	13.5
Costa Rica	5,010	6,564	66	..	−649	610	409	3	4,466	31	33.3
Côte d'Ivoire	3,850	2,860	14	..	64	−47	106	22	12,138	117c	21.9
Croatia	4,659	9,044	73	8	−623	2,451	926	15	12,120	65	51.9
Czech Republic	33,370	36,505	88	8	−2,237	3,299	4,583	43	21,299	43	51.8
Denmark	51,812	45,551	64	21	4,102	..	34,192	..	..	..	56.7
Dominican Republic	5,550	8,870	..	..	−1,026	1,142	953	7	4,598	23	41.7
Ecuador	4,474	5,299	10	6	928	904	710	12	13,281	108	0.0
Egypt, Arab Rep.	4,095	13,060	37	0	−34	1,967	1,235	21	28,957	23	104.6
El Salvador	2,865	5,027	48	6	−418	338	185	29	4,023	29	42.3
Eritrea	..	..	..	..	−325	35	35	43	311	26	..
Estonia	3,505	4,550	73	30	−353	485	387	47	3,280	66	48.0
Ethiopia	410	..	10	0	−264	42	50	11	5,481	52	57.0
Finland	43,304	32,043	85	27	7,859	..	9,125	..	..	..	63.2
France	319,470	322,934	81	24	25,644	..	43,173	..	..	..	108.6
Georgia	290	810	..	..	−209	155	131	34	1,633	42	20.5
Germany	569,584	493,045	85	18	3,815	..	189,178	..	..	..	145.3
Ghana	1,700	3,030	15	14	−314	71	110	32	6,657	81c	40.8
Greece	8,764	27,359	50	9	−9,400	..	1,083	..	..	..	101.8
Guatemala	2,430	5,635	32	8	−1,049	178	230	23	4,622	23	15.4
Guinea	795	1,195	30	..	−155	63	63	21	3,388	80	9.4
Haiti	141	1,036	..	..	..	13	13	26	1,169	17	31.5
Honduras	1,270	2,990	33	2	−204	301	282	70	5,487	54	34.7
Hungary	30,780	33,925	86	26	−1,097	1,721	1,692	25	29,415	63	49.5
India	43,877	50,533	79	4	−3,493	8,771	2,315	1	99,062	0	53.8
Indonesia	56,716	31,170	57	16	7,985	−11,210	−4,550	8	141,803	96	61.1
Iran, Islamic Rep.	26,350	16,450	7	2	12,645	−610	39	2	7,953	7	46.2
Ireland	83,437	50,924	86	48	−1,043	..	22,778	..	..	..	113.1
Israel	29,019	35,123	94	25	−1,730	..	4,392	128	..	..	86.5
Italy	241,257	233,727	88	9	1,591	..	13,175	..	..	..	99.6
Jamaica	1,283	3,409	73	0	−275	898	456	4	4,287	59	23.4
Japan	404,686	350,095	94	28	89,280	..	8,227	..	..	..	308.7
Jordan	2,230	4,945	69	8	−235	455	558	113	8,226	90	89.7
Kazakhstan	8,750	6,445	20	10	158	1,900	1,250	13	6,664	39	11.4
Kenya	1,775	2,890	21	4	−429	53	111	17	6,295	46	45.6
Korea, Rep.	150,653	141,116	91	35	8,617	13,215	9,283	−4	134,417	28	110.4
Kuwait	16,234	6,963	20	1	8,566	..	16	1	..	..	82.2
Kyrgyz Republic	560	475	20	5	−10	−65	−2	44	1,829	109	9.7
Lao PDR	320	437	..	..	90	72	72	53	2,499	72	15.7
Latvia	2,030	3,535	56	4	−758	583	407	38	3,379	46	31.4
Lebanon	890	7,291	..	..	−3,984	2,028	298	45	10,311	61	201.9
Lesotho	260	750	..	..	−151	111	118	20	716	45	5.4
Lithuania	4,630	6,185	60	4	−574	799	379	28	4,855	43	16.0
Macedonia, FYR	1,170	1,630	66	1	−107	187	176	124	1,465	35	14.4
Madagascar	310	780	50	3	−260	83	83	21	4,701	79	16.1
Malawi	310	550	..	..	−524	45	45	43	2,716	89c	9.3
Malaysia	88,521	74,384	80	59	8,409	3,228	1,660	2	41,797	52	156.2
* Taiwan, China	122,902	107,243	95	39	9,316	..	..	0	..	..	..

Note: For data comparability and coverage, see the technical notes. Figures in italics are for years other than those specified.

| | Merchandise trade | | Manufactured exports | High technology exports | Current account balance | Net private capital flows | Foreign direct investment | Official development assistance[a] | External debt | | Domestic credit provided by banking sector |
| | exports | imports | % of total merchandise exports | % of manufactured exports | | | | | Total | Present value | |
	Millions of dollars 2001	Millions of dollars 2001	2000	2000	Millions of dollars 2001	Millions of dollars 2000	Millions of dollars 2000	Dollars per capita 2000	Millions of dollars 2000	% of GNI 2000	% of GDP 2001
Mali	485	770	..	..	..	76	76	33	2,956	58[c]	17.1
Mauritania	280	350	..	..	30	3	5	80	2,500	126	0.5
Mexico	158,542	176,162	83	22	−17,683	11,537	13,286	−1	150,288	28	24.7
Moldova	565	915	33	3	−103	209	128	29	1,233	84	27.5
Mongolia	250	461	..	..	−52	27	30	91	859	59	12.5
Morocco	7,100	10,830	64	12	−352	−293	10	15	17,944	49	87.2
Mozambique	490	1,025	10	2	−764	138	139	50	7,135	32[c]	13.3
Myanmar	1,760	2,461	..	..	−651	188	255	2	6,046	..	35.3
Namibia	1,630	1,720	..	..	204	..	..	86	..	..	48.7
Nepal	646	1,235	77	0	−293	−4	4	17	2,823	27	43.2
Netherlands	229,830	207,858	70	35	12,405	..	54,138	..	..	..	157.5
New Zealand	13,754	13,335	28	10	−1,587	..	3,209	..	..	..	120.0
Nicaragua	606	1,776	8	5	−493	395	254	111	7,019	..	..
Niger	265	430	2	5	−216	13	15	19	1,638	58[c]	8.0
Nigeria	19,150	10,260	0	13	4,926	908	1,082	1	34,134	74	11.3
Norway	57,856	32,361	18	17	24,078	..	5,882	..	..	..	46.5
Pakistan	9,209	10,206	85	0	−1,946	−53	308	5	32,091	45	44.7
Panama	972	3,017	16	0	−499	947	603	6	7,056	77	114.9
Papua New Guinea	1,805	1,072	2	42	−74	128	130	54	2,604	66	24.2
Paraguay	972	2,145	19	3	−202	−16	82	15	3,091	39	29.3
Peru	7,140	8,656	20	3	−1,628	1,553	680	16	28,560	55	25.7
Philippines	33,589	31,373	92	59	4,503	2,459	2,029	8	50,063	64	58.6
Poland	35,500	50,035	80	3	−2,452	13,195	9,342	36	63,561	37	37.3
Portugal	23,730	37,660	85	5	−10,080	..	6,227	..	..	..	152.0
Romania	11,450	15,515	77	6	−1,359	1,900	1,025	19	10,224	27	12.4
Russian Federation	103,210	53,500	22	14	29,156	2,200	2,714	11	160,300	60	24.3
Rwanda	77	260	..	..	−73	14	14	38	1,271	41	12.6
Saudi Arabia	68,200	32,100	7	0	14,502	..	..	1	..	..	68.4
Senegal	1,080	1,510	30	13	−297	106	107	44	3,372	56	24.7
Sierra Leone	28	166	..	..	..	1	1	36	1,273	132	52.1
Singapore	121,731[d]	115,961	86	63	21,797	..	6,390	0	..	..	89.6
Slovak Republic	12,630	14,765	85	4	−694	2,185	2,052	21	9,462	48	63.2
Slovenia	9,331	10,185	90	5	−66	..	176	31	..	..	49.5
South Africa	29,284[e]	28,700[e]	54[e]	1	−166	2,736	961	11	24,861	19	81.0
Spain	110,830	144,467	78	8	−15,082	..	36,023	..	..	..	126.2
Sri Lanka	4,900	6,100	75	3	−1,042	262	173	14	9,065	44	45.1
Sweden	75,198	62,470	85	22	6,696	..	22,125	..	..	..	79.3
Switzerland	82,064	84,077	91	19	32,542	..	17,902	..	..	..	173.3
Syrian Arab Republic	5,410	4,290	8	1	1,062	107	111	10	21,657	128	27.0
Tajikistan	575	775	..	..	−61	64	24	23	1,170	100	..
Tanzania	780	1,660	15	6	−998	182	193	31	7,445	50	10.1
Thailand	64,223	60,190	76	32	6,195	−1,383	3,366	11	79,675	64	112.0
Togo	432	620	31	0	−127	30	30	15	1,435	85	20.5
Tunisia	6,615	9,505	77	3	−937	966	752	23	10,610	57	73.5
Turkey	31,220	40,455	81	5	−9,819	11,416	982	5	116,209	57	71.1
Turkmenistan	2,560	2,105	7	5	412	473	130	6	2,259	..	30.7
Uganda	520	1,430	6	10	−889	231	220	37	3,408	16[c]	10.1
Ukraine	16,615	16,105	..	..	1,402	927	595	11	12,166	38	23.8
United Kingdom	273,462	332,523	82	32	−25,107	..	133,974	..	..	..	142.3
United States	730,897	1,180,497	83	34	−417,440	..	287,680	..	..	..	160.6
Uruguay	2,088	3,119	42	2	−557	574	298	5	8,196	42	54.3
Uzbekistan	2,655	2,715	..	..	−28	18	100	8	4,340	31	..
Venezuela, RB	28,610	18,775	9	3	4,364	5,454	4,464	3	38,196	32	15.5
Vietnam	15,100	16,000	..	..	507	581	1,298	22	12,787	36	39.5
Yemen, Rep.	4,130	2,450	1	0	1,107	−201	−201	15	5,615	48	2.9
Yugoslavia, Fed. Rep.	1,903	4,837	..	..	..	0	0	107[f]	11,960[g]	142	..
Zambia	880	760	..	..	−553	191	200	79	5,730	162	51.4
Zimbabwe	1,770	1,540	28	2	..	29	79	14	4,002	52	52.9
World	6,163,167 t	6,354,719 t	78 w	20 w	.. s	1,167,337 s	.. w	.. s			152.5 w
Low income	219,806	201,634	53	7		4,829	6,812	9	552,095		46.2
Middle income	1,326,040	1,266,001	59	13		207,538	150,572	8	1,798,508[h]		49.0
Lower middle income	705,744	661,566	61	13		92,195	61,925	7	909,722		91.3
Upper middle income	620,295	604,427	57	13		115,344	88,647	8	888,787[h]		46.2
Low & middle income	1,545,853	1,467,974	58	13		212,631	157,408	11	2,356,253[h]		48.4
East Asia & Pacific	531,552	466,380	80	30		52,478	42,847	5	498,536		120.4
Europe & Central Asia	325,397[i]	327,066[i]	53[i]	10		45,446	28,495	23	499,344		37.8
Latin America & Carib.	346,471	375,183	48	16		97,305	75,088	10	774,419		38.3
Middle East & N. Africa	185,847	138,431	16	3		1,074	1,209	16	203,785		72.3
South Asia	65,213	77,339	80	4		9,254	3,093	3	164,375		51.4
Sub-Saharan Africa	91,356	83,102	36	8		7,074	6,676	20	215,794		47.2
High income	4,617,275	4,885,097	83	23		..	1,009,929	..	..		172.1

a. Regional aggregates include data for economies that are not specified elsewhere. World and income group totals include aid not allocated by country or region.
b. Includes Luxembourg. c. Data are from debt sustainability analysis undertaken as part of the Heavily Indebted Poor Countries (HIPC) initiative. d. Includes re-exports.
e. Data on total exports and imports refer South Africa only. Data on export commodity shares refer to the South African Customs Union (Botswana, Lesotho, Namibia, South Africa, and Swaziland). f. Aid to the states of the former Socialist Federal Republic of Yugoslavia that is not otherwise specified is included in regional and income group aggregates. g. Data are estimates and reflect borrowing by the former Socialist Federal Republic of Yugoslavia that are not yet allocated to the successor republics. h. Includes data for Gibraltar not included in other tables. i. Data include the intratrade of the Baltic states and the Commonwealth of Independent States.

Table 1a. Key indicators for other economies

	Population			Gross national income (GNI)[a]		PPP gross national income (GNI)[b]		Gross domestic product per capita % growth 2000–2001	Life expectancy at birth Years 2000	Under-5 mortality rate Per 1,000 2000	Adult illiteracy rate % of people 15 and above 2000	Carbon dioxide emissions Thousands of tons 1998
	Thousands 2001	Avg. annual % growth 1990–2001	density people per sq. km 2001	Millions of dollars 2001	per capita dollars 2001	Millions of dollars 2001	per capita dollars 2001					
Afghanistan	27,248c	3.9	41.8	..	..d	..	..	..	43	279	..	1,037
American Samoa	65	..	327.2	..	..e	..	..	..	..	..	..	282
Andorra	67	..	148.9	..	..f	..	..	..	80	..	..	..
Antigua and Barbuda	68	0.6	155.7	621	9,070	676	9,870	-0.4	75	19	..	337
Aruba	104	4.2	547.4	..	..f	..	..	..	..	..	..	1,883
Bahamas, The	307	1.7	30.7	4,533	14,960	4,969	16,400	..	69	22	5	1,792
Bahrain	714	3.2	1035.3	6,247	9,370	9,605	14,410	..	73	11	12	18,688
Barbados	268	0.4	623.7	2,469	9,250	4,010	15,020	..	75	18	..	1,569
Belize	247	2.4	10.8	718	2,910	1,323	5,350	0.2	74	38	7	399
Bermuda	63	..	1260.0	..	..f	..	..	..	..	..	..	462
Bhutan	828	2.9	17.6	529	640	1,266g	1,530g	4.0	62	..	..	386
Bosnia and Herzegovina	4,060	-0.8	79.6	5,037	1,240	..	..	3.8	73	18	..	4,686
Brunei	345	2.7	65.5	..	..f	..	..	..	76	11	8	5,488
Cape Verde	454	2.6	112.6	596	1,310	2,211g	4,870g	0.4	69	48	26	121
Cayman Islands	35	..	134.6	..	..f	..	..	..	..	..	..	289
Channel Islands	149	0.4	768	..	..f	..	..	..	79	..	..	..
Comoros	572	2.6	256.5	217	380	922g	1,610g	-0.5	61	80	44	70
Cuba	11,222	0.5	102.2	..	..h	..	..	..	76	9	3	24,881
Cyprus	761	1.0	82.3	9,361	12,370	15,734g	20,780g	..	78	9	3	5,918
Djibouti	644	2.9	27.8	572	890	1,369	2,120	-0.3	46	178	35	366
Dominica	73	0.1	97.6	224	3,060	369	5,040	-5.0	76	..	..	84
Equatorial Guinea	469	2.6	16.7	327	700	2,644	5,640	-1.3	51	167	17	253
Faeroe Islands	45	..	32.1	..	..f	..	..	..	..	..	..	641
Fiji	824	1.0	45.1	1,755	2,130	4,231	5,140	1.1	69	21	7	721
French Polynesia	239	1.7	65.2	4,064	17,290	5,486g	23,340g	..	73	13	..	561
Gabon	1,261	2.7	4.9	3,990	3,160	6,890	5,460	0.0	53	89	..	2,820
Gambia, The	1,341	3.3	134.1	440	330	2,319g	1,730g	2.7	53	..	63	227
Greenland	56	..	0.2	..	..f	..	..	..	..	..	..	528
Grenada	99	0.5	291.2	368	3,720	666	6,720	-5.7	72	17	..	183
Guam	157	1.4	285.4	..	..f	..	..	..	78	10	..	4,111
Guinea-Bissau	1,226	2.4	43.6	202	160	872g	710g	-2.0	45	211	62	846
Guyana	766	0.4	3.9	641	840	2,870g	3,750g	0.8	63	73	2	1,649
Iceland	284	1.0	2.8	8,201	28,880	8,470	29,830	1.9	80	6	..	2,083
Iraq	23,750	2.5	54.3	..	..h	..	..	..	61	121	44	82,378
Isle of Man	75	..	131	..	..e	..	..	..	..	..	..	..
Kiribati	93	2.3	127.2	77	830	..	..	-0.8	62	..	..	22
Korea, Dem. Rep.	22,384	1.0	185.9	..	..d	..	..	..	61	90	..	226,149
Liberia	3,216	2.5	33.4	..	..d	..	..	..	47	185	46	353
Libya	5,410	2.1	3.1	..	..e	..	..	..	71	32	20	36,448
Liechtenstein	32	..	200.0	..	..f	..	..	..	..	..	..	..
Luxembourg	444	1.4	172	18,550	41,770	21,352	48,080	3.8	77	6	..	7,678
Macao, China	443	1.6	..	6,385i	14,580i	7,967g	18,190g	..	79	..	6	1,630
Maldives	283	2.6	942.5	578	2,040	1,277g	4,520g	4.5	68	34	3	330
Malta	392	0.8	1225.0	3,559	9,120	6,448g	16,530g	..	78	8	8	1,803
Marshall Islands	53	..	292	115	2,190	..	..	-0.7	65	..	..	..
Mauritius	1,198	1.1	590.1	4,592	3,830	12,468	10,410	6.1	72	20	15	1,726
Mayotte	145	..	388	..	..e	..	..	..	..	..	..	..
Micronesia, Fed. Sts.	120	2.0	171	258	2,150	..	..	-0.9	68	31	..	..
Monaco	32	..	16,410	..	..f	..	..	..	..	..	..	..
Netherlands Antilles	217	1.2	271.0	..	..f	..	..	..	76	16	3	7,753
New Caledonia	216	2.3	11.8	3,203	15,060	4,641	21,820	..	73	11	..	1,746
Northern Mariana Islands	72	..	151	..	..f	..	..	..	..	..	..	..
Oman	2,452	3.7	11.5	..	..e	..	..	..	74	22	28	20,270
Palau	20	..	42.4	131	6,730	..	..	-1.0	70	..	..	242
Puerto Rico	3,950	1.0	445.4	..	..e	..	..	..	76	..	6	17,567
Qatar	598	1.9	54.3	..	..f	..	..	..	75	19	19	46,772
Samoa	171	0.6	60.5	260	1,520	933g	5,450g	9.3	69	..	20	132
San Marino	27	..	450.0	..	..f	..	..	..	80	..	..	..
São Tomé and Principe	151	2.5	157.5	43	280	..	..	0.8	65	62	..	77
Seychelles	82	1.5	183.1	573	7,050	..	..	..	72	14	..	198
Solomon Islands	432	2.8	15.4	253	580	726g	1,680g	-11.5	69	27	..	161
Somalia	9,089	2.2	14.5	..	..d	..	..	..	48	195	..	0
St. Kitts and Nevis	41	-0.2	114.1	283	6,880	482	11,730	1.6	71	..	..	103
St. Lucia	158	1.5	259.2	628	3,970	822	5,200	-4.8	71	19	..	198
St. Vincent and the Grenadines	116	0.7	297.1	312	2,690	608g	5,250g	-1.3	73	20	..	161
Sudan	31,687	2.2	13.3	10,346	330	51,135	1,610	4.0	56	..	42	3,597
Suriname	420	0.4	2.7	709	1,690	1,389g	3,310g	1.2	70	31	..	2,139
Swaziland	1,068	3.0	62.1	1,388	1,300	5,006g	4,690g	-0.6	46	119	20	399
Tonga	101	0.4	139.9	154	1,530	..	..	2.5	71	23	..	117
Trinidad and Tobago	1,310	0.7	255.3	7,249	5,540	11,887	9,080	4.3	73	19	6	22,396
United Arab Emirates	2,976	4.4	35.6	..	..f	..	..	..	75	10	24	88,198
Vanuatu	201	2.8	16.5	212	1,050	546	2,710	-6.1	68	40	..	62
Virgin Islands (U.S.)	122	1.5	360.0	..	..f	..	..	..	78	11	..	11,706
West Bank and Gaza	3,091	4.1	..	4,177	1,350	..	..	-15.5	72	26	..	..

Note: Figures in italics are for years other than those specified.
a. Preliminary World Bank estimates calculated using the World Bank Atlas method. b. Purchasing power parity; see the Technical Notes. c. Estimate does not account for recent refugee flows. d. Estimated to be low income ($745 or less). e. Estimated to be upper middle income ($2,976 to $9,205). f. Estimated to be high income ($9,206 or more). g. The estimate is based on regression; others are extrapolated from the latest International Comparison Programme benchmark estimates. h. Estimated to be lower middle income ($746 to $2,975). i. Refers to GDP and GDP per capita.

Classification of economies by region and income, FY2003[a]

East Asia and the Pacific		Latin America and the Caribbean		South Asia		High income OECD
American Samoa	UMC	Antigua and Barbuda	UMC	Afghanistan	LIC	Australia
Cambodia	LIC	Argentina	UMC	Bangladesh	LIC	Austria
China	LMC	Barbados	UMC	Bhutan	LIC	Belgium
Fiji	LMC	Belize	LMC	India	LIC	Canada
Indonesia	LIC	Bolivia	LMC	Maldives	LMC	Denmark
Kiribati	LMC	Brazil	UMC	Nepal	LIC	Finland
Korea, Dem. Rep.	LIC	Chile	UMC	Pakistan	LIC	France
Lao PDR	LIC	Colombia	LMC	Sri Lanka	LMC	Germany
Malaysia	UMC	Costa Rica	UMC			Greece
Marshall Islands	LMC	Cuba	LMC	Sub-Saharan Africa		Iceland
Micronesia, Fed. Sts.	LMC	Dominica	UMC	Angola	LIC	Ireland
Mongolia	LIC	Dominican Republic	LMC	Benin	LIC	Italy
Myanmar	LIC	Ecuador	LMC	Botswana	UMC	Japan
Palau	UMC	El Salvador	LMC	Burkina Faso	LIC	Korea, Rep.
Papua New Guinea	LIC	Grenada	UMC	Burundi	LIC	Luxembourg
Philippines	LMC	Guatemala	LMC	Cameroon	LIC	Netherlands
Samoa	LMC	Guyana	LMC	Cape Verde	LMC	New Zealand
Solomon Islands	LIC	Haiti	LIC	Central African Republic	LIC	Norway
Thailand	LMC	Honduras	LMC	Chad	LIC	Portugal
Tonga	LMC	Jamaica	LMC	Comoros	LIC	Spain
Vanuatu	LMC	Mexico	UMC	Congo, Dem. Rep.	LIC	Sweden
Vietnam	LIC	Nicaragua	LIC	Congo, Rep.	LIC	Switzerland
		Panama	UMC	Côte d'Ivoire	LIC	United Kingdom
		Paraguay	LMC	Equatorial Guinea	LIC	United States
Europe and Central Asia		Peru	LMC	Eritrea	LIC	
Albania	LMC	Puerto Rico	UMC	Ethiopia	LIC	Other high income
Armenia	LIC	St. Kitts and Nevis	UMC	Gabon	UMC	Andorra
Azerbaijan	LIC	St. Lucia	UMC	Gambia, The	LIC	Aruba
Belarus	LMC	St. Vincent and the		Ghana	LIC	Bahamas, The
Bosnia and Herzegovina	LMC	Grenadines	LMC	Guinea	LIC	Bahrain
Bulgaria	LMC	Suriname	LMC	Guinea-Bissau	LIC	Bermuda
Croatia	UMC	Trinidad and Tobago	UMC	Kenya	LIC	Brunei
Czech Republic	UMC	Uruguay	UMC	Lesotho	LIC	Cayman Islands
Estonia	UMC	Venezuela, RB	UMC	Liberia	LIC	Channel Islands
Georgia	LIC			Madagascar	LIC	Cyprus
Hungary	UMC			Malawi	LIC	Faeroe Islands
Isle of Man	UMC	Middle East and North Africa		Mali	LIC	French Polynesia
Kazakhstan	LMC	Algeria	LMC	Mauritania	LIC	Greenland
Kyrgyz Republic	LIC	Djibouti	LMC	Mauritius	UMC	Guam
Latvia	UMC	Egypt, Arab Rep.	LMC	Mayotte	UMC	Hong Kong, China
Lithuania	UMC	Iran, Islamic Rep.	LMC	Mozambique	LIC	Israel
Macedonia, FYR	LMC	Iraq	LMC	Namibia	LMC	Kuwait
Moldova	LIC	Jordan	LMC	Niger	LIC	Liechtenstein
Poland	UMC	Lebanon	UMC	Nigeria	LIC	Macao, China
Romania	LMC	Libya	UMC	Rwanda	LIC	Monaco
Russian Federation	LMC	Malta	UMC	São Tomé and Principe	LIC	Netherlands Antilles
Slovak Republic	UMC	Morocco	LMC	Senegal	LIC	New Caledonia
Tajikistan	LIC	Oman	UMC	Seychelles	UMC	Northern Mariana Islands
Turkey	LMC	Saudi Arabia	UMC	Sierra Leone	LIC	Qatar
Turkmenistan	LMC	Syrian Arab Republic	LMC	Somalia	LIC	San Marino
Ukraine	LIC	Tunisia	LMC	South Africa	LMC	Singapore
Uzbekistan	LIC	West Bank and Gaza	LMC	Sudan	LIC	Slovenia
Yugoslavia, Fed. Rep.	LMC	Yemen, Rep.	LIC	Swaziland	LMC	Taiwan, China
				Tanzania	LIC	United Arab Emirates
				Togo	LIC	Virgin Islands (U.S.)
				Uganda	LIC	
				Zambia	LIC	
				Zimbabwe	LIC	

This table classifies all World Bank member economies, and all other economies with populations of more than 30,000. Economies are divided among income groups according to 2001 GNI per capita, calculated using the World Bank Atlas method. The groups are: low income (LIC), $745 or less; lower middle income (LMC), $746–2,975; upper middle income (UMC), $2,976–9,205; and high income, $9,206 or more. a. Official World Bank Classification for fiscal year (ending on 30 June).

Source: World Bank data.

Technical Notes

These technical notes discuss the sources and methods used to compile the indicators included in this edition of Selected World Development Indicators. The notes follow the order in which the indicators appear in the tables. Note that the Selected World Development Indicators uses terminology in line with the 1993 System of National Accounts (SNA). For example, in the 1993 SNA *gross national income* replaces *gross national product*. See the technical notes for tables 1 and 3 for other examples.

Sources

The data published in the Selected World Development Indicators are taken from *World Development Indicators 2002*. Where possible, however, revisions reported since the closing date of that edition have been incorporated. In addition, newly released estimates of population and gross national income (GNI) per capita for 2001 are included in table 1.

The World Bank draws on a variety of sources for the statistics published in the *World Development Indicators*. Data on external debt are reported directly to the World Bank by developing member countries through the Debtor Reporting System. Other data are drawn mainly from the United Nations and its specialized agencies, from the International Monetary Fund (IMF), and from country reports to the World Bank. Bank staff estimates are also used to improve currency or consistency. For most countries, national accounts estimates are obtained from member governments through World Bank economic missions. In some instances these are adjusted by staff to ensure conformity with international definitions and concepts. Most social data from national sources are drawn from regular administrative files, special surveys, or periodic censuses.

For more detailed notes about the data, please refer to the World Bank's *World Development Indicators 2002*.

Data consistency and reliability

Considerable effort has been made to standardize the data, but full comparability cannot be assured, and care must be taken in interpreting the indicators. Many factors affect data availability, comparability, and reliability: statistical systems in many developing economies are still weak; statistical methods, coverage, practices, and definitions differ widely; and cross-country and intertemporal comparisons involve complex technical and conceptual problems that cannot be unequivocally resolved. Data coverage may not be complete for economies experiencing problems, such as those deriving from internal or external conflicts, affecting the collecting and reporting of data. For these reasons, although the data are drawn from the sources thought to be most authoritative, they should be construed only as indicating trends and characterizing major differences among economies rather than offering precise quantitative measures of those differences. Also, national statistical agencies tend to revise their historical data, particularly for recent years. Thus, data of different vintages may be published in different editions of World Bank publications. Readers are advised not to compile such data from different editions. Consistent time series are available from the *World Development Indicators 2002* CD-ROM.

Ratios and growth rates

For ease of reference, the tables usually show ratios and rates of growth rather than the simple underlying values. Values in their original form are available from the *World Development Indicators 2002* CD-ROM. Unless otherwise noted, growth rates are computed using the least-squares regression method (see *Statistical methods* below). Because this method takes into account all available observations during a period, the resulting growth rates reflect general trends that are not unduly influenced by exceptional values. To exclude the effects of inflation, constant price economic indicators are used in calculating growth rates. Data in italics are for a year or period other than that specified in the column heading—up to two years before or after for economic indicators and up to three years for social indicators, because the latter tend to be collected less regularly and change less dramatically over short periods.

Constant price series

An economy's growth is measured by the increase in value added produced by the individuals and enterprises operating in that economy. Thus, measuring real growth requires estimates of GDP and its components valued in constant prices.

The World Bank collects constant price national accounts series in national currencies and recorded in the country's original base year. To obtain comparable series of constant price data, it rescales GDP and value added by industrial origin to a common reference year, currently 1995. This process gives rise to a discrepancy between the rescaled GDP and the sum of the rescaled components. Because allocating the discrepancy would give rise to distortions in the growth rate, it is left unallocated.

Summary measures

The summary measures for regions and income groups, presented at the end of most tables, are calculated by simple addition when they are expressed in levels. Aggregate growth rates and ratios are usually computed as weighted averages. The summary measures for social indicators are weighted by population or subgroups of population, except for infant mortality, which is weighted by the number of births. See the notes on specific indicators for more information.

For summary measures that cover many years, calculations are based on a uniform group of economies so that the composition of the aggregate does not change over time. Group measures are compiled only if the data available for a given year account for at least two-thirds of the full group, as defined for the 1995 benchmark year. As long as this criterion is met, economies for which data are missing are assumed to behave like those that provide estimates. Readers should keep in mind that the summary measures are estimates of representative aggregates for each topic and that nothing meaningful can be deduced about behavior at the country level by working back from group indicators. In addition, the estimation process may result in discrepancies between subgroup and overall totals.

Table 1. Key indicators of development

Population is based on the de facto definition, which counts all residents, regardless of legal status or citizenship, except for refugees not permanently settled in the country of asylum, who are generally considered part of the population of the country of origin.

Average annual population growth rate is the exponential rate of change for the period (see the section on statistical methods below).

Population density is midyear population divided by land area. Land area is a country's total area excluding areas under inland bodies of water and coastal waterways. Density is calculated using the most recently available data on land area.

Gross national income (GNI—formerly gross national product or GNP), the broadest measure of national income, measures total value added from domestic and foreign sources claimed by residents. GNI comprises gross domestic product (GDP) plus net receipts of primary income from foreign sources. Data are converted from national currency to current U.S. dollars using the World Bank Atlas method. This involves using a three-year average of exchange rates to smooth the effects of transitory exchange rate fluctuations.

(See the section on statistical methods below for further discussion of the Atlas method.)

GNI per capita is GNI divided by midyear population. It is converted into current U.S. dollars by the Atlas method. The World Bank uses GNI per capita in U.S dollars to classify economies for analytical purposes and to determine borrowing eligibility.

PPP Gross national income, which is GNI converted into international dollars using purchasing power parity (PPP) conversion factors, is included because nominal exchange rates do not always reflect international differences in relative prices. At the PPP rate, one international dollar has the same purchasing power over domestic GNI that the U.S. dollar has over U.S. GNI. PPP rates allow a standard comparison of real price levels between countries, just as conventional price indexes allow comparison of real values over time. The PPP conversion factors used here are derived from the most recent round of price surveys conducted by the International Comparison Programme, a joint project of the World Bank and the regional economic commissions of the United Nations. This round of surveys, completed in 1996 and covering 118 countries, is based on a 1993 reference year. Estimates for countries not included in the survey are derived from statistical models using available data.

PPP GNI per capita is PPP GNI divided by midyear population.

Gross domestic product (GDP) per capita growth is based on GDP measured in constant prices. Growth in GDP is considered a broad measure of the growth of an economy. GDP in constant prices can be estimated by measuring the total quantity of goods and services produced in a period, valuing them at an agreed set of base year prices, and subtracting the cost of intermediate inputs, also in constant prices. See the section on statistical methods for details of the least-squares growth rate.

Life expectancy at birth is the number of years a newborn infant would live if patterns of mortality prevailing at its birth were to stay the same throughout its life.

Under-5 mortality rate is the probability that a child born in the indicated year will die before reaching age 5, if the child is subject to current age specific mortality rates. The probability is expressed as a rate per 1,000.

Adult illiteracy rate is the percentage of persons aged 15 and above who cannot, with understanding, read and write a short, simple statement about their everyday life. The definition here is based on the concept of functional literacy: a person's ability to use reading and writing skills effectively in the context of his or her society. Measuring literacy using such a definition requires census or sample survey measurements under controlled conditions. In practice, many countries estimate the number of illiterate adults from self-reported data or from estimates of school completion rates. Because of these differences in method, comparisons across countries—and even over time within countries—should be made with caution.

Carbon dioxide emissions (CO_2) measures those emissions stemming from the burning of fossil fuels and the manufacture of cement. These include carbon dioxide produced during consumption of solid, liquid, and gas fuels and from gas flaring.

The Carbon Dioxide Information Analysis Center (CDIAC), sponsored by the U.S. Department of Energy, calculates annual anthropogenic emissions of CO_2. These calculations are derived from data on fossil fuel consumption, based on the World Energy Data Set maintained by the UNSD, and from data on world cement manufacturing, based on the Cement Manufacturing Data Set maintained by the U.S. Bureau of Mines. Each year the CDIAC recalculates the entire time series from 1950 to the present, incorporating its most recent findings and the latest corrections to its database. Estimates exclude fuels supplied to ships and aircraft engaged in international transportation because of the difficulty of apportioning these fuels among the countries benefiting from that transport.

Table 2. Poverty and income distribution

Survey year is the year in which the underlying data were collected.

Rural poverty rate is the percentage of the rural population living below the rural poverty line. **Urban poverty rate** is the percentage of the urban population living below the urban poverty line. **National poverty rate** is the percentage of the total population living below the national poverty line. National estimates are based on population weighted subgroup estimates from household surveys.

Population below $1 PPP a day and **$2 PPP a day** are the percentages of the population living on less than $1.08 a day and $2.15 a day at 1993 international prices (equivalent to $1 and $2 in 1985 prices adjusted for purchasing power parity). Poverty rates are comparable across countries, but as a result of revisions in PPP exchange rates, they cannot be compared with poverty rates reported in previous editions for individual countries.

Poverty gap at $1 PPP a day and **Poverty gap at $2 PPP a day** is the mean shortfall below the poverty line (counting the non-poor as having zero shortfall), expressed as a percentage of the poverty line. This measure reflects the depth of poverty as well as its incidence.

International comparisons of poverty data entail both conceptual and practical problems. Different countries have different definitions of poverty, and consistent comparisons between countries can be difficult. Local poverty lines tend to have higher purchasing power in rich countries, where more generous standards are used than in poor countries. Is it reasonable to treat two people with the same standard of living—in terms of their command over commodities—differently because one happens to live in a better-off country? Can we hold the real value of the poverty line constant across countries, just as we do when making comparisons over time?

Poverty measures based on an international poverty line attempt to do this. The $1 a day standard, measured in 1985 international prices and adjusted to local currency using purchasing power parities (PPPs), was chosen for the World Bank's *World Development Report 1990: Poverty* because it is typical of the poverty lines in low-income countries. PPP exchange rates, such as those from the Penn World Tables or

the World Bank, are used because they take into account the local prices of goods and services not traded internationally. But PPP rates were designed not for making international poverty comparisons but for comparing aggregates from national accounts. As a result, there is no certainty that an international poverty line measures the same degree of need or deprivation across countries.

Past editions of the *World Development Indicators* and the Selected World Development Indicators used PPPs from the Penn World Tables. Because the Penn World Tables updated to 1993 are not yet available, this year's edition (like last year's) uses 1993 consumption PPP estimates produced by the World Bank. The international poverty line, set at $1 a day in 1985 PPP terms, has been recalculated in 1993 PPP terms at about $1.08 a day. Any revisions in the PPP of a country to incorporate better price indexes can produce dramatically different poverty lines in local currency.

Problems also exist in comparing poverty measures within countries. For example, the cost of living is typically higher in urban than in rural areas. (Food staples, for example, tend to be more expensive in urban areas.) So the urban monetary poverty line should be higher than the rural poverty line. But it is not always clear that the difference between urban and rural poverty lines found in practice properly reflects the difference in the cost of living. In some countries the urban poverty line in common use has a higher real value—meaning that it allows the purchase of more commodities for consumption—than does the rural poverty line. Sometimes the difference has been so large as to imply that the incidence of poverty is greater in urban than in rural areas, even though the reverse is found when adjustments are made only for differences in the cost of living. As with international comparisons, when the real value of the poverty line varies, it is not clear how meaningful such urban-rural comparisons are.

The problems of making poverty comparisons do not end there. More issues arise in measuring household living standards. The choice between income and consumption as a welfare indicator is one issue. Income is generally more difficult to measure accurately, and consumption accords better with the idea of the standard of living than does income, which can vary over time even if the standard of living does not. But consumption data are not always available, and when they are not there is little choice but to use income. There are still other problems. Household survey questionnaires can differ widely, for example, in the number of distinct categories of consumer goods they identify. Survey quality varies, and even similar surveys may not be strictly comparable.

Comparisons across countries at different levels of development also pose a potential problem, because of differences in the relative importance of consumption of nonmarket goods. The local market value of all consumption in kind (including consumption from own production, particularly important in underdeveloped rural economies) should be included in the measure of total consumption expenditure. Similarly, the imputed profit from production of nonmarket goods should be included in income. This is not always done, though such omissions were a far bigger problem in surveys before the 1980s. Most survey data now include valuations for consumption or income from own production. Nonetheless, valuation methods vary. For example, some surveys use the price in the nearest market, while others use the average farm gate selling price.

Whenever possible, consumption has been used as the welfare indicator for deciding who is poor. When only household income was available, average income has been adjusted to accord with either a survey-based estimate of mean consumption (when available) or an estimate based on consumption data from national accounts. This procedure adjusts only the mean, however; nothing can be done to correct for the difference in Lorenz (income distribution) curves between consumption and income.

Empirical Lorenz curves are weighted by household size, so they are based on percentiles of population, not households. In all cases the measures of poverty have been calculated from primary data sources (tabulations or household data) rather than existing estimates. Estimation from tabulations requires an interpolation method; the method chosen was Lorenz curves with flexible functional forms, which have proved reliable in past work.

Gini index measures the extent to which the distribution of income (or, in some cases, consumption expenditure) among individuals or households within an economy deviates from a perfectly equal distribution. A Lorenz curve plots the cumulative percentages of total income received against the cumulative number of recipients, starting with the poorest individual or household. The Gini index measures the area between the Lorenz curve and a hypothetical line of absolute equality, expressed as a percentage of the maximum area under the line. Thus a Gini index of zero represents perfect equality, while an index of 100 implies perfect inequality.

Percentage share of income or consumption is the share that accrues to subgroups of population indicated by deciles or quintiles.

Inequality in the distribution of income is reflected in the percentage shares of either income or consumption accruing to segments of the population ranked by income or consumption levels. The segments ranked lowest by personal income receive the smallest share of total income. The Gini index provides a convenient summary measure of the degree of inequality.

Data on personal or household income or consumption come from nationally representative household surveys. The data in the table refer to different years between 1985 and 2000. Footnotes to the survey year indicate whether the rankings are based on per capita income or consumption. Each distribution is based on percentiles of population—rather than of households—with households ranked by income or expenditure per person.

Where the original data from the household survey were available, they have been used to directly calculate the income (or consumption) shares by quintile. Otherwise, shares have been estimated from the best available grouped data.

The distribution indicators have been adjusted for household size, providing a more consistent measure of per capita income or consumption. No adjustment has been made for spatial differences in cost of living within countries, because the data needed for such calculations are generally unavail-

able. For further details on the estimation method for low- and middle-income economies see Ravallion and Chen (1996).

Because the underlying household surveys differ in method and in the type of data collected, the distribution indicators are not strictly comparable across countries. These problems are diminishing as survey methods improve and become more standardized, but achieving strict comparability is still impossible.

Two sources of noncomparability should be noted. First, the surveys can differ in many respects, including whether they use income or consumption expenditure as the living standard indicator. The distribution of income is typically more unequal than the distribution of consumption. In addition, the definitions of income used usually differ among surveys. Consumption is usually a better welfare indicator, particularly in developing countries. Second, households differ in size (number of members) and in the extent of income sharing among members. And individuals differ in age and consumption needs. Differences among countries in these respects may bias comparisons of distribution.

World Bank staff have made an effort to ensure that the data are as comparable as possible. Whenever possible, consumption has been used rather than income. The income distribution and Gini indexes for high-income countries are calculated directly from the Luxembourg Income Study database using an estimation method consistent with that applied for developing countries.

Table 3. Economic activity

Gross domestic product is gross value added, at purchasers' prices, by all resident producers in the economy plus any taxes and minus any subsidies not included in the value of the products. It is calculated without deducting for depreciation of fabricated assets or for depletion or degradation of natural resources. Value added is the net output of an industry after adding up all outputs and subtracting intermediate inputs. The industrial origin of value added is determined by the International Standard Industrial Classification (ISIC) revision 3. The World Bank conventionally uses the U.S. dollar and applies the average official exchange rate reported by the International Monetary Fund for the year shown. An alternative conversion factor is applied if the official exchange rate is judged to diverge by an exceptionally large margin from the rate effectively applied to transactions in foreign currencies and traded products.

Gross domestic product average annual growth rate is calculated from constant price GDP data in local currency.

Agricultural productivity refers to the ratio of agricultural value added, measured in constant 1995 U.S. dollars, to the number of workers in agriculture.

Value added is the net output of an industry after adding up all out-puts and subtracting intermediate inputs. The industrial origin of value added is determined by the International Standard Industrial Classification (ISIC) revision 3.

Agriculture value added corresponds to ISIC divisions 1–5 and includes forestry and fishing.

Industry value added comprises mining, manufacturing, construction, electricity, water, and gas (ISIC divisions 10–45).

Services value added correspond to ISIC divisions 50–99.

Household final consumption expenditure (private consumption in previous editions) is the market value of all goods and services, including durable products (such as cars, washing machines, and home computers), purchased by households. It excludes purchases of dwellings but includes imputed rent for owner-occupied dwellings. It also includes payments and fees to governments to obtain permits and licenses. Here, household consumption expenditure includes the expenditures of nonprofit institutions serving households, even when reported separately by the country. In practice, household consumption expenditure may include any statistical discrepancy in the use of resources relative to the supply of resources.

General government final consumption expenditure (general government consumption in previous editions) includes all government current expenditures for purchases of goods and services (including compensation of employees). It also includes most expenditures on national defense and security, but excludes government military expenditures that are part of government capital formation.

Gross capital formation (gross domestic investment in previous editions) consists of outlays on additions to the fixed assets of the economy plus net changes in the level of inventories and valuables. Fixed assets include land improvements (fences, ditches, drains, and so on); plant, machinery, and equipment purchases; and the construction of buildings, roads, railways, and the like, including commercial and industrial buildings, offices, schools, hospitals, and private dwellings. Inventories are stocks of goods held by firms to meet temporary or unexpected fluctuations in production or sales, and "work in progress." According to the 1993 SNA net acquisitions of valuables are also considered capital formation.

External balance of goods and services is exports of goods and services less imports of goods and services. Trade in goods and services comprise all transactions between residents of a country and the rest of the world involving a change in ownership of general merchandise, goods sent for processing and repairs, non-monetary gold, and services.

The **GDP implicit deflator** reflects changes in prices for all final demand categories, such as government consumption, capital formation, and international trade, as well as the main component, private final consumption. It is derived as the ratio of current to constant price GDP. The GDP deflator may also be calculated explicitly as a Paasche price index in which the weights are the current period quantities of output.

National accounts indicators for most developing countries are collected from national statistical organizations and central banks by visiting and resident World Bank missions. Data for high-income economies come from the Organization for Economic Co-operation and Development data files.

Table 4. Trade, aid, and finance

Merchandise exports show the f.o.b. value of goods provided to the rest of the world valued in U.S. dollars.

Merchandise imports show the c.i.f. value of goods (the cost of the goods including insurance and freight) purchased from the rest of the world valued in U.S. dollars. Data on merchandise trade come from the World Trade Organization (WTO) in its annual report.

Manufactured exports comprise the commodities in Standard Industrial Trade Classification (SITC) sections 5 (chemicals), 6 (basic manufactures), 7 (machinery and transport equipment), and 8 (miscellaneous manufactured goods), excluding division 68.

High technology exports are products with high R&D intensity. They include high-technology products such as in aerospace, computers, pharmaceuticals, scientific instruments, and electrical machinery.

Current account balance is the sum of net exports of goods and services, net income, and net current transfers.

Net private capital flows consist of private debt and nondebt flows. Private debt flows include commercial bank lending, bonds, and other private credits; nondebt private flows are foreign direct investment and portfolio equity investment.

Foreign direct investment is net inflows of investment to acquire a lasting management interest (10 percent or more of voting stock) in an enterprise operating in an economy other than that of the investor. It is the sum of equity capital, re-investment of earnings, other long-term capital, and short-term capital, as shown in the balance of payments. Data on the current account balance, private capital flows, and foreign direct investment are drawn from the IMF's *Balance of Payments Statistics Yearbook* and *International Financial Statistics*.

Official development assistance or official aid from the high-income members of the Organisation for Economic Co-operation and Development (OECD) are the main source of official external finance for developing countries, but official development assistance (ODA) is also disbursed by some important donor countries that are not members of OECD's Development Assistance Committee (DAC). DAC has three criteria for ODA: it is undertaken by the official sector; it promotes economic development or welfare as a main objective; and it is provided on concessional terms, with a grant element of at least 25 percent on loans.

Official development assistance comprises grants and loans, net of repayments, that meet the DAC definition of ODA and are made to countries and territories in part I of the DAC list of aid recipients. Official aid comprises grants and ODA-like loans, net of repayments, to countries and territories in part II of the DAC list of aid recipients. Bilateral grants are transfers in money or in kind for which no repayment is required. Bilateral loans are loans extended by governments or official agencies that have a grant element of at least 25 percent and for which repayment is required in convertible currencies or in kind.

Total external debt is debt owed to nonresidents repayable in foreign currency, goods, or services. It is the sum of public, publicly guaranteed, and private non-guaranteed long-term debt, use of IMF credit, and short-term debt.

Short-term debt includes all debt having an original maturity of one year or less and interest in arrears on long-term debt.

Present value of debt is the sum of short-term external debt plus the discounted sum of total debt service payments due on public, publicly guaranteed, and private nonguaranteed long-term external debt over the life of existing loans.

The main sources of external debt information are reports to the World Bank through its Debtor Reporting System from member countries that have received World Bank loans. Additional information has been drawn from the files of the World Bank and the IMF. Summary tables of the external debt of developing countries are published annually in the World Bank's *Global Development Finance*.

Domestic credit provided by banking sector includes all credit to various sectors on a gross basis, with the exception of credit to the central government, which is net. The banking sector includes monetary authorities, deposit money banks, and other banking institutions for which data are available (including institutions that do not accept transferable deposits but do incur such liabilities as time and savings deposits). Examples of other banking institutions include savings and mortgage loan institutions and building and loan associations. Data are from the IMF's *International Finance Statitics*.

Statistical methods

This section describes the calculation of the least-squares growth rate, the exponential (endpoint) growth rate, and the World Bank's Atlas methodology for calculating the conversion factor used to estimate GNI and GNI per capita in U.S. dollars.

Least-squares growth rate

Least-squares growth rates are used wherever there is a sufficiently long time series to permit a reliable calculation. No growth rate is calculated if more than half the observations in a period are missing.

The least-squares growth rate, r, is estimated by fitting a linear regression trendline to the logarithmic annual values of the variable in the relevant period. The regression equation takes the form

$$\ln X_t = a + bt,$$

which is equivalent to the logarithmic transformation of the compound growth equation,

$$X_t = X_o (1 + r)^t.$$

In this equation, X is the variable, t is time, and $a = \log X_o$ and $b = ln (1 + r)$ are the parameters to be estimated. If b^* is the least-squares estimate of b, the average annual growth rate, r, is obtained as $[\exp(b^*)-1]$ and is multiplied by 100 to express it as a percentage.

The calculated growth rate is an average rate that is representative of the available observations over the entire period. It does not necessarily match the actual growth rate between any two periods.

Exponential growth rate

The growth rate between two points in time for certain demographic data, notably labor force and population, is calculated from the equation

$$r = \ln (p_n /p_1)/n,$$

where p_n and p_1 are the last and first observations in the period, n is the number of years in the period, and ln is the natural logarithm operator. This growth rate is based on a model of continuous, exponential growth between two points in time. It does not take into account the intermediate values of the series. Note also that the exponential growth rate does not correspond to the annual rate of change measured at a one-year interval which is given by

$$(p_n - p_{n-1})/p_{n-1}.$$

The Gini index

The Gini index measures the extent to which the distribution of income (or, in some cases, consumption expenditure) among individuals or households within an economy deviates from a perfectly equal distribution. A Lorenz curve plots the cumulative percentages of total income received against the cumulative number of recipients, starting with the poorest individual or household. The Gini index measures the area between the Lorenz curve and a hypothetical line of absolute equality, expressed as a percentage of the maximum area under the line. Thus a Gini index of zero represents perfect equality, and an index of 100 percent implies perfect inequality.

World Bank Atlas method

In calculating GNI and GNI per capita in U.S. dollars for certain operational purposes, the World Bank uses the Atlas conversion factor. The purpose of the Atlas conversion factor is to reduce the impact of exchange rate fluctuations in the cross-country comparison of national incomes.

The Atlas conversion factor for any year is the average of a country's exchange rate (or alternative conversion factor) for that year and its exchange rates for the two preceding years, adjusted for the difference between the rate of inflation in the country, and through 2000, that in the G-5 countries (France, Germany, Japan, the United Kingdom, and the United States). For 2001, these countries include the Euro Zone, Japan, the United Kingdom, and the United States. A country's inflation rate is measured by the change in its GDP deflator.

The inflation rate for G-5 countries (through 2000), or the Euro Zone, Japan, the United Kingdom, and the United States (for 2001), representing international inflation, is measured by the change in the SDR deflator. (Special drawing rights, or SDRs, are the IMF's unit of account.) The SDR deflator is calculated as a weighted average of the G-5 countries' (through 2000, and the Euro Zone, Japan, the United Kingdom, and the United States for 2001) GDP deflators in SDR terms, the weights being the amount of each country's currency in one SDR unit. Weights vary over time because both the composition of the SDR and the relative exchange rates for each currency change. The SDR deflator is calculated in SDR terms first and then converted to U.S. dollars using the SDR to dollar Atlas conversion factor. The Atlas conversion factor is then applied to a country's GNI. The resulting GNI in U.S. dollars is divided by the midyear population to derive GNI per capita.

When official exchange rates are deemed to be unreliable or unrepresentative of the effective exchange rate during a period, an alternative estimate of the exchange rate is used in the Atlas formula (see below).

The following formulas describe the calculation of the Atlas conversion factor for year t:

$$e_t^* = \frac{1}{3}\left[e_{t-2}\left(\frac{p_t}{p_{t-2}} \frac{p_t^{S\$}}{p_{t-2}^{S\$}} \right) + e_{t-1}\left(\frac{p_t}{p_{t-1}} \frac{p_t^{S\$}}{p_{t-1}^{S\$}} \right) + e_t \right]$$

and the calculation of GNI per capita in U.S. dollars for year t:

$$Y_t^\$ = (Y_t / N_t) / e_t^*$$

where e_t^* is the Atlas conversion factor (national currency to the U.S. dollar) for year t, e_t is the average annual exchange rate (national currency to the U.S. dollar) for year t, p_t is the GDP deflator for year t, $p_t^{S\$}$ is the SDR deflator in U.S. dollar terms for year t, $Y_t^\$$ is the Atlas GNI per capita in U.S. dollars in year t, Y_t is current GNI (local currency) for year t, and N_t is the midyear population for year t.

Alternative conversion factors

The World Bank systematically assesses the appropriateness of official exchange rates as conversion factors. An alternative conversion factor is used when the official exchange rate is judged to diverge by an exceptionally large margin from the rate effectively applied to domestic transactions of foreign currencies and traded products. This applies to only a small number of countries, as shown in Primary data documentation table in World Development Indicators 2002. Alternative conversion factors are used in the Atlas methodology and elsewhere in the Selected World Development Indicators as single-year conversion factors.